# Walk-About Guide to Alaska

## The Front Range and the Anchorage Bowl

# VOLUME TWO

## SHAWN R. LYONS
Acknowledged Alaska Hiking Authority

PUBLICATION CONSULTANTS
We Believe In The Power Of Authors

PO Box 221974 Anchorage, Alaska 99522-1974
books@publicationconsultants.com—www.publicationconsultants.com

ISBN 978-1-59433-753-6
eBook ISBN 978-1-59433-754-3
Library of Congress Catalog Card Number: 2018933903

*Photographs* by Shawn R. Lyons

*Maps* by Cameron Kuhle of Mojosa Design

*Cover:* [TOP] On the summit of South Suicide Peak.
[LOWER LEFT]Near Black Lake above Middle Fork Campbell
Creek with Williwaw Peak in the background.
[LOWER RIGHT] Climbing toward Ptarmigan Pass

*Insert:* On the ridge between East Tanaina Peak and West Tanaina Peak

Manufactured in the United States of America.

I dedicate this book to my mother and father:

*To my father, who first took me to the mountains,*
*To my mother, who, though reluctant to let me go,*
*Always lent her support after I had gone.*
*And to them both for instilling in me a love for words.*

# FOREWORD

After too many years since last publishing a Walk-About Guide, friends and readers have convinced me with little difficulty that the time has come to revise and update the old guides as well as add new guides. You now hold the resulting revised version of the second (of four) of these guides in your hands.

The revisions and updates that appear in these books consist of largely adding more detail to the guides that appeared in the first three Walk-About Guides. The Trail Location and Trail Condition for each trail have seen special expansion. Trail Location first indicates any changes in how to reach the beginning of a trail from Anchorage. In addition, the augmentation of Trail Location and Trail Condition of each guide has resulted in more detailed information about how the trails and routes reach various destinations, what landmarks they pass along the way, and what mileage they may have reached at any particular moment, so that hikers can have a better idea as to approximately how far they have come and how far they have to go. It has also resulted in greater care describing the condition of each trail and route in regard to mud, rocks, scree, brush, and snow.

The new guides appear as two types. The first type adds to what already appeared in the first three Walk-About guide books. For instance, what originally appeared in *Volume One: the Kenai Peninsula and Turnagain Arm* now also includes hikes and climbs in Seldovia, Homer, and Seward as well as more hikes, climbs, and ridge walks up and down the lengths of both the Sterling Highway and the Seward Highway. What originally appeared in *Volume Two: The Chugach Mountains* now also includes many more hikes and climbs, such as guides for Indianhouse Mountain, Mount Elliot, and Homicide Peak as well as more traverses through the mountains, including one that follows the skyline along the entire back spine of the Front Range. This volume also includes guides to the bike trails, ski trails, and hiking trails that weave throughout the length and breadth of the Anchorage bowl. The expansion of Volume Two has made it necessary to combine parts of the previous Volumes Two and Three (which covered the northern Chugach Mountains and the Hatcher Pass area) into a new Volume Three, which also contains a number of new hikes and climbs. These include traverses around the Meadow Creek valley, Fourmile Creek valley, and climbs of Mount Rumble and Benign Peak.

The second type of addition includes all the guides previously intended for the unpublished *Walk-About Guide, Volume Four: The Talkeetna Mountains*. For many people the Glenn Highway remains unexplored country. The fourth book in this series, which should help them to explore that country on their own, includes some 65 new guides to trails, climbs, and traverses along the length of the Glenn Highway from Moose Creek to Glenallen. For instance, one can find guides for hikes up drainages such as Moose Creek, Kings River, Purinton Creek, and Crooked Creek; guides for climbs of mountains such as Granite Peak, Lava Mountain, Puddingstone Hill, and Syncline Mountain; and guides for traverses such as Red Mountain Ridge, Anthracite Ridge, and Sheep Mountain, as well as many more hikes, climbs, and traverses. May these guides help the reader discover the wonders of the long, wide valleys, and broad, tall peaks in that country.

As a result of all these inclusions, narratives of this writer's experience on various hikes and climbs do not appear in these pages as they did in previous Walk-About guides. With well over 450 guides in all, no room made itself available for any stories. Perhaps this may compel some former arm-chair travelers to create their own tales of travel to tell others either around some campfire outside a cabin or around some pitcher inside a local watering hole.

# ACKNOWLEDGMENT

Almost every book earmarks the life of the author up to the moment of that book's publication. That certainly remains true of this book. A lifetime of reading, hiking, camping, talking, and listening has gone into the pages contained in this book. So where does one begin in thanking those who helped to produce this book? Instead of going all the way back to family and friends who first piqued my interest in hiking and climbing, it seems best, for brevity's sake, to begin with those who have had the most direct influence on these pages. These include all the people who told me about any of the trails in this book, or kept me informed about the building of new trails and the repairing or rerouting of old trails.

First, I'd like to thank the former Superintendent for Chugach State Park, Al Meiners. Whenever I called him at his office or met him on a trail he spent the time to discuss trail routes and maintenance. Special thanks also go out to the late Chugach State Park Ranger Patrick Murphy. Whenever I called or visited Pat at Independence Mine State Park, he readily took the time to answer my questions about trails, roads, and land ownership and stewardship in the Hatcher Pass area. Pat also kindly took the time to critique the trail guides for the Hatcher Pass area in this book. I'd also like to thank Dave Post, former town planner for the Matanuska Borough. He not only sent me a copy of the "Matanuska-Susitna Borough Trails Plan," an ambitious and comprehensive multi-year plan to update old trails and dedicate and build new trails throughout the entire borough, but also kept me updated as to any progress made about specific trails contained in the plan.

Second, I'd like to thank the other officials and volunteers at Eagle River Nature Center and Independence Mine State Park for their friendly help. In particular, Bill Evans, landscape architect for Alaska

State Parks, took the time to point out the location of new trails at Independence Mine State Historic Site. Next, I'd like to thank the people of the Mountaineering Club of Alaska, the Nordic Ski Club in Anchorage, and the staff at Hatcher Pass Lodge who helped by providing information about trails and shelters in various areas throughout Southcentral Alaska.

Third, I'd also like to thank all the people, both friends and strangers, with whom I have ever swapped ideas and information about trails and routes throughout Southcentral Alaska. Whether we exchanged that information while we walked along some trail in the mountains or leaned over some beer in a bar makes little difference: it all proved helpful. These people include Richard Baranow, Dan and Nancy Dryden, Dan Shearer, and Chuck Spaulding, as well as the people at Hatcher Pass Lodge, Motherlode Lodge, Sheep Mountain Lodge, Majestic Valley Lodge, and Long Rifle Lodge—all frequent rendezvous and refreshment stops on the way to and from the mountains. It remains to thank all the nameless people one meets on a trail or at a slide show who share their ideas about hikes and climbs.

I'd also like to thank all the people who helped in any way specifically with in this book and its predecessors. My special thanks also go to Cameron Kuhle for creating all the maps contained in these volumes. He has shown a profound patience with my erratic judgments and requests for alterations. In addition, his artistic sense and computer skills have resulted in the tidy maps the reader will find accompanying each Walk-About Guide. My thanks also go to the late Richard Larson, whose artistic insight in the creation of the maps, the page layouts, and the overall design of the previous editions has continued to inspire my thoughts in approaching the design and layout of these new volumes. Additional thanks go to my late mother, Marthy Johnson, Sharon Jaeger, and the Pat Murphy (again) who proofread and edited various editions of these volumes. Steve Poirot deserves special thanks for taking time to help me grammatically polish the final version of this newest edition. Many thanks also to Mike Campbell, my former editor at *The Anchorage Daily News*, through whose hands stories that took place on many of the hikes and climbs described in these pages first passed.

Though most of them will never know it, thanks are also due to all the authors of factual and fictional tales about hiking or climbing lining my shelves. These include Dante Alighieri toiling with reverent heart up Mount Purgatory, Petrarch reminiscing about his climb of Mount Ventoux, or W. E. Bowman stumbling with a good-humored grin up Rum Doodle. These and many other authors who have penned tales and accounts of people's journeys into the high places on this planet have all provided entertainment and inspiration.

Finally, but certainly not least, I'd like to thank all the people who've ever gone on hikes with me to anywhere at any time. With this I offer my most sincere thanks to my friends. These include Tucker Spohr, Alan Julliard, Chris Irney, and Paul Berryhill who took me on my first trips into the Chugach Mountains during my first year of living in Anchorage. I would also like to thank all those who have since then regularly accompanied me on trips into the mountains. They put up with my whims of where to go and what route to follow, and at times suffered discomfort as a result, But for their patience in deeming them more adventures than inconveniences, I offer my heartfelt thanks to Tucker and Ginger Spohr, Niles Woods, Steve McKeever, Dave Volper, Jim Sayler, Jim Braham, Dan and Arlene Gerity, Donna Schwirtz, and Bruce Freifeld, as well as various new hiking companions in the Alaska Adventurers Meet-Up group.

The companionship and tolerance of all these has made many a mile all the more enjoyable on those near perfect days, all the more bearable on those less than perfect days, and the memories of both all the more meaningful.

# Table of Contents

**CHAPTER 1**

## CHAPTER 2

## CHAPTER 3

CHAPTER 4

# PROSPECT HEIGHTS TO GLEN ALPS _ _ _ _ _ _ _ _ _ _ _ _ _ 255

## CONNECTING TRAILS

## LOOP TRAILS

CHAPTER 5

# MIDDLE FORK CAMPBELL CREEK VALLEY _ _ _ _ _ _ _ _ 305

## CHAPTER 6

## NORTH FORK CAMPBELL CREEK VALLEY _ _ _ _ _ _ _ _ _ _ 371

## CHAPTER 7

## ARCTIC VALLEY _ _ _ _ _ _ _ _ _ _ _ _ _ _ _ _ _ _ _ _ _ _ _ _ _ 387

## CHAPTER 8

## HILLTOP SKI AREA _ _ _ _ _ _ _ _ _ _ _ _ _ _ _ _ _ _ _ _ _ _ _ _ 401

## CHAPTER 9



## CHAPTER 10



## CHAPTER 11

CHAPTER 12

SINGLE-TRACK BIKING IN THE ANCHORAGE BOWL _ _ _ _ 575

GRAND TOUR OF THE FRONT RANGE _ _ _ _ _ _ _ _ _ _ _ 593

CHAPTER 13

APPENDICES _ _ _ _ _ _ _ _ _ _ _ _ _ _ _ _ _ _ _ _ _ _ _ _ _ _ _ 603

ABOUT THE AUTHOR _ _ _ _ _ _ _ _ _ _ _ _ _ _ _ _ _ _ _ _ _ 608

# INTRODUCTION

This book, the second of four volumes of guides to Southcentral Alaska, journeys through the Front Range of the Chugach Mountains and across the length and breadth of the Anchorage bowl. The Front Range consists of the westernmost mountains in the Chugach. The eastern flank of the Front Range follows the distinct break in the mountains formed by the drainages of Ship Creek and Indian Creek as they flow in opposite directions from the crest of Ship Pass. From that divide the wide Ship Creek valley descends in a long curve around the back of Temptation Peak to where it pours through the wide gap just south of Rendezvous Peak down to Knik Arm, whereas the narrow Indian Creek valley descends a shorter and steeper slope south between the steep slopes of Bird Overlook and Indianhouse Mountain into Turnagain Arm. The western flank of the Front Range borders the Anchorage bowl, thus dominating the skyline on that side of the city. In all, this range extends approximately sixteen miles north to south and approximately 8 miles east to west, including another approximately thirteen miles across the Anchorage bowl to its westernmost point at the tip of Kincaid Park.

Rising so close to Anchorage, one can consider the Front Range and its foothills the playground of the city. On any given day of the week in any season one could very possibly find people climbing Flattop Mountain and Wolverine Peak, skiing up the Ship Pass valley, biking Powerline Trail, or napping alongside Rabbit Lake.

This does not mean the Front Range does not have its remote spots. On any given day of the week in any season one could easily climb Temptation Peak or Mount Elliot, hike alongside Long Lake, or even traverse the ridge directly behind Flattop and not see another human for hours or maybe even days.

Nor does the proximity of the Front Range to Anchorage mean it does not have its dangers. People perish on Flattop almost every year. Others die in avalanches, succumb to hypothermia, break bones in falls, get mauled by bears, or just lose their way.

In addition to the Front Range, the Anchorage bowl also serves as a playground for the city. Threaded by many miles of bike trails, ski trails, and hiking trails, it can satisfy almost any craving for outdoor activity. It even offers a couple of beaches—though these prove far better destinations for beachcombing than swimming.

In the bowl one can find many remote spots. During the summer the longer ski trails at Kincaid and Hillside feel the tread of but few feet. And even the most popular bike trails offer solitude during certain hours of the day or late evening. On such an evening one can even at times watch the alpenglow paint the Front Range pink from the rarely deserted shores of Westchester Lagoon—which can make for a serenely eerie memory.

# GRADING TRAILS

A System to Rate the Hikes

*If you are ready to leave father and mother, brother and sister, and wife and child and friends, and never see them again, —if you have paid your debts, and made your will, and settled all your affairs, and are a free man, then you are ready for a walk.*

H. D. Thoreau, *Walking*

Very few people take their hiking as seriously as did Thoreau. First, not everyone has the inclination, the time, or the energy to spend long hours as Thoreau did wandering the countryside around Concord, hiking on Cape Cod, or climbing Mount Katahdin. Second, most people consider it only a diversion from the everyday working world through which they can relax the mind, boost the morale, or just get a little change of scenery. They don't consider hiking absolutely necessary to the fulfillment of the spirit and the education of the mind.

Like Thoreau, I take my hiking seriously. Like him, I leave all other concerns behind me when I go out on a hike, especially a long hike. We differ, however, in much of the terrain we hike. Thoreau seemed to prefer walking great lengths as opposed to climbing great heights. Except for his climb of Katahdin, Thoreau did little climbing or scrambling. This may result simply from the nature of the terrain in which he lived. The area around Concord and nearby Walden Pond simply did not have terrain that offered a sustained climb of more than a few hundred feet or any need for scrambling. It seems probable that only on the rocky upper slopes of Mount Katahdin, located in the north woods of Maine, did Thoreau ever do any sustained climbing or extensive rock scrambling. Hiking in Alaska usually includes a substantial amount of both, simply because one will find it difficult to go anywhere in the mountains of Alaska without doing at least some climbing or scrambling. Maybe H. D. would have done far more climbing and scrambling if he lived in Alaska, or even near the high mountains of New Hampshire and Maine.

No matter how dedicated the walker traversing any variety of terrain, however, hiking does have its physical and mental limits. For this reason most people want to know the ease or difficulty they may have in hiking a certain trail or climbing a certain mountain. Nobody wants to bite off more than he or she can proverbially chew, no matter how good it tastes, for fear of the gastronomical discomforts it may cause. To prevent one from attempting a climb too high or a hike too long these volumes provide a grading system indicating the level of difficulty for each climb or hike.

In devising such a grading system one first has to ask a number of questions. Should one classify a climb according to its overall elevation gain or according to its steepness? Some elevation gains, like that of Bird Ridge, involve short and steep climbs whereas others, like the climb to Powerline Pass, involve long and shallow climbs. Should one rate the long, shallow climb the same as the short, steep one? The Turnagain Arm Trail gains approximately 1,300 feet in elevation over 9 miles of short ups and downs, whereas Flattop Mountain Trail gains approximately 1,300 feet in 1.5 miles of more or less continuous climbing. Should one rate them the same? And how should one rate the difference between climbing a well-trodden trail and climbing over trackless tundra? O'Malley Peak has a well-beaten track to its summit, whereas Tikishla Peak does not. Should one rate them the same? And should one rate a narrow and rocky trail the same as a wide and smooth trail?

In the end, it seemed best to grade climb difficulty according to three factors: (1) terrain (whether one hikes on-trail or off-trail), (2) elevation gain (how high and how steep one climbs), and (3) length (how far one hikes). All three factors remain important in determining the difficulty and length of any hike or climb.

Then there arises the question of children. Many children between the ages of 8 and 12 years may have the physical ability to the 8-mile round trip to the summit of Wolverine Peak and back, or even the 12 flatter miles to Williwaw Lakes and back. But their physical abilities don't always coincide with their will. I don't have children, but I have many memories of hiking and climbing as a child with my five siblings. Even the long car ride from Boston to the White Mountains of New Hampshire has its memories. Even before leaving Massachusetts the car would start to echo with six voices asking in erratic polyphony "Are we there yet?"

When my father took my younger brother Robert and I on our first hike up Mount Washington, the climb to Tuckerman's Ravine which makes up only the first third of the climb, took much longer than my 10-year-old mind could patiently endure, especially with a 20-pound load. "This takes *forever*," I regaled my father numerous times during that trek, "when will we get there?" We certainly had the physical ability to do it, but it seemed so long! Whether young enough that you must carry them or old enough that they can carry themselves, the distance on some of these climbs may prove more mentally than physically difficult for many children.

Such memories indicate the difficulty in establishing a grading system that works for both parents and children. In the end, one can only suggest that outings with children take less time and cover a shorter distance for both your and their peace of mind.

As to the grading of hikes, these volumes number hikes from 1 to 6, a numbering system similar to the grading system used in rock climbing, with one major difference: In this book Grade 6 entails non-technical rock scrambling and Grade 7 involves technical climbing. (Rock-climbing systems classify levels 5 and 6 as indirect-aid and direct-aid technical climbs, which they then often further differentiate by the use of decimals.) That said, here follows the grading system used in this book and its companion volumes:

**GRADE 1:** This grade denotes a flat, wide trail with a minimum of elevation gain (less than 250 feet per mile). Examples of a Grade 1 hike include Johnson Pass Trail, Eklutna Lake Trail, Upper Willow Creek Trail, and Alascom Road/Knob Hill Trail.

**GRADE 2:** This grade refers to a rougher trail with longer and slightly steeper climbs (250 to 750 feet per mile). Examples of a Grade 2 hike include Middle Fork Loop Trail, Resurrection Pass Trail, Snowbird Mine Trail, Eska Falls Trail, and the climb of Fortress Ridge.

**GRADE 3:** This grade denotes a steep trail with long, continuous climbs (750 or more feet per mile). Examples of a Grade 3 hike include Bird Ridge Trail, Pioneer Ridge Trail, Lazy Mountain Trail, and Belanger Pass Trail.

**GRADE 4:** This grade refers to the lowest level of off-trail hiking. It includes tundra walking with little or no bushwhacking on flat terrain or with only moderate gains in elevation (250 to 750 feet per mile). Examples of a Grade 4 hike, include Ship Lake Pass, Box Lake Overview, Bald Mountain, and Anthracite Ridge.

**GRADE 5:** This grade involves more difficult off-trail hiking. It entails tundra walking or bushwhacking with substantial elevation gain (750 to 1,500 feet per mile). Examples of a Grade 5 hike include The Ramp, Temptation Peak, Government Peak, Snowbird Glacier Overlook, Red Mountain, and Puddingstone Hill.

**GRADE 6:** This grade denotes off-trail hiking that requires extensive use of the hands. A route of this grade crosses very rough and steep terrain of mostly boulders, rocks, and scree in which the climbs are long and steep (1,500 feet or more per mile). The climb or scramble often includes some exposure. Examples of a Grade 6 climb include Hidden Peak, Mount Williwaw, Hurdygurdy Mountain, Bomber Glacier Overlook, Eska Peak, and Lava Peak.

**GRADE 7:** This grade involves technical climbing. A route of this level proves steep and exposed enough to require at least some belayed climbing and even the placement of some protection. Examples of Grade 7 climbing include Montana Peak, the Bomber Glacier Traverse, and rock-climbing the south face of Lions Head. It also include ice-climbing on Matanuska Glacier. Some people may also feel the need for roped protection on such climbs as Eagle Peak, Benign Peak, and Lynx Peak.

But the guides within contain far more than just the grades of various hikes and climbs. They also include the following informational categories to help readers decide which trail or hike best suits them or interests them the most:

**TRAIL LOCATION** appears first in each guide. This section gives driving directions to the trailhead and, if necessary, explains how to get to the trail from the parking area. It then provides a description of the trail or climb. In doing so, it points out landmarks and provides directions through any sections of the trail that may prove confusing because of the crisscrossing of this trail with other trails or roads, or because the trail may all but disappear in tundra or open country.

**TRAIL CONDITION** comes second. This section briefly provides information regarding the state of each trail—whether one may expect to find a rocky, muddy, or overgrown trail or a smooth, dry, and wide trail. Such a category seemed necessary because the difficulty of any hike has to do with more than just how far one walks or how high one climbs. It also has to do with how rough or smooth one finds the ground one walks over. Footing, after all, can slow a person down as much, or more, as climbing.

**TRAIL MILEAGE** appears next. This section includes, wherever applicable, both the one-way and the round-trip mileage for any trail or hike from a specific trailhead. Traverses, on the other hand, list only one-way mileages between two trailheads.

**TOTAL ELEVATION GAIN** comes fourth in the list. This section provides, as close as one can calculate without the use of electronics, the total gain and loss over every little knoll, spur, and hill from the beginning to the end of a particular trail or climb. In some cases, this amounts to little more than the overall difference in height from the beginning of the trail to the top of a pass or the highest point along any trail; in other cases, where the hike may cross over two or more very substantial ridges (or climb two or more summits), it lists the cumulative elevation gain of all the major climbs along a trail or hike. It often, therefore, adds up to a substantially higher total than the simple difference between the elevation of the highest point and the lowest point along any trail or hike.

**HIGHEST POINT** follows next. This section simply lists the highest point above sea level reached in any particular trail or climb.

**NORMAL HIKING TIME** appears sixth in each guide. This section estimates the probable number of hours or days it should take for most people to hike the specific trail or trip. Of course, some people, such as skiers and runners in training, go faster than the time mentioned. Others, such as those who have small children in tow or hike as part of a large party, may proceed more slowly. The times given should accommodate most people's pace. In the end, of course, one remains the best judge of one's own pace.

The category **CAMPSITES** takes up seventh position in each guide. This section includes both cabins and designated places to pitch a tent along the trail as well as other unofficial possibilities. This section also mentions any possible water sources. Of course, one need not camp only in the spots suggested. Keep in mind, however, that some areas, such as private land or Independence Mine State Park, remain closed to overnight camping. In addition, one breaks the law when building a fire in Chugach State Park. But apart from these restrictions, one can camp and build a campfire almost anywhere one chooses in the Kenai Mountains, Chugach Mountains, or Talkeetna Mountains. One should not do so haphazardly, though. Make sure to check fire conditions before building a fire anywhere in the mountains.

**BEST TIME** appears next in each guide. This designates the best time of year in which to do that particular hike or climb, a time frame that hopefully will maximize the enjoyment and minimize the danger of the hike. For instance, one might find some hikes, such as the climb of Rendezvous Peak, more enjoyable in late summer when the blueberries ripen and the tundra turns maroon. One should find other trips, such as the Arctic to Indian traverse, much easier in winter when the otherwise boggy and muddy Ship Creek valley freezes over. One may also find other trips may safer in certain seasons. Devil's Pass Trail, for instance, on the Kenai Peninsula, proves a very easy and safe trail in the summer. In winter, though, it turns into a very hard and dangerous route with many ice dams along its length and many avalanches continually rumbling down the steep-sided gorge the trail slabs through as it climbs up valley. Therefore, the time of year when one hikes a particular trail has as much to do with safety as with enjoyment.

Ninth and last appears the category of **USGS MAPS**. This listing specifies the United States Geological Survey Maps that show the area which the trail or climb passes through. Sometimes, but not very often, the maps even show the trail.

(Besides the USGS maps, one can also find a series of maps called Alaska Road and Recreation Maps, which have as much detail as the USGS maps. These maps also list all the current trails and trailheads, for which they provide short trail descriptions, points of interest, facilities available in nearby towns or villages, fishing spots, and other visitor information. These bigger, two-sided maps also show far more territory at a much lower cost than the USGS maps. The USGS maps, however, remain all-inclusive. Get enough of them and they show every square foot of Alaska in an easily understood grid system that allows one to place maps both side by side and above and below each other to create an ever-larger map.)

Those looking for global positioning system (GPS) coordinates in these guides will look in vain. I have left out such information for two reasons: First, it tends to take away the sense of discovery. Without this sense of discovery one largely loses that personal sense of adventure and involvement that result from bringing one's own powers of observation and calculation to a hike or climb. Many also tend to look down far too often at the tool in their hand rather than at the land ahead.

Second, and more important, it tends to make one over-reliant on technology. A large part of progress involves our ongoing reliance on increasingly complex tools that save us physical and mental labor. The horse-drawn plow and the calculator (and, one must admit, the machine gun) stand as notable examples. As a result, human beings today often compensate for the loss of this physical and mental activity through recreation. Running, biking, swimming, softball, basketball, and soccer replace the physical work we once did while plowing a field or building a cabin. This makes one wonder whether we have a hardwired need to use our bodies and minds. Certainly the widespread desire to visit the outdoors would indicate so. But now technology comes in such small packages that more and more people take it into the wilderness with them.

One wonders how many people need rescuing because of their overreliance on such tools. A friend related a mountain-biking trip he and others made in the Talkeetna Mountains in which someone's GPS indicated that the quickest route back to the Glenn Highway and the car led through a particular valley. This resulted in their wallowing for 3 miles in a boggy landscape. According to the narrator, some simple observations and calculations might have led them to forego the valley and take a slightly longer route that would have taken them along the crest of a much drier ridge back to the car. But the machine pointed straight ahead, and so the majority of the group wanted to forge straight ahead. In the end they spent over two hours pushing their bikes across the low and boggy valley instead of riding for one hour along the high and dry adjacent ridge.

One does need some tools, such as a map and a compass. But such tools still compel one to actively observe and calculate and then reach reasoned deductions, rather than reacting to a stated conclusion provided by an electronic gadget. (Nor do batteries die on a compass.) The gadget states facts; a map and a compass help a thinking person reach conclusions. As Al Meiners, a former superintendent of Chugach State Park used to say, "The best gear is between your ears." Relying too much on GPS we end up using our brain less, much to our own endangerment. Yet many insist on carrying those technologies with them—handy tools for survival, perhaps, but not necessarily helpful tools for hiking.

That said, anyone can certainly add GPS coordinates to these hikes and climbs. Many other hikers and climbers may welcome such information. I will admit to enjoy seeing a GPS outline of a hike over a Google Earth map—but only after the hike. I simply prefer to remain a Luddite for the sheer enjoyment of taking a more active mental role in any trip into the outdoors.

With that said, a quick key should suffice in understanding the maps that accompany each Walk-About Guide. Though most people should find them largely self-explanatory, the reader should note that the shading on the maps indicates changes in elevation. The darkest gray indicates water, and the white indicates permanent snow. Between these two extremes the lighter gray shading indicates areas below tree line while the darker gray areas denote locations above tree line. All the maps in this book also label all other trails found in the vicinity of the highlighted trail that corresponds to that particular Walk-About Guide. One can find the Walk-About Guides and specific maps for many of these secondary labeled trails in other chapters of this book.

Of course, the list of trails in this book remains far from exhaustive. One can find many other trails in the Kenai, Chugach, and Talkeetna mountains not covered in this book. Two reasons lie behind this. First, this book contains guides only for trails and climbs I have personally done. Second, many other trails cross private property. As such, this book contains only guides to trails, hikes, and climbs that the public can legally access. Other hikes and climbs have not found their way into these pages simply because of lack of space. Maybe these various hikes and climbs, as well as new hikes and climbs done in the interim may find their way into future volumes.

Finally, although I have included a chapter on what I carry on my hikes and climbs, I do not, overall, consider this a "how-to" book. One should not look in these pages for tips on how to respond to bears, how to analyze snow conditions, or how to read changes in wind direction and cloud patterns. Nor should one consider this a book on basic wilderness skills such as crossing a river, traversing a glacier, purifying water, and so forth. One can find other books for that, such as *55 Ways to the Wilderness in Southcentral Alaska* by Helen D. Nienhueser and John Wolfe, Jr., *A Naturalist's Guide to Chugach State Park* by Jenny Zimmerman, and *Hiking Alaska* by Dean Littlepage. All three books contain excellent reading on what to carry and wear, how to act and react to terrain and animals, and how to read snow and weather conditions, all important for anyone who wants not just to survive but also to enjoy moving in the mountains of Southcentral Alaska. Nor should one consider this a guide to flora and fauna, knowledge of which this author sorely lacks. Those interested in identifying wildlife and plant life will find many publications to choose from, including *Guide to the Birds of Alaska* by Robert H. Armstrong (who also has written some reference books about fish and fishing in Alaska), *Field Guide to Alaskan Wildflowers* by Verna E. Pratt (one of a number of books on wildflowers in Alaska by the same author), *Alaska Trees and Shrubs* by Leslie A. Vierick and Elbert A. Little, Jr., and *Mammals of Alaska,* published by the Alaska Geographic Society.

Though primarily guides for hiking and climbing, those who want to engage in other outdoor activities apart from hiking may find this and its companion volumes of some use. This holds especially true for people traveling on skis and snowshoes. Not only do many hiking trails of summer also serve as good skiing routes in the winter, but winter even sometimes makes certain dubious summer trips into excellent winter outings. Such winter-only outings include the Ship Creek traverse and the crossing of Portage Lake. Other trips, like Seven Lakes Trail and the Crescent Lake to Carter Lake traverse can prove all the more enjoyable in winter when one can cross frozen lakes and rivers.

Road cyclists and mountain-bikers should find these books of considerable use. Besides describing some of the obvious mountain-biking routes, such as Eklutna Lakeside Trail, Jim Creek Trail, and Matanuska Railroad Grade, they also list most major bike trails and bike parks, including the Bird to Girdwood Bike Trail, the major bike trails in the Anchorage bowl, as well as many parks and locations to mountain-bike, including Mount Alyeska, Kincaid Park, and Government Hill Recreation Area. Many trail guides also specifically list whether one will find a particular trail open to biking. One can also often determine the feasibility of biking any particular trail or route by reading these guides. Those still wishing to read books specifically 'geared' to biking the trails in Alaska should refer to the late Richard Larson's book *Mountain Bike Alaska: 49 Trails in the 49th State* as well as *Mountain Bike Anchorage* by Rosemary Austin.

It probably goes without saying that most canoe, kayak, and pack-raft enthusiasts will find little to glean from these books. They may find information about some trails useful for how to access the upper reaches of a creek or river. For example, if they wish to find a route to access Crescent Creek Trail, Gold Mint Trail, and Chickaloon River Trail, they may find these guides useful. But they should find such trails more the exception than the rule herein.

Snowmachiners, ATVers, and motorcyclists will find even less useful information in these books. For one, most of the trails in these books prohibit motorized traffic. Second, many of the trails also prove too steep and narrow for any motorized vehicle. Admittedly, one can come across a jeep or ATV in the most unexpected places—at the headwaters of Caribou Creek or on a ridge high above the Kenai River—but the rarity of such meetings make them all the more surprising. Many places simply remain more accessible on foot than on machine.

Thus, in the end, regardless of other possible means of travel, this book's intended for those who desire to move through the wilds through bipedal locomotion—whether that locomotion utilizes running shoes, boots, skis, or snowshoes.

# MY PACK

One should not consider a pack a mere accessory. Nor should one consider it a statement of outdoor fashion. One should not imagine it need epitomize the latest advances in outdoor technology. On should not even consider it merely a satchel meant to make a day of hiking more comfortable. One should look upon it as a survival kit.

After more than ten years of use, my pack has faded from a shiny new blue to a scuffed and faded azure. Dirt streaks, water stains, and frayed stitches all give further evidence of its age and long use. This old pack does not have the newest hi-tech strap system to finely balance the weight and size of the load to the body. Nor does it have any detachable pockets or accessory buckles. It consists simply of a non-waterproof bucket with three pockets on the outside.

Yet despite its age, this worn, sagging sack goes on every trip I make. Whether on an hour-long stroll up Flattop Mountain or a 24-hour-long hike through the Talkeetna Mountains, I carry that pack and it often becomes the last buffer between surviving and not surviving. However melodramatic that may sound, it remains the simple truth. Putting on an extra jacket when the temperatures drop or a raincoat when the precipitation falls has staved off hypothermia many times. Donning a headlamp when day deepens into night has lit the way back to the car on many long hikes. Eating that extra candy bar or energy bar can also provide just enough of a boost to finish the last miles after having gone out too far or too deep. Having an extra pair of socks or mittens has saved toes and fingers when the frost began to thicken. The pack becomes one's portable home, containing the possible means of survival for the thin-skinned and weak-stomached human creature that carries it.

Recognizing my pack as the means to survival in the wilds, I try to use some care when deciding what to put into it, first, to keep the load light and, second, to keep the load simple. If weight did not matter, I could obviously carry everything for every occasion: a tent, a stove, a sleeping bag, a sleeping mattress, a fishing rod, a pack raft, and maybe even some binoculars. Too heavy a load, however, often proves as dangerous as too light a load. It tires the body and slows the pace—possibly leading to too long a day, too tiring a hike, and too dulled a brain, all of which could result in any number of problems, including an accident or hypothermia. So instead of carrying everything for anything that could happen, I try to carry only select things for what might happen. And to keep the load simple, my choices remain simple: I do not need to carry three different-weight sweaters or two hats or even a wide choice of food. These things merely add weight and confusion to the pack.

Keeping these goals in mind, I start with the bucket, which I fill with items necessary to the body's survival. First I think of long-term survival. I try to imagine the worst weather I can encounter—the lowest temperature, the hardest precipitation, the highest winds. I try to imagine how these weather conditions could affect me. In order to prepare for the worst, I first stuff a thick fiber pile jacket into the bottom of the pack. Alongside this I push a knee-length rain parka, which even if it makes me sweat, still keeps me warm. Finally, I shove down next to the parka a pair of neoprene gloves that will keep my fingers warm while climbing wet snow or hiking in the rain. Then I start thinking about an emergency food supply which I can turn to if I end up staying out longer than expected. Inside the jacket and parka I nestle a quart-size Tupperware container filled with candy, energy bars, and vitamins. (One could also fill this with a sandwich, dried fruit, and even cut vegetables.) These items take care of most extreme condition changes. Finally, I shove a zip-lock plastic bag containing a roll of toilet paper down the lower outside of the bucket.

Next, I start thinking of lesser changes in air and body temperature. For comfort from hour to hour, I carry a green nylon stuff sack containing smaller items that could easily get lost in the corners and folds of the bucket if packed separately. The stuff sack, on the other hand, remains readily easy, even in the darkest night. In this sack I carry extra mittens with waterproof shells, wool socks, waterproof

over-socks, a wool cap, and a long underwear top. In early spring or
fall I might also put in some long underwear bottoms and a pair of
instep crampons. A small zippered nylon wallet containing my car
keys and some cash also goes in this sack. This may seem strange, but
sometimes one comes out of the woods or mountains far from the
place where one started and the money may then come in handy for a
bus, a taxi, or even just a drink at any nearby convenience store or bar.
(The restaurant on Boretide Road off Seward Highway, for instance,
makes for a wonderful place to stop and sip a hot drink on a cold
winter night after having done the Arctic to Indian traverse.) Next to
this green stuff sack containing extra clothes, I squeeze another red
stuff sack of high-energy food such as hard candies, candy bars, and
some Pop-Tarts.(One might also consider carrying Spirulia tablets
and Cliff Bars in this sack.)

At the top of the bucket I then fold a wind suit. I make the wind
so suit readily accessible because it functions as an all-purpose piece
of clothing that not only protects the body from the wind, but can
also keep in warmth on a cold day or keep out a spitting rain or dry
snow on a gray day. I often find myself donning it on chilly mornings
before even leaving the car at the beginning of a hike. Weighing only a
few ounces, the wind parka and pants have benefits that far outweigh
the effort of carrying them. I never leave home without them. Next
to the wind suit I slip a quart-size plastic water bottle.

Now, having taking care of the body's survival in the main bucket,
I pack the pocket on the back of the pack with the items specifically
needed for each individual trip. First, I put in the appropriate maps for
the hike. I slide these into zip-lock plastic bags for protection and then
lay them as flat as possible along the back of the pocket. In another
zip-lock plastic bag I carry a small notepad, pen, and pencil for taking
notes and jotting down ideas while on the hike. Into this second plastic
bag I also put a wristwatch and a whistle. The whistle warns wildlife
of my whereabouts in thick brush. Then I insert sunglasses and an
extra pair of light gloves into this back pocket.

Finally, I turn my attention to the last essential items. These items
which I do not need very often, but occasionally *really* need, go in
the side pockets. Into one of these pockets I slip a wool cap wrapped

around a multi-tooled, all-purpose, top-of-the-line Swiss army knife. Though a bit heavy, the knife has just about every tool for every emergency; it lacks only the legendary Saint Bernard carrying a flask of brandy under its chin. This pocket also holds a small Tupperware container holding a small bottle of Ibuprofen, some antibiotic cream, a pile of Band-Aids, two or three packets different types of powder juices, and a compass. In the other pocket I stow a metal Sierra Cup for drinking out of springs and streams, and inside the Sierra Cup I tuck a small roll of duct tape and a headlamp. One last item which I also consider essential for every hike hangs off the waist strap of the pack: my camera bag. Besides a camera, this small sack contains a miniature tripod, extra flash cards, and one or two extra batteries.

Though not specifically connected with the pack, what I wear and carry also have some importance on any given day spent in the wilds. Depending on the weather, I start most hikes wearing a pair of shorts, a turtleneck shirt, and a hat with a visor. Depending on the temperature, I may also wear a light sweater and even wear either or both the top and bottom of the wind suit. Depending on where I'm going, I also carry either an ice ax or a walking stick. Although the ice axe has its particular uses in snow, both of these can help in pushing through brush, fording streams, and crossing boulders. Both tools can also be attached to the pack if necessary; so the pack can, in essence, carry everything.

My pack carries within it my wariest anticipations of the worst weather (as in the pile jacket and rain parka I have stuffed in its base) and my fondest expectations for the best weather (as in the sunglasses and shorts I either wear or carry in the back pocket). It also carries the food I need for both the hike itself and any unplanned extra time. My pack also keeps me on a planned route through the maps I carry in the back pocket. These maps also make known other options if the first route does not work out. My pack also allows me to travel after dark with the headlamp stowed under the Sierra Cup. My pack even allows me to keep records of passing fancies and long meditations using the pen and paper stored with the maps.

My pack, in short, remains my closest and most constant companion in the wilds. It has helped me keep off rain, cold, sun, and bugs. It has also helped stave off hypothermia and frostbite. As such, it has probably kept death at a distance many times, although I never knew it simply because I always had the pack on my back, close at hand, with everything I needed for such situations.

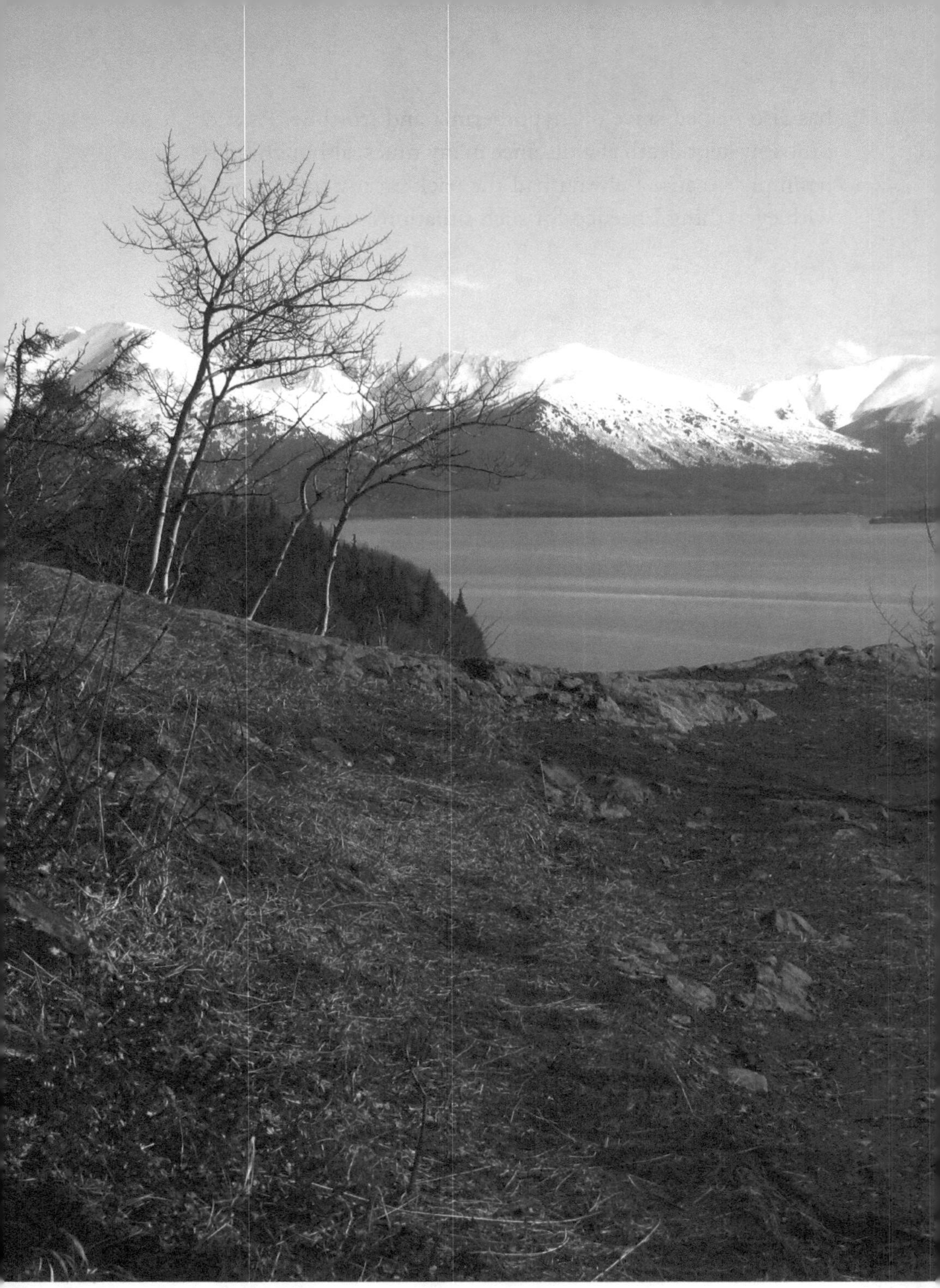

CHAPTER 1

# TURNAGAIN ARM

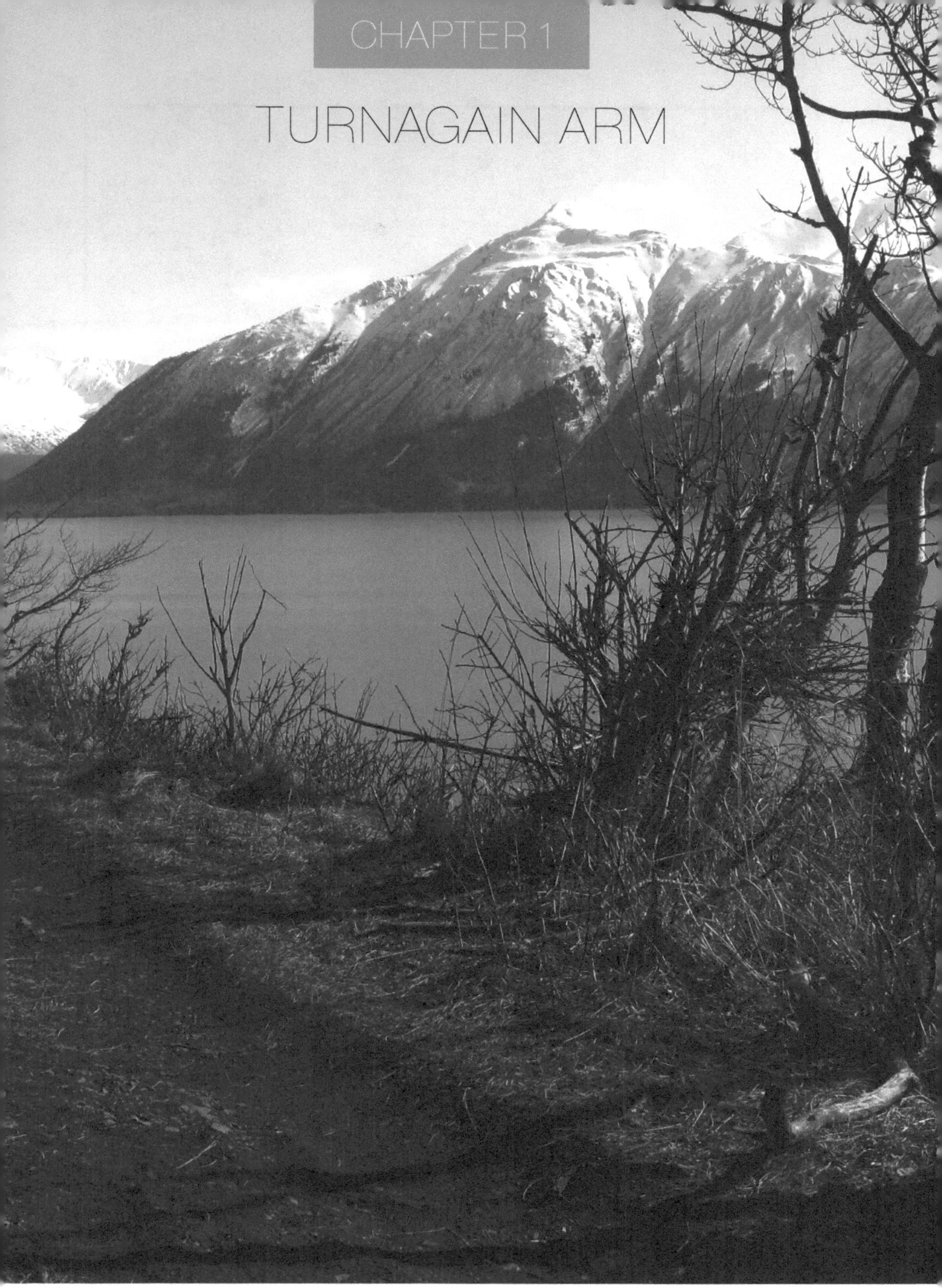

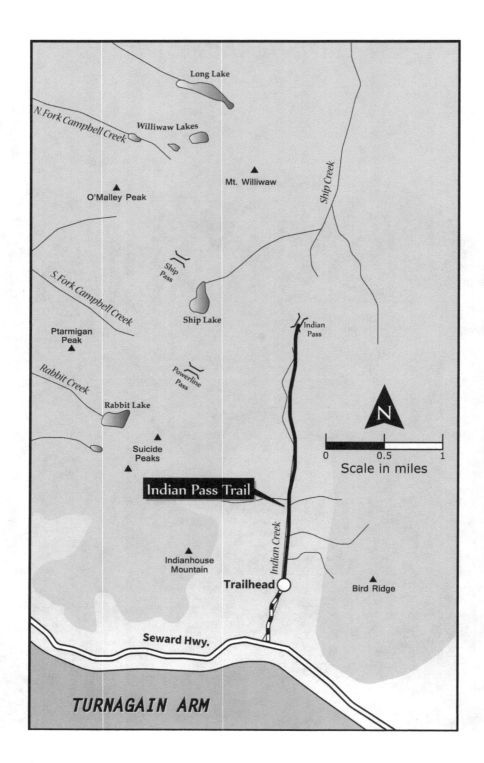

Long Lake

N. Fork Campbell Creek

Williwaw Lakes

Mt. Williwaw

Ship Creek

O'Malley Peak

Ship Pass

S. Fork Campbell Creek

Ship Lake

Indian Pass

Ptarmigan Peak

Powerline Pass

Rabbit Creek

Rabbit Lake

**Indian Pass Trail**

N

0    0.5    1
Scale in miles

Suicide Peaks

Indian Creek

Indianhouse Mountain

**Trailhead**

Bird Ridge

**Seward Hwy.**

**TURNAGAIN ARM**

# Walk-About Guide to Indian Valley Trail

This trail, which climbs from just off Turnagain Arm to Indian Creek Pass forms the southern separation between the Front Range to the west and the Chugach Mountains extending east to Girdwood and beyond. From its uppermost end on the crest of the pass one can look down almost entire length of the spacious Ship Creek valley to where it swings out of sight around the base of Temptation Peak at the northernmost end of the Front Range. Only when looking down this valley from the pass (or up the valley from Rendezvous Peak, located just across the valley from Temptation Peak) does one realize how isolated the Front Range actually seems from the rest of the Chugach.

**TRAIL LOCATION:** Indian Valley Trail begins at the upper end of Boretide Road in the Indian Creek valley. To get there drive 23 miles south from Anchorage on the Seward Highway. There, just past Milepost 104, take a left (north) turn onto Boretide Road next to Turnagain Arm BBQ Pit. Continue on Indian Road for 0.5 miles to a fork in the road. Bear right at this fork and continue for another 0.5 miles to the trailhead. Park wherever possible. The trail starts on the left (west) side of the parking area.

The trail begins by almost immediately by passing under the power lines heading up and over Powerline Pass. In the woods on the far side the trail soon reaches a junction with the beginning of Powerline Trail leading across a bridge on the left (east)*. Keeping to the right, continue along the Indian Valley Trail as it leads away from the bridge

---

* For more information about that trail, which most people access from Glenn Alps parking area, see [31] **Walk-About Guide to Powerline Trail** in Chapter 3.

and deeper into the woods. One soon reaches the right (east) shore of Indian Creek. Turning upstream, follow the trail as it continues alongside the creek's bank. Within 1 mile the trail crosses to the left (west) side of Indian Creek. For the next approximately 4 miles the trail parallels the creek as it slowly ascends the long, wide valley. As it approaches tree line, the trail crosses back over the creek and begins to climb at a steeper angle away from the creek. Approximately 1 mile later it leaves all but spruce trees behind as it nears tree line. After another more gradual 0.25 miles of climbing the trail reaches its uppermost end on the crest of the brush-covered summit of Indian Creek Pass (2,350 feet).

At this point one has three major options. First, one can turn around and return the way they've come. Second, depending on conditions, one can continue ahead, following Ship Creek valley all the way to Arctic Road.* The third option, for the truly ambitious, involves climbing Bird Ridge Overlook (4,600 feet) towering high above immediately to the east and then following its southern ridge back to Bird Ridge and down Bird Ridge Trail**. A possible fourth option, also for the ambitious, entails climbing one of the nearby peaks stretching above the east side of the pass, such as Bidarka (3,835 feet) and Shaman Dome (4,010 feet) or even turning the corner to the left (west) just down valley and climbing over Ship Lake Pass back to Glen Alps***.

**TRAIL GRADE:** This trail rates predominantly Grade 1 as a hike, with some short sections of Grade 2 hiking on the final 1.5 miles to the pass.

**TRAIL CONDITION:** The trail varies little in its condition. The trail crosses many muddy sections in its first 3 miles. As the summer progresses, many chest-high grasses and brush begin to bend over the trail higher

---

\* For more information about that trip, see [2] **OPTION A—Indian to Arctic Traverse** below.

\*\* For more information about that route, see [119] **OPTION A—Bird Ridge Overlook** in Volume One of this series of guidebooks.

\*\*\* For more information about that route, see [37] **OPTION C—Ship Lake Pass** in Chapter 3.

up, slowing the going considerably. During the mid-season, however, some sections make for some quite fine walking. In addition, new trail work has resulted in some fine bridgework across some of the many stream and drainage trenches the trail crosses.

**TRAIL MILEAGE:** To go from the parking area at the trailhead to the crest of Indian Creek Pass entails approximately 5.5 miles of hiking, for a round-trip total of 11 miles.

**TOTAL ELEVATION GAIN:** To hike from the parking area to the crest of Indian Creek Pass entails a total elevation gain of approximately 2,100 feet.

**HIGH POINT:** This trail reaches its highest point of 2,350 feet above sea level at the crest of Indian Creek Pass.

**NORMAL HIKING TIME:** The hike from the parking area to the crest of Indian Creek Pass should take anywhere from 4 to 7 hours, depending on the condition and ambition of the hiker(s) involved.

**CAMPSITES:** One will find no designated campsites along this trail. One will find many fine places on which to pitch a tent, however, both in the open tundra at the pass or tucked among the stunted spruce on the slopes nearby.

**BEST TIME:** Most people should find any time from May to October a good time to do this hike. Many will also find that this trail make for a fine ski or snowshoe outing in the winter*.

**USGS MAPS:** Seward D-7 NW and Anchorage A-7.

-------------------------------------------------------------------

* For more information about this trail as a winter outing, see [2] **OPTION A—Indian to Arctic Traverse** as well as [2] **OPTION A—Arctic to Indian Traverse** in Chapter 1 of Volume Three of this series of guidebooks.

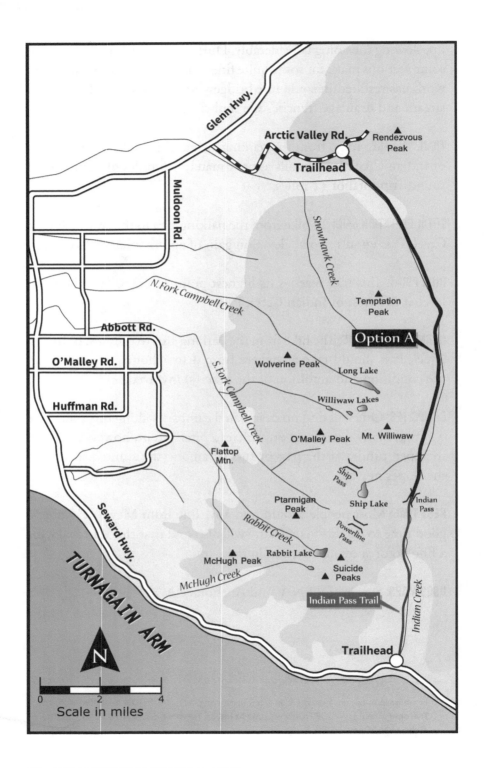

Glenn Hwy.

Arctic Valley Rd.

Rendezvous Peak

Trailhead

Muldoon Rd.

Snowhawk Creek

N. Fork Campbell Creek

Temptation Peak

**Option A**

Abbott Rd.

O'Malley Rd.

Huffman Rd.

S. Fork Campbell Creek

Wolverine Peak

Long Lake

Williwaw Lakes

O'Malley Peak

Mt. Williwaw

Flattop Mtn.

Ship Pass

Ship Lake

Indian Pass

Ptarmigan Peak

Rabbit Creek

Powerline Pass

Seward Hwy.

McHugh Peak

Rabbit Lake

Suicide Peaks

McHugh Creek

Indian Pass Trail

Indian Creek

**TURNAGAIN ARM**

N

Trailhead

0    2    4

Scale in miles

# OPTION A

# Indian to Arctic Traverse

This trip, one of the most popular winter outings for many outdoor aficionados, traverses almost the entire length of the Ship Creek and Indian Creek valleys that mark the back side of the Front Range of the Chugach Mountains. Good reasons underlie this popularity. First, this traverse begins and ends very close to Anchorage. Second, it travels through a largely wide-open and seemingly remote and pristine landscape. Third, it has little to no avalanche danger for almost its entire length.

Though most people prefer to begin this hike on Arctic Valley Road—primarily because traveling north to south requires far more elevation loss than gain—traveling south to north does have some advantages. First, the views predominantly improve the farther one progresses. Second, one can enjoy the long, gradual, near-11-mile slant that follows Ship Creek downstream before the final 1.5 mile climb up to Arctic Valley Road*.

**TRAIL LOCATION:** This traverse begins by following Indian Valley Trail to its uppermost end at Indian Creek Pass (2,350 feet)**. From this point one now begins the long and gradual descent along Ship Creek. Start by heading approximately 1.5 miles down the left (west) side of the valley to where Ship Creek emerges from Ship Pass valley on the

--------------------------------------------------------------------

\* Those still preferring to do this traverse beginning in Arctic Valley, see [ 2 ] **Arctic to Indian Traverse** in Chapter 1 of Volume Three of this series of guidebooks.

\*\* To get there. see [ 1 ] **Walk-About Guide to Indian Valley Trail** above.

left (west). Continue for the next approximately 3.5 miles to where North Fork Ship Creek, flowing out of the wide valley to the right (east), joins Ship Creek in the near center of the wide valley. At this confluence, look for the first available place to cross to the right (east) bank of the creek.

Though no definite trail or route winds down valley, from this point, it generally remains best to remain on the right side of Ship Creek while following it downstream. Where Ship Creek makes a wide bend down and to the left (northwest) toward Knik Arm, look for trail markers indicating the lower end of Ship Creek Trail that climbs up to Arctic Valley Road. If one comes upon no markers, look for tracks in the snow indicating where others have passed. (Usually some evidence of skiers passing this way before should make itself evident by at least a shallow dimple in the snow.) If all else fails look for an obvious opening in the trees and follow it upward.

From Ship Creek Trail one begins the final approximately 1.5-mile climb to Arctic Valley Road. As one approaches the road the trail begins to climb more steeply. But this steeper climbing does not last long. In less than 0.5 miles the trail emerges from the woods onto a long, wide pullout a little more than 0.5 miles below the Alpenglow Ski Area.

For those wanting to spot a car at this pullout, drive north on the Glenn Highway to the Arctic Valley Road exit 6 miles north of Anchorage. (Those coming from Eagle River will want to take the JBER-Richardson exit and, after crossing over the highway, follow the signs to Arctic Valley.) Follow Arctic Valley Road straight past Moose Run Golf Course on the left and the driving range on the right. Continue driving upward as the paved road gives way to gravel and begins winding upward for approximately 5 more miles. A little more than 0.5 miles below the Alpenglow Ski Area the road comes to a long parking area on the right (south). This parking area marks the trailhead for Ship Creek Trail (elevation 1,950 feet).

**TRAIL CONDITION:** The conditions along this winter route vary according to both the weather and frequency of use by other snowshoers and skiers. After a heavy snowfall one should expect to break trail for most of the way. On the other hand, if one undertakes it sometime after the last snowfall, one has a good chance of finding a well-broken trail up the entire valley. Sometimes this trail consists of nothing more than two ski slots in the snow. Sometimes it consists of a wide trough. It all depends on who has traveled the traverse before one and when.

**TRAIL MILEAGE:** To go from the parking area for Indian Valley Trail to the parking area on Arctic Valley Road entails approximately 21 miles of skiing, snowshoeing, or (in exceptional conditions) hiking.

**TOTAL ELEVATION GAIN:** To ski, snowshoe, or hike from the parking area for Indian Valley Trail to the parking area on Arctic Valley Road entails a total elevation gain of approximately 2,800 feet. Whereas to ski, snowshoe, or hike from Arctic Valley Road to the parking area for Indian Valley Trail entails a total elevation gain of approximately 1,250 feet.

**HIGH POINT:** This traverse reaches its highest point of 2,350 feet above sea level at the crest of Indian Creek Pass.

**NORMAL HIKING TIME:** To ski, snowshoe, or hike from the parking area for Indian Valley Trail to the parking area on Arctic Valley Road should take anywhere from 8 hours to 2 days, depending on the condition and ambition of the skier(s), snowshoer(s), or hiker(s) involved.

**CAMPSITES:** One will find no designated campsites along this trail. One will find, however, that almost any spot along the length of this traverse makes a fine place on which to pitch a tent in the winter.

**BEST TIME:** Most people should find any time from late October to late April a good time to do this hike, with late February and March usually considered ideal because of the longer daylight hours and slightly warmer daytime temperatures.

Although this traverse remains popular in the winter, one should think twice about doing it in the summer. In that time of year the route will prove muddy, brushy, boggy, and excessively bug-ridden.

**USGS MAPS:** Seward D-7 and Anchorage A-7.

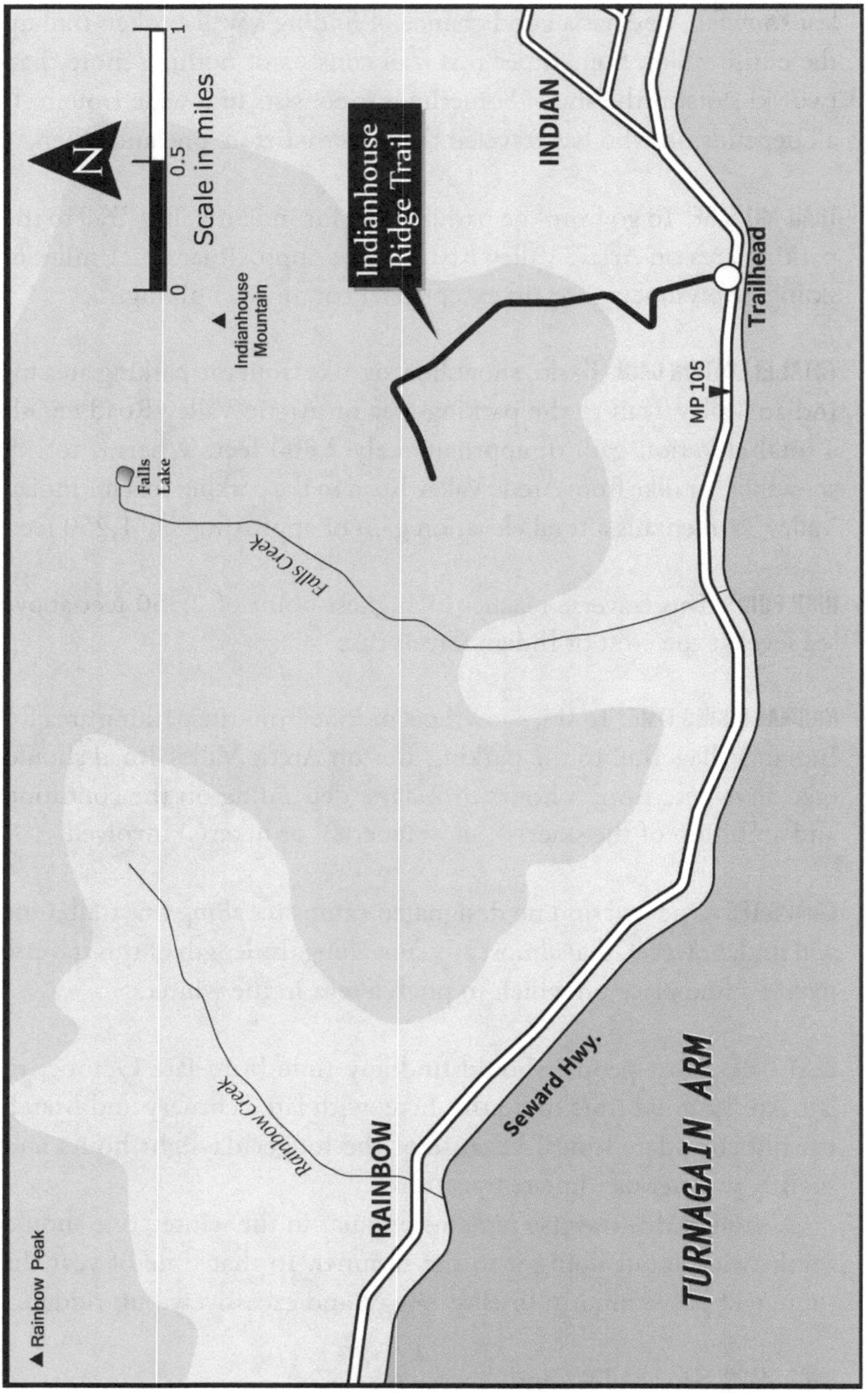
Scale in miles
0
0.5
1
Indianhouse Mountain
Indianhouse Ridge Trail
INDIAN
Trailhead
MP 105
Falls Lake
Falls Creek
Rainbow Peak
Rainbow Creek
RAINBOW
Seward Hwy.
TURNAGAIN ARM

# Walk-About Guide to Indianhouse Ridge Trail

Like Rainbow Peak Trail and McHugh Peak Trail, this unofficial trail provides access to one of the prominent peaks along the north side of Turnagain Arm. Like most other unofficial hiker-forged trails in the Chugach, this narrow trail climbs steeply and directly. But though narrow and steep, this trail, also like other trails of its kind, offers expansive and dramatic views. In this trail's instance, those views extend up and down the length of Turnagain Arm. Finally, like most other trails like it, this trail offers the only access to a summit which otherwise may prove inaccessible to most hikers. If not for the trail, the bushwhacking required and lack of any route to follow in just reaching tree line would discourage most people from even considering climbing such a peak.

**TRAIL LOCATION:** Indianhouse Ridge Trail begins about halfway between Falls Creek Trail and Indian Valley Mine on Seward Highway. To get there drive approximately 22.5 miles south on the Seward Highway from Anchorage to milepost 104.5, located a little over 0.5 miles past a turnout some call "the icebox"—a small grotto into which drips numerous rivulets of spring water. Here one will reach a short and narrow turnout on the left (north) side of the highway. Turn into this pullout and park wherever available. If one finds this parking area too crowded, one can find another pullout on the right (south) side of the highway approximately 200 yards further along the Seward Highway.

From the parking area follow the low-angled trail leading into the woods in the middle of the pullout. A short way into the woods, the trail makes a sharp switchback to the left (west). After a short climb, the trail climbs to the opening below the power lines higher up the slope. Climbing very gently, the trail soon reaches an opening that offers expansive views both up and down Turnagain Arm.

After this easy beginning, the trail reveals its true nature. About halfway across this clearing, look for a second narrow trail that switchbacks up to the right (east) off the main trail. Turn up and onto this trail, which marks the true beginning of Indianhouse Mountain Ridge Trail.

Climbing at a steep angle, this trail begins by cutting up and across the open face of the ridge. At the crest of this open face, the trail eases slightly in its angle before reaching thick wall of downed trees. Though not obvious at first, here the trail continues over a rock outcrop and down into the woods on the right (east) end of the downed trees.

Climbing at a gentler angle the trail winds up through the narrow wall of woods to the more exposed brushy slopes above. There it contours around the right (east) side of the ridge. On the far side of the ridge the trail turns left (north) and begins climbing steeply again. After climbing over a number of short rocky outcrops the trail eventually reaches the obvious crest of the ridge. At this point the climbing, though still steep at times, seems far less exposed.

In another approximately 0.5 miles of climbing the trail reaches the crest of the southeast buttress of Indianhouse Mountain from where one can now look up to the entire impressive east face of the mountain dominating the western sky.

Many people prefer to stop at this fine scenic spot. More ambitious climbers, however, may wish to continue up to the obvious saddle silhouetted by the sky approximately 800 feet higher up on the ridge crest. To reach that saddle, begin by turning left and continuing up the trail. Stay on the trail as it winds up the crest of the buttress to the saddle.

From the saddle one can enjoy dramatic views of Falls Creek valley directly below and the south face of South Suicide Peak off to the right (north).

Experienced climbers at this point may wish to reach the true summit of Indianhouse Mountain[*].

---

[*]  For information about that climb, see [4] **OPTION A—Indianhouse Mountain**.

**TRAIL GRADE:** This trail rates a relentless and difficult Grade 3. At times some of the scrambling should rate a Grade 5, except for the fact that this scrambling takes place on the trail. Well above the last trees, the trail reverts to a more tame Grade 3 hike as it climbs the upper ridge to the crest of the buttress and from there turns up to the saddle on the summit ridge.

**TRAIL CONDITION:** Consisting mostly of gravel interspersed with short rock faces and outcrops, this trail has, despite its steep angle at times, surprisingly firm footing when dry. One might consider avoiding it in wet weather however, when much of the trail turns to slick mud.

**TRAIL MILEAGE:** To hike from the beginning of the trail on the Seward Highway to the saddle on the south ridge of Indianhouse Mountain entails approximately 1.9 miles of hiking, for a round-trip total of 3.6 miles.

**TOTAL ELEVATION GAIN:** To hike from the beginning of the trail in the pullout on the Seward Highway to the scenic spot below the east face of the mountain entails a total elevation gain of approximately 3,100 feet. To hike from the beginning of the trail on the Seward Highway to the saddle in the south ridge of Indianhouse Mountain entails a total elevation gain of approximately 3,400 feet.

**HIGH POINT:** This trail reaches its highest point of approximately 3,450 feet above sea level on saddle on the south ridge of Indianhouse Mountain.

**NORMAL HIKING TIME:** To hike from the beginning of the trail at the pullout on the Seward Highway to either scenic spot below the east face of the mountain or to the saddle on the south ridge of Indianhouse Mountain and back should take anywhere from 2 to 5 hours, depending on the condition and ambition of the hiker(s) involved.

**CAMPSITES:** One will find no designated camping areas on this trail. For the novelty of the location and the magnificence of the views, one could pitch a tent on the first buttress of the ridge, but one will find no readily available water at this height.

**BEST TIME:** Most people should find any time from early June to late September a good time to do this hike. One should avoid this climb in winter, however, when the steepness of the slope and the distinct possibility of avalanches make the climbing dangerous for all but the most experienced mountaineers.

**USGS MAPS:** Seward D-7 and Anchorage A-7.

Indianhouse Ridge Trail

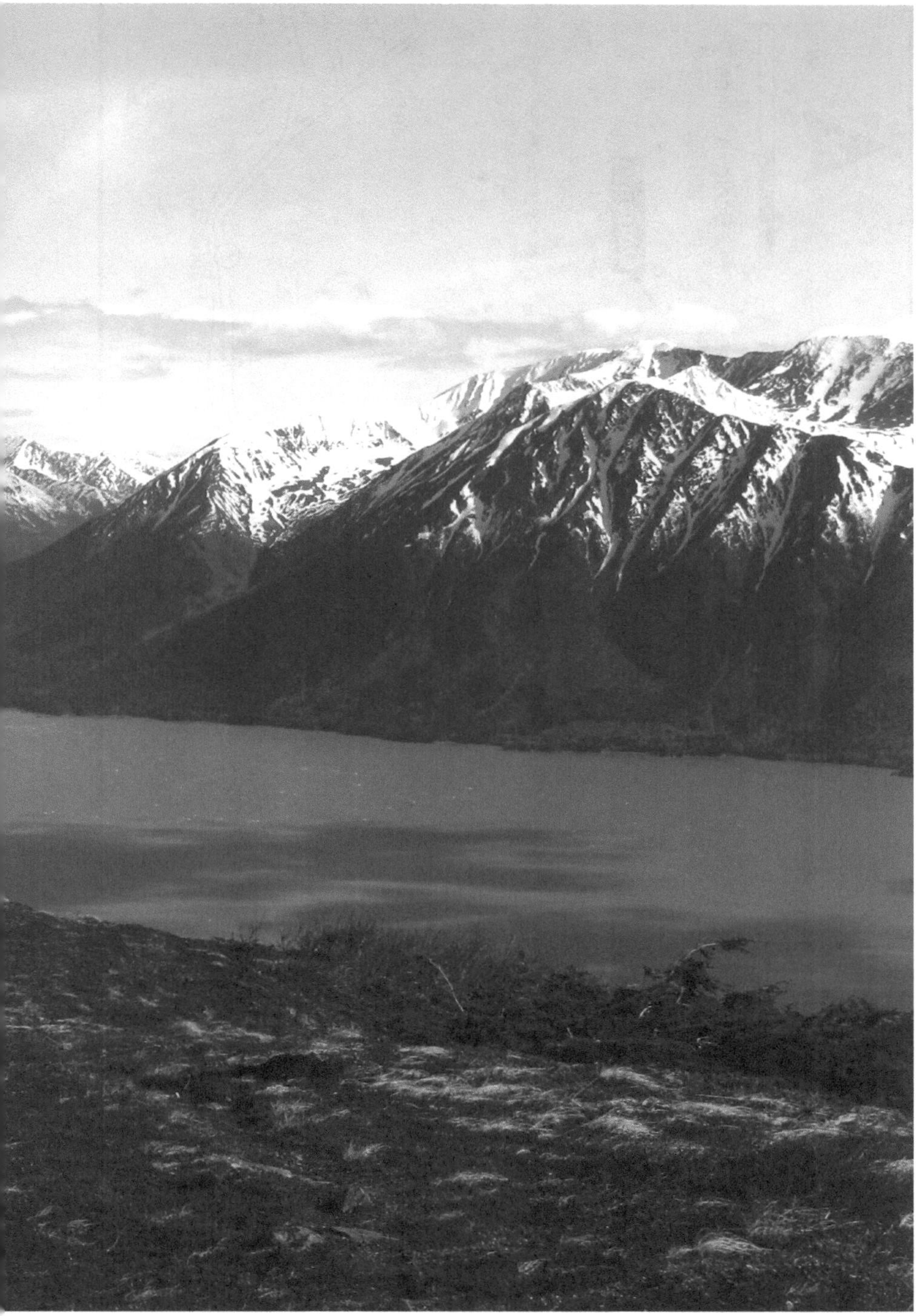

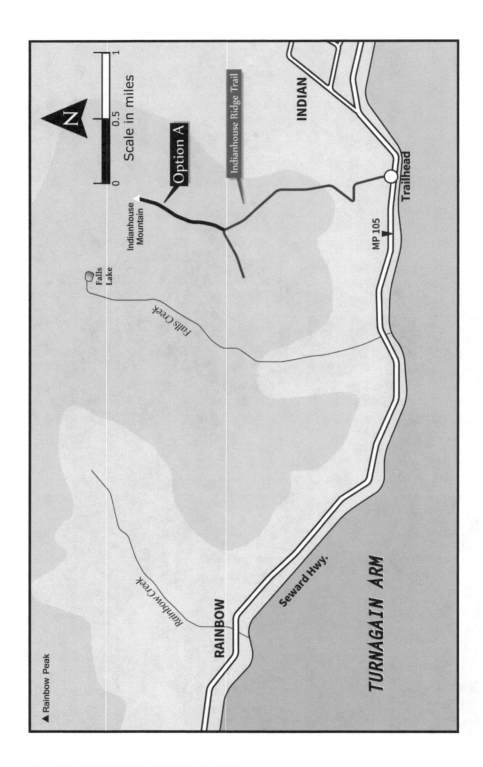

Scale in miles

Option A

Indianhouse Ridge Trail

INDIAN

Indianhouse Mountain

Trailhead

MP 105

Falls Lake

Falls Creek

Rainbow Creek

RAINBOW

Seward Hwy.

TURNAGAIN ARM

▲ Rainbow Peak

# OPTION A

# Indianhouse Mountain

Anyone who has driven from Girdwood to Anchorage on a clear day cannot help but notice this peak. As one rises up out of the Bird Creek drainage and passes Bird Ridge trail parking area, this peak, with its tell-tale notch high on the right-center of the summit ridge, prominent and imposing, rises directly ahead. Considering its obvious position, it should surprise no one that so many hikers and climbers have desired to stand on its summit.

**TRAIL LOCATION:** This climb begins near the uppermost end of Indianhouse Ridge Trail*. Approximately 100 feet from where Indianhouse Ridge Trail reaches its uppermost end at the saddle on the south ridge of Indianhouse Mountain, look for the sheep trail that leads left (north) across the face of the mountain. Follow this sheep trail as it contours across the face for approximately 0.3 miles to a wide, rocky gully angling up and to the left toward the summit. Turn up into this gully. Approximately 100 feet up the gully splits in two, the main gully continuing more or less straight up. But do not continue up the main gully. Instead, bear right (northwest), and follow the narrower gully. In less than 100 feet this gully tops out on the summit ridge. Once on the summit ridge, turn right (north) and continue the final short ascent to the broad summit (4,010 feet).

------------------------------------------------------------

\* For information about that trail, see [3] **Walk-About Guide to Indianhouse Ridge Trail**.

**TRAIL GRADE:** Indianhouse Trail rates a relentless Grade 3 as a hike. At times some of the scrambling should rate a Grade 5, except for the fact that this scrambling takes place on the trail. Well above the last trees, the trail reverts to a more tame Grade 3 hike as it climbs the upper ridge to the crest of the buttress and turns up the last 800 feet to the summit ridge. The climb along the sheep trail rates Grade 3 as a hike. The climb up the gully to the summit ridge rates predominantly Grade 5 as a hike, followed by a final Grade 4 hike up of the ridge crest to the summit.

**TRAIL CONDITION:** Indianhouse Ridge Trail consists mostly of gravel interspersed with rock faces and outcrops that has surprisingly firm footing when dry, despite its steep angle. One might consider avoiding it in wet weather however, when much of the trail turns to slick mud. One will find sheep trail leading across the mountain's east face somewhat rougher and rockier. The climb up the gully to the summit ridge requires a substantial amount of hand-over-hand scrambling, followed by a relatively easy hike along the ridge crest to the summit.

**TRAIL MILEAGE:** To hike from the beginning of the trail in the pullout on the Seward Highway to the summit of Indianhouse Mountain entails approximately 2.9 miles of hiking, for a round-trip total of 5.8 miles.

**TOTAL ELEVATION GAIN:** To hike from the beginning of the trail in the pullout on the Seward Highway to the summit of Indianhouse Mountain entails a total elevation gain of approximately 4,100 feet.

**HIGH POINT:** This trail reaches its highest point of approximately 4,100 feet above sea level at the summit of Indianhouse Mountain.

**NORMAL HIKING TIME:** To hike from the beginning of the trail in the pullout on the Seward Highway to the summit of Indianhouse Mountain and back should take anywhere from 3 to 7 hours, depending on the condition and ambition of the hiker(s) involved.

**CAMPSITES:** One will find no designated camping areas on this trail. For the novelty of the location and the magnificence of the views, one could pitch a tent on the first buttress of the ridge, but one will find no readily available water at this height.

**BEST TIME:** Most people should find any time from early June to late September a good time to do this hike. One should avoid this climb in winter, however, when the steepness of the slope and the distinct possibility of avalanches make the climbing dangerous for all but the most experienced mountaineers.

**USGS MAPS:** Seward D-7 and Anchorage A-7.

Climbing above Turnagain Pass

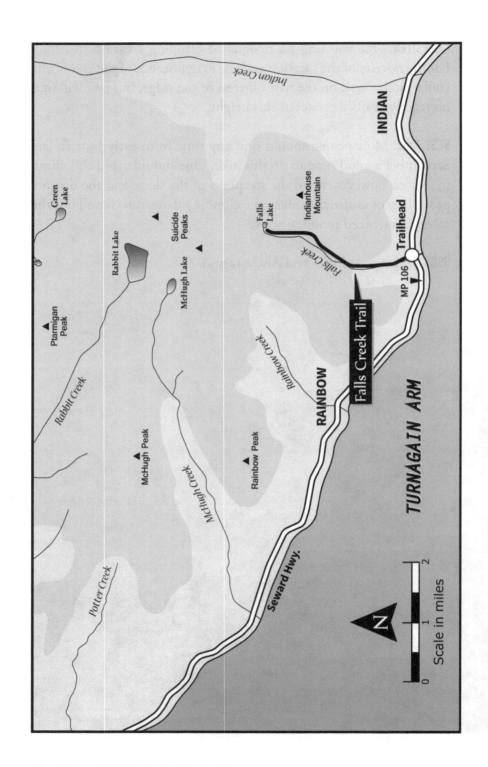

INDIAN

Indian Creek

Green
Lake

Suicide
Peaks

Indianhouse
Mountain

Rabbit Lake

Falls
Lake

Ptarmigan
Peak

McHugh Lake

Trailhead

Falls Creek

MP 106

Rabbit Creek

McHugh Peak

Rainbow Creek

Falls Creek Trail

RAINBOW

McHugh Creek

Rainbow Peak

TURNAGAIN ARM

Potter Creek

Seward Hwy.

N

0    1    2
Scale in miles

# Walk-About Guide to Falls Creek Trail

It seems that most times one drives by this trailhead one sees at least one parked car—a testament to the popularity of this trail. The reason for such popularity makes itself apparent to anyone who has followed this trail up to where it ends in a scenic Alpine cirque. Though a fine end in itself this cirque also marks the beginning of a spectacular ridge-traverse to the summit of South Suicide Peak or a traverse over to McHugh Creek.

**TRAIL LOCATION:** Falls Creek Trail begins in a turnout on the Seward Highway approximately 1 mile south of Windy Corner. To get there drive 21.5 miles south from Anchorage on the Seward Highway. There, between mileposts 106 and 105, look for a small turnout by Falls Creek on the left (north) side of the road. Pull into this turnout and park where possible. The trail starts at the back of the turnout just right (east) of the creek.

The trail begins by climbing alongside the right (east) bank of Falls Creek. Climbing steeply, the trail continues upward with few breaks for the next 1-plus miles. At that point, after passing through some rough-footed sections crowded by alder and willow, the trail continues to follows the creek as it swings up and to the right (west) right around the southwest ridge of Indianhouse Mountain. Although still steadily gaining elevation, the trail now climbs less steeply. Upon reaching tree line the trail climbs onto a shelf. It remains on this shelf as it crosses a cavernous ravine at the base of the intimidating west flank of Indianhouse Mountain. Turning to the left (north) at the upper end of this ravine, the trail enters a broad upper valley. Here the trail terminates at a little tarn in the back right (northeast) corner of the valley.

One need not stop here, though. Ambitious hikers have three major choices. First, one can climb either of the two unnamed summits (3,960 feet and 3,805 feet) on the ridge to the southwest. Second, one can climb to the saddle on the ridge on the upper left (northwest) corner of the valley. Third, one can even climb from that saddle to the summit of South Suicide Peak (5,005 feet)*. From there, one can even continue down a sheep trail hugging the west ridge of South Suicide Peak to the McHugh Creek valley**.

**TRAIL GRADE:** This trail rates Grade 3 as a hike in its lower sections. As it climbs above tree line, however, it relaxes to Grade 2 as a hike.

**TRAIL CONDITION:** This trail varies in its conditions. The lower section of this trail has many muddy and rocky sections. Higher up among the alders and willows, the trail has not only some muddy and rocky sections but also many roots. Once above tree line, however, one will find the trail both drier and smoother.

**TRAIL MILEAGE:** To go from the parking area on the Seward Highway to the tarn at the end of the trail entails 2.5 miles of hiking, for a round-trip total of 5 miles.

**TOTAL ELEVATION GAIN:** To hike from the parking area on the Seward Highway to the tarn at the end of the trail entails a total elevation gain of approximately 2,900 feet.

**HIGH POINT:** This trail reaches its highest point of approximately 3,000 feet above sea level at shore of the tarn at the end of the trail.

**NORMAL HIKING TIME:** Hiking from the parking area on the Seward Highway to the tarn at the end of the trail and back should take

------------------------------------------------------------

\*   For more information about the South Suicide Peak climb, see [6] **OPTION A—South Suicide Peak.**

\*\*   For more information about that trip, see [7] **OPTION B—Traverse from Falls Creek Trail to McHugh Lake Trail Over South Suicide Peak.**

anywhere from 3 to 6 hours, depending on the condition and ambition of the hiker(s) involved.

**CAMPSITES:** One will find no designated campsites along this trail. One will find many fine places on which to pitch a tent, however, both in the open tundra around the tarn at the end of the trail and on the open tundra in the upper valley just beyond.

**BEST TIME:** Most people should find any time from June to September the best time to do this hike. One should think twice about doing this hike in the winter, however, because of the avalanche danger in the upper valley of this trail. Even as late as late May some avalanches may still fall from the valley walls across the trail.

**USGS MAPS:** Seward D-7 and Anchorage A-7.

Climbing above Falls Creek Trail

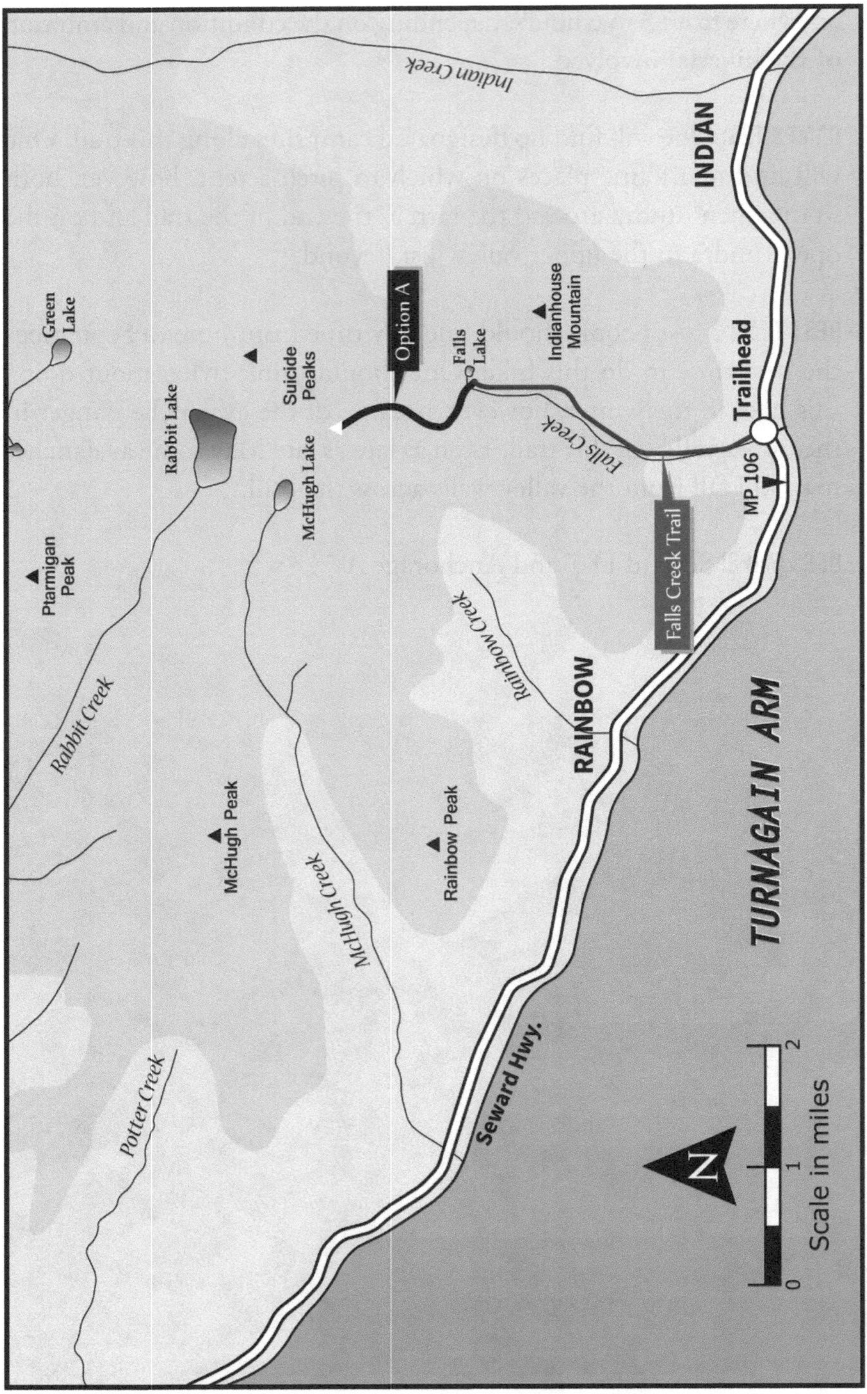
Indian Creek
INDIAN
Green Lake
Option A
Suicide Peaks
Falls Lake
Indianhouse Mountain
Trailhead
Rabbit Lake
McHugh Lake
Falls Creek
MP 106
Falls Creek Trail
Ptarmigan Peak
Rainbow Creek
RAINBOW
Rabbit Creek
TURNAGAIN ARM
McHugh Peak
Rainbow Peak
McHugh Creek
Seward Hwy.
Potter Creek
N
0
1
2
Scale in miles

# OPTION A

# South Suicide Peak

Although this climb entails a considerable amount of elevation gain to reach the summit of South Suicide Peak, most people should find it worth the effort, largely because of the final ridge leading to the summit. Although not especially dangerous if one exercises a modicum of care, this ridge has some exhilarating exposure.

**TRAIL LOCATION:** This climb starts where at the uppermost end of Falls Creek Trail\*. The climb begins by crossing the outlet of Falls Creek flowing from the tarn at the end of Falls Creek Trail. On the far side of this creek, turn and climb toward the saddle approximately 700 feet higher on the left (west) side of valley. From the saddle, turn right (north) and continue up the crest of the ridge. At the top of the first rocky buttress at the uppermost end of the Falls Creek valley, continue climbing along the crest of the suddenly much narrower ridge. Here one may find the need to use the hands while clambering along this rock-crested spine of the ridge. Approximately 0.6 miles from the saddle, this narrow ridge reaches the base of South Suicide Peak's summit cone. On reaching the base, pick any route upward for the last short scramble to the summit (5,005 feet).

---

\*   To get there, see [5] **Walk-About Guide to Falls Creek Trail**.

**TRAIL GRADE:** The first part of this climb on the Falls Creek Trail initially rates Grade 3 as a hike, after which it rates Grade 2 as a hike as the trail turns into the upper valley. The climb from the uppermost end of the trail to the saddle and on to the top of buttress at the upper end of the valley rates Grade 5 as a hike. The following long ridge climb to the summit cone, as well as the last scramble to the summit, rates Grade 6 as a hike.

**TRAIL CONDITION:** This climb varies considerably in its conditions. Falls Creek Trail has many muddy and rocky sections and even root-covered sections. Above tree line, however, the trail becomes both drier and smoother. Upon leaving the trail and crossing the outlet of Falls Creek at the tarn in the upper valley, one has to contend only with an occasional streak of scree and rocks. The final long ridge climb to the summit cone and well as the last scramble to the summit prove both very rocky and steep-sided, requiring considerable of the hands.

**TRAIL MILEAGE:** To go from the parking area on the Seward Highway to the summit of South Suicide Peak entails approximately 4.2 miles of hiking, for a round-trip total of 8.4 miles.

**TOTAL ELEVATION GAIN:** To climb from the parking area on the Seward Highway to the summit of South Suicide Peak entails a total elevation gain of approximately 5,000 feet.

**HIGH POINT:** This trail reaches its highest point of 5,005 feet above sea level at the summit of South Suicide Peak.

**NORMAL HIKING TIME:** To climb from the parking area on the Seward Highway to the summit of South Suicide Peak and back should take anywhere from 6 to 12 hours, depending on the condition and ambition of the hiker(s) involved.

**CAMPSITES:** One will find no designated campsites along this trail. One will find many fine places on which to pitch a tent, however, both in the open tundra around the tarn at the end of the trail and on the open tundra in the upper valley.

**BEST TIME:** Most people should find any time from June to September the best time to do this hike. One should think twice about doing this hike in the winter, however, because of the avalanche danger in the upper valley of this trail. Even as late as early June some avalanches can still fall from the valley walls across the trail and the bowl beyond the trail's end.

**USGS MAPS:** Seward D-7 and Anchorage A-7.

On the ridge leading from Falls Creek
to the summit of South Suicide Peak

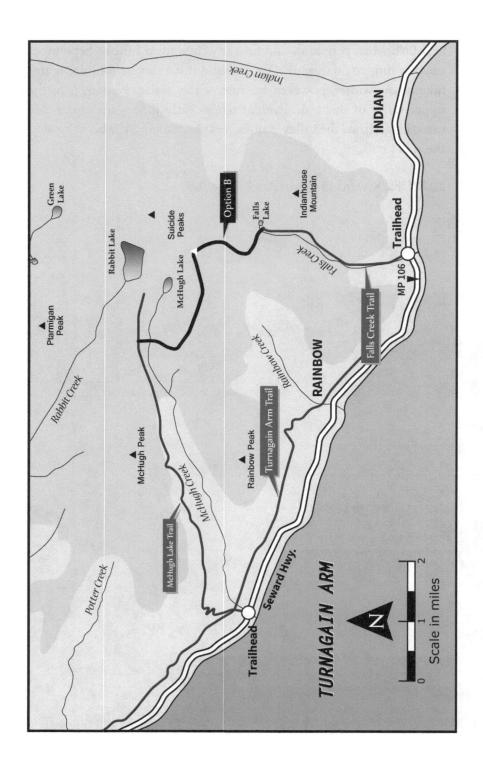

Green
Lake

Rabbit Lake

Ptarmigan
Peak

Suicide
Peaks

McHugh Lake

Rabbit Creek

Option B

Falls
Lake

Indianhouse
Mountain

INDIAN

Indian Creek

Falls Creek

MP 106

Trailhead

Falls Creek Trail

McHugh Peak

McHugh Creek

Rainbow Creek

RAINBOW

Rainbow Peak

Turnagain Arm Trail

McHugh Lake Trail

Potter Creek

Trailhead

Seward Hwy.

TURNAGAIN ARM

N

0       1       2

Scale in miles

# OPTION B

# Traverse from Falls Creek Trail to McHugh Lake Trail Over South Suicide Peak

This traverse across some surprisingly dramatic high country has one small logistic problem: it does not end where it begins. For that reason one might consider spotting a car or bike at the lower parking of McHugh Creek Picnic Area.

**TRAIL LOCATION:** This climb starts where at the uppermost end of Falls Creek Trail*. The climb begins by crossing the outlet of Falls Creek flowing from the tarn at the end of Falls Creek Trail. On the far side of this creek, turn and climb toward the saddle approximately 700 feet higher on the left (west) side of valley. Having reached the saddle, turn right (north) and continue up the crest of the ridge. At the top of the first rocky buttress at the uppermost end of the Falls Creek valley, continue climbing along the crest of the suddenly much narrower ridge. Here one may find the need to use the hands while clambering along this rock-crested spine of the ridge. Approximately 0.6 miles from the saddle, this narrow ridge reaches the base of South Suicide Peak's summit cone. On reaching the base, pick any route upward for the last short scramble to the summit (5.005 feet).

---

* To get there, see [5] **Walk-About Guide to Falls Creek Trail** above.

Continuing the traverse, leave the summit of South Suicide Peak by bearing left down the southwest ridge toward the broad, flat saddle located 700 feet below. The easiest route down entails staying within 20 or 30 feet of the ridge's sheer north side during this descent. Upon reaching the saddle, look for a sheep trail traversing the left (south) side of the ridge. Follow this sheep trail as it almost immediately passes over the next low mound in the ridge crest. Just before reaching two great stone towers located approximately 0.4 miles down the ridge, the sheep trail slants off to the right (north) across the ridge's crest.

Staying on the sheep trail, follow it over to the left (south) side of the ridge. Follow this trail for another approximately 1.5 miles as it slants down the south side of the South Suicide's west ridge. At the end of the ridge, where this west ridge connects with the northern end of the ridge leading to Rainbow Peak, the sheep trail reaches a narrow notch. Pass directly through this notch to its far (northwest) side.

Looking down, one should now see McHugh Lake Trail on the far shore of McHugh Creek in the valley below. After picking a route down the open slope of the ridge, descend into the valley. At the base of the ridge, look for the safest place (*usually* the widest and calmest) to cross McHugh Creek. Then climb the short way up from the creek's far shore to McHugh Lake Trail[*]. On reaching McHugh Lake Trail, turn left (south). Follow this trail for approximately 5 miles down to its junction with Turnagain Arm Trail. On reaching Turnagain Arm Trail, turn left (east)[**]. Then follow Turnagain Arm Trail to the uppermost parking lot at McHugh Creek Picnic Area. From there one can descend the access road down to the lower parking lot.

**TRAIL GRADE:** The first part of this climb on the Falls Creek Trail initially rates Grade 3 as a hike, and then rates Grade 2 as a hike as the trail turns into the upper valley. The climb from the uppermost end of the trail to the saddle and on to the top of buttress at the upper end

- - - - - - - - - - - - - - - - - - - - - - - - - - - - - - - - - - - - - - - - - - - - - - - - - - - - - - -

[*]  For more information about this trail,
    see [11] **Walk-About Guide to McHugh Lake Trail** below.

[**]  For more information about that trail,
    see [8] **Walk-About Guide to Turnagain Arm Trail.**

of the valley rates Grade 5 as a hike. The following long ridge climb to the summit cone, as well as the last scramble to the summit, rates Grade 6 as a hike.

From the summit of South Suicide Peak down to the plateau rates Grade 5 as a climb. From the plateau down to McHugh Lake Trail rates Grade 4 as a hike with very short sections of Grade 5 scrambling. On reaching McHugh Lake Trail, the hike out to McHugh Creek Picnic Area rates Grade 2 as a hike.

**TRAIL CONDITION:** This climb varies considerably in its conditions. Falls Creek Trail has many muddy and rocky sections and even root-covered sections. Above tree line, however, the trail becomes both drier and smoother. Upon leaving the trail and crossing the outlet of Falls Creek at the tarn in the upper valley, one has to contend only with an occasional streak of scree and rocks. The final long ridge climb to the summit cone, however, as well as the last scramble to the summit prove both very rocky and steep-sided, requiring a lot of use of the hands. The hike from South Suicide Peak to the plateau below and to the southwest entails a steep descent over many boulders and much scree. Once on the sheep trail leading off the far side of the plateau, the route still occasionally crosses some scree and boulders but generally remains stable underfoot. The descent from the notch to McHugh Lake Trail also crosses over a predominantly mixed gravel and grass slope with few boulders. Though one must get one's feet wet crossing McHugh Creek, it should not prove a difficult crossing. The following easy descent down McHugh Lake Trail and Turnagain Arm Trail should make the inconvenience of wetting one's feet worthwhile.

**TRAIL MILEAGE:** The entire traverse from the parking area of Falls Creek Trail to the McHugh Creek Picnic Area entails 13.5 miles of hiking.

**TOTAL ELEVATION GAIN:** To hike this entire traverse from the parking area of Falls Creek Trail to the McHugh Creek Picnic Area entails a total elevation gain of approximately 5,300 feet.

**HIGH POINT:** This traverse reaches its highest point of 5,005 feet above sea level at the summit of South Suicide Peak.

**NORMAL HIKING TIME:** To hike from the parking area of Falls Creek Trail to the McHugh Creek Picnic Area should take anywhere from 8 hours to 2 days, depending on the condition and ambition of the hiker(s) involved.

**CAMPSITES:** One will find no designated campsites along this trail. One will find many fine places on which to pitch a tent, however, around the tarn in the upper Falls Creek valley as well as around McHugh Lake and the upper parts of McHugh Creek valley.

Above Falls Creek Trail

**BEST TIME:** Most people should find any time from June to September the best time to do this hike. One should think twice about doing this hike in the winter, however, because of the avalanche danger in the upper Falls Creek valley as well as along the entire descent from the summit of South Suicide Peak to McHugh Lake Trail.

**USGS MAPS:** Seward D-7 and Anchorage A-7.

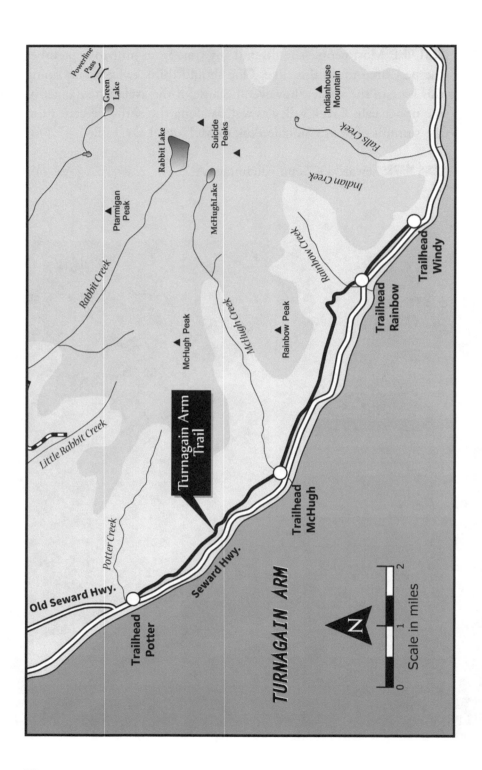

Powerline Pass

Green Lake

Indianhouse Mountain

Falls Creek

Rabbit Lake

Suicide Peaks

Ptarmigan Peak

McHugh Lake

Indian Creek

Rabbit Creek

Rainbow Creek

McHugh Creek

McHugh Peak

Rainbow Peak

Little Rabbit Creek

Turnagain Arm Trail

Trailhead McHugh

Trailhead Rainbow

Trailhead Windy

Potter Creek

Seward Hwy.

Old Seward Hwy.

Trailhead Potter

TURNAGAIN ARM

N

Scale in miles

0    1    2

# Walk-About Guide to Turnagain Arm Trail

This popular 9.4-mile-long trail extends high above the Seward Highway along the north shore of Turnagain Arm. Due to its south-facing exposure it melts out very quickly in the spring, which, in turn, makes it an oft-used destination for early-season hikers wanting to avoid the snow in the high valleys and ridges.

**TRAIL LOCATION:** Turnagain Arm Trail has four access points along its length: one at either end and two in the middle. One can access the westernmost end, which also marks its closest point to Anchorage, just east of Potter Marsh near Anchorage's city limits. To get there drive 11 miles south from Anchorage on the Seward Highway. Less than 0.5 miles past Potter Marsh and just before Milepost 115 look for a parking area and road slanting up into the embankment on the left (north) side of the highway across the highway from Chugach State Park Headquarters. Turn onto this road and follow it up and to the right for 100 yards up to a parking area. (If one finds the gate for the road locked, one can park in the lower parking area by the highway.) Turnagain Arm Trail begins at the upper-left end of this parking area.

One can access the easternmost end of Turnagain Arm Trail near Windy Corners on the Seward Highway. To get there drive 20 miles south from Anchorage on the Seward Highway. There, between mileposts 106 and 107 on the Seward Highway, look for a small turnout on the left (north) side of the highway. Pull into this turnout and park. Turnagain Arm Trail begins at the back of the turnout.

In between these two ends of the trail, lie the other possible access points. The first, at McHugh Creek Picnic Area on the Seward

Highway, has two trailheads. To get these trailheads drive 16 miles south from Anchorage on the Seward Highway. There, just before Milepost 112, turn into the entrance for McHugh Creek Picnic Area on the left (north) side of the highway.

To reach the first trailhead at McHugh Creek for going west toward Potter Marsh, continue straight ahead on entering the picnic area and follow the access road uphill to its uppermost end. Park wherever possible in the last parking area at the edge of the woods. The trail sign indicating access to Turnagain Arm Trail stands at the wood's edge. Approximately 200 feet into the woods, this access trail reaches a junction with Turnagain Arm Trail. Turning left (west) on Turnagain Arm Trail leads one back to Potter Marsh.

To reach the trailhead at McHugh Creek for going east to Windy Corner bear right on entering the paring and drive into the lower area along McHugh Creek. Park wherever possible. The trail begins at the back left corner of the parking area. (Remember that park officials lock the gate at 9 P.M.; so if one plans on a long day hike or overnight camping trip from either of these trailheads, park in the available area directly alongside the highway outside of the gate.)

One can find the final access point for Turnagain Arm Trail at Rainbow. This access point, like McHugh Creek also has two trailheads. To get to this access point drive 19 miles south from Anchorage on the Seward Highway. There, just after the road leading up into Rainbow and just before Milepost 109, one reaches the Rainbow parking area for Turnagain Arm Trail on the left (north) side of the highway. Pull into the parking area and park wherever possible. The trail for going west toward McHugh Creek Picnic Area and Potter Marsh starts at the far right (west) end of the parking area. The trail for going east toward Windy Corner begins on the backside of parking area.

At its westernmost end at Potter Marsh the trail begins almost immediately by climbing to the Old Johnson Road, an old dirt road located higher on the face of the McHugh Peak massif. Turning right (west) on this old trail, the trail then begins contouring along the ridge. For the next approximately 2 miles the trail winds along the wooded face of the ridge, dipping up and down as it goes. At the end of 2 miles it begins a final gradual descent to the McHugh Creek

Picnic Area. After crossing a series of wooden walkways through some bogs, the trail soon afterward reaches a trail junction with McHugh Lake Trail on the left (north)*. Approximately 0.2 miles beyond this junction the trail reaches yet another junction. The trail leading to the right (south) from this junction descends to the uppermost end of the McHugh Creek Picnic Area. Continuing straight ahead from this junction, Turnagain Arm Trail passes through the woods in a sometimes confusing maze of trails. By continuing to bear right, however, one should soon reach the lower parking area of McHugh Creek Picnic Area. (In order to avoid this confusion of trails in the woods around McHugh Creek, some people may find it easier just to turn right at the previously mentioned trail junction and walk down through the picnic area to the back of the lowest parking lot, where one can easily pick up the trail again.)

Climbing out of the back side of the lower parking lot, the trail crosses a bridge and begins climbing gradually. Within 0.5 miles the trail emerges onto an open bench offering wide views up and down Turnagain Arm. For the next 4.2 miles to Rainbow, the trail once more contours along the slope of the ridge before reaching a fine overlook above the southwest side of Rainbow valley. Here one also intersects the lower end of Rainbow Peak Trail**. Just beyond this viewpoint the trail swings left (northeast) to begin a long, gradual descent down a series of long switchbacks to the Rainbow parking area.

On leaving this parking area, the last 1.9 miles of the trail begin by making a short climb. After following the contours of the ridge over a low saddle, the trail then turns sharply right (south) to make its final descent to the Seward Highway at Windy Corner.

**TRAIL GRADE:** This trail, which one can think of as divided into three sections, initially rates Grade 1 as a hike on the section from Potter Marsh to McHugh Creek Picnic Area. The second and longest section

--------------------------------------------------------------

\* For more information about that trail,
  see [11] **Walk-About Guide to McHugh Lake Trail** below.

\*\* For more information about that trail,
  see [9] **Walk-About Guide to Rainbow Peak Trail.**

from McHugh Creek Picnic to Rainbow rates Grade 1 to Grade 2 as a hike. The last section from McHugh Creek Picnic Area to Windy Corners rates Grade 1 as a hike.

**TRAIL CONDITION:** This trail varies in its conditions. It begins at the parking area at Potter Marsh by climbing a wide switch-backed trail. It then follows a wide, gentle old dirt road for much of the way to McHugh Creek Picnic Area. Past McHugh Creek Picnic Area, the trail narrows and becomes rockier, with longer climbs. The final descent to the parking area at Rainbow, however, follows a wide, smooth trail down a series of switchbacks. From Rainbow the trail again follows an old road, but this section often becomes overgrown by midsummer and very rocky at its farther end on its final decent to the highway.

**TRAIL MILEAGE:** To go from the parking area at Potter Marsh to Windy Corners entails 9.4 miles of hiking, for a round-trip total of 18.8 miles. One can further break this total mileage down to the following sectional distances: The section from Potter Marsh to McHugh Creek Picnic Area entails 3.3 miles of hiking, for a round-trip total of 6.6 miles. That from McHugh Creek Picnic Area to Rainbow entails 4.2 miles of hiking, for a round-trip total of 8.4 miles. The final section from Rainbow to Windy Corners entails 1.9 miles of hiking, for a round-trip total of 3.8 miles.

**TOTAL ELEVATION GAIN:** To hike from Potter Marsh to Windy Corners entails a total elevation gain of approximately 1,130 feet. Hiking from Windy Corners to Potter Marsh, on the other hand, entails a total elevation gain of approximately 1,275 feet. One can further break this down to the following sectional gains: To hike from the parking area at Potter Marsh to McHugh Creek Picnic Area entails a total elevation gain of approximately 180 feet, whereas to hike in the opposite direction entails a total elevation gain of approximately 325 feet. To hike from McHugh Creek Picnic Area to the parking at Rainbow entails a total elevation gain of approximately 800 feet, whereas to hike in the opposite direction entails a total elevation gain of approximately 850 feet. To hike from the parking area at Rainbow to Windy Corners entails a total elevation gain of approximately 200 feet, whereas a hike in the opposite direction entails a total elevation gain of also approximately 200 feet.

**HIGH POINT:** This trail reaches its highest point of approximately 900 feet above sea level on the bluffs located approximately 2 miles east of McHugh Creek on the way to Rainbow.

**NORMAL HIKING TIME:** To hike from the parking area at Potter Marsh to Windy Corners should take anywhere from 5 to 9 hours, depending on the condition and ambition of the hiker(s) involved.

**CAMPSITES:** One will find no designated campsites along this trail, nor, given the short length of the trail, is one likely to need any.

**BEST TIME:** Most people should find any time from May to October a good time to do this hike. Many will also find that the first section of this trail from Potter Marsh to the McHugh Creek Picnic Area makes a fine ski or snowshoe trip in the winter. One should think twice about skiing or snowshoeing on much of the trail east of McHugh Creek Picnic Area, however, because of the exposure on some open, wind-blasted slopes that the trail crosses in these sections.

**USGS MAPS:** Anchorage A-8 SE, and Seward D-7 NW and D8.

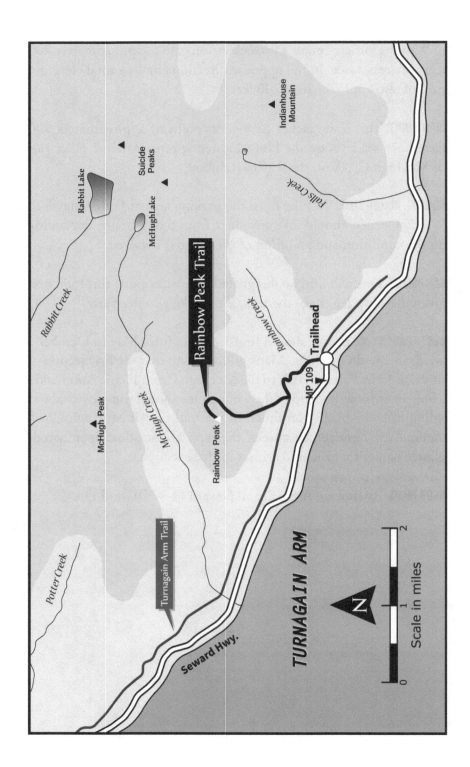

Rainbow Peak Trail

Indianhouse Mountain

Suicide Peaks

Rabbit Lake

McHughLake

Rabbit Creek

McHugh Peak

McHugh Creek

Falls Creek

Rainbow Creek

Rainbow Peak

Trailhead

MP 109

Potter Creek

Turnagain Arm Trail

Seward Hwy.

TURNAGAIN ARM

N

0    1    2
Scale in miles

# Walk-About Guide to Rainbow Peak Trail

Almost everyone driving along Turnagain Arm has seen Rainbow Peak, the triangle-shaped mountain that towers above the westernmost flank of Rainbow Valley. This familiarity enticed some people to forge a makeshift trail up to its summit. This makeshift route has since proved very popular, and for good reason. The challenges of the climb, the sense of adventure, and the views from the summit all make this short but intense climb a favorite of many people.

**TRAIL LOCATION:** Rainbow Peak Trail begins on Turnagain Arm Trail approximately 1 mile west of the Rainbow Valley parking area. To get there drive 19 miles south from Anchorage on the Seward Highway. There, just after the road leading up into Rainbow and just before Milepost 109, one reaches the Rainbow parking area for Turnagain Arm Trail on the left (north) side of the highway. Pull into the parking area and park wherever available. From the parking area, follow the Turnagain Arm Trail left (west) out of the far left (west) end of the parking area back toward McHugh Creek Picnic Area. After approximately 1 mile of steady but gradual climbing, the trail turns around the upper left (west) corner of the valley and levels out. A viewpoint just to the left (south) of the trail also marks this spot. Just after turning this corner the trail reaches a steep, rough swath of scree that drops onto Turnagain Arm Trail from the right (north). This scree marks the beginning of the Rainbow Peak Trail.

The Rainbow Peak Trail begins by scrambling up this steep scree slope at its base. Above the scree, the trail continues to climb steeply through a maze of rocks and roots. Upon reaching tree line, the trail rounds over the crest of a buttress. After a short level respite, the trail again begins to climb a series of rock spines and gullies that drape the ridge crest. At the top of these rock spines and gullies, the trail reaches the base the near-sheer south face of Rainbow Peak. To avoid these cliffs, the trail turns onto a sheep trail leading to the right (east) around the cliffs' base. This sheep trail offers another short respite, but not for long. In less than 0.5 miles this sheep trail reaches the bottom of a wide dirt- and rock-filled gully on the left (west).

Here one leaves behind the last vestiges of trail. Turning up the gully, pick any route than seems best and begin climbing toward the rock-spired ridge far above. Most people find that the best route up this slope hugs the base of the rocks that border the left (south) side of the gully. As one approaches the top of the ridge, begin to bear up and to the left (southwest). Passing through the final rocks at the top of the gully, one soon reaches the rocky spine of the ridge. Here turn left (south) again, and follow the narrow ridge the last 100 or so feet to the summit (3,543 feet).

**TRAIL GRADE:** This climb initially rates Grade 2 as a hike in the first section along the Turnagain Arm Trail. Upon turning off this trail and beginning the scramble up Rainbow Peak Trail, the rate increases to a high Grade 3 as a climb, often requiring the use of hands, as the route scrambles up the through the roots and rocks and then up the rock spine to the base of Rainbow Peak's south face. Upon reaching the sheep trail leading around the base of the summit cliffs, the hike drops to Grade 2 as a hike. On turning up the final trackless wide gully leading to the summit ridge, the rate increases to Grade 5 as a climb. It remains a Grade 5 climb even on the short and rocky traverse along the ridge crest to the summit.

**TRAIL CONDITION:** This route varies in its conditions. Though the Turnagain Arm Trail and the sheep trail around the base of the summit cliffs have good footing, most of the remaining route does not. This route has many rocks and roots on the climb leading up to the base of the cliffs and often requires the use of hands, especially on the rock spine leading up to Rainbow Peak's south face. One then has some relatively easy hiking along the sheep trail leading around to the final slope leading up to the ridge. Upon leaving the sheep trail the remaining climb to the ridge involves scrambling up and over rocks and scree. The rock spines and gullies that drape the upper part of the ridge also frequently require use of the hands to clamber through to the rocky ridge crest above.

**TRAIL MILEAGE:** To go from the parking area on the Seward Highway to the summit of Rainbow Peak entails approximately 3 miles of hiking and scrambling, for a round-trip total of approximately 6 miles.

**TOTAL ELEVATION GAIN:** To climb from the parking area on the Seward Highway to the summit of Rainbow Peak entails a total elevation gain of approximately 3,500 feet.

**HIGH POINT:** This route reaches its highest point of 3,543 feet above sea level at the summit of Rainbow Peak.

**NORMAL HIKING TIME:** To climb from the parking area on the Seward Highway to the summit and back should take anywhere from 3 to 6 hours, depending on the condition and ambition of the hiker(s) involved.

**CAMPSITES:** One will find no designated campsites along this trail, nor, given the short length of the trail, should one need any. Anyone who still wants to camp out can find a fine place on which to pitch a tent along one of the level spots at the top of the first buttress on the ridge or even along the base of the summit cliffs. Such a site would offer a wonderful view and, if early enough in the season, have lingering snow to use as a water source.

**BEST TIME:** Most people should find any time from June to September a good time to do this hike. One should think twice about doing this hike in winter, however, owing to the potential avalanche danger on the climb of the steep ridge line below as well as in the wide gully leading up to the summit ridge.

**USGS MAPS:** Seward D-7 and Anchorage A-7.

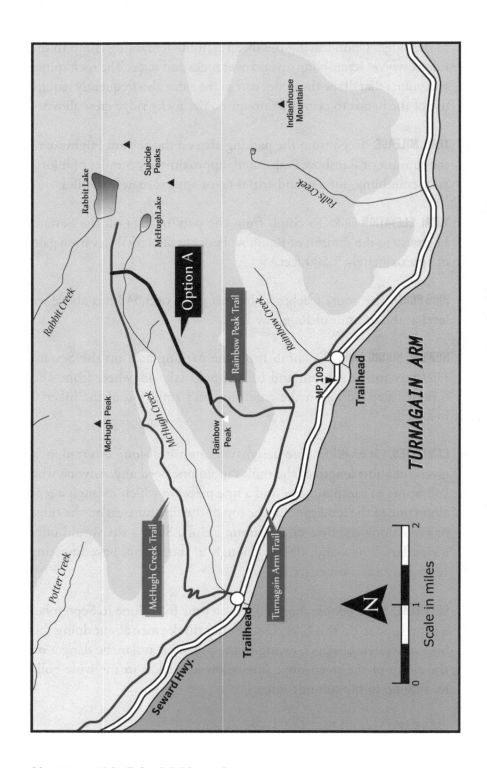

Indianhouse
Mountain

Falls Creek

Suicide
Peaks

Rabbit Lake

McHugh Lake

Rabbit Creek

Option A

Rainbow Peak Trail

Rainbow Creek

McHugh Peak

McHugh Creek

Rainbow
Peak

MP 109

Trailhead

TURNAGAIN ARM

Potter Creek

McHugh Creek Trail

Trailhead

Turnagain Arm Trail

Seward Hwy.

N

Scale in miles

0    1    2

# OPTION A

# Traverse from Rainbow Peak
# to McHugh Lake Trail

**TRAIL LOCATION:** This traverse begins at McHugh Creek Picnic Area*. One can also begin this hike at Rainbow, and thus reduce the length of this hike by approximately 3 miles, but this entails spotting a car at McHugh Creek Picnic Area**. If one starts from McHugh Creek Picnic Area, follow Turnagain Arm Trail east from the lower parking area to where it begins its descent into the Rainbow valley. (One will recognize this spot by the scenic overlook on the right and by the way the trail turns left away from Turnagain Arm to begin its descent into Rainbow valley.) There the trail reaches a steep, rough swath of scree dropping onto Turnagain Arm Trail from the left (north). This scree marks the junction with Rainbow Peak Trail. If, on the other hand, one starts from the Rainbow parking area, follow Turnagain Arm Trail west to where, just after turning around the upper left corner of the valley, it reaches the steep, rough swath of scree now on the right (north) that marks the beginning of the Rainbow Peak Trail***.

The Rainbow Peak Trail begins by scrambling up this steep scree slope at its base. Above the scree, the trail continues to climb steeply through a maze of rocks and roots. Upon reaching tree line, the trail rounds over the crest of a buttress. After a short level respite, the trail again begins to climb a series of rock spines and gullies that drape

---

\*    To get there, see [8] **Walk-About Guide to Turnagain Arm Trail**.

\*\*   To get to the Rainbow parking area, also see [8] **Walk-About Guide to Turnagain Arm Trail**.

\*\*\* For more information about this approach,
see [9] **Walk-About Guide to Rainbow Peak Trail**.

the ridge crest. At the top of these rock spines and gullies, the trail reaches the base the near-sheer south face of Rainbow Peak. To avoid these cliffs, the trail turns onto a sheep trail leading to the right (east) around the cliffs' base. This sheep trail offers another short respite, but not for long. In less than 0.5 miles this sheep trail reaches the bottom of a wide dirt- and rock-filled gully on the left (west).

Here one leaves behind the last vestiges of trail. Turning up the gully, pick any route than seems best and begin climbing toward the rock-spired ridge far above. Most people find that the best route up this slope hugs the base of the rocks that border the left (south) side of the gully. As one approaches the top of the ridge, begin to bear up and to the left (southwest). Passing through the final rocks at the top of the gully, one soon reaches the rocky spine of the ridge. Here turn left (south) again, and follow the narrow ridge the last 100 or so feet to the summit (3,543 feet).

Upon reaching the summit of Rainbow Peak, turn around and backtrack along the ridge. Instead of descending the gully back down to the sheep trail, however, continue straight ahead (north) along the ridge. Follow the ridge for approximately 1 mile to where it broadens into a wide, less rocky hike. Approximately 1.5 miles from the summit of Rainbow Peak the ridge drops into a narrow, steep-sided notch at the base of the South Ridge of South Suicide Peak. One can recognize this slot by the fact that not only does the towering ridge of South Suicide Peak bear off to the right (east) but also many sheep trails intersect in this notch.

From this point one should now see McHugh Lake Trail on the far shore of McHugh Creek in the valley below and to the left (west). After picking a route down the open gravel and grass slope of the ridge, descend to valley below. At the base of the ridge, look for the safest (the widest and calmest) place to cross McHugh Creek. After crossing the creek climb the short way up to McHugh Lake Trail*. Once on McHugh Lake Trail, turns left (south) and follow it for approximately 5 miles down to its junction with the Turnagain Arm

---

\* For more information about this trail, see [11] **Walk-About Guide to McHugh Lake Trail**.

Trail. On reaching the Turnagain Arm Trail, turn left (east)[*]. Then follow Turnagain Arm Trail to the uppermost parking lot at McHugh Creek Picnic Area. From there one can descend the access road down to the lower parking lot.

**TRAIL GRADE:** This climb initially rates Grade 2 as a hike in the first section along the Turnagain Arm Trail. Upon turning of this route and beginning the scramble up Rainbow Peak Trail, the rate increases to a high Grade 3 as a climb, often requiring the use of hands, as the route scrambles up the through the roots and rocks and then up the rock spine to the base of Rainbow Peak's south face. Upon reaching the sheep trail leading around the base of the summit cliffs, the hike drops to Grade 2 as a hike. On turning up the final trackless wide gully leading to the summit ridge, the rate increases to Grade 5 as a climb. It remains a Grade 5 climb even on the short and rocky traverse along the ridge crest to the summit. The backtracking along the ridge and down to McHugh Lake Trail rates Grade 4 as a hike. The final descent along the McHugh Lake Trail and Turnagain Arm Trail rates Grade 1 as a hike.

**TRAIL CONDITION:** This route varies in its conditions. Though the Turnagain Arm Trail and the sheep trail around the base of the summit cliffs have good footing, most of the remaining route does not. This route has many rocks and roots on the climb leading up to the base of the cliffs and often requires the use of hands, especially on the rock spine leading up to Rainbow Peak's south face. One then has some relatively easy hiking along the sheep trail leading around to the final slope leading up to the ridge. Upon leaving the sheep trail the remaining climb to the ridge involves scrambling up and over rocks and scree. The rock spines and gullies that drape the upper part of the ridge also frequently require use of the hands. From the summit of Rainbow Peak, the route along the ridge becomes less rugged as the ridge widens. The descent from the ridge into the McHugh Creek valley entails down-climbing

---

[*]   For more information about that trail, see [8] **Walk-About Guide to Turnagain Arm Trail**.

across mostly firm scree and tundra. Finally, the walk out on the McHugh Lake Trail, though muddy in spots, offers a welcome respite from the rocks on the ridge above. The trail also becomes wider and quicker underfoot as it descends down the valley.

**TRAIL MILEAGE:** The entire traverse beginning and ending at the McHugh Creek Picnic Area entails approximately 14.5 miles of hiking and scrambling. As stated before, one can reduce this total distance by 3 miles by spotting a car at the McHugh Creek Picnic Area and starting at the Turnagain Arm Trail parking area at Rainbow.

**TOTAL ELEVATION GAIN:** The entire traverse beginning and ending at the McHugh Creek Picnic Area entails a total elevation gain of approximately 4,800 feet. The entire traverse from the parking area at Rainbow to the McHugh Creek Picnic Area entails a total elevation gain of approximately 4,000 feet.

**HIGH POINT:** This traverse reaches its highest point of 3,543 feet above sea level at the summit of Rainbow Peak.

**NORMAL HIKING TIME:** The entire traverse beginning and ending at the McHugh Creek Picnic Area should take anywhere from 7 to 12 hours, depending on the condition and ambition of the hiker(s) involved. The entire traverse from the parking area at Rainbow to the McHugh Creek Picnic Area should take anywhere from 5 to 11 hours, depending on the condition and ambition of the hiker(s) involved.

**CAMPSITES:** One will find no designated campsites along this trail. If one wants to camp out, one will find a fine place on which to pitch a tent along one of the level spots at the top of the first buttress on the ridge or even along the base of the summit cliffs. Such a site would provide a wonderful view and, if early enough in the season, have lingering snow to use as a water source. The upper end of McHugh Lake Trail also has many fine places on which to pitch a tent.

**BEST TIME:** Most people should find any time from June to September a good time to do this hike. One should think twice about doing this hike in winter, though, because of the extreme avalanche danger on the climb of the steep ridge line leading up the south face of Rainbow Peak as well as in the wide gully leading up to the summit ridge. The greatest avalanche danger may exist on the slope one must descend to reach McHugh Lake Trail.

**USGS MAPS:** Seward D-7 and Anchorage A-7.

Turnagain Arm Trail and Rainbow Peak

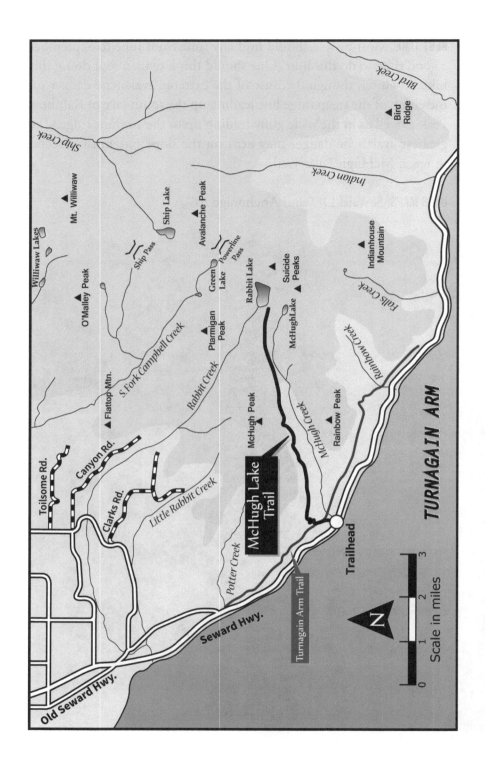

Bird Creek

Bird Ridge

Ship Creek

Indian Creek

Mt. Williwaw

Ship Lake

Williwaw Lakes

Avalanche Peak

Ship Pass

Indianhouse Mountain

O'Malley Peak

Green Lake

Powerline Pass

Suicide Peaks

Falls Creek

Rabbit Lake

S. Fork Campbell Creek

Ptarmigan Peak

McHugh Lake

Rainbow Creek

Flattop Mtn.

Rabbit Creek

McHugh Creek

Toilsome Rd.

Canyon Rd.

McHugh Peak

Rainbow Peak

Clarks Rd.

Little Rabbit Creek

**McHugh Lake Trail**

Potter Creek

Turnagain Arm Trail

Trailhead

**TURNAGAIN ARM**

Seward Hwy.

N

Old Seward Hwy.

0 1 2 3

Scale in miles

# 11

# Walk-About Guide to McHugh Lake Trail

McHugh Lake Trail out of the McHugh Picnic Area offers an alternative way to Rabbit Lake from the more popular route up Rabbit Lakes Trail. Admittedly this route includes a much greater elevation gain, but in doing so also offers a greater variety of views of both Turnagain Arm, the Kenai Peninsula, and nearby peaks such as Rainbow Peak, and the North and South Suicide peaks as it climbs the more secluded McHugh Creek valley

**TRAIL LOCATION:** McHugh Lake Trail begins on the Turnagain Arm Trail just west of the McHugh Creek Picnic Area. To get there drive 16 miles south from Anchorage on the Seward Highway. There, just before Milepost 112, turn into the entrance for McHugh Creek Picnic Area on the left (north) side of the highway. Continue straight ahead on entering the picnic area and follow the access road uphill to its uppermost end at the edge of the woods and park wherever possible. (Remember that park officials lock the gate at 9 P.M.: so if one plans on a long day hike or overnight camping trip from either of these trailheads, leave the car in the parking area alongside the highway and outside of the gate.)

The trail sign indicating access to Turnagain Arm Trail stands at the wood's edge of the uppermost parking area. Follow this access trail approximately 200 feet uphill to where it reaches a junction with Turnagain Arm Trail. Turning left (west) follow Turnagain Arm Trail toward Potter Marsh. Continue on this trail to where just past Milepost 3, one reaches the junction with McHugh Lake Trail on the right (north). Turn right onto McHugh Lake Trail.

McHugh Lake Trail begins by climbing gradually through the woods. As the terrain steepens, the trail begins climbing a series of switchbacks.

At the end of the last switchback the trail swings left around the base of the southernmost ridge of McHugh Peak and crosses an open area far above McHugh Creek, which one can hear far below and to the left. From this point the trail continues up valley, contouring along the slope far above the left (west) side of the creek. Though the trail makes a number of short, steep climbs, these prove exceptions in the otherwise gradual climb. As one continues up valley, though, the trail narrows and roughens under foot. Only on reaching tree line does it begin to flatten and widen again. Approximately 6 miles from its start, the trail reaches McHugh Lake (2,900-plus feet). Approximately 0.5 miles after passing McHugh Lake, the trail bears left (northeast) and crosses over a low saddle. From there the trail and descends to the southeast shore of Rabbit Lake (3,100-plus feet), where it comes to an end.

At this point one has a number of choices. First, one can, after enjoying the scenery, turn around and return the way they have come. Second, one can climb South Suicide Peak towering above and to the left)[*]. Third, one can cross the outlet of Rabbit Lake to reach the uppermost end of Rabbit Creek Trail and follow that out to Canyon Road[**].

**TRAIL GRADE:** This trail rates Grade 2 as a hike, with some sections of Grade 1 hiking where one crosses the open country between McHugh Lake and Rabbit Lake.

**TRAIL CONDITION:** This trail varies little in its condition. With switchbacks leading up out of the lower valley, the trail has few rocks and roots in its lower sections. Only as it climbs past the switchbacks and turns up the McHugh Creek valley proper does the trail turn at all rough and muddy underfoot as it cuts through wide swaths of alder and willow above. Above tree line, the trail begins to flatten and widen as it passes over the low saddle and descends to its uppermost end on the southeast shore of Rabbit Lake.

-----------------------------------------------------------------------

[*]    For more information about that climb, see [12] **OPTION A—South Suicide Peak**.

[**]   For more information about that hike,
       see [14] **OPTION C— McHugh Lake Trail to Rabbit Creek Trail**.

**TRAIL MILEAGE:** To go from McHugh Picnic Area to the southeast shore of Rabbit Lake entails 7 miles of hiking, for a round-trip total of 14 miles.

**TOTAL ELEVATION GAIN:** To hike from the McHugh Creek Picnic Area to the southeast shore of Rabbit Lake entails a total elevation gain of approximately 3,100 feet.

**HIGH POINT:** This trail reaches its highest point of approximately 3,200 feet above sea level on the low saddle between McHugh Lake and Rabbit Lake.

**NORMAL HIKING TIME:** To hike from the McHugh Creek Picnic Area to the end of the trail on the southeast shore of Rabbit Lake should take anywhere from 5 to 8 hours, depending on the condition and ambition of the hiker(s) involved.

**CAMPSITES:** One will find no designated campsites along this trail. One will find many fine places on which to pitch a tent above tree line. Of these, one will find the areas near McHugh Lake or Rabbit Lake particularly fine places for pitching a tent.

**BEST TIME:** Most people should find any time from June to September a good time to do this hike. One should think twice about doing this hike in winter, however, because of the potential avalanche danger where the trail contours up the lower section of the McHugh Creek valley.

**USGS MAPS:** Anchorage A-7 and A-8 SE.

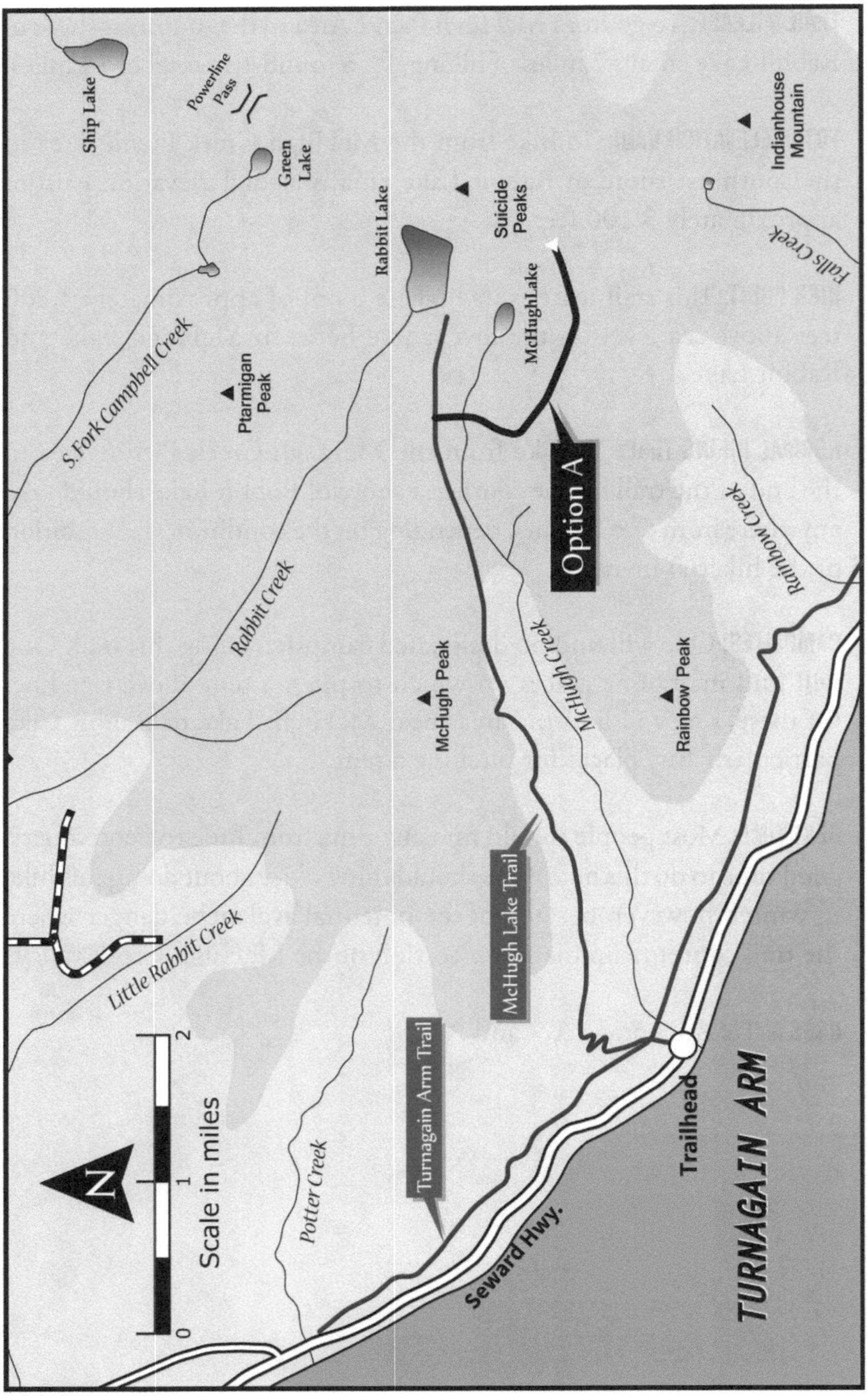
Ship Lake
Powerline Pass
Green Lake
Rabbit Lake
Suicide Peaks
Indianhouse Mountain
Falls Creek
McHughLake
S. Fork Campbell Creek
Ptarmigan Peak
Option A
Rainbow Creek
Rabbit Creek
McHugh Peak
McHugh Creek
Rainbow Peak
McHugh Lake Trail
Little Rabbit Creek
Turnagain Arm Trail
Potter Creek
N
Scale in miles
0
1
2
Seward Hwy.
Trailhead
TURNAGAIN ARM

# OPTION A

# South Suicide Peak

Though difficult, this climb, apart from reaching the summit of the southernmost 5,000-foot-plus peak in the Front Range, has other rewards. First, one has a good chance of seeing more than a few sheep along the south face of mountain. Second, the views down to Turnagain Arm and across to Kenai Peninsula on the high traverse across the south face of the mountain's west ridge make this climb more than worthwhile.

**TRAIL LOCATION:** One can actually approach South Suicide Peak's west ridge from three different directions—all of which begin on McHugh Lake Trail*. Most people will find the first two approaches extremely challenging. The first of these more difficult approaches begins by crossing McHugh Creek within stone-throwing distance of McHugh Lake and climbing up the steep tundra slope to the crest of the ridge. Upon reaching the ridge, turn left (northwest) toward the summit. Going over or around the gendarmes, rock pillars, and scree slopes that block the way, follow the ridge crest to the place where it crosses a wide tundra saddle below the summit cone. On the far side of the saddle, start up the right side of the ridge's crest to the summit. The second of these approaches begins climbing to the crest of the same ridge from near the southern end of Rabbit Lake. Once on the ridge crest, turn left (west). Then continue down the ridge to the summit to

---

\*  To get there, see [11] **Walk-About Guide to McHugh Lake Trail**.

the same saddle below the summit. At the far side of the saddle start up the same route as described in the first approach, namely, following right side of the ridge's crest to the summit.

The third, and easiest of these routes up South Suicide Peak begins by hiking up the McHugh Lake Trail to the place where, approximately 1 mile below McHugh Lake, one can look up to the right (east) and see a small, steep-sided notch on the crest of the ridge where the Rainbow Peak ridge meets the end of South Suicide Peak's west ridge. Here, turn right (east) off McHugh Lake Trail and cross McHugh Creek. Once across the creek climb the 400-some-odd feet to the notch. After reaching the notch, hike straight across it and look for the sheep trail that bears left (east-northeast) out of its far side and contours up the face of South Suicide Peak's west ridge. In approximately 1 mile this sheep trail reaches the wide and broad saddle at the base of the summit cone of South Suicide Peak.

From this saddle, the final portion of this climb follows the same route as the first two approaches: following right side of the ridge's crest to the summit looming approximately 600 feet above. Although the last few feet make for some of the steepest climbing on this hike, it should not prove difficult enough to keep most people from reaching the summit (5,005 feet).

At this point, one has a number of choices. First, one can return the way they have come. Second, ambitious hikers may want to continue down into the very appropriately named Windy Gap (named because of the ferocious south winds that funnel up and through it) and from there continue up to the summit of North Suicide (5,065 feet). One can even continue farther from that summit to traverse down the knife-edged ridge to the east ridge of Ptarmigan Peak, where one can make a gentle descent to Rabbit Lake. This continuation of the climb of South Suicide Peak makes for an incredibly long but spectacular day.

**TRAIL GRADE:** McHugh Lake Trail rates Grade 2 as a hike. Upon leaving this trail, the route rises to Grade 5 as a hike. On the sheep trail at the far side of the notch in the ridge the climb reverts to Grade 3 as a hike. On the summit cone the climb once rises to Grade 5 as a hike, with even some short sections of Grade 6 climbing on the final scramble to the summit of South Suicide Peak.

**TRAIL CONDITION:** This trail varies little in its condition. With switchbacks leading up out of the lower valley, the trail has few rocks and roots in its lower sections. Only as it climbs past the switchbacks and turns up the McHugh Creek valley proper does the trail turn at all rough and muddy underfoot as it cuts through wide swaths of alder and willow above. Above tree line, the trail begins to flatten and widen out. Upon leaving this trail, however, one should expect a very wet stream crossing as well as some steep climbing up scree and tundra to the notch on the ridge. On the sheep trail on the far side of the notch, the climbing becomes surprisingly good underfoot as the trail climbs to the saddle below the summit cone of South Suicide Peak. This final climb to the summit, however, requires some hand-over-hand scrambling.

**TRAIL MILEAGE:** To go from McHugh Picnic Area to the summit of South Suicide Peak entails approximately 8 miles of hiking and climbing, for a round-trip total of approximately 16 miles.

**TOTAL ELEVATION GAIN:** To hike from the McHugh Creek Picnic Area to the summit of South Suicide Peak entails a total elevation gain of approximately 5,000 feet.

**HIGH POINT:** This trail reaches its highest point of 5,005 feet above sea level at the summit of South Suicide Peak.

**NORMAL HIKING TIME:** To hike from the McHugh Creek Picnic Area to the summit of South Suicide Peak and back should take anywhere from 7 to 12 hours, depending on the condition and ambition of the hiker(s) involved.

**CAMPSITES:** One will find no designated campsites along this trail. One will find many fine places on which to pitch a tent above tree line. Of these, the areas in the vicinity of either McHugh Lake or Rabbit Lake offer particularly fine places on which to pitch a tent.

**BEST TIME:** Most people should find any time from June to September a good time to do this climb. One should think twice about doing this hike in winter, however, because of the potential avalanche danger, not only where the trail contours up the lower section of the McHugh Creek valley but also on the climb to the notch above McHugh Creek, and especially where it follows the sheep trail up across the face of the west ridge of South Suicide Peak.

**USGS MAPS:** Anchorage A-7 and A-8 SE.

South Suicide Peak

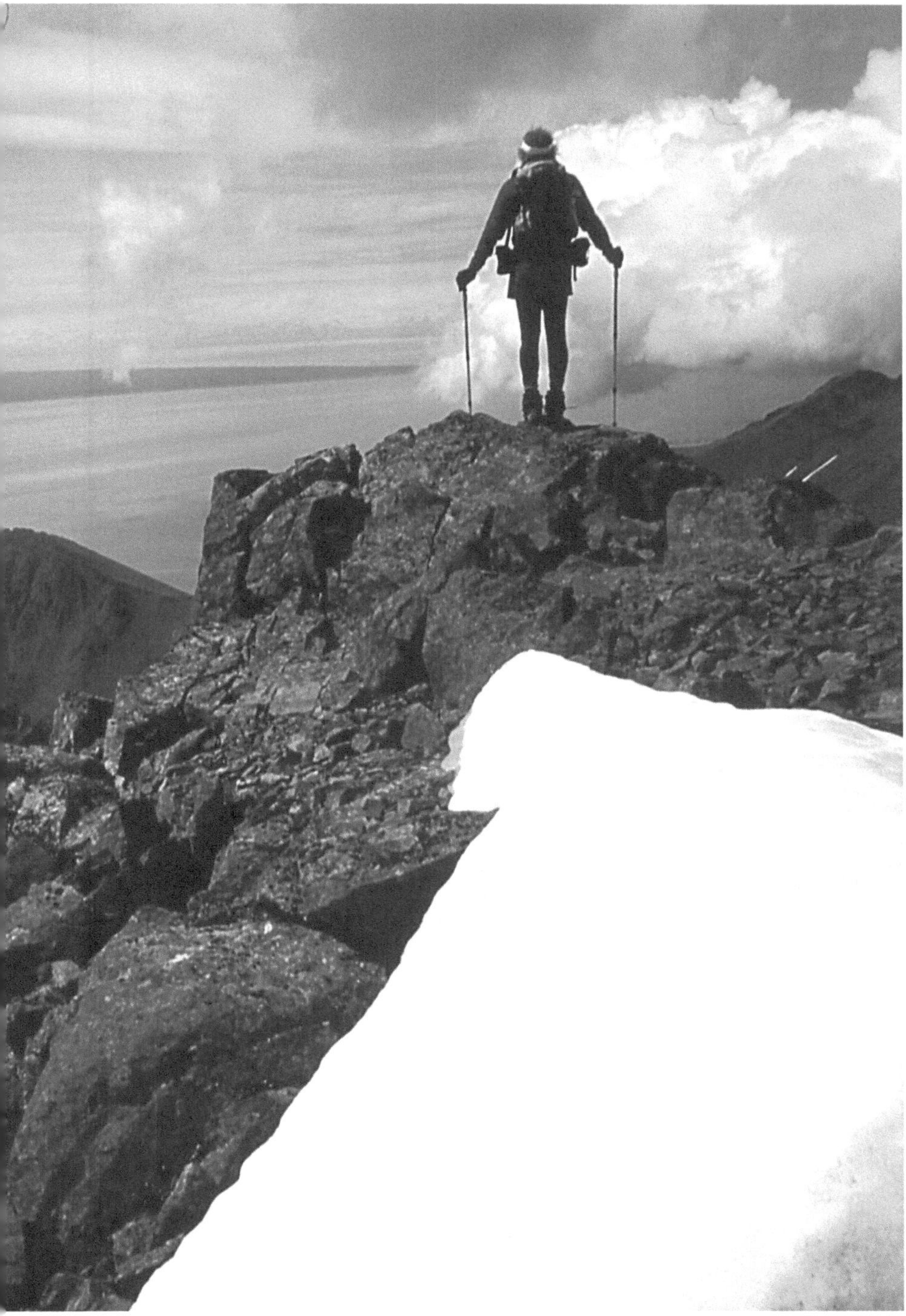

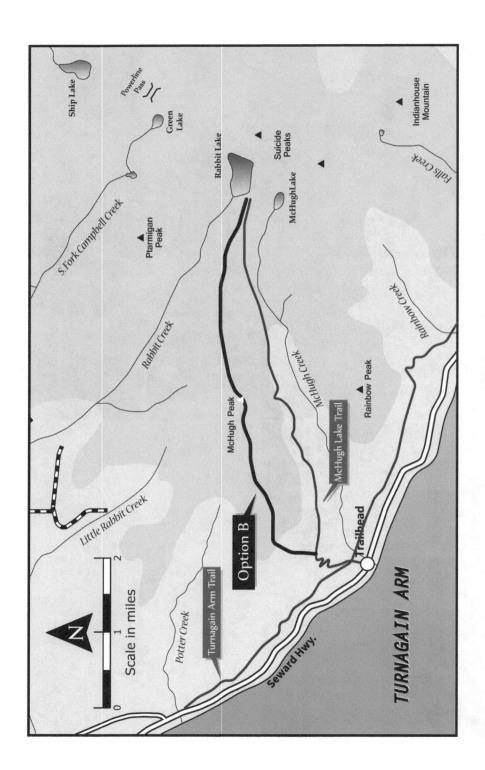

Ship Lake

Powerline Pass

Green Lake

S. Fork Campbell Creek

Ptarmigan Peak

Rabbit Lake

Rabbit Creek

Suicide Peaks

McHugh Lake

Indianhouse Mountain

Falls Creek

McHugh Creek

Rainbow Creek

Rainbow Peak

McHugh Peak

McHugh Lake Trail

Little Rabbit Creek

Option B

Trailhead

Turnagain Arm Trail

Potter Creek

Seward Hwy.

TURNAGAIN ARM

N

Scale in miles

0   1   2

# 13

# OPTION B

# Traverse of McHugh Peak

This climb offers a very scenic, but harder and longer, hike to McHugh Lake than that just hiking up McHugh Lake Trail. Instead of following McHugh Lake Trail to its end, this route loops up and over the crest ridge that parallels the left (northwest) side of the trail before descending to the uppermost end of McHugh Lake Trail near Rabbit Lake. In the process it passes over the summit of McHugh Peak (4,301 feet) and three other lesser peaks.

**TRAIL LOCATION:** This traverse begins approximately 1 mile beyond where McHugh Lake Trail reaches the top of the last switchback in the woods and starts to contour up the McHugh Creek valley*. The trail then makes a short, steep climb through a stand of cottonwood trees onto a more open shelf. Within feet after topping this shelf the trail reaches a junction with a rough unmarked trail leading left and up into the wide cirque that forms a large concave in the face of the south ridge of McHugh Peak. This rough trail marks the beginning of the traverse.

Turning left (northwest) onto this rough trail, follow it as it cuts up and across the center of the cirque to the crest of ridge 1,300 feet above. Once on the crest of the ridge turn right (north) and continue over a steep, narrow hump to the broad ridge just beyond. One should now see the summit pyramid of McHugh Peak rising into the sky at

---

\*   To get there, see [11] **Walk-About Guide to McHugh Lake Trail**.

the far (northern) end of this ridge. Staying on the crest of the ridge, follow it to the summit cone. Here one will find the final climb to the summit blocked by sheer rock walls. To get around these rocks, circle around to the left (west) side of the summit cone. On the far side one will find a series of three gullies leading up the grass and dirt shelf just below the summit. Clambering up the slot on the left (east) of this rock, climb the final few feet to the flat stone summit (4,301 feet).

Apart from continuing the traverse, one now has two other choices. First, one can return the way one came and return to McHugh Creek Picnic Area. Second, one can descend to Bear Valley*. To continue the traverse of the ridge to McHugh Lake first descend the summit cone to the open slopes just below to the north. Having reached these slopes, bear right (east-southeast) around the summit cone to the wide bowl across which one can see the imposing upper slopes of South Suicide Peak. Follow the bowl around to the crest of the ridge on its far side. On the crest of this ridge one should now see far below and to the right the thin line of the McHugh Lake Trail.

One can descend to the trail from many points along this ridge, but the best way entails continuing along the crest of the ridge, following a sporadic sheep trail when possible, to its end. As one continues along the crest of the narrowing ridge, one should soon see Rabbit Creek and Rabbit Creek Trail far below to the left (north). Soon after Rabbit Creek comes into view, the ridge will begin its long descent to the saddle between McHugh Lake and Rabbit Lake. Where the ridge begins to round into a low mound between the two lakes one should reach where the ridge intersects McHugh Lake Trail. Turning right (south) on this trail, one can then follow it for approximately 0.25 miles back to McHugh Lake, and then another approximately 7 miles down to the McHugh Creek Picnic Area.

**TRAIL GRADE:** McHugh Lake Trail rates Grade 2 as a hike, with some sections of Grade 1 hiking. Upon leaving McHugh Lake Trail and beginning the climb up the rough trail to the crest of the south ridge of McHugh

--------------------------------------------------------------------

\* For more information about that trail,
   see [16] **Walk-About Guide to McHugh Peak** in Chapter 2.

Peak, the route rises to Grade 3 as a hike. The ridge walk to the summit of McHugh Peak rates Grade 4 to Grade 5 as a climb for most of its length. The final scramble up the summit cone of McHugh Peak rates Grade 6 as a hike. The remainder of the ridge walk rates Grade 4 as a hike, with some very short sections of Grade 5 down-climbing on the final descent to the saddle between McHugh Lake and Rabbit Lake. Where the traverse rejoins the McHugh Lake Trail, the route rates Grade 1 to Grade 2 as a hike all the way back down to the McHugh Creek Picnic Area.

**TRAIL CONDITION:** This traverse varies in its conditions. The climb on the rough trail to the top of the South Ridge of McHugh Peak crosses both scree and boulders the higher it climbs. On the ridge, the route remains rocky, with only sporadic sections of tundra, all the way to the summit cone of McHugh Peak. Then the short climb up the summit come requires hand-over-hand scrambling. Upon leaving the summit of McHugh Peak and starts down the ridge toward Rabbit Lake, the conditions improve dramatically. Part sheep trail and part open tundra, the conditions remain good until the final, descent back to the McHugh Lake Trail. This descent passes through sections of rock and scree, which may require some use of hands, as well as some gentle stretches of easy tundra walking.

**TRAIL MILEAGE:** This entire traverse from the McHugh Creek Picnic Area to McHugh Lake and back entails approximately 14.5 miles of hiking and climbing.

**TOTAL ELEVATION GAIN:** This entire traverse from the McHugh Creek Picnic Area to McHugh Lake and back entails a total elevation gain of approximately 4,600 feet.

**HIGH POINT:** This traverse reaches its highest point of 4,301 feet above sea level at the summit of McHugh Peak.

**NORMAL HIKING TIME:** This entire traverse from the McHugh Creek Picnic Area to McHugh Lake and back should take anywhere from 7 to 10

**Near the summit of McHugh Peak**

hours, depending on the condition and ambition of the hiker(s) involved.

**CAMPSITES:** One will find no designated campsites along this trail. One will find many fine places on which to pitch a tent, however, both on the broad crest of the ridge just south of the summit of McHugh Peak and on the flat areas that the ridge crosses on the traverse to Rabbit Lake. In addition, one can find many suitable places for pitching a tent in the vicinity of either McHugh Lake or Rabbit Lake.

**BEST TIME:** Most people should find any time from June to September a good time to do this hike. One should think twice about doing this hike in winter, however, because of the potential avalanche danger, both in the section where the McHugh Lake Trail contours up the lower section of the McHugh Creek valley and on the climb up the steep cirque on south ridge of McHugh Peak.

**USGS MAPS:** Anchorage A-7 and A-8 SE.

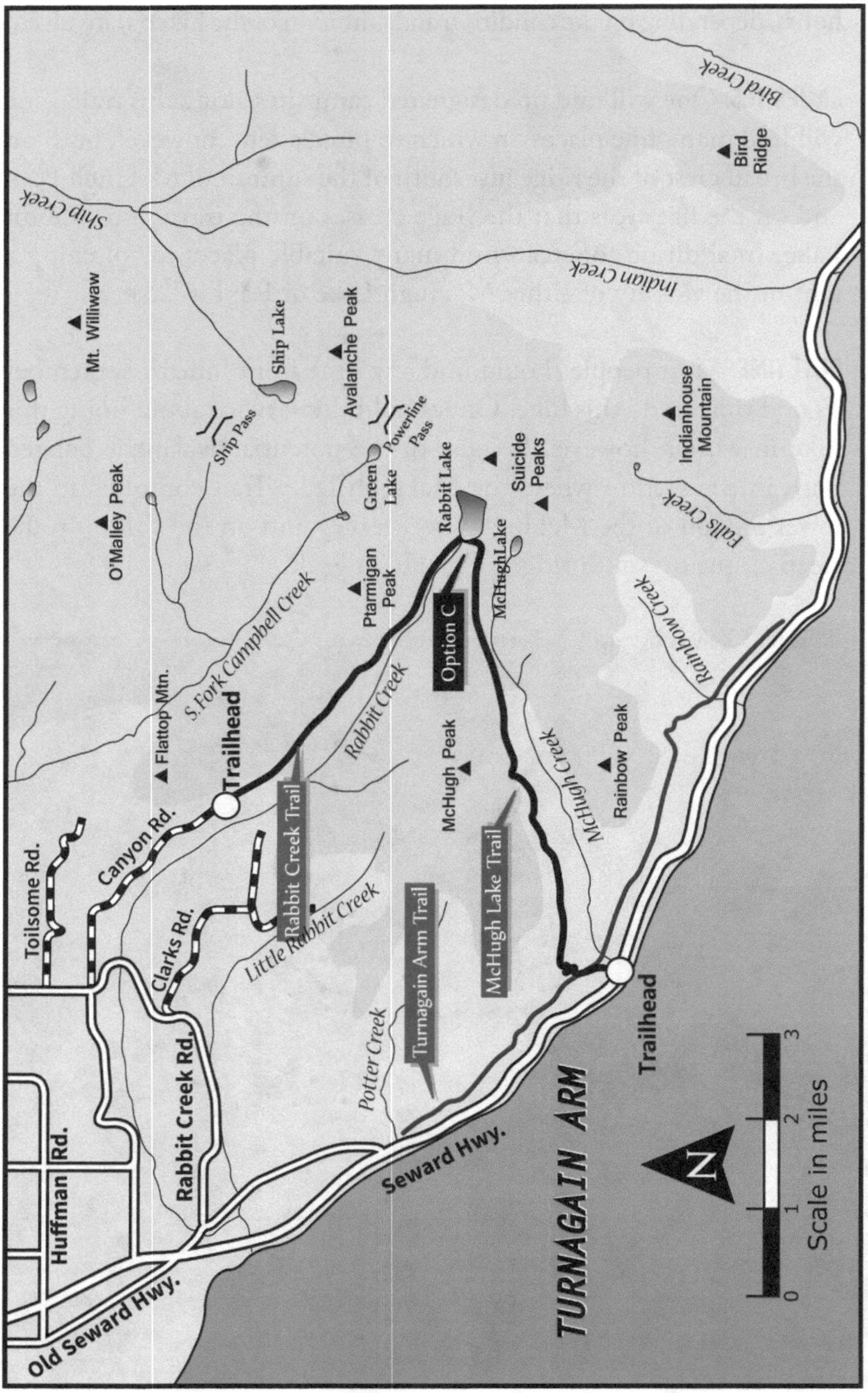
Bird Creek
Bird Ridge
Ship Creek
Indian Creek
Mt. Williwaw
Ship Lake
Avalanche Peak
Ship Pass
Powerline Pass
Green Lake
Rabbit Lake
Suicide Peaks
Indianhouse Mountain
O'Malley Peak
Falls Creek
McHugh Lake
Ptarmigan Peak
S. Fork Campbell Creek
Option C
Rainbow Creek
Flattop Mtn.
Trailhead
Rabbit Creek
McHugh Peak
Rainbow Peak
McHugh Creek
Toilsome Rd.
Canyon Rd.
Rabbit Creek Trail
McHugh Lake Trail
Clarks Rd.
Little Rabbit Creek
Turnagain Arm Trail
Trailhead
Potter Creek
Rabbit Creek Rd.
Huffman Rd.
Seward Hwy.
TURNAGAIN ARM
N
0
1
2
3
Scale in miles
Old Seward Hwy.

# OPTION C

# McHugh Lake Trail to Rabbit Creek Trail

Many should find this one the easier end-to-end hikes in the Front Range, and perhaps in the entire Chugach Mountains. Though relatively easy, it passes through some spectacular country. As it winds up McHugh Creek valley and then down Rabbit Creek valley it passes under the shadows of two 5,000-foot peaks, two 4,000-peaks, as well as numerous other lesser peaks. At its apex, where it crosses from one valley to the next it also passes along the shore of McHugh Lake as well as the broad and wide Rabbit Lake. All in all a very scenic hike for a minimal amount of labor and little worry about the route-finding.

**TRAIL LOCATION:** This traverse of McHugh Lake Trail and Rabbit Creek Trail begins by hiking McHugh Lake Trail to its uppermost end on the southeast shore of Rabbit Lake (3,100-plus feet)*. The upper end of Rabbit Creek Trail lies less than a few hundred yards away from this point. To get there, first follow the shore of Rabbit Lake around to the left (northwest) to the outlet of Rabbit Creek. Cross Rabbit Creek near its outlet where a scattering of conveniently placed stepping stones fill the wide and shallow creek. Once on the far shore of the creek, climb the embankment up to the bluff directly ahead. Near the top of the bluff one should intersect Rabbit Creek Trail. Having reached Rabbit Creek Trail, turn left (west). It only now

--------------------------------------------------------------------

\*   For more information about that trail, see [11] **Walk-About Guide to McHugh Lake Trail**.

remains to follow Rabbit Creek Trail 5.1 miles out to its trailhead on Canyon Road*.

**TRAIL GRADE:** McHugh Lake Trail rates Grade 2 as a hike, with some sections of Grade 1 hiking where one crosses the low, rocky hump between McHugh Lake and Rabbit Lake. The descent along Rabbit Creek Trail rates predominantly Grade 1 as a hike.

**TRAIL CONDITION:** This trail varies little in its condition. On the switchbacks leading up out of the lower valley and through the wide swaths through the alder and willow above, McHugh Lake Trail has few rocks and roots in its lower sections. Only as it climbs up the valley does it turn at all rough and muddy underfoot. Above tree line, the trail flattens and widens as it passes over the low saddle to its end at southeast Rabbit Lake. The following traverse to the upper end of Rabbit Creek Trail involves merely crossing open tundra, followed by a relatively easy stream crossing. The descent along Rabbit Creek Trail predominantly follows an old road, which makes for a wide generally easy trail to follow.

**TRAIL MILEAGE:** To go from McHugh Picnic Area to the trailhead for Rabbit Creek Trail on Canyon Road entails approximately 12.5 miles of hiking.

**TOTAL ELEVATION GAIN:** To hike from McHugh Picnic Area to the trailhead for Rabbit Creek Trail on Canyon Road entails a total elevation gain of approximately 3,600 feet.

-------------------------------------------------------------------------

\* For more information about Rabbit Creek Trail,
see [17] **Walk-About Guide to Rabbit Creek Trail** in Chapter 2.

On the ridge between Rabbit Lake and McHugh Peak

**HIGH POINT:** This trail reaches its highest point of approximately 3,200 feet above sea level on the low saddle between McHugh Lake and Rabbit Lake.

**NORMAL HIKING TIME:** To hike from McHugh Picnic Area to the trailhead for Rabbit Creek Trail on Canyon Road entails should take anywhere from 4 to 8 hours, depending on the condition and ambition of the hiker(s) involved.

**CAMPSITES:** One will find no designated campsites along this trail. One will find many fine places on which to pitch a tent above tree line. Of these, one will find the areas in the vicinity of either McHugh Lake or Rabbit Lake particularly fine places for pitching a tent.

**BEST TIME:** Most people should find any time from June to September a good time to do this hike. One should think twice about doing this hike in winter, however, because of the potential avalanche danger where the trail contours up the lower section of the McHugh Creek valley.

**USGS MAPS:** Anchorage A-7 and A-8 SE.

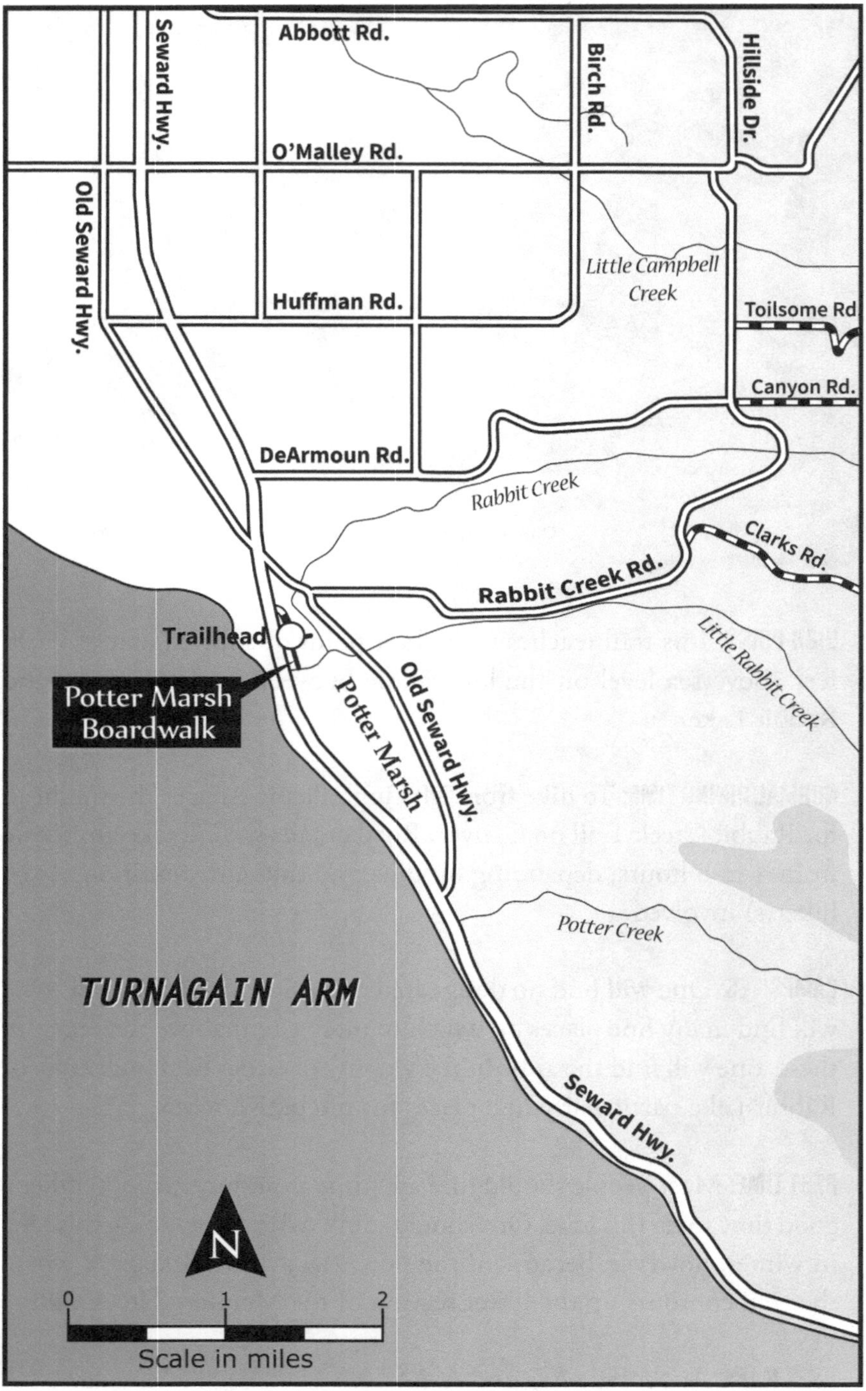
Abbott Rd.
Seward Hwy.
Birch Rd.
Hillside Dr.
O'Malley Rd.
Old Seward Hwy.
Little Campbell Creek
Huffman Rd.
Toilsome Rd
Canyon Rd.
DeArmoun Rd.
Rabbit Creek
Clarks Rd.
Rabbit Creek Rd.
Trailhead
Potter Marsh Boardwalk
Little Rabbit Creek
Potter Marsh
Old Seward Hwy.
Potter Creek
TURNAGAIN ARM
Seward Hwy.
N
0
1
2
Scale in miles

# Walk-About Guide to
# Potter Marsh Boardwalks

Potter Marsh exists as one of those rare places where wildlife has benefited by the intrusion of humankind. Created by the Alaska Railroad stopping the flow of Potter Creek into Cook Inlet, the resulting wetlands have provided a stopping-over place for some birds in mid-migration and a nesting area for other birds. Beginning in early spring, waterfowl of all shapes and sizes begin to appear on the usually placid waters of this marsh. Some, like Canadian geese, trumpeter swans, and assorted ducks come and go. Others, like Arctic Terns, gulls, and waders come and stay. This makes Potter Marsh a sought after location by birders from all over the world. At numerous pullouts along which the Seward Highway sidles the marsh one can see these birders, usually identifiable by their big-lensed cameras, setting up to capture as many of these waterfowls in as many digital pixels as possible.

In addition to these numerous traffic-noisy pullouts, one can watch the vast variety of birds on the marsh from the quieter boardwalks that extend across much of the northern end of the marsh. Besides a fine place from which to bird-watch, these boardwalks make a worthwhile destination for nothing more than a quiet summer-evening stroll with the waters echoing the calls of birds below and the mountains reflecting the quiet gold of the setting sun above.

But this remains more than just a warm-season destination. Come winter, Potter Marsh turns into popular skating spot. Though offering few areas open enough for a game of hockey, the many channels through the frozen grass clumps and mud mounds can transform a simple skating across a pond into a journey through a mile-long maze.

**TRAIL LOCATION:** One can access the boardwalks of Potter Marsh from a parking area just south of Anchorage on the Seward Highway. To get follow there follow Seward Highway south for approximately 9.5 miles from downtown Anchorage to where, at the far end of the Anchorage peninsula, the highway descends to the Turnagain Arm flats. At the bottom of this descent, where the divided highway turns into an undivided highway, one will reach a dirt road on the left (east) and a firing range on the right (west). Turn left onto the dirt road and follow it for approximately 100 yards to a parking area. Park wherever possible. One can access the boardwalks on Potter Marsh on the right (south) side of the parking area.

Once on the boardwalks one can either turn east (left) or right (west). The boardwalk to the east generally remains quieter because of its greater distance from the highway. The boardwalk to the right, however, extends much farther out into the marsh. In doing so it first extends west for approximately 50 feet before turning south for another approximately 100 feet, bringing one closer to far more birds that, surprisingly, seem to remain happily oblivious to the noises from the nearby highway.

**TRAIL GRADE:** These boardwalks rate Grade 1 as a hike for their entire length.

**TRAIL CONDITION:** These boardwalks remain in excellent condition from end to end.

**TRAIL MILEAGE:** To walk the entire length of these boardwalks entails approximately 0.3 miles of hiking.

**TOTAL ELEVATION GAIN:** To walk the entire length of these boardwalks entails virtually no elevation gain.

**HIGH POINT:** This outing reaches its highest point of approximately 20 feet above sea in the parking area.

**NORMAL HIKING TIME:** To walk the entire length of these boardwalks should take anywhere from 20 minutes to an hour, depending on the condition and ambition of the hiker(s) involved.

**CAMPSITES:** One will find no designated camping areas on this trail. Nor should one need one considering the shortness of the hike.

**BEST TIME:** Most people should find any time of year a good time to do this walk.

**USGS MAPS:** Anchorage A-8.

Looking down Turnagain Arm from Kincaid Park

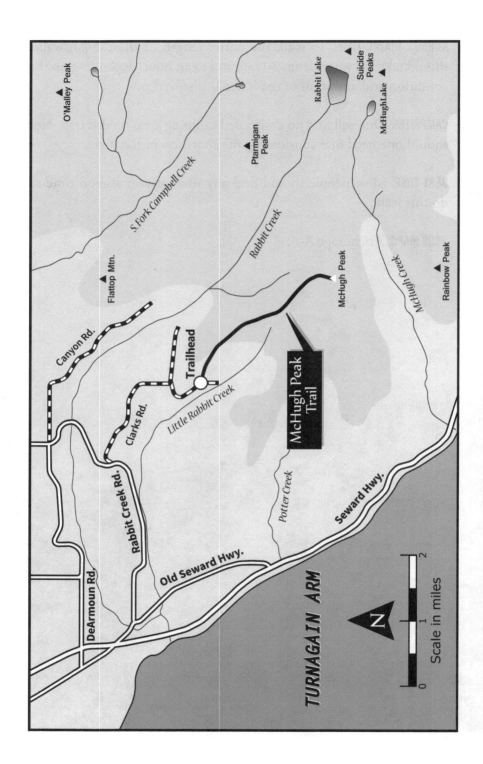

O'Malley Peak

Suicide Peaks

Rabbit Lake

McHugh Lake

S. Fork Campbell Creek

Ptarmigan Peak

Rabbit Creek

Flattop Mtn.

McHugh Peak

McHugh Creek

Rainbow Peak

Canyon Rd.

Trailhead

McHugh Peak Trail

Clarks Rd.

Little Rabbit Creek

Rabbit Creek Rd.

Potter Creek

Seward Hwy.

DeArmoun Rd.

Old Seward Hwy.

TURNAGAIN ARM

N

Scale in miles

0     1     2

## CHAPTER 2

# RABBIT CREEK VALLEY

## Walk-About Guide to McHugh Peak

Though not the tallest mountain in the Front Range of the Chugach Mountains, McHugh Peak can easily lay claim to the title of most massive mountain. Its broad base stretches from Turnagain Arm to the south and Rabbit Creek to the north and from Bear Valley to the west and Rabbit Lake to the east. This geography results in a variety of routes to choose from when climbing it, many of which include a variety of ridge walks. Of all the various routes and ridge walks, however, the climb from Brewster's Drive described below remains the most direct. This also makes a fine destination for any skiers looking for late-season snow, for the snow in the cirque on this side of the mountain, and up which this route climbs to the summit plateau, often lingers well into June.

**TRAIL LOCATION:** The climb of McHugh Peak begins on Brewster's Drive in South Anchorage. To get there drive just over 9 miles south from downtown Anchorage on the Seward Highway to just past Milepost 118, where it reaches the Rabbit Creek Road exit. Take this exit and cross back over the highway onto Rabbit Creek Road. Follow Rabbit Creek Road as it winds up the side of the Anchorage bowl to where it finally levels out as it swings left (north). Just after swinging north, the road passes Storck Park on the right (east). Just past the park, turn right (east) onto Clark's Road. Follow Clark Road to where it turns into King's Way Road. At the next fork in the road bear left (southeast) onto Brewster's Drive. Then follow Brewster's Drive to where it swings south into a higher valley. Approximately halfway up this valley the road reaches a gate. Park wherever possible without blocking the gate.

The hike begins here by continuing past the gate and down the road toward a low rise. Just before reaching this rise, look for a rough trail leaving the road on the left (east). Turning onto this trail, follow it toward the base of the wide 1,100-foot-high cirque formed by the junction of the west and the north ridge directly above.

On reaching the top of the cirque, bear right (southeast) up the rounded slope over the next rise in the ridge. Soon after passing over this rise, one should now clearly see the summit cone rising against the sky on the far side of a wide plateau. Contouring left (east) along a rough trail, circle around the upper side of the plateau to the base of the summit cone. Here a series of steep gullies lead up to a small shelf just below the great rock that makes up summit. Clambering up the slot on the left (east) side of this rock, climb the final few feet to the flat-topped stone summit (4,301 feet).

**TRAIL GRADE:** This climb rates an almost continuous Grade 5 climb from Brewster's Drive to the top of the cirque. Where one crosses the wide plateau from the top of the ravine to the summit cone does the route rates Grade 4 as a hike. The final short climb of the summit cone rates Grade 5 and Grade 6 as a hike.

**TRAIL CONDITION:** This route varies its conditions. The hike up to the base of the cirque crosses through lots of brush and over many muddy and wet spots. Once up the cirque and on the ridge, the climb crosses mostly open tundra mixed with some scree. The final short climb up the summit cone requires a considerable amount of hand-over-hand scrambling.

**TRAIL MILEAGE:** To go from Brewster's Drive to the summit of McHugh Peak entails approximately 2.5 miles of hiking and climbing, for a round-trip total of 5 miles.

**TOTAL ELEVATION GAIN:** The climb from Brewster's Drive to the summit of McHugh Peak entails a total elevation gain of approximately 2,400 feet.

**HIGH POINT:** This hike reaches its highest point of 4,301 feet above sea level at the summit of McHugh Peak.

**NORMAL HIKING TIME:** The climb from Brewster's Drive to the summit of McHugh Peak and back should take anywhere from 3 to 6 hours, depending on the condition and ambition of the hiker(s) involved.

**CAMPSITES:** One will find no designated campsites along this climb. One will find many fine places on which to pitch a tent on the ridge just south of the McHugh Peak's summit. One will find no immediate water sources this high on the mountain, however, unless some snow still lingers from the previous winter.

**BEST TIME:** Most people should find any time from late May to September a good time to do this hike. One should think twice, however, about doing this hike in winter because of the potential avalanche danger on the climb up the ravine to the summit ridge.

**USGS MAPS:** Anchorage A-7 and A-8 SE.

**On McHugh Peak**

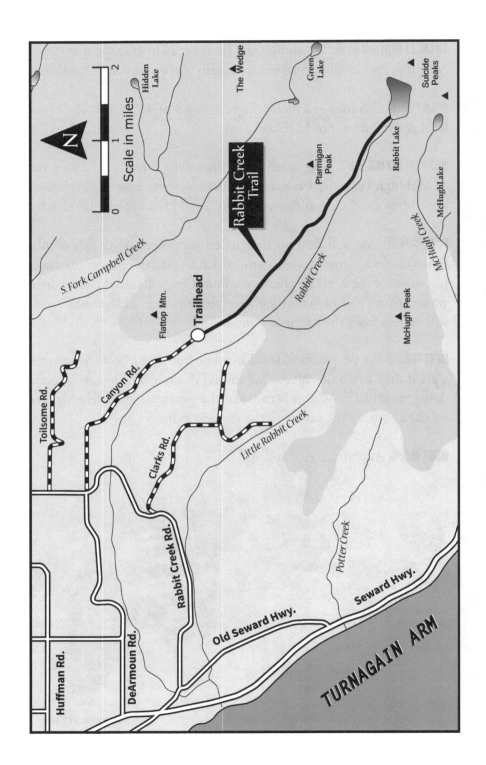

Scale in miles

Hidden Lake

The Wedge

Green Lake

Suicide Peaks

Rabbit Creek Trail

Ptarmigan Peak

Rabbit Lake

McHugh Lake

S. Fork Campbell Creek

Rabbit Creek

McHugh Creek

Flattop Mtn.

Trailhead

McHugh Peak

Toilsome Rd.

Canyon Rd.

Clarks Rd.

Little Rabbit Creek

Rabbit Creek Rd.

Potter Creek

Huffman Rd.

DeArmoun Rd.

Old Seward Hwy.

Seward Hwy.

TURNAGAIN ARM

# Walk-About Guide to Rabbit Creek Trail

A number of years ago, when the first few miles of Rabbit Creek Trail came under private ownership, the owner tried to limit people's use of the trail. To emphasize his intentions, he tore up that part of trail that crossed his property with a backhoe. This resulted in the tortured bit of trail one crosses soon after leaving the parking area. Though the tortured section of trail remains, people can now freely use the trail again without hindrance, and thus again access what some consider the most expansive and picturesque valley in the Front Range.

**TRAIL LOCATION:** Rabbit Creek Trail begins in the shadow of Flattop Mountain on Canyon Road high in Rabbit Creek valley. To get there drive 8.5 miles south on the Seward Highway to just past Milepost 119 where one reaches the DeArmoun Road exit. Take this exit and at the end of the exit ramp turn left (east) and cross back over the highway toward the mountains. After approximately 3.5 miles of steady climbing, DeArmoun Road reaches the lights at the intersection with Hillside Road. Continuing straight through the lights, follow Upper DeArmoun Road as it continues uphill. Approximately 1 mile later the road reaches an intersection with Canyon Road on the right. (One will recognize this road by the row of mailboxes at this junction.) Turning down Canyon Road, follow it for the next 2 miles as it snakes up valley, passing many side streets, along the way. Continuing up valley on Canyon Road, follow it until, after passing one open gate, it dead-ends at a closed gate. This second gate marks the beginning of Rabbit Creek Trail. (Owing to the roughness of the road, some vehicles may have trouble reaching as far as this second gate. If so, one can park at the wide turnaround just below the first gate and walk the short distance up and around the next corner in the road to the second gate.) Park wherever possible without blocking the road and pay the requested fee.

The trail begins by passing around the second gate and continuing up the road beyond it. Within 1 mile the trail reaches the section torn up by the previous owner. Past this section, the trail continues to follow the same road on which it started up valley. After one long and gradual climb the trail finally reaches tree line. From the top of this climb the trail, from which one can now enjoy a wide view of the terrain ahead, then descends onto the flat upper stretches of the valley. Approximately 2 miles later it reaches the west shore of Rabbit Lake (3,000-plus feet) spread out beneath the imposing face of North Suicide Peak. There the trail comes to an end.

At this point one has any number of choices. First, one can turn around and return the way they have come. Second, one can continue over the low pass to the right (south) and follow McHugh Lake Trail down to McHugh Creek Picnic Area*. Third, one can traverse the ridge dividing the headwaters of McHugh Creek and Rabbit back to the summit of McHugh Peak**. Fourth, one can climb South Suicide Peak***. Fifth, they can climb North Suicide Peak****. Finally, a few miles before even reaching Rabbit Lake, one can climb up to the broad expanse of Ptarmigan Pass and there begin a number of other climbs*****.

-------------------------------------------------------------------------------

\* For more information about that trip, see [11] **Walk-About Guide to McHugh Lake Trail** in Chapter 1.

\*\* For more information about that trip, see [18] **OPTION A—McHugh Peak**.

\*\*\* For more information about that climb, see [19] **OPTION B—South Suicide Peak**.

\*\*\*\* For more information about that trip, see [20] **OPTION C—North Suicide Peak**.

\*\*\*\*\*For more information about these climbs, see [21] **OPTION D—Ptarmigan Pass,** [22] **OPTION E—Traverse from Ptarmigan Pass to Flattop Mountain,** [23] **OPTION F— Ptarmigan Peak,** and [24] **OPTION G—Traverse from Ptarmigan Peak to Rabbit Lake.**

**TRAIL GRADE:** This trail rates Grade 2 as a hike for its entire length.

**TRAIL CONDITION:** This trail varies little in its conditions. Following an old road, it remains wide with good footing for almost its entire length. Only in the approximately 1 mile for which it crosses a stretch of formerly privately owned land does it become rough and often muddy underfoot.

**TRAIL MILEAGE:** To go from the parking area on Canyon Road to the shores of Rabbit Lake entails approximately 5.1 miles of hiking, for a round-trip total of approximately 10.2 miles.

**TOTAL ELEVATION GAIN:** To hike from the parking area on Canyon Road to the western end of Rabbit Lake entails a total elevation gain of approximately 1,300 feet.

**HIGH POINT:** This trail reaches its highest point of 3,100-plus feet above sea level at the crest of the bluff one climbs just before reaching Rabbit Lake.

**NORMAL HIKING TIME:** The hike from the parking area on Canyon Road to the shores of Rabbit Lake and back should take anywhere from 3 to 8 hours, depending on the ambition and condition of the hiker(s) involved.

**CAMPSITES:** One will find no designated campsites along this trail. One can, however, still find many fine places on which to pitch a tent almost anywhere above tree line in the upper valley, including by the shores of McHugh Lake, located just up and around the corner to the right (south) from Rabbit Lake.

**BEST TIME:** Most people should find any time from May to September a good time to do this hike. It also makes a fine ski or snowshoe outing in the winter, with only minimal avalanche danger for most of the route up Rabbit Creek valley.

**USGS MAPS:** Anchorage A-7 and A-8 SE.

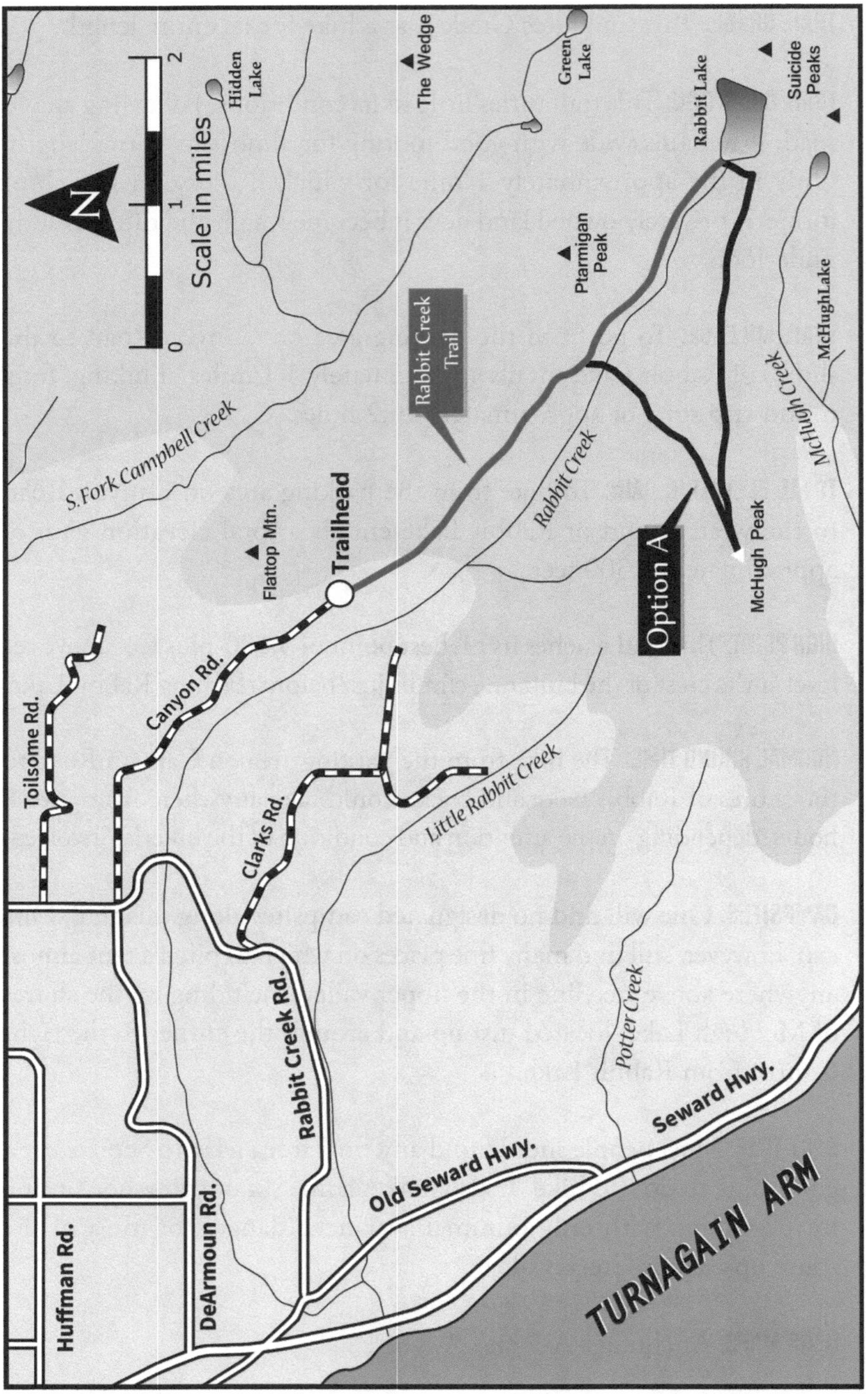
Scale in miles
0
1
2
N
Hidden Lake
The Wedge
Green Lake
Rabbit Lake
Suicide Peaks
Ptarmigan Peak
McHughLake
McHugh Creek
McHugh Peak
Option A
Rabbit Creek
Rabbit Creek Trail
S. Fork Campbell Creek
Flattop Mtn.
Trailhead
Canyon Rd.
Toilsome Rd.
Clarks Rd.
Little Rabbit Creek
Potter Creek
Rabbit Creek Rd.
Huffman Rd.
DeArmoun Rd.
Old Seward Hwy.
Seward Hwy.
TURNAGAIN ARM

# OPTION A

# McHugh Peak

Instead of merely hiking out and back on the Rabbit Creek Trail to Rabbit Lake and back, this option offers a very scenic, but harder, alternative round-trip hike to and from the parking area on Canyon Road via the summit ridge of McHugh Peak. During this traverse the route crosses over four prominent high points on the ridge, concluding with McHugh Peak (4,301 feet), before making an adventurous descent down across Rabbit Creek back to Rabbit Creek Trail for the final short hike back to the parking area.

**TRAIL LOCATION:** This trip starts at the end of Rabbit Creek Trail on the west shores of Rabbit Lake*. From the end of Rabbit Creek Trail, turn right (south) and cross Rabbit Creek. Then climb up to the crest of the low saddle that separates the Rabbit Creek drainage from the McHugh Creek drainage. On the crest of this saddle, turn right (west) and begin climbing directly up the crest of the ridge toward the buttress above.

Upon reaching the buttress, look for the narrow sheep trail that continues along the crest of the ridge. Follow this trail, which requires some rock scrambling in spots, as it winds its long way toward McHugh Peak. Eventually the ridge flattens out into a broad plateau. At the far end of the plateau the ridge suddenly narrows as it circles the wide bowl

--------------------------------------------------------------------

*    To get there, see [17] **Walk-About Guide to Rabbit Creek Trail**.

in front of the summit cone of McHugh Peak. Contouring along the ridge, follow its curve as it bears left (southwest) around the uppermost end of the bowl to the base of the summit cone.

Once where the ridgeline meets the base of the summit cone, contour around the summit cone to the right (north). On the north side of the summit cone, one reaches a series of three gullies leading up to a grass and dirt shelf just below the summit. After climbing one these gullies it only remains to make the final short ascent onto the single rock of the summit. Clambering up the slot on the left (east) of this rock, climb the final few feet to the flat stone summit (4,301 feet).

Upon leaving the summit of McHugh Peak, the route now leads down and to the right (northeast). Begin by first descending back down into the bowl to the right. But instead of contouring back around the bowl, continue at an angle toward the bowl's lower end. Pass over the small rise on the lower right (east) corner of the bowl to where one can look directly down to Rabbit Creek and Rabbit Creek Trail on the slope just above and beyond it. After picking a route down the slope, descend into Rabbit Creek basin. After bushwhacking in and out of the steep-sided Rabbit Creek bed (which into early June may still have a cover of snow over it), climb through the brush on the far side back up to Rabbit Creek Trail. Once on the trail, turn left (west) to hike the approximately 1.5 miles back to the parking area.

**TRAIL GRADE:** While Rabbit Creek Trail and the traverse over to McHugh Lake rate Grade 1 as a hike, once one starts up the long east ridge of McHugh Peak the rate increases to Grade 4 as a hike, with short sections of scrambling rated to Grade 5 as a hike. The final climb to the summit McHugh Peak rates Grade 5 as a hike. The long descent from the summit of McHugh Peak back to Rabbit Creek Trail rates Grade 4 as a hike. The final hike out Rabbit Creek Trail rates Grade 1 as a hike.

**TRAIL CONDITION:** This climb varies considerably in its conditions. It begins on the wide road of Rabbit Creek Trail. Upon starting up the east ridge of McHugh Peak, however, the route crosses steep tundra, scree, and some short boulder fields. The last short climb to the summit of McHugh Peak, also involves scrambling and some low-level rock-climbing.

**TRAIL MILEAGE:** To complete this entire traverse from Canyon Road to the summit of McHugh Peak and back entails approximately 13 miles of hiking and climbing.

**TOTAL ELEVATION GAIN:** To complete this entire traverse from Canyon Road to the summit of McHugh Peak and back entails a total elevation gain of approximately 2,700 feet.

**HIGH POINT:** This climb reaches its highest point of 4,301 feet above sea level at the summit of McHugh Peak.

**NORMAL HIKING TIME:** To complete this entire traverse from Canyon Road to the summit of McHugh Peak and back should take anywhere from 1 to 2 days, depending on the condition and ambition of the hiker(s) involved.

**CAMPSITES:** One will find no designated campsites along this trail. One will, however, find many fine places on which to pitch a tent almost anywhere above tree line in the upper valley, including by the shores of McHugh Lake, which is located just up and around the corner to the right (south) from Rabbit Lake.

**BEST TIME:** Most people should find any time from June to early September a good time to do this hike.

**USGS MAPS:** Anchorage A-7 and A-8 SE.

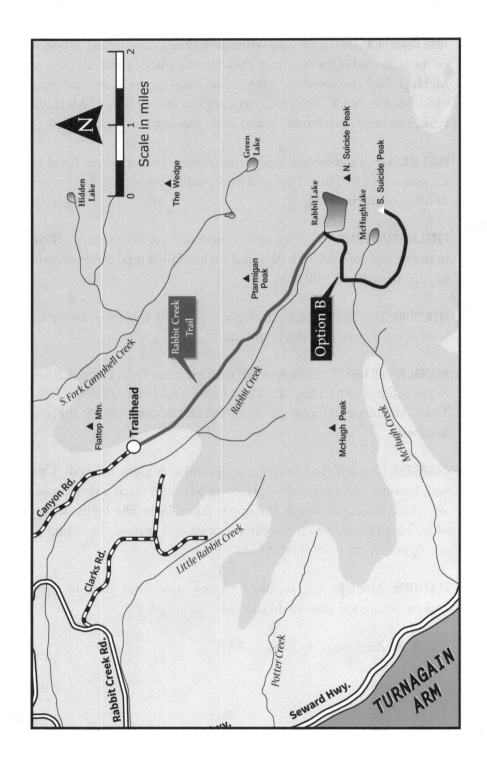

Scale in miles

N

Hidden Lake

The Wedge

Green Lake

N. Suicide Peak

S. Suicide Peak

Rabbit Lake

McHugh Lake

Rabbit Creek Trail

Ptarmigan Peak

Option B

S. Fork Campbell Creek

Rabbit Creek

Flattop Mtn.

Trailhead

McHugh Peak

McHugh Creek

Canyon Rd.

Clarks Rd.

Little Rabbit Creek

Rabbit Creek Rd.

Potter Creek

Seward Hwy.

TURNAGAIN ARM

# OPTION B

# South Suicide Peak

South Suicide Peak, the southernmost 5,000-foot-plus summit in the Front Range, towers over the right (southeast) end of Rabbit Lake. Rising so prominently from the shore of the lake, this massive triangle of rock entices many people to climb it. Few will find it any easy climb, though, requiring as it does much effort and a considerable amount of rock-scrambling. But the view from the summit, a view which extends from the far end of Turnagain Arm to the south and north far across the Chugach Mountains to the Talkeetna Mountains beyond, makes the effort worth it.

**TRAIL LOCATION:** This climb begins at the end of Rabbit Creek Trail at Rabbit Lake*. From the shore of Rabbit Lake turn right (south) and cross Rabbit Creek. Then climb over the low hump directly ahead and descend to follow McHugh Lake Trail the short way down to McHugh Lake. Next, turn left (east) along the far shore of McHugh Lake to where McHugh Creek leaves the lake. Just below the outlet of the lake find a place to cross.

Once on the far side of McHugh Creek one begins the climb proper. Begin the climb by picking a route up the broad but steep tundra slope leading to the buttress of South Suicide Peak's west ridge towering approximately 1,200 feet above. Once on the buttress, turn

--------------------------------------------------

* To get there, see [17] **Walk-About Guide to Rabbit Creek Trail**.

left (east-northeast) to follow the crest of the ridge. Going over or around the gendarmes, rock pillars, and scree slopes that block the way, follow the ridge crest to where it drops into a wide tundra saddle below the summit cone. Descend and cross the saddle.

At the far side of the saddle follow the right (northwest) side of the ridge's crest for the final approximately 600-foot climb to the summit. On this climb make sure to stay as close as possible to the crest of the ridge, keeping the precipitous west face of the mountain on your left. For those who don't want to look down the sheer west face, they can corkscrew up and to the right, making sure not to stray far from the crest of the ridge. At the very top of this climb, one reaches the steep crown of the summit. A few scrambling steps to the right (southeast) one should find a spot to clamber up and over onto the summit (5,005 feet).

Having reached the summit, many will probably want to turn around and return the way they came. More ambitious hikers, however, may want to continue down the opposite side of the mountain into the very appropriately named Windy Gap (so named because of the ferocious south winds that funnel up and through it). From the bottom of this gap one can continue up the opposite side to the summit of North Suicide Peak (5,065 feet). From the top of that summit one can even continue to traverse down the knife-edged ridge on the far side of North Suicide Peak down to where one can make a gentle descent down to the left (west) to the east shores of Rabbit Lake.

Those wanting to continue climbing have yet another two options at this point. First, one can turn left (west) continue along the steep and jagged ridge to the summit of Ptarmigan Peak. From that summit they can then descend down the southwest side of that summit to Ptarmigan Pass. Once in the pass, they can descend off either side. The gentler left (south) side leads down to Rabbit Creek Trail. The steeper right (north) side of the pass drops through the notch at the base of Ptarmigan Peak's west face and down a rocky trail to Powerline Pass. Second, one can continue straight ahead (north) from the knife-edge gap at the bottom of North Suicide Peak's north ridge and continue straight ahead, following a pronounced sheep trail along the backside of the ridge directly ahead to where one can descend straight into Powerline Pass. In the pass, one can hop onto Powerline Trail and follow it out to Glen Alps. Any one of these extensions of the climb up South Suicide Peak makes for a long and spectacular day.

**TRAIL GRADE:** While Rabbit Creek Trail and the traverse over to McHugh Lake rate Grade 1 to Grade 2 as a hike, once one crosses McHugh Creek and begins ascending the face of the west ridge of South Suicide Peak, the rate increases first to Grade 5 as a hike and then increases again to Grade 6 as a hike for most of the remaining climb to the summit.

Those wishing to continue beyond the summit of South Suicide Peak should expect more of the same, and at times a bit more. Though most of the climbing beyond the summit of South Suicide Peak rates between Grade 5 and Grade 6 as a hike, one narrow notch in the saddle between North Suicide Peak and the ridge beyond may seem to some people to rate Grade 7 as a hike. One might, therefore, want to bring a rope. Some may also find a rope useful at times while coming down the rocky north ridge of North Suicide Peak or even along while traversing the jagged east ridge of Ptarmigan Peak.

**TRAIL CONDITION:** This climb varies considerably in its conditions. It begins on the wide road of Rabbit Creek Trail. Once the route crosses McHugh Creek, however, it entails climbing steep, scree-streaked tundra, followed by a considerable amount of rock-scrambling along the crest of the South Suicide Peak's west ridge as well as on the final climb of the summit cone.

**TRAIL MILEAGE:** To go from the parking area on Canyon Road to the summit of South Suicide Peak entails approximately 8.2 miles of hiking and climbing, for a round-trip total of approximately 16.4 miles.

**TOTAL ELEVATION GAIN:** To hike from the parking area on Canyon Road to the summit of South Suicide Peak entails a total elevation gain of approximately 3,105 feet.

**HIGH POINT:** This climb reaches its highest point of 5,005 feet above sea level at the summit of South Suicide Peak.

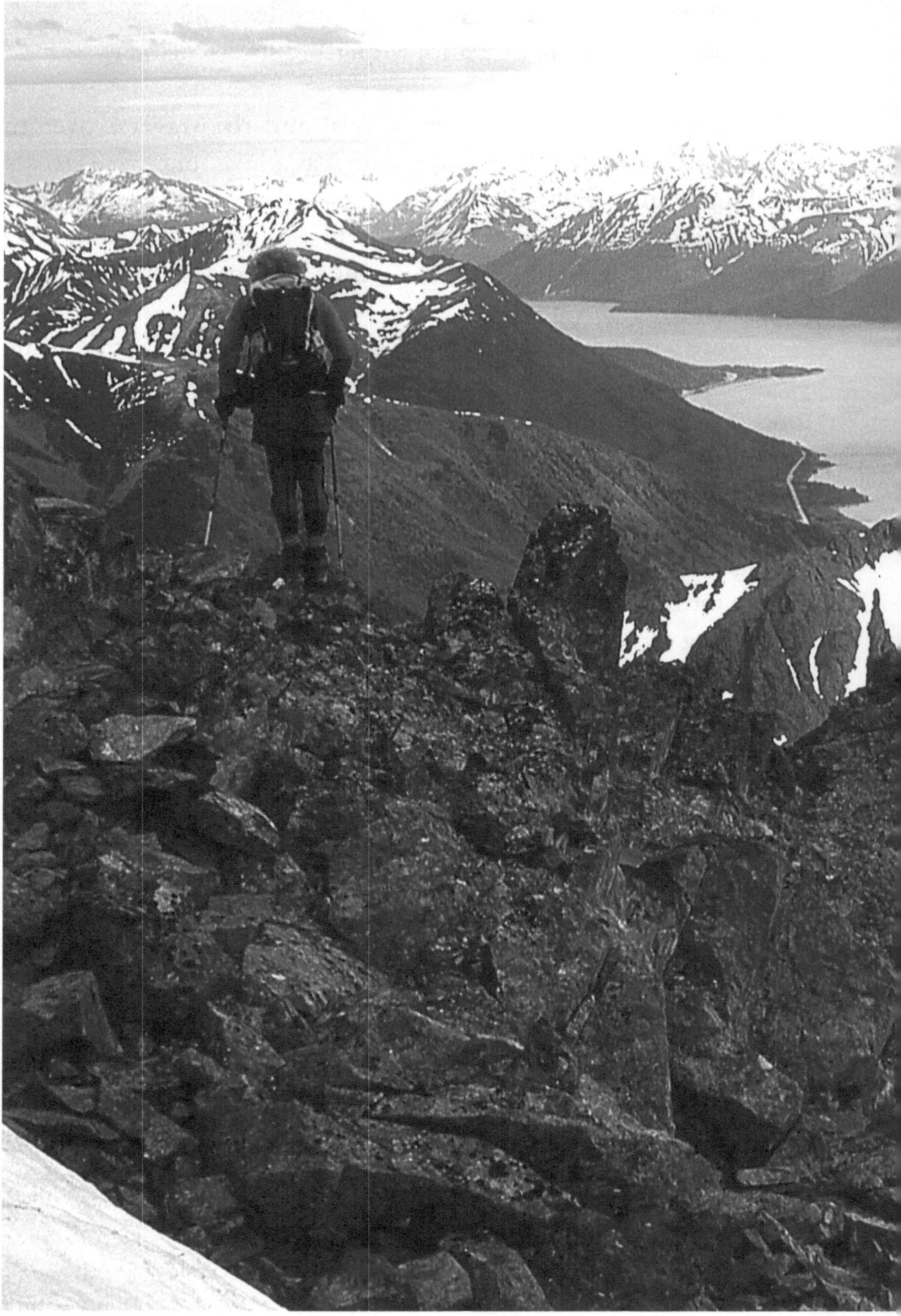

**NORMAL HIKING TIME:** The climb from the parking area on Canyon Road to the summit of South Suicide Peak and back should take anywhere from 1 to 2 days, depending on the condition and ambition of the hiker(s) involved.

**CAMPSITES:** One will find no designated campsites along this trail. One can, however, still find many fine places on which to pitch a tent almost anywhere above tree line in the upper valley, including spots by the shores of McHugh Lake, which is located just up and around the corner to the right (south) from Rabbit Lake.

**BEST TIME:** Most people should find any time from June to early September a good time to do this hike.

**USGS MAPS:** Anchorage A-7 and A-8 SE.

On the ridge between South Suicide Peak and Falls Creek Trail

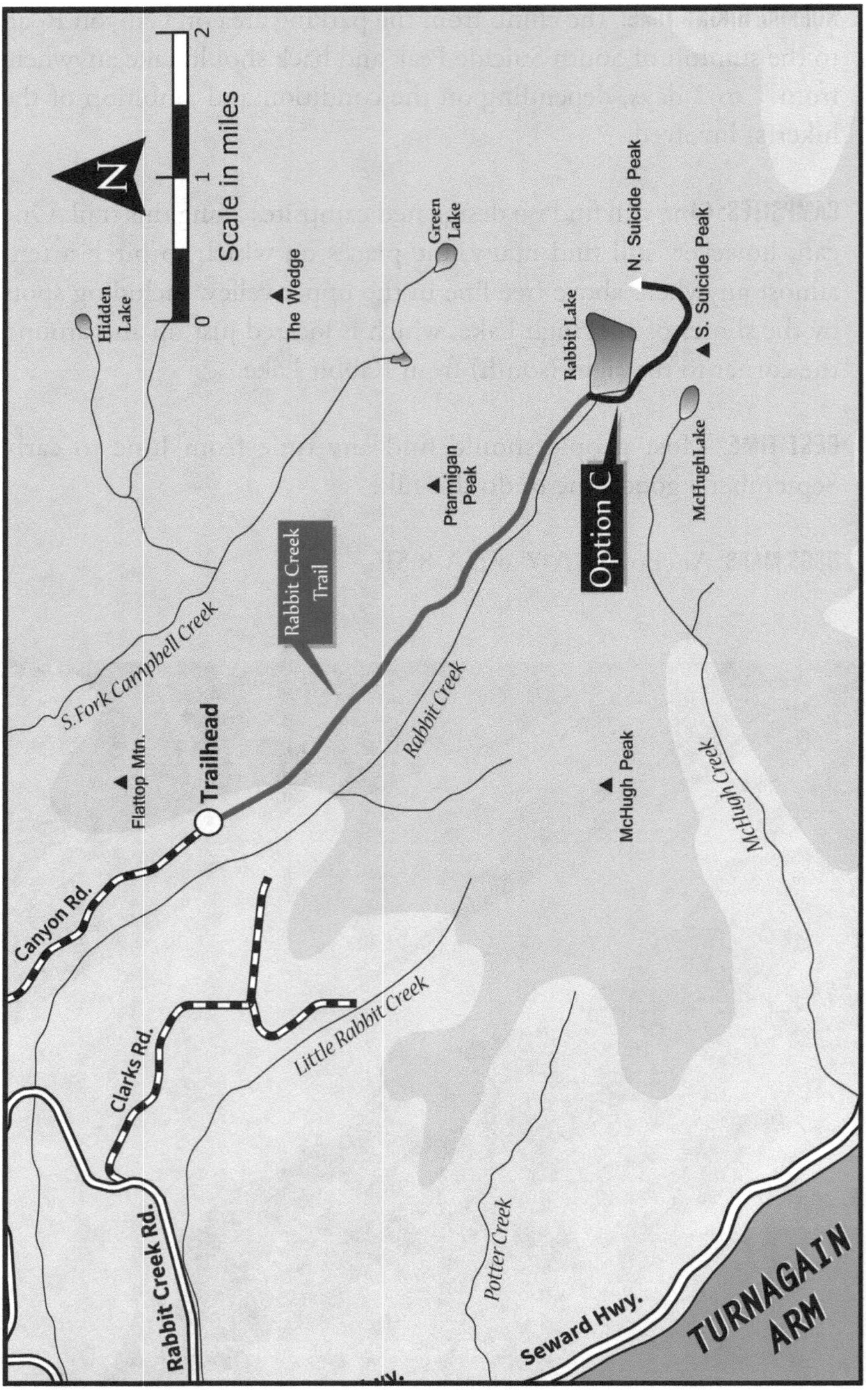
N
Scale in miles
0
1
2
Hidden Lake
The Wedge
Green Lake
N. Suicide Peak
S. Suicide Peak
Rabbit Lake
McHughLake
Option C
Ptarmigan Peak
Rabbit Creek Trail
S.Fork Campbell Creek
Trailhead
Flattop Mtn.
Rabbit Creek
McHugh Peak
McHugh Creek
Canyon Rd.
Clarks Rd.
Little Rabbit Creek
Rabbit Creek Rd.
Potter Creek
Seward Hwy.
TURNAGAIN ARM

# OPTION C

# North Suicide Peak

Although one can climb North Suicide Peak the long way by passing over South Suicide Peak, or the even a longer way by following the ridge from Powerline Pass, the route described below provides the most direct, non-technical way to the summit of North Suicide Peak. Many people, however, might think twice about doing this shorter but labor-intensive climb. Not only does it entail climbing a steep gully, but this steep gully consists almost entirely of loose scree. Although it should not require any roped climbing to scramble up this scree, inexperienced scramblers may find it intimidating. This especially applies anyone who does not like the feeling of lots of earth moving under their feet.

**TRAIL LOCATION:** This climb begins at the end of Rabbit Creek Trail at the western shores of Rabbit Lake*. At this point look straight ahead (east) for the gash that descends from just below the summit of South Suicide Peak along the right (south) side of Windy Gap and all the way down to far shore of Rabbit Lake. The first part of the climb entails reaching the base of that gash. To get there begin by bearing right (south) from the end of Rabbit Creek Trail and crossing the outlet of Rabbit Lake and following the south shore of the lake around to the base of Windy Gap between North Suicide Peak and South Suicide Peak. On

---

\*    To get there, see [17] **Walk-About Guide to Rabbit Creek Trail**.

reaching the base of Windy Gap turn sharply right (southeast) and up. One should now have a clear view of the long, steep gash of loose stones pointing almost directly at the summit of South Suicide Peak.

The base of this gash marks the beginning of the climb proper. From the base of the gully, pick a route and begin climbing the approximately 900 feet leading to the top of the gully. To make this climb a bit easier, one might consider hugging one of the sides of the gully and using the firmer rocks there for some handholds and even footholds.

Upon emerging from the top of this gully on the north face of South Suicide Peak, turn sharply left (north) and descend into Windy Gap. From the gap continue directly ahead and begin climbing the wide, but rocky slope leading to the summit of North Suicide Peak above. At the top of the slope, bear left (northwest) along a short, narrow ridge. Finally, after one last rock-climbing move over an exposed boulder, one can walk final feet to the summit of North Suicide Peak (5,065 feet).

Having reached the summit, many may want to turn around and return the way they have come. Ambitious hikers, however, may want to continue to traverse down the knife-edged ridge on the far side of North Suicide Peak down to where one can make a gentle descent down to the left (west) to the east shores of Rabbit Lake.

Those wanting to continue climbing have yet another two options at this point. First, one can turn left (west) continue along the steep and jagged ridge to the summit of Ptarmigan Peak. From that summit they can then descend down the southwest side of that summit to Ptarmigan Pass. Once in the pass, one can descend off either side. The gentler left (south) side leads down to Rabbit Creek Trail. The steeper right (north) side of the pass drops through the notch at the base of Ptarmigan Peak's west face and down a rocky trail to Powerline Pass. Second, one can continue straight ahead (north) from the knife-edge gap at the bottom of North Suicide Peak's north ridge and continue straight ahead, following a pronounced sheep trail along the backside of the ridge directly ahead to where one can descend straight into Powerline Pass. In the pass, one can hop onto Powerline Trail and follow it out to Glen Alps.

Any one of these extensions of the climb up South Suicide Peak makes for a long and spectacular day.

**TRAIL GRADE:** Rabbit Creek Trail and the traverse over to the base of the gully rate Grade 1 as a hike. Once one begins ascending the gully to the crest of Windy Gap, the climb rates Grade 6 as a scramble. The remainder of the climb to the summit of North Suicide Peak rates between Grade 5 and Grade 6 as a hike.

Though most of the climbing beyond the summit of North Suicide Peak rates between Grade 5 and Grade 6 as a hike, one narrow notch in the saddle between North Suicide Peak and the east ridge of Ptarmigan Peak may seem to some people to rate Grade 7 as a hike. Thus one might consider bringing a rope. Some may also find such a rope useful at times while coming down the rocky north ridge of North Suicide Peak or even along the jagged ridge leading to the summit of Ptarmigan Peak.

**TRAIL CONDITION:** This climb varies considerably in its conditions. It begins on the wide road of Rabbit Creek Trail. Then it crosses open tundra to the base of the gully. Once it starts up the gully to the crest of Windy Gap, the climb entails climbing a very steep scree slope. The climb from Windy Gap to the summit of North Suicide Peak entails more scrambling up scree and over boulders. One must also make a single rock-climbing move over an exposed boulder just before reaching the summit.

**TRAIL MILEAGE:** To go from the parking area on Canyon Road to the summit of North Suicide Peak entails approximately 7.3 miles of hiking and climbing, for a round-trip total of approximately 14.6 miles.

**TOTAL ELEVATION GAIN:** To hike from the parking area on Canyon Road to the summit of North Suicide Peak entails a total elevation gain of approximately 3,100 feet.

**HIGH POINT:** This climb reaches its highest point of 5,065 feet above sea level at the summit of North Suicide Peak.

**NORMAL HIKING TIME:** The climb from the parking area on Canyon Road to the summit of North Suicide Peak and back should take anywhere from 1 to 2 days, depending on the condition and ambition of the hiker(s) involved.

**CAMPSITES:** One will find no designated campsites along this trail. One will find, however, many fine places on which to pitch a tent almost anywhere above tree line in the upper valley, including by the shores of McHugh Lake, which is located just up and around the corner to the right (south) from Rabbit Lake.

**BEST TIME:** Most people should find any time from June to early September a good time to do this hike.

**USGS MAPS:** Anchorage A-7 and A-8 SE.

Descending to Rabbit Lake

Descending North Suicide Peak into Windy Gap

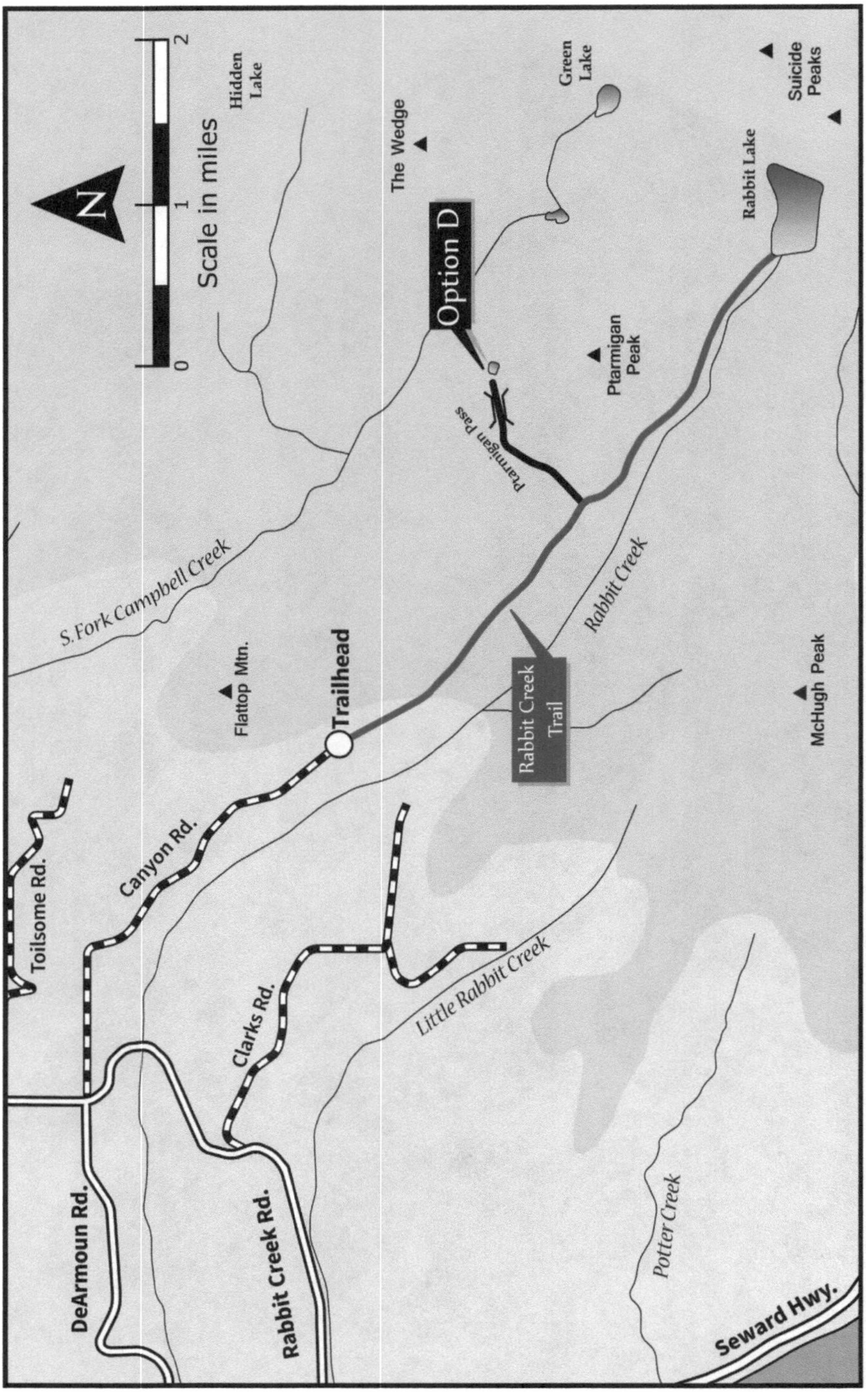
N
Scale in miles
0
1
2
Hidden Lake
The Wedge
Green Lake
Suicide Peaks
Option D
Rabbit Lake
Ptarmigan Peak
Ptarmigan Pass
S. Fork Campbell Creek
Rabbit Creek
Flattop Mtn.
Trailhead
Rabbit Creek Trail
McHugh Peak
Toilsome Rd.
Canyon Rd.
Clarks Rd.
Little Rabbit Creek
DeArmoun Rd.
Rabbit Creek Rd.
Potter Creek
Seward Hwy.

# OPTION D

# Ptarmigan Pass

Most hikers who climb for the first time into this broad pass tucked into the ridge between Rabbit Creek and Campbell Creek wonder why they did not know about it beforehand.

**TRAIL LOCATION:** This hike begins approximately 2.5 miles up Rabbit Creek Trail just after the trail reaches tree line and just before the trail descends to the flats leading to Rabbit Lake*. Here, where a broad gap appears in the ridge above and to the left (north), bear left off the trail and begin climbing the broad tundra slope toward that gap. After approximately 800 feet of climbing, the ridge rolls over the top of the shelf into the long, broad pass. If one then continues diagonally across the pass for approximately 0.5 miles to the far corner, one can reach a tarn in a deep hollow below the sheer west face of Ptarmigan Peak.

Some may choose to make this spot overlooking the tarn their final destination. More ambitious hikers have a number of options at this point. First, one can descend to Powerline Trail via a rough trail dropping down through the slot to the left (northeast) of the tarn. Second, one can climb the ridge to leading west over Flaketop (4,488 feet), Peak Three (3,996 feet), and Peak Two (3,658 feet) to the summit of Flattop Mountain. From there one can take the Flattop Mountain Trail down to Glen Alps parking area or take the Flattop Trail off the

--------------------------------------------------------------------

\*    To get there, see [17] **Walk-About Guide to Rabbit Creek Trail**.

south side of Flattop Mountain that leads down to the parking area for Rabbit Creek Trail on Canyon Road*. Third, one can climb Ptarmigan Peak, the peak towering over the right (east) side of Ptarmigan Pass**. Fourth, one can traverse the ridge between Ptarmigan Peak and Rabbit Lake***. Ptarmigan Pass can thus serve as a destination in itself or as the beginning of a number of other hikes.

**TRAIL GRADE:** Rabbit Creek Trail rates Grade 1 as a hike. On leaving the trail, however, the climb to the crest of Ptarmigan Pass rates Grade 4 as a hike. Crossing the pass also rates Grade 4 as a hike.

**TRAIL CONDITION:** This climb varies little in its conditions. It begins on the wide road of Rabbit Creek Trail. On the slope to Ptarmigan Pass, it crosses mostly tundra and some loose stones. Crossing the pass involves hiking over mostly tundra mixed with some scattered rocks.

**TRAIL MILEAGE:** To go from the parking area to the tarn at the far corner of Ptarmigan Pass entails approximately 3.7 miles of hiking and climbing, for a round-trip total of approximately 7.2 miles.

**TOTAL ELEVATION GAIN:** To hike from the parking area on Canyon Road to the tarn at the far corner of Ptarmigan Pass entails a total elevation gain of approximately 1,900 feet.

**HIGH POINT:** This hike reaches its highest point of 3,600 feet above sea level near the center of Ptarmigan Pass.

**NORMAL HIKING TIME:** The climb from the parking area on Canyon Road to the tarn at the far corner of Ptarmigan Pass and back should take

----

\* For more information about that trail, see [22] **OPTION E—Traverse from Ptarmigan Pass to Flattop Mountain.**

\*\* For more information about that climb, see [23] **OPTION F—Ptarmigan Peak.**

\*\*\* For more information about that climb, see [24] **OPTION G—Traverse from Ptarmigan Peak to Rabbit Lake.**

anywhere from 3 to 6 hours, depending on the condition and ambition of the hiker(s) involved.

**CAMPSITES:** One will find no designated campsites along this trail. One will, however, find many fine places on which to pitch a tent almost anywhere in Ptarmigan Pass as well as farther up the Rabbit Creek valley near Rabbit Lake.

**BEST TIME:** Most people should find any time from June to early September a good time to do this hike.

**USGS MAPS:** Anchorage A-7 and A-8 SE.

Climbing toward Ptarmigan Pass

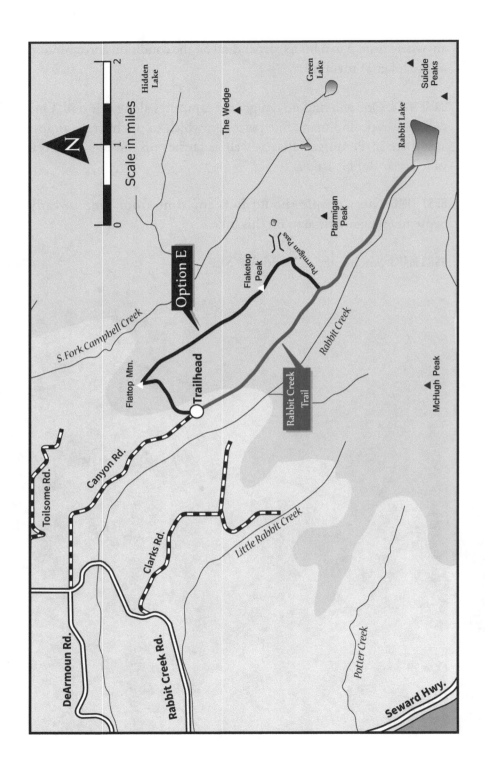

Scale in miles

0   1   2

N

Hidden Lake

The Wedge

Green Lake

Suicide Peaks

Rabbit Lake

Ptarmigan Peak

Ptarmigan Pass

Flaketop Peak

Option E

S. Fork Campbell Creek

Flattop Mtn.

Trailhead

Rabbit Creek

Rabbit Creek Trail

McHugh Peak

Toilsome Rd.

Canyon Rd.

Clarks Rd.

Little Rabbit Creek

DeArmoun Rd.

Rabbit Creek Rd.

Potter Creek

Seward Hwy.

# OPTION E

# Traverse from Ptarmigan Pass to Flattop Mountain

This traverse passes over the same peaks, but in the opposite direction and from a different starting place, as described in the next chapter*.

**TRAIL LOCATION:** This hike begins approximately 2.5 miles up Rabbit Creek Trail just before the trail descends to the flats leading to Rabbit Lake**. Here, where a broad gap appears in the ridge above and to the left (north), bear left off the trail and begin climbing the broad tundra slope toward that gap. After approximately 800 feet of climbing, the ridge rolls over the top of the shelf into long and broad Ptarmigan Pass. Then continue diagonally across the pass for approximately 0.5 miles to the far northeast corner, one can reach a tarn in a deep hollow below the sheer west face of Ptarmigan Peak.

At the tarn turn left (west) and follow, as near as possible, the crest of the ridge as it climbs along the north side of Ptarmigan Pass. At the far end of the pass of look for the dim trail that slants up and to the left up into a small notch. This notch may require some easy hand-over hand scrambling to ascend. Just beyond the notch the route reaches the summit of Flaketop (4,488 feet). From this first summit follow as

---

* For that guide, see [27] **OPTION A—Traverse from Flattop Mountain to Ptarmigan Pass** in Chapter 3.

** To get there, see [17] **Walk-About Guide to Rabbit Creek Trail**.

best as possible the rough sheep and people trail that leads across the many-spired ridge toward Peak Three. This section of the traverse may entail numerous small detours to avoid steep gullies and rock faces if one remains uncertain as to whether they can make a certain descent of a gully or ascent of a face. If this proves true, one usually need only turn down and to the left (south) to make any necessary detour before again continuing along the ridge to the summit of Peak Three (3,996 feet). From Peak Three, the route follows a more easily negotiated trail to Peak Two (3,658 feet). From Peak Two a gravelly trail descends sharply to the next notch where the traverse joins Flattop Trail*.

From the notch Flattop Trail ascends at a relatively gentle angle up and across the east face of Flattop Mountain. Once on the broad summit of Flattop, bear right (northwest) to the small hump of rocks visible at the center of the plateau. This hump of rocks marks the true summit (3,510 feet). Having reached this final summit in the traverse one need only turn around and follow Flattop Trail back down to the previous notch. There, instead of re-climbing Peak Two, bear right (south) and follow Flattop Trail the remainder of the way down to Canyon Road.

**TRAIL GRADE:** Rabbit Creek Trail rates Grade 2 as a hike. Once one leaves the trail and begins the climb to Ptarmigan Pass, the route rates Grade 3 and Grade 4 as a hike. Upon leaving the tarn at the far side of Ptarmigan Pass, the route begins as a grade 4 hike, but soon rises to Grade 5 as a hike as it starts up the backside of Flaketop. It remains mostly a Grade 5 between Flaketop and Peak Three. Past Peak Three, the traverse fluctuates between a Grade 5 and Grade 6 hike. From the summit of Peak Two, the route again rates Grade 3 as it descends a steep trail which connects with Flattop Trail in the next gap. The rest of the route, up Flattop Trail to the summit of Flattop Mountain and then back down to Canyon Road rates Grade 3 as a hike.

--------------------------------------------------------------------

* For more information about that trail, see [25] **Walk-About Guide to Flattop Trail**.

**TRAIL CONDITION:** The first part of this hike entails following the wide Rabbit Creek Trail. The following climb up and across Ptarmigan Pass to the far side crosses mostly open tundra. Upon leaving the tarn and starting up the ridge proper, conditions prove much rougher. The climb up Flaketop follows a very rough trail. The traverse from Flaketop, over Peak Three, and on to Peak Two crosses a very rocky ridge with long sections of scree and boulders. From Peak Two the route descends a steep, rock-strewn trail down to Flattop Trail. The last 2 miles to the summit of Flattop and back down to the parking area on Canyon Road follow the broad Flattop Trail.

**TRAIL MILEAGE:** To complete this traverse from the parking area on Canyon Road along the ridge to Flattop Mountain and back down to Canyon Road entails approximately 8 miles of hiking and scrambling.

**TOTAL ELEVATION GAIN:** To complete this traverse from the parking area on Canyon Road along the ridge to Flattop Mountain and back down to Canyon Road entails a total elevation gain of approximately 3,500 feet.

**HIGH POINT:** This hike reaches its highest point of 4,488 feet above sea level at the summit of Flaketop.

**NORMAL HIKING TIME:** The traverse from the parking area on Canyon Road along the ridge to Flattop Mountain and back down to Canyon Road should take anywhere from 6 to 9 hours, depending on the condition and ambition of the hiker(s) involved.

**CAMPSITES:** One will find no designated campsites on the traverse itself. One will find many fine places on which to pitch a tent, however, in Ptarmigan Pass.

**BEST TIME:** Most people should find any time from June to early September a good time to do this hike.

**USGS MAPS:** Anchorage A-7 and A-8 SE.

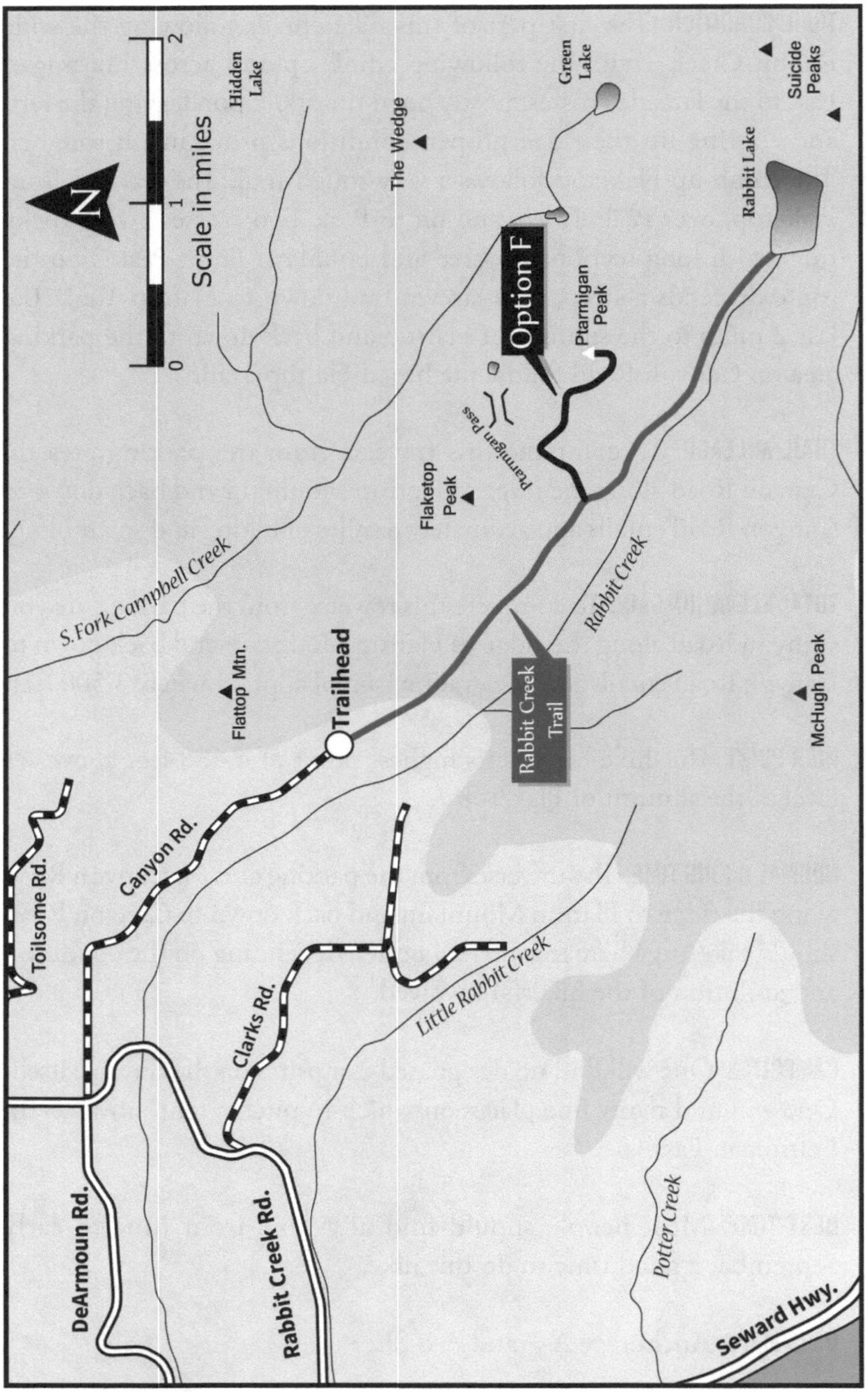
N
Scale in miles
0
1
2
Hidden Lake
The Wedge
Green Lake
Suicide Peaks
Rabbit Lake
Option F
Ptarmigan Peak
Ptarmigan Pass
Flaketop Peak
S. Fork Campbell Creek
Rabbit Creek
Flattop Mtn.
Trailhead
Rabbit Creek Trail
McHugh Peak
Toilsome Rd.
Canyon Rd.
Clarks Rd.
Little Rabbit Creek
DeArmoun Rd.
Rabbit Creek Rd.
Potter Creek
Seward Hwy.

# OPTION F

# Ptarmigan Peak

This mountain has claimed more than a few lives. A number of these deaths resulted from people straying onto the sheer west face of the mountain. But this peak need not prove a particularly dangerous climb as long as one makes certain to stay on the southwest slope of the mountain. By thus staying well to the right (south) of the west face, one still has to do some rock scrambling, but no rock climbing, which should make the going much safer for all concerned.

**TRAIL LOCATION:** This climb begins approximately 2.5 miles up Rabbit Creek Trail just before the trail descends to the flats leading to Rabbit Lake*. Here, where a broad opening appears in the ridge above and to the left (north), bear left off the trail and begin climbing the broad tundra slope towards that opening. Approximately 800 feet up the ridge, the slope rolls over the top of the shelf into Ptarmigan Pass.

Upon reaching Ptarmigan Pass, bear left (east) toward the right (southwest) ridge of Ptarmigan Peak, the prominent peak towering above the east side of the pass. At the base of this ridge, look for the faint trail leading upward. If one finds no obvious trail, begin angling up and to the right across the south face toward the summit. During this climb make sure not to stray to the right (southwest) onto the sheer west face of the mountain. If one feels oneself getting

----------------------------------------------------------------

* To get there, see [17] **Walk-About Guide to Rabbit Creek Trail**.

too close to the cliffs on that face, simply keep slanting up and to the right.

With or without trail, as long as one persists upward, one should not miss the summit. Even if one swings too far to the right, as long as one continues climbing, one should at least reach the summit ridge. From there one can backtrack the short way to the summit. Most people, however, usually reach the short summit ridge on the western side of the summit. If so, then turn right (east) and climb the short distance to the register and plaque that mark the summit (4,880 feet).

**TRAIL GRADE:** Rabbit Creek Trail rates Grade 1 as a hike. Once one leaves the trail, however, this climb rates Grade 4 as a hike. The final climb of Ptarmigan Peak initially rates Grade 5 as a hike. This rises to Grade 6 as a climb the closer one gets to the summit.

**TRAIL CONDITION:** This climb varies considerably in its conditions, which become rougher, rockier, and steeper the higher one climbs. It begins on the wide road of Rabbit Creek Trail. On the climb up to and Ptarmigan Pass, it crosses mostly tundra and some loose stones. Once on Ptarmigan Peak proper, the route initially climbs over tundra and loose stones, which give way to more scree and rocks the higher one climbs.

**TRAIL MILEAGE:** To go from the parking area on Canyon Road to the summit of Ptarmigan Peak entails approximately 4.5 miles of climbing, for a round-trip total of 9 miles.

**TOTAL ELEVATION GAIN:** To climb from the parking area on Canyon Road to the summit of Ptarmigan Peak entails a total elevation gain of 3,100 feet.

**HIGH POINT:** This climb reaches its highest point of 4,880 feet above sea level at the summit of Ptarmigan Peak.

**NORMAL HIKING TIME:** To climb from the parking area on Canyon Road to the summit of Ptarmigan Peak and back should take anywhere

Ptarmigan Pass

from 6 to 10 hours, depending on the condition and ambition of the hiker(s) involved.

**CAMPSITES:** One will find no designated campsites along this trail. One will find many fine places on which to pitch a tent in Ptarmigan Pass, as well as almost anywhere above tree line in the Rabbit Lake valley.

**BEST TIME:** Most people should find any time from June to early September a good time to do this hike.

**USGS MAPS:** Anchorage A-7 and A-8 SE.

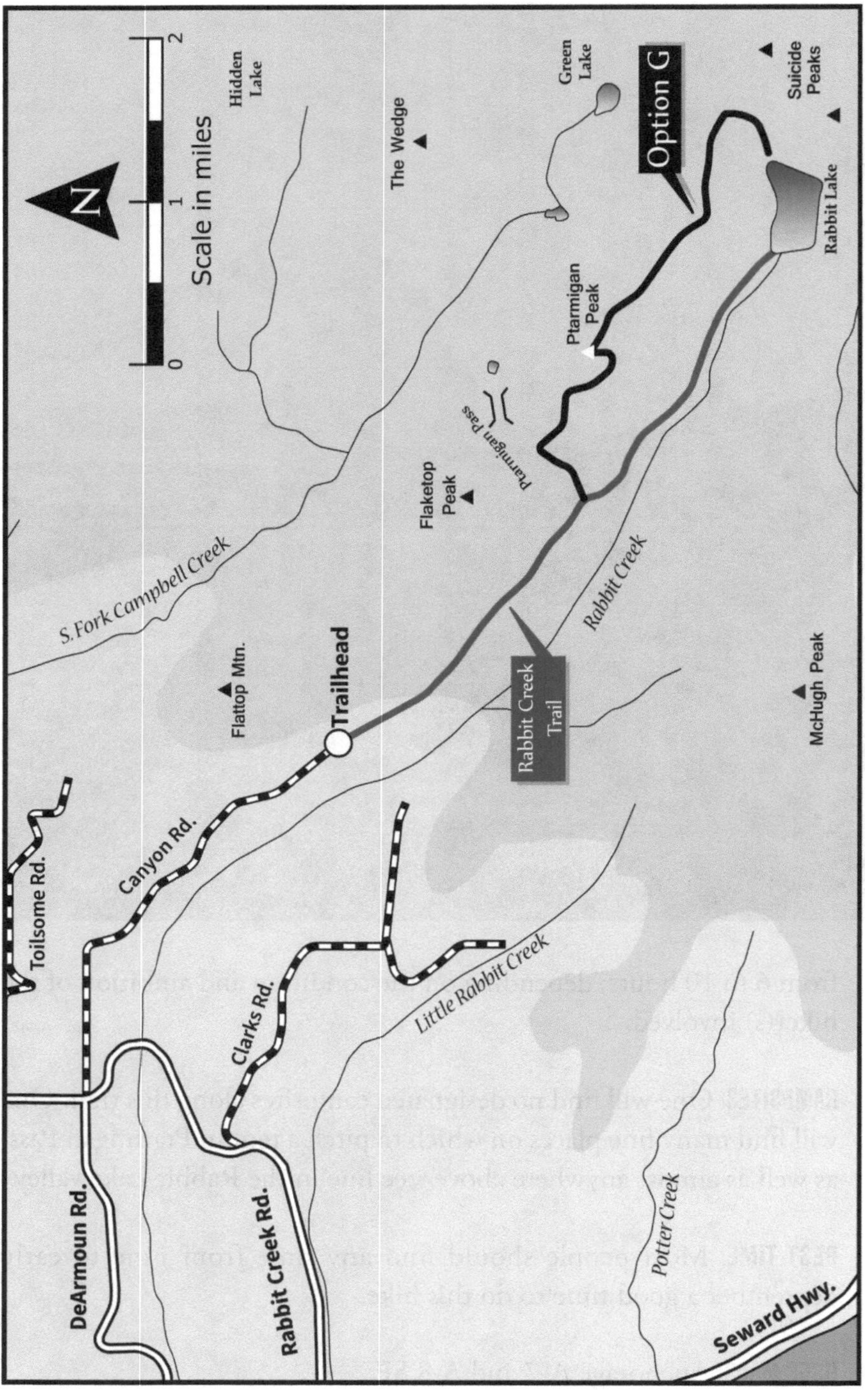
N
Scale in miles
0
1
2
Hidden Lake
The Wedge
Green Lake
Option G
Suicide Peaks
Rabbit Lake
Ptarmigan Peak
Ptarmigan Pass
Flaketop Peak
S. Fork Campbell Creek
Rabbit Creek
Flattop Mtn.
Trailhead
Rabbit Creek Trail
McHugh Peak
Toilsome Rd.
Canyon Rd.
Clarks Rd.
Little Rabbit Creek
DeArmoun Rd.
Rabbit Creek Rd.
Potter Creek
Seward Hwy.

# OPTION G

# Traverse from Ptarmigan Peak to Rabbit Lake

If one likes to scramble over rocks and slide down gullies, one should delight in this airy traverse. Some hikers have even said that it reminds them of the children's game *Chutes and Ladders*. A destination in and of itself, the point of this traverse lies not in getting anywhere but simply in having fun doing the traverse.

**TRAIL LOCATION:** This climb begins approximately 2.5 miles up Rabbit Creek Trail just before the trail descends to the flats leading to Rabbit Lake*. Here, where a broad gap appears in the ridge above and to the left (north), bear left off the trail and begin climbing the broad tundra slope toward that gap. After approximately 800 feet of climbing, the ridge rolls over the top of the shelf into Ptarmigan Pass.

Upon reaching Ptarmigan Pass, bear left (east) toward the right (southwest) ridge of Ptarmigan Peak, the prominent peak towering above the east side of the pass. At the base of this ridge, look for the faint trail leading upward. If one finds no obvious trail, begin angling up and to the right across the south face toward the summit. During this climb make sure not to stray to the right (southwest) onto the sheer west face of the mountain. If one feels oneself getting too close to the cliffs on that face, simply keep slanting up and to the right.

---

\* To get there, see [17] **Walk-About Guide to Rabbit Creek Trail**.

With or without trail, as long as one persists upward, one should not miss the summit. Even if one swings too far to the right, as long as one continues climbing, one should at least reach the summit ridge. From there one can backtrack the short way to the summit. Most people, however, usually reach the short summit ridge on the western side of the summit. If so, then turn right (east) and climb the short distance to the register and plaque that mark the summit (4,880 feet).

From the summit of Ptarmigan Peak, continue east down the ridge, staying as close to the crest as possible. Some places will require 100 to 200 feet down-climbing onto the right (south) face of the ridge in order to avoid cliffs. In other places, to avoid some rock ledges, requires down-climbing onto the left (north) face of the ridge. Generally, however, one can stay within easy shouting distance of the top of the ridge.

Upon reaching the grass slopes just beyond Hope Mountain (4,630 feet) approximately 1.5 miles from the summit of Ptarmigan Peak, one should have a clear view down a long open slope to Rabbit Lake. Here turn right (south) and begin the long descent to the eastern end of Rabbit Lake. At the shore of the lake, look for the trail leading right (northwest) along its north shore. This trail, after circling the north shore of the lake, leads out to a junction with Rabbit Creek Trail on the western end of the lake. Once on Rabbit Creek Trail turn left and follow it for approximately 5 miles out to the parking area on Canyon Road.

**Note** One can also descend into Powerline Pass off the end of this traverse[*].

**TRAIL GRADE:** Rabbit Creek Trail rates Grade 1 as a hike. Upon leaving the trail, however, this climb rates Grade 4 as a hike. The final climb of Ptarmigan Peak initially rates Grade 5 as a hike. This rises to Grade 6 as a climb the closer one gets to the summit. On the traverse to the far side of Hope Mountain the route rates between Grade 5 and Grade 6 as a climb, with considerably more of the latter than the former. On the last section of ridge, the rate drops to Grade 4 as a climb. It remains

---

[*] For more information about that route choice, see [28] **OPTION B—Traverse from Flattop Mountain to Powerline Pass** in Chapter 3.

Grade 4 as a hike all the way down to the eastern end of Rabbit Lake. On the trail leading around the lake to Rabbit Creek Trail, the rate drops again to Grade 1 as a hike. It continues to rate Grade 1 as a hike for the remainder of the hike out to the parking area on Canyon Road.

**TRAIL CONDITION:** This climb varies considerably in its conditions. It begins on the wide road of Rabbit Creek Trail. On the slope to Ptarmigan Pass it crosses mostly tundra and some loose stones. From Ptarmigan Peak proper, the route initially climbs over tundra and loose stones, which give way to scree and boulders the higher one climbs. Past the summit of Ptarmigan Peak, the ridge becomes a series of rocky spires and gendarmes, interspersed with many ledges and gullies, which results in constant climbing and scrambling up and down and back and forth across the ridge as one makes their way along the ridge. Eventually, just after passing over Hope Mountain, the ridge widens and becomes less rocky. From this point down to the eastern end of Rabbit Lake, the route mostly crosses tundra mixed with some loose stones and some scree. Along the shore of the lake, the route follows a well-defined trail all the way out to Rabbit Creek Trail and to the parking area on Canyon Road.

**TRAIL MILEAGE:** To complete this traverse from the parking area on Canyon Road and back entails approximately 13.5 miles of hiking and climbing.

**TOTAL ELEVATION GAIN:** To complete this traverse from the parking area on Canyon Road and back entails a total elevation gain of approximately 4,000 feet.

**HIGH POINT:** This climb reaches its highest point of 4,880 feet above sea level at the summit of Ptarmigan Peak.

**NORMAL HIKING TIME:** This traverse from the parking area on Canyon Road and back should take anywhere from 9 to 13 hours, depending on the condition and ambition of the hiker(s) involved.

**CAMPSITES:** One will find no designated campsites along this trail. One can, however, still find many fine places on which to pitch a tent in Ptarmigan Pass, as well as almost anywhere above tree line in the Rabbit Lake valley.

**BEST TIME:** Most people should find any time from June to early September a good time to do this hike.

**USGS MAPS:** Anchorage A-7 and A-8 SE.

Ptarmigan Pass

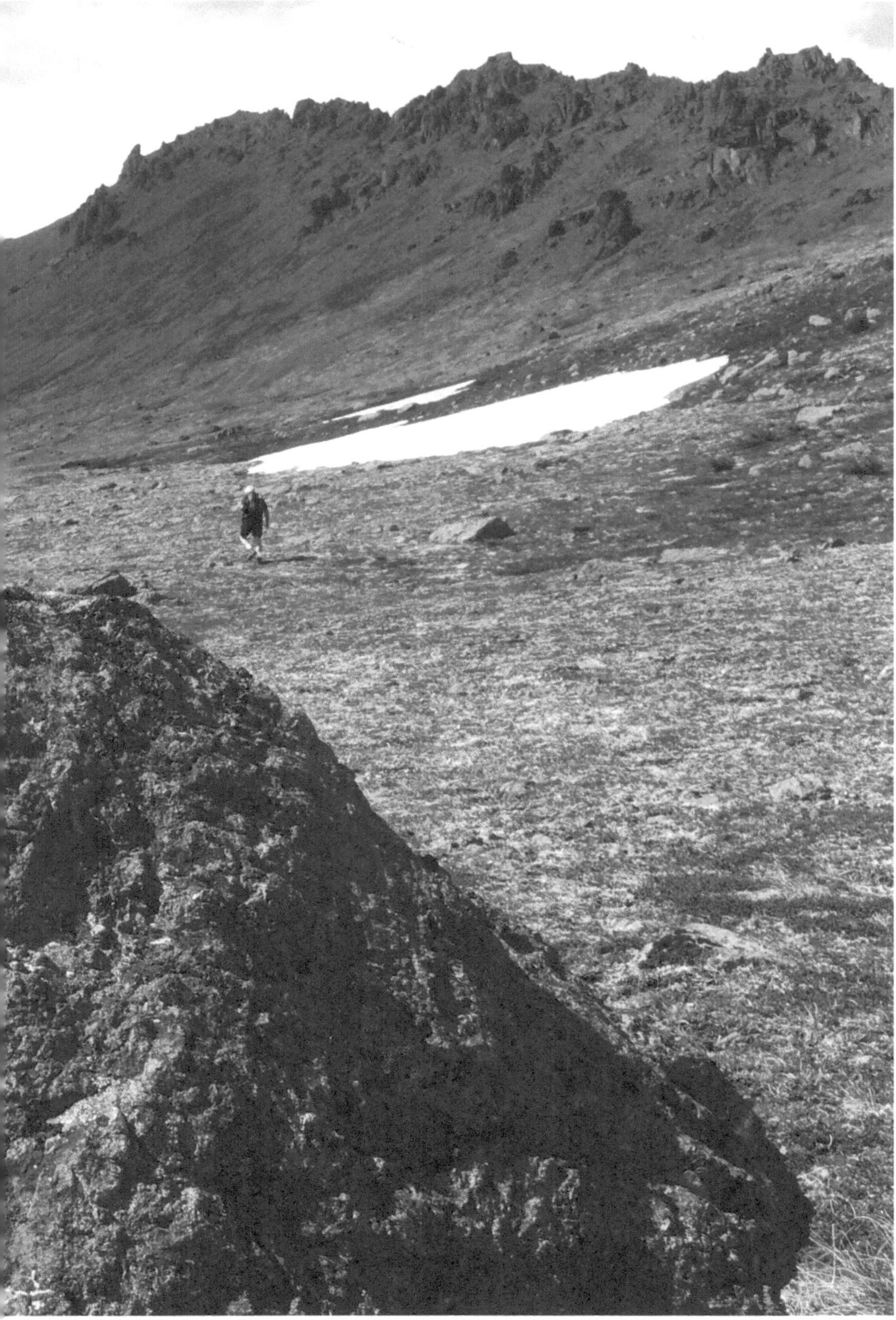

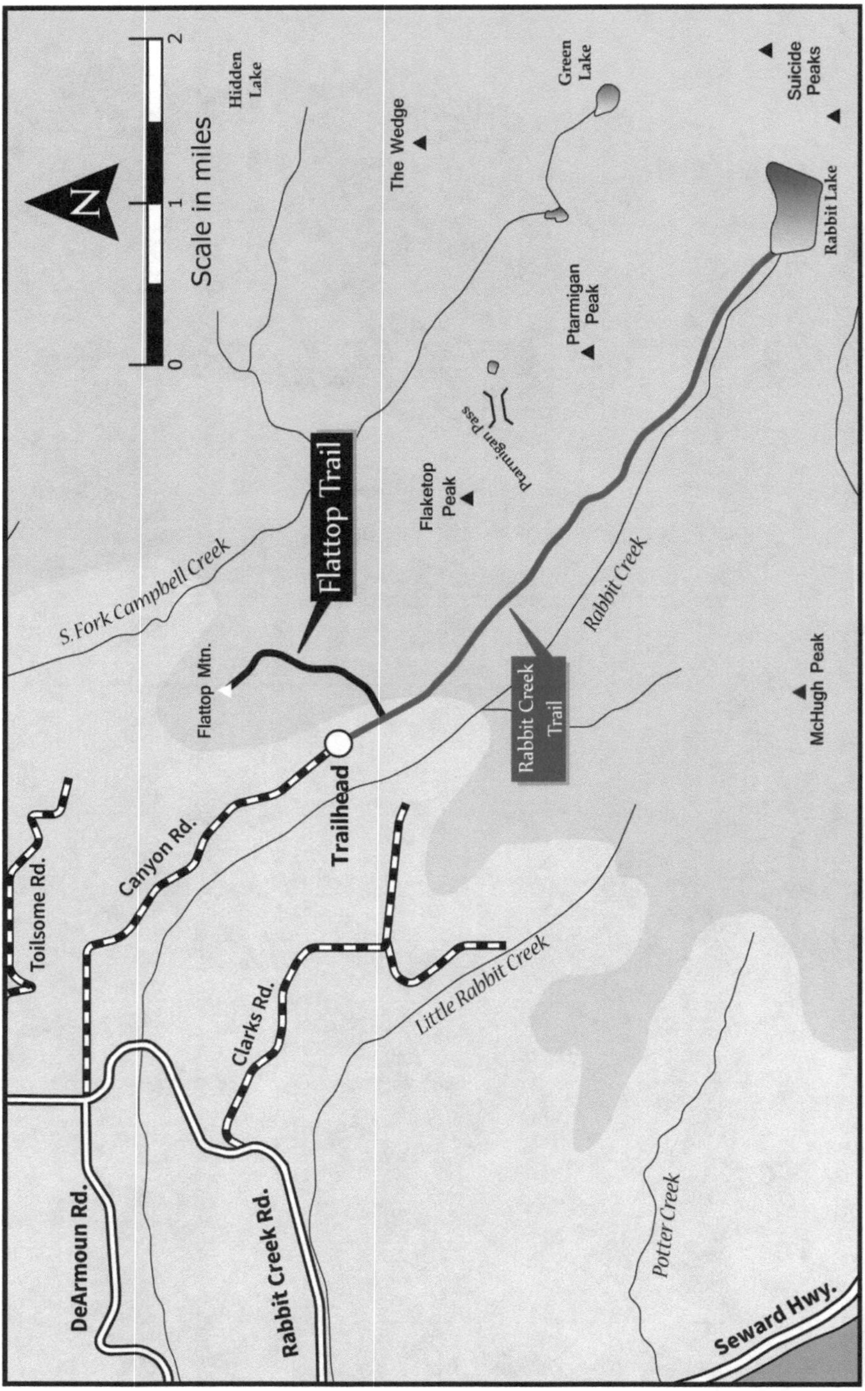
N
Scale in miles
0
1
2
Hidden Lake
The Wedge
Green Lake
Suicide Peaks
Rabbit Lake
Ptarmigan Peak
Ptarmigan Pass
Flaketop Peak
Flattop Trail
S. Fork Campbell Creek
Flattop Mtn.
Rabbit Creek
Rabbit Creek Trail
McHugh Peak
Trailhead
Canyon Rd.
Toilsome Rd.
Clarks Rd.
Little Rabbit Creek
DeArmoun Rd.
Rabbit Creek Rd.
Potter Creek
Seward Hwy.

# Walk-About Guide to Flattop Trail

Due to the increasing popularity of climbing Flattop Mountain from Rabbit Creek, which has resulted in a confusion of unofficial trails leading to the summit from that side, park officials deemed it necessary to construct an official trail. As a result, many people now find this well-conceived and well-constructed trail more satisfying than the climb from Glen Alps. The preference for this trail may result from a variety of reasons. First, one usually finds far fewer people on this alternate trail. Second, this climb arguably has better views of the surrounding landscape than the climb from Glen Alps, including wide view up Rabbit Creek to the summits of North Suicide Peak and South Suicide Peak.

**TRAIL LOCATION:** This hike begins less than 100 feet up Rabbit Creek Trail on Canyon Road. To get there drive 8.5 miles south on the Seward Highway to just past Milepost 119 where one reaches the DeArmoun Road exit. Take this exit and at the end of the exit ramp turn left (east) and cross back over the highway toward the mountains. After approximately 3.5 miles of steady climbing, DeArmoun Road reaches the lights at the intersection with Hillside Road. Continuing straight through the lights, follow Upper DeArmoun Road as it continues uphill. Approximately 1 mile later the road reaches an intersection with Canyon Road on the right. (One will recognize this road by the row of mailboxes at this junction.) Turning down Canyon Road, follow it for the next 2 miles as it snakes up valley, passing many side streets, along the way. Continuing up valley on Canyon Road, follow it until, after passing one open gate, it dead-ends at a closed gate. This second gate marks the beginning of Rabbit Creek Trail. (Owing to the roughness of the road, some vehicles may have trouble reaching as far as this second gate. If so, one can park at the wide turnaround just below the first gate and walk the short distance up and around the next corner in the road to the second gate.)

To reach the beginning of Flattop Trail hike approximately 100 feet up Rabbit Creek Trail. At that point, one should see a stone marker with a small plaque on it marking the beginning of the trail. Leaving Rabbit Creek Trail, Flattop Trail begins by zigzagging up to the left (north) on two long switchbacks. Above these switchbacks the trail climbs more directly, but not steeply, up through some brush. Above the brush the trail angles up the right (east) side of a broad hollow. The trail then bears left (west) and crosses the top of the hollow. At the far side of the hollow, the trail begins climbing Flattop proper. Climbing at a long slant across the east face of the mountain, the wide trail climbs to the far left (south) side of Flattop's broad summit. Once on the summit plateau, bear right (northwest) to the small hump of rocks visible at the center of the plateau. This hump of rocks marks the true summit of Flattop Mountain (3,510 feet).

**TRAIL GRADE:** This climb rates Grade 3 as a hike.

**TRAIL CONDITION:** This climb varies little in its overall good condition. It begins and ends on a trail that has some sections of both some loose gravel and scree and few boulders along its entire length.

**TRAIL MILEAGE:** To go from the parking area to the summit of Flattop Mountain entails approximately 1.5 miles of hiking and climbing, for a round-trip total of approximately 3 miles.

**TOTAL ELEVATION GAIN:** To hike the parking area on Canyon Road to the summit of Flattop Mountain entails a total elevation gain of approximately 1,650 feet.

**HIGH POINT:** This hike reaches its highest point of 3,510 feet above sea level at the summit of Flattop Mountain.

**NORMAL HIKING TIME:** The climb from the parking area on Canyon Road to the summit of Flattop Mountain and back should take anywhere from 1 to 3 hours, depending on the condition and ambition of the hiker(s) involved.

**CAMPSITES:** One will find no designated campsites along this trail. Nor should one need one considering the shortness of the hike. Many people, however, find that the summit of Flattop Mountain makes for a novel place on which to pitch a tent.

**BEST TIME:** Most people should find any time from June to early September a good time to do this hike.

**USGS MAPS:** Anchorage A-8 SE.

Flattop Mountain Trail

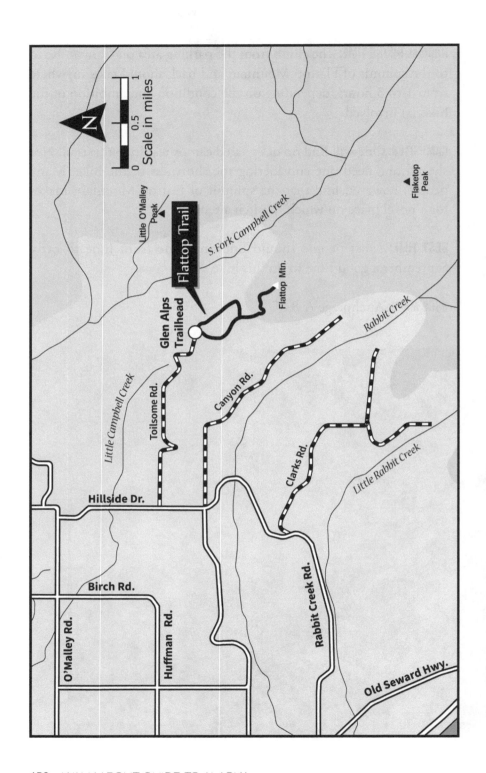

Scale in miles

Little O'Malley Peak

Flattop Trail

S. Fork Campbell Creek

Flaketop Peak

Flattop Mtn.

Glen Alps Trailhead

Rabbit Creek

Little Campbell Creek

Toilsome Rd.

Canyon Rd.

Clarks Rd.

Little Rabbit Creek

Hillside Dr.

Birch Rd.

O'Malley Rd.

Huffman Rd.

Rabbit Creek Rd.

Old Seward Hwy.

## CHAPTER 3

# CAMPBELL CREEK VALLEY

## Walk-About Guide to Flattop Mountain Trail

This little mountain, the rump of a 6-mile long ridge extending from the backbone of the Front Range, has proved to the most popular climb in all of Alaska. People looking for an evening hike after work in the summer, mountain runners looking for a good workout, families and friends looking to get some fresh air together on a weekend afternoon, and even climbers looking for a place to lug heavy loads up and down in training for a climb of Denali have all made Flattop Mountain their preferred choice for a climb. Some people even go so far as to climb Flattop every day.

The primary reason for such popularity results from the fact that it rises right next door to Anchorage, which has the highest concentration of people in Alaska. In addition, unlike Wolverine Peak, McHugh Peak, and O'Malley Peak, all of which also rise right next door to Anchorage, most people find the climb of Flattop Mountain neither too high nor too long for a little outdoor exercise. It also, apart from the last few feet to the summit, has trails easily negotiated by most any person capable of walking. Finally, on a clear day it also affords wide-angle views of Turnagain Arm and Knik Arm and all the way to the distant, hazy horizon stretching from Mount Redoubt to Denali.

Many ambitious hikers also use Flattop as a starting point for other climbs. Some continue along the ridge for approximately 3 miles to Ptarmigan Pass, climbing Peak Two (3,658 feet), Peak Three (3,996 feet), and Flaketop (4,488 feet) in the process[*]. Other more determined hikers continue along the ridge even farther, climbing Ptarmigan Peak (4,880 feet) and Hope Mountain (4,630 feet), and from there continuing all the way to Powerline Pass[**].

Despite its popularity, however, one should not take Flattop Mountain lightly. The same high winds, smothering clouds, and blistering blizzards that assail the mountains nearby do not ignore this mountain. In addition, the rock cliffs that border the last 100 feet of the trail to the summit, as well as those that drop off the edges of the broad, flat summit itself, have claimed the lives of more than a few people. Thus, while climbing Flattop Mountain, one would do well to remember that, although it rises right next door to Anchorage, it has the same dangers as other mountains.

**TRAIL LOCATION:** Flattop Mountain Trail begins at Glen Alps parking area, located just below tree line in the foothills of the Front Range. To get there drive 6.2 miles south from Anchorage on the Seward Highway. There, just after Milepost 121, turn right (west) onto the O'Malley Road exit. At the end of the ramp, turn left (east) and cross back under the highway. Continuing straight on O'Malley Road, ascend past Lake Otis Parkway and the Anchorage Zoo. Approximately 3 miles from the Seward Highway O'Malley Road reaches a junction with Hillside Road on the right (south). Turn onto Hillside Road and follow it for another 1 mile to just past a sign for Chugach State Park one reaches Upper Huffman Road on the left (east). Turn left onto Upper Huffman Road and follow it for 0.75 miles to appropriately named Toilsome Hill Drive on the right (south). Turning onto Toilsome Hill Drive, follow it as it switchbacks and winds its way upward.

---

[*]   For information about this hike,
      see [27] **OPTION A—Traverse from Flattop Mountain to Ptarmigan Pass**.

[**]  For information about this trip,
      see [28] **OPTION B—Traverse from Flattop Mountain to Powerline Pass**.

In approximately 2 miles Toilsome Hill Drive reaches the entrance to Glen Alps parking area on the left (east) side of the road at the top of one last short, steep hill. Park wherever possible (which may prove easier said than done on any given summer weekend) and pay the parking fee. (If one finds the main parking area full they may find extra parking in the overflow parking area located just downhill from the ranger's station.) Flattop Mountain Trail begins a short way up the wide trail to the right of the ranger station at the back right (southeast) end of the parking area.

Only a few feet after climbing onto the trail at the end of the parking area, turn right and back onto the switch-backed trail marked "Flattop Trail." (Though this main trail climbs with relative ease, one can find an even shallower graded trail approximately 200 yards farther down the dirt trail from the parking area.) Flattop Trail begins by climbing gradually, first passing under some low spruce before emerging into an open area just below Blueberry Hill. After a very short climb, the trail reaches a junction on the north slope of Blueberry Hill with Blueberry Loop Trail. The trail sign here points to the right (west) away from Flattop Mountain as it begins its one-way circumnavigation around the front of Blueberry Hill. Turning away from Flattop Mountain, follow the trail as it swings around the western end of Blueberry Hill before turning back to the east toward Flattop Mountain once more.

On the far side of Blueberry Hill, the trail begins to climb with some determination up a mixed series of steps and open slopes to the notch at the base of Flattop Mountain. Here Flattop Mountain Trail reaches a junction with Blueberry Loop Trail. While the latter trail swings to the left (northwest), Flattop Mountain Trail turns right (east) to begin the final ascent of Flattop Mountain now looming directly above.

Dropping off Blueberry Loop Trail, Flattop Mountain Trail immediately crosses the base of the notch, after which it starts up a series of wide switchbacks. At the top of these switch-backs the trail reaches the hardest section of the climb. The trail clambers up a series of steep ledges and gullies. At the top of these ledges and gullies the trail comes to one last short gully. Just above this last gully lies the summit plateau. Once on the plateau, bear right (southwest) to the little mound of rocks that mark the actual summit (3,501 feet).

**TRAIL GRADE:** The lower portions of this trail rate Grade 1 as a hike. As it starts up the back side of Blueberry Hill, the trail rises to Grade 2 as a hike. It remains Grade 2 as a hike up the switchbacks. Up on the final rock ledges and gullies to the summit, the hiking becomes substantially more difficult, often requiring the use of hands. But the fact that one still climbs a trail means that this section rates only Grade 3 as a hike. The short walk across the plateau to the summit rates Grade 1 as a hike.

**TRAIL CONDITION:** With the completion of the new trail in 1996, the trail conditions on Flattop Mountain have improved dramatically. Unlike the steep, scree and dirt trail that climbed the northwest face of the mountain, the new wider and far less steep trail even has steps up some of the steeper sections. Even on the summit cone, the trail follows wide and gradual switchbacks. Only in the last 100 feet to the summit, where one must clamber over ledges and up some steep gullies before standing on the wide and flat summit plateau, does any evidence of the old trail's difficulty remain.

**TRAIL MILEAGE:** To go from Glen Alps parking area to the summit entails 1.6 miles of hiking, for a round-trip total of 3.2 miles.

**TOTAL ELEVATION GAIN:** The climb from Glen Alps parking area to the summit entails a total elevation gain of approximately 1,260 feet.

**HIGH POINT:** This trail reaches its highest point of 3,510 feet above sea level at the summit of Flattop Mountain.

**NORMAL HIKING TIME:** The climb from Glen Alps parking area to the summit and back should take anywhere from 45 minutes to 5 hours, depending on the condition and ambition of the hiker(s) involved.

**CAMPSITES:** One will find no designated campsites along this trail. Many people, however, find that the summit of Flattop Mountain makes fine place on which to pitch a tent.

**BEST TIME:** Most people should find any times from June to early September a good time to do this hike. Many people also climb Flattop Mountain regularly in the winter. But one should beware of taking this popular mountain lightly. Many avalanches do tumble down the upper slopes of this mountain, making it a very dangerous mountain to climb not only in the winter, but even into early May.

**USGS MAPS:** Anchorage A-8 SE.

Flattop Mountain

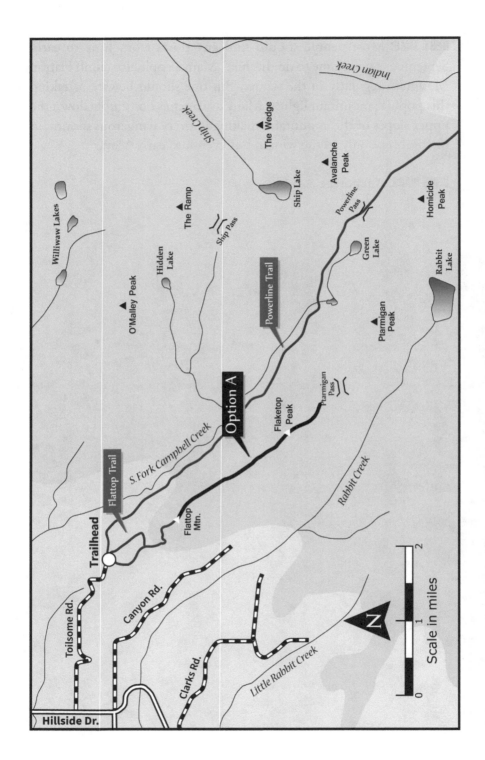

Indian Creek

The Wedge

Ship Creek

Avalanche Peak

Ship Lake

Powerline Pass

Homicide Peak

The Ramp

Ship Pass

Green Lake

Rabbit Lake

Hidden Lake

O'Malley Peak

Powerline Trail

Ptarmigan Peak

Williwaw Lakes

Option A

Ptarmigan Pass

Flaketop Peak

S. Fork Campbell Creek

Rabbit Creek

Flattop Trail

Flattop Mtn.

Trailhead

Toilsome Rd.

Canyon Rd.

Clarks Rd.

Little Rabbit Creek

Hillside Dr.

N

Scale in miles

0     1     2

# OPTION A

# Traverse from Flattop Mountain to Ptarmigan Pass

This hike entails climbing over the next three summits behind Flattop Mountain. In doing so, it takes one away from the usual crowds on Flattop Mountain while traversing some quite spectacular alpine country. One can also do this same traverse from Rabbit Creek Trail*.

**TRAIL LOCATION:** This hike starts at the summit of Flattop Mountain**. Begin this traverse by hiking over to right back (southwest) corner of Flattop Mountain toward Peak Two (3,568 feet), the next peak rising 1 mile farther and 100 feet higher along the ridge. Once at the far southeastern side of Flattop Mountain's summit, follow Flattop Trail as it slants down to the left (northeast) to the saddle below. From the saddle begin the next relatively steep climb up the crest of the ridge to the summit of Peak Two (3,658 feet).

To then reach the long, thin summit ridge of Peak Three located 2 miles farther along the ridge requires considerable more energy. Descending off the far eastern end of Peak Two, continue along the crest of the ridge as it winds over a number of rock spires, outcrops, and ledges. In this section one may have to do a considerable amount

-----------------------------------------------------------------------

\* For this traverse in the opposite direction and beginning and ending on Rabbit Creek Trail, see [22] **OPTION E—Traverse from Ptarmigan Pass to Flattop Mountain** in Chapter 2.

\*\* To get there, see [26] **Walk-About Guide to Flattop Mountain Trail**.

of rock scrambling. Despite the difficulty of the climbing, though, the exposure remains minimal. The views should also make the scrambling seem worthwhile once one reaches the summit of Peak Three (3,996 feet).

To reach Flaketop, the next peak on the ridge, should seem relatively easy compared to the climbing done to this point. Descending off the far end of Peak Three, continue along the crest of the now less rocky ridge for just about 1 mile to the summit of Flaketop (4,488 feet). From the far side of this last summit one begins the descent into Ptarmigan Pass (3,585 feet).

Once in Ptarmigan Pass, one has four choices. First, one can retrace one's steps back down the ridge. Second, one can turn right (south) and descend off the broad and gentle fan of the ridge into the Rabbit Creek valley. From there one can walk out Rabbit Creek Trail to the parking area on Canyon Road*. Third, one can continue along the ridge, which means climbing Ptarmigan Peak, the imposing peak which rises above the opposite side of the pass**.

Fourth, for the quickest way back to Gen Alps parking area, one can descend into the Powerline Pass valley and follow Powerline Trail back out to Glen Alps parking area.

If one chooses this last option, begin by following the crest of the ridge from the summit of Flaketop all the way down to Ptarmigan Pass. Once in the pass, descend to the rim of the tarn located in a deep hollow at the left (northeast) corner of the pass. Upon reaching the tarn one should come in sight of a notch just to the left (north) of the tarn. Hike around the rim of the tarn toward this notch. From the northwest corner of the tarn, continue down into this notch keeping a lookout for Ptarmigan Pass Trail that follows the left (west) side of the tarn's outlet out onto the face of the ridge***.

--------------------------------------------------------------------

* For more information about that trail,
  see [17] **Walk-About Guide to Rabbit Creek Trail** in Chapter 2.

** For more information about that hike,
  see [28] **OPTION B—Traverse from Flattop to Powerline Pass.**

*** For more information about that trail, see [40] **Walk-About Guide to Ptarmigan Pass Trail.**

Having reached the ridge, continue following the trail down for approximately 1,000 vertical feet to its junction with Powerline Trail weaving along south side of the valley floor*. Once on Powerline Trail turn left (west) onto it and follow it out to Glen Alps parking area.

**TRAIL GRADE:** The trail to the summit of Flattop Mountain rates Grade 1 and Grade 2 as a hike. Upon dropping off the back side of Flattop Mountain, the hike remains Grade 1 as a hike down to the next saddle. The climb of Peak Two rates Grade 3 as a hike. Past Peak Two the route rises to Grade 5 as a hike, interspersed with a quite a few sections of Grade 6 scrambling. After Peak Three the route rates a more consistent Grade 5 as a hike. It fluctuates between Grade 3 and Grade 4 as a hike during the crossing of Ptarmigan Pass and the descent into the Powerline Pass valley. Upon reaching Powerline Trail, it drops to Grade 1 as a hike for the last 3 miles out to Glen Alps parking area.

**TRAIL CONDITION:** Outside of the last 100 feet to its summit, the first part of this climb over Flattop Mountain consists of hiking up a wide trail. Beyond the summit of Flattop Mountain, however, the conditions become much rougher. The traverse from Flattop Mountain to Peak Two follows a rough trail. Between Peak Two and Peak Three the route, though it still sporadically follows a sheep trail, traverses a very rocky ridge with long sections of scree and boulders. Past Peak Three, the route becomes less and less rocky as it passes over Flaketop and descends into Ptarmigan Pass. After crossing the tundra and loose gravel in the pass, the route descends a rough trail to Powerline Pass valley. From there the last 3 miles of the route follow the broad and predominantly flat Powerline Trail out to Glen Alps parking area.

**TRAIL MILEAGE:** This entire traverse from Glen Alps parking area to Ptarmigan Pass and back out Powerline Trail entails approximately 10 miles of hiking.

--------------------------------------------------------------------

\*    For more information about that trail, see [31] **Walk-About Guide to Powerline Trail**.

**TOTAL ELEVATION GAIN:** This entire traverse from Glen Alps parking area to Ptarmigan Pass and back out Powerline Trail entails a total elevation gain of approximately 3,300 feet.

**HIGH POINT:** This traverse reaches its highest point of 4,488 feet above sea level at the summit of Flaketop.

**NORMAL HIKING TIME:** This entire traverse from Glen Alps parking area to Ptarmigan Pass and back out Powerline Trail should take anywhere from 5 to 10 hours, depending on the condition and ambition of the hiker(s) involved.

**CAMPSITES:** One will find no designated campsites along this trail. Many people, however, find that the summit of Flattop Mountain makes a fine place on which to pitch a tent. Ptarmigan Pass makes even a finer place on which to pitch a tent, however. Not only does it offer more seclusion, but it also has the tarn as a water supply.

**BEST TIME:** Most people should find any time from June to early September a good time to do this traverse.

**USGS MAPS:** Anchorage A-7 and A-8.

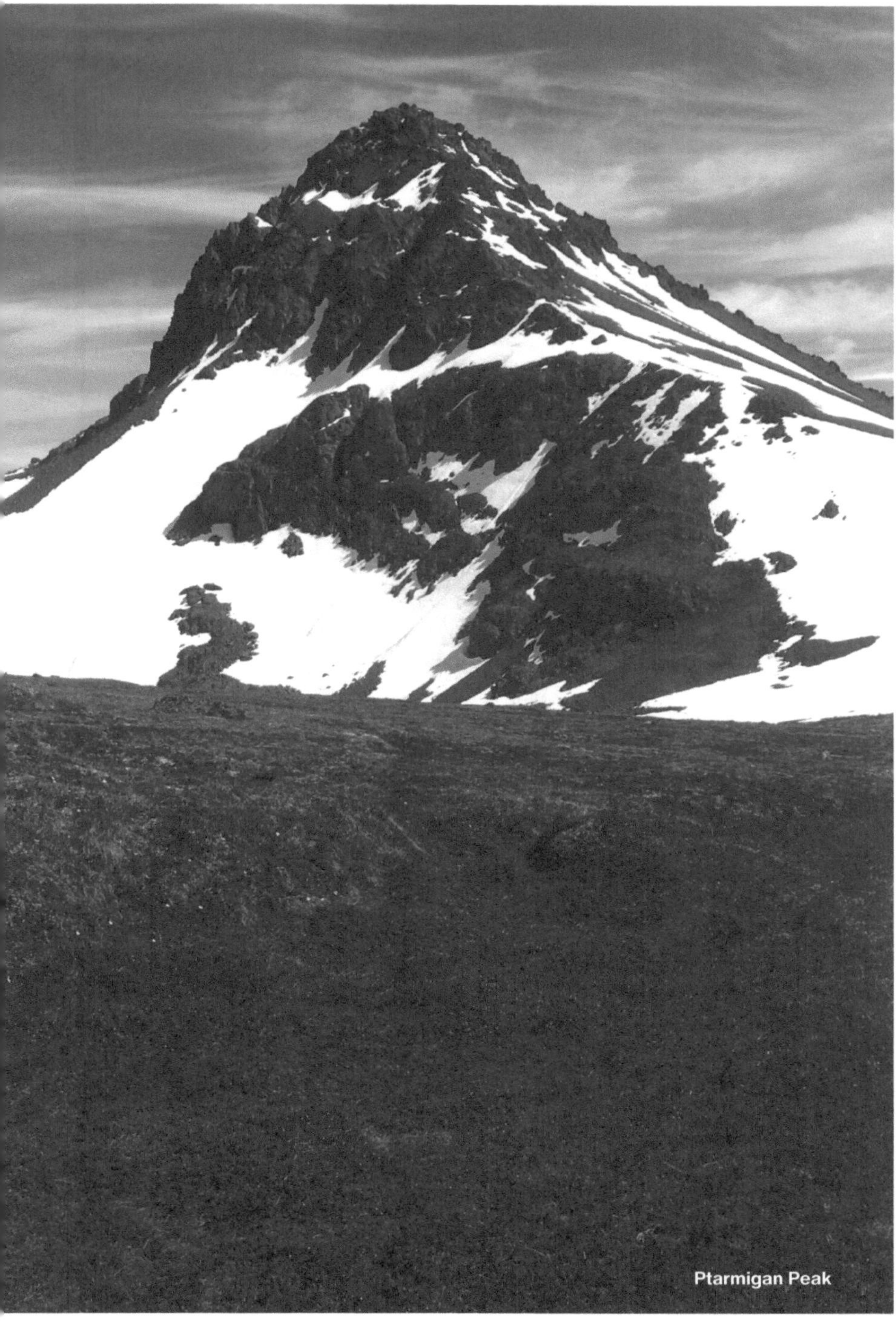
Ptarmigan Peak

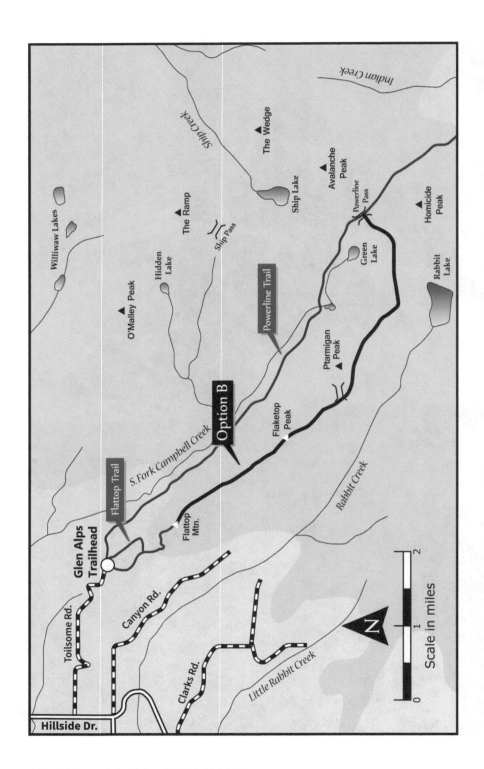

Indian Creek

The Wedge

Ship Creek

Avalanche Peak

Ship Lake

The Ramp

Homicide Peak

Powerline Pass

Ship Pass

Williwaw Lakes

Hidden Lake

Green Lake

Rabbit Lake

O'Malley Peak

Powerline Trail

Flattop Trail

Ptarmigan Peak

Option B

S. Fork Campbell Creek

Flaketop Peak

Rabbit Creek

Glen Alps Trailhead

Flattop Mtn.

Toilsome Rd.

Canyon Rd.

Little Rabbit Creek

Clarks Rd.

Hillside Dr.

N

Scale in miles

0    1    2

# OPTION B

# Traverse from Flattop Mountain to Powerline Pass

This traverse combines [27] **OPTION A—Traverse from Flattop Mountain to Ptarmigan Pass** above and much of [24] **OPTION G—Traverse from Ptarmigan Peak to Rabbit Lake** in Chapter2. This makes it a long and exciting climb for any one with some scrambling skills and lots of stamina.

**TRAIL LOCATION:** This hike starts at the summit of Flattop Mountain[*]. Begin this traverse by hiking over to right back (southwest) corner of Flattop Mountain toward Peak Two (3,568 feet), the next peak rising 1 mile farther and 100 feet higher along the ridge. At the far southeastern side of Flattop Mountain's summit, follow the trail slanting down to the left (northeast) to the saddle immediately below. From the saddle begin the next relatively easy climb up the crest of the ridge to the summit of Peak Two (3,658 feet).

To next reach the long, thin summit ridge of Peak Three located 2 miles farther along the ridge requires considerable more energy. Descending off the far eastern end of Peak Two, continue along the crest of the ridge as it winds over a number of rock spires, outcrops, and ledges. In this section one may have to do a considerable amount of rock scrambling. Despite the difficulty of the climbing, though, the exposure remains minimal. The views should also make the

-------------------------------------------------------------------

[*]   To get there, see [26] **Walk-About Guide to Flattop Mountain Trail**.

scrambling seem worthwhile once one reaches the summit of Peak Three (3,996 feet).

To reach Flaketop, the next peak on the ridge, should seem relatively easy compared to the climbing done to this point. Descending off the far end of Peak Three, continue along the crest of the now less rocky ridge for just about 1 mile to the summit of Flaketop (4,488 feet). From the far side of this last summit one begins the descent into Ptarmigan Pass (3,585 feet).

Once in Ptarmigan Pass, bear left (east) toward the right (southwest) ridge of Ptarmigan Peak, the prominent peak towering above the east side of the pass. At the base of this ridge, look for the faint trail leading upward. If one finds no obvious trail, begin angling up and to the right across the south face toward the summit. During this climb make sure not to stray to the right (southwest) onto the sheer west face of the mountain. If one feels oneself getting too close to the cliffs on that face, simply keep slanting up and to the right.

With or without trail, as long as one persists upward, one should not miss the summit. Even if one swings too far to the right, as long as one continues climbing, one should at least reach the summit ridge. From there one can backtrack the short way to the summit. Most people, however, usually reach the short summit ridge on the western side of the summit. If so, then turn right (east) and climb the short distance to the register and plaque that mark the summit (4,880 feet).

From the summit of Ptarmigan Peak, continue east down the ridge, staying as close to the crest as possible. Some places will require 100 to 200 feet down-climbing onto the right (south) face of the ridge in order to avoid cliffs. In other places, to avoid some rock ledges, requires down-climbing onto the left (north) face of the ridge. Generally, however, one can stay within easy shouting distance of the top of the ridge.

Upon reaching the grass slopes just beyond Hope Mountain (4,630 feet) and approximately 1.5 miles from the summit of Ptarmigan Peak, bear left and continue along the crest of the ridge. After passing over a small rib of rocks, continue climbing along the ridge past the last cliffs to where one has a clear view down a 0.25-mile long scree slope on the left (north) to Powerline Pass. With the route down to the pass clearly in sight, descend into the pass. Then hike over to Powerline Trail on the far side. Having reached this trail turn left (west) onto it and follow it for 6 miles back out to Glen Alps parking area.

**TRAIL GRADE:** The trail to the summit of Flattop Mountain rates Grade 1 and Grade 2 as a hike. On the trail down the back side of Flattop Mountain, the hike remains Grade 1 as a hike. The climb of Peak Two rates Grade 3 as a hike Past Peak Two the route rises to Grade 5 as a hike, interspersed with a quite a few sections of Grade 6 scrambling. After Peak Three the route rates a more consistent Grade 5 as a hike. It fluctuates between Grade 3 and Grade 4 as a hike during the crossing of Ptarmigan Pass. The rate then rises to Grade 5 as a climb once the route begins the ascent of Ptarmigan Peak. On leaving Ptarmigan Peak the rate increases to a near-consistent Grade 6 as a scramble until one passes the summit of Hope Mountain. The climb over the next saddle rates Grade 4 as a hike, followed by a Grade 4 hike down to Powerline Pass. Once on Powerline Trail the rate drops to Grade 1 to Grade 2 as a hike all the way out to Glen Alps parking area.

**TRAIL CONDITION:** Outside of the last 100 feet to the summit of Flattop Mountain, the first part of this climb consists of hiking up a wide trail. Flattop Trail off the backside of Flattop Mountain also remains wide on the descent to the next saddle. Once one begins the climb of Peak Two, the conditions become much rougher. The traverse between Peak Two and Peak Three the route traverses a very rocky ridge with long sections of scree and boulders. Past Peak Three, the route becomes less and less rocky as it passes over Flaketop and descends into Ptarmigan Pass.

After crossing the tundra and loose gravel in the pass, the route becomes rockier as it approaches the summit of Ptarmigan Peak. Past Ptarmigan Peak the route becomes a maze of rock spires, ledges, and gullies. It remains so until it reaches the other side of Hope Mountain. Then, after a short section of tundra and gravel, it crosses one last rocky ridge before making the rock- and scree-covered descent to Powerline Pass. Once on Powerline Trail the route again follows a wide road that becomes less and less rocky as it winds 6 miles down the valley back to Glen Alps parking area.

**TRAIL MILEAGE:** The traverse from Glen Alps parking area to Powerline Pass and back via Powerline Trail entails approximately 16.5 miles of hiking.

**TOTAL ELEVATION GAIN:** To complete the traverse from Glen Alps parking area to Powerline Pass and back entails a total elevation gain of approximately 5,900 feet.

**HIGH POINT:** This traverse reaches its highest point of 4,880 feet above sea level at the summit of Ptarmigan Peak.

**NORMAL HIKING TIME:** This traverse should take anywhere from 10 hours to 2 days, depending on the condition and ambition of the hiker(s) involved.

On the ridge east of Flattop Mountain

**CAMPSITES:** One will find no designated campsites along this traverse. Many people however, find that the summit of Flattop Mountain makes a fine place on which to pitch a tent. The upper end of Powerline Trail below the pass also offers many fine places on which to pitch a tent, including around the two lakes just below the pass. Finally, Ptarmigan Pass makes even a finer place on which to pitch a tent. Not only does it offer more seclusion, but it also has the tarn as a water supply.

**BEST TIME:** Most people should find any time from June to early September a good time to do this traverse.

**USGS MAPS:** Anchorage A-7 and A-8.

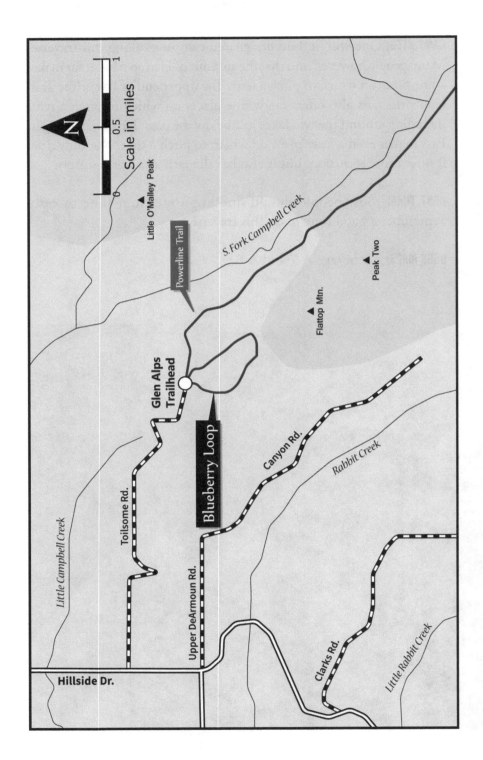

Scale in miles

N

Little O'Malley Peak

Powerline Trail

S. Fork Campbell Creek

Peak Two

Flattop Mtn.

Glen Alps Trailhead

Blueberry Loop

Canyon Rd.

Rabbit Creek

Toilsome Rd.

Little Campbell Creek

Upper DeArmoun Rd.

Clarks Rd.

Little Rabbit Creek

Hillside Dr.

# Walk-About Guide to Blueberry Loop Trail

**TRAIL LOCATION:** Blueberry Loop Trail, which circumnavigates Blueberry Hill, the lower knoll on the ridge just west of Flattop Mountain, begins at the first trail junction on Flattop Mountain Trail. To get there drive 6.2 miles south from Anchorage on the Seward Highway. There, just after Milepost 121, turn right (west) onto the O'Malley Road exit. At the end of the ramp, turn left (east) and cross back under the highway. Continuing straight on O'Malley Road, ascend past Lake Otis Parkway and the Anchorage Zoo. Approximately 3 miles from the Seward Highway O'Malley Road reaches a junction with Hillside Road on the right (south). Turn onto Hillside Road and follow it for another 1 mile to just past a sign for Chugach State Park one reaches Upper Huffman Road on the left (east). Turn left onto Upper Huffman Road and follow it for 0.75 miles to appropriately named Toilsome Hill Drive on the right (south). Turning onto Toilsome Hill Drive, follow it as it switchbacks and winds its way upward. In approximately 2 miles Toilsome Hill Drive reaches the entrance to Glen Alps parking area on the left (east) side of the road at the top of one last short, steep hill. Park wherever possible (which may prove easier said than done on any given summer weekend) and pay the parking fee. (If one finds the main parking area full they may find extra parking in the overflow parking area located just downhill from the ranger's station.) Flattop Mountain Trail begins a short way up the wide trail to the right of the ranger station at the back right (southeast) end of the parking area.

Only a few feet after climbing onto the trail at the end of the parking area, turn right and back onto the switch-backed trail marked "Flattop Trail." (Though this main trail climbs with relative ease, one can find an even shallower graded trail approximately 200 yards farther down the dirt trail from the parking area.) Flattop Trail begins by climbing gradually, first passing under some low spruce before emerging into an open area just below Blueberry Hill. After a very short climb, the trail reaches a junction on the north slope of Blueberry Hill with Blueberry Loop Trail. The trail sign here points to the right (west) away from Flattop Mountain as it begins its one-way circumnavigation around the front of Blueberry Hill. On this circumnavigation Flattop Mountain Trail and Blueberry Loop Trail exist as one and the same trail.

Turning right onto this trail, follow it around to the west and south sides of the mountain. Halfway across the south slope of Blueberry Hill the trail begins climbing gradually. After climbing a series of wood steps the trail reaches a notch between Blueberry Hill and Flattop Mountain. Here Blueberry Hill Trail and Flattop Mountain Trail diverge as Flattop Mountain Trail turns right (east) and descends into a shallow notch before beginning its ascent of Flattop Mountain proper.

Blueberry Hill Trail continues straight ahead (north) through the notch. On the far side of the notch, the trail swings left (west) and down to continue its circumnavigation of Blueberry Hill. Approximately 0.25 miles after leaving the notch, the trail reaches the junction with Flattop Mountain Trail, and thus completes the circumnavigation of Blueberry Hill. Turning right (northwest) and down follow Flattop Mountain Trail the short distance back down to Glen Alps parking area.

**TRAIL GRADE:** This wide, easy, and predominantly flat trail rates Grade 1 as a hike.

**TRAIL CONDITION:** Cut by a bulldozer, and then covered with loose gravel, this trail remains wide and smooth underfoot for almost its entire length.

**TRAIL MILEAGE:** The climb from Glen Alps parking area and around the entire Blueberry Loop Trail entails approximately 1 mile of hiking.

**TOTAL ELEVATION GAIN:** The climb from Glen Alps parking area and around the entire Blueberry Loop Trail entails a total elevation gain of approximately 400 feet.

**HIGH POINT:** This trail reaches its highest point of approximately 2,500 feet above sea level in the notch between Blueberry Hill and Flattop Mountain.

**NORMAL HIKING TIME:** The climb from the Glen Alps and around the entire Blueberry Loop Trail should take anywhere from 20 minutes to 1 hour, depending on the condition and ambition of the hiker(s) involved.

**CAMPSITES:** One will find no designated campsites along this trail. Nor, given the short length of the trail, should one need any.

**BEST TIME:** Most people should find any time from June to early September a good time to do this hike. Many people also find that it makes a fine winter ski, snowshoe, or hiking outing as well.

**USGS MAPS:** Anchorage A-8 SE.

Trail work on Flattop Mountain

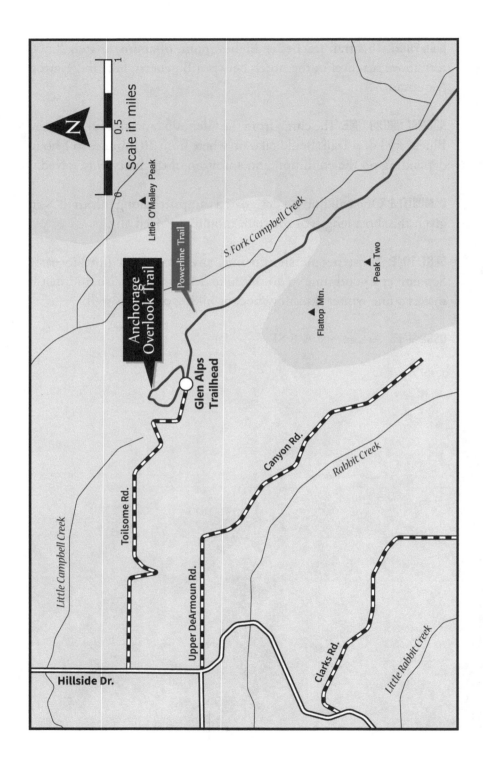

Scale in miles

N

Little O'Malley Peak ▲

S. Fork Campbell Creek

Powerline Trail

Anchorage Overlook Trail

Peak Two ▲

Flattop Mtn. ▲

Glen Alps Trailhead

Canyon Rd.

Rabbit Creek

Little Campbell Creek

Toilsome Rd.

Upper DeArmoun Rd.

Clarks Rd.

Little Rabbit Creek

Hillside Dr.

# Walk-About Guide to Anchorage Overlook Trail

Handicap accessible, this short, entirely paved trail proves an ideal destination for anyone physically unable to walk any great distance and yet still wants to enjoy a wide, spacious view of Anchorage.

**TRAIL LOCATION:** Anchorage Overlook Trail begins in Glen Alps parking area. To get there drive 6.2 miles south from Anchorage on the Seward Highway. There, just after Milepost 121, turn right (west) onto the O'Malley Road exit. At the end of the ramp, turn left (east) and cross back under the highway. Continuing straight on O'Malley Road, ascend past Lake Otis Parkway and the Anchorage Zoo. Approximately 3 miles from the Seward Highway O'Malley Road reaches a junction with Hillside Road on the right (south). Turn onto Hillside Road and follow it for another 1 mile to just past a sign for Chugach State Park one reaches Upper Huffman Road on the left (east). Turn left onto Upper Huffman Road and follow it for 0.75 miles to appropriately named Toilsome Hill Drive on the right (south). Turning onto Toilsome Hill Drive, follow it as it switchbacks and winds its way upward. In approximately 2 miles Toilsome Hill Drive reaches the entrance to Glen Alps parking area on the left (east) side of the road at the top of one last short, steep hill. Park wherever possible (which may prove easier said than done on any given summer weekend) and pay the parking fee. (If one finds the main parking area full they may find extra parking in the overflow parking area located just downhill from the ranger's station.) Anchorage Overlook Trail starts on the left (northeast) side of the parking lot near the outhouse.

Anchorage Overlook Trail begins by bearing left off the northeast corner of the parking area. Winding slowly upward, it soon turns up and around the top of the small knoll rising above the left (north) side of the parking area. At the top of this same knoll it reaches its end at a wind-screened viewing platform.

**TRAIL GRADE:** This short and easy trail rates a very easy Grade 1 as a hike.

**TRAIL CONDITION:** Paved from end to end, this trail remains excellent underfoot for its entire length.

**TRAIL MILEAGE:** To go from Glen Alps parking area to the viewing platform and back entails approximately 0.2 miles of hiking.

**TOTAL ELEVATION GAIN:** The walk from Glen Alps parking area to the viewing platform entails a total elevation gain of approximately 50 feet.

Taking a break on Flattop Mountain

**HIGH POINT:** Anchorage Overlook Trail reaches its highest point of 2,258 feet above sea level at the viewing platform.

**NORMAL HIKING TIME:** The walk from Glen Alps parking area to the viewing platform and back should take anywhere from 10 to 30 minutes, depending on the ambition and condition of the hiker(s) involved.

**CAMPSITES:** One will find no designated campsites along this trail. Given the short length of the trail, however, one is not likely to need any.

**BEST TIME:** Most people should find any time from June to early September a good time to do this hike. Many people also find that it makes a fine winter outing as well.

**USGS MAPS:** Anchorage A-8 SE.

Middle Powerline Trail
Middle Fork Campbell Creek
Williwaw Lakes
O'Malley Peak
Hidden Lake
The Ramp
Ship Pass
The Wedge
Ship Lake
Avalanche Peak
Powerline Pass
Homicide Peak
Green Lake
Rabbit Lake
Suicide Peaks
McHughLake
Ptarmigan Peak
S. Fork Campbell Creek
Powerline Trail
Rabbit Creek
McHugh Peak
McHugh Creek
Flattop Mtn.
Glen Alps Trailhead
Little Campbell Creek
Toilsome Rd.
Canyon Rd.
Clarks Rd.
Little Rabbit Creek
Hillside Dr.
Birch Rd.
Rabbit Creek Rd.
Potter Creek
O'Malley Rd.
Huffman Rd.
Seward Hwy.
Old Seward Hwy.
Seward Hwy.
TURNAGAIN ARM
N
0
1
2
Scale in miles

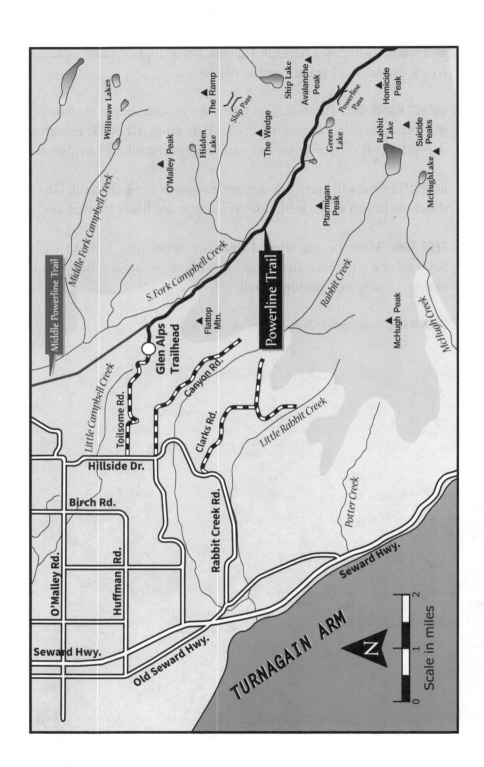

# Walk-About Guide to Powerline Trail

Though the actual western end of Powerline Trail begins at Prospect Heights parking area, most people prefer to begin hiking this trail from Glen Alps parking area. For this reason this book designates this higher and more popular section of Powerline Trail by its usual title of Powerline Trail, as opposed to what this book will refer to as Middle Powerline Trail that extends from Prospect Heights parking area to Glen Alps, and the unofficial trail, which this guide refers to as Lower Powerline Trail, which extends from Foothills subdivision in East Anchorage near the corner of Tudor Road and Muldoon Road to State Parks parking area on Basher Road*. From this highest trailhead at Glen Alps, many people use this trail as a quiet place for an afternoon run, an evening walk, or a weekend bike ride.

Other more ambitious hikers find it a useful way to access many hikes and climbs in the ridges and hanging valleys surrounding Campbell Creek valley. To such hikers it often seems a momentous moment when first stepping off the trail to begin a climb or when stepping back onto the trail at the end of a climb. Whether going to or coming from O'Malley Peak, The Ramp, Hidden Peak, Ship Lake Pass, The Wedge, Avalanche Mountain, Ptarmigan Peak, or Homicide Peak, or any other place in the isolated heights in the South Fork Campbell Creek valley, Powerline Trail serves as the primary link between these many climbs and home. Once on Powerline Trail it seems only a matter of an easy walk to finish the day.

These many uses, from the casual walker out for an hour to the ambitious hiker out for an entire day, give the trail has an air of

---

\*    For more information about these trails, see [46] **Walk-About Guide to Middle Powerline Trail** and [91] **Walk-About Guide to Lower Powerline Trail** in Chapter 9.

familiarity that may often lead one to take it for granted. One may not do so when caught in a blizzard, a thunderstorm, a windstorm, or fog, or simply feel exhausted after too long a day on their feet. Then they discover the trail a lifeline back to Glen Alps parking area.

**TRAIL LOCATION:** One can access Powerline Trail from either its western end at Glen Alps or its eastern end in Indian. Access to western end of Powerline Trail begins at Glen Alps parking area*. To get there drive 6.2 miles south from Anchorage on the Seward Highway. There, just after Milepost 121, turn right (west) onto the O'Malley Road exit. At the end of the ramp, turn left (east) and cross back under the highway. Continuing straight on O'Malley Road, ascend past Lake Otis Parkway and the Anchorage Zoo. Approximately 3 miles from the Seward Highway O'Malley Road reaches a junction with Hillside Road on the right (south). Turn onto Hillside Road and follow it for another 1 mile to just past a sign for Chugach State Park one reaches Upper Huffman Road on the left (east). Turn left onto Upper Huffman Road and follow it for 0.75 miles to appropriately named Toilsome Hill Drive on the right (south). Turning onto Toilsome Hill Drive, follow it as it switchbacks and winds its way upward. In approximately 2 miles Toilsome Hill Drive reaches the entrance to Glen Alps parking area on the left (east) side of the road at the top of one last short, steep hill. Park wherever possible (which may prove easier said than done on any given summer weekend) and pay the parking fee. (If one finds the main parking area full they may find extra parking in the overflow parking area located just downhill from the ranger's station.) From the parking area one can access Powerline Trail via the trail that begins at the far left (southeast) end of that parking area a trail and leads 0.5 miles out to Powerline Trail.

Access to the eastern end of Powerline Trail begins in the parking area for the Indian Valley Trail. To get there drive 23 miles south from Anchorage on the Seward Highway. There, just past Milepost 104, take a left (north) turn onto Indian Road. Continue on this road for

--------------------------------------------------------------------

\*    For information about how to access the lower end of Powerline Trail,
     see [46] **Walk-About Guide to Middle Powerline Trail.**

0.5 miles to the fork in the road. Go right and continue for another approximately 0.5 miles to the trailhead. Park wherever possible. Indian Valley Trail leading to Powerline Trail starts on the left (west) side of the parking area. Indian Valley Trail begins by almost immediately coming to a junction with Powerline Trail. Powerline Trail then begins by crossing the substantial bridge just to the left (east) of the trail junction.

Upon leaving Glen Alps parking area, follow the wide, alder-lined 0.5-mile trail out to an intersection where Middle Powerline Trail and Powerline Trail meet on a wide dirt road on a crest underneath the power lines. Here Powerline Trail bears right (east), following the wide dirt road as it parallels the power lines down a short hill. At the bottom of the hill the road levels off for a short distance before beginning its long, very gradual climb to Powerline Pass visible in the distance. As it winds up valley, the trail rolls over a series of small rises. Despite some slight downhill sections over this rolling section, the trail continues to trend slowly upwards.

Approximately 4 miles from the parking area the trail climbs up and around the north buttress of Ptarmigan Peak and enters the wide cirque of the upper valley. After descending a short hill to pass cross Campbell Creek the trail begins a determined 1.5-mile climb to Powerline Pass. Contouring up the north side of the valley, the trail passes beneath the west face of Avalanche Mountain before making the last steep climb to the crest of Powerline Pass (3,550 feet).

After crossing the broad pass the trail begins its long descent across the western flank of Indian Creek valley to the parking area at its eastern end in Indian. During this descent it continues to follow the access road for the power lines. At times this road drops quite steeply (making one wonder what kinds of vehicles used this road). Crossing below the eastern bases of Homicide Peak and Indianhouse Mountain, the trail eventually crosses a substantial bridge over Indian Creek. Just beyond the bridge Powerline Trail merges with Indian Valley Trail. Bearing right (south) in Indian Valley Trail follow it the last approximately 100 feet out to the parking area.

**TRAIL GRADE:** This trail rates Grade 1 as a hike for the first 4.5 miles from Glen Alps parking area. The following 1.5-mile-long climb from Campbell Creek to Powerline Pass rates Grade 2 as a hike. The descent to the Indian parking area rates Grade 1 as a hike and sometimes even Grade 2 as a hike on the steeper portions of the descent.

From the parking area in Indian, this trail rates Grade 3 as a hike on the climb from the Indian parking area to Powerline Pass. Once over the pass, the trail rates Grade 1 as a hike almost the entire way out to Glen Alps parking area.

**TRAIL CONDITION:** The trail varies little in its conditions. As the trail follows a wide road for its entire length, the conditions underfoot remain good for almost the entire length. One should remain aware, however, that sometimes even as late as early July one might have to kick steps across a steep snowfield on the last 100 feet of the climb to the pass, making an otherwise easy trail dangerous at times.

**TRAIL MILEAGE:** To hike from Glen Alps parking area to the top of Powerline Pass entails approximately 5.5 miles of hiking, for a round-trip total of 11 miles. From Powerline Pass down to the Indian parking area entails approximately 13 miles of hiking for a round-trip total of approximately 26 miles.

**TOTAL ELEVATION GAIN:** To hike from Glen Alps parking area to the top of Powerline Pass and down to the Indian parking area entails a total elevation gain of approximately 1,400 feet. To hike from the parking area at Indian to Glen Alps parking area entails a total elevation gain of approximately 3,300 feet.

**HIGH POINT:** This trail reaches its highest point of 3,550 feet above sea level at the top of Powerline Pass.

**NORMAL HIKING TIME:** To hike from Glen Alps parking area to the top of Powerline Pass and back should take anywhere from 4 to 8 hours, depending on the condition and ambition of the hiker(s) involved. To hike one-way from Glen Alps parking area to the Indian parking area should take anywhere from 5 to 9 hours.

**CAMPSITES:** One will find no designated campsites along this traverse. Many people, however, find that the cirque that Powerline Trail enters before the climb up to the pass offers many fine places for pitching a tent, including around the two lakes just below the pass. Powerline Pass also makes even a finer place on which to pitch a tent, though, apart from some possible patch of snow, it has no ready water supply.

**BEST TIME:** Most people should find any time from June to early September a good time to do this traverse. Much of the trail on the Glen Alps side of the pass also makes a fine ski or snowshoe outing in winter. One should think twice, however, of venturing too far up toward the pass because of the extreme avalanche danger during the last 1-mile-long climb to the pass across the lower face of the appropriately named Avalanche Mountain.

**USGS MAPS:** Anchorage A-7 and A-8 SE.

**Powerline Pass Trail in early April**

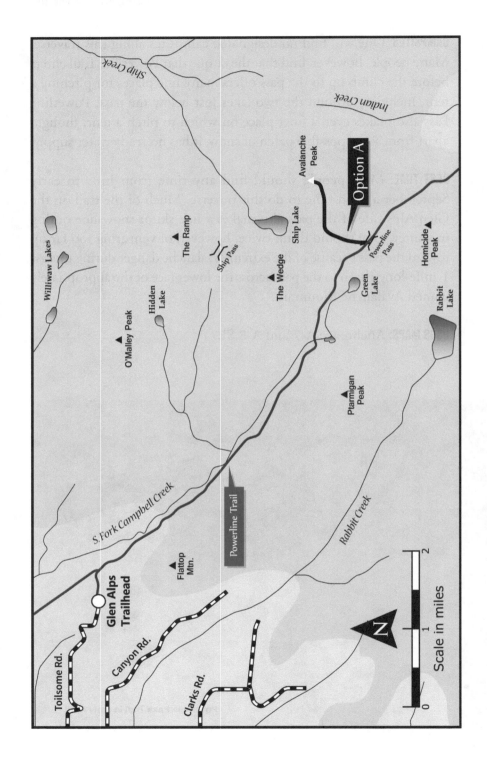

Ship Creek

Indian Creek

Williwaw Lakes

The Ramp

Avalanche Peak

**Option A**

Ship Lake

Ship Pass

Powerline Pass

Homicide Peak

Hidden Lake

O'Malley Peak

The Wedge

Green Lake

Rabbit Lake

Ptarmigan Peak

S. Fork Campbell Creek

Rabbit Creek

Powerline Trail

Flattop Mtn.

**Glen Alps Trailhead**

Toilsome Rd.

Canyon Rd.

Clarks Rd.

N

Scale in miles

0        1        2

# OPTION A

# Avalanche Mountain

Avalanche Mountain (which some also refer to as Powerline Pass Peak) towers above the north side of Powerline Pass. As one of the twelve 5,000-foot peaks in the Front Range, Avalanche Mountain often has at least one or two climbers on its flanks on most week-end days.

**TRAIL LOCATION:** This climb begins just past the power station in the near left (northwest) corner at the top of Powerline Pass on Powerline Trail*. After passing this power station in the near corner of the pass, turn left (north) toward the broad tundra and scree slope directly above. Then staying relatively close to the ridge line on the left (east) side of the slope where one can find generally firmer footing as one climbs higher, begin climbing.

Having reached the ridge at the top of the slope turn right (east). Continuing down the long ridge crest, follow it as it swings to the left away from Powerline Pass. As one continues down the ridge, passing over a number of smaller knolls and false summits along the way, one should have fine views in all directions. Far below to the left, at the base of the precipitous north wall of the mountain one should see the turquoise waters of Ship Lake. Far below to the right (south) one can see both Indian Creek Pass and Turnagain Arm far beyond that. Approximately 1 mile after reaching the top of the ridge a short sharp climb brings one to the spired summit of Avalanche Mountain (5,050 feet).

---------------------------------------------------------------------

* To get there, see [31] **Walk-About Guide to Powerline Trail**.

**TRAIL GRADE:** Powerline Trail rates Grade 1 as a hike for the first 4.5 miles from Glen Alps parking area. The following 1.5-mile climb from Campbell Creek to Powerline Pass rates Grade 2 as a hike. On leaving the trail and beginning climbing up the south face of Avalanche Mountain, the climb rises to Grade 5 as a hike. In the final 1 mile along the ridge this route rates between Grade 4 and Grade 5 as a hike all the way to the summit.

**TRAIL CONDITION:** This climb varies in its conditions. Considering Powerline Trail follows a wide road for its entire length, the conditions underfoot remain good for almost the entire length. One should, however, expect to encounter snow in the last section leading up to the pass early in the season. Though the climb from Powerline Pass up to the west ridge of Avalanche Mountain does not follow a trail, the footing generally remains good, especially on the part of the lower slope, which remains covered by a fair amount of tundra. The higher one climbs, though, the more scree covers the ridge, making the footing more unstable. Travel along the top of the ridge consists almost entirely of hiking over firmer scree and boulders, making it easier to negotiate than the climb up to the ridge.

**TRAIL MILEAGE:** To go from Glen Alps parking area to the summit of Avalanche Mountain entails approximately 7 miles of hiking, for a round-trip total of approximately 14 miles.

**TOTAL ELEVATION GAIN:** The climb from Glen Alps parking area to the summit of Avalanche Mountain entails a total elevation gain of approximately 3,200 feet.

**HIGH POINT:** This climb reaches its highest point of 5,050 feet above sea level at the summit of Avalanche Mountain.

**NORMAL HIKING TIME:** The climb from Glen Alps parking area to the summit of Avalanche Mountain and back should take anywhere from 6 to 10 hours, depending on the ambition and condition of the hiker(s).

**CAMPSITES:** One will find no designated campsites on this climb. The cirque at the upper end of Powerline Trail before the climb up to the pass, however, offers many fine places on which to pitch a tent, including around the two lakes just below the pass. Finally, the meadows just beyond the crest of Powerline Pass also offer many fine places upon which to pitch a tent. Not only do these meadows offer more seclusion, but lingering snowfields can also make for a convenient water supply.

**BEST TIME:** Most people should find any time from June to late August a good time to do this climb. One should think twice about doing this climb in winter, however, owing to the extreme avalanche danger on the open slopes leading up to Powerline Pass as well as on the slope leading up to the summit ridge of Avalanche Mountain.

**USGS MAPS:** Anchorage A-7 and A-8.

Avalanche Mountain

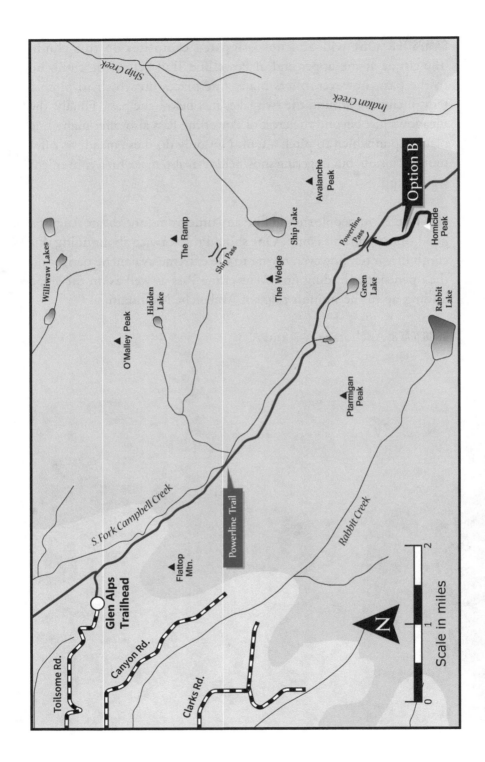

Ship Creek

Indian Creek

Williwaw Lakes

Avalanche Peak

The Ramp

Ship Pass

Ship Lake

Powerline Pass

Option B

Homicide Peak

O'Malley Peak

Hidden Lake

The Wedge

Green Lake

Rabbit Lake

Ptarmigan Peak

S. Fork Campbell Creek

Rabbit Creek

Powerline Trail

Flattop Mtn.

Glen Alps Trailhead

Toilsome Rd.

Canyon Rd.

Clarks Rd.

N

Scale in miles

0          1          2

# OPTION B

# Homicide Peak

Homicide Peak towers above the south side of Powerline Pass, making it seem a Scylla to Avalanche Mountain's Charybdis. This seems especially so despite it rising far fewer feet above the pass than Avalanche Mountain. Most will even look up at much more imposing considering its first impression. From the pass one does not look up a long slope like that on Avalanche Mountain, but up a near-vertical wall of broken rocks and cracked columns. It makes one wonder how to climb it without ropes. One can do it, though, and with only minimal exposure.

**TRAIL LOCATION:** This climb begins at the crest of Powerline Pass on Powerline Trail*. From the crest of the pass one looks directly up the intimidating north face of Homicide Peak on the right (west), making it appear an intimidating rock-climb up an unstable face—which some climbers may welcome. Most people, however, may prefer to follow the far easier route leading around to backside of the mountain.

This easier route begins by following Powerline Trail across Powerline Pass to the southern end of Homicide Peak's massif. Once there, look right (south) and down across the hollow. There one should see the faint outline of a sheep trail as it crosses the rocks below and climbs around the left base of the peak. Follow this sheep trail as it corkscrews up and around the back of the mountain. On the backside of the

---

\*   To get there, see [31] **Walk-About Guide to Powerline Trail**.

mountain, continue along the sheep trail for as long as one can up and across the mountain's southern flank. When after approximately 0.5 miles the sheep trail finally fades away in the rocks, continue climbing at a slightly steeper angle toward the summit. This last bit of climbing entails crossing a number of gullies and winding up and over boulders and scree. But these obstacles do not last long. Within 0.25 miles after leaving the uppermost end of the sheep trail one should reach the wide summit of Homicide Peak (4,660 feet).

**TRAIL GRADE:** Powerline Trail rates Grade 1 as a hike for the first 4.5 miles from Glen Alps parking area. The 1.5-mile-long climb from Campbell Creek to Powerline Pass rates Grade 2 as a hike. On starting up the sheep trail around the back side of the mountain the climb rates Grade 3 as a climb. From the end of the sheep trail the final push to the summit over boulders and scree rates Grade 5 as a climb.

**TRAIL CONDITION:** This climb varies in its conditions. Considering that Powerline Trail follows a wide road for its entire length, the conditions underfoot remain good for almost the entire length. One should, however, expect to encounter snow in the last section leading up to the pass early in the season. The sheep trail around the back side of the mountain also has surprisingly good footing. The higher up one goes, though, the more boulders and scree one encounters, making the footing more and more unstable. The last push to the summit entails climbing almost entirely up scree and over boulders.

**TRAIL MILEAGE:** To go from Glen Alps parking area to the summit of Homicide Peak entails approximately 7.5 miles of hiking, for a round-trip total of approximately 15 miles.

**TOTAL ELEVATION GAIN:** To climb from Glen Alps parking area to the summit of Homicide Peak entails a total elevation gain of approximately 2,800 feet.

**HIGH POINT:** Thus climb reaches its highest point of 4,660 feet above sea level at the summit of Homicide Peak.

**NORMAL HIKING TIME:** To climb from Glen Alps parking area to the summit of Homicide Peak and back should take anywhere from 6 to 10 hours, depending on the ambition and condition of the hiker(s).

**CAMPSITES:** One will find no designated campsites on this climb. The cirque at upper end of Powerline Trail before the climb up to the pass, however, offers many fine places on which to pitch a tent, including around the two lakes just below the pass. Finally, the meadows just beyond the crest of Powerline Pass also offer many fine places for pitching a tent. Not only do these meadows offer more seclusion, but lingering snowfields also often provide a water supply.

**BEST TIME:** Most people should find any time from June to late August a good time to do this climb. One should think twice about doing this climb in winter, however, owing to the extreme avalanche danger on the open slopes leading up to Powerline Pass as well as on the slopes on the back side of Homicide Peak.

**USGS MAPS:** Anchorage A-7 and A-8.

On Homicide Peak

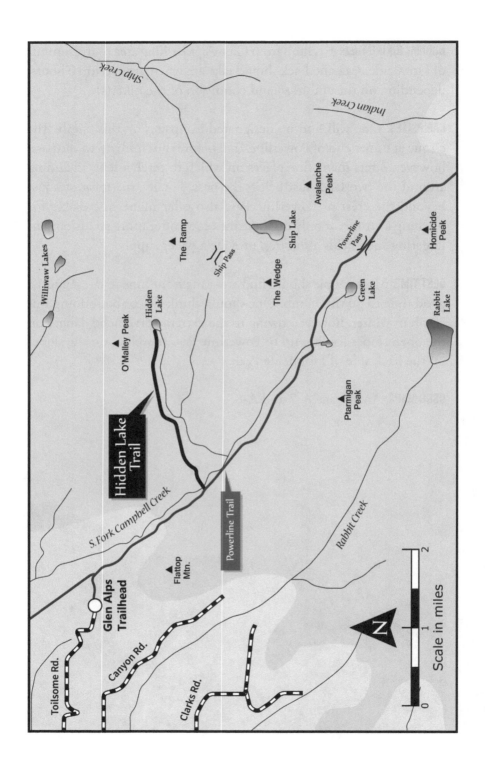

Ship Creek

Indian Creek

Williwaw Lakes

The Ramp

Ship Pass

Avalanche Peak

Ship Lake

Powerline Pass

Homicide Peak

O'Malley Peak

Hidden Lake

The Wedge

Green Lake

Rabbit Lake

**Hidden Lake Trail**

S. Fork Campbell Creek

Ptarmigan Peak

**Powerline Trail**

Flattop Mtn.

Rabbit Creek

Glen Alps Trailhead

Toilsome Rd.

Canyon Rd.

Clarks Rd.

N

Scale in miles

0    1    2

# Walk-About Guide to Hidden Lake Trail

Hidden Lake Trail, one of the two trails that branch off Powerline Trail, leads one up into Ship Pass valley to Hidden Lake, a small tarn tucked into a secluded niche at the southern base of Hidden Peak. Apart from hiking to Hidden Lake, one can also use this trail to access a number of other trips. The most popular of these destinations include the summits of The Wedge (4,660 feet), Ship Lake Pass (4,050 feet), and The Ramp (5,240 feet)*. Another little-known option entails traversing the sheep trail on the back of The Wedge back to Powerline Trail**. An even more ambitious trip entails climbing Hidden Peak from Hidden Lake and following the ridge out and over O'Malley Peak back to Glen Alps parking area***.

**TRAIL LOCATION:** Hidden Lake Trail begins approximately 2.5 miles up Powerline Trail from Glen Alps parking area. To get there drive 6.2 miles south from Anchorage on the Seward Highway. There, just after Milepost 121, turn right (west) onto the O'Malley Road exit. At the end of the ramp, turn left (east) and cross back under the highway. Continuing straight on O'Malley Road, ascend past Lake Otis Parkway and the Anchorage Zoo. Approximately 3 miles from the Seward Highway O'Malley Road reaches a junction with Hillside Road on the right (south). Turn onto Hillside Road and follow it

---

\* For information about these trips, see [35] **OPTION A—The Wedge,**
  [37] **OPTION C—Ship Lake Pass**, and [38] **OPTION D—The Ramp**.

\*\* For information about this trip, see [36] **OPTION B—Circumnavigation of the Wedge.**

\*\*\* For information about this trip, see [39] **OPTION E—Hidden Peak.**

for another 1 mile to just past a sign for Chugach State Park one reaches Upper Huffman Road on the left (east). Turn left onto Upper Huffman Road and follow it for 0.75 miles to appropriately named Toilsome Hill Drive on the right (south). Turning onto Toilsome Hill Drive, follow it as it switchbacks and winds its way upward. In approximately 2 miles Toilsome Hill Drive reaches the entrance to Glen Alps parking area on the left (east) side of the road at the top of one last short, steep hill. Park wherever possible (which may prove easier said than done on any given summer weekend) and pay the parking fee. (If one finds the main parking area full they may find extra parking in the overflow parking area located just downhill from the ranger's station.) From the parking area one can access Powerline Trail via the trail that begins at the far left (southeast) end of that parking area a trail and leads 0.5 miles out to Powerline Trail.

Leaving Glen Alps parking area, follow this access trail out to the intersection with Powerline Trail underneath the power lines. From here, Powerline Trail bears right (east) to continue for another 2.5 miles up valley to where it reaches the well-marked intersection with Hidden Lake Trail on the left (north).

Begin the hike on Hidden Lake Trail by dropping off Powerline Trail and crossing the bridge over Campbell Creek. On the far side of the creek the trail starts its climb to Hidden Lake. This climb begins by winding up to the top of the high shelf on the opposite side of the creek. After topping the shelf the trail turns right (east) to follow its crest. Approximately 0.25 miles later the trail reaches the Ship Creek basin. Turning left (northeast) the trail next follows the right side of the basin upwards to a fork. One trail crosses the stream and continues up Ship Creek valley. Hidden Lake Trail remains on the left (west) side of the stream, which it follows up through brush to the tundra beyond.

As it approaches Hidden Lake, the trail swings around the base of a low buttress dropping down from the right (east). Just beyond the base of the buttress the trail enters the lower end of a dramatic, high-walled cirque. Approximately 100 feet later the trail reaches its uppermost end at the western shore of Hidden Lake.

**TRAIL GRADE:** Hidden Lake Trail rates Grade 2 as a hike from end to end.

**TRAIL CONDITION:** The conditions on this trail vary little. Though wide and flat for much of its length, it often has many very muddy sections on is lower end. Only after it climbs above tree line does the trail begin to dry out. It remains relatively dry for the last climb up into the cirque to the edge of Hidden Lake.

**TRAIL MILEAGE:** To go from Glen Alps parking area to the junction with Hidden Lake Trail entails approximately 2.5 miles of hiking. From this junction to the western shore of Hidden Lake entails approximately 2.3 miles of hiking. This makes for a round-trip total of approximately 9.6 miles from Glen Alps parking area to Hidden Lake and back.

**TOTAL ELEVATION GAIN:** To hike from Glen Alps parking area to the western shore of Hidden Lake entails a total elevation gain of approximately 1,500 feet.

**HIGH POINT:** This trail reaches its highest point of approximately 3,650 feet above sea level at the western shore of Hidden Lake.

**NORMAL HIKING TIME:** To hike from Glen Alps parking area to the western shore of Hidden Lake and back should take anywhere from 4 to 6 hours, depending on the condition and ambition of the hiker(s) involved.

**CAMPSITES:** One will find no designated campsites on this climb. One will find many fine places on which to pitch a tent, however, anywhere along the western shore of Hidden Lake and along the final plateau leading up to the lake.

**BEST TIME:** Most people should find the time from May to September a good time to do this hike. It will also make a relatively safe ski or snowshoe outing in the winter, as long as one remains alert to the avalanche dangers both along Powerline Trail and in the Hidden Lake cirque.

**USGS MAPS:** Anchorage A-7 and A-8 SE.

Ship Creek
Indian Creek
Williwaw Lakes
The Ramp
Avalanche Peak
Ship Lake
Ship Pass
The Wedge
Powerline Pass
Homicide Peak
Hidden Lake
O'Malley Peak
Green Lake
Rabbit Lake
Option A
Ptarmigan Peak
Hidden Lake Trail
S.Fork Campbell Creek
Powerline Trail
Rabbit Creek
Flattop Mtn.
Glen Alps Trailhead
Toilsome Rd.
Canyon Rd.
Clarks Rd.
N
0
1
2
Scale in miles

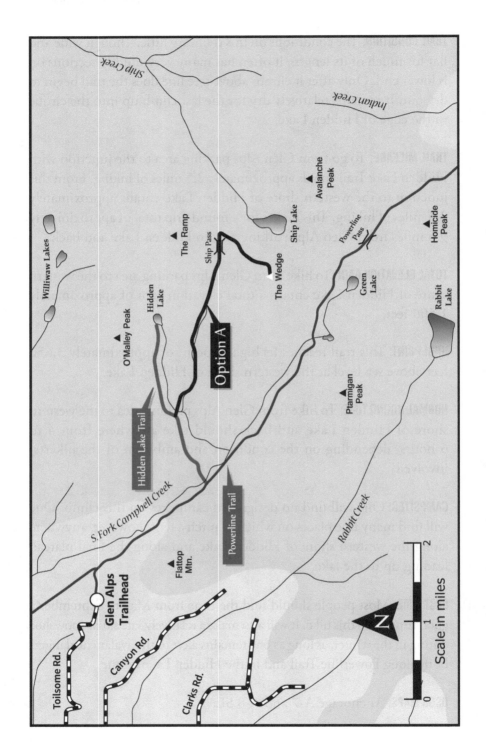

# OPTION A

# The Wedge

The Wedge, while not the highest peak, may appear the most obvious peak in Campbell Creek valley. This impression results from its solitary position in the center of the upper valley between the drainages of Ship Creek and Campbell Creek. The steep west face it initially presents to all who first step onto Powerline Trail from Glen Alps Parking area further enhances this impression. But these first impressions need not intimidate anyone. Its gentler backside makes for a hike that most anyone with a modicum of endurance can complete.

**TRAIL LOCATION:** This hike begins near the upper end of Hidden Lake Trail*. Soon after turning up Ship Creek basin, Hidden Lake Trail reaches a fork. One trail crosses the stream and continues up valley. The other trail, Hidden Lake Trail proper, remains on the left (west) side of the stream. Turning off Hidden Lake Trail follow the fork leading across the stream. Continue on this trail as it leads up through the last brush in the valley to the wide and broad expanse of the upper basin. Here, though faint, the trail leads across the tundra directly toward Ship Pass. If one does lose the trail in this open country, one need not worry. Simply continue up valley toward the pass. Upon reaching the bottom of the pass, pick a route up the open tundra and scree-streaked slope and climb to the crest

--------------------------------------------------

*    To get there, see [34] **Walk-About Guide to Hidden Lake Trail**.

WALK-ABOUT GUIDE TO ALASKA   **201**

(4,000-plus feet). From this point one should have a fine view looking down to Ship Lake.

On reaching the crest of the pass, turn right (south) and hike to the southern end. Here the ridge line bears to the right (southwest) and turns steeply upward. Here one should see a faint trail. Staying on face of the ridge, follow this faint trail up to where it rolls over onto the broad summit ridge. Staying in the center of this high ridge, follow it all the way up to the small rocky mounds that mark the rounded summit of The Wedge (4,460 feet).

**TRAIL GRADE:** Hidden Lake Trail rates Grade 2 as a hike from end to end. On leaving the end of the trail, this route rises to Grade 4 as a hike. It remains Grade 4 as a hike for the remainder of the climb to the summit of The Wedge.

**TRAIL CONDITION:** The conditions on this trail vary little. Though wide and flat for much of its length, Hidden Lake Trail often has many very muddy sections on is lower end. Only when the route crosses Ship Creek and climbs above tree line does the trail begins to dry out. The route remains largely dry, apart from any lingering snowfields, as it climbs the mostly tundra slope up to Ship Lake Pass and the summit of The Wedge.

**TRAIL MILEAGE:** To go from Glen Alps parking area to the summit of The Wedge entails approximately 6.5 miles of hiking, for a round-trip total of approximately 13 miles.

**TOTAL ELEVATION GAIN:** From Glen Alps parking area to the summit of The Wedge entails a total elevation gain of approximately 2,550 feet.

**HIGH POINT:** This route reaches its highest point of 4,460 feet above sea level at the summit of The Wedge.

**NORMAL HIKING TIME:** To hike from Glen Alps parking area to the summit of The Wedge should take anywhere from 4 to 9 hours, depending on the condition and ambition of the hiker(s) involved.

**CAMPSITES:** One will find no designated campsites on this climb. One will find many fine places on which to pitch a tent, however, in the wide, broad bowl below Ship Lake Pass.

**BEST TIME:** Most people should find any time from May to September a good time to do this hike. Depending on conditions, this could also make a fine ski or snowshoe outing in the winter. Even when conditions seem fine, however, one should remain alert to the avalanche dangers along Powerline Trail as well as on the climb to the crest of Ship Lake Pass and the summit of The Wedge.

**USGS MAPS:** Anchorage A-7 and A-8 SE.

The Wedge from Hidden Lake Trail

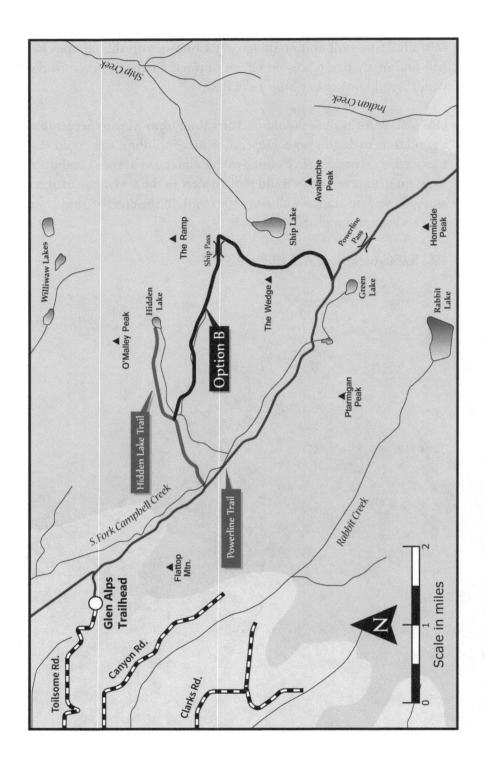

Ship Creek

Indian Creek

Williwaw Lakes

The Ramp

Avalanche Peak

Ship Pass

Ship Lake

Powerline Pass

Homicide Peak

Hidden Lake

O'Malley Peak

The Wedge

Green Lake

Rabbit Lake

Option B

Hidden Lake Trail

Ptarmigan Peak

S. Fork Campbell Creek

Powerline Trail

Rabbit Creek

Glen Alps Trailhead

Flattop Mtn.

Toilsome Rd.

Canyon Rd.

Clarks Rd.

N

Scale in miles

0     1     2

# OPTION B

# Circumnavigation of the Wedge

Some sheep trails seem better than many human trails. After centuries, and maybe millenniums, of searching out the right route across a ridge or along a mountain's flank that sheds snow early and still provides the most efficient route from any two points, sheep seem to have forged many routes that need little, if any improvement. This well-trod trail seems just such an example of a sheep's cognizance in trail blazing. If one ever follows this trail, make sure to say a silent thank-you to the sheep that have made this circumnavigation possible.

**TRAIL LOCATION:** This hike begins near the upper end of Hidden Lake Trail*. Soon after turning up Ship Creek basin, Hidden Lake Trail reaches a junction. Here, an unofficial trail crosses the stream and continues up valley while the other trail, Hidden Lake Trail proper, remains on the left (west) side of the stream. Turning off Hidden Lake Trail follow the trail leading across the stream. Continue on this trail as it leads up through the last brush in the valley to the wide and broad expanse of the upper basin. Here, though faint, the trail leads across the tundra directly toward Ship Pass. If one loses the trail, one need not worry. Simply continue up valley toward the pass. Upon reaching the bottom of the pass, pick a route up the open tundra and scree-streaked slope and climb to the crest (4,000-plus

------------------------------------------------------------

*    To get there, see [34] **Walk-About Guide to Hidden Lake Trail**.

feet). From this point one should have a fine view looking down to Ship Lake.

At the crest of the pass, turn right (south) and follow it to the southern end of the pass. Upon reaching the southern end of the pass, where the slope begins to climb more steeply toward the summit of The Wedge, look for a sheep trail contouring down and to the left (southeast) across the backside of The Wedge. Descending onto this trail, follow it all the way across the back flank of The Wedge to where it rejoins the ridge crest at the far side. Here one should have an expansive view of the upper cirque of Powerline Pass valley, including a clear view down to Powerline Trail winding up its near flank. From this point, the fastest route back down to Powerline Trail entails descending off the ridge to the right (south) down the relatively steep tundra slope to Powerline Trail visible far below. Once on Powerline Trail turn right (west) and follow it for approximately 4.5 miles back to Glen Alps parking area.

Those not wishing to descend from the ridge so quickly can continue with care along the ridge, following the sheep trail for the next 0.25 miles as it passes over a very rough ridge that will require extensive use of the hands to cross, to the base of Avalanche Mountain's northwest buttress. At the end of this short, jagged ridge turn right (south) and descend the relatively gentle but rocky slope to Powerline Trail visible below. On reaching Powerline Trail turn right (west) and follow it for approximately 4.7 miles back to Glen Alps parking area.

**TRAIL GRADE:** Hidden Lake Trail rates Grade 2 as a hike from end to end. On leaving the end of the trail, this route rises to Grade 4 as a hike. It remains a Grade 4 as a hike for the remainder of the climb to Ship Lake Pass. The traverse around the back side of The Wedge along the sheep trail rates Grade 3 as a hike. The descent to Powerline Trail rates Grade 4 as hike because of the steepness of the descent. The final walk out Powerline Trail back to the parking area at Glen Alps rates Grade 1 as a hike.

**TRAIL CONDITION:** This route varies little in its conditions. Though wide and flat for much of its length, Hidden Lake Trail often has many very muddy sections on its lower end. Only after the route climbs above tree line does the trail begin to dry out. The route remains largely dry as it climbs the mostly tundra slope, marked by only sporadic patches of scree, up to Ship Lake Pass. The sheep trail across the back side of The Wedge remains surprisingly wide and flat for most of its length. The descent to Powerline Trail on the far side of The Wedge reverts again to open tundra. Though this descent is steep with some scree, the footing remains generally good.

**TRAIL MILEAGE:** This circumnavigation from Glen Alps parking area around The Wedge and back entails approximately 11.5 miles of hiking.

**TOTAL ELEVATION GAIN:** To complete the circumnavigation from Glen Alps parking area around The Wedge and back entails a total elevation gain of approximately 1,900 feet.

**HIGH POINT:** This traverse reaches its highest point of approximately 4,150 feet above sea level on the sheep trail behind The Wedge.

**NORMAL HIKING TIME:** To complete the circumnavigation from Glen Alps parking area around The Wedge and back should take anywhere from 5 to 9 hours, depending on the condition and ambition of the hiker(s) involved.

**CAMPSITES:** One will find no designated campsites along this traverse. One will find many fine places on which to pitch a tent, however, including the open tundra all across the upper valley below Ship Lake Pass as well as the tundra at the base of the Powerline Pass side of the traverse.

**BEST TIME:** Most people should find any time from June to September a good time to do this hike. One should think twice, however, about traversing the back side of The Wedge or even making the steep descent into the Powerline Pass valley in the winter on account of the potential avalanche danger.

**USGS MAPS:** Anchorage A-7 and A-8 SE.

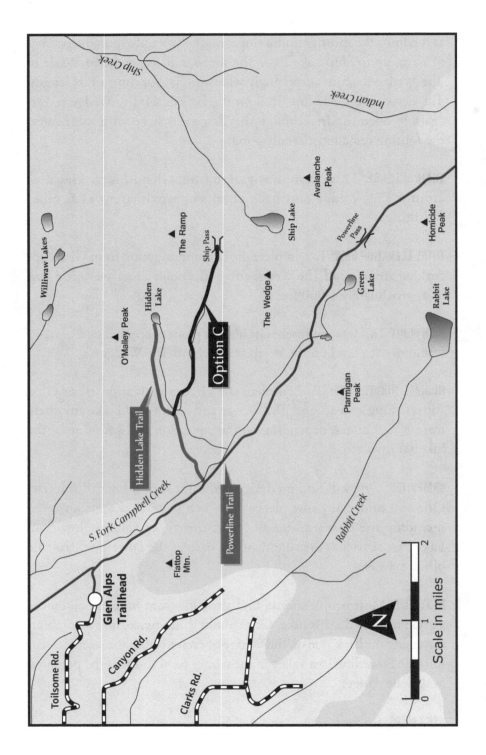

Ship Creek

Indian Creek

Williwaw Lakes

The Ramp

Avalanche Peak

Ship Lake

Powerline Pass

Homicide Peak

O'Malley Peak

Hidden Lake

Ship Pass

**Option C**

The Wedge

Green Lake

Rabbit Lake

Hidden Lake Trail

Ptarmigan Peak

S. Fork Campbell Creek

Powerline Trail

Rabbit Creek

Flattop Mtn.

Glen Alps Trailhead

Toilsome Rd.

Canyon Rd.

Clarks Rd.

N

Scale in miles

0    1    2

# OPTION C

# Ship Lake Pass

**TRAIL LOCATION:** This hike begins near the upper end of Hidden Lake Trail[*]. Soon after turning up Ship Creek basin, Hidden Lake Trail reaches a junction. Here, an unofficial trail crosses the stream and continues up valley while the other trail, Hidden Lake Trail proper, remains on the left (west) side of the stream. Turning off Hidden Lake Trail follow the trail leading across the stream. Continue on this trail as it leads up through the last brush in the valley to the wide and broad expanse of the upper basin. Here, though faint, the trail leads across the tundra directly toward Ship Pass. If one loses the trail, one need not worry. Simply continue up valley toward the pass. Upon reaching the bottom of the pass, pick a route up the open tundra and scree-streaked slope and climb to the crest of Ship Pass (4,000-plus feet).

From this point one should have a fine view not only down to Ship Lake, but also across a Ship Creek valley and far into the Chugach Mountains stretching to Bird Peak and beyond to the east and northeast as far as Pioneer Peak.

At this point one also has a number of options. First, they can turn right and climb The Wedge[**]. Second, they can turn right and follow the sheep trail around the backside of The Wedge[***]. Third, they can turn left (north) and climb The Ramp[****].

---

[*] To get there, see [34] **Walk-About Guide to Hidden Lake Trail**.

[**] For more information about that trip, see [35] **OPTION A—The Wedge**.

[***] For more information about that trip, see [36] **OPTION B—Circumnavigation of the Wedge**.

[****] For more information about that trip, see [38] **OPTION D—The Ramp**.

**TRAIL GRADE:** Hidden Lake Trail rates Grade 2 as a hike from end to end. On leaving the end of Hidden Lake Trail, the route rises to Grade 4 as a hike. It remains Grade 4 as a hike for the remainder of the climb to Ship Lake Pass.

**TRAIL CONDITION:** The conditions on this trail vary little. Though wide and flat for much of its length, Hidden Lake Trail often has many very muddy sections on its lower end. Only after the route climbs above tree line does the trail begin to dry out. Once off Hidden Lake Trail, first cross the sometimes boggy bottom of Ship Pass valley. The route then becomes largely dry as it climbs the mostly tundra slope, marked by only sporadic patches of scree, up to Ship Lake Pass.

**TRAIL MILEAGE:** To go from Glen Alps parking area to the summit of Ship Lake Pass entails approximately 6 miles of hiking, for a round-trip total of approximately 12 miles.

**TOTAL ELEVATION GAIN:** To hike from Glen Alps parking area to the crest of Ship Lake Pass entails a total elevation gain of approximately 2,050 feet.

**HIGH POINT:** This route reaches its highest point of 4,000-plus feet above sea level at crest of Ship Lake Pass.

**NORMAL HIKING TIME:** To hike from Glen Alps parking area to the crest of Ship Lake Pass and back should take anywhere from 4 to 8 hours, depending on the condition and ambition of the hiker(s) involved.

**CAMPSITES:** One will find no designated campsites on this climb. One will find many fine places on which to pitch a tent, however, in the wide, flat bowl below Ship Lake Pass.

**BEST TIME:** Most people should find any time from May to September a good time to do this hike. Depending on conditions, this could also make a fine ski or snowshoe outing in the winter. Even when conditions seem fine, however, one should remain alert to the avalanche dangers both along Powerline Trail and on the climb to the crest of Ship Lake Pass.

**USGS MAPS:** Anchorage A-7 and A-8 SE.

Cooling off in Ship Pass valley

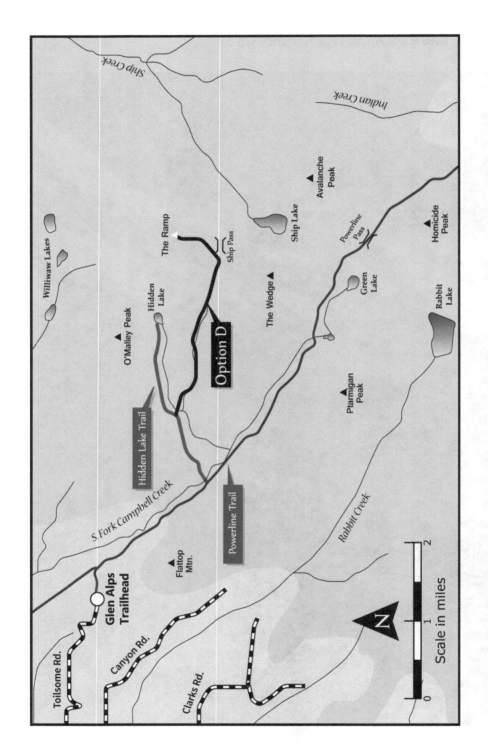

Ship Creek

Indian Creek

Williwaw Lakes

Avalanche Peak ▲

Ship Lake

Homicide Peak ▲

The Ramp ▲

Ship Pass

Powerline Pass

Hidden Lake

O'Malley Peak ▲

The Wedge ▲

Green Lake

Rabbit Lake

**Option D**

Hidden Lake Trail

Ptarmigan Peak ▲

S. Fork Campbell Creek

Powerline Trail

Rabbit Creek

Glen Alps Trailhead

Flattop Mtn. ▲

Toilsome Rd.

Canyon Rd.

Clarks Rd.

N

Scale in miles

0    1    2

# OPTION D

# The Ramp

**TRAIL LOCATION:** This hike begins near the upper end of Hidden Lake Trail*. Soon after turning up Ship Creek basin, Hidden Lake Trail reaches a junction. Here, an unofficial trail crosses the stream and continues up valley while the other trail, Hidden Lake Trail proper, remains on the left (west) side of the stream. Turning off Hidden Lake Trail follow the trail leading across the stream. Continue on this trail as it leads up through the last brush in the valley to the wide and broad expanse of the upper basin. Here, though faint, the trail leads across the tundra directly toward Ship Pass. If one loses the trail, one need not worry. Simply continue up valley toward the pass. Upon reaching the bottom of the pass, pick a route up the open tundra and scree-streaked slope and climb to the crest of Ship Pass (4,000-plus feet).

At the crest of the pass, turn left (north) along the faint trail leading along across the top of the pass. If one does not see the trail, follow the crest of the pass to where the ridge turns steeply upward at the northern end of the pass. Here one should more easily find the now more obvious trail leading up the steep ridge face. Continue climbing the faint trail to where the flat western ridge above joins the summit cone. On reaching the crest of this west ridge, bear right (east) and continue up the rough trail toward the summit. Continue up the ridge as it narrows more and more into a rocky rib with some exposure on both sides. After one final exposed move around the left (west) side of the ridge, one reaches the narrow summit of The Ramp (5,240 feet).

---

\* To get there, see [34] **Walk-About Guide to Hidden Lake Trail**.

**TRAIL GRADE:** Hidden Lake Trail rates Grade 2 as a hike from end to end. On leaving the end of Hidden Lake Trail, the route rises to Grade 4 as a hike. It remains a Grade 4 as a hike for the remainder of the climb to the crest of the pass. On starting up the summit cone the rate gradually increase to Grade 5 and then Grade 6 as a hike the higher one climbs.

**TRAIL CONDITION:** The conditions on this trail vary considerably. Though wide and flat for much of its length, Hidden Lake Trail often has many very muddy sections on its lower end. As the route climbs above tree line does the trail begins to dry out. Once off Hidden Lake Trail, first cross the sometimes boggy bottom of Ship Pass valley. The route then becomes largely dry as it climbs the mostly tundra slope, marked by sporadic patches of scree, up to Ship Lake Pass. From Ship Lake Pass to the summit of The Ramp the route becomes rockier and steeper the higher one climbs. The final climb of the summit cone also features some eye-opening exposure on the northwest side of the ridge dropping precipitously into the Middle Fork Campbell Creek valley.

**TRAIL MILEAGE:** To go from Glen Alps parking area to the summit of The Ramp entails approximately 6.75 miles of hiking, for a round-trip total of almost 13.5 miles.

**TOTAL ELEVATION GAIN:** To hike from Glen Alps parking area to the summit of The Ramp entails a total elevation gain of approximately 3,100 feet.

**HIGH POINT:** This climb reaches its highest point of 5,240 feet above sea level at the summit of The Ramp.

**NORMAL HIKING TIME:** To hike from Glen Alps parking area to the summit of The Ramp and back should take anywhere from 5 to 9 hours, depending on the condition and ambition of the hiker(s) involved.

**CAMPSITES:** One will find no designated campsites on this climb. One will find many fine places on which to pitch a tent, however, in the wide, flat bowl below Ship Lake Pass as well as around Hidden Lake.

**BEST TIME:** Most people should find any time from June to September a good time to do this hike. One should think twice about doing this climb in the winter, however, owing to the avalanche danger along much of the route as well as the technical expertise one would need in icy conditions on the climb of the final summit cone.

**USGS MAPS:** Anchorage A-7 and A-8 SE.

On the summit
of The Ramp

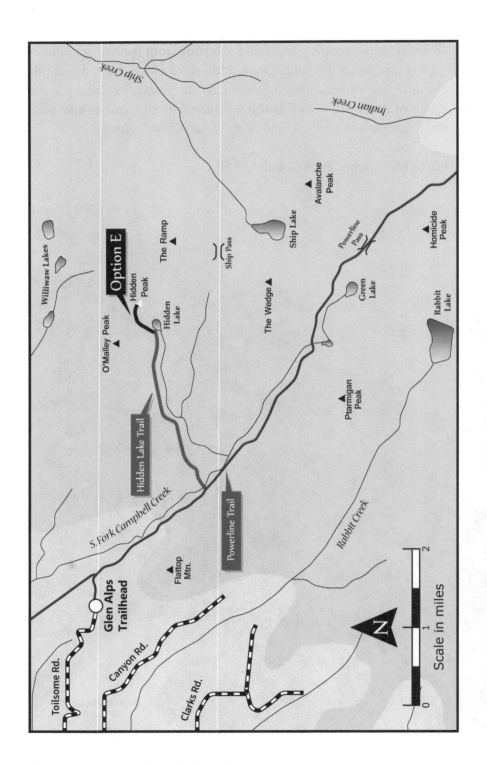

Ship Creek

Indian Creek

Avalanche Peak ▲

Ship Lake

Homicide Peak ▲

Powerline Pass

Green Lake

Rabbit Lake

**Option E**

The Ramp ▲

Hidden Peak

Ship Pass

The Wedge ▲

Williwaw Lakes

O'Malley Peak ▲

Hidden Lake

Ptarmigan Peak ▲

Hidden Lake Trail

S. Fork Campbell Creek

Rabbit Creek

Powerline Trail

Flattop Mtn. ▲

**Glen Alps Trailhead**

Toilsome Rd.

Canyon Rd.

Clarks Rd.

N

Scale in miles

0    1    2

# OPTION E

# Hidden Peak

Though very easy to describe, this climb proves very difficult to do. Many may find the climb so steep that they might prefer not to go down the way they had come up. For this reason this guide offers an alternative route down via O'Malley Peak.

**TRAIL LOCATION:** This hike begins at the uppermost end of Hidden Lake Trail at Hidden Lake*. At the end of Hidden Lake Trail, continue around the left (north) side of Hidden Lake. Approximately halfway around the lake, turn left (north) and look for a wide gully that looks to provide best access to the slopes above. Then begin climbing, picking out firm steps wherever possible as one scrambles upward. On the more open slopes above, bear very slightly to the left (northwest) so as to avoid the extremely steep slopes to the east of the summit. Eventually, after clambering up the steep scree and rocks below, one should reach the base of the sharp rock ribs dropping off the ridge crest. Scrambling more directly up the fall line between two of these ribs, climb onto the ridge top.

Once on the rocky ridge, turn right (east) toward the summit, which one can recognize by its huge block-like shape. As one scrambles along the ridge, make sure to stay below and to the right (south) wherever the ridge becomes impassable. In this way one can avoid

--------------------------------------------------------------------

\*   To get there, see [34] **Walk-About Guide to Hidden Lake Trail**.

the sheer north face of the ridge. On reaching the block-like summit cap, a final scramble up its right side leads to the surprisingly broad summit (5,105 feet).

Upon making the summit one has two choices. First, one can return the way one came. Second, those not wishing to pick their way back down the steep slope they have just climbed have the alternative of returning via O'Malley Peak. This safer and more scenic route begins by turning west off the summit of Hidden Peak and following the rocky ridge back toward Anchorage. Approximately 0.75 miles later, after crossing one major saddle, a final climb leads to the summit of O'Malley Peak (5,150 feet). From there one can follow O'Malley Peak Trail back down to Glen Alps parking area[*].

**TRAIL GRADE:** Hidden Lake Trail rates Grade 2 as a hike from end to end. On leaving the end of the trail and beginning the climb from the shore of Hidden Lake to the summit of Hidden Peak, it rises dramatically to Grade 6 as a hike. It remains Grade 6 as a hike all the way to the summit of Hidden Peak. For those wishing to follow the route over O'Malley Peak, the traverse between the two summits initially rates Grade 6 as a scramble but rates Grade 5 as a climb on the final ascent to the summit of O'Malley Peak. O'Malley Peak Trail rates Grade 3 as a hike, with sections of Grade 2 hiking across "The Ballpark" and in the last 0.5 miles across Campbell Creek and along Powerline Trail back to Glen Alps parking area.

**TRAIL CONDITION:** The conditions on this trail vary considerably. Though wide and flat for much of its length, Hidden Lake Trail has many very muddy sections on is lower end. Once above tree line, the trail begins to dry out and remains largely dry for the last climb to the western shore of Hidden Lake. On beginning the climb from Hidden Lake the route becomes steep and rocky with lots of scree and loose stones to clamber over. It remains this way for almost the entire climb to the summit of Hidden Peak as well as on the traverse out and over

--------------------------------------------------------------------------

[*]   For more information about that trail, see [43] **Walk-About Guide to O'Malley Peak Trail.**

O'Malley Peak. On O'Malley Peak Trail the footing improves, with only two steep sections, on the steep descents to "The Ballpark" and to the Campbell Creek valley floor.

**TRAIL MILEAGE:** To go from Glen Alps parking area to the summit of Hidden Peak entails approximately 5.8 miles of hiking, for a round-trip total of approximately 11.6 miles. To continue the traverse out and over O'Malley Peak and down O'Malley Peak Trail to Glen Alps parking area entails approximately 11.3 miles of hiking.

**TOTAL ELEVATION GAIN:** To hike from Glen Alps parking area to the summit of Hidden Peak and back entails a total elevation gain of approximately 2,900 feet. To hike from Glen Alps parking area to the summit of Hidden Peak and out over O'Malley Peak and down the O'Malley Peak Trail back to Glen Alps parking area entails a total elevation gain of approximately 3,400 feet.

**HIGH POINT:** This climb reaches its highest point of 5,105 feet above sea level at the summit of Hidden Peak. If one continues the traverse out and over O'Malley Peak and down O'Malley Peak Trail to Glen Alps parking area this climb reaches a yet higher point of 5,150 feet above sea level at the summit of O'Malley Peak.

**NORMAL HIKING TIME:** To hike from Glen Alps parking area to the summit of Hidden Peak and back should take anywhere from 5 to 9 hours, depending on the condition and ambition of the hiker(s) involved. To hike from Glen Alps parking area to the summit of Hidden Peak and then back out over O'Malley Peak and down O'Malley Peak Trail to Glen Alps parking area should also take anywhere from 5 to 9 hours, again depending on the condition and ambition of the hiker(s) involved.

**CAMPSITES:** One will find no designated campsites on this climb. One will, however, find many fine places on which to pitch a tent both anywhere along the western shore of Hidden Lake and along the final plateau leading up to the lake.

**BEST TIME:** Most people should find any time from June to September a good time to do this climb. One should think twice about doing this climb in the winter, however, due to the avalanche danger along much of the route.

**USGS MAPS:** Anchorage A-7 and A-8 SE.

A ridge-walk in the clouds

Climbing above Hidden Lake

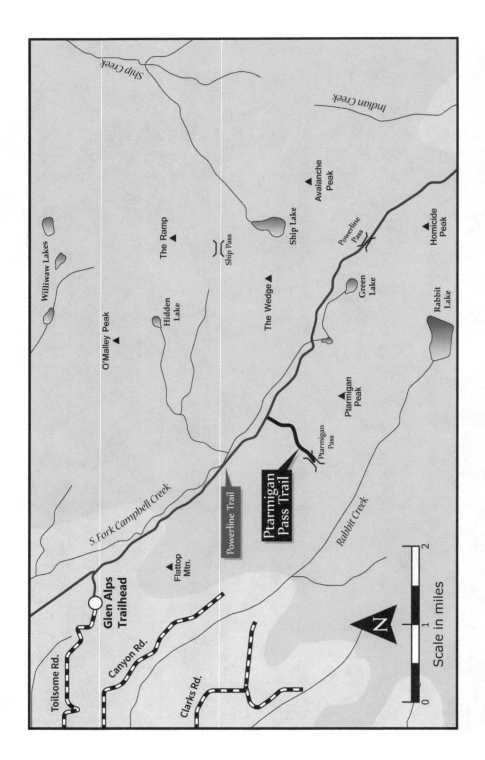

Ship Creek

Indian Creek

Williwaw Lakes

The Ramp ▲

Avalanche Peak ▲

Ship Pass )(

Ship Lake

Powerline Pass

Homicide Peak ▲

O'Malley Peak ▲

Hidden Lake

The Wedge ▲

Green Lake

Rabbit Lake

S. Fork Campbell Creek

Ptarmigan Peak ▲

Ptarmigan Pass

Powerline Trail

**Ptarmigan Pass Trail**

Rabbit Creek

Flattop Mtn. ▲

Glen Alps Trailhead

Toilsome Rd.

Canyon Rd.

Clarks Rd.

N

Scale in miles

0    1    2

# Walk-About Guide to Ptarmigan Pass Trail

This unofficial trail climbs the south side of Campbell Creek valley to Ptarmigan Pass between Flaketop and Ptarmigan Peak. It thus allows one to complete a circle after first traversing the ridge from Flattop Mountain to Ptarmigan Pass*. It also allows one to climb Ptarmigan Peak from Glen Alps parking area. But then it also makes for an adventurous climb to a scenic spot in and of itself.

**TRAIL LOCATION:** Ptarmigan Pass Trail begins approximately 3.8 miles up Powerline Trail from Glen Alps parking area. To get there drive 6.2 miles south from Anchorage on the Seward Highway. There, just after Milepost 121, turn right (west) onto the O'Malley Road exit. At the end of the ramp, turn left (east) and cross back under the highway. Continuing straight on O'Malley Road, ascend past Lake Otis Parkway and the Anchorage Zoo. Approximately 3 miles from the Seward Highway O'Malley Road reaches a junction with Hillside Road on the right (south). Turn onto Hillside Road and follow it for another 1 mile to just past a sign for Chugach State Park one reaches Upper Huffman Road on the left (east). Turn left onto Upper Huffman Road and follow it for 0.75 miles to appropriately named Toilsome Hill Drive on the right (south). Turning onto Toilsome Hill Drive, follow it as it switchbacks and winds its way upward. In approximately 2 miles Toilsome Hill Drive reaches the entrance to Glen Alps parking area on the left (east)

---

\*    For more information about that trip,
see [27] **OPTION A—Traverse from Flattop Mountain to Ptarmigan Pass**.

side of the road at the top of one last short, steep hill. Park wherever possible (which may prove easier said than done on any given summer weekend) and pay the parking fee. (If one finds the main parking area full they can find extra parking in the overflow parking area located just downhill from the ranger's station.) From the parking area one can access Powerline Trail via the trail that begins at the far left (southeast) end of that parking area a trail and leads 0.5 miles out to Powerline Trail.

Leaving Glen Alps parking area, follow this access trail out to the intersection with Powerline Trail underneath the power lines. From here, bear right (east) and follow Powerline Trail for approximately 3.3 miles, to where, just as the trail begins to pass under the west face of Ptarmigan Peak towering high above, one reaches a faint in an opening in the brush on the right (south) This opening marks the beginning of Ptarmigan Pass Trail. (If one reaches the small creek tumbling down from the right out of Ptarmigan Pass, one has gone a too far. Turn around and look for the trail now on the left.)

Begin the hike on Ptarmigan Pass Trail by climbing through the opening to the steeper slope above. Continuing up the slope, follow the trail as it angles slight to the left (east) and aims for the pronounced gully near the top of the ridge. Once in the gully, the trail climbs along the left (west) side of the streams. At the top of the notch, follow the trail as it swings up and to the right onto the open tundra of the pass. As the trail comes over the last rise above the tarn located at that corner of the pass, it peters out in the open tundra.

At this point one has a number of choices. First, they can return the way they have come. Second, they can turn sharply right and follow the route as described in [27] **OPTION A—Traverse from Flattop Mountain to Ptarmigan Pass** in reverse back to Flattop. Third, they can pick up in the middle, thus saving much climbing, and continue the traverse to Powerline Pass[*].

**TRAIL GRADE:** Powerline Trail rates Grade 1 as a hike for the first 3 miles from Glen Alps parking area. The following 1.3-mile-long climb from Powerline Trail to Ptarmigan Pass rates Grade 3 as a hike.

---------------------------------------------------------------------

[*]    For more information about that trip, see [28] **OPTION B—Traverse from Flattop Mountain to Powerline Pass.**

**TRAIL CONDITION:** The trail varies little in its conditions. Climbing more or less straight up the fall line, it remains steep and often quite rocky the entire way. Only where the trail swings up and on the far northeast end of Ptarmigan Pass does the trail climb less steeply through less rock.

**TRAIL MILEAGE:** From Powerline Trail to the top of Ptarmigan Pass entails approximately 1.3 miles of hiking, for a round-trip total of 2.6 miles. To hike from Glen Alps parking area to the top of Ptarmigan Pass entails approximately 4.3 miles of hiking for a round-trip total of approximately 8.6 miles.

**TOTAL ELEVATION GAIN:** To hike from Powerline Trail to the top of Ptarmigan Pass entails a total elevation gain of approximately 1,300 feet. To hike from Glen Alps parking area to the top of Ptarmigan Pass entails a total elevation gain of approximately 1,700 feet.

**HIGH POINT:** This trail reaches its highest point of 3,585 feet above sea level at the top of Ptarmigan Pass.

**NORMAL HIKING TIME:** To hike from Glen Alps parking area to the top of Ptarmigan Pass and back should take anywhere from 3 to 7 hours, depending on the condition and ambition of the hiker(s) involved.

**CAMPSITES:** One will find no designated campsites on this trail. Many people, however, find that Ptarmigan Pass also makes a fine place on which to pitch a tent, though, with a ready-available supply of water at the tarn located in the northeast corner.

**BEST TIME:** Most people should find any time from June to early September a good time to do this hike. One should think twice, however, of hiking this trail in the winter due to the extreme avalanche danger.

**USGS MAPS:** Anchorage A-7.

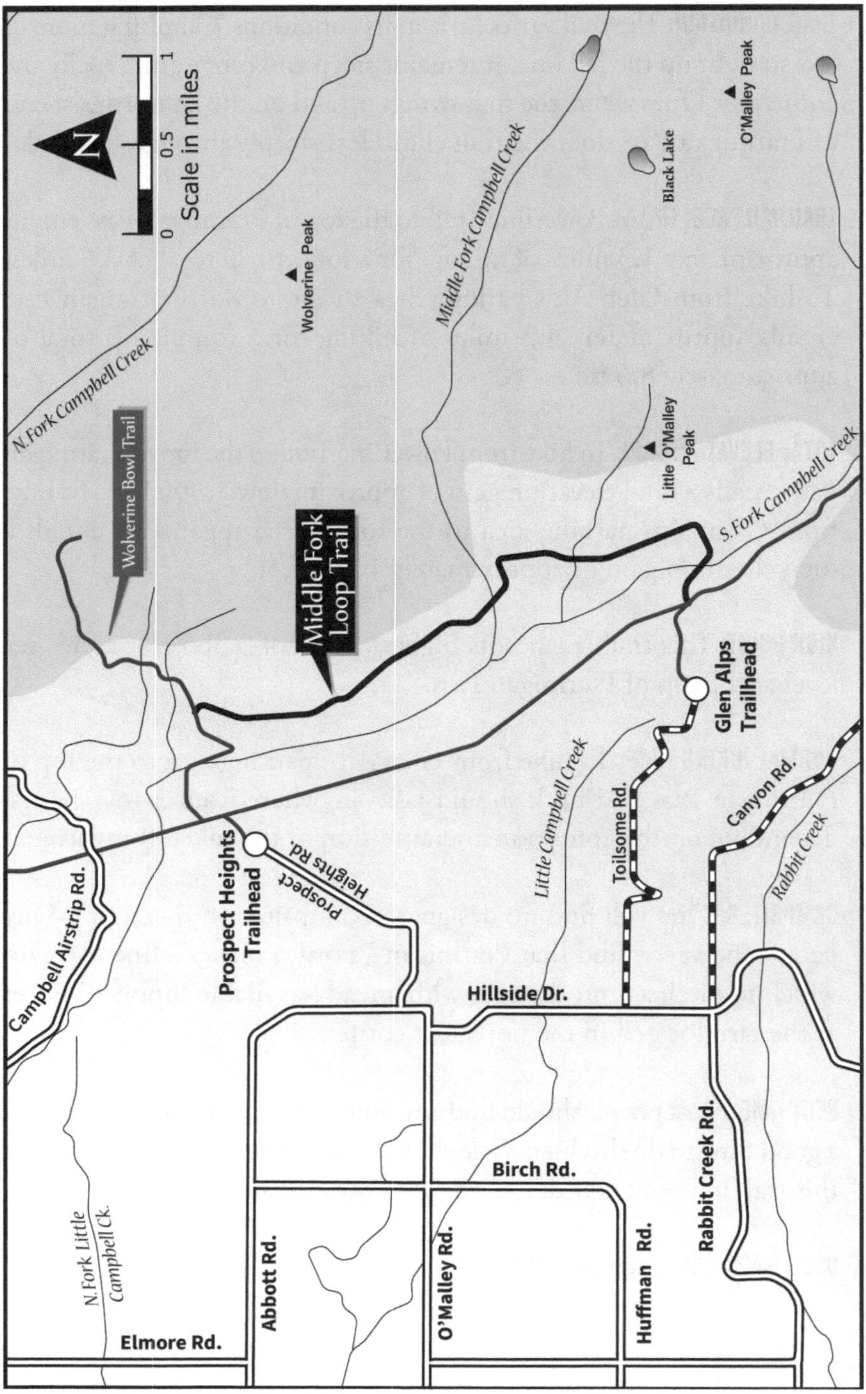

N
0
0.5
1
Scale in miles
N.Fork Campbell Creek
Wolverine Bowl Trail
Wolverine Peak
Middle Fork Campbell Creek
Black Lake
O'Malley Peak
Middle Fork Loop Trail
Little O'Malley Peak
S.Fork Campbell Creek
Glen Alps Trailhead
Toilsome Rd.
Little Campbell Creek
Canyon Rd.
Rabbit Creek
Prospect Heights Trailhead
Prospect Heights Rd.
Campbell Airstrip Rd.
Hillside Dr.
Birch Rd.
N.Fork Little Campbell Ck.
Elmore Rd.
Abbott Rd.
O'Malley Rd.
Huffman Rd.
Rabbit Creek Rd.

# Walk-About Guide to Middle Fork Loop Trail

This trail may see more use than all other trails in the Front Range apart from Flattop Mountain Trail. Regardless of the day of the week, the time of day, or the time of year, this trail usually has some travelling its length. Hikers, runners, bikers, skiers, and snowshoers all leave their marks on this trail. For all this use the trail neither begins nor ends at a parking area. Instead one can only access it by means of other trails. This, however, may explain its popularity. Through its connection to other trails, this trail serves as part of a popular loop that one can begin or end either from Prospect Heights parking area or Glenn Alps parking area. This loop, though it travels into the high country, remains easily accessible all year round and avalanche-free in the winter, all of which makes it all the more popular. One can even hike or run this well-trodden on most days in the winter.

**TRAIL LOCATION:** One can start this trail from two different trailheads. The south end of Middle Fork Loop Trail begins approximately 0.5 miles along Powerline Trail from Glen Alps parking area. To get there drive 6.2 miles south from Anchorage on the Seward Highway. There, just after Milepost 121, turn right (west) onto the O'Malley Road exit. At the end of the ramp, turn left (east) and cross back under the highway. Continuing straight on O'Malley Road, ascend past Lake Otis Parkway and the Anchorage Zoo. Approximately 3 miles from the Seward Highway O'Malley Road reaches a junction with Hillside Road on the right (south). Turn onto Hillside Road and follow it for another 1 mile to just past a sign for Chugach State Park one reaches

Upper Huffman Road on the left (east). Turn left onto Upper Huffman Road and follow it for 0.75 miles to appropriately named Toilsome Hill Drive on the right (south). Turning onto Toilsome Hill Drive, follow it as it switchbacks and winds its way upward. In approximately 2 miles Toilsome Hill Drive reaches the entrance to Glen Alps parking area on the left (east) side of the road at the top of one last short, steep hill. Park wherever possible (which may prove easier said than done on any given summer weekend) and pay the parking fee. (If one finds the main parking area full they can find extra parking in the overflow parking area located just downhill from the ranger's station.) From the parking area one can access Powerline Trail and Middle Fork Loop Trail via the trail that begins at the far left (southeast) end of that parking area a trail and leads 0.5 miles out to Powerline Trail.

The northern end of Middle Fork Loop Trail begins approximately 1 mile along Wolverine Bowl Trail from Prospect Heights parking area. To get there drive 6.2 miles south from Anchorage on the Seward Highway. There, just after Milepost 121, take a right (west) on the O'Malley Road exit. At the end of the ramp, turn left (east) back under the highway. Continue straight on this road as it ascends past Lake Otis Parkway and the Anchorage Zoo. Approximately 3 miles from the highway O'Malley Road passes the junction with Hillside Road leading right (south). Staying on O'Malley Road, follow it as it swings left to become the continuation of Hillside Drive leading north. Almost immediately after Hillside Road straightens out, it reaches the junction with Upper O'Malley Road on the right (east). Turn right onto Upper O'Malley Road. Approximately 0.5 miles later, this road ends at a T-intersection with Prospect Drive. Turn left (north) on Prospect Drive and follow it for 1 mile to a stop sign. Bear left through the stop sign onto Siderof Lane. Approximately 200 yards later this road reaches the entrance to Chugach State Park on the right (north). Turn into this parking area. Wolverine Bowl Trail leading to Middle Fork Loop Trail begins at the fire gate just to the right of the outhouse and signboard at the far end of the parking area*. Follow

-------------------------------------------------------------

\* For more information about that trail,
  see [57] **Walk-About Guide to Wolverine Bowl Trail** in Chapter 5.

Wolverine Bowl Trail for approximately 1 mile to where, after crossing Campbell Creek, it follows a wide switchback up to a junction with Middle Fork Loop Trail on the right (south).

Leaving the southern trailhead at Glen Alps parking area, follow this access trail out to the intersection with Powerline Trail underneath the power lines. From here, bear right (east) and follow the Powerline Trail for less than 100 yards to where it starts down a long and shallow hill. A short way down this hill Powerline Trail reaches the junction with Middle Fork Loop Trail on the left (north).

Turning left (northeast) onto Middle Fork Loop Trail, follow it downhill. After first descending the few hundred feet to the valley floor, Middle Fork Loop Trail then crosses bridge over South Fork Campbell Creek. On the far side of the bridge, the trail climbs a series of wooden walkways to the tundra above. Approximately 100 yards beyond far end of these wooden walkways, Middle Fork Loop Trail reaches a junction with O'Malley Peak Trail*.

Turn right (northwest) and continue following Middle Fork Loop Trail as it swings around the western base of O'Malley Peak. On the far side of O'Malley Peak the trail reaches another junction with Williwaw Lakes Trail**. Bearing left (northeast) from this junction the trail crosses over a long bench and swings down the far side to cross a bridge over Middle Fork Campbell Creek. After contouring along the far side of creek for approximately 0.25 miles, the trail angles up and to the right and crosses the hump at the base of Wolverine Peak's southwest ridge. Once over this hump, the trail begins a gradual descent for the next 1.5 miles to where it ends at a junction with Wolverine Bowl Trail.

From this northern end of the trail one has two primary options. First, one can turn right (northeast) on Wolverine Bowl Trail to climb Wolverine Peak or Near Point. Second, one can turn left (west) on Wolverine Bowl Trail and follow it out to Prospect Heights parking area. This second option also offers an option of its own. As one nears

---

\*      To get there, see [43] **Walk-About Guide to O'Malley Peak Trail**.

\*\*    For more about this trail see [61] **Walk-About Guide to Williwaw Lakes Trail** in Chapter 5.

the parking lot, one can turn onto Powerline Trail and follow it back up to Glen Alps parking area[*].

**TRAIL GRADE:** This trail rates Grade 1 as a hike.

**TRAIL CONDITION:** The conditions along this trail vary little. Wide and flat for much of its length, Middle Fork Loop Trail only has a few muddy sections along its length.

**TRAIL MILEAGE:** To go from Glen Alps parking area to the end of Middle Fork Loop Trail at its junction with Wolverine Bowl Trail entails approximately 3.8 miles of hiking, for a round-trip total of approximately 7.2 miles. To continue the traverse out to Prospect Heights parking area entails approximately 5.3 miles of hiking, for a round-trip total of approximately 10.6 miles. To complete the entire loop of Middle Fork Loop Trail and Middle Powerline Trail back to Glen Alps parking area entails approximately 8 miles of hiking.

**TOTAL ELEVATION GAIN:** To hike from Glen Alps parking area to the end of Middle Fork Loop Trail at its junction with Wolverine Bowl Trail entails a total elevation gain of approximately 400 feet. It entails another approximately 150-plus feet of elevation gain to continue the traverse out to Prospect Heights parking area. To hike the entire loop of Middle Fork Loop Trail and Middle Powerline Trail back to Glen Alps parking area entails a total elevation gain of approximately 1,600 feet.

**HIGH POINT:** This hike reaches its highest point of approximately 2,150 feet above sea level at the junction with O'Malley Peak Trail.

**NORMAL HIKING TIME:** To hike from Glen Alps parking area to the end of Middle Fork Loop Trail at its junction with Wolverine Bowl Trail

---------------------------------------------------------------------

[*] For more about these trips see [57] **Walk-About Guide to Wolverine Bowl Trail** and [60] **Walk-About Guide to Wolverine Peak Trail** in Chapter 5, and [46] **Walk-About Guide to Middle Powerline Trail** in Chapter 4.

and back should take anywhere from 2 to 4 hours, depending on the condition and ambition of the hiker(s) involved. To hike from Glen Alps parking area to Prospect Heights parking should take anywhere from 2.5 to 4.5 hours. It should take anywhere from 3 to 6 hours to hike the entire loop of Middle Fork Loop Trail and Middle Powerline Trail back Glen Alps parking area.

**CAMPSITES:** One will find no designated campsites on this climb. One will find many fine places on which to pitch a tent, however, in the tundra surrounding the junction of this trail with Williwaw Lakes Trail.

**BEST TIME:** Most people should find any time from June to September a good time to do this climb. It also makes a fine ski or snowshoe trip in the winter, although one should remain wary of potential avalanches while skirting below the faces of O'Malley Peak and Wolverine Peak.

**USGS MAPS:** Anchorage A-7 and A-8 SE.

Biking on Middle Fork Loop Trail

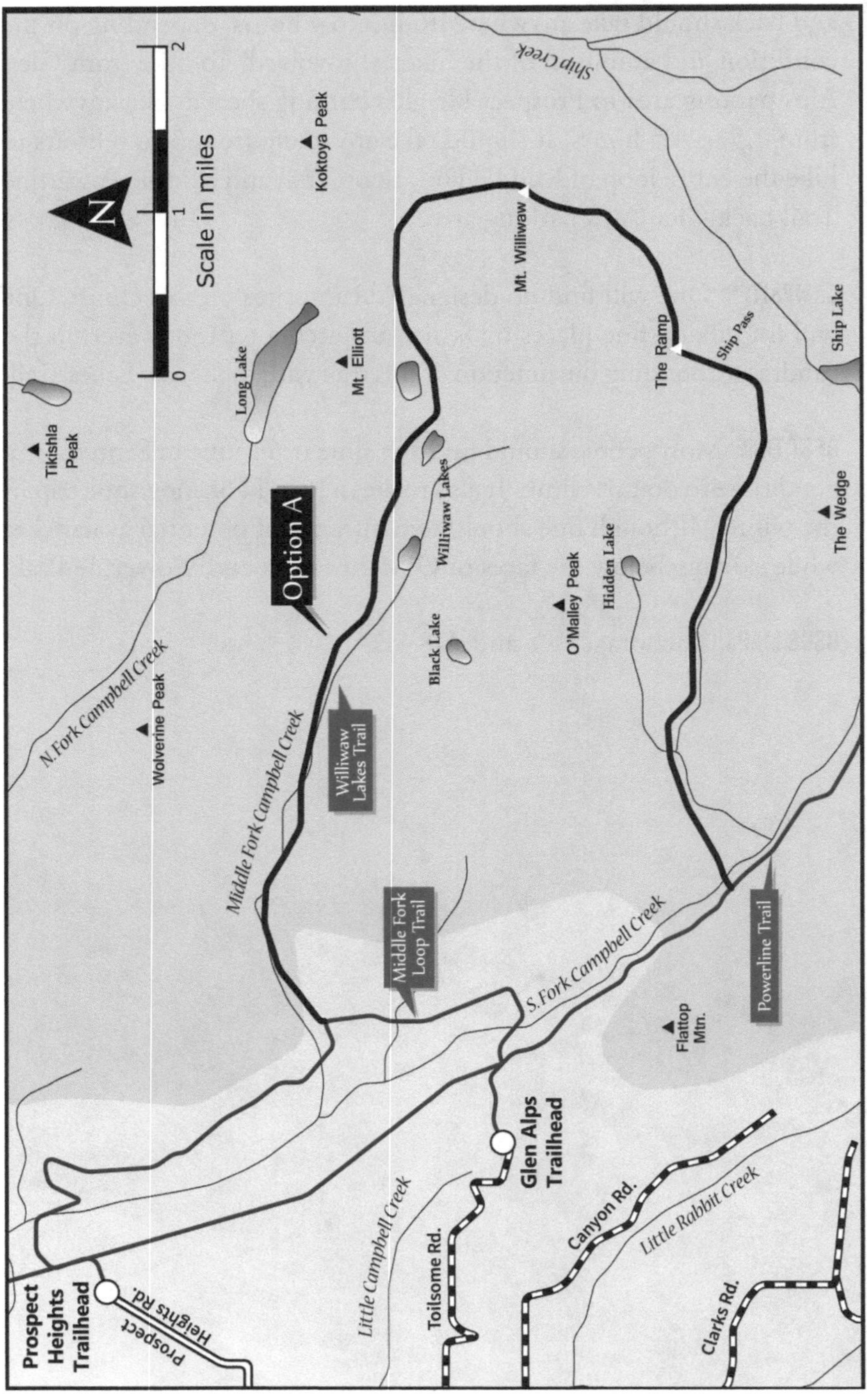
Scale in miles
0
1
2
N
Koktoya Peak
Ship Creek
Mt. Williwaw
Mt. Elliott
Long Lake
Tikishla Peak
The Ramp
Ship Pass
Ship Lake
Option A
Williwaw Lakes
The Wedge
Hidden Lake
O'Malley Peak
Black Lake
N. Fork Campbell Creek
Wolverine Peak
Middle Fork Campbell Creek
Williwaw Lakes Trail
Middle Fork Loop Trail
S. Fork Campbell Creek
Powerline Trail
Flattop Mtn.
Glen Alps Trailhead
Prospect Heights Trailhead
Prospect Heights Rd.
Little Campbell Creek
Toilsome Rd.
Canyon Rd.
Little Rabbit Creek
Clarks Rd.

# OPTION A

## Traverse from Mount Williwaw to the Ramp

Many experienced hikers and scramblers consider this the most challenging and spectacular traverse in the Front Range. Crossing one of the highest and most remote ridges in the Front Range, it certainly does have an airy danger about it that warns away all but those with considerable stamina and audacity.

**TRAIL LOCATION:** This traverse begins on the saddle between Koktoya Peak and Williwaw Peak at the uppermost end of the North Fork Campbell Creek valley. To get there from Glen Alps parking area, first follow Powerline Trail approximately 0.5 miles out to its intersection with Middle Fork Loop Trail. Turning left (north) onto Middle Fork Loop Trail, follow it for approximately 1.5 miles to its junction with Williwaw Lakes Trail. Then turn right (east) onto Williwaw Lakes Trail and follow it to its very end at the shore of the uppermost lake in the valley*. On reaching the end of Williwaw Lakes Trail, bear left (north) and cross the stream feeding into the last lake.

One now has two options in climbing Mount Williwaw. The first, and more dangerous, option entails turning upstream to the right (east)

---

* For more information about these trails, see [31] **Walk-About Guide to Powerline Trail** in Chapter 3, [41] **Walk-About Guide to Middle Fork Loop Trail**, and [61] **Walk-About Guide to Williwaw Lakes Trail** in Chapter 5.

and following the creek back into the great cirque below the south slopes of Mount Williwaw. From there, one can climb the very steep gully at the back left (northeast) corner of the cirque up and onto the wide plateau just below the summit cone of Mount Williwaw. Once there, turn left (north) and continue to climb to the summit of Mount Williwaw. Many, however, find this climb out of the cirque far too steep for them to consider it an option.

The second, and longer but easier, option begins by continuing north around the far end of the uppermost Williwaw Lake. Upon passing the last lake, continue up the series of benches leading into the big gap between Mount Elliot on the left (west) and Mount Williwaw on the right (east). (One can also begin this ascent earlier along the Williwaw Lakes Trail. Just look for a place to cross the valley before the lowest Williwaw Lake and start up around the base of Mount Elliot toward the pass.) Staying to the left (west) side of the pass, one should soon find a path to follow up and around the left side of each lake one passes on each higher bench in the "rosary-bead" of lakes that have formed on the north side of the pass.

After approximately 1 mile of climbing from the valley, the route reaches the final, and steepest, section of the climb out of the Middle Fork Campbell Creek valley. Staying in the main gully of the pass's headwall, climb toward the saddle above. On reaching the crest of the pass (approximately 3,750 feet), one should have a fine view of the upper end of the North Fork Campbell Creek valley on the far side.

With Mount Williwaw now towering just overhead to the right (east), one should also now have a clear view of the narrow alley leading up to the saddle on the left (north) end of Mount Williwaw's jagged north ridge. To get to the bottom of that saddle with the least amount of elevation loss, turn right (east) at the pass and follow the crest of the ridge for approximately 100 yards to where two lakes come into sight below and to the left (northwest). Descending from the ridge, pass around the left (north) side of both lakes, making sure to cross the second lake's outlet as close to the lake as possible. Once past the second lake, turn right (east) up the narrow alley way that leads up towards the daylight at top of the ridge above.

At the crest of ridge, which offers a panoramic view of Ship Creek valley below, turn right (south) and follow the well-pronounced sheep trail up the ridge. After approximately 1 mile of steady climbing, the route reaches the summit of Mount Williwaw (5,446 feet), the highest peak in the Front Range.

From the summit of Mount Williwaw continue straight ahead. At the far side of the summit descend the broad and rocky southern slope of the summit cone that drops to the wide plateau below. (This plateau marks where this longer option rejoins the first more dangerous option mentioned earlier.) Continuing straight across the plateau, follow the crest of the ridge as it swings to the right (southwest). Staying on the crest wherever possible, or just off the right (west) of the crest when necessary, continue straight ahead. In another approximately 1.2 miles, after an excessive amount of rock scrambling and clambering to negotiate the long, spired, fluted, trackless crest, the ridge makes a last short and steep climb to the summit of The Ramp (5,240 feet).

From here, follow the steep trail down the southwest ridge of The Ramp to the large Ship Pass bowl below. Once in the bowl, turn right (west) and follow the faint trail that follows the small creek down the center of the valley out to Hidden Lake Trail. On reaching Hidden Lake Trail, turn left (southwest) and follow it out to Powerline Trail. Then turn right (west) onto that trail and follow Powerline Trail out to Glen Alps parking area*.

**TRAIL GRADE:** Powerline Trail, Middle Fork Loop Trail, and Williwaw Lakes Trail all rate Grade 1 as a hike. On leaving the end of Williwaw Lakes Trail and beginning the climb to the pass below Mount Williwaw, this traverse rates Grade 4 as a hike interspersed with short climbs, such as the last one to the pass, that rated Grade 5 as a hike.

The next section of the hike past the lakes and up to the saddle north of Mount Williwaw rates Grade 4 as a hike. The climb up to the summit of Williwaw Peak rates Grade 5 as a hike with even some short sections of Grade 6 climbing as one nears the summit.

-------------------------------------------------------------------

\* For more information about these last two trails see [34] **Walk-About Guide to Hidden Lake Trail** and [31] **Walk-About Guide to Upper Powerline Trail**.

The ridge walk from the summit of Mount Wiliwaw over to The Ramp initially rates Grade 4 as a hike but quickly rises to Grade 5 and Grade 6 as the route climbs past the plateau on the south side of Mount Williwaw. It remains a Grade 5 and Grade 6 hike all the way to the summit of The Ramp. The descent from The Ramp rates Grade 4 as a hike. This lessens to Grade 2 as a hike on the trail leading down Ship Pass valley and Hidden Lake Trail. The hike out Powerline Trail to Glen Alps parking area rates Grade 1 as a hike.

**TRAIL CONDITION:** This trail varies greatly in its conditions. Powerline Trail and Middle Fork Loop Trail remain relatively flat and dry for their entire lengths. In contrast, the predominantly flat first 2 miles of Williwaw Lakes Trail has many boggy and muddy sections. Only after winding through 1.5 miles of swamp and scrub spruce does the trail reach higher and drier ground. The trail then passes over some boulder fields as it contours past the lower lakes. It then pushes through some low brush as it approaches its end at the fat shore of the uppermost Williwaw Lake. On leaving Williwaw Lakes Trail, it crosses mostly open tundra. It even follows bits of a trail as it winds over the pass below Mount Williwaw.

The next section of the hike down the far side of the pass, past the lakes, up to the saddle between Mount Elliot and Mount Williwaw and then up the narrow alley to the ridge crest north of Mount Williwaw entails crossing mostly mixed tundra and scree. The climb along the ridge to the summit of Mount Williwaw follows a sheep trail of more tundra and scree. The following descent to the plateau entails crossing a mix of loose rocks and scree. Beyond the plateau on the far side of Mount Williwaw, the route turns extremely rugged with numerous rock gendarmes, ledges, and boulders, and lots of scree as well as some airy gullies as it winds its way to The Ramp.

From summit of The Ramp route initially descends through extensive rock fields before reaching the open tundra in the Ship Pass bowl below. The conditions on the trail leading down Ship Pass valley and then onto Hidden Lake Trail and Powerline Trail the, though muddy in some sections, only get better and better on the hike out to Glen Alps parking area.

**TRAIL MILEAGE:** To go from Glen Alps parking area over both Mount Williwaw and The Ramp and then back to the parking area entails approximately 22 miles of hiking and scrambling.

**TOTAL ELEVATION GAIN:** To hike this traverse from Glen Alps parking area over both Mount Williwaw and The Ramp and then back to the parking area entails a total elevation gain of approximately 4,500 feet.

**HIGH POINT:** This traverse reaches its highest point of 5,445 feet above sea level at the summit of Mount Williwaw.

**NORMAL HIKING TIME:** To hike this traverse from Glen Alps parking area over both Mount Williwaw and The Ramp and then back to the parking area should take anywhere from 1 long day to 2 days.

**CAMPSITES:** One will find designated camp sites along this trail. One can find some fine places for pitching a tent, however, in the many open areas around any of the Williwaw Lakes as well as around any of the "rosary-bead" lakes leading up to the pass between Mount Elliot and Mount Williwaw. The two lakes one passes on the far side of the pass offer a particularly secluded place for camping. The bowl one reaches after descending from The Ramp also makes a fine place on which to pitch a tent.

**BEST TIME:** Most people should find any time from June to September a good time to do this traverse. One should think twice about doing this hike in winter, however, owing to the avalanche danger on climbing over the pass between Williwaw Lakes and Long Lake as well as anywhere along the ridge and all the way down to the bowl on the southwestern side of The Ramp.

**USGS MAPS:** Anchorage A-7, A-8 NE, and A-8 SE.

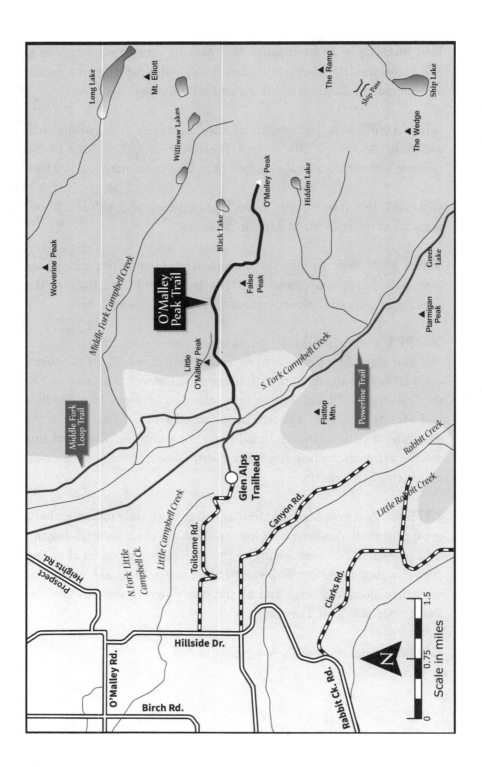

Long Lake

Mt. Elliott ▲

The Ramp ▲

Ship Pass

Ship Lake

Williwaw Lakes

The Wedge ▲

O'Malley Peak ▲

Hidden Lake

Wolverine Peak ▲

Black Lake

**O'Malley Peak Trail**

False Peak ▲

Green Lake

Middle Fork Campbell Creek

Ptarmigan Peak ▲

Little O'Malley Peak ▲

S. Fork Campbell Creek

**Powerline Trail**

**Middle Fork Loop Trail**

Flattop Mtn. ▲

Rabbit Creek

Glen Alps Trailhead ○

Little Rabbit Creek

Little Campbell Creek

Canyon Rd.

Prospect Heights Rd.

N. Fork Little Campbell Ck.

Toilsome Rd.

Clarks Rd.

Hillside Dr.

O'Malley Rd.

Rabbit Ck. Rd.

Birch Rd.

N

Scale in miles

0    0.75    1.5

# 43

# Walk-About Guide to O'Malley Peak Trail

Along with the broad triangle shape of Wolverine Peak, the spired summit of O'Malley Peak remains one of the most recognizable sights of the Front Range. Too many, the peak may appear from afar as far from easy to climb. Yet O'Malley Peak remains but one of a handful of peaks, including Flattop Mountain, Wolverine Peak, Near Point, and Ice Cream Cone, in the Front Range that has a trail leading all the way to its summit. This trail may take a lot of work to climb, but the fact that one can follow a trail saves the trouble of route-finding and minimizes the possibility of getting lost.

**TRAIL LOCATION:** O'Malley Peak Trail, which leads to the top of O'Malley Peak, begins approximately 0.6 miles along Middle Fork Loop Trail from Glen Alps parking area. To get there drive 6.2 miles south from Anchorage on the Seward Highway. There, just after Milepost 121, turn right (west) onto the O'Malley Road exit. At the end of the ramp, turn left (east) and cross back under the highway. Continuing straight on O'Malley Road, ascend past Lake Otis Parkway and the Anchorage Zoo. Approximately 3 miles from the Seward Highway O'Malley Road reaches a junction with Hillside Road on the right (south). Turn onto Hillside Road and follow it for another 1 mile to just past a sign for Chugach State Park one reaches Upper Huffman Road on the left (east). Turn left onto Upper Huffman Road and follow it for 0.75 miles to appropriately named Toilsome Hill Drive on the right (south). Turning onto Toilsome Hill Drive, follow it as it switchbacks and winds its way upward. In approximately 2 miles Toilsome Hill Drive reaches the entrance to Glen Alps parking area on the left (east) side of the road at the top of one last short, steep hill. Park wherever possible (which may prove easier said than done on any given summer weekend) and pay the parking fee. (If one finds the main parking area full they can find extra parking in the overflow parking area located just downhill from the ranger's station.) From the parking area one can access Powerline Trail and Middle Fork Loop Trail via the trail that begins at the far left (southeast) end of that parking area a trail and leads 0.5 miles out to Powerline Trail.

Leaving Glen Alps parking area, follow this access trail out to the intersection with Powerline Trail underneath the power lines. From here, bear right (east) and follow the Powerline Trail for less than 100 yards to where it starts down a long and shallow hill. A short way down this hill Powerline Trail reaches the junction with Middle Fork Loop Trail on the left (north).

Turning left (northeast) onto Middle Fork Loop Trail, follow it downhill. After first descending the few hundred feet to the valley floor, Middle Fork Loop Trail then crosses bridge over South Fork Campbell Creek. Once across the bridge, the trail climbs a series of wooden walkways to the tundra above. Approximately 100 yards beyond far end of these wooden walkways, Middle Fork Loop Trail reaches the junction with O'Malley Peak Trail on the right (northeast).

Upon turning onto O'Malley Peak Trail one begins by climbing gradually. The trail soon climbs more steeply as it begins to climb the wide, shallow dirt gully leading up to the shoulder of the lower west ridge of O'Malley Peak. The crest of this shoulder often has a shelf of snow at its crest that blocks the trail well into June. To get past this shelf, one can either kick steps up its face or circle around either end.

Upon reaching the ridge crest just to the right (east) of Little O'Malley Peak (3,278 feet), the trail bears right (east) and down across the right side of the "The Ballpark," the wide and broad plateau that spreads out below the summit spires of O'Malley Peak. (Highly visible, The Ballpark is what makes O'Malley Peak so easily recognizable from Anchorage.)

Approximately 1 mile up The Ballpark, the trail bears right (south) again and climbs gradually to the base of the wide, scree-and-dirt slope leading up to the summit ridge of O'Malley Peak. Picking any feasible, and possibly firm-footed, route up the slope, climb to the summit ridge. On the ridge, the trail bears left (east) and follows the rocky crest of the ridge upward. After passing over one false summit (4,630 feet) the trail winds up through a short maze of more boulders and scree to the true summit of O'Malley Peak (5,150 feet).

**TRAIL GRADE:** This climb varies considerably in its grades. From Glen Alps parking area to the beginning of O'Malley Peak Trail rates Grade 2 as a hike. The steep climb to ridge at lower end of The Ballpark rates Grade 3 as a climb. The gradual climb across The Ballpark rates Grade 2 as a hike. The rate increases to a Grade 5 as a hike on the climb up the scree gully to the summit ridge. On the summit ridge the rate remains a relatively constant Grade 3 as a hike for the rest of the way to the summit.

**TRAIL CONDITION:** The trail conditions also vary considerably on this climb. From Glen Alps parking area to the beginning of the O'Malley Peak Trail one follows a wide, dirt trail. The steep climb to the edge of the Ballpark entails crossing loose dirt, rocks, and even some snow. Then one makes a long, gradual climb along a firm and rock-strewn trail across The Ballpark. The scramble up the gully to summit ridge entails a laborious climb up loose dirt and scree. On the summit ridge the trail again becomes relatively firm as it winds upward among boulders and across scree to the summit.

**TRAIL MILEAGE:** To climb from Glen Alps parking area to the summit of O'Malley Peak entails approximately 4.7 miles of hiking, for a round-trip total of approximately 9.5 miles.

**TOTAL ELEVATION GAIN:** The hike from Glen Alps parking area to the summit of O'Malley Peak entails a total elevation gain of approximately 3,150 feet.

**HIGH POINT:** This climb reaches its highest point of 5,150 feet above sea level at the summit of O'Malley Peak.

**NORMAL HIKING TIME:** To hike from Glen Alps parking area to the summit of O'Malley Peak and back should take anywhere from 5 to 10 hours, depending on the condition and ambition of the hiker(s) involved.

**CAMPSITES:** One will find no designated campsites on this climb. One will find many fine places on which to pitch a tent in The Ballpark, however, and especially around Deep Lake, a tarn located in the upper eastern corner of the plateau.

**BEST TIME:** Most people should find any time from June to September a good time to do this climb. One should think twice about doing this climb in the winter, however, because of the avalanche danger on both the climb to the Ballpark and the climb to the summit ridge.

**USGS MAPS:** Anchorage A-7 and A-8 SE.

The Ballpark below O'Malley Peak

In The Ballpark on O'Malley Peak Trail

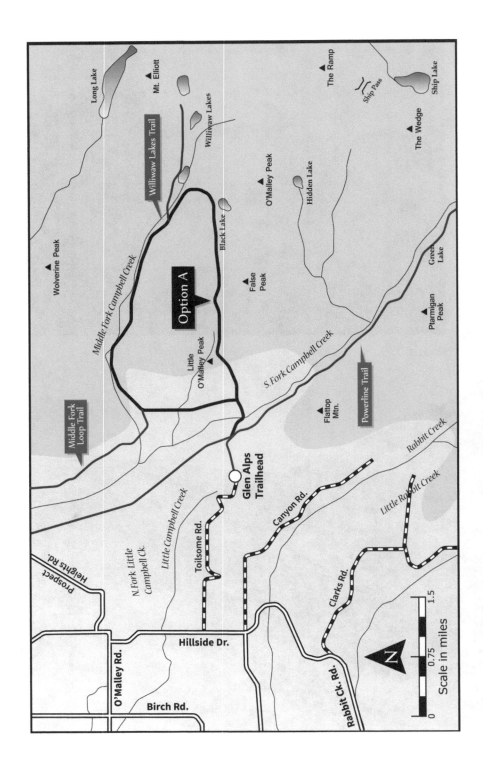

Long Lake

Mt. Elliott

The Ramp

Ship Pass

Ship Lake

Williwaw Lakes

Williwaw Lakes Trail

The Wedge

O'Malley Peak

Hidden Lake

Wolverine Peak

Middle Fork Campbell Creek

Black Lake

Green Lake

Option A

False Peak

Ptarmigan Peak

Middle Fork Loop Trail

Little O'Malley Peak

S. Fork Campbell Creek

Powerline Trail

Flattop Mtn.

Rabbit Creek

Glen Alps Trailhead

Little Campbell Creek

Little Rabbit Creek

Canyon Rd.

Prospect Heights Rd.

N. Fork Little Campbell Ck.

Toilsome Rd.

Clarks Rd.

O'Malley Rd.

Hillside Dr.

N

Scale in miles

0    0.75    1.5

Rabbit Ck. Rd.

Birch Rd.

# 44

# OPTION A

# Traverse from O'Malley Peak Trail to Williwaw Lakes Trail

Though it crosses over no summits, this traverse has a devoted number of followers who hike it least once a summer. One can understand the reasons why. The remote and dramatic settings of both Deep Lake and Black Lake provide this hike with a real sense of wilderness. At the same time, the manageable length and elevation gain also prove far less intimidating than other longer and higher traverses.

**TRAIL LOCATION:** This traverse begins on O'Malley Peak Trail as accessed from Glen Alps parking area*. Once on O'Malley Peak Trail, follow it up to the ridge crest just to the east of Little O'Malley Peak. From there, continue following O'Malley Peak Trail up an across The Ballpark.

Approximately 1 mile up The Ballpark, the traverse diverges from O'Malley Peak Trail. Where the O'Malley Peak Trail bears right (south) toward the scree slope leading to the summit ridge of O'Malley Peak, this traverse continues climbing gently east toward the saddle in the upper left (northeast) corner of The Ballpark. Just before reaching the saddle one reaches the rim of the depression containing appropriately named Deep Lake. Continue around the left (west) shore of the lake to the saddle on the far side.

------------------------------------------------------------

\* To get to the parking area and the trail, see [43] **Walk-About Guide to O'Malley Peak Trail**.

Upon reaching the saddle, one should take a few moments to climb the ledges up to the right of the saddle from which one can partake an expansive view of not only the Middle Fork Campbell Creek valley below but also far into the Chugach.

When done viewing, continue over the saddle's far side and start down the slot leading to Black Lake, located some 800 feet below. Here one should find a pronounced trail leading down the left side of the slot onto the open slopes beyond. Follow this trail down to Black Lake. On reaching the shores of Black Lake, the route skirts around the left (west) side of the lake and follows another trail along its outlet and down into the Williwaw Lakes valley beyond. If one happens to lose the trail on the open slopes dropping down into valley, slant down and to left (west) until one reaches Williwaw Lakes Trail*.

Turning left (west) on Williwaw Lakes Trail, follow it for approximately 2.5 miles to its junction with Middle Fork Loop Trail**. At this junction turn left (south) to follow Middle Fork Loop Trail for its entire length to Powerline Trail. On reaching Powerline Trail, turn right (west) and follow that trail out the last approximately 0.5 miles back to Glen Alps parking area.

**TRAIL GRADE:** This climb varies considerably in its grades. From Glen Alps parking area to the beginning of O'Malley Peak Trail rates Grade 2 as a hike. The steep climb to the edge of The Ballpark rates Grade 3 as a climb. The gradual climb across The Ballpark rates Grade 2 as a hike. The descent to Black Lake then rates Grade 3 as a hike. The trail leading down to Williwaw Lakes Trail rates Grade 2 as a hike. The hike out Williwaw Lakes Trail begins as Grade 2 as a hike, but reverts to Grade 1 as a hike the closer one gets to Glen Alps parking area.

**TRAIL CONDITION:** The trail conditions vary very little in this traverse. Although one follows official trails for only about half of this traverse,

------------------------------------------------------------

\*  For more information about that trail,
   see [61] **Walk-About Guide to Williwaw Lakes Trail** in Chapter 5.

\*\*  For more information about that trail,
   see [41] **Walk-About Guide to Middle Fork Loop Trail**.

one still follows at least some semblance of a trail for almost this entire traverse. From Glen Alps parking area to the beginning of O'Malley Peak Trail one follows a wide, flat trail. The steep climb to the edge of The Ballpark entails clambering up dirt, rocks, and even some snow. Then one makes a long, gradual climb along a firm trail across The Ballpark. The descent to Black Lake follows a steep, rocky trail. Just past the lake, the trail occasionally fades out in places as it descends to Williwaw Lakes Trail. Williwaw Lakes Trail usually crosses many soggy and muddy spots on its lower section. Back on Middle Fork Loop Trail, the trail again becomes firm and wide and remains so for the last approximately 2 miles back to Glen Alps parking area.

**TRAIL MILEAGE:** To complete this traverse from Glen Alps parking area to Williwaw Lakes Trail and then back to Glen Alps parking area via Middle Fork Loop Trail entails approximately 8.2 miles of hiking.

**TOTAL ELEVATION GAIN:** To complete this traverse from Glen Alps parking area to Williwaw Lakes Trail and then back to Glen Alps parking area via Middle Fork Loop Trail entails a total elevation gain of approximately 2,200 feet.

**HIGH POINT:** This traverse reaches its highest point of approximately 3,750 feet above sea level at the uppermost eastern corner of The Ballpark just before one begins the descent to Black Lake.

**NORMAL HIKING TIME:** To complete this traverse from Glen Alps parking area to Williwaw Lakes Trail and then back to Glen Alps parking area via Middle Fork Loop Trail should take anywhere from 4 to 8 hours, depending on the condition and ambition of the hiker(s) involved.

**CAMPSITES:** One will find no designated campsites on this climb. One will find many fine places on which to pitch a tent in The Ballpark, however, and especially around Deep Lake in the upper eastern corner of the plateau, as well as around Black Lake.

**BEST TIME:** Most people should find any time from June to September a good time to do this climb. One should think twice about doing this climb in the winter, however, due to the avalanche danger on the climb to the Ballpark and the descent to Black Lake.

**USGS MAPS:** Anchorage A-7 and A-8 SE.

In The Ballpark below O'Malley Peak

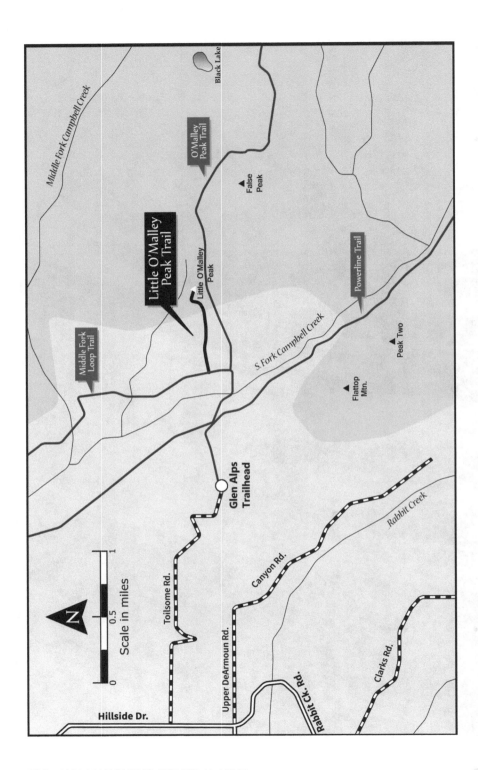

Black Lake

Middle Fork Campbell Creek

O'Malley Peak Trail

▲ False Peak

Little O'Malley Peak Trail

Little O'Malley Peak

Powerline Trail

Middle Fork Loop Trail

S. Fork Campbell Creek

▲ Peak Two

▲ Flattop Mtn.

Glen Alps Trailhead

Rabbit Creek

N

Scale in miles

0    0.5    1

Toilsome Rd.

Canyon Rd.

Upper DeArmoun Rd.

Rabbit Ck. Rd.

Clarks Rd.

Hillside Dr.

# 45

# Walk-About Guide to Little O'Malley Peak Trail

This unofficial trail provides a direct route to the summit of Little O'Malley Peak, a peak that many people by-pass, thinking it a mere buttress of the ridge instead of an actual peak. Yet from this seemingly inconsequential summit one can partake of a long and wide view of Anchorage and Cook Inlet beyond as well as north and south across the western slopes of the Front Range and even west through various gaps to the back of the Front Range and beyond.

**TRAIL LOCATION:** Little O'Malley Peak Trail begins approximately 0.3 miles along Middle Fork Loop Trail. To get there drive 6.2 miles south from Anchorage on the Seward Highway. There, just after Milepost 121, turn right (west) onto the O'Malley Road exit. At the end of the ramp, turn left (east) and cross back under the highway. Continuing straight on O'Malley Road, ascend past Lake Otis Parkway and the Anchorage Zoo. Approximately 3 miles from the Seward Highway O'Malley Road reaches a junction with Hillside Road on the right (south). Turn onto Hillside Road and follow it for another 1 mile to just past a sign for Chugach State Park one reaches Upper Huffman Road on the left (east). Turn left onto Upper Huffman Road and follow it for 0.75 miles to appropriately named Toilsome Hill Drive on the right (south). Turning onto Toilsome Hill Drive, follow it as it switchbacks and winds its way upward. In approximately 2 miles Toilsome Hill Drive reaches the entrance to Glen Alps parking area on the left (east) side of the road at the top of one last short, steep hill. Park wherever possible (which may prove easier said than done on any given summer weekend) and pay the parking fee. (If one finds the main parking area full they can find extra parking in the overflow parking area located just downhill from the ranger's station.) From the parking area one can access Powerline Trail and Middle Fork Loop Trail via the trail that begins at the far left (southeast) end of that parking area a trail and leads 0.5 miles out to Powerline Trail.

Leaving Glen Alps parking area, follow this access trail out to the intersection with Powerline Trail underneath the power lines. From here, bear right (east) and follow the Powerline Trail for less than 100 yards to where it starts down a long and shallow hill. A short way down this hill Powerline Trail reaches the junction with Middle Fork Loop Trail on the left (north).

Turning left (northeast) onto Middle Fork Loop Trail, follow it downhill. After first descending the few hundred feet to the valley floor, Middle Fork Loop trail then crosses bridge over South Fork Campbell Creek. Once across the bridge, the trail climbs a series of wooden walkways to the tundra above. Approximately 100 yards beyond far end of these wooden walkways, Middle Fork Loop Trail reaches the junction with O'Malley Peak Trail on the right (northeast).

Continue on Middle Fork Loop Trail as it swings left (northwest) toward the front of O'Malley Peak. Approximately 0.2 miles past the junction with O'Malley Peak Trail, Middle Fork Loop Trail reaches a partially open area with an unmarked trail on the right (north). This unmarked trail marks the beginning of Little O'Malley Peak Trail.

Turning onto Little O'Malley Peak Trail, follow it as it begins it climb of Little O'Malley Peak almost immediately. After climbing through some low brush on the lower flank of the ridge, the trail turns more steeply upward as it starts up the face of the mountain. As the trail approaches the rock spires blocking direct access to the ridge, it bears left (northwest) to circle up and onto the ridge crest. On the crest of the ridge the trail turns sharply right (east). Climbing steeply at first over a series of large boulders and low ledges, the trail soon reaches the more gradual upper summit ridge of the mountain. After a few short ups and downs along this high ridge, the trail reaches the summit proper (3,278 feet).

From this point one has two major options. First, one can return the way they have come. Second, one can continue straight ahead and drop off the summit's far side to O'Malley Peak Trail. Once on

O'Malley Peak Trail one can either turn left (northeast) and follow it across The Ballpark or turn right (south) and follow it down into the South Fork Campbell Creek valley and back to Glen Alps parking area[*].

**TRAIL GRADE:** This trail rates Grade 3 as a hike.

**TRAIL CONDITION:** The conditions along this trail vary little. Steep and gravelly, it makes for a slow climb up to the ridge top. On the ridge boulders and scree continue to make for slow climbing to the summit.

**TRAIL MILEAGE:** To go from Glen Alps parking area to the summit of Little O'Malley Peak entails approximately 2.25 miles of hiking, for a round-trip total of approximately 4.5 miles.

**TOTAL ELEVATION GAIN:** To hike from Glen Alps parking area to the summit of Little O'Malley Peak entails a total elevation gain of approximately 1,325 feet.

**HIGH POINT:** This hike reaches its highest point of 3,278 feet above sea level at the summit of Little O'Malley Peak.

**NORMAL HIKING TIME:** To hike from Glen Alps parking area to the summit of Little O'Malley Peak and back should take anywhere from 2 to 4 hours, depending on the condition and ambition of the hiker(s) involved.

**CAMPSITES:** One will find no designated campsites on this climb. One will find many fine places on which to pitch a tent, however, farther long Middle Fork Loop Trail in the tundra surrounding its junction with Williwaw Lakes Trail or out on The Ballpark of O'Malley Peak.

**BEST TIME:** Most people should find any time from June to September a good time to do this climb.

**USGS MAPS:** Anchorage A-7 and A-8 SE.

-----------------------------------------------------------------------

[*]    For more information about that trail, see [43] **Walk-About Guide to O'Malley Peak Trail**.

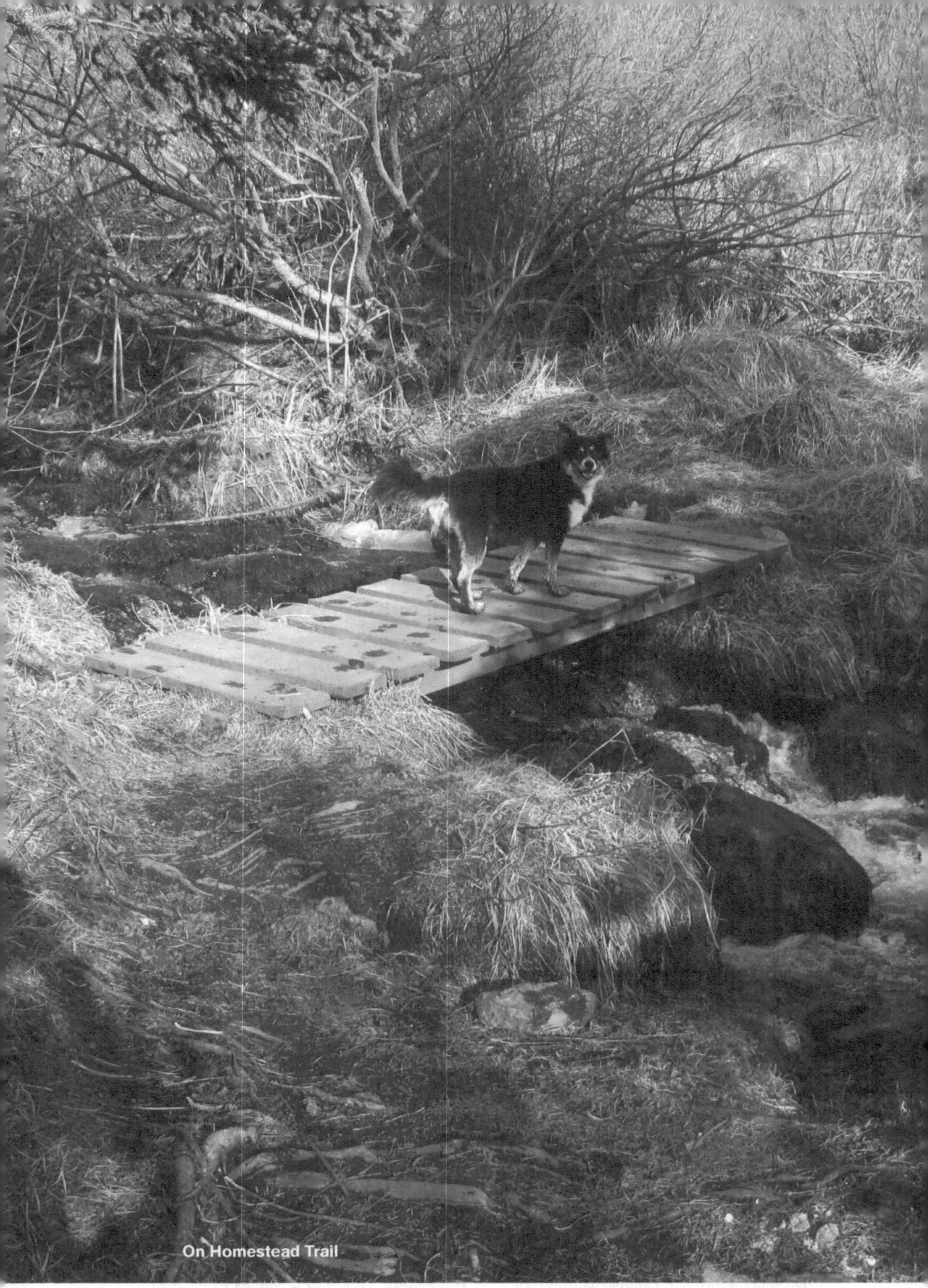
On Homestead Trail

## CHAPTER 4

# PROSPECT HEIGHTS
# TO GLEN ALPS

## Overview of the Hillside Trails Between Prospect Heights and Glen Alps

As Middle Powerline Trail climbs the approximately 3 miles from Prospect Heights parking area up to Glen Alps parking area it passes through a crisscrossing maze of other trails and nearby one other trailhead at Upper Huffman parking area. Some might find this coming and going of different trails a bit bewildering. In order to give some order to this maze of trails, it may help to have an overall picture of their layout.

First, one should realize that this complex of trails has a hierarchy. Of all these trails, regardless of the many other trails one may pass, Middle Powerline Trail remains the central artery of this trail system. Next to Middle Powerline Trail, Upper Gasline Trail, the upper section of which more or less parallels Middle Powerline Trail before connecting with it approximately 0.3 miles below Glen Alps, functions as an another major through artery. Off these two trails come and go all the other lesser trails.

One can divide these lesser trails into two major groups. The first of these groups consists of connecting trails. These connecting trails consist of two types. The first type of these trails connects a parking area with one of the two major trails. For instance, Silver Fern Trail connects Upper Huffman parking area with Upper Gasline Trail. The second type of connecting trails, which includes trails such as Hemlock Knob Trail, connects Upper Gasline Trail with Middle Powerline Trail. Some second type of connecting trails, such as White Spruce Trail,

Early summer in Powerline Pass

continue even farther to connect with South Fork Rim Trail. But more than just means of connecting the two major trails, these shorter trails allow one to create a variety of circular hikes while often pass by some wide-ranging views. One need only consider the title of one of these trails—Panorama View Trail—to imagine the extent of some of the views offered along these trails.

The second large group of trails consists of loop trails. All these loop trails begin and end at various points along Middle Powerline Trail. Varying in length, each of these trails circles east from Middle Powerline Trail to skirt the rim along the 600-foot-deep canyon of South Fork Campbell Creek. In the process they offer some surprisingly long views up Campbell Creek and into the nearby mountains.

In conclusion, these many trails on Hillside offer a surprising number of options as to how to connect various points together in a variety of ways. Those who have not hiked these trails should find them a pleasant discovery to which one can return again and again all year round.

# THE CONNECTING TRAILS

Apart from Silver Fern Trail, which begins at Upper Huffman parking area, the following descriptions of these various connecting trails and loop trails begin at Prospect Heights parking area*. In this way these guides follow the same direction in which one would pass them during the hike up Middle Powerline Trail from Prospect Heights parking area up to Glen Alps parking area.

---

\* For information as to how to get there,
see [46] **Walk-About Guide to Middle Powerline Trail**.

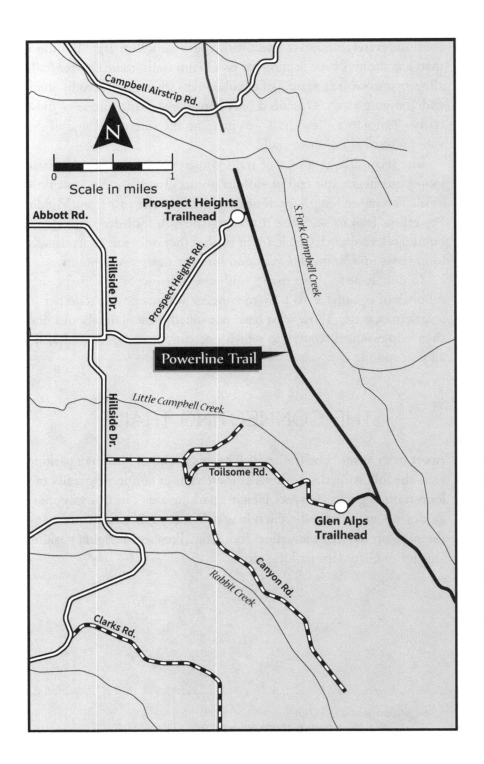

Campbell Airstrip Rd.

N

Scale in miles
0                    1

Abbott Rd.

Prospect Heights
Trailhead

Hillside Dr.

Prospect Heights Rd.

S. Fork Campbell Creek

Powerline Trail

Little Campbell Creek

Hillside Dr.

Toilsome Rd.

Glen Alps
Trailhead

Canyon Rd.

Rabbit Creek

Clarks Rd.

# 46

# Walk-About Guide to Middle Powerline Trail

The entirety of Powerline Trail extends from Prospect Heights to Indian. But people rarely hike or bike its entire length. In fact, people rarely hike the entire distance just from Prospect Heights to Powerline Pass. Instead, most people begin their hike to Powerline Pass and the surrounding valleys from Glen Alps parking area. On the other hand, most people who access Middle Powerline Trail from Prospect Heights usually turn around at the side trail leading to Glen Alps parking area or use Middle Powerline Trail to access the maze of smaller trails that crisscross from Middle Powerline Trail and Gasline Trail. For this reason it seemed best to take the liberty of differentiating between these two parts of Powerline Trail and refer to them as Powerline Trail and Middle Powerline Trail. In addition to these two sections of Powerline Trail, this book has includes information about Lower Powerline Trail, a designation this book uses for the unofficial trail that climbs from Chugach Foothills subdivision in East Anchorage near the corner of Tudor Road and Muldoon Road up to State Parks parking area on Basher Road, which for many serves as largely an end in itself*.

**TRAIL LOCATION:** One can access the lower end of Middle Powerline Trail from Prospect Heights parking area. (This parking area also provides access the true beginning of the whole length of Powerline Trail.) To get there drive 6.2 miles south from Anchorage on the Seward Highway.

---

\* For more information about that trail, see [91] **Walk-About Guide to Lower Powerline Trail** in Chapter 9.

There, just after Milepost 121, turn right (west) on the O'Malley Road exit. At the end of the ramp, turn left (east) and cross back under the highway. Continue straight on this road as it ascends past Lake Otis Parkway and the Anchorage Zoo. Approximately 3 miles from the Seward Highway, this road passes the junction with Hillside Road leading right (south). Staying on O'Malley Road, follow it to where, in less than 100 yards, it swings left north) onto the continuation of Hillside Drive. Almost immediately after Hillside Road straightens out, it reaches the junction with Upper O'Malley Road on the right (east). Turn right onto Upper O'Malley Road. Approximately 0.5 miles later, this road ends at a T intersection with Prospect Drive. Turn left (north) on Prospect Drive and follow it for approximately 1 mile to a stop sign. Bear left through the stop sign onto Sider of Lane. Approximately 200 yards later this road reaches the entrance to Chugach State Park on the right (north). Turn into this parking area and look for the sign board and fee station in the middle right (east) of the parking area. An access trail leading to Middle Powerline Trail begins just to the left of the fee station.

One can also access the upper end of Middle Powerline Trail at Glen Alps parking area[*].

From Prospect Heights parking area follow the access trail by the fee station as it contours upward for approximately 0.2 miles to a junction with Middle Powerline Trail underneath the power lines. Turn up Middle Powerline Trail as it climbs over the first rise above. Beyond the first four power line poles the trail climbs more gradually. It continues to climb gradually as it follows the power lines uphill. During this long climb, it sometimes follows the open swath under the power lines and sometimes winds up through the trees on the left (north) side of the swath. Finally, after emerging from the trees one last time, this trail reaches a junction with Upper Gasline Trail. After this junction Middle Powerline Trail climbs one last hill before reaching the trail leading right (west) out to Glen Alps parking area.

------------------------------------------------------------

[*]    To get there, see [26] **Walk-About Guide to Flattop Mountain Trail** in Chapter 3.

**TRAIL GRADE:** This trail rates Grade 2 as a hike.

**TRAIL CONDITION:** Though often wet and muddy in late spring, this wide trail generally remains in fine condition for most of the season. Even in winter it sees so much travel that one can easily hike it.

**TRAIL MILEAGE:** To hike from Prospect Heights parking area to the access trail leading out to Glen Alp parking area entails approximately 3 miles of hiking, for a round-trip total of 6 miles. To hike from Prospect Heights the top of Powerline Pass entails approximately 9 miles of hiking, for a round-trip total of 18 miles. To hike from Prospect Heights parking area to the southern end of the trail in Indian entails approximately 14 miles of hiking, for a round-trip total of 28 miles.

**TOTAL ELEVATION GAIN:** To hike from Prospect Heights parking area to the access trail leading out to Glen Alp parking area entails a total elevation gain of approximately 1,200 feet. To hike from Prospect Heights parking area to the top of Powerline Pass and down to southern end of the trail at Indian entails a total elevation gain of approximately 2,400 feet. To hike the same route in the opposite direction, from Indian to Prospect Heights parking area, entails a total elevation gain of approximately 4,300 feet.

**HIGH POINT:** Middle Powerline Trail reaches its highest point of approximately 1,200 feet above sea level at the side trail leading 0.5 miles out to Glen Alps parking area. For those continuing along Powerline Trail to Powerline Pass, this trail reaches its highest point of 3,550 feet above sea level at Powerline Pass.

**NORMAL HIKING TIME:** To hike from Prospect Heights parking area to the access trail leading out to Glen Alp parking area should take anywhere from 2 to 3 hours, depending on the condition and ambition of the hiker(s) involved. To hike from Prospect Heights parking area to the top of Powerline Pass and back should take anywhere from 8 to 12 hour, depending on the condition and ambition of the hiker(s) involved. To hike from Prospect Heights parking area to Indian parking area and back should take anywhere from 1 long day to 3 days, again depending on the condition and ambition of the hiker(s) involved.

**CAMPSITES:** One will find no designated campsites along this traverse. The cirque that Powerline Trail passes through before the climb up to the pass also offers many fine places for pitching a tent, including around the two lakes just below the pass.

**BEST TIME:** Most people should find any time from June to early September a good time to do this traverse. Much of the trail on the Glen Alps side of the pass also makes a fine ski or snowshoe outing in winter. One should think twice, however, of venturing too far up the pass along Powerline Trail, however, because of the extreme avalanche danger during the last 1.5-mile-long climb to the pass.

**USGS MAPS:** Anchorage A-8.

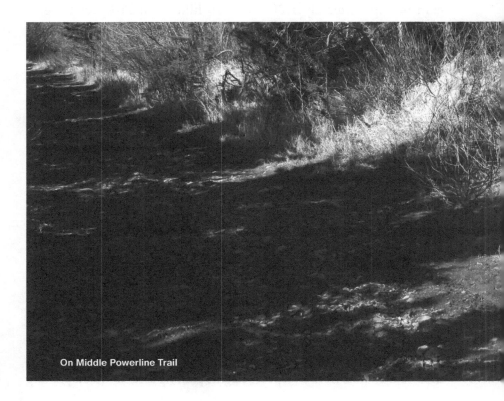

On Middle Powerline Trail

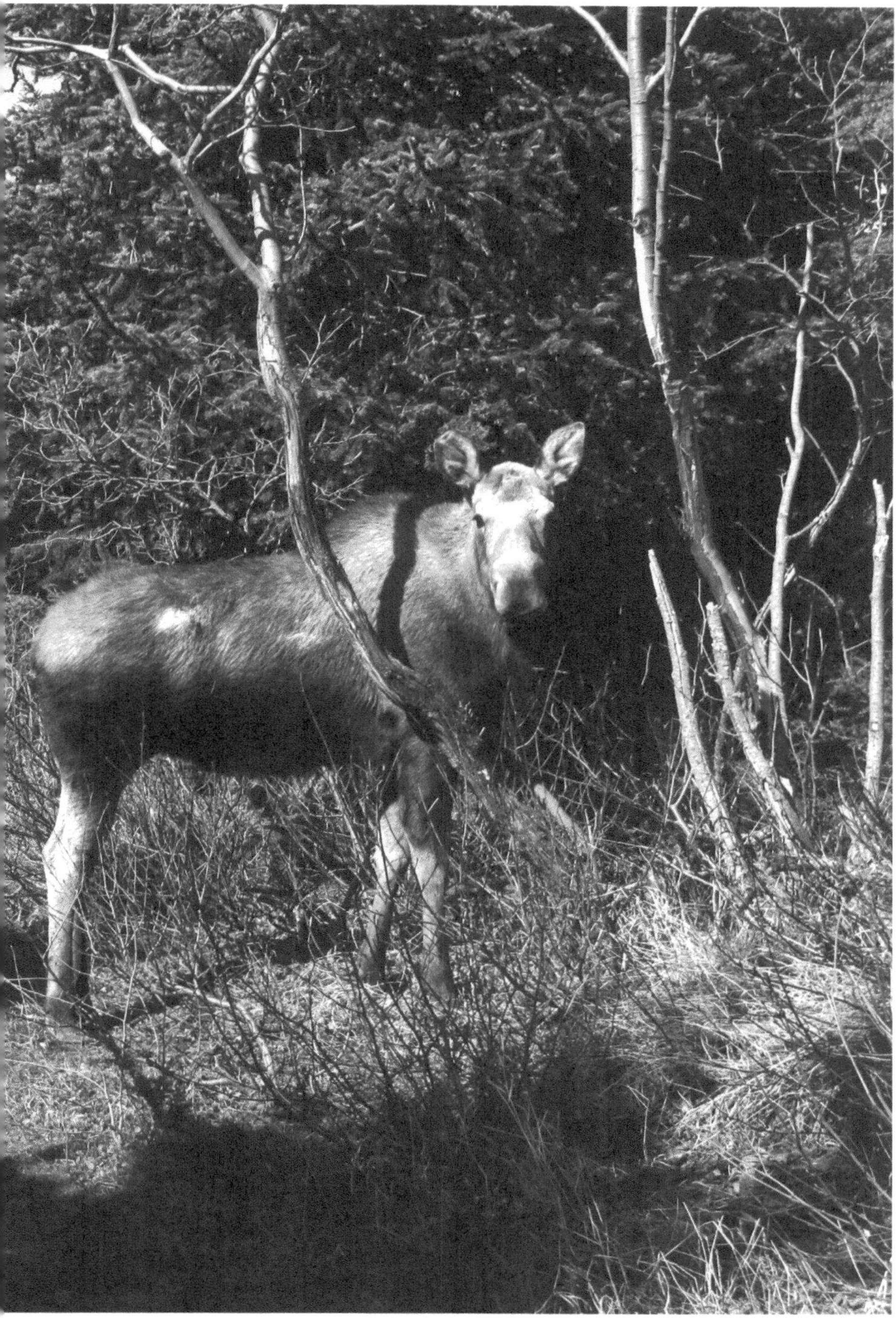

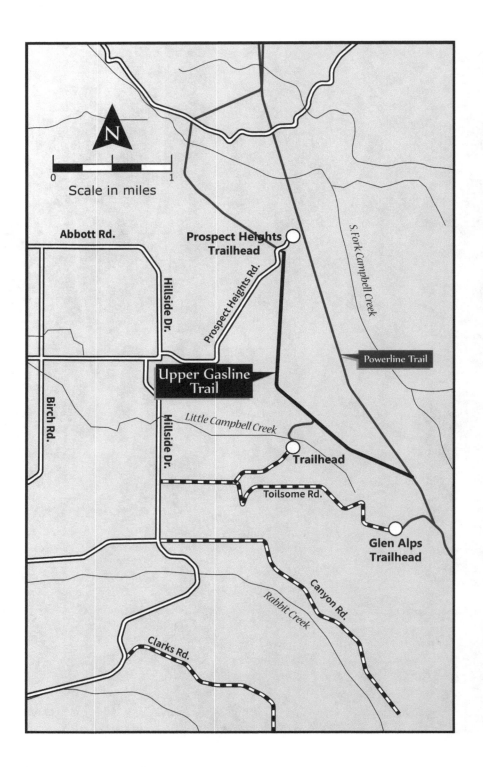

N

0      1
Scale in miles

Abbott Rd.

Prospect Heights
Trailhead

S. Fork Campbell Creek

Hillside Dr.

Prospect Heights Rd.

Powerline Trail

Upper Gasline
Trail

Birch Rd.

Hillside Dr.

Little Campbell Creek

Trailhead

Toilsome Rd.

Glen Alps
Trailhead

Canyon Rd.

Rabbit Creek

Clarks Rd.

# 47

# Walk-About Guide to Upper Gasline Trail

Like Powerline Trail, Gasline Trail also consists of two distinct sections. The first climbs from Hilltop Ski Area to Prospect Heights parking area. The second climbs from Prospect Heights parking area toward Glen Alps where, approximately 0.5 miles shy of the access trail leading out to Glen Alps parking area, it ends at a junction with Middle Powerline Trail. As also with Middle Powerline Trail and Powerline Trail, very few people hike, bike, or ski both sections of Gasline Trail as a continuous whole. Instead, they either choose one or other as an end in itself or part of a larger loop. For this reason, it seems appropriate to offer exclusive guides for each section of Gasline Trail. The guide for Upper Gasline Trail from Prospect Heights up toward Glen Alps begins below.

**TRAIL LOCATION:** This trail begins at Prospect Heights parking area. To get there drive 6.2 miles south from Anchorage on the Seward Highway. There, just after Milepost 121, turn right (west) onto the O'Malley Road exit. At the end of the ramp, turn left (east) back under the highway. Continue straight on this road as it ascends past Lake Otis Parkway and the Anchorage Zoo. Approximately 3 miles from the Seward Highway one passes Hillside Road leading right (south). Less than 100 yards later O'Malley Road swings left and turns into Hillside Drive leading north. Almost immediately after Hillside Road straightens out, it reaches the junction with Upper O'Malley Road on the right (east). Turn right onto Upper O'Malley Road. Approximately 0.5 miles later, this road ends at a T-intersection with Prospect Drive. Turn left (north) on Prospect Drive and follow it for approximately 1 mile to a stop sign. Bear left through the stop sign onto Siderof Lane. Approximately 200 yards later this road reaches the entrance to Chugach State Park on the right (north). Turn into the parking area and park. After parking, walk back toward the parking area entrance. Upper Gasline Trail begins at the fire gate just to the right (east) of the entrance.

Passing around the gate, begin following Upper Gasline Trail as it trends steadily upward with Chugach State Park on the left (east) and Siderof Lane on the right (west). Approximately 1.3 miles up from Prospect Heights, Upper Gasline Trail reaches Upper O'Malley parking area on Shebanof Avenue.

Just past this trailhead, Upper Gasline Trail bears left (southeast). Approximately 0.4 miles later it passes through a junction with Silver Fern Trail on the right (southwest), which leads out to Upper Huffman parking area, and Hemlock Trail on the left (northeast), which leads over to Middle Powerline Trail*.

Approximately 1.6 miles later, after passing some snowmobile access trails on the left (southwest), Upper Gasline Trail reaches its uppermost end at a junction with Middle Powerline Trail.

At this point one has three main choices. First, they can return the way they have come. Second, they can return via Middle Powerline Trail to Prospect Heights. Third, they can continue the approximately 0.3 miles further up Middle Powerline Trail to where one reaches the access trail leading right (south) to Glen Alps parking area**.

**TRAIL GRADE:** This trail rates Grade 2 as a hike.

**TRAIL CONDITION:** Though often wet and muddy in late spring, this wide trail generally remains in fine condition for most of the season.

**TRAIL MILEAGE:** To hike from the lower end of this trail at Prospect Heights parking area to its upper end at the junction with Middle Powerline Trail entails approximately 2.8 miles of hiking, for a round-trip total of 5.6 miles. To hike from Prospect Heights and then continue past the

---

\* For more information about these trails, see [48] **Walk-About Guide to Silver Fern Trail** and [53] **Walk-About Guide to Hemlock Knob Trail.**

\*\* For more information about this trail, see [46] **Walk-About Guide to Middle Powerline Trail.**

upper end of this trail to follow Powerline Trail all the way to Powerline Pass entails approximately 9 miles of hiking, for a round-trip total of 18 miles. To hike from Prospect Heights to the Indian parking area entails approximately 14 miles of hiking, for a round-trip total of 28 miles.

**TOTAL ELEVATION GAIN:** To hike from Prospect Heights parking area to the junction with Middle Powerline Trail entails a total elevation gain of approximately 1,000 feet. To hike from Prospect Heights to the top of Powerline Pass entails a total elevation gain of approximately 2,400 feet. To hike from Prospect Heights to Indian entails a total elevation gain of approximately 2,500 feet, whereas to hike this route in entails a total elevation gain of approximately 4,300 feet.

**HIGH POINT:** This trail reaches its highest point of approximately 2,000 feet above sea level at the junction with the Middle Powerline Trail.

**NORMAL HIKING TIME:** To hike from Prospect Heights parking area to the junction with Middle Powerline Trail and back either trail should take anywhere from 2 to 5 hours, depending on the condition and ambition of the hiker(s) involved. To hike from Prospect Heights to the top of Powerline Pass and back should take anywhere from 8 to 12 hour, also depending on the condition and ambition of the hiker(s) involved. To hike one-way from Prospect Heights parking area to Indian parking area should take anywhere from 7 to 10 hours.

**CAMPSITES:** One will find no designated campsites along this traverse. Many people, however, that the cirque at the far end of Powerline Trail before the climb up to the pass also offers many fine places for pitching a tent, including around the two lakes just below the pass.

**BEST TIME:** Most people should find any time from June to early September a good time to hike this trail. This trail also makes a fine ski or snowshoe outing in winter with little or no danger of avalanches, unless one decides to venture past Glen Alps toward Powerline Pass.

**USGS MAPS:** Anchorage A-8.

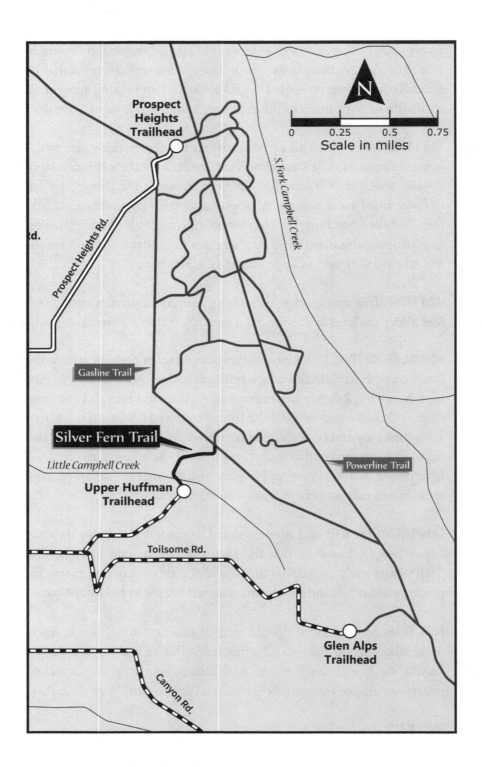

Prospect
Heights
Trailhead

N

0        0.25         0.5          0.75
Scale in miles

S. Fork Campbell Creek

Prospect Heights Rd.

Rd.

Gasline Trail

Silver Fern Trail

Little Campbell Creek

Powerline Trail

Upper Huffman
Trailhead

Toilsome Rd.

Glen Alps
Trailhead

Canyon Rd.

# CONNECTING TRAILS

# Walk-About Guide to Silver Fern Trail

**TRAIL LOCATION:** This short trail connects Upper Huffman parking area with Upper Gasline Trail. To get to Upper Huffman parking area drive 6.2 miles south from Anchorage on the Seward Highway. There, just after Milepost 121, turn right (west) onto the O'Malley Road exit. At the end of the ramp, turn left (east) and cross back under the highway. Continuing straight on this road, ascend past Lake Otis Parkway and the Anchorage Zoo. Approximately 3 miles from the Seward Highway this road reaches a junction with Hillside Road on the right (south). Turn onto Hillside Road and follow it for another 1 mile to where just past a sign for Chugach State Park, one reaches Upper Huffman Road on the left (east). Turn left onto Upper Huffman Road and follow it for 0.75 miles to appropriately named Toilsome Hill Drive on the right (south). At that point, instead of turning right up Toilsome Hill Drive to Glen Alps, bear left and continue straight ahead for approximately 0.5 miles to the marked parking area. The trail begins at the fire gate by an information board at the back left (northwest) side of the parking area.

After passing around the gate follow the wide trail as it dips to cross a stream. On the far side it climbs to a viewpoint where it turns right (north) into the trees. Trending slowly upward as it makes a wide U-turn through the open woods, the trail reaches its end at a T-junction with Upper Gasline Trail. At this point, one has three major. First, they can turn around and return the way they have come. Second, they can continue straight ahead and follow Hemlock Knob Trail to its junction with Middle Powerline Trail*. Third, they can turn right (south) on Upper Gasline Trail and follow it to its junction with Powerline Trail at Glen Alps and from there even continue farther to Powerline Pass or all the way to Indian**.

**TRAIL GRADE:** This trail rates Grade 1 as a hike.

**TRAIL CONDITION:** This wide trail remains in excellent condition from end to end.

**TRAIL MILEAGE:** To go from Upper Huffman parking to the junction with Upper Gasline Trail entails approximately 0.6 miles of hiking for a round-trip total of 1.2 miles. To hike from Upper Huffman parking area to the beginning of Powerline Trail at Glen Alps entails approximately 1.2 miles of hiking, for a round-trip total of 2.4 miles. To hike from Upper Huffman parking area to the top of Powerline Pass entails approximately 7.8 miles of hiking, for a round-trip total of 15.6 miles. To hike from Upper Huffman parking area to the southern end of the trail at Indian parking area entails approximately 12.8 miles of hiking, for a round-trip total of 25.6 miles.

**TOTAL ELEVATION GAIN:** To hike from Upper Huffman parking area to the junction with Upper Gasline Trail entails a total elevation gain of approximately 175 feet. To hike from Upper Huffman parking area to the beginning of Powerline Trail at Glen Alps entails a total elevation gain of approximately 500 feet. To hike from Upper Huffman parking area to the top of Powerline Pass entails a total elevation gain of approximately 2,200 feet, To hike from Upper Huffman parking area to Indian parking area entails a total elevation gain of approximately 2,300 feet, whereas to hike this route in reverse entails a total elevation gain of approximately 4,100 feet.

---------------------------------------------------------------------

\*    For more information about that trail, see [53] **Walk-About Guide to Hemlock Knob Trail**.

\*\*    For more information about these trails, see [47] **Walk-About Guide to Upper Gasline Trail above** and [31] **Walk-About Guide to Powerline Trail** in Chapter 3.

**HIGH POINT:** This trail reaches its highest point of 1,600 feet above sea level at the junction with Upper Gasline Trail.

**NORMAL HIKING TIME:** To hike from Upper Huffman parking area to the junction with Upper Gasline Trail and back should take anywhere from 30 minutes to 1 hour, depending on the condition and ambition of the hiker(s) involved. To hike from Upper Huffman parking area to the beginning of Powerline Trail at Glen Alps should take anywhere from 1 to 3 hours, depending on the condition and ambition of the hiker(s) involved. To hike from Upper Huffman parking area to the top of Powerline Pass and back should take anywhere from 6 to 10 hour, also depending on the condition and ambition of the hiker(s) involved. To hike one-way from Upper Huffman to Indian parking area should take anywhere from 6 to 10 hours.

**CAMPSITES:** One will find no designated campsites along this trail.

**BEST TIME:** Most people should find that any time of year a good time to do this hike. It also makes a fine bike ride or ski tour.

**USGS MAPS:** Anchorage A-8.

Silver Fern Trail

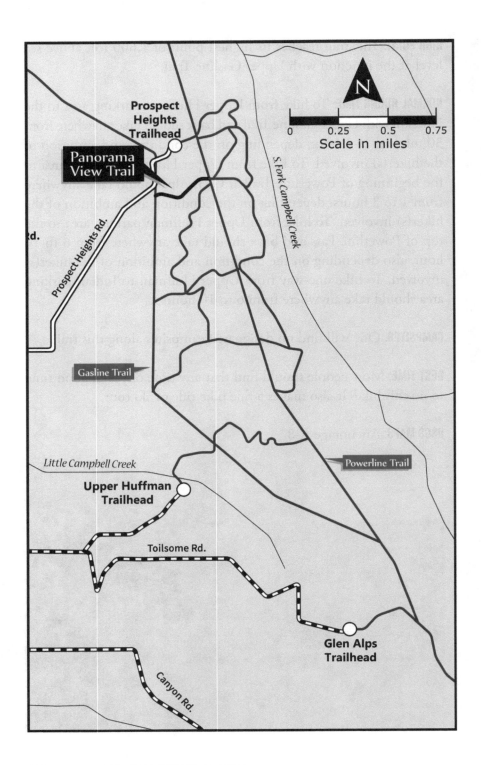

Prospect
Heights
Trailhead

Panorama
View Trail

S. Fork Campbell Creek

N

Scale in miles
0      0.25      0.5      0.75

Prospect Heights Rd.

Rd.

Gasline Trail

Little Campbell Creek

Powerline Trail

Upper Huffman
Trailhead

Toilsome Rd.

Glen Alps
Trailhead

Canyon Rd.

# 49

# Walk-About Guide to Panorama View Trail

**TRAIL LOCATION:** This trail, which connects to Upper Gasline Trail and South Fork Rim Trail, begins approximately 0.3 miles up Upper Gasline Trail from Prospect Heights parking area. To get there drive 6.2 miles south from Anchorage on the Seward Highway. There, just after Milepost 121, turn right (west) onto the O'Malley Road exit. At the end of the ramp, turn left (east) back under the highway. Continue straight on this road as it ascends past Lake Otis Parkway and the Anchorage Zoo. Approximately 3 miles from the Seward Highway one passes Hillside Road leading right (south). Less than 100 yards later O'Malley Road swings left and turns into Hillside Drive leading north. Almost immediately after Hillside Road straightens out, it reaches the junction with Upper O'Malley Road on the right (east). Turn right onto Upper O'Malley Road. Approximately 0.5 miles later, this road ends at a T-intersection with Prospect Drive. Turn left (north) on Prospect Drive and follow it for approximately 1 mile to a stop sign. Bear left through the stop sign onto Siderof Lane. Approximately 200 yards later this road reaches the entrance to Chugach State Park on the right (north). Turn into the parking area and park. After parking, walk back toward the parking area entrance. Upper Gasline Trail begins at the fire gate just to the right (east) of the entrance.

Passing around the gate, follow Upper Gasline Trail as it trends steadily upward with Chugach State Park on the left (east) and Siderof Lane on the right (west). Approximately 0.4 miles from Prospect Heights, Upper Gasline Trail reaches a junction with Panorama View Trail on the left (north).

Turning onto Panorama View Trail follow it as it slants up through a wooded slope. After zigzagging upward for approximately 0.3 miles, it reaches an open area providing expansive views to the west and north. Soon after passing these views the trail descends gradually for another 0.3 miles to a junction with Middle Powerline Trail directly

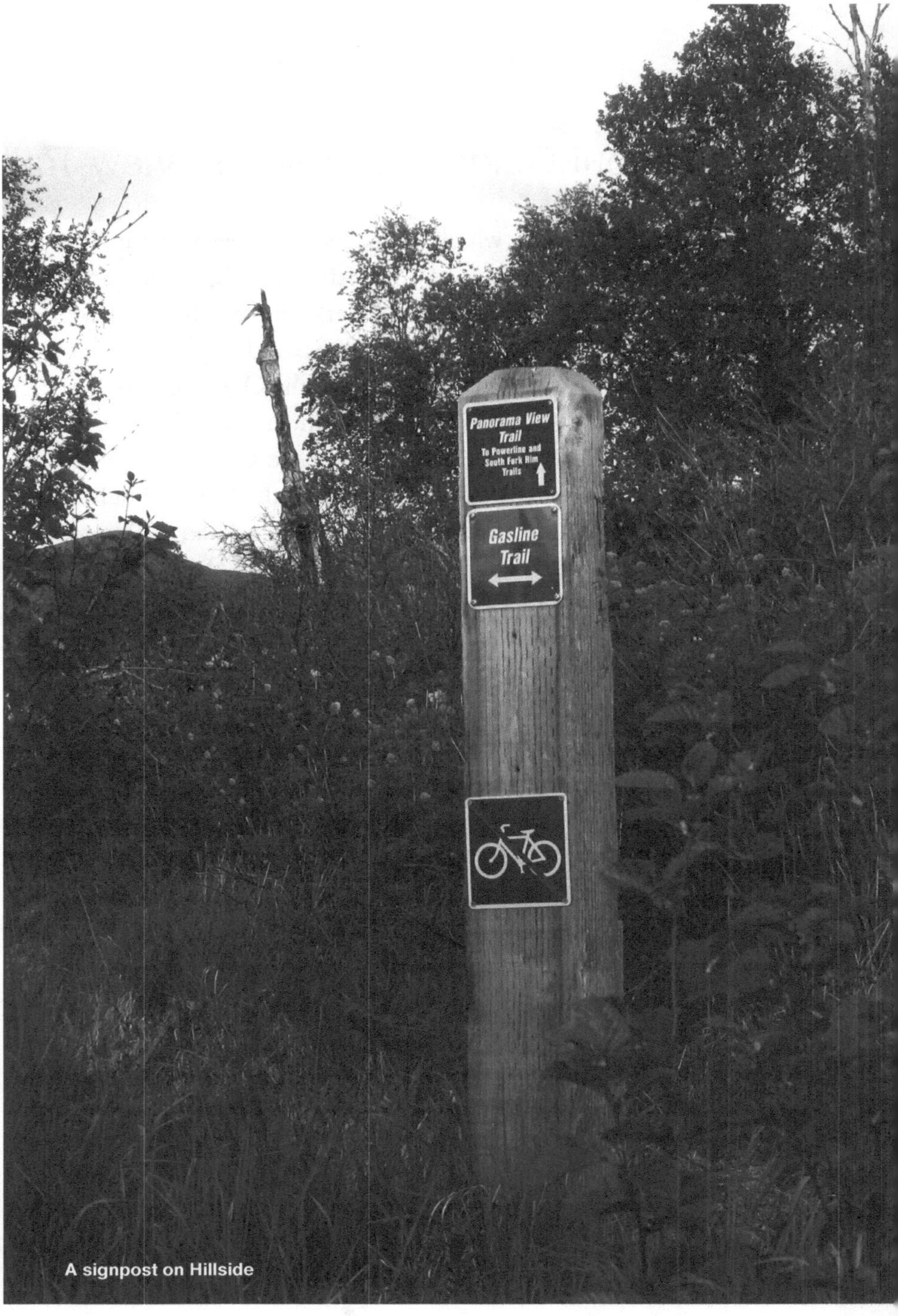
Panorama View Trail
To Powerline and South Fork Rim Trails
Gasline Trail

A signpost on Hillside

beneath the power lines. Continuing straight through this intersection, the trail trends downhill for another 0.3 miles to where it ends at a junction with South Fork Rim Trail*.

**TRAIL GRADE:** This trail rates Grade 1 as a hike.

**TRAIL CONDITION:** This trail remains in good condition from end to end.

**TRAIL MILEAGE:** To go from Prospect Heights parking area to the junction with Middle Powerline Trail entails approximately 1.3 miles of hiking for a round-trip total of 2 miles.

**TOTAL ELEVATION GAIN:** To hike from Prospect Heights parking area to the junction with Middle Powerline Trail entails a total elevation gain of approximately 350 feet.

**HIGH POINT:** This trail reaches its highest point of 1,350 feet above sea level at the viewpoints approximately half-way along Panorama View Trail.

**NORMAL HIKING TIME:** To hike from Prospect Heights parking area to the junction with Middle Powerline Trail and back should take anywhere from 45 minutes to 1.5 hours, depending on the condition and ambition of the hiker(s) involved.

**CAMPSITES:** One will find no designated campsites along this trail.

**BEST TIME:** Most people should find that any time of year a good time to do this hike. It also makes a fine bike ride or ski tour.

**USGS MAPS:** Anchorage A-8.

--------------------------------------------------------------------

\*    For more information about that trail, see [55] **Walk-About Guide to South Fork Rim Trail**.

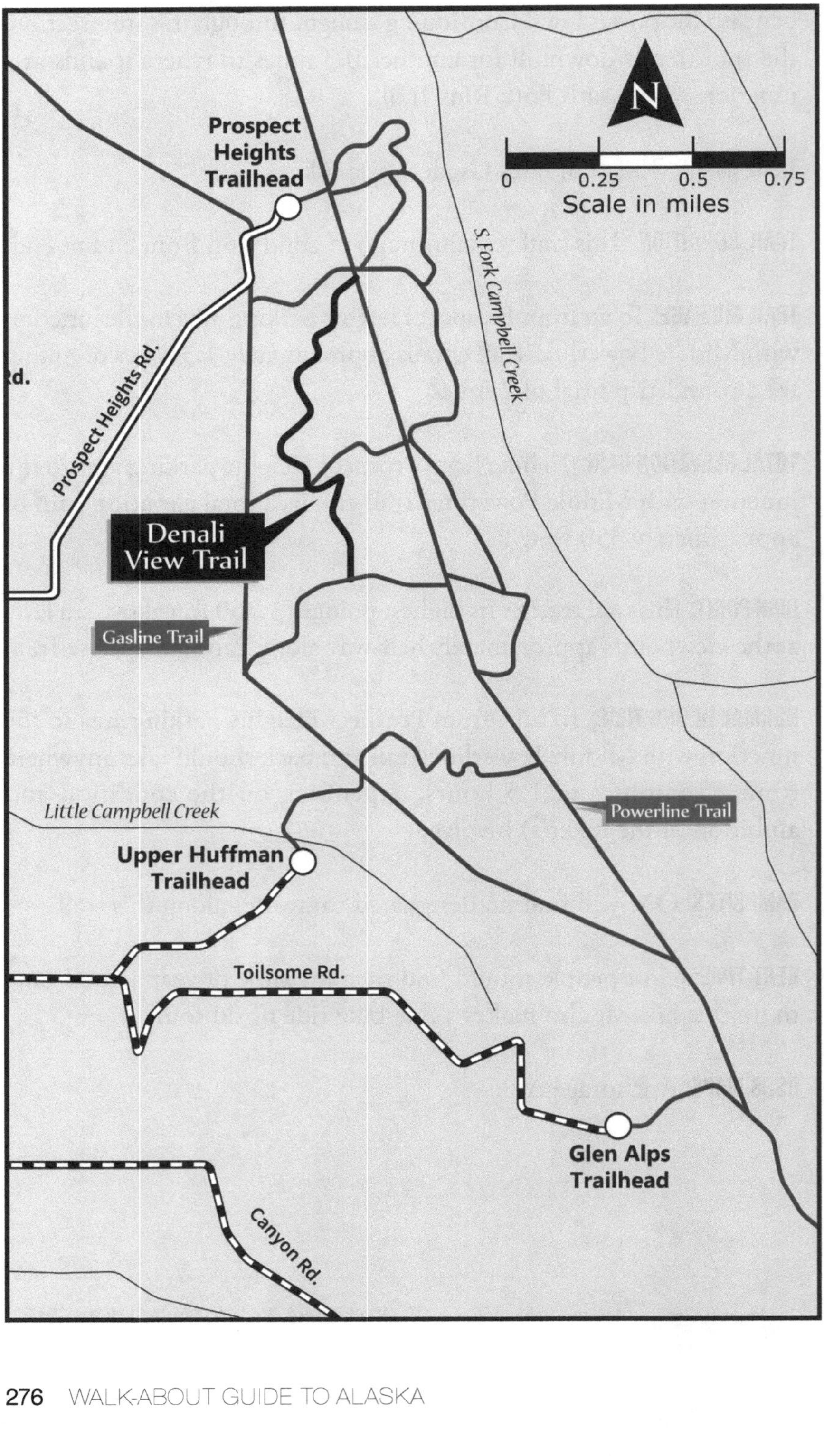
Prospect Heights Trailhead
N
0
0.25
0.5
0.75
Scale in miles
S. Fork Campbell Creek
Prospect Heights Rd.
Denali View Trail
Gasline Trail
Little Campbell Creek
Powerline Trail
Upper Huffman Trailhead
Toilsome Rd.
Glen Alps Trailhead
Canyon Rd.

# 50

# Walk-About Guide to Denali View Trail

**TRAIL LOCATION:** Denali View Trail, which connects Middle Powerline Trail to White Spruce Trail, begins approximately 0.3 miles up Middle Powerline Trail. To get there drive 6.2 miles south from Anchorage on the Seward Highway. There, just after Milepost 121, turn right (west) on the O'Malley Road exit. At the end of the ramp, turn left (east) and cross back under the highway. Continue straight on this road as it ascends past Lake Otis Parkway and the Anchorage Zoo. Approximately 3 miles from the Seward Highway, this road passes the junction with Hillside Road leading right (south). Staying on O'Malley Road, follow it to where, in less than 100 yards, it swings left north) onto the continuation of Hillside Drive. Almost immediately after Hillside Road straightens out, it reaches the junction with Upper O'Malley Road on the right (east). Turn right onto Upper O'Malley Road. Approximately 0.5 miles later, this road ends at a T intersection with Prospect Drive. Turn left (north) on Prospect Drive and follow it for approximately 1 mile to a stop sign. Bear left through the stop sign onto Siderof Lane. Approximately 200 yards later this road reaches the entrance to Chugach State Park on the right (north). Turn into this parking area and look for the sign board and fee station in the middle right (east) of the parking area. An access trail leading to Middle Powerline Trail begins just to the left of the fee station.

Follow the access trail by the fee station as it contours upward for approximately 0.2 miles to a junction with Middle Powerline Trail underneath the power lines. Turn up Middle Powerline Trail as it climbs over the first rise above. Approximately 0.4 miles up Middle Powerline Trail one reaches a junction with both Denali View Trail and Panorama View Trail on the right (west). Turn right onto Denali View Trail, the upper of these two trails, and follow it as it weaves up a slope to some fine viewpoints. Approximately 0.6 miles from

**April on Powerline Trail**

Middle Powerline Trail it crosses Alder Trail, another connecting trail\*. Approximately 0.3 miles beyond the Alder Trail the trail reaches a T-intersection with White Spruce Trail, yet another connecting trail\*\*. This intersection marks the end Denali View Trail.

**TRAIL GRADE:** This trail rates Grade 1 as a hike.

**TRAIL CONDITION:** This wide trail remains in excellent condition from end to end.

**TRAIL MILEAGE:** To go from the beginning of this trail at its junction with Middle Powerline Trail to where it ends at its junction with White Spruce Trail entails approximately 0.9 miles of hiking, for a round-trip total of 1.8 miles.

**TOTAL ELEVATION GAIN:** To hike from the beginning of this trail at its junction with Middle Powerline Trail to where it ends at its junction with White Spruce Trail entails a total elevation gain of approximately 325 feet.

**HIGH POINT:** This trail reaches its highest point of 1,650 feet above sea level where it ends at the junction with White Spruce Trail.

**NORMAL HIKING TIME:** To hike from the junction with Middle Powerline Trail to the junction with White Spruce Trail and back should take anywhere from 30 minutes to 1 hour, depending on the condition and ambition of the hiker(s) involved.

**CAMPSITES:** One will find no designated campsites along this trail.

**BEST TIME:** Most people should find that any time of year a good time to do this hike or ski tour. It remains, however, closed to mountain-biking.

**USGS MAPS:** Anchorage A-8.

------------------------------------------------------------------

\*   For more information about that trail, see [51] **Walk-About Guide to Alder Trail**.

\*\*  For more information about that trail, see [52] **Walk-About Guide to White Spruce Trail**.

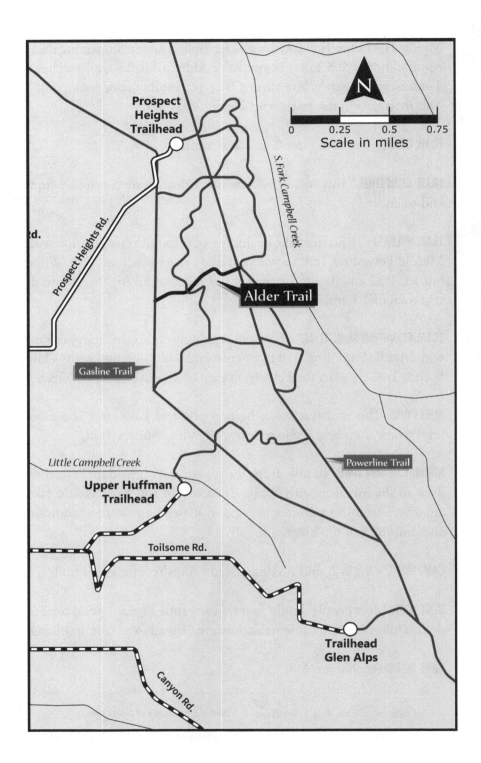

Prospect
Heights
Trailhead

N

0    0.25    0.5    0.75
Scale in miles

S. Fork Campbell Creek

Alder Trail

Gasline Trail

Little Campbell Creek

Powerline Trail

Upper Huffman
Trailhead

Toilsome Rd.

Prospect Heights Rd.

Rd.

Trailhead
Glen Alps

Canyon Rd.

# 51

# Walk-About Guide to Alder Trail

**TRAIL LOCATION:** This trail, which connects to Middle Powerline Trail and South Fork Rim Trail, begins on Upper Gasline Trail. To get there drive 6.2 miles south from Anchorage on the Seward Highway. There, just after Milepost 121, turn right (west) on the O'Malley Road exit. At the end of the ramp, turn left (east) and cross back under the highway. Continue straight on this road as it ascends past Lake Otis Parkway and the Anchorage Zoo. Approximately 3 miles from the Seward Highway, this road passes the junction with Hillside Road leading right (south). Staying on O'Malley Road, follow it to where, in less than 100 yards, it swings left north) onto the continuation of Hillside Drive. Almost immediately after Hillside Road straightens out, it reaches the junction with Upper O'Malley Road on the right (east). Turn right onto Upper O'Malley Road. Approximately 0.5 miles later, this road ends at a T intersection with Prospect Drive. Turn left (north) on Prospect Drive and follow it for approximately 1 mile to a stop sign. Bear left through the stop sign onto Siderof Lane. Approximately 200 yards later this road reaches the entrance to Chugach State Park on the right (north). Turn into this parking area and look for the sign board and fee station in the middle right (east) of the parking area. An access trail leading to Middle Powerline Trail begins just to the left of the fee station.

After parking, walk back toward the entrance to the parking area and look for the gate in the woods just to the left (south) of the entrance. Upper Gasline Trail begins just behind this gate.

From the gate follow Upper Gasline Trail as it climbs for 0.8 miles to a junction with Alder Trail on the left (east). Turn left onto Alder Trail and follow it as it weaves up a slope to some fine viewpoints. Approximately 0.3 miles from Upper Gasline Trail it crosses Denali View Trail, another connecting trail*. Approximately 0.6 miles beyond the

---

\*   For more information about that trail, see [50] **Walk-About Guide to Denali View Trail**.

Alder Trail the trail reaches a 4-way-intersection with Middle Powerline Trail*. Continuing straight through this intersection, Alder Trail ends approximately 20 feet at a junction with South Fork Rim Trail.

**TRAIL GRADE:** This trail rates Grade 1 as a hike.

**TRAIL CONDITION:** This trail remains in good condition from end to end.

**TRAIL MILEAGE:** To go from the beginning of this trail at its junction with Upper Gasline Trail to where it ends at its junction with South Fork Rim Trail entails approximately 0.2 miles of hiking for a round-trip total of 0.4 miles.

**TOTAL ELEVATION GAIN:** To hike from go from the beginning of this trail at its junction with Upper Gasline Trail to where it ends at its junction with South Fork Rim Trail entails a total elevation gain of approximately 100 feet.

**HIGH POINT:** This trail reaches its highest point of 1,650 feet above sea level just before it reaches the junction with Denali View Trail.

**NORMAL HIKING TIME:** To hike from the junction with Upper Gasline Trail to where it ends at its junction with South Fork Rim Trail and back should take anywhere from 10 to 30 minutes, depending on the condition and ambition of the hiker(s) involved.

**CAMPSITES:** One will find no designated campsites along this trail.

**BEST TIME:** Most people should find that any time of year a good time to do this hike or ski tour. Unfortunately, it remains un-open to mountain-biking.

**USGS MAPS:** Anchorage A-8.

--------------------------------------------------------------------

* For more information about that trail, see [47] **Walk-About Guide to Upper Gasline Trail**.

Rutting season below O'Malley Peak

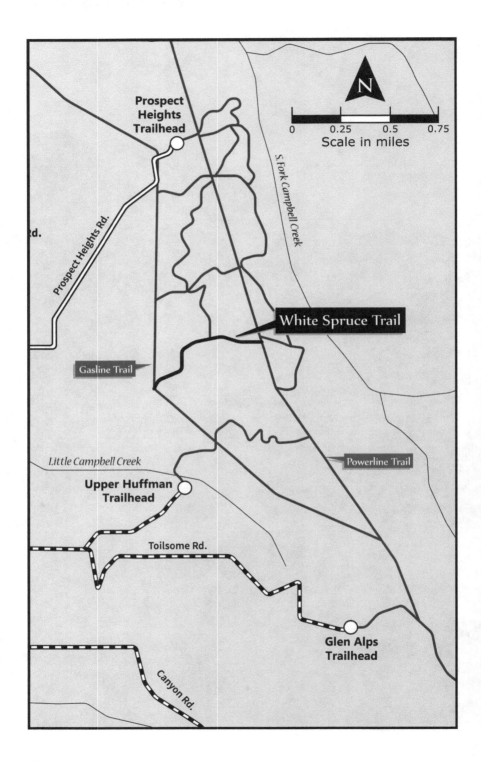

Prospect
Heights
Trailhead

N

| 0 | 0.25 | 0.5 | 0.75 |

Scale in miles

S. Fork Campbell Creek

Prospect Heights Rd.

d.

White Spruce Trail

Gasline Trail

Little Campbell Creek

Powerline Trail

Upper Huffman
Trailhead

Toilsome Rd.

Glen Alps
Trailhead

Canyon Rd.

# Walk-About Guide to White Spruce Trail

**TRAIL LOCATION:** This trail, which connects to Middle Powerline Trail and South Fork Rim Trail, begins on Upper Gasline Trail. To get there drive 6.2 miles south from Anchorage on the Seward Highway. There, just after Milepost 121, turn right (west) on the O'Malley Road exit. At the end of the ramp, turn left (east) and cross back under the highway. Continue straight on this road as it ascends past Lake Otis Parkway and the Anchorage Zoo. Approximately 3 miles from the Seward Highway, this road passes the junction with Hillside Road leading right (south). Staying on O'Malley Road, follow it to where, in less than 100 yards, it swings left north) onto the continuation of Hillside Drive. Almost immediately after Hillside Road straightens out, it reaches the junction with Upper O'Malley Road on the right (east). Turn right onto Upper O'Malley Road. Approximately 0.5 miles later, this road ends at a T intersection with Prospect Drive. Turn left (north) on Prospect Drive and follow it for approximately 1 mile to a stop sign. Bear left through the stop sign onto Siderof Lane. Approximately 200 yards later this road reaches the entrance to Chugach State Park on the right (north). Turn into this parking area and look for the sign board and fee station in the middle right (east) of the parking area. An access trail leading to Middle Powerline Trail begins just to the left of the fee station.

After parking, walk back toward the entrance to the parking area and look for the gate in the woods just to the left (south) of the entrance. Upper Gasline Trail begins just behind this gate.

From the gate follow Upper Gasline Trail as it climbs approximately 1.2 miles to a junction with White Spruce Trail on the left (east). Turn left onto White Spruce Trail. Follow the trail as it weaves up a slope to an intersection with the uppermost end of Denali View Trail*. Continuing straight across this intersection, the trail begins its

---

\* For more information about that trail, see [50] **Walk-About Guide to Denali View Trail**.

approximate 0.4-mile descent to a 4-way-intersection with Middle Powerline Trail*. Continuing straight past this intersection, follow White Spruce Trail as it trends downward for another approximately 0.2 miles where it ends at a 4-way intersection with Blueberry Hollow Trail and South Fork Rim Trail**.

**TRAIL GRADE:** This trail rates Grade 1 as a hike.

**TRAIL CONDITION:** This trail remains in good condition from end to end.

**TRAIL MILEAGE:** To go from the beginning of this trail at its junction with Upper Gasline Trail to where it ends at the junction with Blueberry Hollow Trail and South Fork Rim Trail entails approximately 0.8 miles of hiking for a round-trip total of 1.6 miles.

**TOTAL ELEVATION GAIN:** To hike from the beginning of this trail at its junction with Upper Gasline Trail to where it ends at the junction with Blueberry Hollow Trail and South Fork Rim Trail entails a total elevation gain of approximately 100 feet.

**HIGH POINT:** This trail reaches its highest point of 1,675 feet above sea level just before it reaches the junction with Denali View Trail.

**NORMAL HIKING TIME:** To hike from the junction with Upper Gasline Trail to where it ends at the junction with Blueberry Hollow Trail and South Fork Rim Trail and back should take anywhere from 45 minutes to 1 hour, depending on the condition and ambition of the hiker(s) involved.

--------------------------------------------------------------------

\* For more information about that trail,
  see [46] **Walk-About Guide to Middle Powerline Trail**.

** For more information about these trails,
  see [56] **Walk-About Guide to Blueberry Hollow Trail** and [55] **South Fork Rim Trail**.

**CAMPSITES:** One will find no designated campsites along this trail.

**BEST TIME:** Most people should find that any time of year a good time to do this hike. It also makes a fine bike ride or ski tour.

**USGS MAPS:** Anchorage A-8.

Looking down Middle Powerline Trail

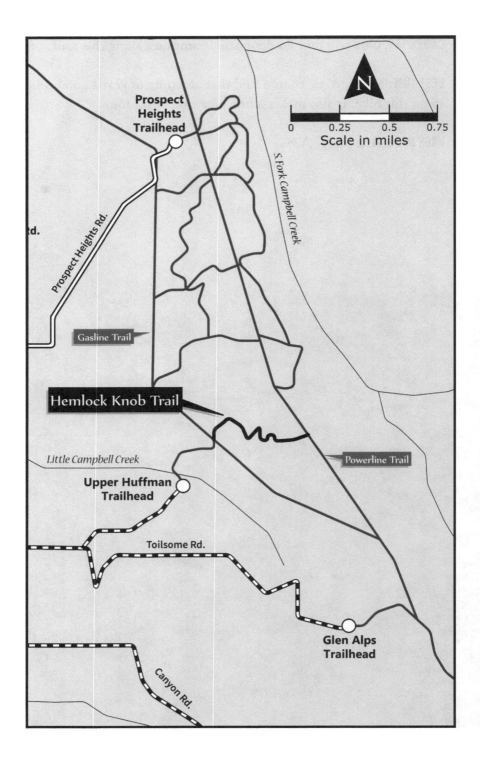

Prospect
Heights
Trailhead

Scale in miles

0    0.25    0.5    0.75

S. Fork Campbell Creek

Prospect Heights Rd.

Rd.

Gasline Trail

Hemlock Knob Trail

Little Campbell Creek

Powerline Trail

Upper Huffman
Trailhead

Toilsome Rd.

Glen Alps
Trailhead

Canyon Rd.

# Walk-About Guide to Hemlock Knob Trail

**TRAIL LOCATION:** This trail, which connects Upper Gasline Trail with Middle Powerline Trail, begins at the end of Silver Fern Trail. To get to Upper Huffman parking area drive 6.2 miles south from Anchorage on the Seward Highway. There, just after Milepost 121, turn right (west) onto the O'Malley Road exit. At the end of the ramp, turn left (east) and cross back under the highway. Continuing straight on this road, ascend past Lake Otis Parkway and the Anchorage Zoo. Approximately 3 miles from the Seward Highway this road reaches a junction with Hillside Road on the right (south). Turn onto Hillside Road and follow it for another 1 mile to where just past a sign for Chugach State Park, one reaches Upper Huffman Road on the left (east). Turn left onto Upper Huffman Road and follow it for 0.75 miles to appropriately named Toilsome Hill Drive on the right (south). At that point, instead of turning right up Toilsome Hill Drive to Glen Alps, bear left and continue straight ahead for approximately 0.5 miles to Upper Huffman parking area. Silver Fern Trail begins at the fire gate by an information board at the back left (northwest) side of the parking area.

After passed around the gate follow the wide trail as it dips to cross a stream. On the far side it climbs to a viewpoint where it turns right (north) into the trees. Trending slowly upward as it makes a wide U-turn through the open woods, the trail reaches its end at a 4-way-junction with Upper Gasline Trail*, begins on Upper Gasline Trail near Upper Huffman parking area. Hemlock Knob Trail begins at the far side of this intersection.

Hemlock Knob Trail begins by climbing steadily toward the hemlock stand one can see on the low rise directly ahead. Follow the

---

\* For more information about that trail, see [47] **Walk-About Guide to Upper Gasline Trail**.

Starting up Hemlock Knob Trail

trail as it weaves up the slope to the top of rise. From the crest of this ridge it then trends downward through a series of twists and turn to where it ends at a T-intersection with Middle Powerline Trail, which crosses the intersection at a right angle,

**TRAIL GRADE:** This trail rates Grade 1 as a hike.

**TRAIL CONDITION:** This trail remains in good condition from end to end.

**TRAIL MILEAGE:** To go from the beginning of this trail at its junction with Silver Fern Trail to where it ends at its junction with Middle Powerline Trail entails approximately 0.8 miles of hiking for a round-trip total of 1.6 miles.

**TOTAL ELEVATION GAIN:** To hike from go from the beginning of this trail at its junction with Middle Powerline Trail to where it ends at its junction with Middle Powerline Trail entails a total elevation gain of approximately 300 feet.

**HIGH POINT:** This trail reaches its highest point of 1,880 feet above sea level approximately 0.2 miles from its beginning at the junction with Silver Fern Trail.

**NORMAL HIKING TIME:** To hike from the junction with Silver Fern Trail to the junction with Middle Powerline Trail and back should take anywhere from 45 minutes to 1 hour, depending on the condition and ambition of the hiker(s) involved.

**CAMPSITES:** One will find no designated campsites along this trail.

**BEST TIME:** Most people should find that any time of year a good time to do this hike or ski tour. Unfortunately, it remains un-open to mountain-biking.

**USGS MAPS:** Anchorage A-8.

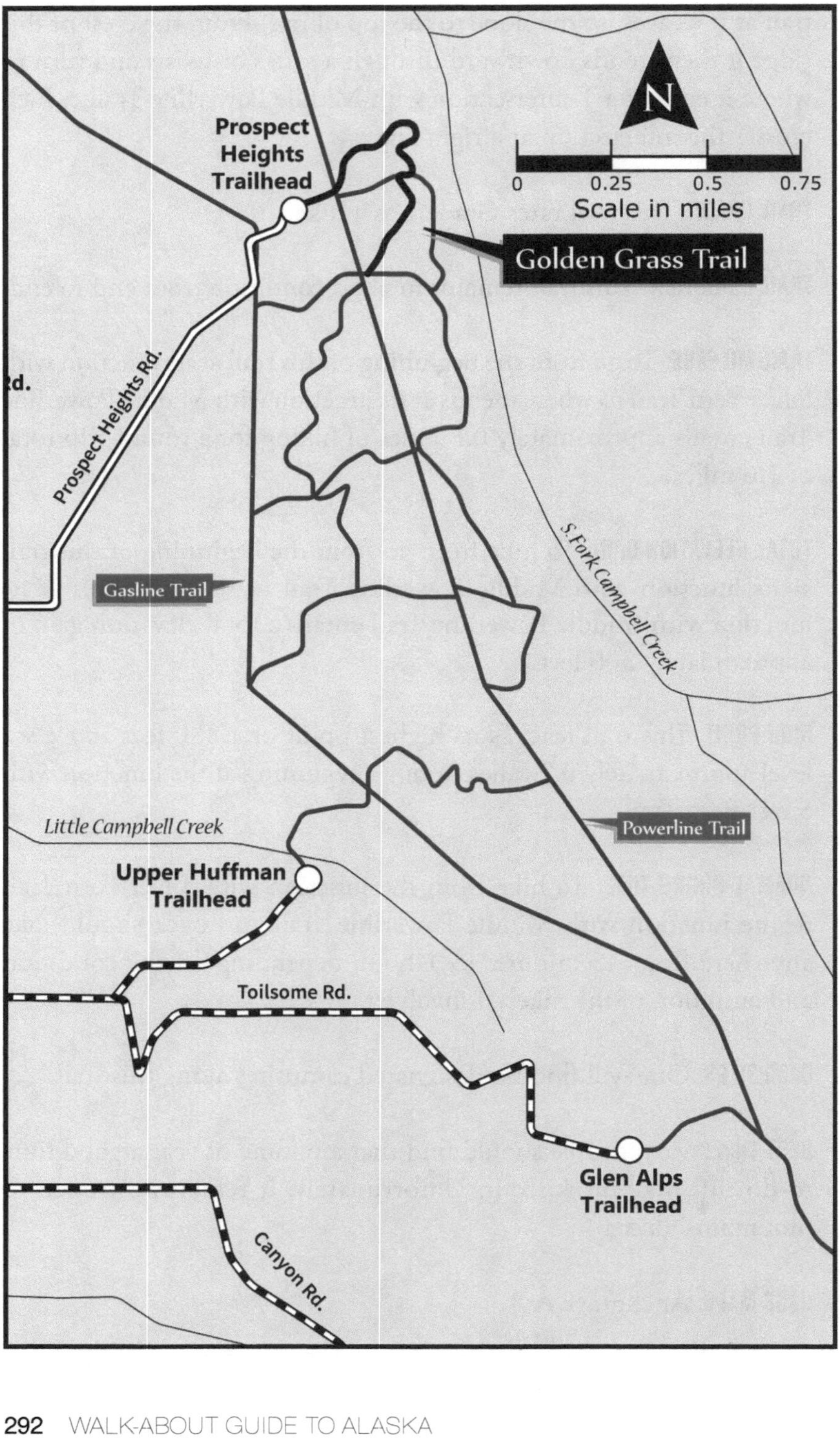
N
0
0.25
0.5
0.75
Scale in miles
Prospect Heights Trailhead
Golden Grass Trail
Rd.
Prospect Heights Rd.
Gasline Trail
S. Fork Campbell Creek
Little Campbell Creek
Powerline Trail
Upper Huffman Trailhead
Toilsome Rd.
Glen Alps Trailhead
Canyon Rd.

# Walk-About Guide to Golden Grass Trail

**TRAIL LOCATION:** This trail begins at the lower end of Middle Powerline Trail. To get there drive 6.2 miles south from Anchorage on the Seward Highway. There, just after Milepost 121, turn right (west) on the O'Malley Road exit. At the end of the ramp, turn left (east) and cross back under the highway. Continue straight on this road as it ascends past Lake Otis Parkway and the Anchorage Zoo. Approximately 3 miles from the Seward Highway, this road passes the junction with Hillside Road leading right (south). Staying on O'Malley Road, follow it to where, in less than 100 yards, it swings left north) onto the continuation of Hillside Drive. Almost immediately after Hillside Road straightens out, it reaches the junction with Upper O'Malley Road on the right (east). Turn right onto Upper O'Malley Road. Approximately 0.5 miles later this road ends at a T intersection with Prospect Drive. Turn left (north) on Prospect Drive and follow it for approximately 1 mile to a stop sign. Bear left through the stop sign onto Siderof Lane. Approximately 200 yards later this road reaches the entrance to Chugach State Park on the right (north). Turn into this parking area and drive to its far end. There Wolverine Bowl, which accesses Golden Grass Trail, begins at the gate to the right of the outhouse.

Begin by following Wolverine Bowl Trail for approximately 150 yards to a four-way intersection. There Middle Powerline Trail turns up the dirt road to the right and Wolverine Bowl Trail turns down the dirt road to the left. Golden Grass Trail begins continuing straight across this intersection and entering the trees on the far side. Upon entering the woods, the trail winds about while trending steadily upward, offering views of South Fork Campbell Creek hollow below and the southwest ridge of Wolverine Peak above as it climbs.

Approximately 0.25 miles from Powerline Trail this trail reaches a junction with South Fork Rim Trail*. Passing straight through this intersection, the trail continues to climb steadily. As it approaches its upper end, Golden Grass Trail bears right (south) back toward Middle Powerline Trail and passes over its highest point along the way. Golden Grass Trail reaches its uppermost end at approximately 0.4 miles up Middle Powerline Trail.

**TRAIL GRADE:** This trail rates Grade 1 as a hike.

**TRAIL CONDITION:** This trail remains in good condition from end to end.

**TRAIL MILEAGE:** To go from the beginning of this trail at its lower junction with Middle Powerline Trail to where it ends at its upper junction with Middle Powerline Trail entails approximately 0.8 miles of hiking for a round-trip total of 1.6 miles.

**TOTAL ELEVATION GAIN:** To hike from the beginning of this trail at its lower junction with Middle Powerline Trail to where it ends at its upper junction with Middle Powerline Trail entails a total elevation gain of approximately 275 feet.

**HIGH POINT:** This trail reaches its highest point of 1,375 feet above sea level approximately 0.1 miles before its upper junction with Middle Powerline Trail.

**NORMAL HIKING TIME:** To hike from the beginning of this trail at its lower junction with Middle Powerline Trail to where it ends at its upper junction with Middle Powerline Trail and back should take anywhere from 30 minutes to 1 hour, depending on the condition and ambition of the hiker(s) involved.

---------------------------------------------------------------------

\* For more information about that trail, see [55] **Walk-About Guide to South Fork Rim Trail.**

**CAMPSITES:** One will find no designated campsites along this trail.

**BEST TIME:** Most people should find that any time of year a good time to do this hike or ski tour. Unfortunately, it remains un-open to mountain-biking.

**USGS MAPS:** Anchorage A-8.

Ptarmigan on Hillside

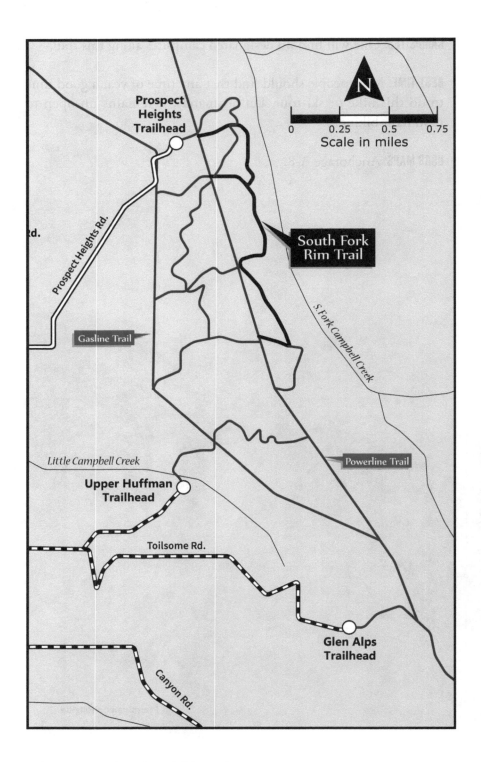

Prospect
Heights
Trailhead

N

0    0.25    0.5    0.75
Scale in miles

South Fork
Rim Trail

Prospect Heights Rd.

.d.

Gasline Trail

S. Fork Campbell Creek

Little Campbell Creek

Powerline Trail

Upper Huffman
Trailhead

Toilsome Rd.

Glen Alps
Trailhead

Canyon Rd.

# 55

# Walk-About Guide to South Fork Rim Trail

**TRAIL LOCATION:** South Fork Rim Trail begins approximately 0.1 miles up Middle Powerline Trail. To get there drive 6.2 miles south from Anchorage on the Seward Highway. There, just after Milepost 121, turn right (west) on the O'Malley Road exit. At the end of the ramp, turn left (east) and cross back under the highway. Continue straight on this road as it ascends past Lake Otis Parkway and the Anchorage Zoo. Approximately 3 miles from the Seward Highway, this road passes the junction with Hillside Road leading right (south). Staying on O'Malley Road, follow it to where, in less than 100 yards, it swings left north) onto the continuation of Hillside Drive. Almost immediately after Hillside Road straightens out, it reaches the junction with Upper O'Malley Road on the right (east). Turn right onto Upper O'Malley Road. Approximately 0.5 miles later, this road ends at a T intersection with Prospect Drive. Turn left (north) on Prospect Drive and follow it for approximately 1 mile to a stop sign. Bear left through the stop sign onto Siderof Lane. Approximately 200 yards later this road reaches the entrance to Chugach State Park on the right (north). Turn into this parking area and look for the sign board and fee station in the middle right (east) of the parking area. An access trail leading to Middle Powerline Trail begins just to the left of the fee station.

Follow the access trail by the fee station as it contours upward for approximately 0.2 miles to a junction with Middle Powerline Trail. Here Middle Powerline Trail follows the power lines to the left and right.

South Fork Rim begins by entering the brush edge directly across Middle Powerline Trail. In less than 0.2 miles it reaches an intersection with Golden Grass Trail*. Continuing straight through this intersection,

---

*     For more information about that trail, see [54] **Walk-About Guide to Golden Grass Trail**.

the trail soon bears right (southeast) to follow the rim of South Fork Campbell Creek upstream. As it climbs steadily, it crosses many open meadows offering fine views both of Wolverine Peak and O'Malley Peak on the far side of South Fork Campbell Creek as well as far up the creek toward Flattop and beyond. Near the upper end of this section the trail reaches a particularly expansive viewpoint with a bench upon which to rest while enjoying the view.

Soon after passing this viewpoint South Fork Rim Trail passes a junction with Panorama View Trail on the left (west)*. Approximately 0.7 miles up the rim from the viewpoint the trail swings right back toward Powerline Trail to circle a hollow. Here it reaches a junction with Alder Trail almost directly below the power lines**. On winding out to the rim again, the trail continues for another approximately 0.5 miles to an intersection with Blueberry Hollow Trail and White Spruce Trail***. Passing straight through this intersection, the trail soon bears right away from the rim once more as it trends back to Middle Powerline Trail. One reaches the end of South Fork Rim Trail at approximately mile 1.3 miles of Middle Powerline Trail.

**TRAIL GRADE:** This trail rates Grade 1 as a hike.

**TRAIL CONDITION:** This trail remains in good condition from end to end.

**TRAIL MILEAGE:** To go from the beginning of this trail at its lower junction with Middle Powerline Trail to where it ends at its upper junction with Middle Powerline Trail entails approximately 2.2 miles of hiking for a round-trip total of 4.4 miles.

**TOTAL ELEVATION GAIN:** To hike from the beginning of this trail at its lower junction with Middle Powerline Trail to where it ends at its upper

---

\*    For more information about that trail, see [49] **Walk-About Guide to Panorama View Trail**.

\*\*    For more information about that trail, see [51] **Walk-About Guide to Alder Trail**.

\*\*\*    For more information about these trails, see [52] **Walk-About Guide to White Spruce Trail** above and [56] **Walk-About Guide to Blueberry Hollow Trail**.

junction with Middle Powerline Trail entails a total elevation gain of approximately 250 feet.

**HIGH POINT:** This trail reaches its highest point of 1,750 feet above sea level at its upper junction with Middle Powerline Trail.

**NORMAL HIKING TIME:** To hike from the beginning of this trail at its lower junction with Middle Powerline Trail to where it ends at its upper junction with Middle Powerline Trail and back should take anywhere from 1.5 to 2.5 hour, depending on the condition and ambition of the hiker(s) involved.

**CAMPSITES:** One will find no designated campsites along this trail.

**BEST TIME:** Most people should find that any time of year a good time to do this hike. It also makes a fine bike ride or ski tour.

**USGS MAPS:** Anchorage A-8.

O'Malley Peak from South Fork Rim Trail

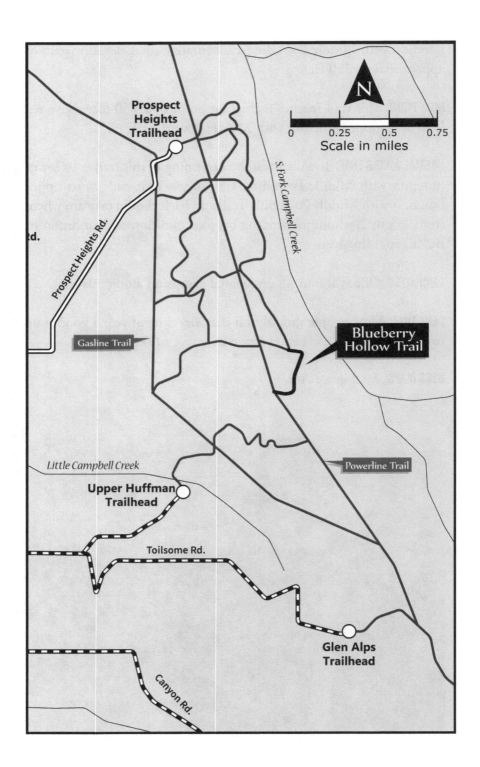

Prospect
Heights
Trailhead

S. Fork Campbell Creek

N

0        0.25        0.5        0.75
Scale in miles

Prospect Heights Rd.

Rd.

Gasline Trail

Blueberry
Hollow Trail

Little Campbell Creek

Powerline Trail

Upper Huffman
Trailhead

Toilsome Rd.

Glen Alps
Trailhead

Canyon Rd.

# 56

# Walk-About Guide to Blueberry Hollow Trail

**TRAIL LOCATION:** Blueberry Hollow Trail begins at a trail junction approximately 2 miles up Middle Powerline Trail. To get there drive 6.2 miles south from Anchorage on the Seward Highway. There, just after Milepost 121, turn right (west) on the O'Malley Road exit. At the end of the ramp, turn left (east) and cross back under the highway. Continue straight on this road as it ascends past Lake Otis Parkway and the Anchorage Zoo. Approximately 3 miles from the Seward Highway, this road passes the junction with Hillside Road leading right (south). Staying on O'Malley Road, follow it to where, in less than 100 yards, it swings left north) onto the continuation of Hillside Drive. Almost immediately after Hillside Road straightens out, it reaches the junction with Upper O'Malley Road on the right (east). Turn right onto Upper O'Malley Road. Approximately 0.5 miles later, this road ends at a T intersection with Prospect Drive. Turn left (north) on Prospect Drive and follow it for approximately 1 mile to a stop sign. Bear left through the stop sign onto Siderof Lane. Approximately 200 yards later this road reaches the entrance to Chugach State Park on the right (north). Turn into this parking area and look for the sign board and fee station in the middle right (east) of the parking area. An access trail leading to Middle Powerline Trail begins just to the left of the fee station.

Follow the access trail by the fee station as it contours upward for approximately 0.2 miles to a junction with Middle Powerline Trail underneath the power lines. Turn up Middle Powerline Trail as it climbs over the first rise above. In the next 1.5-mile-plus of hiking Middle Powerline Trail passes numerous trail junctions. After one long passage through the trees on the left (north) of the power lines,

Middle Powerline Trail bears left out onto the open swath beneath the power lines. In another approximately 100 yards it reaches the junction with Blueberry Hollow Trail

Blueberry Hollow Trail begins by turning sharply left (east) off Middle Powerline Trail. Almost immediately after leaving Middle Powerline Trail, Blueberry Hollow Trail begins a gradual descent to the rim South Fork Campbell Creek. Upon reaching the rim with its wide views across the creek to Wolverine Peak and O'Malley Peak on the far side as well as far up valley toward Flattop, Blueberry Hollow Trail bears left to follow the rim downstream. In approximately 1.3 miles the trail reaches an intersection with South Fork Rim Trail and White Spruce Trail where it reaches its lower end*.

Here one has two major choices. First they can follow White Spruce Trail on the left (west) and follow it for approximately 0.2 miles to Middle Powerline Trail. Second, they can bear right (northwest) onto South Fork Rim Trail and follow it down valley to where it eventually reaches Middle Powerline Trail just opposite the access trail leading 0.2 miles back down to Prospect Heights Parking area.

**TRAIL GRADE:** This trail rates Grade 1 as a hike.

**TRAIL CONDITION:** This trail remains in good condition from end to end.

**TRAIL MILEAGE:** To go from the beginning of this trail at its junction with Middle Powerline Trail to where it ends at its lower junction with South Fork Rim Trail entails approximately 1.2 miles of hiking for a round-trip total of 2.4 miles. To continue from that point down South Fork Rim Trail and back to Prospect Heights parking area entails another approximately 1.4 miles of hiking.

**TOTAL ELEVATION GAIN:** To hike from the beginning of this trail it ends at its lower junction with South Fork Rim Trail entails a total elevation

-------------------------------------------------------------------

\* For more information about these trails, see [52] **Walk-About Guide to White Spruce Trail** and [55] **Walk-About Guide to South Fork Rim Trail**.

gain of approximately 100 feet. To continue from that point down South Fork Rim Trail and back to Prospect Heights parking area entails a total elevation gain of approximately 200 feet.

**HIGH POINT:** This trail reaches its highest point of 2,050 feet above sea level at its junction with Middle Powerline Trail.

**NORMAL HIKING TIME:** To hike from the beginning of this trail at its junction with Middle Powerline Trail to where it ends at its lower junction with South Fork Rim Trail and back should take anywhere from 45 minutes to 1 hour, depending on the condition and ambition of the hiker(s) involved. To hike from the beginning of this trail at its junction with Middle Powerline Trail back down South Fork Rim Trail to Prospect Heights parking area should take anywhere from 1 to 1.5 hour, depending on the condition and ambition of the hiker(s) involved.

**CAMPSITES:** One will find no designated campsites along this trail.

**BEST TIME:** Most people should find that any time of year a good time to do this hike or ski tour. Unfortunately it remains un-open to mountain-biking.

**USGS MAPS:** Anchorage A-8.

Bunning on Hillside

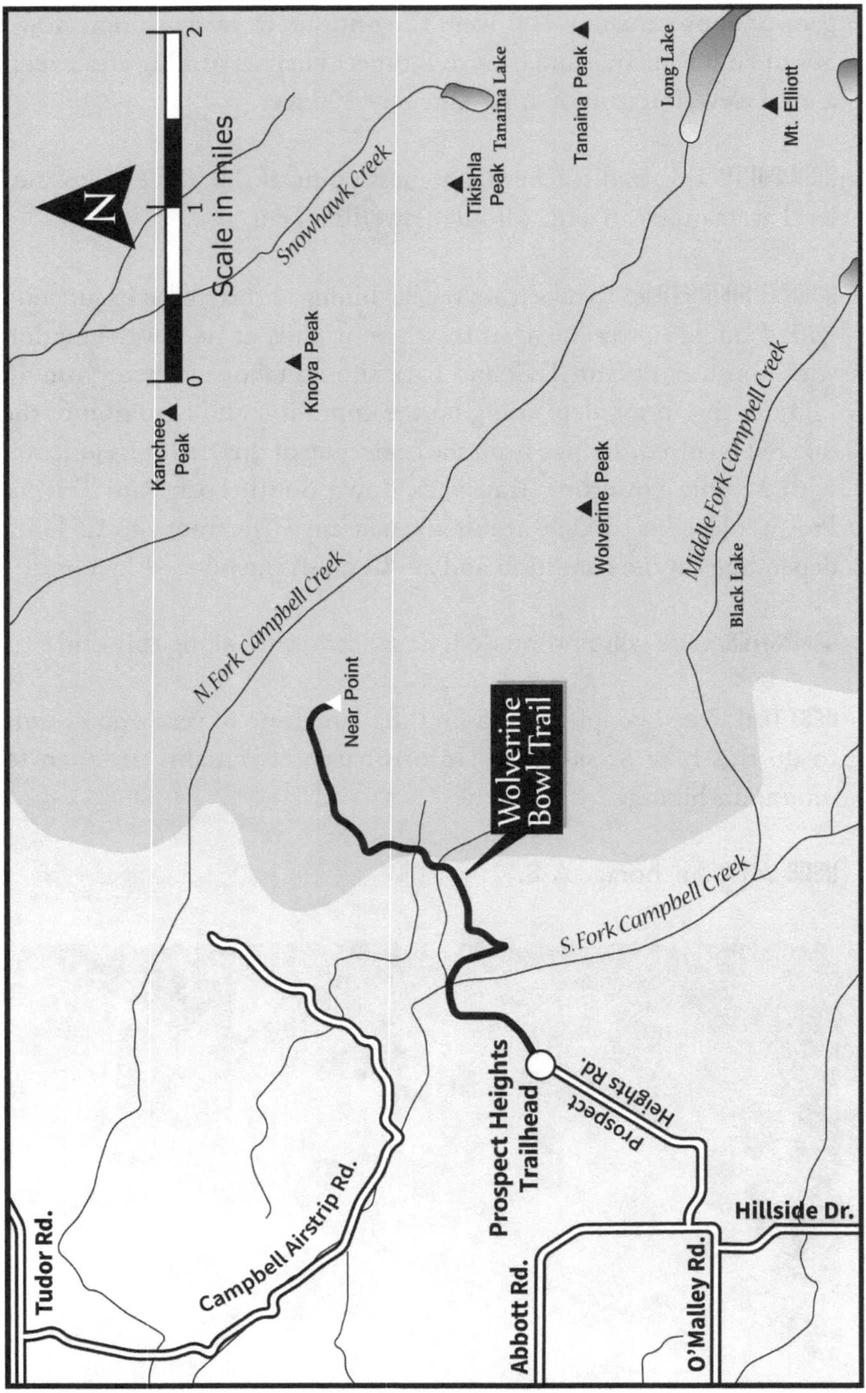
N
Scale in miles
0
1
2
Kanchee Peak
Knoya Peak
Snowhawk Creek
Tikishla Peak
Tanaina Lake
Tanaina Peak
Long Lake
Mt. Elliott
N. Fork Campbell Creek
Near Point
Wolverine Peak
Middle Fork Campbell Creek
Black Lake
Wolverine Bowl Trail
S. Fork Campbell Creek
Prospect Heights Trailhead
Prospect Heights Rd.
Campbell Airstrip Rd.
Tudor Rd.
Abbott Rd.
O'Malley Rd.
Hillside Dr.

## CHAPTER 5

# MIDDLE FORK CAMPBELL CREEK VALLEY

## 57

## Walk-About Guide to Wolverine Bowl Trail

Though not exceptionally long or high, this trail not only provides access to a number of other trails that extend farther, deeper, and higher into the mountains, but also opens up on some very wide and lengthy views the higher one climbs toward the summit of Near Point, which marks the uppermost end of this trail. The trails which this trail accesses both directly and indirectly along its length include Middle Fork Loop Trail, Williwaw Lakes Trail, and Wolverine Peak Trail*. As for views, at various points along the trail one can look out over Cook Inlet, the Alaska Range, and Knik Arm to the west and north. From the summit of Near Point, one can look deep into Chugach to the east as far as Long Lake, and the summits of Knoya Peak and Williwaw Peak that rise well above and beyond it.

**TRAIL LOCATION:** Wolverine Bowl Trail begins at Prospect Heights parking area. To get there drive 6.2 miles south from Anchorage on the Seward Highway. There, just after Milepost 121, turn right (west) on the

---

\*   For more information about those trails, see [41] **Walk-About Guide to Middle Fork Loop Trail** in Chapter 3 above, and [61] **Walk-About Guide to Williwaw Lakes Trail** and [60] **Walk-About Guide to Wolverine Peak Trail**.

O'Malley Road exit. At the end of the ramp, turn left (east) and cross back under the highway. Continue straight on this road as it ascends past Lake Otis Parkway and the Anchorage Zoo. Approximately 3 miles from the Seward Highway, this road passes the junction with Hillside Road leading right (south). Staying on O'Malley Road, follow it to where, in less than 100 yards, it swings left north) onto the continuation of Hillside Drive. Almost immediately after Hillside Road straightens out, it reaches the junction with Upper O'Malley Road on the right (east). Turn right onto Upper O'Malley Road. Approximately 0.5 miles later, this road ends at a T intersection with Prospect Drive. Turn left (north) on Prospect Drive and follow it for approximately 1 mile to a stop sign. Bear left through the stop sign onto Siderof Lane. Approximately 200 yards later this road reaches the entrance to Chugach State Park on the right (north). Turn into this parking area and drive to its far end. There Wolverine Bowl begins at the gate to the right of the outhouse.

Begin by following Wolverine Bowl Trail for approximately 150 yards to a four-way intersection. There Middle Powerline Trail begins by turning up the dirt road to the right and Golden Grass Trail begins by continuing straight across this intersection*. Turn left (north) at this intersection and follow the trail for another approximately 1 mile around the north end of a low ridge to where it descends and crosses Middle Fork Campbell Creek over a sturdy bridge. The trail then swings up and across the face of a low ridge on the opposite bank where it reaches a junction with Middle Fork Loop Trail on the right (south)**.

Continuing straight past this junction, Wolverine Bowl Trail contours in a big semicircle up and to the left across the base of Wolverine Peak. Soon after crossing one small bridge it reaches a

--------------------------------------------------------------------

\* For more information about those trails, see [46] **Walk-About Guide to Middle Powerline Trail** and [54] **Walk-About Guide to Golden Grass Trail** in Chapter 4.

\*\* For more information about that trail, see [41] **Walk-About Guide to Middle Fork Loop Trail** in Chapter 3.

junction with Wolverine Peak Trail on the right (east)*. Continuing once more straight ahead past this junction, the trail swings right (west) to begin the ascent of Near Point. Switch-backing at first up the southwest side of the mountains, the next trail passes an unofficial trail on the right leading more directly and steeply to the summit. Soon after passing this trail, Wolverine Bowl Trail swings up and onto the west face. After initially climbing through the last brush the trail emerges onto the broad open face above. Less than 0.5 miles later it reaches the rounded summit of Near Point (3,050 feet).

**TRAIL GRADE:** This trail rates Grade 2 as a hike for much of its length. Upon beginning the ascent of Near Point it rises to Grade 3 as a hike.

**TRAIL CONDITION:** This trail varies little in its conditions. For much of its length it follows an old road, which has only some muddy sections along its length. Once one begins to climb Near Point, however, the trail narrows as it crosses more and wider mud holes. On reaching tree line, the trail dries out and remains dry for most of the last 0.5 miles to the summit.

**TRAIL MILEAGE:** To go from Prospect Heights parking area to the summit of Near Point entails approximately 4 miles of hiking, for a round-trip total of approximately 8 miles.

**TOTAL ELEVATION GAIN:** From Prospect Heights parking area to the summit of Near Point entails a total elevation gain of approximately 2,050 feet.

**HIGH POINT:** This hike reaches its highest point of 3,050 feet above sea level at the summit of Near Point.

**NORMAL HIKING TIME:** To hike from Prospect Heights parking area to the summit of Near Point and back should take anywhere from 3 to 6 hours, depending on the condition and ambition of the hiker(s) involved.

-----------------------------------------------------------------------

\* For more information about that trail, see [57] **Walk-About Guide to Wolverine Peak Trail**.

**CAMPSITES:** One will find no designated campsites along this trail. Nor should one need any, given that most people do it as a day hike. One can find some decent places on which to pitch a tent, however, in some of the meadows just off the trail near tree line.

**BEST TIME:** Most people should find any time from May to October a good time to do this hike. It also makes a fine ski or snowshoe outing in the winter, with only minimal avalanche danger on the upper slopes of Near Point.

**USGS MAPS:** Anchorage A-7 and A-8 NE.

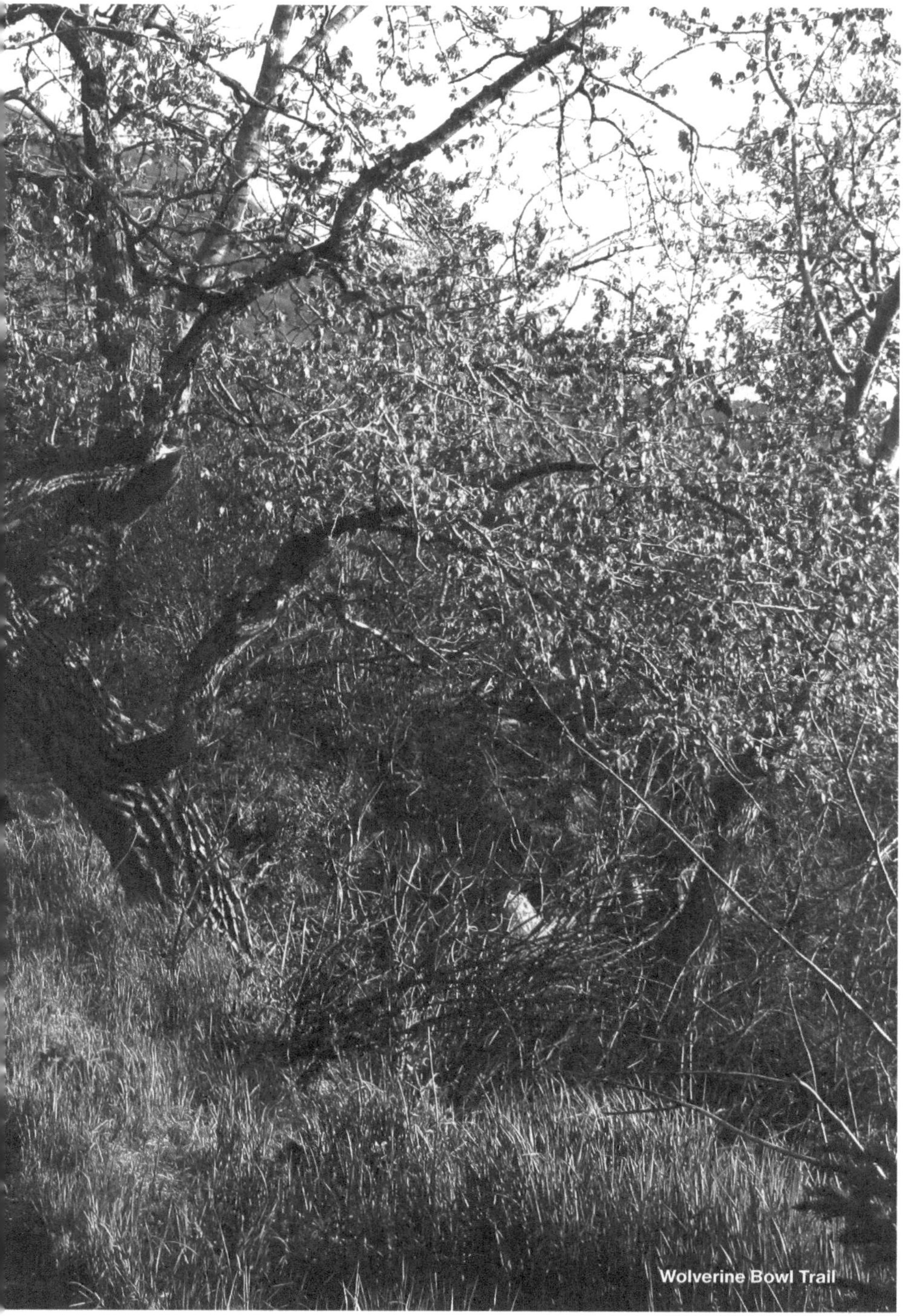
Wolverine Bowl Trail

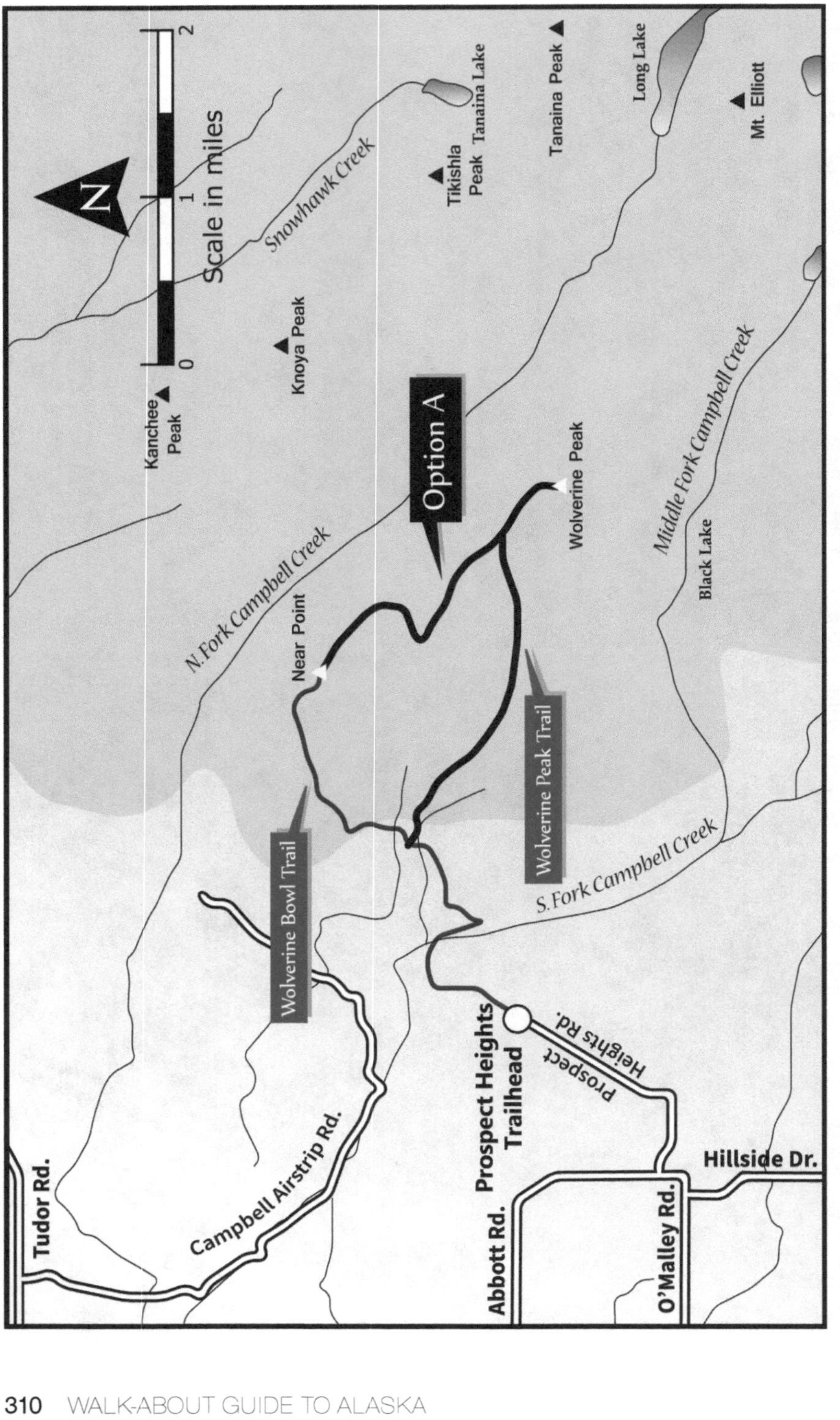
N
Scale in miles
0
1
2
Kanchee Peak
Knoya Peak
Snowhawk Creek
Tikishla Peak
Tanaina Lake
Tanaina Peak
Long Lake
Mt. Elliott
Option A
N. Fork Campbell Creek
Near Point
Wolverine Peak
Middle Fork Campbell Creek
Black Lake
Wolverine Peak Trail
Wolverine Bowl Trail
S. Fork Campbell Creek
Prospect Heights Trailhead
Prospect Heights Rd.
Campbell Airstrip Rd.
Tudor Rd.
Abbott Rd.
O'Malley Rd.
Hillside Dr.

# OPTION A

# Traverse from Near Point to Wolverine Peak

This trip has a simple concept: follow the ridge off the back side of Near Point to the summit of Wolverine Peak. By connecting these two summits via the ridge between them, one can turn an out-and-back trip into a loop traverse, which includes the added adventure of climbing off trail along a scenic ridge with expansive views.

**TRAIL LOCATION:** This traverse begins at the summit of Near Point[*]. From the top of Near Point continue along the faint trail leading straight ahead (east-southeast) along the ridge. In the first 0.5 mile the ridge occasionally narrows dramatically as weaves along the ridge crest. But none of these narrow sections last long or prove excessively dangerous.

Approximately 0.6 miles from Near Point the trail winds over a prominent bump (2,963 feet), on the far side of which it drops 300 feet into a wide saddle. Continue straight across this saddle to the base of the broad slope rising directly above its opposite side. The base of this broad slope marks the beginning of the northwest buttress of Wolverine Peak. Once at the base of this buttress, begin climbing any route that seems feasible to the ridge top 800 feet above. Though steep at first, this climb gradually becomes less arduous as the crest of the ridge rounds over to reach the crest.

-----------------------------------------------------------------------

[*]  To get there, see [57] **Walk-About Guide to Wolverine Bowl Trail.**

From the top of the buttress one should now have a clear view of the summit of Wolverine Peak located approximately 1 mile farther up the ridge to the left (southeast). Turning toward the summit, continue up the crest of ridge, following the sporadic sheep trails that wind up the ridge wherever possible. Approximately 0.75 miles up the ridge this route reaches Wolverine Peak Trail. Hopping onto this trail, follow it the last 0.25 miles up to the summit of Wolverine Peak (4,455 feet).

From the summit one can then turn around and follow Wolverine Peak Trail 3 miles down to Wolverine Bowl Trail. Upon reaching Wolverine Bowl Trail turn left (south). Then follow this trail for approximately 2 miles back to Prospect Heights parking area.

**TRAIL GRADE:** This traverse rates Grade 2 and Grade 3 as a hike on the climb to the summit of Near Point. On the far side of the summit, this traverse crosses a short section of Grade 5 scrambling. The route then fluctuates between grades 4 and 5 as a hike as it ascends the ridge to the buttress of Wolverine Peak. Where this route joins Wolverine Peak Trail the route lowers to Grade 3 as a hike. The route then drops to Grade 2 as a hike where, after descending Wolverine Peak, it turns onto Wolverine Bowl Trail.

**TRAIL CONDITION:** This traverse varies but little in its conditions. For much of its length the Wolverine Bowl Trail follows an old road, which has only some muddy sections along its length. On beginning to climb Near Point, however, the trail narrows as it crosses more and wider mud holes. Beyond the summit of Near Point, one has to push through some brush and scramble alongside the rock-ledged ridge crest. From the saddle and up to the top of the buttress of Wolverine Peak, one traverses mostly rocky tundra mixed with scattered patches of scree. Along Wolverine Peak's ridge the route follows some sporadic sheep trails until it reaches Wolverine Peak Trail. From the summit back to Prospect Heights parking area, one again follows trail, which widens and flattens the nearer one gets to the parking area.

**TRAIL MILEAGE:** This entire traverse from Prospect Heights parking area and back entails approximately 12 miles of hiking.

Overlooking the Anchorage Bowl
from the ridge behind Wolverine Peak

**TOTAL ELEVATION GAIN:** To hike this entire traverse from Prospect Heights parking area and back entails a total elevation gain of approximately 4,000 feet.

**HIGH POINT:** This traverse reaches its highest point of 4,455 feet above sea level at the summit of Wolverine Peak.

**NORMAL HIKING TIME:** To hike this entire traverse from Prospect Heights parking area and back entails approximately should take anywhere from 6 to 10 hours, depending on the condition and ambition of the hiker(s) involved.

**CAMPSITES:** One will find no designated campsites along this trail. Nor should one need any, given that most people do this as a day hike. One can find some decent places on which to pitch a tent, however, in the saddle between Near Point and Wolverine Peak as well as in some of the meadows just off the trails below tree line.

**BEST TIME:** Most people should find any time from June to September a good time to do this traverse. One should think twice about doing this traverse in the winter, however, because of the avalanche danger between Near Point and the upper ridge of Wolverine Peak.

**USGS MAPS:** Anchorage A-7 and A-8 NE.

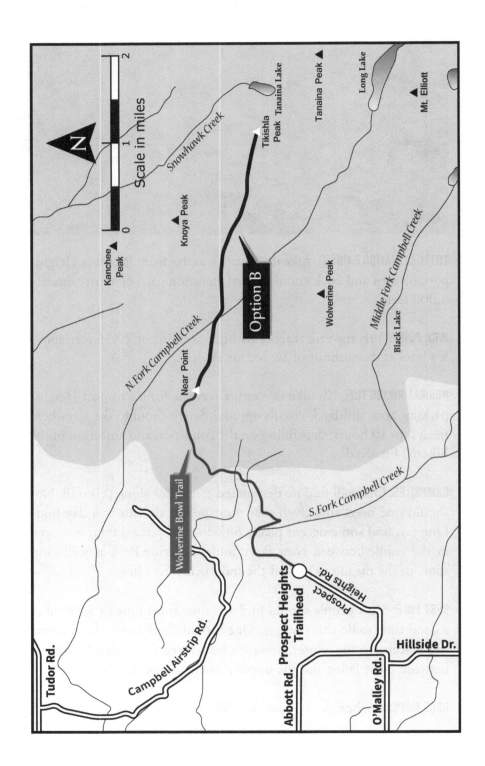

Scale in miles

N

Kanchee Peak ▲

Knoya Peak ▲

Snowhawk Creek

Tikishla Peak ▲

Tanaina Lake

Tanaina Peak ▲

Long Lake

Mt. Elliott ▲

N. Fork Campbell Creek

Option B

Near Point

Wolverine Peak ▲

Middle Fork Campbell Creek

Black Lake

Wolverine Bowl Trail

S. Fork Campbell Creek

Tudor Rd.

Campbell Airstrip Rd.

Prospect Heights Trailhead

Prospect Heights Rd.

Abbott Rd.

Hillside Dr.

O'Malley Rd.

# OPTION B

# Tikishla Peak from Near Point

This guide describes just one of a number of different routes to the summit of Tikishla Peak. This volume, for instance, contains two other routes to Tikishla Peak. The first, [68] **OPTION G—Tikishla Peak from Williwaw Lakes Trail** found below, describes the hardest and longest route to Tikishla Peak. The other, [71] **OPTION B—Tikishla Peak** found in Chapter 6, describes arguably the easiest and shortest route to Tikishla Peak. That makes the description below the middle choice, containing as it does a relatively long route, but one that follows well-established trails for much of the way.

**TRAIL LOCATION:** This hike begins at the summit of Near Point[*]. From the top of Near Point continue along the faint trail leading straight ahead (east-southeast) along the ridge. In the first 0.5 miles the ridge occasionally narrows to stay close to the ridge crest. But none of these narrow sections last long or prove excessively dangerous.

Approximately 0.6 miles from Near Point the trail winds over a prominent bump (2,963 feet) and immediately drops 300 feet into a wide saddle. From the center of this saddle turn left (north) to descend the broad slope into the North Fork Campbell Creek. Continue descending all the way to the shore of the North Fork Campbell Creek and ford the creek. After fording the creek, slant up and into the long,

--------------------------------------------------

[*]   To get there, see [57] **Walk-About Guide to Wolverine Bowl Trail**.

wide, hanging valley that drops down from the opposite ridge from the convergence of the northwest and south ridge of Tikishla Peak.

Once in the hanging valley, follow it to its uppermost end. Then bear left (north) and climb to the crest of the ridge looming above. On reaching the crest of the ridge turn right (northeast) up the crest to the summit of Tikishla Peak (5,150 feet), the tallest of the numerous spires on the ridge.

At this point, one has little choice but to return the way they have come. Continuing along the ridge to West Tanaina Peak requires some very serious climbing, making most people opt to descend a long way into the North Fork Campbell Creek valley before turning back up to the ridge. Continuing along the ridge in the opposite direction to Knoya Peak also requires some steep ridge walking as well, followed by a very brushy crossing North Fork Campbell Creek valley back to Near Point or else coming out via Ice Cream Cone Trail to Basher Road*. Most people will therefore choose to simply return the way they have come and hike back to Prospect Heights parking area.

**TRAIL GRADE:** This climb initially rates Grade 2 and Grade 3 as a hike on the climb to the summit of Near Point. Past the summit of Near Point this traverse crosses a short section of Grade 5 scrambling along the ridge just east of Nar Point. The route then fluctuates between grades 4 and 5 as it descends into the North Fork Campbell Creek valley and climbs into the hanging valley below Tikishla. On the climb out of the hanging valley to the ridge above the rate increases to Grade 5 as a hike. Finally, one must pass through short sections rated Grade 6 as a hike along the summit ridge and on the final scramble up the summit spire.

**TRAIL CONDITION:** This traverse varies considerably in its conditions. For much of its length the Wolverine Bowl Trail follows an old road, which has only some muddy sections along its length. On beginning the climb to Near Point, however, the trail narrows as it crosses more and wider mud holes. Beyond the summit of Near Point, one has to push through some brush and scramble along the rock-ledged ridge crest before descending to the

--------------------------------------------------------------

* For more information about that trail, see [69] **Walk-About Guide to Ice Cream Cone Trail** in Chapter 6.

saddle. Upon descending from the saddle into the North Fork Campbell Creek valley, one crosses mostly rocky tundra mixed with scattered patches of scree. One must then push through some minor brush when crossing the North Fork Campbell Creek, but this soon gives way to more tundra and scree on the climb into the bowl below Tikishla Peak.

The climb to the summit of Tikishla Peak then includes first climbing through the boulder and scree of the lower bowl and then skirting around lots of boulders, ledges, and scree once one is on the summit ridge. The climb ends with a last scramble up the summit spire.

**TRAIL MILEAGE:** To go from Prospect Heights to Tikishla Peak entails 9 miles of hiking, for a round-trip total of 18 miles.

**TOTAL ELEVATION GAIN:** To hike from the Prospect Heights parking area to the summit of Tikishla Peak and back entails a total elevation gain of approximately 5,000 feet.

**HIGH POINT:** This hike reaches its highest point of 5,150 feet above sea level at the summit of Tikishla Peak.

**NORMAL HIKING TIME:** To hike from Prospect Heights parking area to the summit of Tikishla Peak and back should take 1 to 2 days, depending on the condition and ambition of the hiker(s) involved.

**CAMPSITES:** There are no designated camp sites along this route. One should find some fine places on which to pitch a tent, however, in the North Fork Campbell Creek valley as well as in the bowl below the summit of Tikishla Peak.

**BEST TIME:** Most people should find any time from June to September a good time to do this hike. One should think twice about doing this hike in winter, however, because of the high avalanche danger both in the descent into the North Fork Campbell Creek valley and in the final climb from the bowl to the summit of Tikishla Peak.

**USGS MAPS:** Anchorage A-7 and A-8 NE.

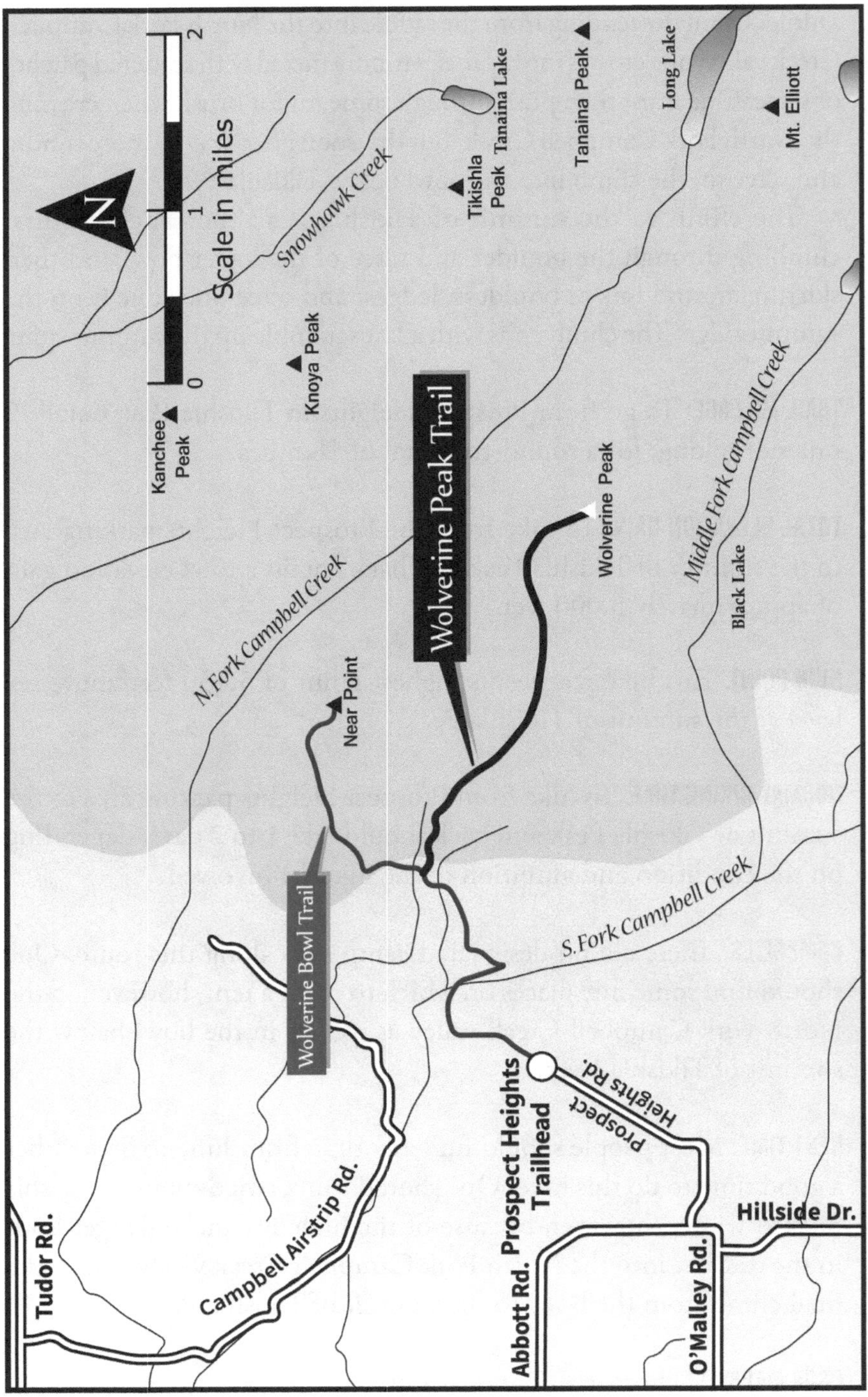

N
Scale in miles
0
1
2
Kanchee Peak
Knoya Peak
Snowhawk Creek
Tikishla Peak
Tanaina Lake
Tanaina Peak
Long Lake
Mt. Elliott
Wolverine Peak Trail
Wolverine Peak
Middle Fork Campbell Creek
Black Lake
N. Fork Campbell Creek
Near Point
Wolverine Bowl Trail
S. Fork Campbell Creek
Prospect Heights Trailhead
Prospect Heights Rd.
Campbell Airstrip Rd.
Tudor Rd.
Abbott Rd.
O'Malley Rd.
Hillside Dr.

# Walk-About Guide to Wolverine Peak Trail

After Flattop Mountain, Wolverine Peak may rank second as the most climbed peak in the Front Range. Yet this mountain requires one to hike considerably farther and climb significantly higher, making it more of a challenge. It also makes standing on the summit more rewarding—both for the effort required and the view rewarded.

**TRAIL LOCATION:** Wolverine Peak Trail begins 2 miles along Wolverine Bowl Trail*. To get there drive 6.2 miles south from Anchorage on the Seward Highway. There, just after Milepost 121, take a right (west) onto the O'Malley Road exit. At the end of the ramp, turn left (east) and cross back under the highway. Continue straight on O'Malley Road as it ascends past Lake Otis Parkway and the Anchorage Zoo. Approximately 3 miles from the Seward Highway this road reaches a junction with Hillside Road leading right (south). Staying on O'Malley Road, follow it to where in less than 100 yards it swings left and turns into Hillside Drive leading north. Almost immediately after Hillside Drive straightens out, it reaches the junction with Upper O'Malley Road on the right (east). Turn right onto Upper O'Malley Road. Approximately 0.5 miles later, this road ends at a T-intersection with Prospect Drive. Turn left (north) on Prospect Drive and follow it for 1 mile to a stop sign. Bear left through the stop sign onto Siderof Lane. In approximately 200 yards this road reaches the entrance to Chugach State Park on the right (north). Turn into the parking area and park wherever available. Wolverine Bowl Trail begins just to the

* For more information about that trail, see [57] **Walk-About Guide to Wolverine Bowl Trail**.

right of an outhouse and signboard at the fire gate at the far end of the parking area.

From Prospect Heights parking area follow Wolverine Bowl Trail for approximately 2 miles, crossing over Middle Fork Campbell Creek and passing by the junction with Middle Fork Loop Trail, to where it swings up and across the base of Wolverine Peak. Just after crossing a wide short bridge over a small stream, the trail reaches the marked junction with Wolverine Peak Trail on the right (east).

Wolverine Peak Trail begins its climb to the summit of Wolverine Peak almost immediately. After first ascending through some spruce, the trail climbs into a series of open meadows. Just beyond the meadows the trail bears right (southeast) as it turns more sharply upward to begin climbing the flank of the central buttress of the mountain that extends out from the face of the mountain. Contouring upward along the buttress's left (north) side, the trail reaches the crest near the far (east) end of the buttress. The trail next bears left (east) up the crest of the buttress for the climb to the summit ridge. Though not long, this climb may seem to take a long time as it winds upward in that the view changes only very slowly as one climbs above the nearby ridges. As it nears the crest of the summit ridge, the trail turns right (southeast) for the last 0.25 miles of scenic climbing to the summit of Wolverine Peak (4,455 feet).

**TRAIL GRADE:** Wolverine Peak Trail rates a consistent Grade 3 as a hike for its entire length.

**TRAIL CONDITION:** This trail varies little in its conditions. Though muddy in spots, the trail generally remains wide and easy to follow, with only loose dirt and scattered rocks and scree even on the upper mountain.

**TRAIL MILEAGE:** To go from the beginning of Wolverine Peak Trail to the summit of Wolverine Peak entails approximately 3 miles of hiking, for a round-trip total of 6 miles. This means that from the Prospect Heights parking area to the summit of Wolverine Peak entails approximately 5 miles of hiking, for a round-trip total of 10 miles.

**TOTAL ELEVATION GAIN:** To hike from Prospect Heights parking area to the summit of Wolverine Peak entails a total elevation gain of approximately 3,350 feet.

**HIGH POINT:** This trail reaches its highest point of 4,455 feet above sea level at the summit of Wolverine Peak.

**NORMAL HIKING TIME:** To hike from Prospect Heights parking area to the summit of Wolverine Peak and back should take anywhere from 5 to 8 hours, depending on the condition and ambition of the hiker(s) involved.

**CAMPSITES:** One will find no designated campsites along this trail. Nor should one need any, given that most people do this as a day hike. One can find some decent places on which to pitch a tent, however, on the central buttress of the mountain as well in some of the meadows just off the trail below tree line.

**BEST TIME:** Most people should find any time from June to September a good time to do this traverse. This climb also makes a fine ski or snowshoe outing in the winter.

**USGS MAPS:** Anchorage A-7 and A-8 NE.

Just below the summit of Wolverine Peak

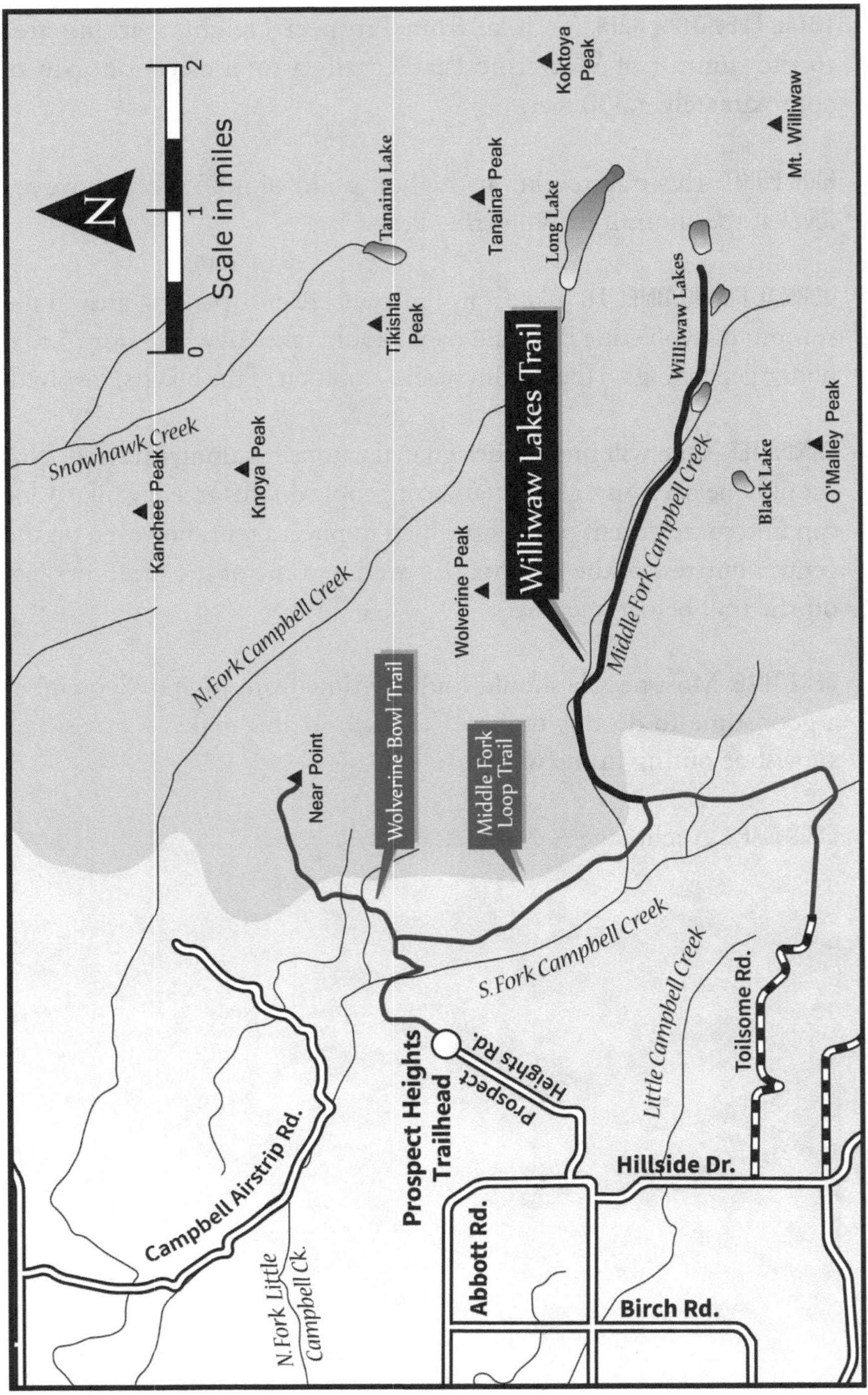
N
Scale in miles
0
1
2
Snowhawk Creek
Kanchee Peak
Knoya Peak
Tikishla Peak
Tanaina Lake
Tanaina Peak
Koktoya Peak
Long Lake
Mt. Williwaw
Williwaw Lakes
Williwaw Lakes Trail
Wolverine Peak
N. Fork Campbell Creek
Middle Fork Campbell Creek
Black Lake
O'Malley Peak
Near Point
Wolverine Bowl Trail
Middle Fork Loop Trail
S. Fork Campbell Creek
Little Campbell Creek
Toilsome Rd.
Prospect Heights Trailhead
Prospect Heights Rd.
Campbell Airstrip Rd.
Hillside Dr.
Abbott Rd.
Birch Rd.
N. Fork Little Campbell Ck.

# Walk-About Guide to Williwaw Lakes Trail

This relatively flat trail ends at the shores of the numerous Williwaw Lakes. One need not end one's hike at the lakes, though. The end of the trail marks the beginning of a number of more adventurous off-trail hikes and climbs. The most popular of these hikes first continues over the pass just west of Mount Williwaw and down to Long Lake, and then follows North Fork Campbell Creek down valley to where a final climb over Near Point (or Wolverine Peak) connects back to the beginning of Middle Fork Loop Trail*. This first option leads to yet other options, including a traverse from Mount Elliot to Wolverine Peak, as well as climbs of Koktoya Peak, East Tanaina Peak and West Tanaina Peak, and Tikishla Peak**. Thus, like so many other hikes in the Chugach Mountains, this trail makes available a number of options, which often branch out into other options, and other options, and so on and so on.

**TRAIL LOCATION:** Williwaw Lakes Trail begins approximately 2 miles from the northern end of Middle Fork Loop Trail at its junction with Wolverine Bowl Trail. To get there drive 6.2 miles south from Anchorage on the Seward Highway. There, just after Milepost 121, take a right (west) onto the O'Malley Road exit. At the end of the

---

\* For more information about this hike, see [63] **OPTION B—Traverse from Williwaw Lakes Trail to the North Fork Campbell Creek**.

\*\* For more information about these climbs, see [64] **OPTION C—Mount Williwaw,** [65] **OPTION D—Traverse from Mount Elliot to Wolverine Peak,** [66] **OPTION E—Ship Creek Overlook and Koktoya Peak,** [67] **OPTION F—East and West Tanaina Peaks,** and [68] **OPTION G—Tikishla Peak from Williwaw Lakes Trail**.

ramp, turn left (east) and cross back under the highway. Continue straight on O'Malley Road as it ascends past Lake Otis Parkway and the Anchorage Zoo. Approximately 3 miles from the Seward Highway this road reaches a junction with Hillside Road leading right (south). Staying on O'Malley Road, follow it to where in less than 100 yards it swings left and turns into Hillside Drive leading north. Almost immediately after Hillside Drive straightens out, it reaches the junction with Upper O'Malley Road on the right (east). Turn right onto Upper O'Malley Road. Approximately 0.5 miles later, this road ends at a T-intersection with Prospect Drive. Turn left (north) on Prospect Drive and follow it for 1 mile to a stop sign. Bear left through the stop sign onto Siderof Lane. In approximately 200 yards this road reaches the entrance to Chugach State Park on the right (north). Turn into the parking area and park wherever available. Wolverine Bowl Trail begins just to the right of an outhouse and signboard at the fire gate at the far end of the parking area.

From Prospect Heights parking area follow Wolverine Bowl Trail for approximately 1.2 miles to its junction with Middle Fork Loop Trail*. Turn right (south) on Middle Fork Loop Trail and follow it for approximately 2 miles until, just after it crosses the Middle Fork Campbell Creek and contours up and around a low buttress, it reaches the junction with Williwaw Lakes Trail on the left (east).

Williwaw Lakes Trail begins by climbing shallowly up a wide hollow. Upon nearing the right (south) shore of Middle Fork Campbell Creek it bears right (east) to follow the creek up valley. In the next 2 miles of this hike upstream one has to dodge or leap many excessively muddy sections. Eventually the trail mounts a bench higher above the creek. The trail remains on this bench during its climb above tree line. At about the same time as one reaches tree line, the lowest of the Williwaw Lakes should come into view.

Staying above the right (south) side of the lakes, the trail continues past two more smaller lakes before reaching the largest of the lower Williwaw Lakes. (Other lakes, which one cannot see from this trail,

---

\* For more information about that trail,
see [41] **Walk-About Guide to Middle Fork Loop Trail** in Chapter 3.

forming what geologists call "rosary bead" lakes, continue in a series of steps up to the pass high in the valley to the upper northeast that separates the Middle Fork Campbell Creek from the North Fork Campbell Creek.)

Once past this large lake, the trail crosses a boulder field and descends through some thick, waist-high brush to where it ends at a small waterfall feeding the upper end of the uppermost lake. From the end of this trail one has a number of options from which to choose. First one can continue the traverse over the pass to the north and descend the North Fork Campbell Creek valley to where one can climb over Near Point or Wolverine Pea back to Prospect Heights parking area[*]. Second, one can climb Williwaw Peak via the pass leading over into North Fork Campbell Creek[**]. Third, one can climb toward the pass leading to North Fork Campbell Creek and then turn left (west) to climb Mount Elliot and from there continue along the ridge to Wolverine Peak[***]. Fourth, one can cross the pass leading over into North Fork Campbell Creek and there turn right (east) to climb to the overlook between Mount Williwaw and Koktoya Peak and from there climb Koktoya Peak[****]. Fifth, one can cross the pass leading over into North Fork Campbell Creek and there cross the valley to climb East and West Tanaina peaks[*****]. Sixth, one can cross the pass leading over into North Fork Campbell Creek and there continue down the valley to climb Tikishla Peak[******].

-------------------------------------------------------------------------

[*]    For more information about this hike, see [63] **OPTION B—Traverse from Williwaw Lakes Trail to The North Fork Campbell Creek**.

[**]   For more information about this climb, see [64] **OPTION C—Williwaw Peak**.

[***]  For more information about this trip,
       see [65] **OPTION D—Traverse from Mount Elliot to Wolverine Peak**.

[****] For more information about that hike,
       see [66] **OPTION E—Ship Creek Overlook and Koktoya Peak**.

[*****] For more information about that trip,
       see [67] **OPTION F—East and West Tanaina Peaks**.

[******] For more information about that climb,
       see [68] **OPTION G—Tikishla Peak from Williwaw Lakes Trail**.

**TRAIL GRADE:** The Williwaw Lakes Trail rates Grade 1 as a hike, with sections of Grade 2 hiking as one climbs past the uppermost lakes to the end of the trail.

**TRAIL CONDITION:** This trail varies little in its conditions. Though predominantly flat, the first miles of this trail cross some long boggy and muddy sections. Only after winding through approximately 2 miles of swamp and scrub spruce does the trail finally reach higher and drier ground. It then passes over some boulder fields as it contours past the lower Williwaw Lakes. As it approaches its end, where it passes around the upper end of the last lower lake, it again encounters much brush.

**TRAIL MILEAGE:** To go from the junction with Middle Fork Loop Trail to the end of Williwaw Lakes Trail just beyond the uppermost Williwaw Lake entails 4 miles of hiking, for a round-trip total of 8 miles. This means that to go from the Prospect Heights parking area to the end of Williwaw Lakes Trail entails approximately 7 miles of hiking, for a round-trip total of 14 miles.

**TOTAL ELEVATION GAIN:** To hike from the junction with Middle Fork Loop Trail to the end of Williwaw Lakes Trail just beyond the uppermost Williwaw Lake entails a total elevation gain of approximately 1,000 feet. This means that to hike from the Prospect Heights parking area to the end of Williwaw Lakes Trail entails a total elevation of approximately 1,700 feet.

**HIGH POINT:** This trail reaches its highest point of approximately 2,800 feet above sea level at the end of Williwaw Lakes Trail just beyond the uppermost Williwaw Lake.

**NORMAL HIKING TIME:** To hike from the junction with Middle Fork Loop Trail to the end of Williwaw Lakes Trail just beyond the uppermost Williwaw Lake should take anywhere from 1.5 to 3 hours, depending on the condition and ambition of the hiker(s) involved. This means that to hike from Prospect Heights parking area to the end of Williwaw

Lakes Trail and back should take anywhere from 5 to 10 hours, also depending on the hiker(s) involved.

**CAMPSITES:** One will find no designated camp sites along this trail. One can find some fine places on which to pitch a tent, however, in the open tundra around the junction of Middle Fork Loop Trail and Williwaw Lakes Trail as well as on many of the tundra bluffs around Williwaw Lakes.

**BEST TIME:** Most people should find anytime from May to early October the best time to do this hike. It also makes a fine ski or snowshoe outing in the winter, although one should remain wary of potential avalanches in the upper valley around the lakes.

**USGS MAPS:** Anchorage A-7 and A-8.

Williwaw Lakes Trail

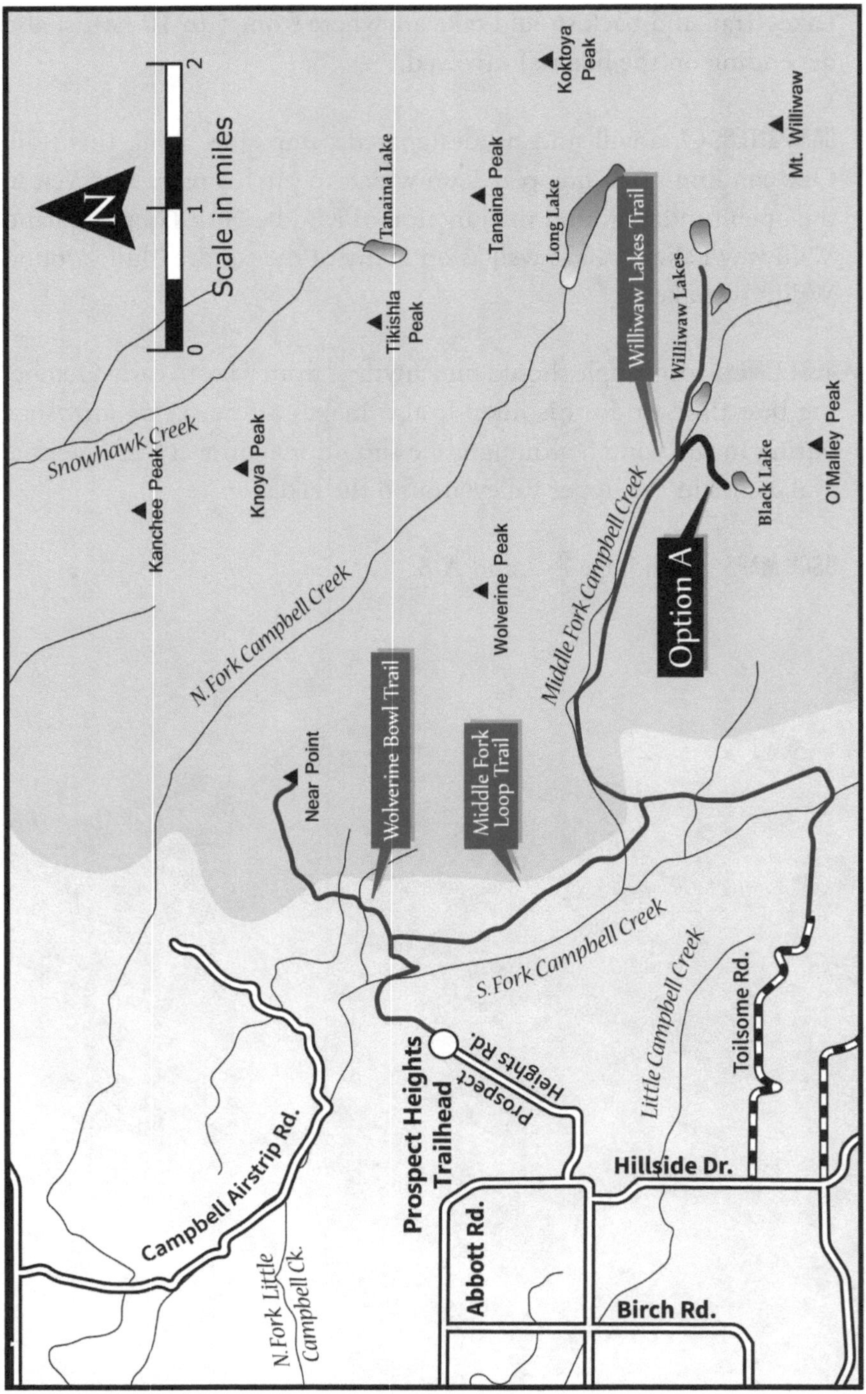
N
Scale in miles
0
1
2
Koktoya Peak
Mt. Williwaw
Tanaina Lake
Tanaina Peak
Long Lake
Williwaw Lakes Trail
Williwaw Lakes
Tikishla Peak
Snowhawk Creek
Kanchee Peak
Knoya Peak
O'Malley Peak
Black Lake
Option A
Middle Fork Campbell Creek
N. Fork Campbell Creek
Wolverine Peak
Wolverine Bowl Trail
Near Point
Middle Fork Loop Trail
S. Fork Campbell Creek
Little Campbell Creek
Toilsome Rd.
Prospect Heights Trailhead
Prospect Heights Rd.
Campbell Airstrip Rd.
Hillside Dr.
Abbott Rd.
Birch Rd.
N. Fork Little Campbell Ck.

# OPTION A

# Black Lake

The name of this small body of water tucked in a cirque below O'Malley Peak's northeast shoulder seems both wrong and right. Because it has no creek or stream entering it, it should technically have the name of Black Tarn. But apart from this technical quibble the name seems poetically right. The word 'black' fits it in two ways. First, its opaque waters at time shine like obsidian. Second, the cirque which encloses it allows very little sunlight to reflect on its waters. Throughout most of the winter it receives no direct sunlight and even during the summer it receives only some direct sunlight in the early morning and late afternoon. No matter what its name, though, this lake occupies a wondrous little corner of the Front Range. With only a small opening to the north by which to enter the cirque and the 5,000-foot summits of O'Malley Peak and Hidden Peak towering directly above its southern shore, it makes for a quite a dramatic destination.

**TRAIL LOCATION:** The rough trail leading up to Black Lake begins approximately 2.75 miles up Williwaw Lakes Trail[*]. There, just as one approaches the first of the Williwaw Lakes, one should see up to the right (south) a large gap in the ridge. A little way farther along the trail, and just before reaching the narrow creek spilling out of that gap, one should come upon a trail on the right (south) that climbs

--------------------------------------------------------------------

[*]    To get there, see [61] **Walk-About Guide to Williwaw Lakes Trail**.

up the slope toward that gap. This trail leads to Black Lakes. (One will know they have missed this trail if they reach the narrow creek cascading down the same slope. If this does occur, one can just easily climb up along the creek as opposed to turning back and looking for the trail.)

Turning right onto this trail, follow it up the open slope toward the gap in the ridge directly above. In approximately 0.25 miles the trail begins to roll over the top of the slope and level out. In another approximately 0.2 miles the trail curls over a small rise and drops to the north shore of Black Lake.

At this point, one has two major options. First, they can turn around and return the way they have come. Second, they can follow the trail winding up the slope behind the far right (southwest) corner of the lake up to The Ballpark and out O'Malley Peak Trail to Glen Alps parking area*.

**TRAIL GRADE:** Williwaw Lakes Trail to the junction with the trail leading to Black Lake rates Grade 1 as a hike. The trail up to Black Lake rates 2 as a hike.

**TRAIL CONDITION:** This route varies little in its conditions. Though predominantly flat, the first miles of Williwaw Lakes Trail crosses numerous boggy and muddy sections. Only after winding through approximately 2 miles of swamp and scrub spruce does the trail finally reach higher and drier ground. From Williwaw Lakes Trail to Black Lake, on the other hand, remains firm underfoot.

**TRAIL MILEAGE:** To go from the beginning of Williwaw Lakes Trail to Black Lake entails 3.5 miles of hiking, for a round-trip total of 7 miles. This means that to go from Prospect Heights parking area to Black Lake entails approximately 6.5 miles of hiking, for a round-trip total of 13 miles.

--------------------------------------------------------------------

\* For information about that route, see [44] **OPTION A—Traverse from O'Malley Peak Trail to Williwaw Lakes Trail** in Chapter 3.

**TOTAL ELEVATION GAIN:** To hike from the beginning of Williwaw Lakes Trail to the shores of Black Lake entails a total elevation gain of approximately 1,200 feet. This means that to hike from Prospect Heights parking area to the shore of Black Lake entails a total elevation of approximately 2,300 feet.

**HIGH POINT:** This trail reaches its highest point of approximately 2,800 feet above sea level at the shores of Black Lake.

**NORMAL HIKING TIME:** To hike from the beginning of Williwaw Lakes Trail to the shore of Black Lake and back should take anywhere from 3 to 5 hours, depending on the condition and ambition of the hiker(s) involved. This means that to hike from Prospect Heights parking area to the shore of Black Lake and back should take anywhere from 6 to 11 hours, also depending on the hiker(s) involved.

**CAMPSITES:** One will find no designated camp sites along this trail. One can find some fine places on which to pitch a tent, however, in the open tundra near the beginning Williwaw Lakes Trail and especially along the shore of Black Lake.

**BEST TIME:** Most people should find anytime from May to early October the best time to do this hike. It also makes a fine ski or snowshoe outing in the winter, although one should remain wary of potential avalanches in the upper valley around the lake.

**USGS MAPS:** Anchorage A-7 and A-8.

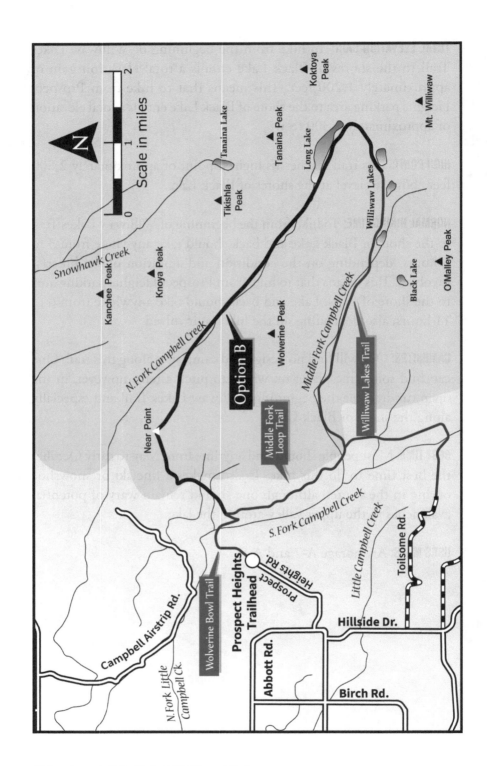

Koktoya Peak

Mt. Williwaw

Tanaina Lake

Tanaina Peak

Long Lake

Tikishla Peak

Williwaw Lakes

Kanchee Peak

Knoya Peak

Snowhawk Creek

O'Malley Peak

Black Lake

N. Fork Campbell Creek

Middle Fork Campbell Creek

Option B

Wolverine Peak

Near Point

Williwaw Lakes Trail

Middle Fork Loop Trail

S. Fork Campbell Creek

Campbell Airstrip Rd.

Wolverine Bowl Trail

Prospect Heights Trailhead

Prospect Heights Rd.

Little Campbell Creek

Toilsome Rd.

Hillside Dr.

Abbott Rd.

Birch Rd.

N. Fork Little Campbell Ck.

Scale in miles

N

0    1    2

## OPTION B

# Traverse from Williwaw Lakes Trail to North Fork Campbell Creek

**TRAIL LOCATION:** This hike begins where Williwaw Lakes Trail ends*. Upon reaching the end of Williwaw Lakes Trail just beyond the uppermost Williwaw Lake, bear left (north) and cross the stream feeding into the lake. Then begin to climb the series of benches leading up through the wide gap between Mount Elliot on the left (west) and Mount Williwaw on the right (east). (One can also begin this ascent earlier along the Williwaw Lakes Trail. Just look for a place to cross the valley below the lowest of the Williwaw Lakes and start up around the base of Mount Elliot toward the pass.) As one climbs, angle toward the left (west) side of the pass to find a path leading up and around the left side of the "rosary-bead" string of lakes that fill the basin of each consecutively higher bench.

After approximately 1 mile of climbing the route reaches the final, and steepest, section of the climb up to the pass separating Middle Fork Campbell Creek from North Fork Campbell Creek. Starting up the main gully of the wall, climb to the pass above. On reaching the pass (approximately 3,750 feet) one should now have a fine view of the upper end of the North Fork Campbell Creek valley 600 feet below.

From this point many may find the direct descent down the far side of the pass too steep for their liking. If so, bear right (east) along the crest of the ridge and descend the shallower slope to the tarn just below the northeast side of pass. (This tarn lies at the base of a textbook example of a rock glacier.) Once at the shore of the tarn, follow its

---

\* To get there, see [61] **Walk-About Guide to Williwaw Lakes Trail**.

outlet down to the eastern end of Long Lake. Here one find evidence of a rough trail leading down the entire left (south) side of Long Lake to the open tundra beyond. From the far end of Long Lake, continue down the left (south) side of the valley.

One now has two choices regarding how to ascend the ridge looming above the left (south) side of the valley. The first, though requiring a greater amount of climbing, offers the option of coming out over the high and scenic summit of Wolverine Peak. The second comes out over lower summit of Near Point.

To come out over the summit of Wolverine Peak, first continue approximately 1 mile down valley from the western end of Long Lake. Then, having passed the rockiest sections of the ridge above and to the left (south), look for the wide grassy slope leading up to the low point on the ridge. Angling up the slope, climb to ridge's crest. Once on the ridge bear right (west) and follow the faint sheep trail along the ridge. In approximately 1 mile of increasingly steeper climbing, the ridge reaches the summit of Wolverine Peak (4,455 feet). From the summit descend the Wolverine Peak Trail 3 miles down the front of the mountain to the Wolverine Bowl Trail. On reaching the Wolverine Bowl Trail turn left (south) and hike the last 2 miles back to Prospect Heights parking area[*].

To come out over the summit of Near Point, first continue approximately 2 miles down valley from the western end of Long Lake. Then look up and to the left (southwest) for the saddle between the northwest buttress of Wolverine Peak and the summit of Near Point. When this saddle comes into view, begin contouring up to it, crossing numerous gullies on the way. Once on the saddle bear right (west) and follow the rough trail along the sometimes narrow ridge for approximately 0.5 miles to the summit of Near Point (3,050 feet). From the summit follow the Wolverine Bowl Trail the 4 miles back to Prospect Heights parking area[**].

--------------------------------------------------------------------------

[*]   For more information about those trails, see [60] **Walk-About Guide to Wolverine Peak Trail** and [57] **Walk-About Guide to Wolverine Bowl Trail**.

[**]  For more information about that trail, see [57] **Walk-About Guide to Wolverine Bowl Trail**.

**TRAIL GRADE:** Wolverine Bowl Trail, Middle Fork Loop Trail, and Williwaw Lakes Trail all rate predominantly Grade 1 as a hike, with some very short rough or steep sections that rate Grade 2 as a hike. On leaving the end of Williwaw Lakes Trail and beginning the climb to the pass, the traverse rates Grade 4 as a hike, with short climbs, such as the last one to the pass, rated Grade 5 as a hike. The descent of the North Fork Campbell Creek valley rates Grade 4 as a hike. The climb out of the valley to the summit of Wolverine Peak or Near Point the traverse once more rates Grade 5 as a hike. It remains Grade 5 as a hike until one begins the descent on either mountain back to Prospect Heights parking area, at which time the route again rates Grade 1 to Grade 2 as a hike.

**TRAIL CONDITION:** This trail varies greatly in its conditions. Wolverine Bowl Trail and Middle Fork Loop Trail remain relatively flat and dry for their entire lengths. In comparison, the first 2 miles of Williwaw Lakes Trail often has long boggy and muddy sections. After winding through these first miles of swamp and scrub spruce does the trail reach higher and drier ground. The trail then passes over some boulder fields as it contours past the lower lakes, after which it pushes through some low brush as it approaches its end at the upper end of the last lake. On leaving the uppermost end of Williwaw Lakes Trail, the route crosses mostly open tundra. It then follows a relatively well-pronounced trail up to base of the pass between Mount Elliot and Mount Williwaw. From that point, one crosses mostly trackless tundra down to the rough trail along the south shore of Long Lake to the tundra beyond.

If one comes out over the summit of Wolverine Peak, the traverse crosses mostly open tundra. Along the ridge, one follows a sheep trail that becomes more pronounced the closer one gets to the summit. From the summit of Wolverine Peak the trails leading back down the front of the mountain only get better and better as one nears Prospect Heights parking area.

If one comes out over the summit of Near Point, the traverse crosses a number of gullies to reach the saddle between Wolverine Peak and Near Point. The climb to the summit of Near Point requires traversing a sometimes narrow ridge. From the summit of Near Point, however, the trail leading back down the front of the mountain only gets better and better as it nears Prospect Heights parking area.

**TRAIL MILEAGE:** This entire traverse from Prospect Heights parking area and back entails approximately 18 miles of hiking. This mileage remains largely the same regardless of whether one comes over the summit of Wolverine Peak or Near Point.

**TOTAL ELEVATION GAIN:** To hike this entire traverse from Prospect Heights parking area and back entails a total elevation gain of approximately 5,000 feet if one chooses to come out over the summit of Wolverine Peak and approximately 3,550 feet if one comes out over the summit of Near Point.

**HIGH POINT:** This traverse reaches its highest point of 4,455 feet above sea level at the summit of Wolverine Peak if one chooses to come out over Wolverine Peak. This traverse reaches its highest point of approximately 3,750 feet above sea level at the top of the pass between Mount Williwaw and Mount Elliot if one comes out over the summit of Near Point.

**NORMAL HIKING TIME:** To hike this entire traverse from Prospect Heights parking area and back should take anywhere from 8 hours to 2 days, depending on the condition and ambition of the hiker(s) involved.

**CAMPSITES:** One will find no designated campsites along this trail. One can find some fine places on which to pitch a tent, however, in the many open areas around any of the Williwaw Lakes, around any of the "rosary-bead" lakes leading up to the pass, and along almost the entire length of the North Fork Campbell Creek valley.

**BEST TIME:** Most people should find any time from June to September a good time to do this traverse. It also can make fine ski or snowshoe trip in the winter, although one should remain very wary of the avalanche danger on climbing over the pass between Williwaw Lakes and Long Lake as well as on the north flank of Near Point.

**USGS MAPS:** Anchorage A-7 and A-8 NE, and A-8 SE.

Descending into the North Fork Campbell Creek valley

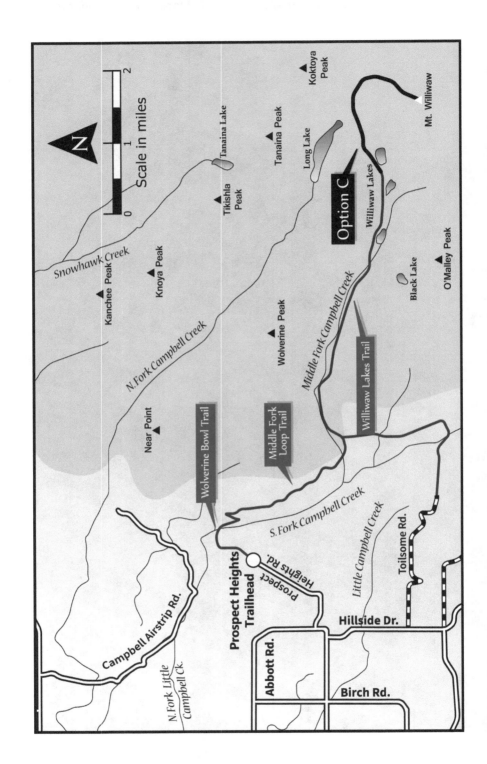

Scale in miles

N

Koktoya Peak

Mt. Williwaw

Tanaina Lake

Tanaina Peak

Long Lake

Option C

Williwaw Lakes

Tikishla Peak

O'Malley Peak

Snowhawk Creek

Kanchee Peak Creek

Knoya Peak

Black Lake

Middle Fork Campbell Creek

N. Fork Campbell Creek

Wolverine Peak

Williwaw Lakes Trail

Near Point

Wolverine Bowl Trail

Middle Fork Loop Trail

S. Fork Campbell Creek

Little Campbell Creek

Toilsome Rd.

Campbell Airstrip Rd.

Prospect Heights Trailhead

Prospect Heights Rd.

N. Fork Little Campbell Ck.

Hillside Dr.

Abbott Rd.

Birch Rd.

# OPTION C

# Mount Williwaw

This guide offers an alternative way than that offered in Chapter 3 to approach and climb Mount Williwaw, the highest peak in the Front Range.

**TRAIL LOCATION:** This hike begins where Williwaw Lakes Trail ends[*]. Upon reaching the end of Williwaw Lakes Trail just beyond the uppermost Williwaw Lake, bear left (north) and cross the stream feeding into the lake. Then begin climbing the series of benches leading up through the wide gap between Mount Elliot on the left (west) and Mount Williwaw on the right (east). (One can also begin this ascent earlier along the Williwaw Lakes Trail. Just look for a place to cross the valley below the lowest of the Williwaw Lakes and start up around the base of Mount Elliot toward the pass.) As one climbs, angle toward the left (west) side of the pass to find a path leading up and around the left side of the "rosary-bead" string of lakes that fill the basin of each consecutively higher bench.

After approximately 1 mile of climbing the route reaches the final, and steepest, section of the climb up to the pass separating Middle Fork Campbell Creek from North Fork Campbell Creek. Starting up the main gully of the wall, climb to the pass above. On reaching the pass (approximately 3,750 feet) one should now have a fine view of the upper end of the North Fork Campbell Creek valley 600 feet below.

------------------------------------------------------------

[*]    To get there, see [61] **Walk-About Guide to Williwaw Lakes Trail**.

Up to this point this route has followed the same route as that followed in [63] **OPTION B—Traverse from Williwaw Lakes Trail to North Fork Campbell Creek** above. But now it diverges from that route.

With Mount Williwaw now towering overhead just to the right (east), one should also now have a clear view of the narrow alley leading up and to the left (north) to Mount Williwaw's jagged north ridge. This alley provides the easiest access to the saddle on that ridge. To get to that saddle with the least amount of elevation loss, turn right (east) from the pass and follow the crest of the ridge for approximately 100 yards to where two lakes come into sight below and to the left (northeast).

Descending from the ridge, pass around the left (north) side of both lakes, making sure to cross the second lake's outlet as close to the lake as possible. Having passed the second lake, turn right (east) up the alley way that leads up towards the top of the ridge. On reaching the saddle of the ridge (with its panoramic view of Ship Creek valley below) turn right (south) and follow the well-pronounced sheep trail up the ridge. After approximately 1 mile of steady climbing, the trail reaches the summit of Mount Williwaw (5,446 feet), the highest peak in the Front Range.

From the summit of Mount Williwaw one has three choices. First, one can go back the way one came. Second, one can continue straight ahead*. Third, and far more interesting, one can return to Prospect Heights parking area by descending the North Fork Campbell Creek valley and coming out over either Wolverine Peak or Near Point.

To begin this last option, first descend back down the ride and past the alley one has just ascended to the wide saddle below Koktoya Peak. From there turn left (west) off the ridge and descend the wide head of the valley down to the left (south) end of Long Lake. Here one should find the rough foot trail leading down the entire left (south) side of Long Lake to the open tundra beyond**.

------------------------------------------------------------------------

\*    For more information about that hike, see [42] **OPTION A—Traverse from Mount Williwaw to The Ramp** in Chapter 3.

\*\*   For information about the remainder of this route out, see [63] **OPTION B—Traverse from Williwaw Lakes Trail to North Fork Campbell Creek**.

**TRAIL GRADE:** Wolverine Bowl Trail, Middle Fork Loop Trail, and Williwaw Lakes Trail all rate predominantly Grade 1 as a hike, with some rough or steep sections rated to Grade 2 as a hike. On leaving the end of Williwaw Lakes Trail and beginning the climb to the saddle between Mount Elliot and Mount Williwaw, the traverse rates Grade 4 as a hike, with some short climbs, such as the last one to the pass, rising to Grade 5 as a hike. The next section leading past the lakes and up to saddle north of Mount Williwaw rates Grade 4 as a hike. The final climb up the sheep trail to the summit rates Grade 4 as a hike.

**TRAIL CONDITION:** This hike varies greatly in its conditions. Wolverine Bowl Trail and Middle Fork Loop Trail remain relatively flat and dry for their entire lengths. In comparison, the predominantly flat first 2 miles of Williwaw Lakes Trail crosses numerous boggy and muddy sections. Only after winding through 1.5 miles of boggy and scrubby terrain does the trail reach higher and drier ground. The trail then passes over some boulder fields as it contours past the lower lakes. Then after pushing through some low brush, approaches its end at the upper end of the last Williwaw Lake. On leaving Williwaw Lakes Trail, the route crosses mostly open tundra. It then follows a relatively well-pronounced primitive trail as it winds to the crest of the pass between Mount Elliot and Mount Williwaw.

The next section of the hike past the lakes and up to the saddle north of Mount Williwaw entails crossing mostly mixed tundra and scree. The final climb to the summit of Mount Williwaw follows a sheep trail over mostly tundra and scree.

**TRAIL MILEAGE:** To go from Prospect Heights parking area to the summit of Mount Williwaw entails approximately 13 miles of hiking, for a round-trip total of 26 miles.

**TOTAL ELEVATION GAIN:** Hiking from Prospect Heights parking area to the summit of Mount Williwaw entails a total elevation gain of approximately 5,700 feet.

**HIGH POINT:** This hike reaches its highest point of 5,446 feet above sea level at the summit of Mount Williwaw.

**NORMAL HIKING TIME:** To hike this entire traverse from Prospect Heights parking area to the summit of Mount Williwaw and back should take anywhere from 12 hours to 2 days depending on the ambition and condition of the hiker(s) involved.

**CAMPSITES:** One will find no designated campsites along this trail. One can find some fine places on which to pitch a tent, however, in the many open areas around any of the Williwaw Lakes, around any of the "rosary-bead" lakes leading up to the pass, and along almost the entire length of the North Fork Campbell Creek valley. The two secluded tarns just over the pass at the beginning of the climb up to the saddle north of Mount Williwaw have many particularly remote and dramatic places on which to pitch a tent near their shores. Some may even choose to pitch a tent at the crest of the pass north of Mount Williwaw, although one would have to rely on any possible lingering snowfields for a water source.

**BEST TIME:** Most people should find any time from June to September a good time to do this traverse. One should think twice about doing this hike in winter, however, because of the avalanche danger on climbing over the pass between Williwaw Lakes and Long Lake as well as on the climb to Mount Williwaw.

**USGS MAPS:** Anchorage A-7, A-8 NE, and A-8 SE.

On the ridge between Mount Williwaw and The Ramp

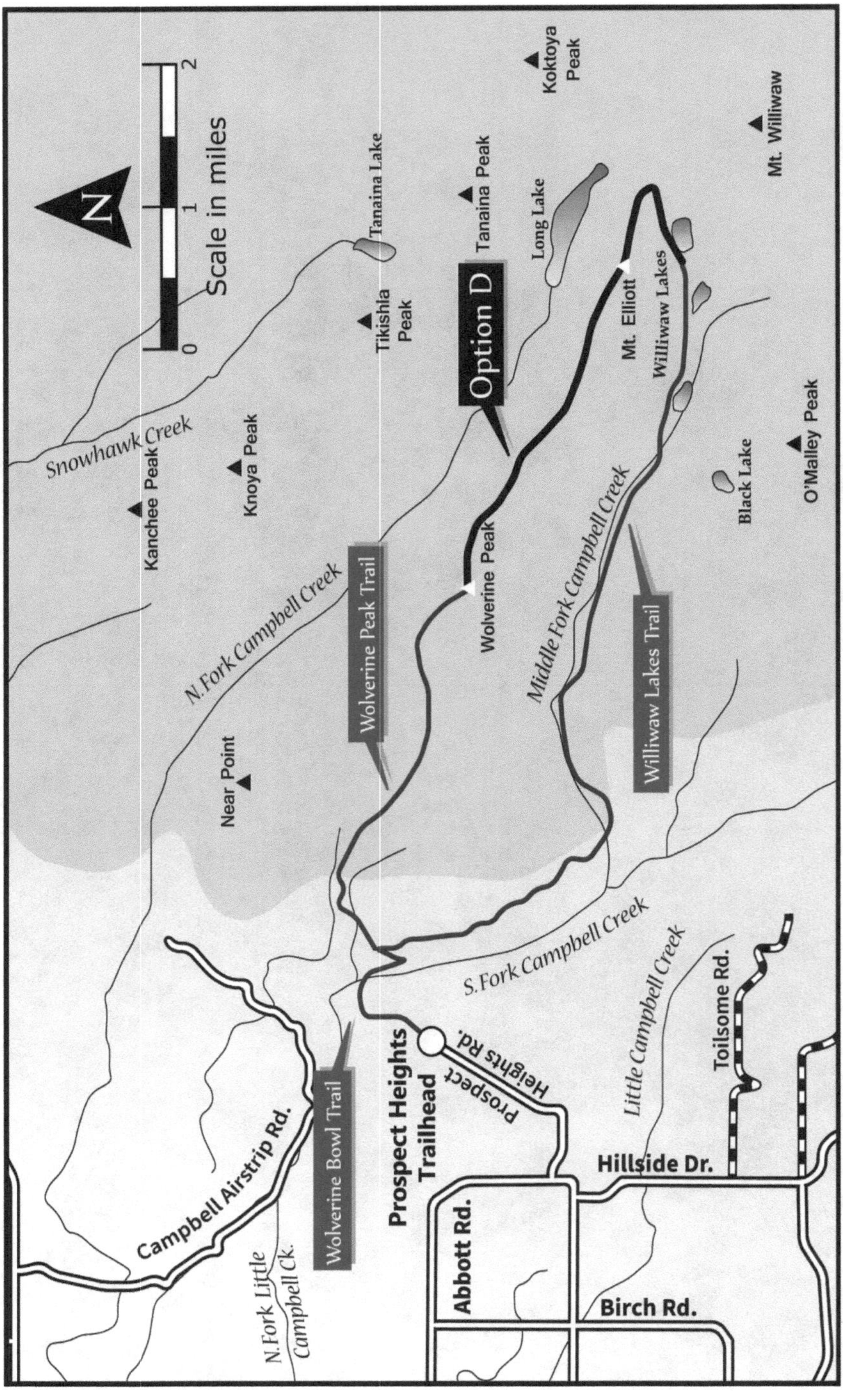
N
Scale in miles
0
1
2
Snowhawk Creek
Kanchee Peak
Knoya Peak
Tanaina Lake
Tikishla Peak
Tanaina Peak
Koktoya Peak
Long Lake
Option D
Mt. Elliott
Williwaw Lakes
Mt. Williwaw
O'Malley Peak
Black Lake
Wolverine Peak
Middle Fork Campbell Creek
Williwaw Lakes Trail
Wolverine Peak Trail
N. Fork Campbell Creek
Near Point
S. Fork Campbell Creek
Little Campbell Creek
Toilsome Rd.
Prospect Heights Trailhead
Prospect Heights Rd.
Hillside Dr.
Wolverine Bowl Trail
Campbell Airstrip Rd.
Abbott Rd.
Birch Rd.
N. Fork Little Campbell Ck.

# OPTION D

# Traverse from Mount Elliot to Wolverine Peak

Though not as popular as many other traverses in the Front Range this traverse has much to recommend it. It does take an excessive amount of time or effort to complete, but during the course of completion it includes some very adventuresome route-finding and rock scrambling. It also provides expansive views of both the Front Range and Anchorage. From some vantage points one can even look deeper into Chugach as well as far as the Kenai Peninsula to the south and the Talkeetna Mountains to the north.

**TRAIL LOCATION:** This hike begins where Williwaw Lakes Trail ends*. Upon reaching the end of Williwaw Lakes Trail just beyond the uppermost Williwaw Lake, bear left (north) and cross the stream feeding into the lake. Then begin to climb the series of benches leading up through the wide gap between Mount Elliot on the left (west) and Mount Williwaw on the right (east). (One can also begin this ascent earlier along the Williwaw Lakes Trail. Just look for a place to cross the valley below the lowest of the Williwaw Lakes and start up around the base of Mount Elliot toward the pass.) As one climbs, angle toward the left (west) side of the pass to find a path leading up and around the left side of the "rosary-bead" string of lakes that fill the basin of each consecutively higher bench.

-----------------------------------------------------------------------

* To get there, see [61] **Walk-About Guide to Williwaw Lakes Trail**.

After approximately 1 mile of climbing the route reaches the shores of the highest and largest of these lakes at the base of the final and steepest climb up to the pass separating Middle Fork Campbell Creek from North Fork Campbell Creek. At this point where the traverse begins, one has two choices. The first choice entails turning left (south) and directly climbing the long and broad boulder-strewn slope to the ridge above. On reaching the ridge, bear left (southwest) and climb the short remaining distance along the rocky spine of the ridge toward the summit of Mount Elliot. The second choice, which requires approximately 0.5 miles more of hiking along a very rocky ridge, begins by continuing straight ahead (north) and climbing to the crest of the pass (3,750 feet) leading into the North Fork Campbell Creek valley. Once on the pass turn left (west) and begin climbing the entire length of the very rocky ridge back toward the summit of Mount Elliot. Either choice involves some effort in reaching the ridge crest leading to the summit of Mount Elliot. Rock spires, gullies, and loose stones create obstacle courses that take some time to negotiate.

If one chooses the first option, one can, by bearing predominantly to the left (southeast) of the ridge's crest, find a relatively easy way through the chaos of rocks. Eventually, just where the ridge begins to bear slightly to the right (west), one reaches three rocky rises within 100 feet of each other and of very nearly the same height. Though very nearly the same height, the last one marks the true summit (4,710 feet), which also provides a small patch of grass on which to take a break. If one chooses the second option, expect to do some hand-over-hand climbing before reaching the ridge and the true summit.

From the summit of Mount Elliot continue following the rough and rocky ridge as it swings around to the right (west-northwest). Though the ridge walk now becomes broken up by more extensive patches of open slope, it also still crosses numerous ledges which require considerable up and down climbs of steep gullies. Some sheer-sided rises in the ridge may even seem impassable. But by continuing to follow the faint sheep trail that follows just below the left (south) side of the ridge crest, one can find a way around every obstacle. Approximately 1 mile past Mount Elliot the route descends a long gully down the left (south) side of the last and largest bump in Mount Elliot's west ridge and emerges onto the welcome grassy saddle that marks the middle of the traverse between Mount Elliot and Wolverine Peak. Here, up until late June, one may still find snow patches that may provide some welcome water.

From this grassy saddle at nadir of the ridge, continue following the sheep trail along the crest of the ridge. In less than 0.25 miles it passes through some rocky bumps. Though far easier than the ridge-scrambling leading to and from the summit of Mount Elliot, these bumps still require some care to climb over or around. By staying on the increasingly obvious sheep trail, though, one can avoid most questionable obstacles. After rounding the last bump in the ridge, the last climb up the back side of Wolverine Peak remains. Although it does not seem like much of a climb, it does provide a sudden dramatic panorama of the entire Anchorage bowl when one emerges from the shadows of the back ridge and finally stands on the summit (4,455 feet).

From the summit descend Wolverine Peak Trail 3 miles to the Wolverine Bowl Trail. On reaching Wolverine Bowl Trail turn left (south) to follow it for the 2.5 miles back to Prospect Heights parking area*.

**TRAIL GRADE:** Wolverine Bowl Trail, Middle Fork Loop Trail, and Williwaw Lakes Trail all rate predominantly Grade 1 as a hike. When one leaves the end of Williwaw Lakes Trail and begins climbing to the pass, the route rises to Grade 4 as a hike. On beginning the climb up the back side of Mount Elliot, the grade quickly rises to Grade 5 as a hike intermixed with sections of Grade 6 hiking. The route continues to fluctuate between Grade 5 and Grade 6 as a hike as the route continues over the summit of Mount Elliot. Only when one reaches the grassy saddle halfway along the ridge between Mount Elliot and Wolverine Peak does the rate drop to Grade 4 as a hike. From this saddle to the summit of Wolverine Peak the route fluctuates between Grade 4 and Grade 5 as a hike, with some very short sections of Grade 6 scrambling as one nears the summit of Wolverine Peak. The descent from the summit of Wolverine Peak back to Prospect Heights parking area rates between Grade 1 and Grade 2 as a hike.

------------------------------------------------------------------------

\* For more information about those trails, see [60] **Walk-About Guide to Wolverine Peak Trail** and [57] **Walk-About Guide to Wolverine Bowl Trail**.

**TRAIL CONDITION:** This route varies greatly in its conditions. Wolverine Bowl Trail and Middle Fork Loop Trail remain relatively flat and dry for their entire lengths. In comparison, the predominantly flat first 2 miles of Williwaw Lakes Trail often has long boggy and muddy sections. Only after winding through 1.5 miles of swamp and scrub spruce does the trail reach higher and drier ground. The route then passes over some boulder fields as it contours past the lower lakes. It then pushes through some low brush as it approaches its end at the upper end of the last of the Williwaw Lakes. Once one steps off Williwaw Lakes Trail, the route crosses mostly open tundra. As it enters the lower part of the pass the route follows a relatively well-pronounced primitive trail that winds over the pass between Mount Elliot and Mount Williwaw.

On leaving leaves this faint trail, however, and begins climbing the back side of Mount Elliot, the trail condition deteriorates quickly. Broken up by only small and sporadic patches of tundra, the entire climb to the summit of Mount Elliott as well the first 1 mile past the summit remains very rough with many boulders and much scree. One also has to climb up and down many gullies, skirt along many ledges, and slip around many rock spires. Halfway between Mount Elliot and Wolverine Peak, however, the route descends onto a broad, grassy saddle that provides excellent footing and easy going for about 0.5 miles.

The trail conditions up the back side of Wolverine Peak include some more short sections of rock scrambling and climbing around rocks and scree. But if one follows the sheep trail that becomes more pronounced the closer one gets to the summit, this section should prove quite manageable. From the summit of Wolverine Peak the trails leading down the front side of the mountain only get better and better as one nears Prospect Heights parking area.

**TRAIL MILEAGE:** This entire traverse from Prospect Heights parking area over Mount Elliot and Wolverine Peak and back entails approximately 17 miles of hiking and scrambling.

**TOTAL ELEVATION GAIN:** To hike the entire traverse from Prospect Heights parking area over Mount Elliot and Wolverine Peak and back entails a total elevation gain of approximately 4,800 feet.

**HIGH POINT:** This traverse reaches its highest point of 4,710 feet above sea level at the summit of Mount Elliot.

**NORMAL HIKING TIME:** To hike this entire traverse from Prospect Heights parking area over Mount Elliot and Wolverine Peak and back should take anywhere from 8 hours to 2 days, depending on the condition and ambition of the hiker(s) involved.

**CAMPSITES:** One will find no designated campsites along this trail. One can find some fine places on which to pitch a tent, however, in the many open areas around any of the Williwaw Lakes and around any of the "rosary-bead" lakes leading up to the pass between Mount Elliot and Mount Williwaw. Truly ambitious campers may also find the grass saddle located on the ridge approximately halfway between Mount Elliot and Wolverine Peak a scenic campsite. If one goes early enough in the season, lingering snowfields often provide enough water for these campsites.

**BEST TIME:** Most people should find any time from June to September a good time to do this traverse. One should think twice about doing it in the winter, however, because of the avalanche danger not only on the climb to the summit of Mount Elliot, but also along many portions of the ridge where the snow can bundle into large and unstable cornices and snow slabs.

**USGS MAPS:** Anchorage A-7, A-8 NE, and A-8 SE.

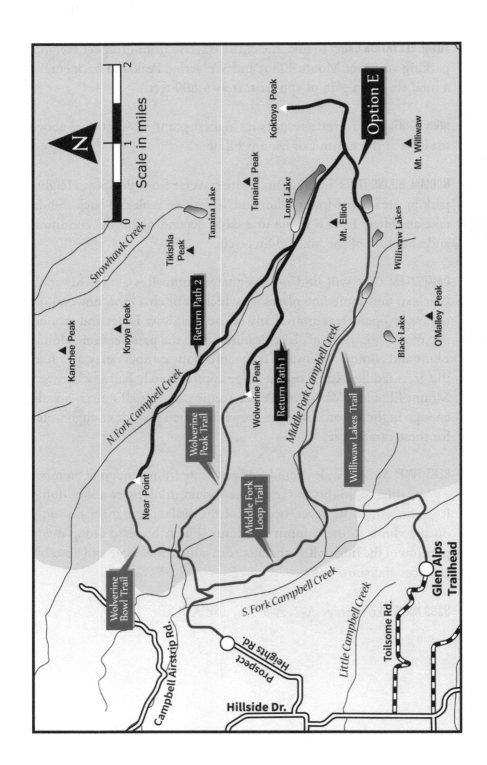

Scale in miles

N

Option E

Koktoya Peak

Mt. Williwaw

Tanaina Peak

Long Lake

Williwaw Lakes

Tikishla Peak

Tanaina Lake

Mt. Elliot

Snowhawk Creek

Knoya Peak

Black Lake

O'Malley Peak

Kanchee Peak

Return Path 2

N. Fork Campbell Creek

Middle Fork Campbell Creek

Wolverine Peak

Return Path 1

Wolverine Peak Trail

Williwaw Lakes Trail

Near Point

Wolverine Bowl Trail

Middle Fork Loop Trail

Campbell Airstrip Rd.

S. Fork Campbell Creek

Prospect Heights Rd.

Little Campbell Creek

Hillside Dr.

Toilsome Rd.

Glen Alps Trailhead

# OPTION E

# Ship Creek Overlook and Koktoya Peak

Although Ship Creek Overlook does not appear as a title on any maps, this guide gives it that title because of the fine view it provides of the Ship Creek valley. It marks the crest of the pass between Mount Williwaw and Koktoya Peak.

**TRAIL LOCATION:** This hike begins where Williwaw Lakes Trail ends*. Upon reaching the end of Williwaw Lakes Trail just beyond the uppermost Williwaw Lake, bear left (north) and cross the stream feeding into the lake. Then begin climbing the series of benches leading up through the wide gap between Mount Elliot on the left (west) and Mount Williwaw on the right (east). (One can also begin this ascent earlier along the Williwaw Lakes Trail. Just look for a place to cross the valley below the lowest of the Williwaw Lakes and start up around the base of Mount Elliot toward the pass.) As one climbs, angle toward the left (west) side of the pass to find a path leading up and around the left side of the "rosary-bead" string of lakes that fill the basin of each consecutively higher bench.

After approximately 1 mile of climbing the route reaches the final, and steepest, section of the climb up to the pass separating Middle Fork Campbell Creek from North Fork Campbell Creek. Starting up the main gully of the wall, climb to the pass above. On reaching the

---

\*   To get there, see [61] **Walk-About Guide to Williwaw Lakes Trail**.

pass (approximately 3,750 feet) one should now have a fine view of the upper end of the North Fork Campbell Creek valley 600 feet below.

Up to this point this route has followed the same route as that followed in [63] **OPTION B—Traverse From Williwaw Lakes Trail to North Fork Campbell Creek** above. But now it diverges from that route.

With Mount Williwaw now towering overhead just to the right (east), one should also now have a clear view of the narrow alley leading up and to the left (north) to Mount Williwaw's jagged north ridge. This alley provides the easiest access to the saddle on that ridge. To get to that saddle with the least amount of elevation loss, turn right (east) from the pass and follow the crest of the ridge for approximately 100 yards to where two lakes come into sight below and to the left (northeast).

Descending from the ridge, pass around the left (north) side of both lakes, making sure to cross the second lake's outlet as close to the lake as possible. Past the second lake, turn right (east) up the alley way leading to the top of the ridge.

Up to this point this route has followed the same route as that followed in [64] **OPTION C—Mount Williwaw** above. But now it diverges from that route. As one nears the top of the ridge after a steady 0.5 miles of climbing, bear left across the flats near the top of the climb and angle toward the lowest point in the saddle approximately 200 yards up and to the left (northeast). In reaching saddle, one has also reached Ship Creek Overlook (4,455 feet). From this overlook one can look both up and down the length of the Ship Creek valley as well as farther inland to the great peaks and perpetual snowfields of the inner Chugach. On a really clear day, one can even see as far as Mount Marcus Baker, the highest peak in the Chugach Mountains.

One need not turn around here, though. With a little more effort one can reach the summit of Koktoya Peak located approximately 1 mile up and to the left (north) of the saddle. To get there, first turn left (north) from the saddle. Following the ridge's crest, begin climbing toward the summit. The higher one climbs, the more rock gendarmes and cliffs one has to maneuver around. By drifting toward the shallower slopes to the left (west), however, one can avoid most of these obstacles. Nevertheless, one still has to clamber up much scree the higher one climbs. Eventually the ridge rounds off for the final stretch to the summit (approximately 5,150 feet).

From the summit of Koktoya one has two choices. First, one can go back the way they have come. Second, and far more interesting, one can return to Prospect Heights parking area by descending into the North Fork Campbell Creek valley and coming out over either Wolverine Peak or Near Point.

One begins this second option by descending back to the overlook. From there turn right (west) off the ridge and descend to the near end of Long Lake. Here one should find the rough foot trail leading down the entire left (south) side of Long Lake to the open tundra beyond*.

**TRAIL GRADE:** Wolverine Bowl Trail, Middle Fork Loop Trail, and Williwaw Lakes Trail all rate predominantly Grade 1 as a hike, with some very short rough or steep sections that rate Grade 2 as a hike. On leaving the end of Williwaw Lakes Trail and beginning the climb to the pass, this climb rates Grade 4 as a hike, with short climbs, such as the last one to the pass, rising to Grade 5 as a hike.

The next section of the hike past the lakes and up to Ship Creek Overlook rates Grade 4 as a hike. The climb up to the summit of Koktoya Peak rises to Grade 5 as a hike with some short sections even rated to Grade 6 as a hike as one nears the summit.

**TRAIL CONDITION:** This hike varies greatly in its conditions. Wolverine Bowl Trail and Middle Fork Loop Trail remain relatively flat and dry for their entire lengths. In comparison, the predominantly flat first 2 miles of Williwaw Lakes Trail often has long boggy and muddy sections. Only after winding through 1.5 miles of swamp and scrub spruce does the trail reach higher and drier ground. The trail then passes over some boulder fields as it contours past the lower lakes. After pushing through some low brush, it then approaches its end at the upper end of the last Williwaw Lake. On leaving Williwaw Lakes Trail, the route crosses mostly open tundra. As the route climbs past

--------------------------------------------------------------------

\* For information about the remainder of this route out, see [63] **OPTION B—Traverse from Williwaw Lakes Trail to North Fork Campbell Creek.**

the "rosary-bead" lakes to the crest of the pass it follows a relatively well-pronounced primitive trail as it winds over the pass between Mount Elliot and Mount Williwaw.

The next section of the hike past the lakes and up to Ship Creek Overlook entails crossing mostly mixed tundra and scree. The climb to the summit of Koktoya Peak entails scrambling up boulders and scree intermixed with short sections of tundra.

**TRAIL MILEAGE:** To go from Prospect Heights parking area to Ship Creek Overlook and back over either Wolverine Peak or Near Point entails approximately 11 miles of hiking, for a round-trip total of 22 miles. To go from Prospect Heights parking area to the summit of Koktoya Peak and back over either Wolverine Peak or Near Point entails approximately 12 miles of hiking, for a round-trip total of 24 miles of hiking.

**TOTAL ELEVATION GAIN:** Hiking from Prospect Heights parking area to Ship Creek Overlook and back over either Wolverine Peak or Near Point entails a total elevation gain of approximately 4,750 feet. Hiking from Prospect Heights parking area to the summit of Koktoya Peak and back over either Wolverine Peak or Near Point entails a total elevation gain of approximately 5,400 feet.

**HIGH POINT:** This traverse reaches its highest point of 4,455 feet above sea level at crest of Ship Overlook Pass or a higher point of approximately 5,150 feet above sea level at the summit of Koktoya Peak.

**NORMAL HIKING TIME:** To hike this entire traverse from Prospect Heights parking area to the summit of Koktoya Peak and back over either Wolverine Peak or Near Point back to Prospect Heights parking area should take anywhere from 11 hours to 2 days, depending on the ambition and condition of the hiker(s) involved.

**CAMPSITES:** One will find no designated campsites along this trail. One can find some fine places on which to pitch a tent, however, in the many open areas around any of the Williwaw Lakes and around any of the "rosary-bead" lakes leading up to the pass, as well as along almost the entire length of the North Fork Campbell Creek valley. The two secluded tarns just over the pass at the beginning of the climb up to Ship Creek Overlook provide particularly remote and dramatic places for pitching a tent. Some may even choose to pitch a tent at the crest of Ship Creek Overlook, where lingering snowfields can often provide a water source.

**BEST TIME:** Most people should find any time from June to September a good time to do this traverse. One should think twice about doing this hike in winter, however, owing to the avalanche danger on climbing over the pass between Williwaw Lakes and Long Lake as well as on the climbs to Ship Creek Overlook and Koktoya Peak.

**USGS MAPS:** Anchorage A-7, A-8 NE, and A-8 SE.

On the ridge between Koktoya Peak and east Tanaiana Peak

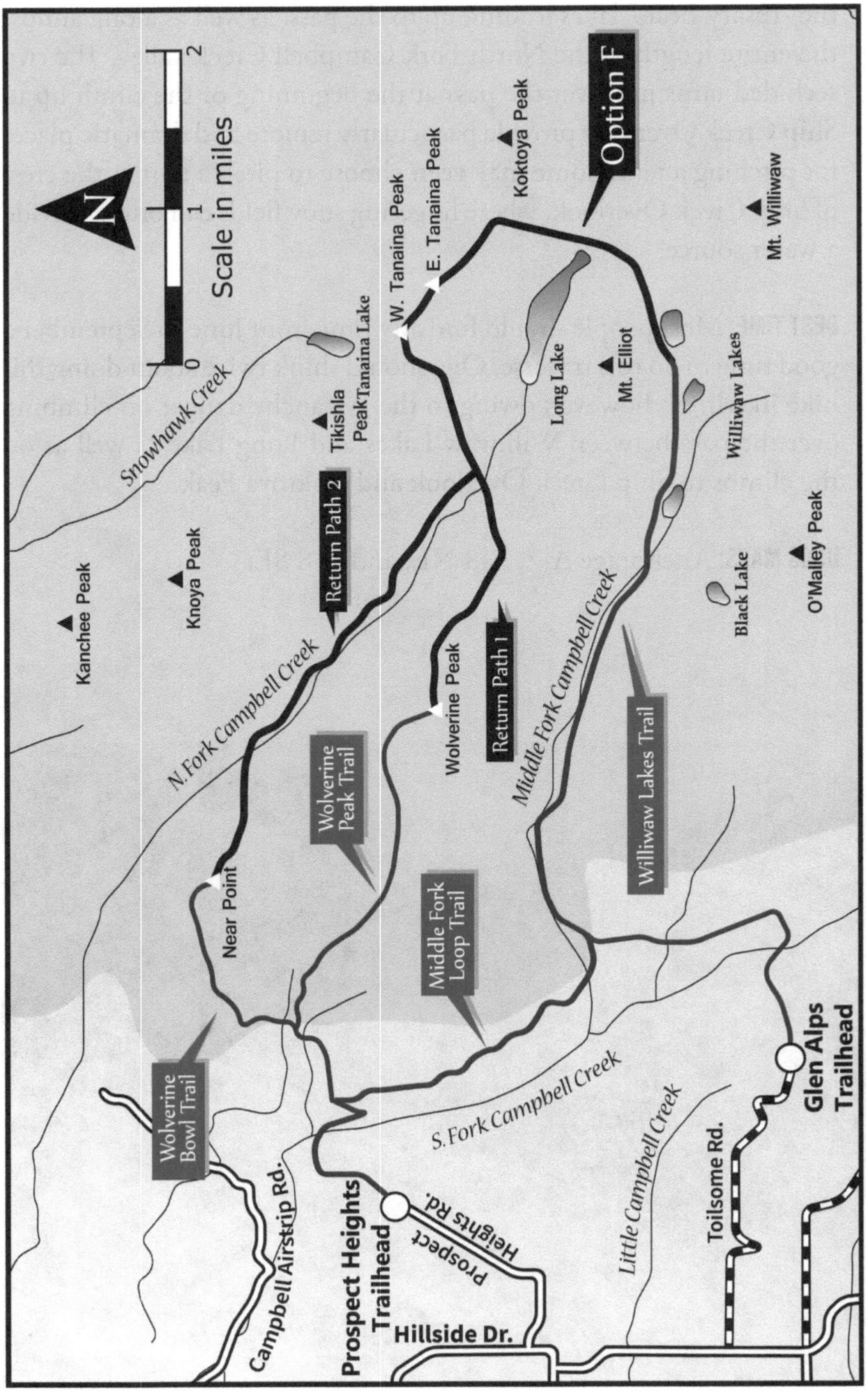

N
Scale in miles
0
1
2
Option F
Koktoya Peak
Mt. Williwaw
E. Tanaina Peak
W. Tanaina Peak
Tanaina Lake
Tikishla Peak
Snowhawk Creek
Long Lake
Mt. Elliot
Williwaw Lakes
Return Path 2
Knoya Peak
Kanchee Peak
O'Malley Peak
Black Lake
Return Path 1
Middle Fork Campbell Creek
N. Fork Campbell Creek
Wolverine Peak
Wolverine Peak Trail
Williwaw Lakes Trail
Near Point
Middle Fork Loop Trail
Wolverine Bowl Trail
S. Fork Campbell Creek
Little Campbell Creek
Glen Alps Trailhead
Toilsome Rd.
Campbell Airstrip Rd.
Prospect Heights Trailhead
Prospect Heights Rd.
Hillside Dr.

# OPTION F

# East and West Tanaina Peaks

Most people ignore these twin summits as possible destinations because of their lack of prominence when looked for from Anchorage, or even from many locations in the Front Range. Nor does this seem surprising seeing as they rise amidst the more popular climbs of Tikishla Peak, Mount Williwaw, and Temptation Peak. Yet these summits make fine destinations for anyone looking for a path less traveled in the Front Range.

**TRAIL LOCATION:** This hike begins where Williwaw Lakes Trail ends[*]. Upon reaching the end of Williwaw Lakes Trail just beyond the uppermost Williwaw Lake, bear left (north) and cross the stream feeding into the lake. Then begin climbing the series of benches leading up through the wide gap between Mount Elliot on the left (west) and Mount Williwaw on the right (east). (One can also begin this ascent earlier along the Williwaw Lakes Trail. Just look for a place to cross the valley below the lowest of the Williwaw Lakes and start up around the base of Mount Elliot toward the pass.) As one climbs, angle toward the left (west) side of the pass to find a path leading up and around the left side of the "rosary-bead" string of lakes that fill the basin of each consecutively higher bench.

After approximately 1 mile of climbing the route reaches the final, and steepest, section of the climb up to the pass separating Middle

---------------------------------------------------------------------

[*]   To get there, see [61] **Walk-About Guide to Williwaw Lakes Trail**.

Fork Campbell Creek from North Fork Campbell Creek. Starting up the main gully of the wall, climb to the pass above. On reaching the pass (approximately 3,750 feet) one should now have a fine view of the upper end of the North Fork Campbell Creek valley 600 feet below.

From this point many may find the direct descent down the far side of the pass too steep for their liking. If so, bear right (east) along the crest of the ridge and descend the shallower slope to the tarn just below the northeast side of pass. (This lake lies at the base of a textbook example of a rock glacier.) From the shore of this lake follow its outlet down to the eastern end of Long Lake.

Up to this point this route has followed the same route as that followed in [63] **OPTION B—Traverse from Williwaw Lakes Trail to North Fork Campbell Creek** above. But now it diverges from that route.

Instead of turning along left (south) side of the lake as described in OPTION B, follow the shore of the lake in the opposite direction around to the right (north) to its easternmost end. From the end of the lake, continue straight ahead and hike toward the steep and narrow notch in the ridge between Koktoya Peak to the right (northeast) and east of East Tanaina Peak to the left (northwest). Once at the base of this notch, follow the faint sheep trail up the steep, scree-covered left (northwest) side of the gully to the ridge above. On reaching the ridge proper, turn left (northwest) and follow it upward. After approximately 0.5 miles of working one's way around boulders and along scree, one reaches the summit of East Tanaina Peak (5,354 feet).

To continue on to West Tanaina Peak, stay on the ridge crest as it continues northwest. Approximately 0.5 miles from East Tanaina Peak the ridge swings left (west) and dips into a saddle. At the far end of the saddle the ridge swings right (northwest) and climbs the last 0.5 miles to the summit of West Tanaina Peak (5,200-plus feet).

From the summit of West Tanaina Peak one has two choices. First, one can go back the way one came. Second, and far more interesting, and shorter, one can hike out by descending the North Fork Campbell Creek valley and come out over either Wolverine Peak or Near Point*.

--------------------------------------------------------------------

* As described in [63] **OPTION B—Traverse from Williwaw Lakes Trail to North Fork Campbell Creek**.

Begin this second option by turning right (south) off the summit of West Tanaina Peak and picking a way down to the open slopes below. Bearing right (southwest) when possible, descend all the way to the floor of the North Fork Ship Creek valley. Having reached the valley floor, ford North Fork Campbell Creek and climb onto the bench above the opposite shore.

One now has two choices as to where to ascend the ridge looming above the left (south) side of the valley. The first, although it requires a greater amount of climbing, offers the option of coming out over the summit of Wolverine Peak. The second offers the option of coming out over Near Point.

To come out over the summit of Wolverine Peak, first continue approximately 1 mile down valley from the western end of Long Lake. Then, having passed the rockiest sections of the ridge to the left (south), look for the wide grassy slope leading up to the low point on the ridge. Angling up the slope, climb to ridge's crest. Once on the ridge (from which one can now look down to into Middle Fork Campbell Creek valley) turn right (west) and follow the faint sheep trail up the ridge. In approximately 1 mile of increasingly steeper climbing, the ridge reaches the summit of Wolverine Peak (4,455 feet). From this summit descend the Wolverine Peak Trail 3 miles down the front of the mountain to the Wolverine Bowl Trail. On reaching the Wolverine Bowl Trail turn left (south) and hike the last 2 miles back to Prospect Heights parking area*.

To come out over the summit of Near Point, first continue approximately 2 miles down valley from the western end of Long Lake. Then look up and to the left (southwest) for the saddle between the northwest buttress of Wolverine Peak and Near Point. Once this saddle comes into view, contour up to it, crossing numerous gullies on the way. Once on the saddle turn right (west) and follow the rough trail along the sometimes narrow ridge for approximately 0.5 miles to the summit of Near Point (3,050 feet). From this summit follow the Wolverine Bowl Trail the 4 miles back to Prospect Heights parking

-------------------------------------------------------------------

\* For more information about those trails, see [60] **Walk-About Guide to Wolverine Peak Trail** and [57] **Walk-About Guide to Wolverine Bowl Trail**.

area*.

**TRAIL GRADE:** Wolverine Bowl Trail, Middle Fork Loop Trail, and Williwaw Lakes Trail all rate predominantly Grade 1 as a hike, with some very short rough or steep sections that rate Grade 2 as a hike. On leaving the end of Williwaw Lakes Trail and begins climbing to the pass, the traverse rates Grade 4 as a hike, with short climbs, such as the last one to the pass, rising to Grade 5 as a hike.

The descent down the far side of the pass and around the northern side of Long Lake rates Grade 4 as a hike. The climb to the summit of East Tanaina Peak and West Tanaina Peak initially rates Grade 6 as a hike on the scramble up to the crest of the ridge. Once on the ridge, the route rates Grade 5 as a hike for remainder of the climb to both summits.

The descent into the North Fork Campbell Creek valley rates Grade 4 as a hike. But on beginning the climb out of the valley to the summit of Wolverine Peak or Near Point the route rises to a Grade 5 as a hike. Once one starts down either Wolverine Peak Trail or Wolverine Bowl Trail, the route drops initially to Grade 2 as a hike and then to Grade 1 as a hike as one approaches Prospect Heights parking area.

**TRAIL CONDITION:** This route varies greatly in its conditions. Wolverine Bowl Trail and Middle Fork Loop Trail remain relatively flat and dry for their entire length. In comparison, the first 2 miles of Williwaw Lakes Trail often has long boggy and muddy sections. Only after winding through 1.5 miles of swamp and scrub spruce does the trail reach higher and drier ground. The trail then passes over some boulder fields as it contours past the lower lakes. It then pushes through some low brush as it approaches its end at the upper end of the last lake. On leaving Williwaw Lakes Trail, the route crosses mostly open tundra. It then follows a relatively well-pronounced primitive trail as it winds past the "rosary-bead" lakes and over the pass between Mount Elliot and Mount Williwaw.

The next section of the hike down and around the eastern end of

-------------------------------------------------------------------

\*     For more information about that trail, see [57] **Walk-About Guide to Wolverine Bowl Trail.**

Long Lake entails crossing mostly mixed tundra and scree. The climb to the summit of East Tanaina Peak involves climbing a steep scree slope up to the ridge, followed by skirting around some rock gendarmes, ledges, and boulders on the climb over both East Tanaina Peak and West Tanaina Peak. The hike back down and across the North Fork Campbell Creek valley crosses over mostly open tundra.

If one comes out over the summit of Wolverine Peak, the route initially crosses mostly open tundra. On the ridge leading up and over the back side of Wolverine Peak, the route includes some scrambling over rocks and scree. But if one follows the sheep trail that becomes more pronounced the closer one gets to the summit, this section should prove quite manageable. From the summit of Wolverine Peak the trails only get better and better as one nears Prospect Heights parking area.

If one comes out over the summit of Near Point, the traverse crosses a number of gullies to reach the saddle between Wolverine Peak and Near Point. The climb to the summit of Near Point requires pushing through some low brush as well as traversing a sometimes very narrow ridge. From the summit of Near Point, though, the trail steadily improves as one nears Prospect Heights parking area.

**TRAIL MILEAGE:** To go from Prospect Heights parking area to the summits of West Tanaina Peak and East Tanaina Peak and back over either Wolverine Peak or Near Point entails approximately 22 miles of hiking.

**TOTAL ELEVATION GAIN:** Hiking from Prospect Heights parking area to the summits of East Tanaina and West Tanaina and back over Wolverine Peak entails a total elevation gain of approximately 7,700 feet. Hiking from Prospect Heights parking area to the summits of East Tanaina and West Tanaina and back over Near Point to the parking area entails a total elevation gain of approximately 6,300 feet.

**HIGH POINT:** This traverse reaches its highest point of 5,354 feet above sea level at the summit of East Tanaina Peak.

**NORMAL HIKING TIME:** To hike this entire traverse from Prospect Heights parking area to the summits of West Tanaina Peak and East Tanaina Peak and back over either Wolverine Peak or Near Point should take anywhere from 11 hours to 2 days, depending on the ambition and condition of the hiker(s) involved.

**CAMPSITES:** One will find no designated campsites along this trail. One can find some fine places on which to pitch a tent, however, in the many open areas around any of the Williwaw Lakes, around any of the "rosary-bead" lakes leading up to the pass, and along almost the entire length of the North Fork Campbell Creek valley.

**BEST TIME:** Most people should find any time from June to September a good time to do this traverse. One should think twice about doing this hike in winter, however, because of the avalanche danger both on climbing over the pass between Williwaw Lakes and Long Lake and on the climbs to East Tanaina Peak and West Tanaina Peak.

**USGS MAPS:** Anchorage A-7, A-8 NE, and A-8 SE.

On the ridge between East Tanaina Peak and West Tanaina Peak

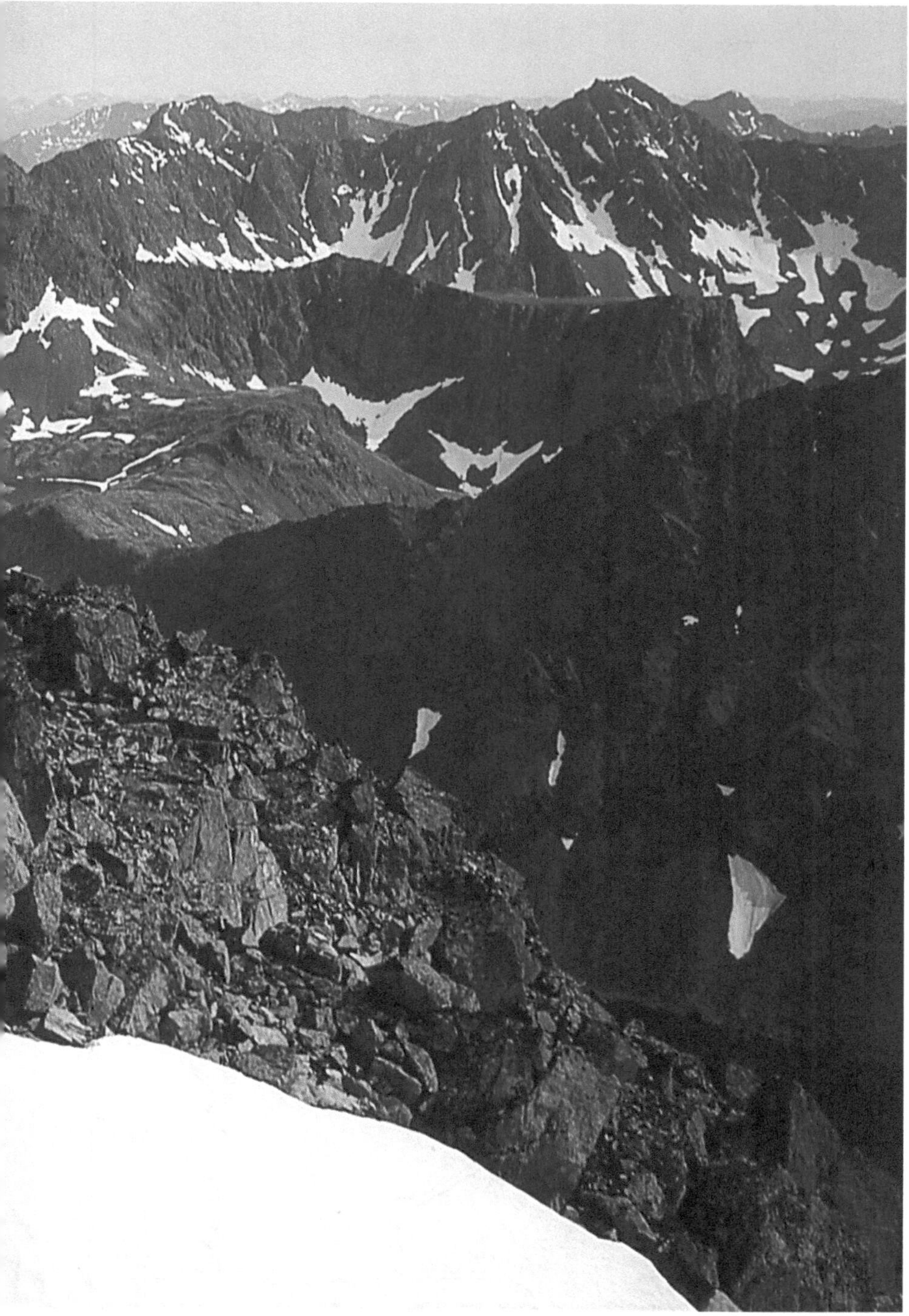

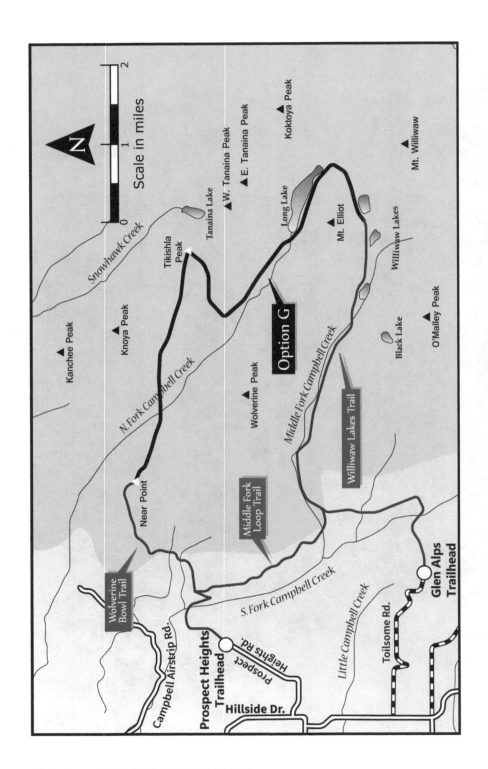

Scale in miles

0  1  2

N

Snowhawk Creek

Kanchee Peak

Knoya Peak

Tikishla Peak

Tanaina Lake

W. Tanaina Peak

E. Tanaina Peak

Koktoya Peak

Mt. Williwaw

Long Lake

Mt. Elliot

Williwaw Lakes

Option G

Wolverine Peak

N. Fork Campbell Creek

Middle Fork Campbell Creek

O'Malley Peak

Black Lake

Williwaw Lakes Trail

Middle Fork Loop Trail

Near Point

Wolverine Bowl Trail

S. Fork Campbell Creek

Campbell Airstrip Rd.

Prospect Heights Trailhead

Prospect Heights Rd.

Hillside Dr.

Little Campbell Creek

Toilsome Rd.

Glen Alps Trailhead

# OPTION G

# Tikishla Peak from Williwaw Lakes Trail

Though long, this approach to Tikishla Peak allows one to include the climb as part of the scenic circumnavigation of the Wolverine Peak and Mount Elliot massif.

**TRAIL LOCATION:** Upon reaching the end of Williwaw Lakes Trail just beyond the uppermost Williwaw Lake, bear left (north) and cross the stream feeding into the lake\*. Then begin to climb the series of benches leading up through the wide gap between Mount Elliot on the left (west) and Mount Williwaw on the right (east). (One can also begin this ascent earlier along the Williwaw Lakes Trail. Just look for a place to cross the valley below the lowest of the Williwaw Lakes and start up around the base of Mount Elliot toward the pass.) If one starts this climb by leaning toward the left (west) side of the pass, one should soon find a path to follow up and around the left side of the "rosary-bead" string of lakes that fill the basin each consecutively higher bench.

After approximately 1 mile of climbing from the valley the route reaches the final, and steepest, section of the climb up to the pass separating Middle Fork Campbell Creek from North Fork Campbell Creek. Starting up the main gully of the wall, climb to the pass above. On reaching the pass (approximately 3,750 feet) one should now have a fine view of the upper end of the North Fork Campbell Creek valley 600 feet below.

------------------------------------------------------------

\*    To get there, see [61] **Walk-About Guide to Williwaw Lakes Trail**.

From this point many may find the direct descent down the far side of the pass too steep for their liking. If so, bear right (east) along the crest of the ridge and descend the shallower slope to the tarn just below the northeast side of pass. (This lake lies at the base of a textbook example of a rock glacier.) Once at the shore of this lake, follow its outlet down to the eastern end of Long Lake. Here one should also find evidence of a rough foot trail that leads down the entire left (south) side of Long Lake to the open tundra beyond.

Upon reaching the western end of Long Lake, continue down valley for another 1 to 1.5 miles to a suitable approach to Tikishla Peak above and to right (north). In finding this approach to the summit, one must not to climb too early. Doing so will put one on the wrong side of the notch in the ridge between the East and West Tanaina peaks and Tikishla Peak. Therefore, to make certain about finding a route summit, continue down valley until the great southwestern-hanging bowl that opens up just after one has passed under the summit opens up above and to the right (north). At that point do a wide U-turn and climb into the bowl and follow it to its uppermost end. Then bear left (north) and climb to the crest of the ridge looming above. On reaching the crest of the ridge turn right (northeast) up the crest to the summit (5,150 feet), the tallest of the numerous spires on the ridge's crest.

From the summit descend back into the valley again by going straight down the ridge one just came up then back down into the great bowl in the southwest side of the peak. Once in the bowl follow it back out to the North Fork Campbell Creek valley. Then descend into that valley and cross back over the North Fork Campbell Creek.

After crossing the creek climb to the saddle between the northwest buttress of Wolverine Peak and Near Point. Then turn right (west) from the saddle and climb the sometimes narrow ridge for approximately 0.5 miles to the summit of Near Point (3,050 feet). From the summit of Near Point follow the Wolverine Bowl Trail the 4 miles back to Prospect Heights parking area[*].

--------------------------------------------------------------------------

[*]    For more information about that trail, see [57] **Walk-About Guide to Wolverine Bowl Trail**.

**TRAIL GRADE:** Wolverine Bowl Trail, Middle Fork Loop Trail, and Williwaw Lakes Trail all rate predominantly Grade 1 as a hike, with some very short rough or steep sections that rate Grade 2 as a hike. Upon leaving the end of Williwaw Lakes Trail and beginning climbing to the pass, the traverse rates Grade 4 as a hike, with short climbs, like the last one to the pass, rising to Grade 5 as a hike.

The descent out of the bowl into the North Fork Campbell Creek valley rates Grade 4 as a hike. The climb out of the valley into the bowl below Tikishla Peak also rates Grade 4 as a hike. On turning up to climb out of the bowl to the ridge above, the rate increases to Grade 5 as a hike. This even includes some short sections rated to Grade 6 as a hike on the climb along the summit ridge as well as up the final summit spire.

The descent back to the bowl also rates between Grade 5 and Grade 6 as a hike. The hike out of the bowl and then across North Fork Campbell Creek valley rates Grade 4 as a hike. The climb to the saddle between Wolverine Peak and Near Point the traverse rises to Grade 5 as a hike. It remains Grade 5 as a hike until one reaches the uppermost end of Wolverine Bowl Trail at the summit of Near Point. From there back to Prospect Heights parking area, the route again rates between Grade 1 and Grade 2 as a hike.

**TRAIL CONDITION:** This trail varies greatly in its conditions. Wolverine Bowl Trail and Middle Fork Loop Trail remain relatively flat and dry for their entire length. In comparison, the predominantly flat first 2 miles of Williwaw Lakes Trail often has long boggy and muddy sections. Only after winding through 1.5 miles of swamp and scrub spruce does the trail reach higher and drier ground. The trail then passes over some boulder fields as it contours past the lower lakes, and then pushes through some low brush as it approaches its end at the upper end of the last lake. On leaving Williwaw Lakes Trail, the route crosses mostly open tundra. It even follows a relatively well-pronounced trail as it winds over the pass between Mount Elliot and Mount Williwaw and down to Long Lake.

The next section of the hike past Long Lake and down the North Fork Campbell Creek valley entails crossing mostly mixed tundra and scree. The climb to the summit of Tikishla Peak, however, includes first climbing the boulder and scree of the lower bowl, then skirting around lots of boulders, ledges, and, once on the summit ridge, scree, followed by a last scramble up the summit spire.

The descent across the North Fork Campbell Creek valley entails mostly just crossing some tundra, fording the stream, and then climbing a long tundra and scree-streaked slope to the saddle between Wolverine Peak and Near Point. From the saddle, the climb to the summit of Near Point requires pushing through some low brush as well as traversing a sometimes very narrow ridge. From the summit of Near Point, though, Wolverine Bowl Trail only gets better and better as one nears Prospect Heights parking area.

**TRAIL MILEAGE:** To go from Prospect Heights parking area to the summit of Tikishla Peak and back over Near Point entails approximately 22 miles of hiking.

**TOTAL ELEVATION GAIN:** To hike from Prospect Heights parking area to the summit of Tikishla Peak and back over Near Point entails a total elevation gain of approximately 4,300 feet.

**HIGH POINT:** This traverse reaches its highest point of 5,150 feet at the summit of Tikishla Peak.

**NORMAL HIKING TIME:** To hike this entire traverse from Prospect Heights parking area to the summit of Tikishla Peak and back over Near Point should take anywhere from 11 hours to 2 days depending on the ambition and condition of the hiker(s) involved.

**CAMPSITES:** One will find no designated campsites along this trail. One can find some fine places on which to pitch a tent, however, in the many open areas around any of the Williwaw Lakes, around any of the "rosary-bead" lakes leading up to the pass, and along almost the entire length of the North Fork Campbell Creek valley.

**BEST TIME:** Most people should find any time from June to September a good time to do this traverse. One should think twice about doing this hike in winter, however, because of the avalanche danger on climbing over the pass between Williwaw Lakes and Long Lake as well as on the steep climb out of the valley to the summit of Tikishla Peak.

**USGS MAPS:** Anchorage A-7, A-8 NE, and A-8 SE.

Climbing toward Tikishla Peak

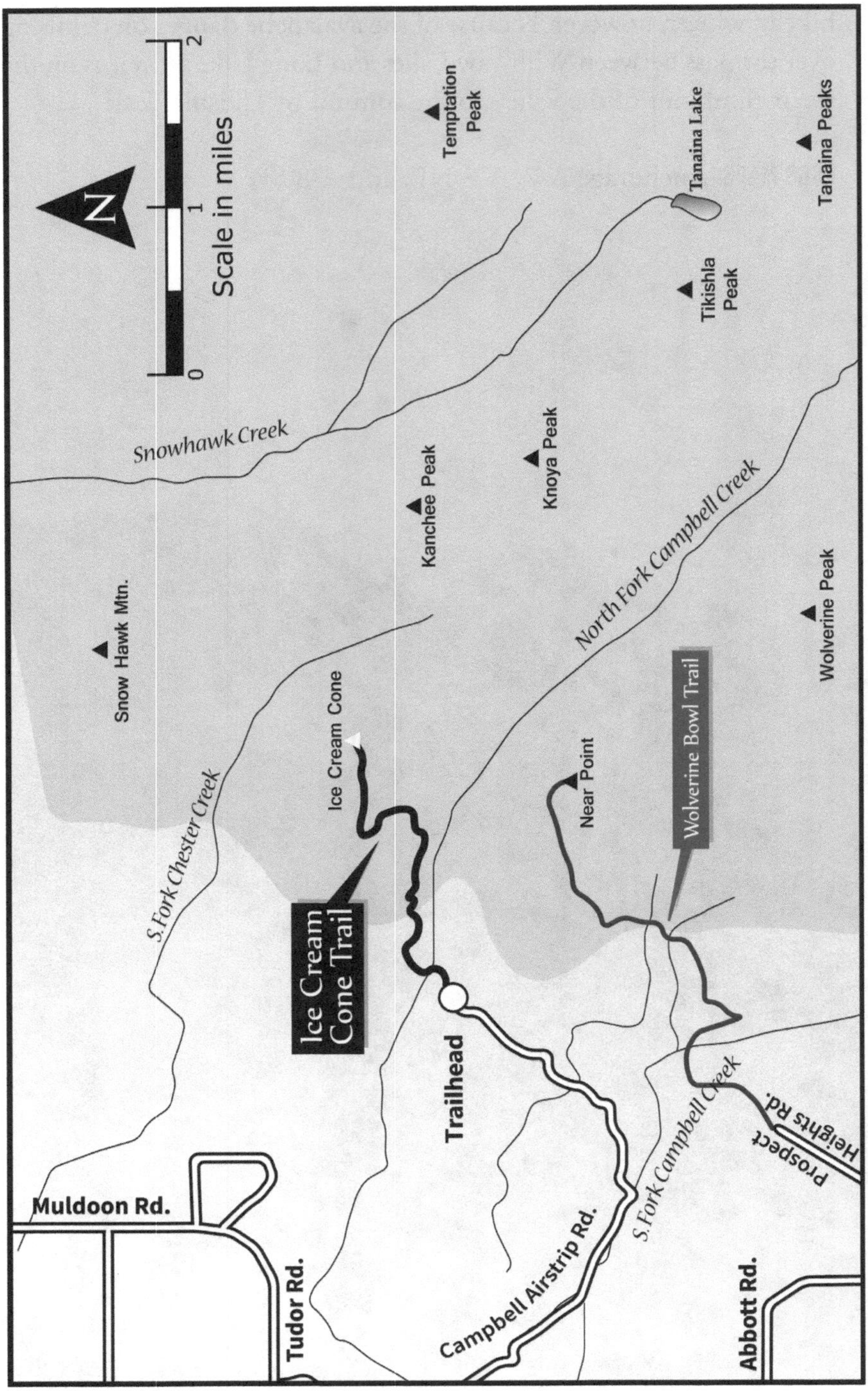
N
Scale in miles
0
1
2
Temptation Peak
Tanaina Lake
Tanaina Peaks
Tikishla Peak
Snowhawk Creek
Kanchee Peak
Knoya Peak
North Fork Campbell Creek
Wolverine Peak
Snow Hawk Mtn.
Ice Cream Cone
Wolverine Bowl Trail
Near Point
S.Fork Chester Creek
Ice Cream Cone Trail
Trailhead
Prospect Heights Rd.
S.Fork Campbell Creek
Muldoon Rd.
Tudor Rd.
Campbell Airstrip Rd.
Abbott Rd.

## CHAPTER 6

# NORTH FORK CAMPBELL CREEK VALLEY

69

## Walk-About Guide to Ice Cream Cone Trail

More the buttress at the end of a ridge than a summit, Ice Cream Cone (which some refer to as Baldy) makes for a scenic destination. From its summit one also continue on a number of longer hikes and climbs, including climbs of Kanchee Peak, Knoya Peak and Tikishla Peak, as well as the longer climb of Temptation Peak in the Snow Hawk Creek valley to the northeast. Thus, though many will find Ice Cream Cone a worthwhile destination in itself, others may find it but a rest area before pushing deeper into the Front Range.

This trail crosses military land, and therefore one needs to obtain a permit from JBER-Richardson to hike it. To obtain this permit, see Appendix 3 at the end of the book.

**TRAIL LOCATION:** Ice Cream Cone Trail to the summit of Ice Cream Cone begins at the uppermost end of Basher Road in Stuckagain Heights. To get there drive 3.2 miles south of downtown Anchorage on the Seward Highway. There, just after Milepost 124, take the Tudor Road exit. At the end of the ramp, turn left (east) and cross back over the highway. Continue straight on Tudor Road as it gradually ascends past Lake Otis Parkway and Elmore Drive. Approximately 3.2 miles from the Seward Highway Tudor Road reaches a set of lights with Campbell Airstrip

Road leading right (south). Turn right on Campbell Airstrip Road. In approximately 1 mile this road becomes Basher Road. Stay on Basher Road as it continues to wind upward. Approximately 2.5 miles from Tudor Road the road passes the Bivouac Trail parking areas on either side of the road. In another approximately 0.8 miles the road passes State Park parking area on the right (south). Approximately 5.5 miles from Tudor Road the road ends at a small area on the fenced border of military land. Park wherever possible without blocking any private drive.

Ice Cream Cone Trail begins by following the fence bordering the private property on the right (east) of the parking area. After initially hugging the fence for approximately 100 feet, the trail turns left (northeast) and drops steeply into the North Fork Campbell Creek gorge. Approximately 0.2 miles later the trail levels out and crosses the North Fork Campbell Creek via a narrow bridge.

On the far side of the creek the trail begins its long and relatively steady climb to the summit of Ice Cream Cone. It begins this climb by switch backing to the crest of a low ridge. There it reaches a junction with Ice Cream Cone Cut-off coming in from the left (west)[*]. Staying to the right at this junction, the trail continues to wind up the ridge. Eventually the trail bends left (north) and begins climbing some long switchbacks toward the open ridge above. At the top of these switchbacks the trail turns left (north) and begins its last steep and direct climb to the ridge's mounded, bald top that marks the summit of Ice Cream Cone (approximately 2,800 feet).

From the summit of Ice Cream Cone one has a number of choices. First, one can return the way they have come. Second, one can continue along the trail leading up the ridge and from there bear northeast to climb Kanchee Peak, Knoya Peak, or Temptation Peak[**]. Third, one can continue along the trail leading up the ridge and from there continue straight ahead (east) to climb Tikishla Peak[***].

-----------------------------------------------------------------------

[*]    For more information about that trail, see [88] **Walk-About Guide to Ice Cream Cone Cut-Off** in Chapter 9.

[**]   For more information about these climbs, see [70] **OPTION A—Traverse of Kanchee Peak and Knoya Peak** and [72] **OPTION C—Temptation Peak**.

[***]  For more information about that climb, see [71] **OPTION B—Tikishla Peak**.

**TRAIL GRADE:** This climb rates Grade 2 as a hike for almost its entire length. Only for the final 0.4 miles to the summit of Ice Cream Cone does it climb steeply enough to rate Grade 3 as a hike.

**TRAIL CONDITION:** Although it does have some muddy spots, this trail generally remains good to excellent.

**TRAIL MILEAGE:** To go from the parking area to the summit of Ice Cream Cone entails approximately 2.5 miles of hiking, for a round-trip total of 5 miles.

**TOTAL ELEVATION GAIN:** To hike from the parking area to the summit of Ice Cream Cone entails a total elevation gain of approximately 1,600 feet.

**HIGH POINT:** This hike reaches its highest point of approximately 2,800 feet above sea level at the summit of Ice Cream Cone.

**NORMAL HIKING TIME:** This hike should take anywhere from 2 to 4 hours depending on the condition and ambition of the hiker(s) involved.

**CAMPSITES:** One will find no designated campsites along this trail. Nor, given the short length of the trail, should one need any.

**BEST TIME:** Most people should find any time from early May to September a good time to do this hike. This also makes a fine ski or snowshoe trip in the winter, although the last climb to the ridge may prove a bit treacherous underfoot in icy conditions.

**USGS MAPS:** Anchorage A-8.

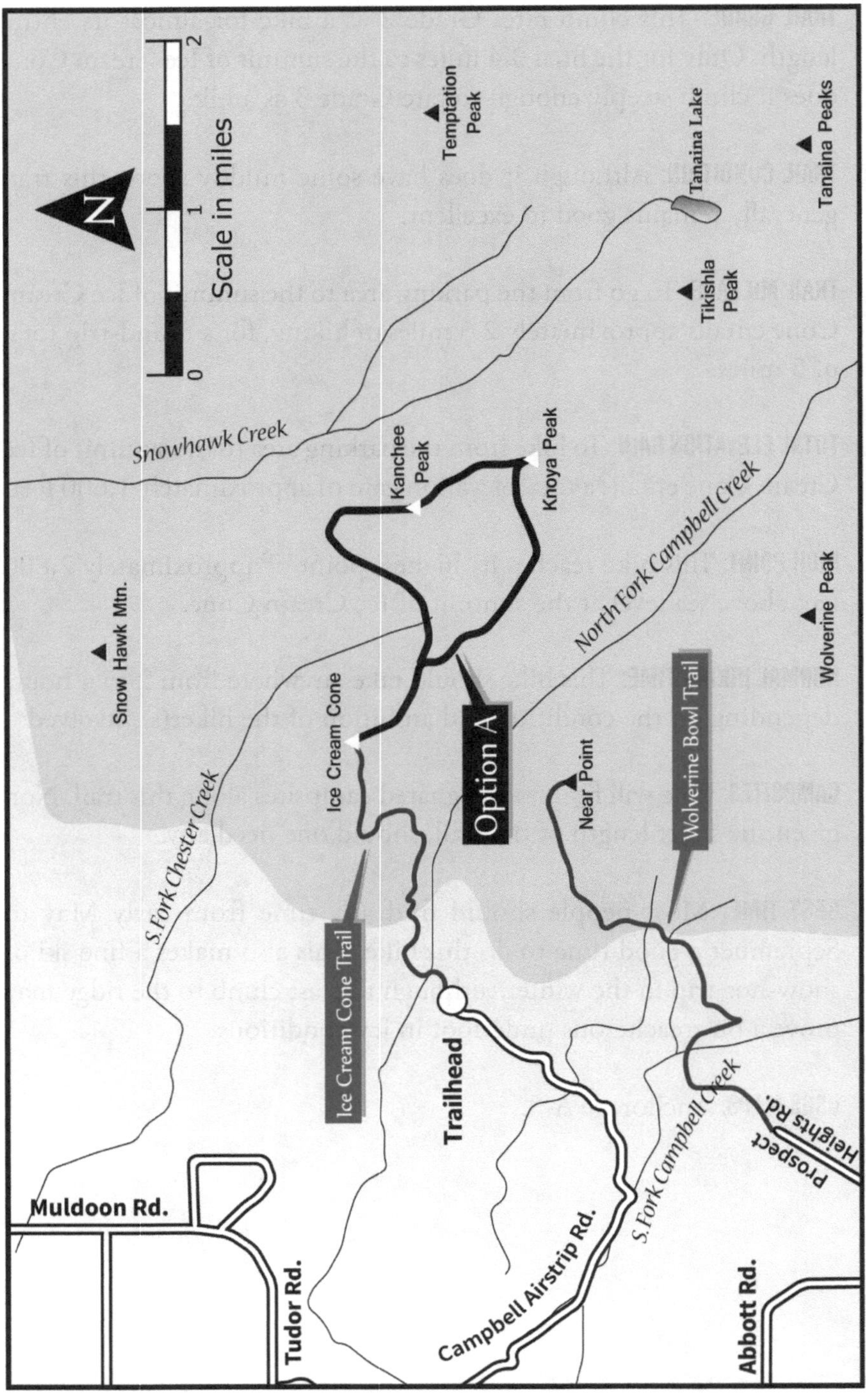
Scale in miles
0
1
2
N
Temptation Peak
Tanaina Lake
Tanaina Peaks
Tikishla Peak
Snowhawk Creek
Knoya Peak
Kanchee Peak
North Fork Campbell Creek
Snow Hawk Mtn.
Wolverine Peak
Ice Cream Cone
Option A
Wolverine Bowl Trail
Near Point
S. Fork Chester Creek
Ice Cream Cone Trail
Trailhead
S. Fork Campbell Creek
Prospect Heights Rd.
Muldoon Rd.
Campbell Airstrip Rd.
Tudor Rd.
Abbott Rd.

# OPTION A

# Traverse of Kanchee Peak
# and Knoya Peak

Despite the fact that this traverse stays almost entirely within sight of the city, it has an oddly incongruous sense of remoteness about it. Perhaps this perception results from so much of this traverse following little or no trail. Or perhaps it results from the mere fact that it does stay in sight of the city, which gives one the feeling of pleasant isolation.

Despite its sense of remoteness, this route does cross military land, and therefore one needs to obtain a permit from JBER-Richardson to hike it. To obtain this permit, see Appendix 3 at the end of the book.

**TRAIL LOCATION:** This traverse begins on the summit of Ice Cream Cone at the upper end of Ice Cream Cone Trail*. From the summit of Ice Cream Cone follow the wide trail on the right (east) as it climbs to of the next knoll on the ridge. At the top of this knoll bear left (northeast) off the trail and drop into the wide upper end of the Chester Creek valley that spreads out underneath the west facing Kanchee Peak and Knoya Peak. After crossing the stream bed at the base of the valley, climb through the brush to the low saddle to the left (northwest) of Kanchee Peak.

The true traverse begins at this saddle. Begin this traverse from the saddle by turning left (southeast) up the ridge line. Passing over the first

------------------------------------------------------------

\*    To get there see [69] **Walk-About Guide to Ice Cream Cone Trail** above or
     [88] **Walk-About Guide to Ice Cream Cone Cut-Off** in Chapter 9.

spire in the ridge, descends and cross the saddle on its far side. From this higher saddle continue up the ridge through the maze of rocks and tundra until one reaches the summit of Kanchee Peak (4,393 feet).

From the summit of Kanchee Peak continue straight ahead (southwest) as the ridge winds its relatively short way toward Knoya Peak. Halfway across this traverse the route follows a sheep trail across the steep flank of the bowl between the two peaks. Just beyond this slope one can again climb back onto the ridge crest for the final climb to the summit of Knoya Peak (4,668 feet).

From the summit of Knoya Peak one must exercise some care to find the right way down. If any clouds obscure the view, one can easily turn down the ridge leading to Tikishla Peak. So make sure not to continue straight ahead from the summit. Instead bear right (west-southwest) onto the faint trail leading down the southwest ridge of the mountain. In a short time this trail should become more pronounced as it contours just below the right side of ridge crest in a wide curve back down toward Ice Cream Cone. Upon reaching the flat plateau at the base of the ridge, the trail soon passes a tarn on the right. The trail then climbs over two humps in the ridge before arriving back at the top of Ice Cream Cone. Here one can rejoin Ice Cream Cone Trail and follow it back to the parking area at Stuckagain Heights.

**TRAIL GRADE:** This hike rates initially Grade 2 as a hike on Ice Cream Cone Trail. On leaving the summit of Ice Cream Cone, however, it rises to Grade 4 as a hike. It rises to Grade 5 as a hike as it leaves the saddle above the far side of the Chester Creek valley for the traverse over the summits of Kanchee Peak and Knoya Peak. Upon reaching down the trail on the far side of Knoya Peak, it reverts to Grade 2 as a hike. It remains Grade 2 as a hike the entire way back to the Stuckagain Heights parking area.

**TRAIL CONDITION:** Although one may have to cross some muddy spots, Ice Cream Cone Trail generally remains good to excellent. On leaving the summit of Ice Cone, however, one has to hike through some knee-high to waist-high brush in order to reach the saddle across the Chester

Creek valley. On the ridge line of Kanchee Peak, one should have an easier time climbing up rocky tundra. These conditions continue until one starts down the ridge on the far side of the traverse, where the trail only gets better and better as it approaches Ice Cream Cone.

**TRAIL MILEAGE:** To complete this traverse from the parking area at Stuckagain Heights and back entails approximately 10.5 miles of hiking.

**TOTAL ELEVATION GAIN:** To complete this traverse from the parking area at Stuckagain Heights and back entails a total elevation gain of approximately 4,300 feet.

**HIGH POINT:** This traverse reaches its highest point of 4,668 feet above sea level at the summit of Knoya Peak.

**NORMAL HIKING TIME:** To complete this traverse from the parking area at Stuckagain Heights and back should take anywhere from 6 to 11 hours depending on the condition and ambition of the hiker(s) involved.

**CAMPSITES:** One will find no designated campsites along this traverse. One will find a fine place on which to pitch a tent, however, on the flats around on the tarn on the far end of the traverse. There are also some fine places for pitching a tent on the saddle to the left (northwest) of Kanchee Peak, although these places lack any obvious source of water.

**BEST TIME:** Most people should find any time from early May to September a good time to do this hike. Parts of this traverse also make for a fine ski or snowshoe trip in the winter, although one should remain very wary of avalanche conditions along the entire length of the ridge.

**USGS MAPS:** Anchorage A-7 and A-8.

N
Scale in miles
0
1
2
Temptation Peak
Tanaina Lake
Tanaina Peaks
Tikishla Peak
Snowhawk Creek
Knoya Peak
Kanchee Peak
North Fork Campbell Creek
Wolverine Peak
Snow Hawk Mtn.
Ice Cream Cone
Option B
Wolverine Bowl Trail
Near Point
S.Fork Chester Creek
Ice Cream Cone Trail
Trailhead
Prospect Heights Rd.
S.Fork Campbell Creek
Muldoon Rd.
Campbell Airstrip Rd.
Tudor Rd.
Abbott Rd.

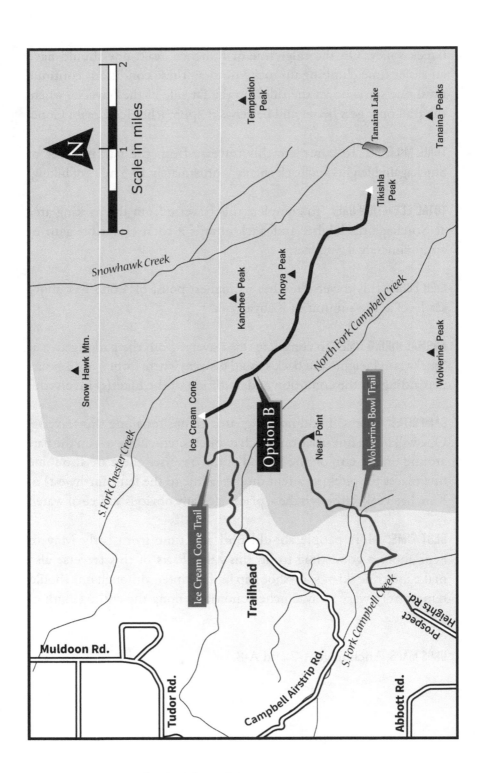

# 71

# OPTION B

# Tikishla Peak

Of all the various routes up Tikishla Peak offered in this volume, the route described below remains the most efficient. Shortest in length with the least elevation gain it gets to and from the summit of Tikishla Peak in the least amount of time with the least amount of effort.

This climb crosses military land, and therefore one needs to obtain a permit from JBER-Richardson to hike it. To obtain this permit, see Appendix 3 at the end of the book.

**TRAIL LOCATION:** This climb begins at the summit of Ice Cream Cone*. Turning right (east) off the summit of Ice Cream Cone follow the wide trail as it climbs over the next two humps in the ridge. After passing a tarn on the left (north), the trail begins climbing the southwest ridge of Knoya Peak. Where the trail bears right near the top of the ridge, continue straight over the crest and bear down and left (northeast) in the wide hanging valley on the far side. (If one chooses to avoid any excess elevation gain they can detour around the climb to the top of the ridge by contouring around the right, or south, side of the ridge. This means having to do some rocky and brushy side-hilling before one can turn into the hanging valley. Whichever way one chooses, keep in mind that the end result entails reaching the hanging valley just on the other side of the ridge.)

---

\* To get there see [69] **Walk-About Guide to Ice Cream Cone Trail** above or [88] **Walk-About Guide to Ice Cream Cone Cut-Off** in Chapter 9.

Once in the hanging valley, hike to its uppermost end. At the top of the valley bear left (north) and climb to the crest of the ridge looming above. On reaching the crest of the ridge turn right (northeast) up the crest to the summit (5,150 feet), the tallest of the numerous spires on the ridge's crest.

**TRAIL GRADE:** This hike initially rates Grade 2 as a hike on Ice Cream Cone Trail. Upon leaving the summit of Ice Cream Cone the trail rises to Grade 3 as a hike. It rises again to Grade 4 as a hike on the traverse into the hanging valley. The hike to the uppermost end of the hanging valley also rates Grade 4 as a hike. The climb to the ridge above the hanging valley rises to Grade 6 as a hike and remains so until one reaches the summit.

**TRAIL CONDITION:** This route varies considerably in its conditions. Although one may have to cross some muddy spots on Ice Cream Cone Trail, it generally remains good to excellent. Hiking remains good to excellent until one leaves the trail leading up the southwest ridge of Knoya Peak and crosses into the hanging valley between Knoya Peak and Tikishla Peak. Here one must do some relatively easy bushwhacking through some waist-high brush to reach the upper end of the bowl. The ascent to the summit ridge includes climbing over some loose rocks and up scree. Along the summit ridge the route consists almost entirely of loose rocks and scree all the way to the summit.

**TRAIL MILEAGE:** To go from the parking area at Stuckagain Heights to the summit of Tikishla Peak entails 7 miles of hiking, for a round-trip total of 14 miles.

**TOTAL ELEVATION GAIN:** From the parking area at Stuckagain Heights to the summit of Tikishla Peak entails an elevation gain of approximately 5,000 feet. The return trip entails up to another approximately 1,000 feet of climbing, for a round-trip total of approximately 6,000 feet.

**HIGH POINT:** This climb reaches its highest point of 5,229 feet above sea level at the summit of Tikishla Peak.

**NORMAL HIKING TIME:** To hike from the parking area at Stuckagain Heights to the summit of Tikishla Peak and back should take anywhere from 10 hours to 2 days, depending on the condition and ambition of the hiker(s) involved.

**CAMPSITES:** One will find no designated campsites along this trail. One will find a fine place on which to pitch a tent, however, on the flats around the tarn below Knoya Peak as well as in the hanging valley between Knoya Peak and Tikishla Peak.

**BEST TIME:** Most people should find any time from early May to September a good time to do this hike. One should think twice about doing this climb in the winter, however, because of the avalanche danger in the hanging valley between Knoya Peak and Tikishla Peak as well as on the final climb to the summit of Tikishla Peak.

**USGS MAPS:** Anchorage A-7 and A-8.

Tarn above Ice Cream Cone

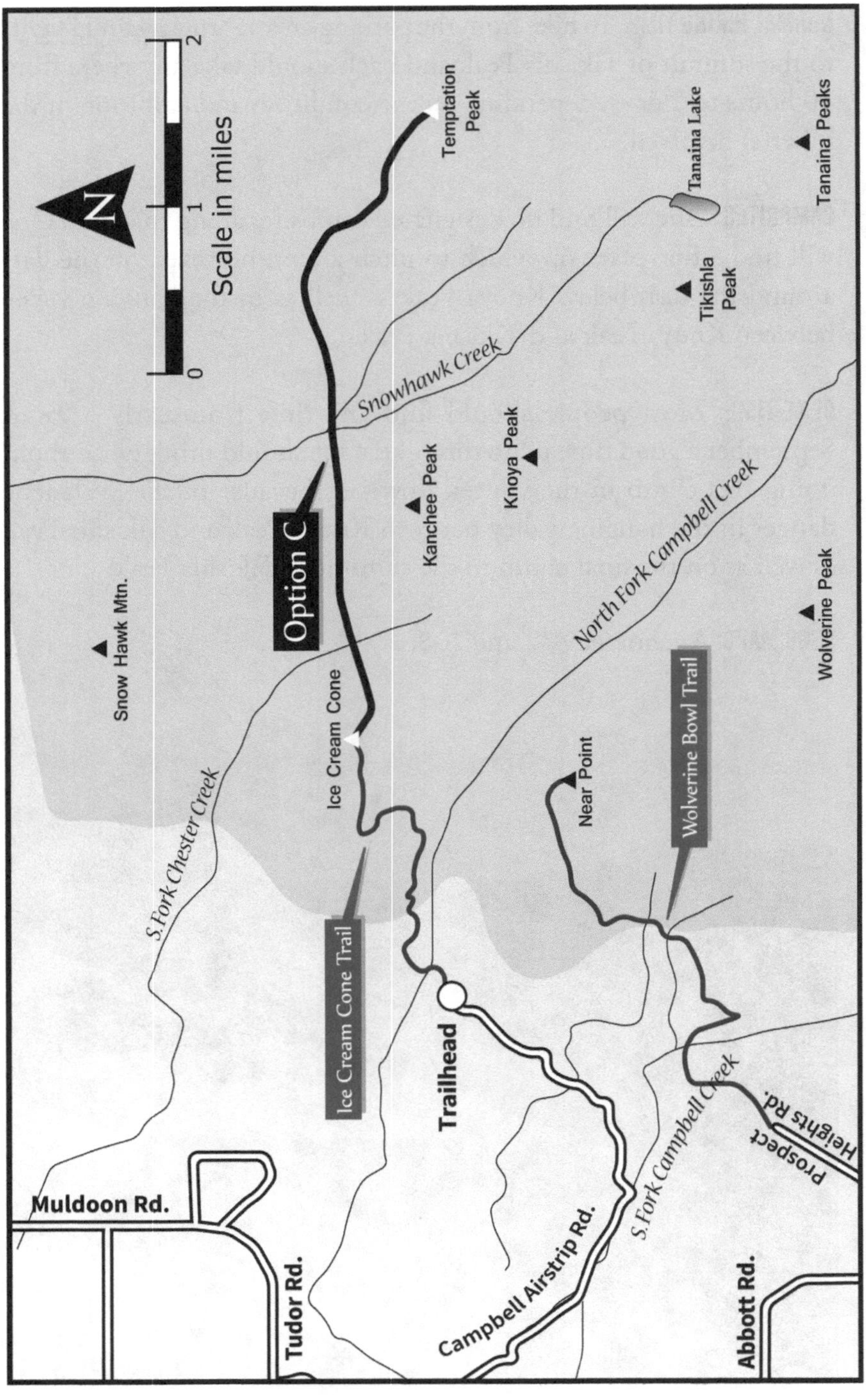
N
Scale in miles
0
1
2
Temptation Peak
Tanaina Lake
Tanaina Peaks
Tikishla Peak
Snowhawk Creek
Knoya Peak
Kanchee Peak
Option C
Snow Hawk Mtn.
North Fork Campbell Creek
Wolverine Peak
Ice Cream Cone
Wolverine Bowl Trail
Near Point
S. Fork Chester Creek
Ice Cream Cone Trail
Trailhead
Prospect Heights Rd.
S. Fork Campbell Creek
Muldoon Rd.
Campbell Airstrip Rd.
Tudor Rd.
Abbott Rd.

# 72

# OPTION C

# Temptation Peak

One of the most remote 5,000-foot peaks in the Front Range to reach, Temptation Peak makes for a long of climbing for anyone with some ambition. One can access this peak via Snow Hawk Creek valley\*. Though easier than the one described below, that route does not cross nearly so dramatic terrain. Nor, considering how much of it follows trail lacks the sense of adventure the route described below offers. Both, however, end with the same open climb to the summit.

This climb crosses military land, and therefore one needs to obtain a permit from JBER-Richardson to hike it. To obtain this permit, see Appendix 3 at the end of the book.

**TRAIL LOCATION:** This climb begins at the summit of Ice Cream Cone\*\*. From the summit of Ice Cream Cone, follow the wide trail to the right (east) as it climbs to the crest of the next knoll on the ridge. On reaching the crest, bear left (northeast) off the trail and descend into the wide valley that spreads out underneath the west faces Kanchee Peak and Knoya Peak. After crossing the stream bed at the base of this valley, climb through the brush to the low saddle to the left (northwest) of Kanchee Peak. The crest of the saddle provides a magnificent first view of Temptation Peak as well as the valley one has to cross to reach it.

---------------------------------------------------------------------------

\*    For more information about that route,
     see [73] **Walk-About Guide to Snow Hawk Valley Trail** in Chapter 7.

\*\*   To get there see [69] **Walk-About Guide to Ice Cream Cone Trail** above or
     [88] **Walk-About Guide to Ice Cream Cone Cut-Off** in Chapter 9.

From the saddle (which begins the traverse of Knoya Peak and Kanshee Peak by turning right up the ridge), continue straight (northeast) to the far side of the saddle. On the far side of the saddle descend into the Snow Hawk Creek valley spread out below. During this descent direct your steps as best as possible toward Snow Hawk Cabin visible just above the confluence of the two streams that divides the upper valley. Once at the base of the valley, turn upstream to where a low ridge divides these two streams. Here bear left (northeast) toward Temptation Peak and cross the lower creek. Just beyond the convergence of the two streams, one arrives at the doorstep of Upper Snow Hawk Cabin. Just beyond the cabin the route crosses the upper stream and continues right up to the base of the southeast ridge, the large buttress extending down from the summit toward the cabin.

At the base of this ridge the actual climb of Temptation Peak begins. One should find nothing extreme about this climb, though. Climbing steadily up the wide ridge, it just takes time and effort. Neither should one easily get lost on this climb. Simply stay just to the right (southeast) of the ridge's crest as it rises past the secluded tarn located in the narrow vale below and to the left toward the summit ridge. As long as one does not stray too far out onto the windswept open slopes to the right or try to maneuver through the rocks on the left, in approximately 100 yards one should soon reach the summit (5,383 feet).

**TRAIL GRADE:** This hike initially rates Grade 2 as a hike on Ice Cream Cone Trail. On the climb to the knoll past Ice Cream Cone it rises to Grade 3 as a hike. On leaving the trail summit of this knoll it rises Grade 4 as a hike for the entire way up and over the saddle west of Kanchee Peak and down to Upper Snow Hawk Cabin. Only when the climb up the southwest ridge begins, does the route rise to Grade 5 as a climb. It remains Grade 5 as a climb all the way to the summit.

**TRAIL CONDITION:** This route varies considerably in its conditions. Although one may have to cross some muddy spots, Ice Cream Cone Trail generally remains good to excellent. Hiking remains good to excellent until one leaves the trail at the knoll above Ice Cream Cone and descends across and up the other side of the valley to the saddle leading into the Snow

Hawk Creek valley. On reaching the next valley's floor, one almost always has at least some brush to push through on the route up valley. Past Snow Hawk Cabin the route climbs mostly open slope with only a few skids of scree to cross or climb even on the highest reaches of the summit.

**TRAIL MILEAGE:** To go from the parking area at Stuckagain Heights to the summit of Temptation Peak entails approximately 9 miles of hiking, for a round-trip total of 18 miles.

**TOTAL ELEVATION GAIN:** To hike from the parking area at Stuckagain Heights to the summit of Temptation Peak entails a total elevation gain of approximately 5,400 feet. To hike from the summit of Temptation Peak back to the parking area at Stuckagain Heights entails another elevation gain of approximately 1,000 feet. This makes for a round-trip total of approximately 6,400 feet.

**HIGH POINT:** This climb reaches its highest point of 5,383 feet above sea level at the summit of Temptation Peak.

**NORMAL HIKING TIME:** This climb should take anywhere from 12 hours to 2 days depending on the condition and ambition of the hiker(s) involved.

**CAMPSITES:** One will find no designated campsites along this trail. One will find many a fine place on which to pitch a tent, however, throughout the entire valley between Tikishla Peak and Temptation Peak, almost all of which have readily available sources of water. Upper Snow Hawk Cabin is also a fine place to stay, but one should make arrangements with the proper authorities on JBER-Richardson before doing so*.

**BEST TIME:** Most people should find that any time from early May to September the best time to do this hike.

**USGS MAPS:** Anchorage A-7 and A-8.

---

\* For information as to how to reach them, see [Appendix 3] at the end of the book.

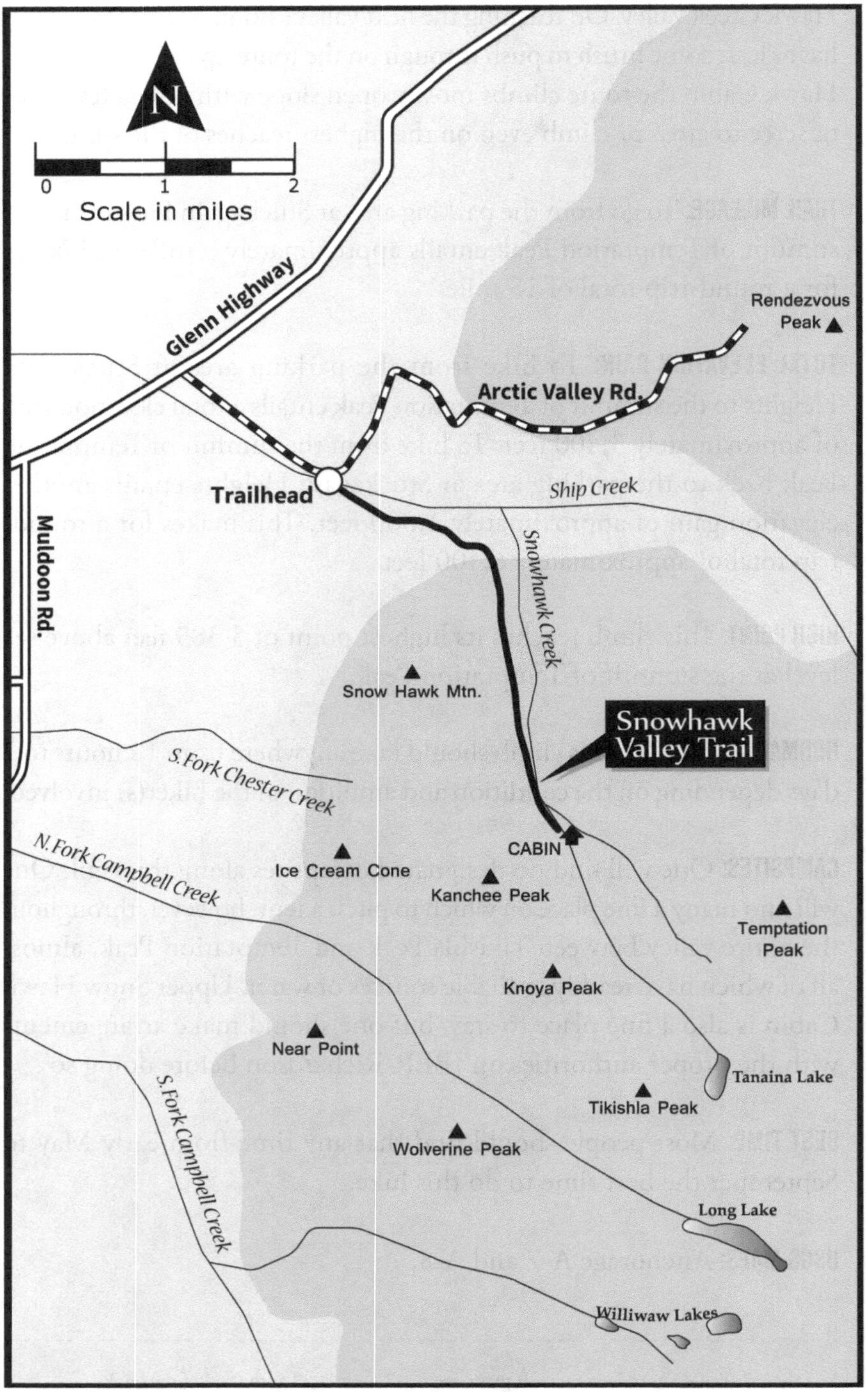
N
0
1
2
Scale in miles
Glenn Highway
Rendezvous Peak
Arctic Valley Rd.
Trailhead
Ship Creek
Muldoon Rd.
Snowhawk Creek
Snow Hawk Mtn.
Snowhawk Valley Trail
S. Fork Chester Creek
CABIN
N. Fork Campbell Creek
Ice Cream Cone
Kanchee Peak
Temptation Peak
Knoya Peak
Near Point
Tanaina Lake
Tikishla Peak
S. Fork Campbell Creek
Wolverine Peak
Long Lake
Williwaw Lakes

## CHAPTER 7

# ARCTIC VALLEY

## Walk-About Guide to Snow Hawk Valley Trail

This trail offers a backdoor entry into the Front Range. In climbing this trail one can access climbs of the not-very-often-climbed Temptation Peak and the even-lesser-climbed Snow Hawk Peak. The latter of these two climbs makes for a particularly unique experience, opening a new perspective of the Anchorage bowl from its summit. Of course, one's idea of a wilderness experience may not include a broad view of a major city. But the view does not just include the city. It also includes Turnagain Arm, Knik Arm, Cook Inlet, and all the surrounding mountain ranges, all of which put that city in its proper perspective as a small enclave of sheltered humanity in a very large wilderness. Bear in mind, however, that one needs an access permit from JBER to do this hike[*].

**TRAIL LOCATION:** The little-used Snow Hawk Valley Trail begins on a side road off Arctic Valley Road. To get there drive 6 miles north from Anchorage on the Glenn Highway. There, at Milepost 6, turn right (east) on the Arctic Valley Road exit. At the end of the ramp, continue

---

[*]    For information as to how to obtain such a permit, see [Appendix 3] **Permits and Fees** at the end of this volume.

following the road as it straightens out. (Southbound traffic should take the JBER-Richardson exit. Then, after taking a left at the top of the exit ramp and crossing back over the highway, follow this road as it continues along the opposite side of the highway for approximately 1.5 miles to where it intersects with Arctic Valley Road. Then turn left [east] on Arctic Valley Road.)

After turning onto Arctic Valley Road follow it for just under 1.5 miles past the golf course. After passing Moose Run Golf Course, the road climbs a small hill. Just beyond the crest of this hill one passes a sign for Snow Hawk Cabins. Just beyond the sign a gravel road that drops into the wood on the right (south). Turn right on this gravel road and follow for less than 100 feet to the first Y intersection. There go left. Then continue down the road until one reaches a gate just shy of the bridge spanning Ship Creek. There turn into the parking area down and to the left (north) off the road and park wherever convenient.

To reach the trailhead proper, one must now continue on foot. After hiking through the gate, continue up the road to another intersection. Bear left (northeast) at this intersection and follow it up the southeast side of Ship Creek. In approximately 0.25 miles the trail turns sharply right and uphill. After one large switchback it approaches Ship Creek dam. Just before the final short turn to the dam it passes a rough dirt road climbing into the brush on the right (south). Turn right onto this road and follow it up through the trees. (If one passes this dirt road and reaches the dam, which one will do in less than 100 feet, back track the short way back to the road leading off the main road on the left.) In less than 100 feet this rough road reaches an intersection with a marked footpath on the left (east).

This marked trail junction indicates the beginning of Snow Hawk Valley Trail. Follow this trail as it winds upward. The trail, though rough in places, remains generally easy to follow. Only at one place might one lose the trail. One reaches this spot approximately 0.8 miles after turning up the dirt road by the dam. Here another trail continues straight ahead to where it soon peters out in the brush. Instead of following this false trail, turn right (south) onto the main trail (marked by a trail sign on a tree up to the right as well as some marking tape hanging on a number of trees) and follow it as climbs a small rise. At the top of the rise, the trail swings left (east) to contour the slope. As it contours along the slope, the trail rounds the first large buttress of the mountain above and to the right. Within 0.25 miles past the base of the buttress the trail crosses a wide plateau well above the confluence of Ship Creek and Snow Hawk Creek. At the far end of this plateau one reaches the ruins of Lower Snow Hawk Cabin, which burned down a number of years ago.

After passing these ruins the trail swings right (southwest) and turns into the Snow Hawk Creek valley. The trail continues up valley paralleling Snow Hawk Creek. As one approaches tree line, it passes through some thick patches of alder. Then it emerges onto more open tundra slopes. Approximately 1 mile later the trail dips in and out of a deep trough with a pleasantly surprising copse of cottonwoods growing in its wide hollow. Approximately 0.25 miles past this trough the trail crosses a low ridge and descends to the wide flats of the upper end of this valley.

After continuing through the low brush for another approximately 1 mile, the trail comes to a confluence of Snow Hawk Creek with a tributary creek flowing down the left (southeast) side of a low rise in the middle of the valley. Continuing along the right shore of Snow Hawk Creek follow it for approximately 50 feet past this tributary. There turn left and cross the creek. Once on the far shore, follow the right (southeast) bank of the tributary stream approximately 100 yards upstream to the doorstep of Upper Snow Hawk Cabin, located in a small open meadow at the base of Temptation Peak. Here the trail reaches its uppermost end.

At this point one has a number of choices. First, one can return the way they have come. Second, one can explore the upper Snow Hawk Creek valley beyond the cabin, a wide but enclosed area that few people visit. Ambitious hikers may especially find Tanaina Lake, located at the uppermost end of the valley in the shadows of East and West Tanaina Peaks. Third, one can backtrack Snow Hawk Valley Trail to where they can turn left (west) off the trail and climb Snow Hawk Peak*. Fourth, one can climb Temptation Peak towering high

--------------------------------------------------------

\* For more information about that hike, see [75] **OPTION B—Snowhawk Peak**.

to the left behind Upper Snow Hawk Cabin*. Other options include climbing Kanchee Peak, Knoya Peak, and Tikishla Peak, all standing in a row high above the opposite side of the valley**.

**TRAIL GRADE:** Relatively gentle in its long climb of the valley, Snow Hawk Valley Trail rates Grade 2 as a hike for its entire length.

**TRAIL CONDITION:** Because of military restrictions this trail sees little use. As a result, not only does it have many muddy and rocky sections, but it also many weeds and brush encroach upon it by midsummer, making it sometimes difficult to follow.

**TRAIL MILEAGE:** To go from the parking area at Ship Creek to Upper Snow Hawk Cabin entails approximately 5.5 miles of hiking for a round-trip total of 11 miles.

**TOTAL ELEVATION GAIN:** To hike from the parking area at Ship Creek to Upper Snow Hawk Cabin entails a total elevation gain of approximately 2,300 feet.

**HIGH POINT:** This trail reaches its highest point of approximately 2,650 feet above sea level at Upper Snow Hawk Cabin.

**NORMAL HIKING TIME:** To hike from the parking area at Ship Creek to Upper Snow Hawk Cabin should take anywhere from 4 to 8 hours, depending on the condition and ambition of the hiker(s) involved. Extending this time to 2 days, however, allows hikers to enjoy the clean and comfortable solitude of the cabin for a night.

------------------------------------------------------------

* For more information about that hike, see [74] **OPTION A—Temptation Peak** below.

** This guide does not include climbs of these peaks from this valley. But for more information about climbing these peaks from North Fork of Campbell Creek valley, see [70] **OPTION A—Traverse of Kanchee Peak and Knoya Peak** and [71] **OPTION B—Tikishla Peak** in Chapter 6.

**CAMPSITES:** One will find no designated campsites along this trail. One will find many fine places on which to pitch a tent, however, throughout the entire upper valley between Tikishla Peak and Temptation Peak, most of which have readily available sources of water. One will find also find Upper Snow Hawk Cabin a fine place to stay. If one does plan to stay there, however, be sure to make arrangements with the proper authorities on JBER-Richardson before doing so.*

**BEST TIME:** Most people should find that any time from early May to September remains the best time to do this hike. This also makes a fine ski or snowshoe outing in the winter, although one should remain wary of potential avalanche danger in the upper valley.

**USGS MAPS:** Anchorage A-7 and A-8.

---

\*     For information as to how to reach them, see [Appendix 3] at the end of the book.

Upper Snowhawk Valley with Tikishla Peak on the right and Temptation Peak on the left

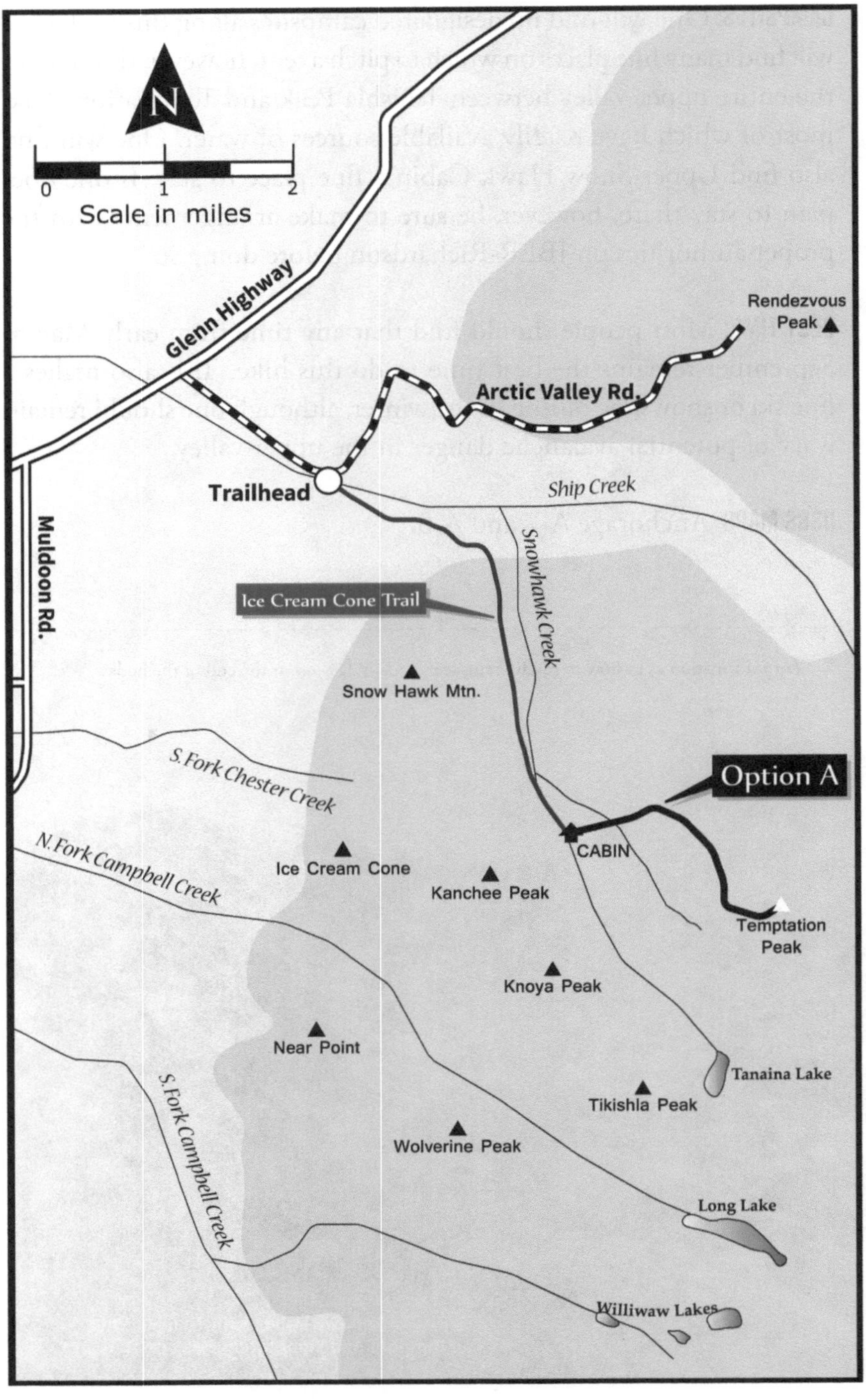
N
0
1
2
Scale in miles
Glenn Highway
Arctic Valley Rd.
Rendezvous Peak
Trailhead
Muldoon Rd.
Ship Creek
Snowhawk Creek
Ice Cream Cone Trail
Snow Hawk Mtn.
S. Fork Chester Creek
Option A
CABIN
N. Fork Campbell Creek
Ice Cream Cone
Kanchee Peak
Temptation Peak
Knoya Peak
Near Point
Tanaina Lake
Tikishla Peak
Wolverine Peak
S. Fork Campbell Creek
Long Lake
Williwaw Lakes

# OPTION A

# Temptation Peak

**TRAIL LOCATION:** This climb begins at Upper Snow Hawk Cabin located at the uppermost end of Snow Hawk Valley Trail*. From the doorstep of Upper Snow Hawk Cabin follow the creek up the southeastern slope of Mount Temptation through a mix of low brush, tundra, and scree. Although the open slope offers many routes, most people should find that the best way follows the ridge line directly above the cabin. This route also offers some fine views of the tarn squeezed into a couloir below and to the left (west) of the mountain if one takes a few moments to peak through openings in the rocks on the left side of the climb.

This route, besides being efficient and scenic, should also make it difficult to get lost. Staying just to the right (southeast) of the ridge's crest, follow it as it rises past the secluded tarn on the left toward the summit ridge. If one does not stray too far out onto the windswept open slopes to the right or try to maneuver through the rocks on the left, one should eventually, as long as they continue upward, reach the crest of the jagged summit ridge. One now has but a short scramble up the summit ridge, streaked with loose scree and rocks, to reach the summit (5,383 feet).

**TRAIL GRADE:** The relatively gentle Snow Hawk Valley Trail rates Grade 2 as hike for its entire length. Only when the route begins to climb the southwest ridge does the route rise to Grade 5 as a hike. It continues to rate Grade 5 as a hike for almost the entire way to the summit.

---

\*   To get there, see [73] **Walk-About Guide to Snow Hawk Valley Trail**.

**TRAIL CONDITION:** Because of military restrictions Snow Hawk Valley Trail sees little use. As a result, not only does it have many muddy and rocky sections, but many weeds and brush also encroach upon it by midsummer. This sometimes makes it difficult to follow. Past Upper Snow Hawk Cabin, however, the route soon clears of brush, leaving but a few skids of scree to cross or climb near the summit.

**TRAIL MILEAGE:** To go from Upper Snow Hawk Cabin to the summit of Temptation Peak entails approximately 3 miles of hiking, for a round-trip total of 6 miles. This means that to go from the parking area at Ship Creek to the summit of Temptation Peak entails approximately 8.5 miles of hiking, for a round-trip total of 17 miles.

**TOTAL ELEVATION GAIN:** To hike from the parking area by Ship Creek to the summit of Temptation Peak entails a total elevation gain of approximately 4,800 feet.

**HIGH POINT:** This climb reaches its highest point of approximately 5,383 feet above sea at the summit of Temptation Peak.

**NORMAL HIKING TIME:** The round-trip hike from the parking area by Ship Creek to the summit of Temptation Peak should take anywhere from 12 hours to 2 days, depending on the condition and ambition of the hiker(s) involved.

**CAMPSITES:** One will find no designated campsites along this trail. One will find, however, many a fine place on which to pitch a tent throughout the entire valley between Tikishla Peak and Temptation Peak, almost all of which have readily available sources of water. One will find also find Upper Snow Hawk Cabin a fine place to stay. If one does plan to stay there, however, be sure to make arrangements with the proper authorities at JBER-Richardson before doing so*.

--------------------------------------------------------------------

\*    For information as to how to reach them, see [Appendix 3] at the end of the book.

**BEST TIME:** Most people should find any time from June to September the best time to do this hike. One can also make the hike to Upper Snow Hawk Cabin in the winter. The avalanche dangers on Temptation Peak itself, however, should make anyone think twice about climbing it in the winter.

**USGS MAPS:** Anchorage A-7 and A-8.

On Temptation Peak

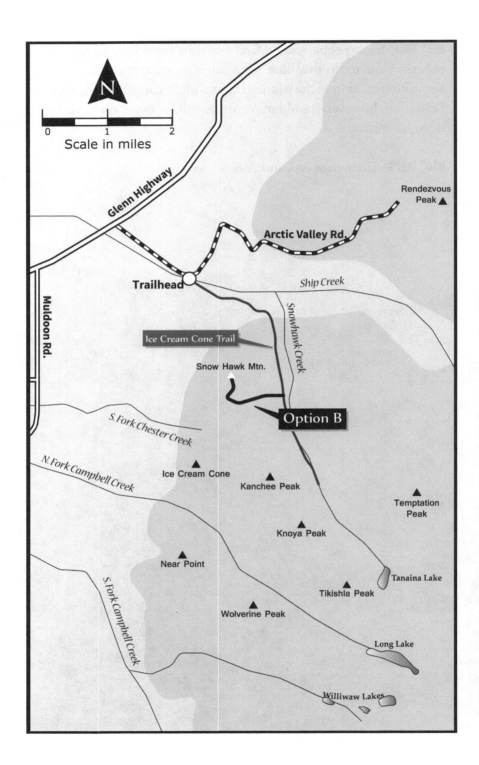

75

# OPTION B

# Snow Hawk Peak

From almost any location in the Anchorage bowl one can look up and see this peak but not notice it. Located at the far north end of the Front Range, this summit, a low-angled pyramid, rises from the short ridge extending from Kanchee Peak to the Ship Creek basin. Yet despite rising in plains sight, rarely does anyone climb it. An old tank trail scars its south face, but the tanks that trained this high on Fort Richardson land have long since retreated to the lowlands. People, in the meantime, come and go along the Snow Hawk Valley Trail or pass by it on their way from the upper end of Ice Cream Cone Trail to Kanchee Peak or Temptation Peak, but hardly anyone visits this summit. They should, though. The gentle climb to the summit of Snow Hawk Peak, and any continuation south along its ridge toward Kanchee Peak, offers wide views not only of the higher mountains above it the north, east, and south but also of the city below to the west.

**TRAIL LOCATION:** This climb begins approximately halfway up Snow Hawk Valley Trail*. At that point the trail should begin its climb through the last alder, spruce, and brush to tree line. Once past the thickets of alder and low spruce marking of tree line, one can begin looking for an optimal place to turn right (west) off the trail and begin climbing to the summit of Snow Hawk Peak. One need not look for any landmarks for

---

* To get there see [73] **Walk-About Guide to Snow Hawk Valley Trail.**

the precise place to begin this climb. As long as one has climbed above tree line and sees mostly open tundra leading up to the ridge top above the right (west) side of the trail, they can begin the climb. If one does reach a relatively large, cottonwood-filled trough approximately 3.5 miles up Snow Hawk Valley Trail one has gone too far. One does not have to back-track along the trail, though. Simply begin at that point the climb toward the ridge. Once on the ridge, bear right (northwest) and climb the gentle slope the last approximately 0.3 miles to the summit.

If one still remains uncertain as to where to begin the climb off Snow Hawk Valley Trail, then continue to the far side of the trough and there turn right (west) and climb to the saddle above. From the saddle turn right (northwest) and follow ridge crest back toward the summit. Upon reaching the ridge, one need only revel in a little more than 0.5 miles of gentle climbing northwest up the open and scenic to reach the summit of Snow Hawk Peak (3,215 feet).

From the summit one has two major choices. First, one can turn around and return the way they have come. Second, one can backtrack south along the ridge, passing some dramatic clefts on the western face of the ridge, to the notch below Kanchee Peak, from which point one can either drop down the slope to the left (northeast) to the upper end of Snow Hawk Valley Trail near Upper Snow Hawk Cabin, plainly visible just above the confluence of Snow Hawk Creek and another creek in the valley below or climb Kanchee Peak before returning to the valley below.

**TRAIL GRADE:** Relatively gentle in its long climb of the valley, Snow Hawk Valley Trail rates Grade 2 as a hike for its entire length. Once off trail the climb to the summit of Snow Hawk Peak rates Grade 4 as a hike.

**TRAIL CONDITION:** Because of military restrictions Snow Hawk Valley Trail sees little use. As a result, not only does it have many muddy and rocky sections, but many weeds and brush also encroach upon it by midsummer. Off the trail, the walking, despite some tufted tundra in the lower sections, steadily improves as one climbs higher with the summit ridge walk mostly across gravel mixed with tundra and rock.

**TRAIL MILEAGE:** To go from the parking area at Ship Creek to the summit of Snow Hawk Peak entails approximately 4.25 miles of hiking for a round-trip total of 9.5 miles.

**TOTAL ELEVATION GAIN:** To hike from the parking area at Ship Creek to the summit of Snow Hawk Peak entails a total elevation gain of approximately 2,850 feet.

**HIGH POINT:** This trail reaches its highest point of 3,215 feet above sea level at the summit of Snow Hawk Peak.

**NORMAL HIKING TIME:** To hike from the parking area at Ship Creek to the summit of Snow Hawk Peak and back should take anywhere from 4 to 7 hours, depending on the condition and ambition of the hiker(s) involved.

**CAMPSITES:** One will find no designated campsites along this trail. One will find many fine places on which to pitch a tent, however, above tree line on either side of Snow Hawk Valley Trail. One will find also find Upper Snow Hawk Cabin located at the uppermost end of Snow Hawk Valley Trail a fine place to stay. If one does plan to stay there, however, be sure to make arrangements with the proper authorities on JBER-Richardson before doing so*.

**BEST TIME:** Most people should find any time from early May to September a good time to do this hike. This hike also makes a fine ski or snowshoe outing in the winter, although one should remain wary of potential avalanche danger if one ventures very far up valley beyond this climb.

**USGS MAPS:** Anchorage A-7 and A-8.

---------------------------------------------------------------------

*   For information as to how to reach them, see [Appendix 3] at the end of the book.

Spenser Loop at Hilltop Ski Area

## CHAPTER 8

# HILLTOP SKI AREA

## THE ANCHORAGE BOWL

Apart from the last chapter, the remaining Walk-About Guides in this volume all describe hiking and biking trips in the Anchorage bowl. Some might think that this makes them tame and picturesque. This may prove true for some of these trips, but not for most. As John McPhee points out that Anchorage differs little from other cities. This may lull some into thinking Anchorage differs little from other cities. But McPhee qualifies his statement by adding that though it may seem like other cities, it lies right next door to Alaska. Consider it McPhee's observation a subtle reminder. On any give morning in Anchorage one can wake to see moose grazing in the garden or a bear scrounging in the garbage. A friend looked out one day to see her dog playing with a fox on the lawn, while another friend had to protect her cat from a bald eagle. In the spring snow geese pass through on their way north and in the fall Canadian geese stream through on their way south. In the summer beluga whales steam up Turnagain Arm and in winter ravens play far above the ice floes creaking at the base of Point Woronzof.

Nor should one consider Anchorage entirely urban. Besides 10,946 acres of municipal parkland, Anchorage has 223 parks with 82 playgrounds, 250 miles of trails (including 135 miles of paved bike trails, 87 miles of non-paved hiking trails, 105 miles of groomed ski trails, 36 miles of mushing trails, and 6-plus miles of equestrian trails) 110 athletic fields, and numerous greenbelts linking neighborhoods with surrounding wild lands and wildlife habitats. This makes Anchorage a place worth exploring in and of itself—apart from the lure of the Alaska next door.

The following Walk-About Guides for trails and routes in the major parks and rides along major bike trails, though hardly comprehensive as to all the outdoor opportunities in the Anchorage bowl, will at least introduce new-comers and tourists to Alaska to a variety of mountain and ocean scenery in both popular and secluded places throughout the bowl. Some guides may even allow some long-time residents to discover a new trail or route maybe but a short distance from their doorstep.

# OVERVIEW OF HILLTOP SKI AREA

For those lacking either the desire or the time to drive to Alyeska, Hilltop Ski Area often serves as a nearby alternative. Besides groomed downhill ski and snowboard slopes, it also offers 32 kilometers of groomed cross-country ski trails that draw considerably large crowds on winter weekends. It even has a ski jump. On most weekday afternoons, local grade-school students flock to its slopes to slice their way down Hillside's slopes while high school and college cross-country ski teams in training join recreational skiers on the various cross-country loops in the surrounding woods.

Remarkably, despite all the skiers coming and going this way and that, some of these trails remain open to all users—runners, bikers, skijorgers, and even equestrians—all year round. These include South Gasline Trail (also known as Multi-Use Corridor), Gasline Trail, and the appropriately named Multi-Use Trail. At the end of the ski season, though, runners, bikers, hikers, and horseback riders can also reclaim all the ski trails for their own use. Only when the first substantial snowfall of the next late autumn must they again relinquish them to the skiers and snowboarders.

Besides serving as a winter alternative to Alyeska, Hilltop Ski Area also serves as an important all-season link between Anchorage bowl below and the Front Range of the Chugach Mountains above. Lower Gasline Trail, various single-lane bike trails, and even Spenser Loop (when ski season ends) link the bowl below with the mountains above, thus providing contiguous routes allowing the hiker or biker to experience the changes in flora and fauna that occur as one climbs higher and higher into the open high country above the city.

Spenser Loop on Hillside

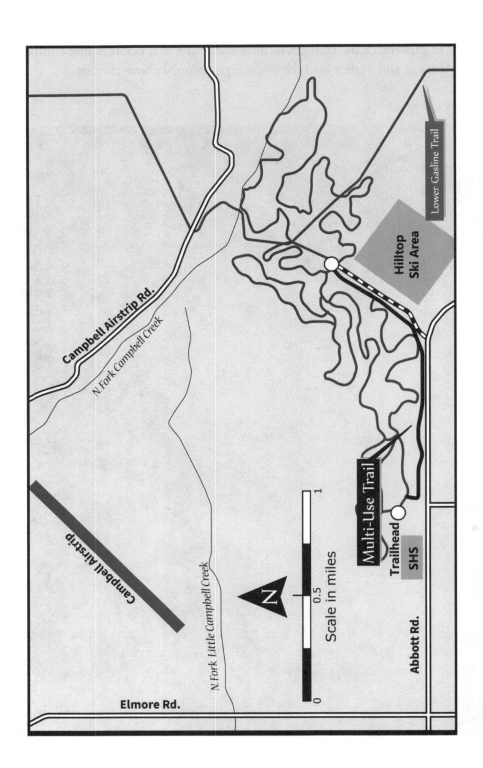

Lower Gasline Trail

Hilltop Ski Area

Campbell Airstrip Rd.

N. Fork Campbell Creek

Campbell Airstrip

N. Fork Little Campbell Creek

Multi-Use Trail

Trailhead

SHS

Abbott Rd.

Elmore Rd.

N

Scale in miles

0    0.5    1

# 76

# Walk-About Guide to Multi-Use Trail

Just one of the many trails used by runners, bikers, hikers, and horseback riders in the summer, this trail takes a more important role in winter. At that time, when most other trails on Hillside close to all but ski travel, Multi-Use Trail remains open to all users. Thus through the use of this trail and its extension, South Gasline Trail (also known as Multi-Use Corridor), and South Bivouac Trail a non-skier can connect Abbott Road with Basher Road. This trail thus allows non-skiers to also connect any number of loops, such as the Circumnavigation of Campbell Tract described later in this chapter.

**TRAIL LOCATION:** Multi-Use Trail begins a short way up the bike trail that begins at the northeast corner behind Service High School. To get there drive south on the Seward Highway from 5th Avenue in downtown Anchorage for approximately 5.5 miles to the Dimond Boulevard exit. Turn off the highway at this exit. At the bottom of the ramp, turn left and cross back under the highway. In less than 100 yards Dimond Boulevard turns into Abbott Road as it swings in a broad curve to the left. Follow Abbott Road as it swings first around this curve to the right (south) and then to the (left) north. Approximately 1 mile from the Seward Highway Abbott Road reaches a set of lights at Lake Otis Parkway. Continue straight through these lights and follow Abbott Road uphill toward the mountains for another approximately 1 mile to another set of lights. Continue straight through these lights as well and continue for another 0.75 miles uphill.

At that point one should come in sight of Service High School on the left (north) side of Abbott Road. Continue along Abbott Road past the school's main building to its far end. There turn left (north) into the parking area. Follow this parking area back to the far right (northeast) corner of the school and park where available.

Access to Multi-Use Trail begins on the bike trail that leaves the parking area to the right (east) of the football/soccer field and to the left (west) of the windowless sports building on the right (east). Follow the bike trail down a very short hill to the edge of the woods where it swings up to the right. Approximately 0.2 miles From Service High School the bike trail approaches a large walking bridge over Abbott Road. At that point look for a dirt trail climbing of the bike to the left (east). This dirt trail marks the beginning Multi-Use Trail.

Turn left onto Multi-Use Trail and follow it up the first rise to where it drops steeply into the woods. For the next approximately 1 mile Multi-Use Trail winds through the woods over a series of short climbs and descents to a parking area for the Hilltop Ski Area cross-country ski trails. Continue straight across the edge of the parking area to its far end where Multi-Use Trail slants up into the woods on the left (northeast). In another 0.3 miles the trail reaches a trailhead for some of the many cross-country ski trails in Hilltop Ski Area. Pass straight across the opening by the trailhead to the narrow opening in the trees on the far side. In approximately 0.1 miles the trail emerges from the trees where it reaches its easternmost end on southern end of the broad Gasline Multi-Use Corridor.

At this point one has at least three choices. First, one can turn around and return the way they have come. Second, one can continue along Gasline Multi-Use Corridor and then South Bivouac Trail to South Bivouac Trailhead on Basher Road*. Third, they can continue in a big loop that circumnavigates Campbell Tract**.

**TRAIL GRADE:** This entire trail, despite its many short, sharp ups and downs, rates Grade 1 as a hike.

- - - - - - - - - - - - - - - - - - - - - - - - - - - - - - - - - - - - - - - - - - - - - - - - - - - - - -

\*    For more information about that route, see [77] **Walk-About Guide to South Gasline Trail** and [78] **Walk-About Guide to South Bivouac Trail**.

\*\*   For more information about that route,
see [86] **OPTION A—Circumnavigation of Campbell Tract** in Chapter 8.

**TRAIL CONDITION:** This wide trail, despite some and roots and seasonal mud holes remains in generally excellent condition for its entire length.

**TRAIL MILEAGE:** To complete the entire length of Multi-Use Trail from Service High School to its end where it merges with the broad South Gasline Trail entails approximately 1.6 miles of hiking or biking for a round-trip total of 3.2 miles.

**TOTAL ELEVATION GAIN:** To hike the entire length of Multi-Use Trail and back entails a total elevation gain of approximately 400 feet.

**HIGH POINT:** This trail reaches its highest point of approximately 520 feet above sea level on the last hill before one reaches the first parking area for Hilltop Ski Area.

**NORMAL HIKING TIME:** To hike the entire length of Multi-Use Trail from Service High School to its end and back should take anywhere from 1.5 to 3 hours, depending on the condition and ambition of the hiker(s) involved.

**CAMPSITES:** One will find no designated campsites along this trail. Nor, given the short length of the trail, should one need any.

**BEST TIME:** Most people should find any time of year a good time to do this hike, bike, or ski. In winter it also makes a fine hike or bike because it remains usually well-packed through much use.

**USGS MAPS:** Anchorage A-8.

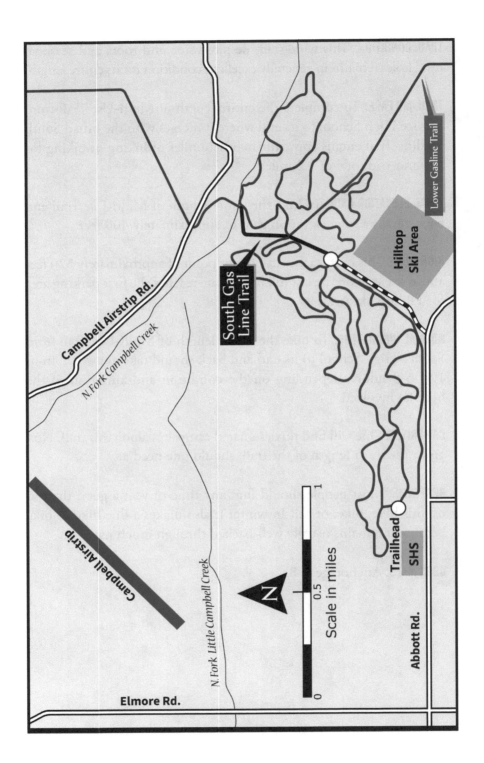

Lower Gasline Trail

Hilltop Ski Area

South Gas Line Trail

Campbell Airstrip Rd.

N. Fork Campbell Creek

Campbell Airstrip

N. Fork Little Campbell Creek

Elmore Rd.

Trailhead

SHS

Abbott Rd.

N

Scale in miles

0    0.5    1

# 77

# Walk-About Guide to South Gasline Trail (Multi-Use Corridor)

This trail, combined with Multi-Use Trail and South Bivouac Trail, allows the only way a non-skier can cross Hilltop Ski Area in winter months. During these months one could very well share the trail with not only skiers, but runners, hikers, and bikers, along with parents pushing baby strollers and people walking their dogs, and anyone else wanting to cross from Abbott Road to Basher Road without going all the way down and around through Camp bell Tract.

This trail also provides access via Lower Gasline Trail and Upper Gasline Trail to the Front Range above. Thus, though short, this trail sees not only multi-uses, but also serves multi-purposes.

**TRAIL LOCATION:** South Gasline Trail begins where Multi-Use Trail ends in Hilltop Ski Area. To get there drive south on the Seward Highway from 5th Avenue in downtown Anchorage for approximately 5.5 miles to the Dimond Boulevard exit. Turn off the highway at this exit. At the bottom of the ramp, turn left and cross back under the highway. In less than 100 yards Dimond Boulevard turns into Abbott Road as it swings in a broad curve to the left. Follow Abbott Road as it swings first around this curve to the right (south) and then to the (left) north. Approximately 1 mile from the Seward Highway Abbott Road reaches a set of lights at Lake Otis Parkway. Continue straight through these lights and follow Abbott Road uphill toward the mountains for another approximately 1 mile to another set of lights. Continue straight through these lights as well and continue for another 0.75 miles uphill.

At that point one should come in sight of Service High School on the left (north) side of Abbott Road.

Continuing straight past Service High School, follow Abbott Road as it passes under a walking bridge. Approximately 0.5 miles after the bridge, the road reaches a parking area for the lighted cross-country ski loop of Hillside Park. Continue along Abbott Road to the far end of the parking area. There one should reach a road on the left (north) marked by a large sign for Hilltop Ski Area. Turn left onto this road. Follow this road for approximately 0.3 miles past Hilltop Chalet to the far (northern) end of the parking area. Park where available. Access to South Gasline (Multi-Use Corridor) begins at the ski trailhead just to the left (west) upper end of the parking area.

Upon leaving the parking area, bear right (northeast) across the opening behind the information board and look for a break in the trees on the right where begins the very last section of Multi-Use Trail. Turn onto this tail end of Multi-Use Trail*. In less than 0.1 miles Multi-Use Trail emerges onto the broad south end of South Gasline Trail (Multi-Use Corridor). Bearing left (north) onto South Gasline Trail (Multi-Use Corridor), follow it for approximately 0.1 miles to where it reaches the intersection with Lower Gasline Trail, which climbs the wide, steep opening in the trees to the right**. Approximately 0.2 miles past this trail junction, South Gasline Trail (Multi-Use Corridor) reaches the edge of the bluff overlooking Campbell Creek. Here, just to the right, one should see a post marking the southern end of South Bivouac Trail dropping into the woods on the right***. At this point, continue straight ahead down the face of the bluff. South Gasline Trail (Multi-Use Corridor) ends 0.2 miles from the top of the bluff at a t-intersection with Rover's Run on the south shore of Campbell Creek.

At this point one has three choices. First, they can return the way they have come. Second, they can turn right (east) and follow

---

\*   For more information about that trail, see [76] **Walk-About Guide to Multi-Use Trail.**

\*\*  For more information about that trail, see [79] **Walk-About Guide to Lower Gasline Trail.**

\*\*\* For more about that trail, which forms the last section of the multi-use corridor across hillside, see [78] **Walk-About Guide to South Bivouac Trail.**

Rover's Run for 0.1 miles into the woods to a junction with South Bivouac Trail. Third, they can turn left (west) and follow Rover's Run downstream on a circumnavigation of Campbell Tract\*.

**TRAIL GRADE:** The entirety of this wide trail rates Grade 1 as a hike.

**TRAIL CONDITION:** This trail remains in excellent condition for its entire length.

**TRAIL MILEAGE:** To hike the entire length of this trail from the Hilltop parking area to edge of Campbell Creek entails approximately 0.7 miles of hiking or biking for a round-trip total of 1.4 miles.

**TOTAL ELEVATION GAIN:** To hike the entire length of this trail from the Hilltop parking area to the edge of Campbell Creek and back entails a total elevation gain of approximately 100 feet.

**HIGH POINT:** This trail reaches its highest point of approximately 525 feet above sea level on the bluff overlooking Campbell Creek.

**NORMAL HIKING TIME:** To hike the entire length of this trail from the Hilltop parking area to the edge of Campbell Creek and back again should take anywhere from 45 minutes to 1.5 hours, depending on the condition and ambition of the hiker(s) involved.

**CAMPSITES:** One will find no designated campsites along this trail. Nor, given the short length of the trail, should one need any.

**BEST TIME:** Most people should find any time of year a good time to do this hike, bike, or ski. In winter it also makes a fine hike or bike because it usually becomes well packed through being so well used.

**USGS MAPS:** Anchorage A-8.

----------------------------------------------------------------

\* For more information about that trail, see [85] **Walk-About Guide to Rover's Run** in Chapter 9.

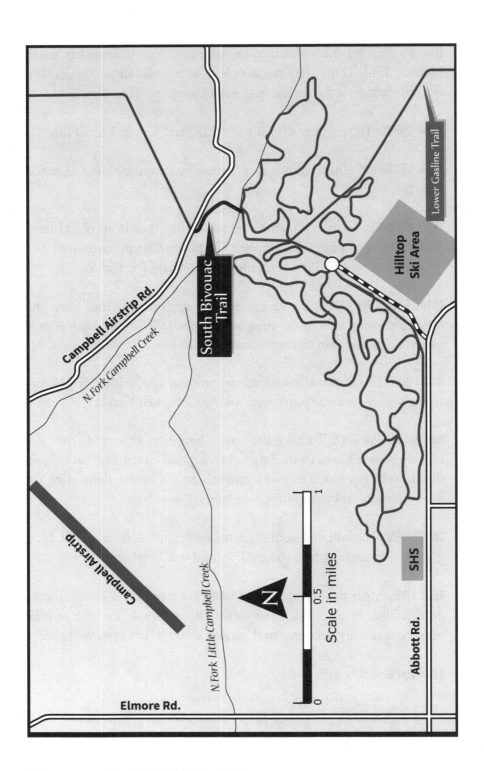

Campbell Airstrip Rd.

N. Fork Campbell Creek

South Bivouac Trail

Lower Gasline Trail

Hilltop Ski Area

Campbell Airstrip

N. Fork Little Campbell Creek

N

Scale in miles

0    0.5    1

SHS

Abbott Rd.

Elmore Rd.

# 78

# Walk-About Guide to South Bivouac Trail

This trail, though short, has some important roles. First, it completes the northern end of a multi-use corridor across Hilltop Ski Area. Though this fact has little importance in the summer, it has great importance in winter. At that time when all the adjacent trails remain closed to all but ski traffic, the multi-use corridor allows hikers, runners, bikers, and skijorgers a means by which to connect Abbott Road with Basher Road through Hilltop Ski Area. Second, in the non-skiing seasons, South Bivouac Trail allows easy access to Spenser Loop, the most spectacular cross-country ski trail in the Hilltop Ski Area complex of trails, making it a popular destination for hikers, bikers, and runners.

**TRAIL LOCATION:** South Bivouac Trail begins at South Bivouac parking area on Basher Road. To get there drive 3.2 miles south of downtown Anchorage on the Seward Highway. Then, just after Milepost 124, take a right (west) on the Tudor Road exit. At the end of the ramp, turn left (east) and cross back over the highway. Continue straight on this road as it gradually climbs past Lake Otis Parkway and Elmore Drive. Approximately 3.2 miles from the Seward Highway, Tudor Road reaches a set of lights at Campbell Airstrip Road leading right (south). Turn right on Campbell Airstrip Road. In approximately 1 mile this road turns into Basher Road. Stay on Basher Road as it continues to wind upward. Approximately 2.5 miles from Tudor Road the road reaches North Bivouac parking area to the left (north) and South Bivouac parking area to the right (south). Turn right into South Bivouac parking area and park wherever available. South Bivouac Trail begins at the far upper (east) end of the parking area.

The trail begins by following a wide and level old road through the woods for 0.1 miles. There it reaches a fork at the crest of a hill dropping into the Campbell Creek hollow. Bear right at this fork (the "downhill" trail) and follow it down for another 0.1 miles to where it rejoins the "uphill" fork. Approximately 0.1 miles later the trail crosses a substantial bridge over Campbell Creek. At the far end of the bridge the trail reaches another fork. Bear right (southwest) at this junction. In another 0.1 miles the trail passes a junction with Rover's Run on the right (west)*. Immediately after this junction, the trail begins a short, steep climb. Approximately 0.2 miles later the trail emerges onto the wide and open edge of South Gasline Trail (Multi-Use Corridor)**.

At this point one has a number of choices. First, one can turn around and return the way they have come. Second, to complete a short balloon loop, one can turn right (north) on South Gasline Trail (Multi-Use Corridor) and follow it down to Rover's Run. One can then turn right (east) on Rover's Run and follow it back to South Bivouac Trail and there turn left (north) and follow it back to South Bivouac parking area. Third, one can bear left (south) and follow South Gasline Trail (Multi-Use Corridor) and then Multi-Use Trail out to Hilltop Ski Area parking area or continue along Multi-Use Trail to Hillside Park parking area***.

**TRAIL GRADE:** The entirety of this wide trail rates Grade 1 as a hike.

**TRAIL CONDITION:** This trail remains in generally excellent condition for its entire length.

---

\*    For more information about that trail, see [85] **Walk-About Guide to Rover's Run** in Chapter 9.

\*\*   For more information about this trail, see [77] **Walk-About Guide to South Gasline Trail**.

\*\*\*  For more information about those trails that complete the multi-use corridor, see [77] **Walk-About Guide to South Gasline Trail** and [76] **Multi-Use Trail**.

**TRAIL MILEAGE:** To hike the entire length of this trail from the South Bivouac parking area to the northern end of South Gasline Trail entails approximately 0.6 miles of hiking or biking for a round-trip total of 1.2 miles.

**TOTAL ELEVATION GAIN:** To hike the entire length of this trail from the South Bivouac parking area to where it ends at a junction with South Gasline Trail (Multi-Use Corridor) and back entails a total elevation gain of approximately 100 feet.

**HIGH POINT:** This trail reaches its highest point of approximately 530 feet above sea level a few feet past the information board one reaches just after leaving South Bivouac parking area.

**NORMAL HIKING TIME:** To hike the entire length of this trail from the South Bivouac parking area to where it ends at a junction with South Gasline Trail (Multi-Use Corridor) and back again should take anywhere from 30 minutes to 1 hour, depending on the condition and ambition of the hiker(s) involved.

**CAMPSITES:** One will find no designated campsites along this trail. Nor, given the short length of the trail, should one need any.

**BEST TIME:** Most people should find any time of year a good time to do this hike, bike, or ski. In winter it also makes a fine hike or bike because it usually becomes well packed through being so well used.

**USGS MAPS:** Anchorage A-8.

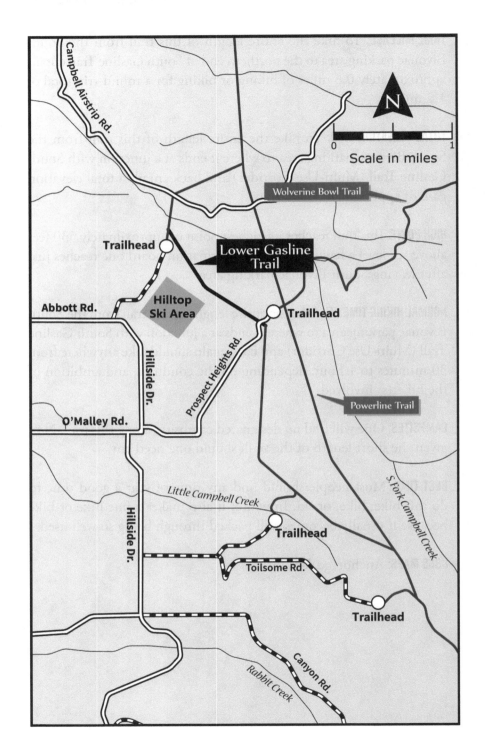

Campbell Airstrip Rd.

N

Scale in miles

0                    1

Wolverine Bowl Trail

Trailhead

Lower Gasline Trail

Hilltop Ski Area

Abbott Rd.

Hillside Dr.

Prospect Heights Rd.

Trailhead

O'Malley Rd.

Powerline Trail

Little Campbell Creek

Hillside Dr.

S. Fork Campbell Creek

Trailhead

Toilsome Rd.

Trailhead

Canyon Rd.

Rabbit Creek

# 79

# Walk-About Guide to Lower Gasline Trail

Though often referred to as just Gasline Trail, this book has adopted the name Lower Gasline Trail to differentiate it from Upper Gasline Trail and South Gasline Trail (Multi-Use Corridor). These differentiations seem justified by the fact that, like the different sections of Powerline Trail, very few people hike all of Gasline Trail in its entirety. Instead, most people use the various sections as part of longer hikes, runs, and ski trips. In doing so, it functions as one of the few means south of Basher Road that to access the Front Range from lower Hillside. It does this without any fooling around. Following a wide, right-of-way cut for an underground pipe it climbs in a straight line up the side of the Anchorage bowl. In doing so, it climbs up and down some steep slopes as it trends upward. This makes it especially exciting to ski or bike down it, but hard work for anyone hiking, biking, or skiing up it.

**TRAIL LOCATION:** The lower end of this trail begins approximately 0.1 miles from the beginning of South Gasline Trail (Multi Use Corridor). (One can also access the lower end of this trail via South Bivouac Trail and South Gasline Trail from South Bivouac parking area on Basher Road, but the easier access begins at Hilltop Park parking area.) To get there drive south on the Seward Highway from 5th Avenue in downtown Anchorage for approximately 5.5 miles to the Dimond Boulevard exit. Turn off the highway at this exit. At the bottom of the ramp, turn left and cross back under the highway. In less than 100 yards Dimond Boulevard turns into Abbott Road as it swings in a broad curve to the left. Follow Abbott Road as it swings first around this curve to the right (south) and then to the (left) north. Approximately 1 mile from the Seward Highway Abbott Road reaches a set of lights at Lake Otis Parkway. Continue straight through these lights and follow Abbott Road uphill toward the mountains for another approximately 1 mile to another set of lights. Continue straight through these lights as well and continue for another 0.75 miles uphill.

At that point one should come in sight of Service High School on the left (north) side of Abbott Road.

Continuing straight past Service High School, follow Abbott Road as it passes under a walking bridge. Approximately 0.5 miles after the bridge, the road reaches a parking area for the lighted cross-country ski loop of Hillside Park. Continue along Abbott Road to the far end of the parking area. There one should reach a road on the left (north) marked by a large sign for Hilltop Ski Area. Turn left onto this road. Follow this road for approximately 0.3 miles past Hilltop Chalet to the far (northern) end of the parking area. Park where available. Access to South Gasline (Multi-Use Corridor) begins at the ski trailhead just to the left (west) upper end of the parking area.

Upon leaving the parking area, bear right (northeast) across the opening behind the information board and look for a break in the trees on the right marking the very last section of Multi-Use Trail. Turn onto this tail end of Multi-Use Trail*. In less than 0.1 miles Multi-Use Trail emerges onto the broad south end of South Gasline Trail (Multi-Use Corridor). Bearing left (north) onto South Gasline Trail (Multi-Use Corridor), follow it for approximately 0.1 miles to where it reaches the intersection with Lower Gasline Trail at the base of a wide, steep opening in the trees to the right.

Turning right onto Lower Gasline Trail at this junction, follow it as almost immediately begins climbing directly up the steep slope above. At the top of the slope, the angle of the climb decreases dramatically, but the climbing doesn't stop. For the next approximately 1 mile Lower Gasline Trail climbs with few breaks, passing one major intersection of various single-lane bike trails and ski trails along the way. Near the

--------------------------------------------------------------------

\*    For more information about that trail, see [76] **Walk-About Guide to Multi-Use Trail.**

top of this climb the trail reaches another major intersection of single-track bike trails. Continuing past this intersection, the trail dips in and out of one last hollow before dropping off the embankment into the entrance road for Prospect Heights parking area on the left (north). This marks the upper end of Lower Gasline Trail.

At this point, one has a number of choices. First, one can return the way they have come, perhaps descending via one of the three bike trails branching off the trail just below its upper end. Second, one can continue climbing toward Flattop Mountain and the trails of Campbell Creek valley via Upper Gasline Trail or Middle Powerline Trail*. Third, one can climb either Near Point or Wolverine via Wolverine Bowl Trail**.

**TRAIL GRADE:** This wide but often steep trail rates Grade 2 as a hike.

**TRAIL CONDITION:** This trail remains in generally excellent condition for its entire length.

**TRAIL MILEAGE:** To go the entire length of this trail from Hilltop Ski Area to Prospect Heights parking area entails approximately 1.2 miles of hiking. To then continue on Upper Gasline Trail to where it ends at a junction with Middle Powerline Trail entails approximately 4.0 miles of hiking or biking for a round-trip total of 8.0 miles.

**TOTAL ELEVATION GAIN:** To hike the entire length of this trail from Hilltop Ski Area to Prospect Heights parking area entails a total elevation gain of approximately 650 feet. To then continue on Upper Gasline Trail to where it ends at the junction with Powerline Trail entails a total elevation gain of approximately 1,700 feet.

**HIGH POINT:** This trail reaches its highest point of approximately 1,100

---------------------------------------------------------------------------

\* For more information about these two trails, see [47] **Walk-About Guide to Upper Gasline Trail** and [46] **Walk-About Guide to Middle Powerline Trail** in Chapter 4.

\*\* For more information about that trail, see [57] **Walk-About Guide to Wolverine Bowl Trail** and [60] **Walk-About Guide to Wolverine Peak Trail** in Chapter 5.

feet at the small rise just near the very end of the trail just before it drops onto the entrance road for Prospect Heights parking area. If continuing on Upper Gasline Trail, this reaches its highest point of approximately 2,100 feet above sea level at its uppermost end at the junction with Powerline Trail.

**NORMAL HIKING TIME:** To hike the entire length of this trail from Hilltop Ski Area to Prospect Heights parking area and back entails from 1 to 2.5 hours of hiking, depending on the condition and ambition of the hiker(s) involved. To hike from Hilltop Ski Area parking area to where Upper Gasline Trail ends at the junction with Powerline Trail and back again should take anywhere from 2 to 6 hours, also depending on the

Lower Gasline Trail

condition and ambition of the hiker(s) involved.

**CAMPSITES:** One will find no designated campsites along this trail. Nor, given the short length of the trail, should one need any.

**BEST TIME:** Most people should find any time of year a good time to do this hike, bike, or ski. In winter it also makes a fine hike or bike because it usually becomes well packed through being so well used.

**USGS MAPS:** Anchorage A-8.

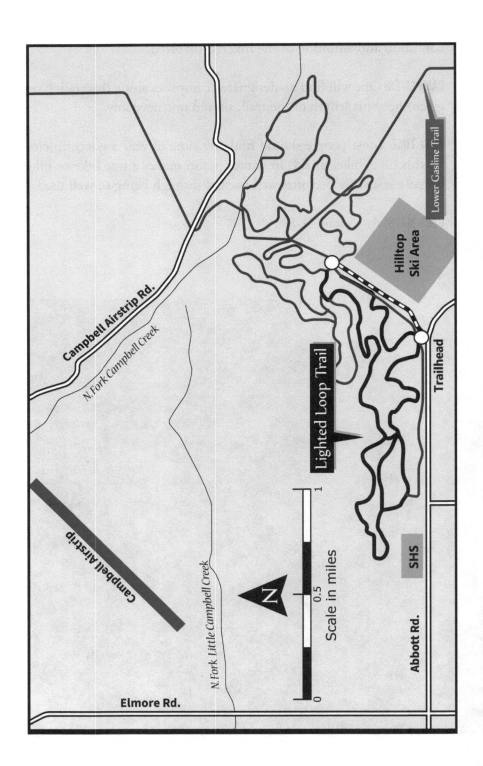

Lower Gasline Trail

Hilltop Ski Area

Campbell Airstrip Rd.

N. Fork Campbell Creek

Lighted Loop Trail

Trailhead

Campbell Airstrip

N. Fork Little Campbell Creek

N

Scale in miles

0    0.5    1

SHS

Abbott Rd.

Elmore Rd.

# Walk-About Guide to Lighted Loop Trail

Though not particularly long (1.5 miles) this ski trail forms the central hub for many trails branching off it in all directions. This, along with its ease of access, makes it a popular trail in the months when it opens to non-skiers. At the top of some of the low hills this trail passes over one can even look out over some wide view of the Chugach Mountains to the east and the city and ocean to the west.

**TRAIL LOCATION:** Lighted Loop Trail begins in a parking area just east of Service High School on lower Hillside. To get there drive south on the Seward Highway from 5th Avenue in downtown Anchorage for approximately 5.5 miles to the Dimond Boulevard exit. Turn off the highway at this exit. At the bottom of the ramp, turn left and cross back under the highway. In less than 100 yards Dimond Boulevard turns into Abbott Road as it swings in a broad curve to the left. Follow Abbott Road as it swings first around this curve to the right (south) and then to the (left) north. Approximately 1 mile from the Seward Highway Abbott Road reaches a set of lights at Lake Otis Parkway. Continue straight through these lights and follow Abbott Road uphill toward the mountains for another approximately 1 mile to another set of lights. Continue straight through these lights as well and continue for another 0.75 miles uphill.

At that point one should come in sight of Service High School on the left (north) side of Abbott Road. Continuing straight past Service High School, Abbott Road next passes under a walking bridge. Approximately 0.5 miles later, Abbott Road reaches a Hillside Park parking area on the left. Pull into this parking area and park wherever possible. Lighted Loop Trail begins just behind the information board at the left (east) backside of the parking area.

Just past the information board, turn right (east) onto the wide Lighted Loop Trail. As one begins this trail, keep in mind that though many trails converge with Lighted Loop Trail one need only continue straight ahead, passing to left of every intersecting trail to stay on Lighted Loop Trail. (The sharp left-hand turns onto the two ends of Coach's Cutoff, located at miles 0.4 and 1.3, remains the one main exception to this rule.) At mile 0.8 the trail reaches broad Conversation Corner, where the two trails to the left lead toward Service High School. Just past Conversation Corner, the trail begins its hilliest section. In rapid succession, the trail climbs over three short, sharp hills. At the top of the second hill (mile 1.1) the trail passes a well-placed bench offering a rest with a fine view. At mile 1.3, where Coach's Cutoff turns sharply to the left, the main trail turns to the right (south). After climbing over two last hills, it descends to an intersection. There it turns left (east) toward the mountains and enters the woods where it reaches yet another intersection. Staying on the main trail by bearing to the right follow it out to where it emerges from the woods on the east end of the parking area, which marks the beginning and end of this loop trail (mile 1.5).

**TRAIL CONDITION:** This trail remains in excellent condition for its entire length.

**TRAIL MILEAGE:** To complete the entire length of Light Loop Trail entails approximately 1.5 miles of hiking or biking.

**TOTAL ELEVATION GAIN:** To hike the entire length of Lighted Loop Trail entails a total elevation gain of approximately 300 feet.

**HIGH POINT:** This trail reaches its highest point of approximately 525 feet above sea level within 0.2 miles from the parking area on the far eastern end of the loop before it descends to a major intersection.

**NORMAL HIKING TIME:** To hike the entire length of Lighted Loop Trail should take anywhere from 45 minutes to 1.5 hours, depending on the condition and ambition of the hiker(s) involved.

**CAMPSITES:** One will find no designated campsites along this trail. Nor, given the short length of the trail, should one need any.

**BEST TIME:** Most people should find any time of year but winter, when the trail remains off-limits to all but skiers, proves a good time to hike or bike this trail.

**USGS MAPS:** Anchorage A-8.

On Lighted Loop Trail

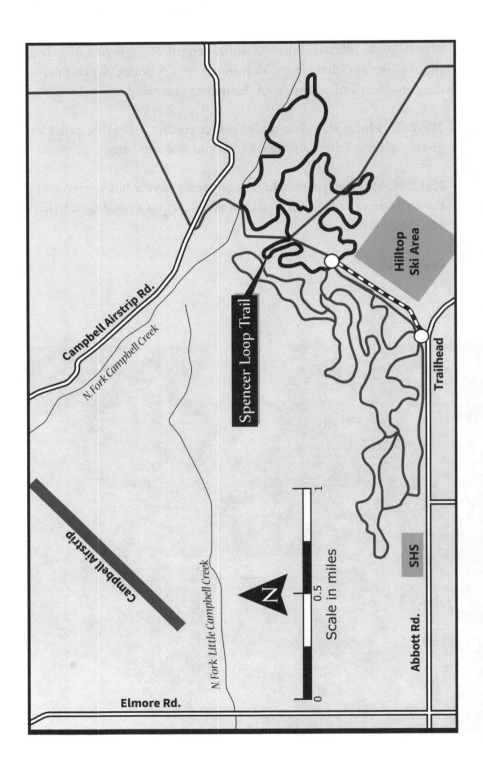

Campbell Airstrip Rd.

N. Fork Campbell Creek

Spencer Loop Trail

Hilltop Ski Area

Trailhead

Campbell Airstrip

N. Fork Little Campbell Creek

N

Scale in miles

0    0.5    1

SHS

Abbott Rd.

Elmore Rd.

# Walk-About Guide to Spenser Loop

As the most challenging cross-country ski trail in Hilltop Ski Area, this trail makes any hiker, biker, or runner work much harder than usual for their miles. It thus serves as an honest measure of one's strength and stamina. But this work does have its rewards in the wide views of Anchorage and Cook Inlet the trail offers at various points along its length. Biker also can enjoy some thrilling descents after some climbs. Unfortunately, this trail remains closed to all but skiers after the first substantial snow fall.

**TRAIL LOCATION:** To get there drive south on the Seward Highway from 5th Avenue in downtown Anchorage for approximately 5.5 miles to the Dimond Boulevard exit. Turn off the highway at this exit. At the bottom of the ramp, turn left and cross back under the highway. In less than 100 yards Dimond Boulevard turns into Abbott Road as it swings in a broad curve to the left. Follow Abbott Road as it swings first around this curve to the right (south) and then to the (left) north. Approximately 1 mile from the Seward Highway Abbott Road reaches a set of lights at Lake Otis Parkway. Continue straight through these lights and follow Abbott Road uphill toward the mountains for another approximately 1 mile to another set of lights. Continue straight through these lights as well and continue for another 0.75 miles uphill. At that point one should come in sight of Service High School on the left (north) side of Abbott Road.

Continuing straight past Service High School, follow Abbott Road as it passes under a walking bridge. Approximately 0.5 miles after the bridge, the road reaches a parking area for the lighted cross-country ski loop of Hillside Park. Continue along Abbott Road to the far end of the parking area. There one should reach a road on the left (north) marked by a large sign for Hilltop Ski Area. Turn left onto this road. Follow this road for approximately 0.3 miles past Hilltop Chalet to the far (northern) end of the parking area. Park where available. Access to South Gasline (Multi-Use Corridor) begins at the ski trailhead just to the left (west) upper end of the parking area.

To reach Spenser Loop first bike or hike straight past (west) the information board at the edge of the parking area. Upon reaching the far end of the clearing behind the information board bear right (north) onto Double Bubble ski trail. At mile 0.4 the trail veers very close to South Gasline Trail (Multi-Use Corridor) before turning back into the woods. Just after mile 0.8 Spenser Loop crosses the north end of South Gasline Trail (Multi-Use Corridor)*. Staying to the right of the upper end of South Bivouac Trail, it next drops into the woods on the far side of the corridor and descends to the right (south) shore of South Fork Campbell Creek.

Now, 1.3 miles from the parking area, the hill-climbing begins in earnest. Initially the trail climbs gradually as it follows Campbell Creek up steam. After turning away from the creek, the trail starts its first climb to a bench. Then after one relatively long downhill back to the edge of South Fork Campbell Creek the trail begins its real climbing to the shelf above the right (south) side of the canyon. At mile 2.2, after one last, long switchback, the trail reaches the crest of the canyon.

From this highest point of the trail it descends sharply. At the bottom of this first steep hill the trail flattens out somewhat while still consistently trending downhill over a series of bumps. At the bottom of this first loop on the face of the slope Spenser Loop passes a trail on the right (west) that drops down to South Gasline Trail (Multi-Use Corridor). Unless one wants a short-cut back the where they started, ignore this side trail and continue straight ahead to where the trail turns left (east) and begins climbing again. At the top of this climb, it turns right and starts down again.

At mile 3.7 Spenser Loop reaches a junction Lower Gasline Trail** Continuing straight across this trail, Spenser Loop soon begins to climb

--------------------------------------------------------------

\*   For more information about that trail, see [77] **Walk-About Guide to South Gasline Trail**.

\*\*   For more information about that trail, see [79] **Walk-About Guide to Lower Gasline Trail**.

to the top of another loop. There, at the top of the final loop, it passes close to the uppermost end of the Hilltop Ski Area chairlift. From this high point, it starts down a series of twists and turns, which include a number of short ascents followed by longer descents to where the trail finally comes out once more to South Gasline Trail (Multi-Use Corridor). At this point, continue straight across the corridor to the information board where one first started and where Spenser Loop now ends.

**TRAIL CONDITION:** This trail remains in generally excellent condition for its entire length.

**TRAIL MILEAGE:** To hike the entire length of Spenser Loop entails approximately 4.9 miles of hiking or biking.

**TOTAL ELEVATION GAIN:** To hike the entire length of Spenser Loop entails a total elevation gain of approximately 1000 feet.

**HIGH POINT:** This trail reaches its highest point of approximately 925 feet above sea level at the top of the long climb up and out of the Campbell Creek canyon.

**NORMAL HIKING TIME:** To hike the entirety of Spenser Loop should take anywhere from 2 to 4 hours, depending on the condition and ambition of the hiker(s) involved.

**CAMPSITES:** One will find no designated campsites along this trail. Nor, given the short length of the trail, should one need any.

**BEST TIME:** Most people should find any time of year but winter, when the trail remains off-limits to all but skiers, proves a good time to hike or bike this trail.

**USGS MAPS:** Anchorage A-8.

Crossing Campbell Creek

## CHAPTER 9

# FAR NORTH BICENTENNIAL PARK

## OVERVIEW OF FAR NORTH BICENTENNIAL PARK

Far North Bicentennial Park extends across the foothills of the northern Front Range. Starting in the lowlands of the Anchorage bowl on its easternmost side, the park extends high up the flanks of the mountains. As the northeastern frontier of the city, it has its very wild side. On any given day one can cross paths with moose, bears, wolves, and even wolverines in any part of the park. In winter, ravens pass back and forth in their daily migration from their roosts in the mountains above to the city below. In early spring and late fall Canadian Geese pass over the park on their long journeys to the arctic and back again. During the same periods salmon migrate to and from their spawning grounds along the numerous branches of Campbell Creek that descend through the park.

Yet for all the wild animals that come and go, the also has its very tame side. Its extensive maze of trails draws all kind of people for all kinds of recreation. On any given hour of any given day, one crosses paths hikers, runners, bikers, skiers, and even horseback riders. This maze of trails varies in types, from a wide and level path to a narrow and rooted rut. Apart from its maze of trails, the park also contains the highly developed Hilltop Ski Area for downhill skiing and snowboarding in its upper southeast corner as well as the Campbell Creek Environmental Education Center (also known simply as the Campbell Creek Science Center) on the flats on the northwest corner

On The Ballpark above Black Lake

of the park. So no matter what non-motorized recreation one chooses, one can find a place to do it in Far North Bicentennial Park.

Considering the near book-length guide it would take to describe all the trails in Far North Bicentennial Park, it seemed best for this guide to focus on the most popular trails and options. Nevertheless, despite this focus, these few guides, along with the **Walk-About Guide to Tour of Anchorage Route** in Chapter 11, should provide enough information to offer a number of fine adventures in the park without anyone getting too misplaced in the process.

Winter trail in Bicentennial Park

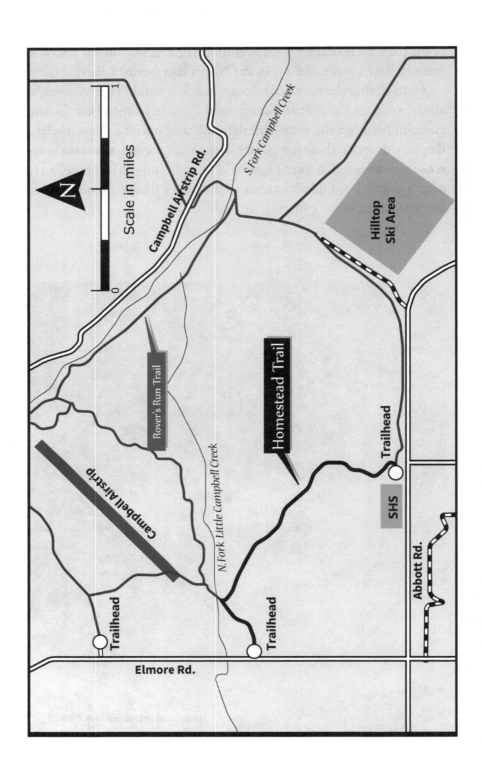

Scale in miles

Campbell Airstrip Rd.

S. Fork Campbell Creek

Hilltop Ski Area

Rover's Run Trail

Homestead Trail

Campbell Airstrip

N. Fork Little Campbell Creek

Trailhead

SHS

Abbott Rd.

Trailhead

Trailhead

Elmore Rd.

# Walk-About Guide to Homestead Trail

Along with Moose Track Trail, described next in this chapter, this trail probably sees more use than any other trail in Far North Bicentennial Park. The primary reason for this may lie in the simple fact that this trail connects Service High School and the Hilltop Ski Area with Campbell Tract. This trail thus makes it possible to hike, run, or ski some large loops in the area. In addition, both ends of this trail lie within close proximity to two large neighborhoods. These reasons may account for all the people hiking, biking, running, skiing, horseback riding, and dog-walking on this trail.

**TRAIL LOCATION:** Homestead Trail begins at Abbott Loop Community Park located at the southwest corner of Far North Bicentennial Park. To get there drive south on the Seward Highway from 5th Avenue in downtown Anchorage for approximately 2.75 miles to the Tudor Road exit. At the upper end of the ramp turn left (east) on Tudor Road and cross back over the highway. Continue along Tudor Road for approximately 1.75 miles to its intersection with Bragaw Street on the left (north) and Elmore Drive on the right (south). Turn right (south) on Elmore Drive. Continue for approximately 2.4 miles to where, just after the top of a short hill one reaches Abbott Loop Community Park on the left (east). Turn left into the parking area and park wherever available. Homestead Trail begins just beyond the boulders on the upper left (northeast) corner of the parking area.

The trail begins by descending a short sharp hill behind the boulders. Approximately 0.3 miles later, Homestead Trail reaches a T-junction with Coyote Trail. While Coyote Trail continues straight ahead onto BLM land, Homestead Trail bears right (east) to begin climbing a series of short hills as it makes a long steady gain in elevation. Approximately 1.3 miles later, the trail reaches a 4-way junction. Continue straight past this junction. In another 0.1 miles the trail reaches another 4 way junction. Here turn right (west) and follow the wide dirt trail down a short hill onto a paved bike trail. Bearing right onto the bike trail, follow it the short way up to the parking area at the back of Service High School where the trail ends.

At this point, one has two major options. First, they can turn and around and return the way they have come. Second, they can backtrack to the first 4-way intersection at the bottom of the trail and turn right (south) to continue a circumnavigation of Campbell Tract*.

**TRAIL GRADE:** This trail rates Grade 1 as a hike for its entire length.

**TRAIL CONDITION:** This trail remains in excellent condition from the beginning to end.

**TRAIL MILEAGE:** To go from the beginning of this trail at Abbott Loop Community Park to Service High School parking area entails approximately 1.9 of hiking, for a round-trip total of 3.6 miles.

**TOTAL ELEVATION GAIN:** To hike from the beginning of this trail at Abbott Loop Community Park to Service High School parking area entails a total elevation gain of approximately 130 feet.

**HIGH POINT:** This trail reaches its highest point of approximately 350 feet above sea level where the trail ends at Service High School.

**NORMAL HIKING TIME:** To hike from the beginning of this trail at Abbott Loop Community Park to Service High School and back should take anywhere from 1.5 to 3 hours, depending on the condition and ambition of the hiker(s) involved.

-------------------------------------------------------------------------

\*   For more information about that route,
    see [86] **OPTION A—Circumnavigation of Campbell Tract**.

**CAMPSITES:** One will find no designated camping areas on this trail. Nor should one need one considering the shortness of the hike.

**BEST TIME:** Most people should find any time of year a good time to do this hike.

**USGS MAPS:** Anchorage A-8.

Biking in Bicentennial Park

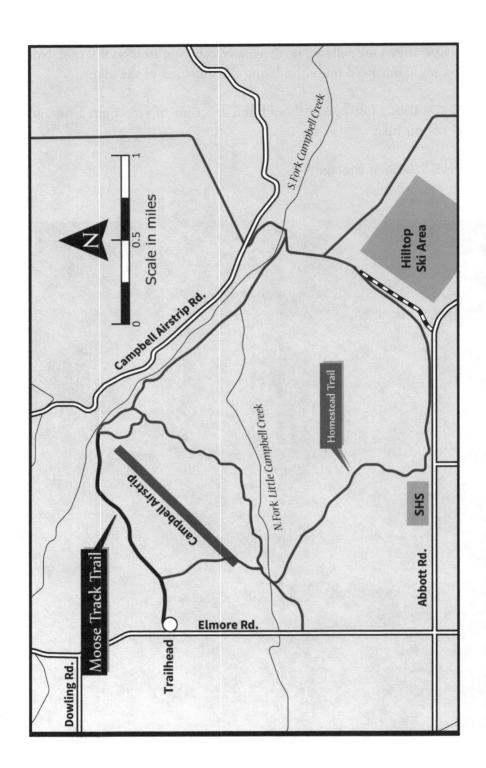

N

Scale in miles
0    0.5    1

S. Fork Campbell Creek

Hilltop
Ski Area

Campbell Airstrip Rd.

Homestead Trail

N. Fork Little Campbell Creek

SHS

Campbell Airstrip

Moose Track Trail

Abbott Rd.

Dowling Rd.

Trailhead

Elmore Rd.

# Walk-About Guide to Moose Track Trail

This popular trail serves as both an end in itself for those out for a short mid-day walk or an evening walk with the dog as well as the beginning of many longer walks or runs routes in Far North Bicentennial Park.

**TRAIL LOCATION:** This hike begins at Smokejumper parking area located on BLM land on the east side of Anchorage. To get there drive south on the Seward Highway from 5th Avenue in downtown Anchorage for approximately 2.75 miles to the Tudor Road exit. At the upper end of the ramp turn left (east) on Tudor Road and cross back over the highway. Continue along Tudor Road for approximately 1.75 miles to its intersection with Bragaw Street on the left (north) and Elmore Drive on the right (south). Turn right (south) on Elmore Drive. Continue for approximately 1.6 miles to where, just past the second set of lights on Elmore, one reaches a junction with BLM Drive on the left (east) and the sign on its far side reading "Campbell Tract Facility (Administrative Site)". Here turn left (east) onto BLM Drive. Follow BLM Drive for 0.1 to the Smokejumper parking area on the left (north). Park wherever available. Moose Track Trail begins beside the large information board located in the middle parking area's backside.

Upon entering the woods this graveled trail soon comes in sight of the road leading from BLM Drive to Campbell Creek Environmental Education Center. For its entire length this trail rarely strays far from this road. Winding almost imperceptibly uphill the trail continues in a northeast direction. A little less than 1 mile from its start this trail passes within sight of the parking area for Campbell Creek Environmental Education Center. Just beyond the parking area passes through a junction with a trail leading from the parking area. Only a few dozen feet after this junction Moose Track Trail reaches its end at a junction with Old Rondy Trail, a trail which forms part of the Tour of Anchorage route*.

At this point one has three choices. First, one can turn around and return the way they have come. Second, one can continue straight across Old Rondy Trail and follow the trail on the far side out to the shore of Campbell Creek. Third, one can turn right (east) up Old Rondy Trail and complete the popular circumnavigation of Campbell Airstrip**.

**TRAIL GRADE:** This trail rates Grade 1 as a hike for its entire length.

**TRAIL CONDITION:** Despite its many twists and turns through the woods this trail remains wide and flat with virtually no roots and rocks to trip over.

**TRAIL MILEAGE:** To go from the beginning of this route on BLM Drive to its intersection Old Rondy Trail entails approximately 1.2 miles of hiking, for a round-trip total of 2.4 miles.

**TOTAL ELEVATION GAIN:** To hike from the beginning of this route on BLM Drive to its intersection Old Rondy Trail entails a total elevation gain of approximately 50 feet.

**HIGH POINT:** This trail reaches its highest point of approximately 250 feet above sea at its end where it intersects with Old Rondy Trail.

**NORMAL HIKING TIME:** To hike from the beginning of this trail on BLM Drive to its intersection Old Rondy Trail and back entails back should take anywhere from 1 to 3 hours, depending on the condition and ambition of the hiker(s) involved.

---------------------------------------------------------------

* For more information about that trail,
    see [106] **Walk-About Guide to Tour of Anchorage Route** in Chapter 11.

** For more information about that route,
    see [84] **OPTION A—Circumnavigation of Campbell Airstrip**.

**CAMPSITES:** One will find no designated camping areas on this trail. Nor should one need one considering the shortness of the hike.

**BEST TIME:** Most people should find any time of year a good time to do this hike.

**USGS MAPS:** Anchorage A-8.

Tour of Anchorage route

N
Scale in miles
0
0.5
1
Campbell Airstrip Rd.
S.Fork Campbell Creek
Hilltop
Ski Area
Option A
Homestead Trail
Trailhead
Campbell Airstrip
Moose Track Trail
N.Fork Little Campbell Creek
SHS
Abbott Rd.
Trailhead
Elmore Rd.
Trailhead
Dowling Rd.

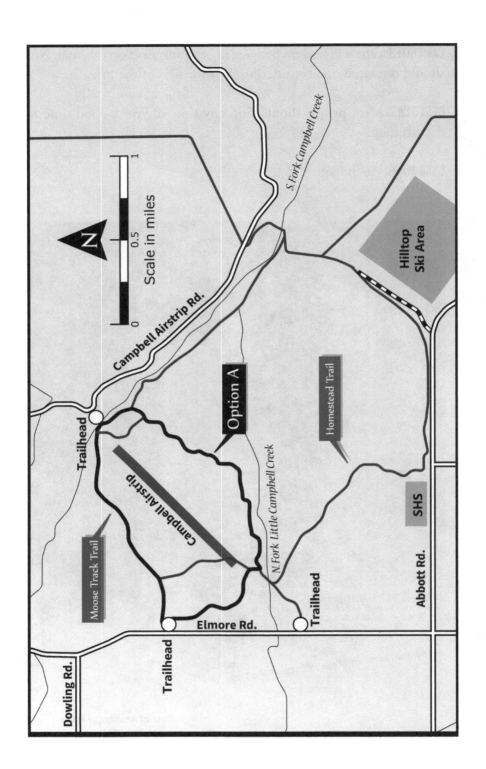

## OPTION A

# Circumnavigation of Campbell Airstrip

This former military airstrip now owned by BLM sees very little use. On rare occasions a government plane or helicopter might land or take off from the strip. On rarer occasions it also sees use for emergency landings. The various trails that circle around the airstrip, on the other hand, see lots of use by all kinds of non-motorized traffic. Hikers, runners, bikers, skiers, horseback riders, and dog mushers all use this maze of trails as they come and go from all points of the compass. But though many people have preferred loops among this maze of trails, the most popular follows a four-mile loop through the woods around the airstrip. This loop utilizes all or part of five different trails: Moose Track Trail, Old Rondy Trail, Viewpoint Trail, Coyote Trail, and Lynx Trail.

For those not familiar with Campbell Tract and its maze of trails this loop serves as a good introduction to the area. Learning this loop makes it possible to branch off in various directions. Familiarity with this loop also makes it possible to explore a number of shorter loops around the airstrip. One should, after all, arrive back on this loop somewhere along its length no matter how short or long the loop within it. One should thus feel free to explore with confidence knowing that though you might feel misplaced at one point or another, you need not feel lost.

**TRAIL LOCATION:** Though one can begin this circumnavigation at the parking areas at either Campbell Airstrip Road or Abbott Loop Community Park (which entail hiking a short connecting trail to reach this loop) this trail description begins at Smokejumpers parking area[*].

From Smokejumpers parking area follow Moose Track Trail for its entire length to where less than 100 yards past Campbell Creek Environmental Education Center parking area, it reaches a junction with Old Rondy Trail. Turn right (east) on Old Rondy Trail. Follow this trail for approximately 0.3 miles to the right (south) end of a large footbridge over Campbell Creek. (The trail over the footbridge leads the short way out to the parking area on Campbell Airstrip Road.)

Continuing straight past the end of the bridge, follow the next trail, Viewpoint Trail, into the woods just beyond. Continue following Viewpoint Trail as it first climbs gradually to the fire gate marking the beginning of Rover's Run[**]. After winding through the woods Viewpoint Trail soon passes straight through a junction with Moose Meadow Trail on the left (east). Approximately 200 feet beyond this junction, the trail curves into a clearing with a fork in the trail. Bearing right (northwest) at the fork follow the trail as it makes a short and sharp climb to the crest of a bluff. At the top of the bluff the trail turns sharply left (south) and crosses the top of the other fork. At the end of the bluff the trail turns right (west) and begins a rollercoaster ride downhill. Approximately 0.25 miles later, at the bottom of the last little hump in the ride, it reaches a T-intersection with Coyote Trail.

Turning right (north) on Coyote Trail, follow it for less than 0.2 miles to its junction with Lynx Trail, the final trail of this loop, on the left (south). Turn onto Lynx Trail and follow it as it weaves through the woods, passing a junction in a small clearing with Lore Road Trail on the left (south). Approximately 0.25 miles past this junction, Lynx Trail pops out of the woods onto BLM Drive directly

--------------------------------------------------------

[*]   To get there, see [83] **Walk-About Guide to Moose Track Trail.**

[**]   For more information about that trail, see [85] **Walk-About Guide to Rover's Run.**

across BLM Drive from Smokejumpers parking area and the end of the loop.

**TRAIL GRADE:** This entire circumnavigation rates Grade 1 as a hike.

**TRAIL CONDITION:** This remains in excellent condition for its entire length.

**TRAIL MILEAGE:** To hike this entire circumnavigation of Campbell Airstrip entails approximately 4 miles of hiking.

**TOTAL ELEVATION GAIN:** To hike this entire circumnavigation of Campbell Airstrip entails a total elevation gain of approximately 150 feet

**HIGH POINT:** This trail reaches its highest point of approximately 325 feet above sea level at the crest of the bluff one climbs about 1.5 miles along Viewpoint Trail.

**NORMAL HIKING TIME:** To hike this entire circumnavigation of Campbell Airstrip should take anywhere from 1.5 to 4 hours, depending on the condition and ambition of the hiker(s) involved.

**CAMPSITES:** One will find no designated campsites along this trail. Nor, given the short length of the trail, should one need any.

**BEST TIME:** Most people should find any time of year a good time to do this hike, bike, or ski. In winter it also makes for a fine hike or run because it usually becomes well packed through so much use.

**USGS MAPS:** Anchorage A-8.

Trailhead
Trailhead
Campbell Airstrip Rd.
N
0
0.5
1
Scale in miles
S. Fork Campbell Creek
Hilltop Ski Area
Rover's Run Trail
Homestead Trail
N. Fork Little Campbell Creek
Campbell Airstrip
SHS
Abbott Rd.
Elmore Rd.
Dowling Rd.

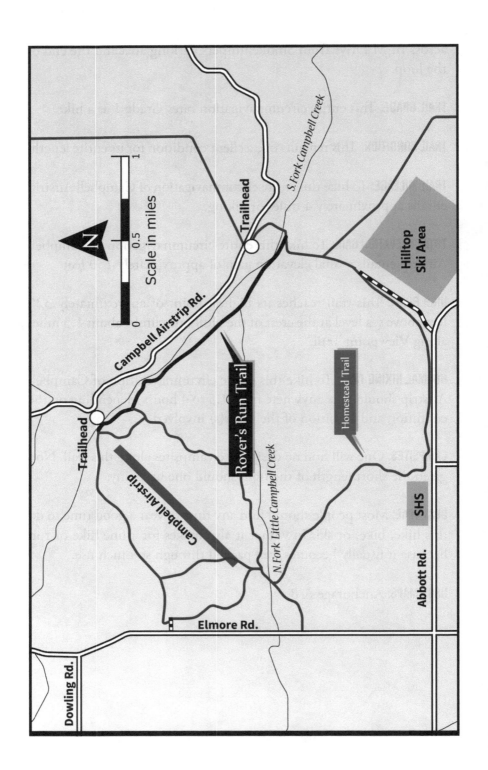

# Walk-About Guide to Rover's Run

This trail, along with Moose Meadow Trail and Homestead Trail, allows one to connect Campbell Airstrip with the Hilltop Ski Area. This makes this trail quite popular. One should, however, avoid it during late summer when the salmon run. For with the salmon come the bears. Despite warning signs, some people still venture up this trail during this season. If the trail traveled through open country with wide views, this may not seem so imprudent. But this trail's tight corners and close trees, which allow for only limited visibility in any direction, makes almost any encounter between bear and human very close and, therefore, very dangerous. As a result, bears have mauled more than a few people along this trail.

**TRAIL LOCATION:** Rover's Run begins a short way from the beginning of Viewpoint Trail in Campbell Tract. To get there drive 3.2 miles south of downtown Anchorage on the Seward Highway. There, just after Milepost 124, take a right (west) on the Tudor Road exit. At the end of the ramp, turn left (east) and cross back over the highway. Continue straight on Tudor Road as it gradually ascends past Lake Otis Parkway and Elmore Drive. Approximately 3.2 miles from the Seward Highway Tudor Road reaches a set of lights at Campbell Airstrip Road leading right (south). Turn right on Campbell Airstrip Road. In approximately 1.2 miles, just after passing over a low dog-mushing bridge the road reaches the entrance to a parking area on the right (west). Turn into this parking area and park where ever possible, which sometimes proves more easily said than done on a nice week-end day.

Access to Rover's Run begins at the right (west) corner of the parking area. From the parking area follow the trail across the substantial bridge just ahead. Immediately past the bridge one reaches a 4-way intersection with Viewpoint Trail. Turn left (east) on Viewpoint Trail and follow it up stream into the nearby woods. Approximately 100 yards into the woods, the trail reaches a fire gate with a sign posted on it about the dangers of encountering bears during salmon run. This gate marks the lower end of Rover's Run.

Rover's Run begins by following an old dirt road. Approximately 100 yards from its beginning the trail narrows and turns rougher with many roots, rocks, and small dips. Though Campbell Creek remains largely out of sight of the trail in this section, one can often hear its murmuring through the trees and brush on the left.

Approximately 1 mile from its beginning the trail reaches a junction with Moose Meadow Trail on the left. Here Rover's Run bears left (east). (For those interested, the Moose Meadow Trail circles around to the right, where it eventually rejoins Viewpoint Trail.) Still following Campbell Creek up stream, Rover's Run soon begins to cross more open country. Here during or just after a rain the trail may prove quite slick under foot. At the far end of this open area the trail enters a short stand of woods. Less than 100 yards later it emerges out of the woods into the open right-of-way for an underground gas line. Here the trail crosses the T-intersection with South Gasline Trail (Multi-Use Corridor)*. At the far side of the cut the trail again enters the woods. Approximately 100 feet later it reaches its uppermost end at a T-intersection with South Bivouac Trail**.

Here one has a number of choices. First, one can turn around and return the way they have come. Second, one can turn left (north) and follow South Bivouac Trail out to South Bivouac parking area on Basher Road. Third, one can also turn left (north) on South Bivouac Trail and follow it just as far as the bridge over Campbell Creek to where just up the creek past the bridge one can hop onto Spenser

-----------------------------------------------------------------------------

\*    For more information about this trail, see [77] **Walk-About Guide to South Gasline Trail** in Chapter 8.

\*\*    For more information about this trail, see [78] **Walk-About Guide to South Bivouac Trail** in Chapter 8.

Loop*. Fourth, one can turn right (south) on South Bivouac Trail and follow it up to South Gasline Trail (Multi-Use Corridor). From there one can continue along the Multi-Use Trail back to Hillside Park and eventually down into Campbell Tract**.

**TRAIL GRADE:** This trail rates Grade 1 as a hike.

**TRAIL CONDITION:** Sections of Rover's Run has a considerable number of roots and mud holes along its length.

**TRAIL MILEAGE:** To hike this entire trail from the parking area on Campbell Airstrip Road to the junction with South Bivouac Trail entails approximately 1.5 miles of hiking or biking, for a round-trip total of 3 miles.

**TOTAL ELEVATION GAIN:** To hike this entire trail from the parking area on Campbell Airstrip Road to the junction with South Bivouac Trail entails a total elevation gain of approximately 200 feet.

**HIGH POINT:** This trail reaches its highest point of approximately 450 feet above sea at its uppermost end where it reaches the junction with South Bivouac Trail.

**NORMAL HIKING TIME:** To hike this entire trail from the parking area on Campbell Airstrip Road to the junction with South Bivouac Trail and back should take anywhere from 1 to 2 hours, depending on the condition and ambition of the hiker(s) involved.

**CAMPSITES:** One will find no designated campsites along this trail. Nor, given the short length of the trail, should one need any.

---------------------------------------------------------------------

\*    For more information about these trails, see [78] **Walk-About Guide to South Bivouac Trail** and [81] **Walk-About Guide to Spenser Loop** in Chapter 8.

\*\*    For more information about these trails, see [77] **Walk-About Guide to South Gasline Trail** and [76] **Walk-About Guide to Multi-Use** in Chapter 8.

Getting acquainted in Bicentennial Park

**BEST TIME:** Most people should find almost any time of year a good time to do this hike, bike, or ski, except in late summer when the salmon run brings more than a few bears to the shores of Campbell Creek. In winter it also makes a fine hike or bike because it usually becomes well packed through so much use.

**USGS MAPS:** Anchorage A-8.

Taking a break above Hidden Lake

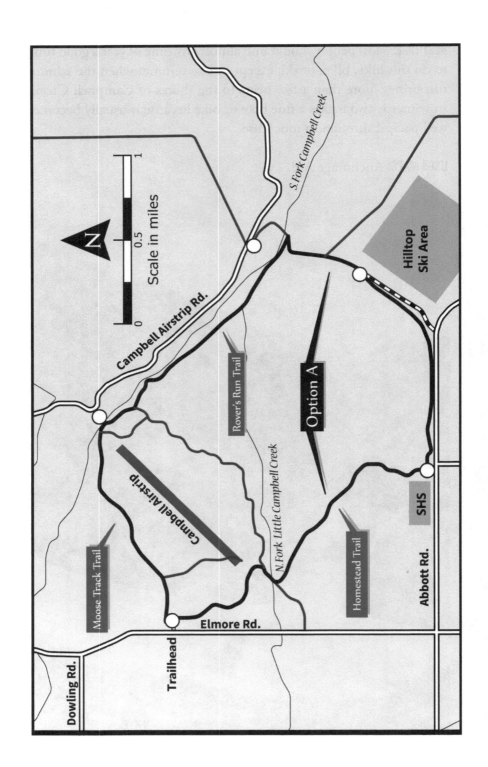

S. Fork Campbell Creek

Hilltop Ski Area

Campbell Airstrip Rd.

Rover's Run Trail

Option A

N. Fork Little Campbell Creek

Campbell Airstrip

Moose Track Trail

Homestead Trail

SHS

Abbott Rd.

Elmore Rd.

Trailhead

Dowling Rd.

N

Scale in miles

0    0.5    1

# 86

# OPTION A

# Circumnavigation of Campbell Tract

This option greatly expands the circumnavigation of Campbell Airstrip described immediately above by climbing well up the flank of Hillside before returning to complete the circuit around Campbell Airstrip. In doing so, it climbs past Service High School to Hilltop Ski Area and beyond before dropping back down to the Campbell Airstrip area.

For those not familiar with the trails in Campbell Tract this loop serves as another good introduction. Learning this larger loop makes it possible to branch off in various directions without too much worry about finding one's way back. Familiarity with this loop also makes it possible to explore a number of shorter loops in Campbell Tract without worry of finding one's way back. In addition, this circumnavigation passes by some trails that lead up into the Front Range. With knowledge of these trails, such as Lower Gasline Trail and Lost Cabin Trail, one can begin hiking or biking in the Anchorage bowl and climb well into the mountains before returning. Finally, this guide describes this larger circumnavigation in the opposite direction of [84] **OPTION A—Circumnavigation of Campbell Airstrip** (above) so that those just learning their way around Campbell Tract can see some of the same trails from a different perspective.

Upon completion of this route one should feel more confident about exploring the entire lower Hillside area without a guide such as this one in hand. Thus one can have the surprising and happy satisfaction of making personal discoveries.

**TRAIL LOCATION:** Like [84] **OPTION A—Circumnavigation of Campbell Airstrip** described immediately above, this route description begins at Smokejumpers parking area*. To begin this circumnavigation from the parking area, first cross BLM Drive to where Lynx Trail begins on the edge of the woods opposite the parking area. Follow this trail for approximately 0.25 miles to its junction with Lore Road Trail. Passing directly through this junction, follow Lynx Trail for another 0.2 miles to its junction with Coyote Trail. Turn right (east) on Coyote Trail and follow it for approximately 0.2 miles to where it reaches a T-intersection with Viewpoint Trail. At this point, this larger loop diverges from the shorter loop described in [84] **OPTION A—Circumnavigation of Campbell Airstrip** above.

Continue straight ahead at this junction and follow Coyote Trail over a wide bridge crossing a narrow stream. A few feet past the far side of this bridge, Coyote Trail reaches a junction with Homestead Trail. Turning left (east) on Homestead Trail, follow it for approximately 1.5 miles up a series of hills to a 4-way intersection. Continue straight past this intersection to a paved bike trail. Bearing left (southeast) onto the bike trail follow it down past a playing field on the right and some dirt trails on the left and up to the near end of a footbridge crossing Abbott Road. Just before the bridge look for Multi-Use Trail on the left (east). Turn left off the pavement onto Multi-Use Trail. Follow this trail for approximately 1 mile to where it reaches a parking area for the Hillside Park cross-country ski trails. At this point one has just about reached the top of this circumnavigation.

Continuing straight across the right (north) side of the parking area, follow Multi-Use Trail as it contours up and to the left into the trees on the far side of the parking area. Approximately 0.5 miles later Multi-Use Trail reaches the upper end of another parking area for Hilltop Ski Area. Continuing straight across the opening where a number of cross-country ski trails branch off in all directions, follow Multi-Use Trail into the trees on the far side of the opening. In another less than 0.1 miles Multi-Use Trail leaves the wood behind as it reaches the broad, open southern end of South Gasline Trail (also

--------------------------------------------------------------------

\*　To get there, see [83] **Walk-About Guide to Moose Track Trail**.

known as Multi-Use Corridor). Bearing left (north) up South Gasline Trail, follow it for approximately 0.2 miles to where it reaches the edge of a bluff overlooking the Campbell Creek hollow. Continuing straight ahead, follow South Gasline Trail down the face of the bluff to the shore of Campbell Creek. At the edge of Campbell Creek turn left (west) onto Rover's Run and follow it into the wood beside the creek. This marks the beginning of the backside of this circumnavigation.

Staying on Rover's Run, follow it for approximately 1.3 miles, passing an intersection with Moose Meadow Trail in the process, to its lower end at a T-intersection with Viewpoint Trail. Bearing right (northwest) on Viewpoint Trail, follow it down and out of the woods to the left (south) of a large footbridge over Campbell Creek. Continuing straight past the end of the bridge, at which point Viewpoint Trail turns into Old Rondy Trail, follow Old Rondy Trail for approximately 0.3 miles its junction with Moose Track Trail leading (left) south to Campbell Creek Science Center.

Turning left (south) onto Moose Track Trail, follow it through the woods for 100 yards to the right (southwest) around the parking area for the Campbell Creek Science Center. Past the Campbell Creek Science Center, continue following Moose Track Trail for approximately 1 mile out to Smokejumpers parking area and the end of the circumnavigation.

**TRAIL GRADE:** This entire circumnavigation rates Grade 1 as a hike.

**TRAIL CONDITION:** Other than Rover's Run, which has many roots and mud holes along its length, this route remains in excellent condition for its entire length.

**TRAIL MILEAGE:** To hike this entire circumnavigation of Campbell Tract entails approximately 8.6 miles of hiking or biking.

**TOTAL ELEVATION GAIN:** To hike this entire circumnavigation of Campbell Tract entails a total elevation gain of approximately 500 feet.

**HIGH POINT:** This trail reaches its highest point of approximately 525 feet above sea level on the bluff at the end of South Gasline Trail overlooking Campbell Creek hollow.

**NORMAL HIKING TIME:** To hike this entire circumnavigation of Campbell Tract should take anywhere from 3 to 6 hours, depending on the condition and ambition of the hiker(s) involved.

**CAMPSITES:** One will find no designated campsites along this trail. Nor, given the short length of the trail, should one need any.

**BEST TIME:** Most people should find any time of year a good time to do this hike, bike, or ski. In winter it also makes a fine hike or bike as it usually remains well packed through being so well used.

**USGS MAPS:** Anchorage A-8.

On the flank of Wolverine Peak

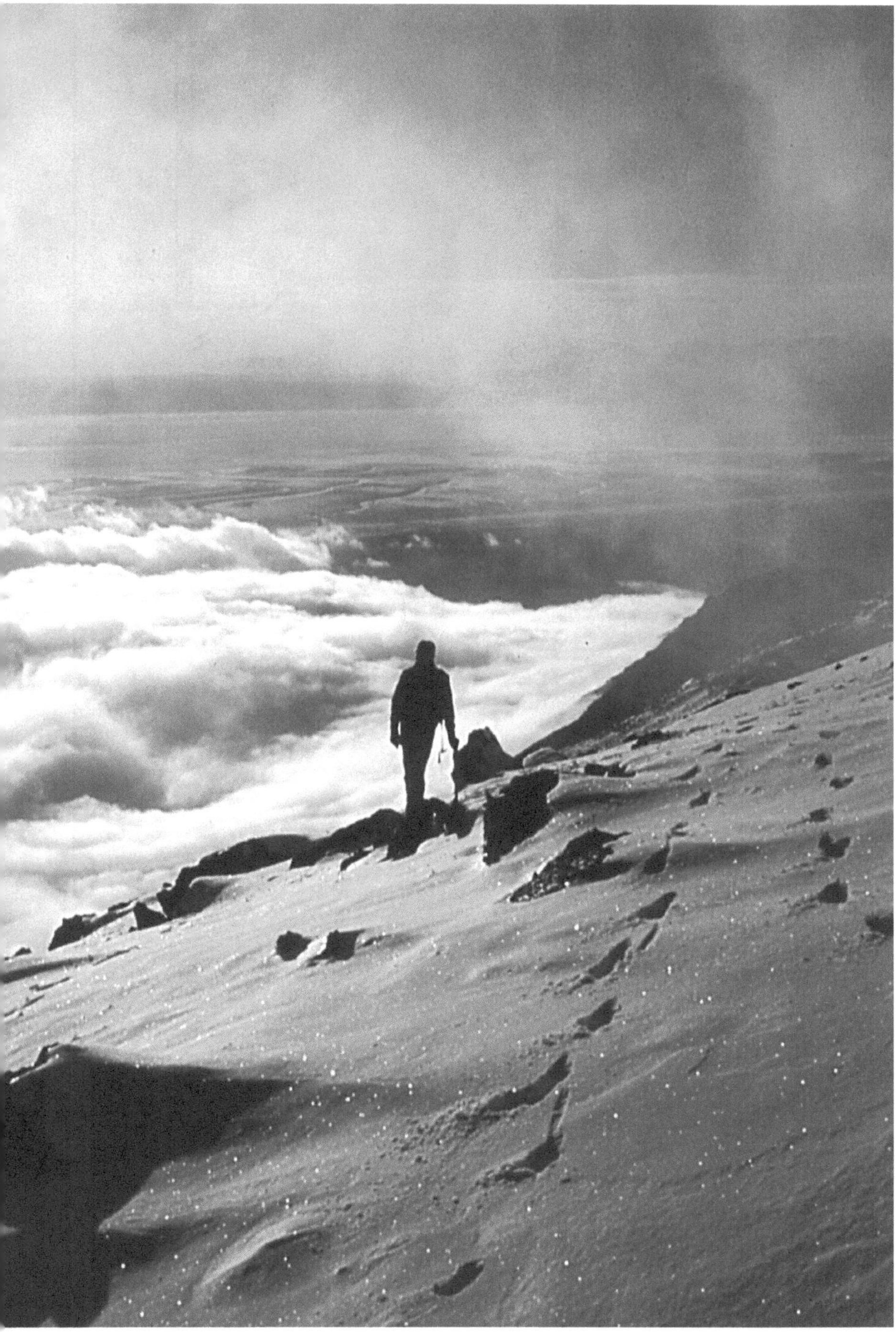

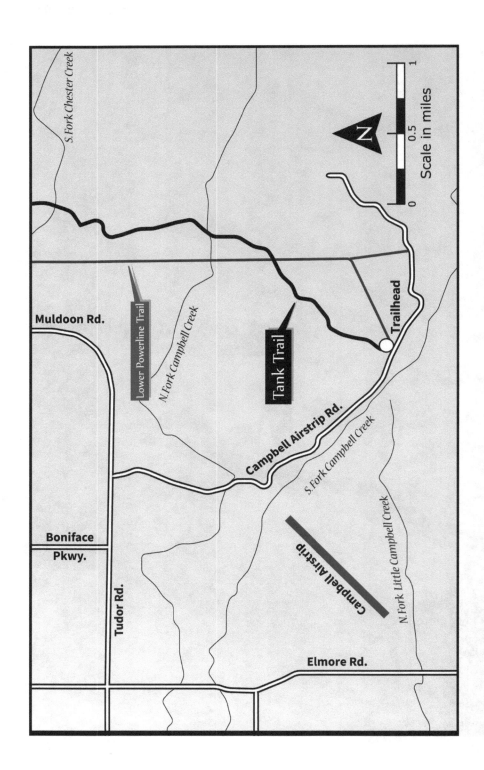

Scale in miles
0   0.5   1

N

S. Fork Chester Creek

Muldoon Rd.

Lower Powerline Trail

N. Fork Campbell Creek

Tank Trail

Trailhead

Campbell Airstrip Rd.

S. Fork Campbell Creek

N. Fork Little Campbell Creek

Boniface
Pkwy.

Tudor Rd.

Campbell Airstrip

Elmore Rd.

# 87

# Walk-About Guide to Tank Trail

This trail functions as the central artery of the largest off-leash dog park in the Anchorage bowl. Though the two other popular dog parks, University Lake and Connors Lake Park, may draw more people because of their convenient locations, Tank Trail and the network of trails attached to it offers dog owners a much larger territory in which they can exercise their dogs.

Yet for all the tame animals that come and go with their owners along these trails, the area also has its wild side. During salmon run many bears also haunt the shores of the creeks that cross the lower end of the trail. And during all seasons of the year, moose move along the usually packed trail to avoid the surrounding deeper snow. One acquaintance even mentioned the novelty of seeing a wolverine lumbering along a lower portion of this trail.

But besides the comings and goings of both domestic and wild animals, Tank Trail also serves as a starting place for a number of hikes. One can make longer climbs of Ice Cream Cone, Knoya Peak, Kanshee Peak, Near Point, and Wolverine Peak from both Lower Powerline Trail and Ice Cream Cone Cut-off that intersect this trail. It also makes a fine place to bike and ski any time of the year.

**TRAIL LOCATION:** This hike begins at North Bivouac parking area located approximately 2.5 miles up Basher Road in Far North Bicentennial Park in Anchorage. To get there drive 3.2 miles south of downtown Anchorage on the Seward Highway. There, just after Milepost 124, turn right (west) onto the Tudor Road exit. At the end of the ramp, turn left (east) and cross back over the highway. Continue straight on this road as it gradually ascends past Lake Otis Parkway and then Elmore Drive. Approximately 3.2 miles from the Seward Highway, Tudor Road reaches a set of lights at Campbell Airstrip Road leading right (south). Turn right onto Campbell Airstrip Road. In approximately 1 mile this road becomes Basher Road. Stay on Basher Road as it continues to wind upward. Approximately 2.5 miles from Tudor Road one reaches North Bivouac parking area to the left (north) and South Bivouac parking area to the right (south). Turn left into North Bivouac parking area and park wherever available. Tank Trail begins by going straight through the gate at the backside of the parking area.

Beyond the gate the trail follows the wide, dirt road trail. Continue following the wide trail straight by numerous side trails. Posts at many of these side trails give the name of the trail and a map as to where they go. (Of these rougher side trails, any of the trails leading down to Bog Lakes, located downhill to the left, remain very popular.)

Approximately 1 mile from the parking area, Tank Trail climbs a short hill and passes under the power lines. In the middle of this clearing it reaches a 4-way intersection with Lower Powerline Trail. Continuing straight past this intersection into the wood on the far side of the power lines, the trail next crosses a very narrow creek. It then comes to a metal fence marking the edge of Fort Richardson. (To continue beyond this point, one needs a permit from JBER-Richardson. To obtain this permit, see Appendix 3 at the end of the book.)

From the gate the trail continues straight ahead through the trees. Less than 0.25 miles from the gate, the trail descends a short hill to a narrow bridge over North Fork of Campbell Creek—a popular feeding ground for bears during salmon run. On the far side of the bridge the trail reaches the upper end of a wide gravel road. With a JBER – Richardson permit in hand, one can continue down this trail-road. In approximately 0.5 miles one passes the junction with Ice Cream Cone Cut-off on the right (east). Approximately 0.5 miles after this junction, the trail climbs up and over a low bluff. Approximately 0.5 miles later the trail reaches a yet larger bridge over South Fork Chester Creek.

Though the road does continue beyond this point for another almost 4 miles, one should stop here because beyond this point the military has built a number of shooting pits at which they use live ammunition. For this reason the military prefers no one continue beyond this point.

At this point, one has a number of choices. First, they can return the entire way they have come. Second, they can return approximately 1 mile to the junction with Ice Cream Cone Cut-off and follow it to summit of Ice Cone*. Third, they can return to the power lines and follow Lower Powerline Trail up to Campbell Creek gorge**. Fourth, they can explore one of the other trails leading west (on the right going back) out to the power lines, under which one follow Lower Powerline Trail back to an intersection with Tank Trail.

**TRAIL GRADE:** This trail rates Grade 1 as a hike.

**TRAIL CONDITION:** This entire trail, apart from some flooding and mud in the spring, remains in excellent condition.

**TRAIL MILEAGE:** To hike from the beginning of Tank Trail at the North Bivouac parking area to the second and larger bridge on military land entails approximately 3.5 miles of hiking, for a round-trip total of 7 miles.

**TOTAL ELEVATION GAIN:** To hike from the beginning of Tank Trail at the North Bivouac parking area to the second and larger bridge on military land and back entails a total elevation gain of approximately 400 feet.

**HIGH POINT:** This route reaches its highest point of approximately 600 feet above sea level almost exactly at the gate marking the border of Fort Richardson.

**NORMAL HIKING TIME:** To hike from the beginning of Tank Trail at the North Bivouac parking area to the second and larger bridge on military land and back should take anywhere from 2.5 to 4 hours, depending on the condition and ambition of the hiker(s) involved.

--------------------------------------------------------------------------------

* For more information about that trail,
  see [88] **Walk-About Guide to Ice Cream Cut-Off Trail.**

** For more information about that trail, see [91] **Walk-About Guide to Lower Powerline Trail.**

**CAMPSITES:** One will find no designated campsites along this route. Nor, given the short length of the trail, should one need any.

**BEST TIME:** Most people should find any time of year a good time to hike or bike this trail. In winter it also makes a fine hike or bike as it usually remains well packed through being so well used.

**USGS MAPS:** Anchorage A-8.

Tank Trail in April

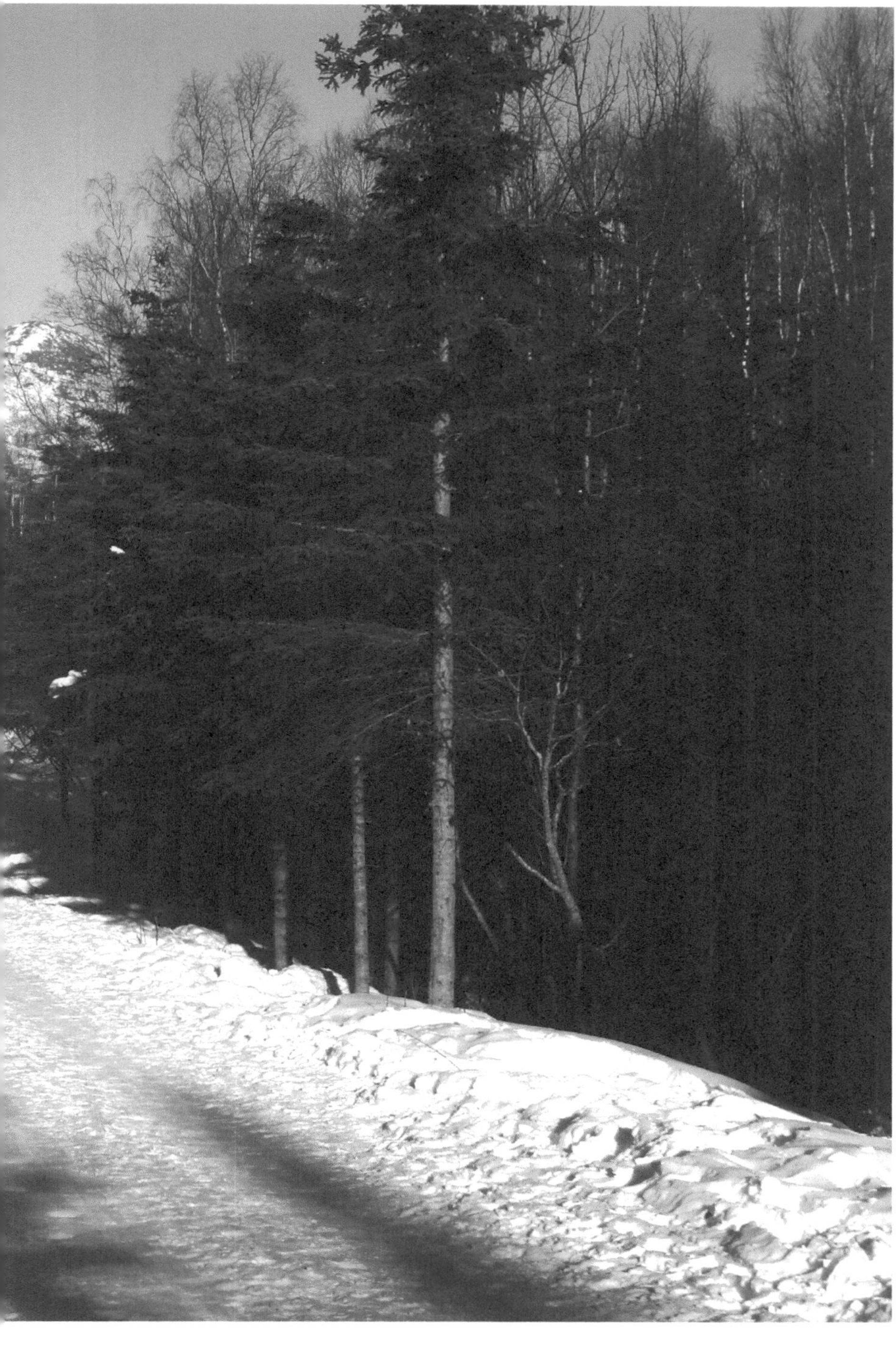

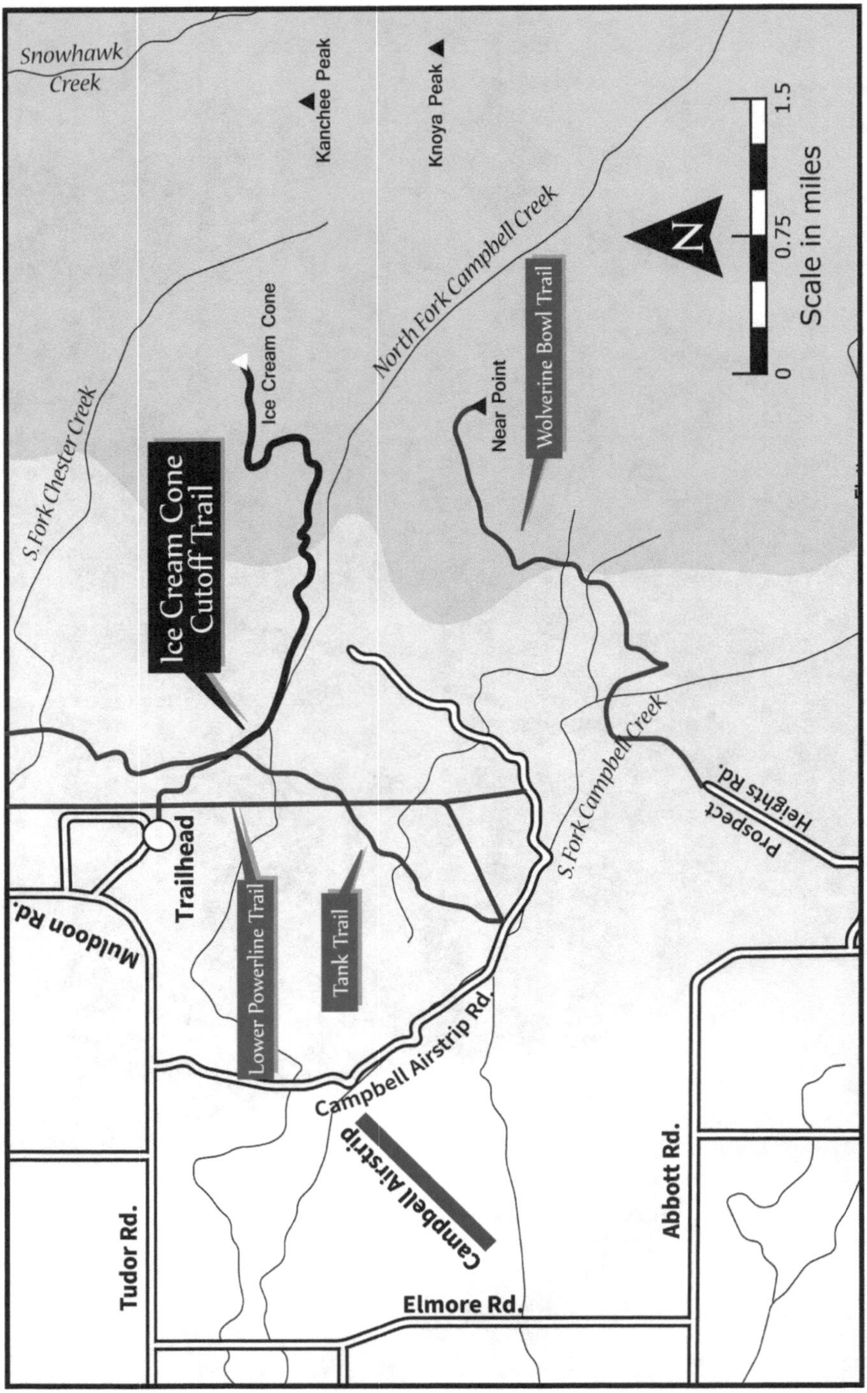
Snowhawk Creek
Kanchee Peak
Knoya Peak
S. Fork Chester Creek
Ice Cream Cone Cutoff Trail
Ice Cream Cone
North Fork Campbell Creek
Near Point
Wolverine Bowl Trail
N
0
0.75
1.5
Scale in miles
Trailhead
Lower Powerline Trail
Tank Trail
S. Fork Campbell Creek
Prospect Heights Rd.
Muldoon Rd.
Campbell Airstrip Rd.
Campbell Airstrip
Tudor Rd.
Elmore Rd.
Abbott Rd.

# Walk-About Guide to Ice Cream Cone Cut-off

Since this route crosses military land, one does need a permit from JBER- Richardson. To obtain this permit, see Appendix 3 at the end of the book.

**TRAIL LOCATION:** This alternate route to the summit of Ice Cream Cone (which some also refer to as Baldy) begins in the Chugach Foothills subdivision in East Anchorage. To get there drive 3.2 miles south of downtown Anchorage on the Seward Highway. There, just after Milepost 125, turn right (west) on the Tudor Road exit. At the end of the ramp, turn left (east) and cross back over the highway. Continue straight on this road as it gradually ascends past Lake Otis Parkway and Elmore Drive. Approximately 3.8 miles from the Seward Highway, Tudor Road swings left (north) and becomes into Muldoon Road. Just where the Muldoon Road begins to straighten after this wide curve, turn right (east) onto East 36th Avenue. Then turn right on Pioneer Drive. Follow Pioneer Drive until it winds its way to Klutina Drive, a dead end street on the right. Turn right (south) onto Klutina and park anywhere near the gate at the far end of this dead-end road without blocking access through the gate or parking on people's lawns and driveways.

The route begins by hiking through the gate. Immediately after passing through the gate, follow the dirt road as it swings left (east) under the right-of-way of the power lines. Approximately 100 yards later this dirt road reaches a clearing under a larger set of power lines. Turning right (south-southeast), follow the dirt road up the right-of way of the power lines toward the small, fenced-in electric station that one can see approximately 0.5 miles ahead. Just beyond this station bear left and follow the trail that hugs the boundary fence on the left (east). In another 100 yards or so one should reach a small opening in this fence leading left (east). Turning onto this trail, follow it into the woods. In another approximately 200 yards this trail reaches a wide gravel road (an obvious reminder that you are now hiking on JBER-Richardson military reservation land). Turning left (north) on this road, follow it for another approximately 0.25 miles to where an unmarked opening on the left indicates the beginning of Ice Cream Cone Cut-off.

Turning right (east) onto the Ice Cream Cone Cut-off follow it as it leads into the woods. Within 100 feet the trail begins to wind steadily upward. Eventually, after topping a wooded ridge, it reaches a junction with Ice Cream Cone Trail*. Bearing left on Ice Cream Cone Trail follow it as it continues winding up the ridge crest. Eventually this trail bends left (north) and begin climbing some long switchbacks toward the higher, open ridge above. At the top of these switchbacks the trail turns left (north) again and begins its last steep and direct climb to the ridge's mounded, bald top that marks the summit of Ice Cream Cone (approximately 2,800 feet).

**TRAIL GRADE:** This hike rates Grade 1 as a hike for the first approximately 1 mile. On leaving the military road and starting up Ice Cream Cutoff proper the route rates Grade 2 as a hike. It remains Grade 2 as a hike for almost the entire rest of the hike. Only at the very end does it climb steeply enough, though for less than 0.5 mile, to rate Grade 3 as a hike.

**TRAIL CONDITION:** Although one may have to cross some muddy spots on the section from the military road to the summit, conditions on this trail generally remain good to excellent.

**TRAIL MILEAGE:** To go from the parking area on Klutina Drive to the summit of Ice Cream Cone entails approximately 4 miles of hiking, for a round-trip total of 8 miles.

-------------------------------------------------------------------

\* For information about that trail see [69] **Walk-About Guide to Ice Cream Cone Trail** in Chapter 6.

**TOTAL ELEVATION GAIN:** To hike from the parking area on Klutina Drive to the summit of Ice Cream Cone entails a total elevation gain of approximately 2,700 feet

**HIGH POINT:** This hike reaches its highest point of approximately 2,800 feet above sea level at the summit of Ice Cream Cone.

**NORMAL HIKING TIME:** To hike from the parking area on Klutina Drive to the summit of Ice Cream Cone and back should take anywhere from 3 to 6 hours, depending on the condition and ambition of the hiker(s) involved.

**CAMPSITES:** One will find no designated campsites along this trail. Nor, given the short length of the trail, is one likely to need any.

**BEST TIME:** Most people should find any time from early May to September a good time to do this hike. This also makes a fine ski or snowshoe trip in the winter, although the last climb to the ridge may prove very arduous in icy conditions.

**USGS MAPS:** Anchorage A-8.

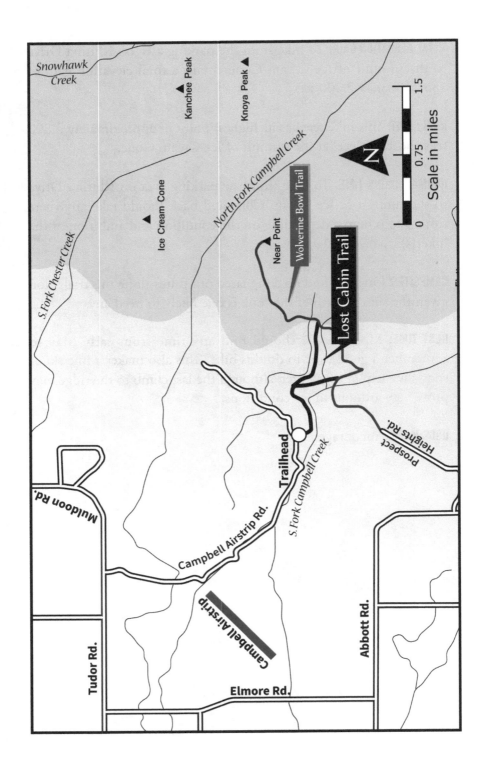

Snowhawk Creek

Kanchee Peak ▲

Knoya Peak ▲

Ice Cream Cone ▲

S. Fork Chester Creek

North Fork Campbell Creek

Near Point

Wolverine Bowl Trail

Lost Cabin Trail

N

Scale in miles

0    0.75    1.5

Trailhead

S. Fork Campbell Creek

Prospect Heights Rd.

Muldoon Rd.

Campbell Airstrip Rd.

Campbell Airstrip

Tudor Rd.

Elmore Rd.

Abbott Rd.

# Walk-About Lost Cabin Trail

Some people may traditionally know this trail as Homestead Trail. Upon the building of State Park parking area, it now goes by the name Lost Cabin Trail. This differentiates it from Homestead Trail found lower in Far North Bicentennial Park off Elmore Drive described above.

**TRAIL LOCATION:** Lost Cabin Trail begins at State Park parking area located approximately 3.2 miles up Basher Road in Far North Bicentennial Park. To get there drive 3.2 miles south of downtown Anchorage on the Seward Highway. Then, just after Milepost 124, turn right (west) on the Tudor Road exit. At the end of the exit ramp, turn left (east) and cross back over the highway. Continue straight on Tudor Road as it gradually ascends past Lake Otis Parkway and Elmore Drive. Approximately 3.2 miles from the Seward Highway Tudor Road reaches a set of lights at Campbell Airstrip Road leading right (south). Turn right on Campbell Airstrip Road. In approximately 1 mile this road becomes Basher Road. Stay on Basher Road as it continues to wind upward. Approximately 2.5 miles from Tudor Road the road passes the Bivouac Trail parking areas on either side of the road. Approximately 0.8 miles later the road passes under power lines. Immediately after passing under the power lines the road reaches State Park parking area on the right (south). Turn into this parking area. Lost Cabin Trail begins at the back of the parking area.

The trail begins by following an old access road for the power lines over two short steep hills. Approximately 0.4 miles from the parking area, at the crest of the second hill, which overlooks the North Fork Campbell Creek gorge, the trail turns sharply left (east). Climbing a very short and steep embankment, the trail climbs past the base of a power line tower before leveling off on the wooded bench above. For the next 0.5 miles the trail winds along the crest of the bench, allowing sporadic views of the gorge dropping away steeply on the right (south). At the far end of the bench the trail drops down a steep bank. At the bottom of the bank it reaches a trail junction.

Both trails eventually lead to Wolverine Bowl Trail. The trail to the right (south) descends a shallow, wooded slope down to the edge of North Fork Campbell Creek. At the creek's edge, it turns left (southeast) and follows the creek upstream for approximately 0.5 miles to where it reaches a T intersection with Wolverine Bowl Trail at the east end of the bridge over North Fork Campbell Creek.

The longer Lost Cabin Trail leading left (north) almost immediately climbs a short, steep hill before swinging right (east). For the next 1 mile it winds gradually upward through woods and meadows. Approximately 200 yards after crossing a short bridge it reaches its uppermost end at a T intersection with Wolverine Bowl Trail directly across from where Wolverine Peak Trail begins.

Here one has three choices. First, one can return the way they came. Second, one can climb Wolverine Peak*. Third, one can climb Near Point**. Fourth, one can follow Wolverine Bowl Trail 2.5 miles out to Prospect Heights parking area. Fifth, one can complete the circumnavigation of Campbell Creek Gorge***.

**TRAIL GRADE:** Lost Cabin Trail rates Grade 1 as a hike, with some extremely short sections rated Grade 2 as a hike on the first short steep climbs at the beginning of the trail.

**TRAIL CONDITION:** This trail varies little in its conditions. After following a wide access road for its first 0.5 mile, it then turns onto a narrower trail. This trail, though sometimes rough and muddy underfoot, generally has good footing. This remains true of both branches of the trail leading to Wolverine Bowl Trail, although the lower trail sometimes floods in the spring as it approaches the bridge over Campbell Creek.

-------------------------------------------------------------------

\* For more information about that hike, see [60] **Wolverine Peak Trail** in Chapter 5.

\** For more information about that hike, see [57] **Wolverine Bowl Trail** in Chapter 5.

\*** For more information about that trip,
see [90] **OPTION A—Circumnavigation of Campbell Creek Gorge**.

**TRAIL MILEAGE:** To go from State Park parking area to Wolverine Bowl Trail where it reaches the bridge over Campbell Creek entails approximately 1.3 miles of hiking, for a round trip total of 2.6 miles. To go from State Park parking area to Wolverine Bowl Trail across from Wolverine Peak Trail entails approximately 2.1 miles of hiking, for a round-trip total of approximately 4.2 miles.

**TOTAL ELEVATION GAIN:** To hike from State Park parking area to Wolverine Bowl Trail where it reaches the bridge over Campbell Creek entails a total elevation gain of approximately 150 feet. To hike from State Park parking area to Wolverine Bowl Trail across from Wolverine Peak Trail a total elevation gain of approximately 500 feet

**HIGH POINT:** This trail reaches its highest point of approximately 1,400 feet above sea level where it reaches its junction with Wolverine Bowl Trail across from Wolverine Peak Trail.

**NORMAL HIKING TIME:** To hike from State Park parking area to Wolverine Bowl Trail to where the trail reaches the bridge over Campbell Creek and back should take anywhere from 1 to 2 hours, depending on the condition and ambition of the hiker(s) involved. To hike from the parking area to Wolverine Bowl Trail across from Wolverine Peak Trail and back should take anywhere from 1.5 to 3 hours, depending on the condition and ambition of the hiker(s) involved.

**CAMPSITES:** One will find no designated campsites along this trail. Nor, given the short length of the trail, should one need any.

**BEST TIME:** Most people should find any time from May to early October the best time to do this hike. In addition, it makes a fine ski or snowshoe outing in the winter. In winter it also makes a fine hike or bike as it usually remains well packed through being so well used.

**USGS MAPS:** Anchorage A-8.

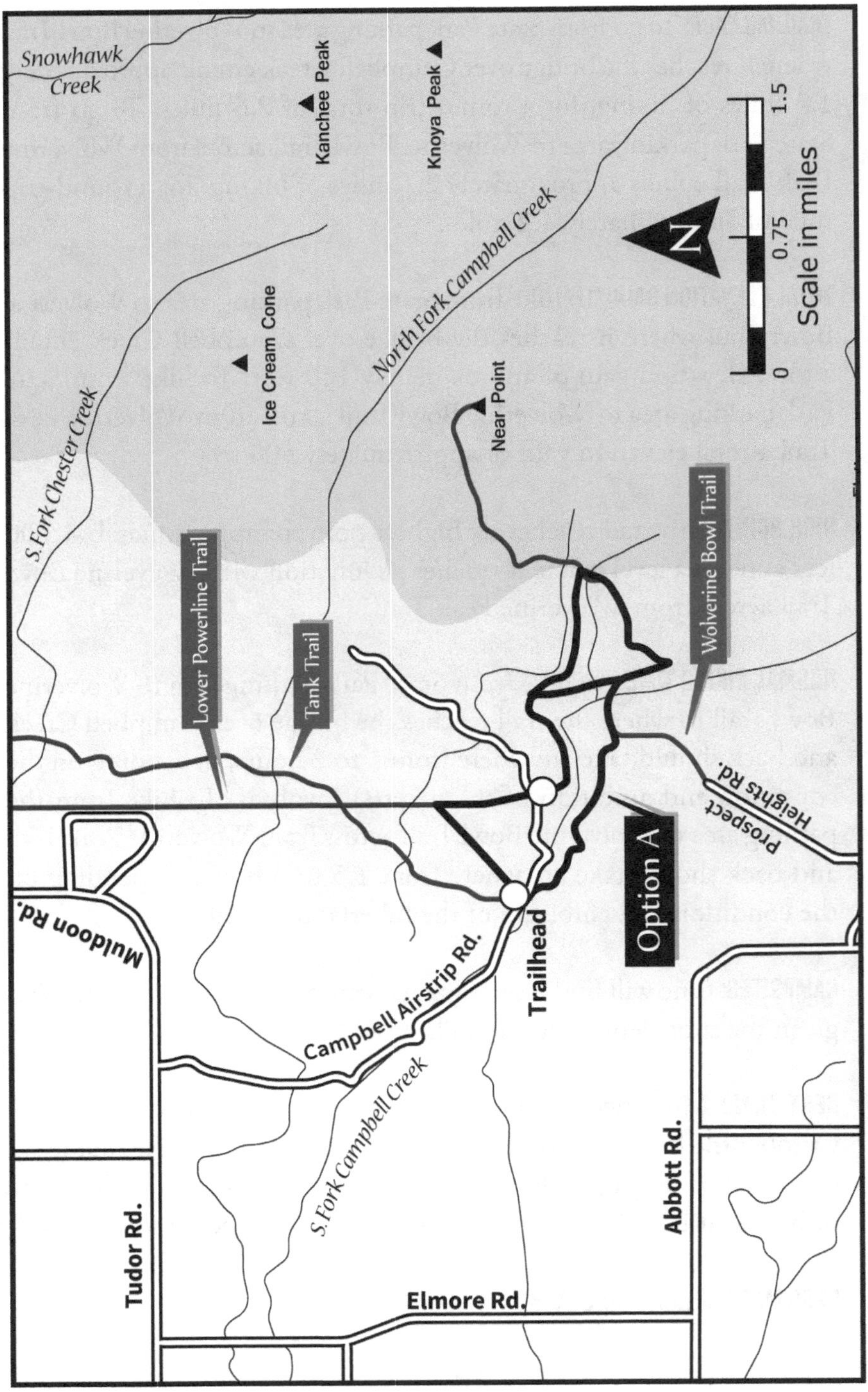
Snowhawk Creek
Kanchee Peak
Knoya Peak
North Fork Campbell Creek
Ice Cream Cone
Near Point
S. Fork Chester Creek
Lower Powerline Trail
Tank Trail
Wolverine Bowl Trail
N
0
0.75
1.5
Scale in miles
Muldoon Rd.
Prospect Heights Rd.
Option A
Trailhead
Campbell Airstrip Rd.
S. Fork Campbell Creek
Abbott Rd.
Tudor Rd.
Elmore Rd.

# OPTION A

# Circumnavigation of
# Campbell Creek Gorge

This hike, although it utilizes the entire length of Lost Cabin Trail, does not begin on that trail. Instead it starts lower at North Bivouac parking area. In doing so it finishes most of the climbing in the first half of the hike on the north side of Campbell Creek. Thus it makes for a more aesthetically pleasing loop that starts and finishes at its lower end.

**TRAIL LOCATION:** This hike begins in South Bivouac parking area approximately 2.5 miles up Basher Road in Far North Bicentennial Park. To get there drive 3.2 miles south of downtown Anchorage on the Seward Highway. Then, just after Milepost 124, turn right (west) on the Tudor Road exit. At the end of the ramp, turn left (east) and cross back over the highway. Continue straight on Tudor Road as it gradually ascends past Lake Otis Parkway and Elmore Drive. Approximately 3.2 miles from the Seward Highway Tudor Road reaches a set of lights at Campbell Airstrip Road leading right (south). Turn right on Campbell Airstrip Road. In approximately 1 mile this road becomes Basher Road. Stay on Basher Road as it continues to wind upward. Approximately 2.5 miles from Tudor Road the road reaches the Bivouac Trail parking areas on either side of the road. Turn left (north) into North Bivouac parking area. The beginning of the circumnavigation begins on the narrow trail just to the right of signboard at the far right (southeast) corner of the parking area.

Bearing right past the signboard, follow this relatively narrow trail as it winds into the woods. In approximately 0.2 miles this trail emerges into the open swath of the underground gas pipeline. Bearing left (east-northeast) up the swath, follow the trail as it climbs over two low hills in the next 0.5 miles. At the top of the second hill it reaches a trail junction underneath the power lines. Here turn right (south) onto the trail climbing up the embankment to the right (southeast). Follow this trail as it climbs the right-of-way for the power lines. In approximately 0.4 miles the trail pushes through some low brush to the embankment on Basher Road. Descend the embankment and bear left into State Park parking area on the far side of the road.

The circumnavigation now follows Lost Cabin Trail out the back side of the parking area. Lost Cabin Trail begins by climbing over two short steep hills. Approximately 0.4 miles from the parking area, at the crest of far hill overlooking North Fork Campbell Creek gorge, the trail turns sharply left (east).

Climbing a very short and steep embankment, the trail climbs past the base of a power line tower and levels off on the wooded bench above. For the next 0.5 miles the trail winds along the crest of the bench, allowing sporadic views of the gorge dropping away steeply on the right (south). At the far end of the bench the trail drops down a steep bank. At the bottom of the embankment it reaches a trail junction.

One can follow either trail to complete the circumnavigation. The shorter trail to the right (south) descends a shallow, wooded slope down to the edge of North Fork Campbell Creek. At the creek's edge the trail turns left (southeast) and follows the creek upstream for approximately 0.5 miles to where it reaches a T intersection with Wolverine Bowl Trail at the east end of the bridge over North Fork Campbell Creek. There turn right on Wolverine Bowl Trail to complete the circumnavigation.

The longer route follows Lost Cabin Trail to left (north) almost immediately climbs a short, steep hill before swinging right (east). For the next 1 mile it winds gradually upward through woods and meadows. Approximately 200 yards after crossing a short bridge it reaches its uppermost end at a T intersection with Wolverine Bowl Trail directly across from where Wolverine Peak Trail begins*.

The circumnavigation continues at this point by turning right (south) onto Wolverine Bowl Trail and following it back down to the bridge over North Fork Campbell Creek. Here it rejoins the shorter trail described above. Continuing over the bridge, the trail climbs up and around a low buttress as it heads back toward Prospect Heights parking area. Before reaching the parking area, however, look for where the trail comes again in sight of the power lines to the right. At that point, look for a wide trail leading off to the right (west) from Wolverine Bowl Trail. Turn onto this trail and follow it as it descends an open meadow under the power lines. There bear right (north) and follow the trail down toward the gorge just visible ahead.

At the base of the meadow one reaches another trail junction. Though both trails ultimately go to the same place, the more scenic of the two continues straight ahead toward the gorge. Bearing left (west) into the trees as it nears the gorge, this slightly longer trail soon reaches a dramatic overlook at the top of some sheer cliffs above the gorge. As the trail continues down the south side of the gorge, it passes a number of other scenic overlooks before turning sharply left (south) away from the gorge and rejoining the other trail. On rejoining the trail from which it parted in the meadow below the power lines, turn right (west) and continue the short way down to the wide Spencer Loop.

On reaching Spenser Loop, turn right (northwest) and follow it for approximately 1 mile down to a bridge crossing North Fork Campbell Creek. After crossing the creek, follow the trail up to South Bivouac parking area. Continue through the parking area out to Basher Road. Now just cross the road back to North Bivouac parking area where this circumnavigation began.

**TRAIL GRADE:** This entire circumnavigation rates Grade 1 as a hike, with some sporadic sections in the few short hills that one climbs to where one reaches Wolverine Bowl Trail rated Grade 2 as a hike.

- - - - - - - - - - - - - - - - - - - - - - - - - - - - - - - - - - - - - - - - - - - - - - - - - - -

*   For more information about these trails, see [57] **Wolverine Bowl Trail** and [60] **Wolverine Peak Trail** in Chapter 5.

**TRAIL CONDITION:** This route varies little in its conditions. After following some fine trails out of the parking area and up to the power lines, it then crosses probably its muddiest section on the climb under the power lines to Basher Road. On the far side of Basher Road it follows an access road for its first 0.4 miles before turning onto a narrower trail. This trail, though sometimes rough and muddy underfoot, generally has good footing. This remains true of both branches of the trail leading to Wolverine Bowl Trail. One then follows the wide and predominantly flat Wolverine Trail. On leaving Wolverine Bowl Trail the route down the power lines to Spencer Loop often becomes overgrown by midsummer. On Spenser Loop, the route again follows a wide dirt trail, all the way back to the parking area.

**TRAIL MILEAGE:** To complete this circumnavigation from North Bivouac parking area on and back via the shorter route along Campbell Creek entails approximately 3.4 miles of hiking To complete this circumnavigation from North Bivouac parking area and back via the longer route entails approximately 4.9 miles of hiking.

**TOTAL ELEVATION GAIN:** To complete this circumnavigation from North Bivouac parking area and back via the shorter route entails a total elevation gain of approximately 300 feet. To complete this circumnavigation from North Bivouac parking area and back via the longer route entails a total elevation gain of approximately 650 feet.

**HIGH POINT:** This trail reaches its highest point of approximately 1,400 feet above sea level where the longer route reaches the junction with Wolverine Bowl Trail where the latter begins its ascent of Near Point.

**NORMAL HIKING TIME:** To complete this circumnavigation from North Bivouac parking area and back via the shorter route should take anywhere from 1.5 to 3 hours, depending on the condition and ambition of the hiker(s) involved. To complete this circumnavigation from North Bivouac parking area and back via the longer route should take anywhere from 2 to 4 hours, again depending on the condition and ambition of the hiker(s) involved.

**CAMPSITES:** One will find no designated campsites along this trail. Nor, given the short length of the trail, should one need any.

**BEST TIME:** Most people should find any time from May to early October the best time to do this hike. In addition, much of it makes a fine ski or snowshoe outing in the winter, except for the fact that Spenser Loop remains off-limits to foot travel in the winter.

**USGS MAPS:** Anchorage A-8.

In Campbell Creek gorge

S. Fork Chester Creek
Lower Powerline Trail
N
0
0.5
1
Scale in miles
Trailhead
Trailhead
Muldoon Rd.
N. Fork Campbell Creek
Tank Trail
Campbell Airstrip Rd.
S. Fork Campbell Creek
Boniface
Pkwy.
Tudor Rd.
Campbell Airstrip
N. Fork Little Campbell Creek
Elmore Rd.

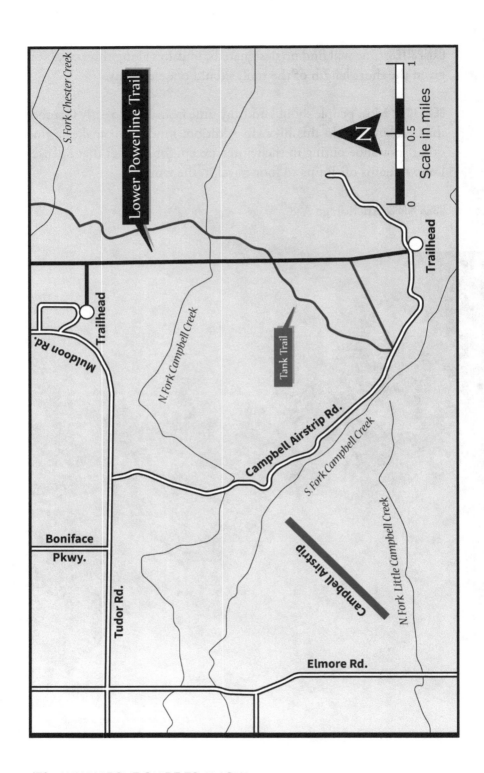

# Walk-About Guide to
# Lower Powerline Trail

This trail, which begins in a popular dog park in East Anchorage, follows the power lines up Hillside to Basher Road. From there one can cross the road continue up Lost Cabin Trail into the Chugach Mountains. And while other routes do this as well, they usually involve changing directions at many trail junctions. This trail connects the Anchorage bowl with the Front Range in a single sweep upward.

**TRAIL LOCATION:** This trail begins in the Chugach Foothills subdivision in East Anchorage. To get there drive 3.2 miles south of downtown Anchorage on the Seward Highway. There, just after Milepost 125, turn right (west) on the Tudor Road exit. At the end of the ramp, turn left (east) and cross back over the highway. Continue straight on this road as it gradually ascends past Lake Otis Parkway and Elmore Drive. Approximately 3.8 miles from the Seward Highway, Tudor Road swings left (north) and becomes into Muldoon Road. Just where the Muldoon Road begins to straighten after this wide curve, turn right (east) onto East 36th Avenue. Then turn right on Pioneer Drive. Follow Pioneer Drive until it winds its way to Klutina Drive, a dead end street on the right. Turn right (south) onto Klutina and park anywhere near the gate at the far end of this dead-end road without blocking access through the gate or parking on people's lawns and driveways.

The route begins by hiking through the gate. Immediately after passing through the gate, follow the dirt road as it swings left (east) under the right-of-way of the power lines. Approximately 100 yards later this dirt road reaches a clearing under a larger set of power lines.

Turning right (south-southeast), follow the dirt road up the right-of way of the power lines toward the small, fenced-in electric station that one can see approximately 0.5 miles ahead.

Just beyond this station Lower Powerline Trail reaches a junction with a trail that bears left and follows the trail that hugs the boundary fence on the left for approximately 100 yards to small opening leading left (east). This trail through the fence leads to both Tank Trail and Ice Cream Cone Cut-off*.

Continuing straight up the power lines, follow the main trail to where, approximately 0.5 beyond the electric station, it reaches the shore of North Fork Campbell Creek. One can either ford the creek or turn left (northeast) or follow the creek upstream to where a sturdy steel girder allows passage to the far shore. Once on the far side of the creek, continue up the main trail beneath the power lines toward the prominent bluff ahead. As one nears the bluff, the trail splits apart as it enters the lower end of an oft-soggy section of trail. One can follow either trail up either side of the bluff. At the top of the bluff one reaches an intersection with Tank Trail**.

Continuing past Tank Trail, the trail plunges down a small dip as it continues to follow the power lines up toward the mountains. The next approximately 1 mile of trail often proves especially soggy. Many side trails split from the main trail to avoid the puddles and the mud. Approximately 0.5 miles after passing Tank Trail, the trail drops into another, deeper dip and crosses a wide, shallow stream. On the climb out of this big hole, the trail crosses another narrow stream. Just after crossing the stream the trail reaches another junction with a trail that follows the right-of-way for the gas line back toward Basher Road and North Bivouac parking areas.

On the far side of this junction the trail climbs a small embankment and heads toward the next high hill ahead up the power lines. Upon reaching the crest of this hill, one can turn and enjoy a wide and long

--------------------------------------------------------------------

\*  For more information about these trails see [88] **Walk-About Guide to Ice Cream Cone Cut-Off** and [87] **Walk-About Guide to Tank Trail.**

\*\*  For more information about that trail, see [87] **Walk-About Guide to Tank Trail.**

view of the Anchorage bowl and Knik Arm, Denali, and the Talkeetna Mountains beyond. From the crest of this last hill, the trail slants downward for another 50 yards to the embankment of Basher Road. This marks the upper end of Lower Powerline Trail.

At this point one has two major choices. First, one can turn around and return the way they have come. Second, one can continue straight across Basher Road to Basher Road parking area and where one can start up Lost Cabin Trail as it continues following the power lines up to the edge of Campbell Creek Gorge and beyond*.

**TRAIL GRADE:** This trail initially rates Grade 1 as a hike. From the climb of the first bluff to the end the trail at Basher Road it rises to Grade 2 as a hike.

**TRAIL CONDITION:** Although one may have to cross some muddy spots, this trail generally remains good to excellent.

**TRAIL MILEAGE:** To go from the parking area at Klutina Drive to the end of the trail at the edge of Basher Road entails approximately 2.5 miles of hiking for a round-trip total of 5 miles.

**TOTAL ELEVATION GAIN:** To hike this traverse from the parking area at Klutina Drive to the end of the trail at the edge of Basher Road and back entails a total elevation gain of approximately 600 feet.

**HIGH POINT:** This hike reaches its highest point of 800 feet above sea level at the summit of the last hill before reaching Basher Road.

**NORMAL HIKING TIME:** To hike this trail from the parking area at Klutina Drive to the end of the trail at the edge of Basher Road and back should take anywhere from 2 to 4 hours depending on the condition and ambition of the hiker(s) involved.

----------------------------------------------------------------------

\* For more information about that trail, see [89] **Walk-About Guide to Lost Cabin Trail.**

**CAMPSITES:** One will find no designated campsites along this trail. Nor should one need one considering the shortness of the hike.

**BEST TIME:** Most people should find any time of the year a good time to hike, bike, run, or ski.

**USGS MAPS:** Anchorage A-8.

On Lower Hillside

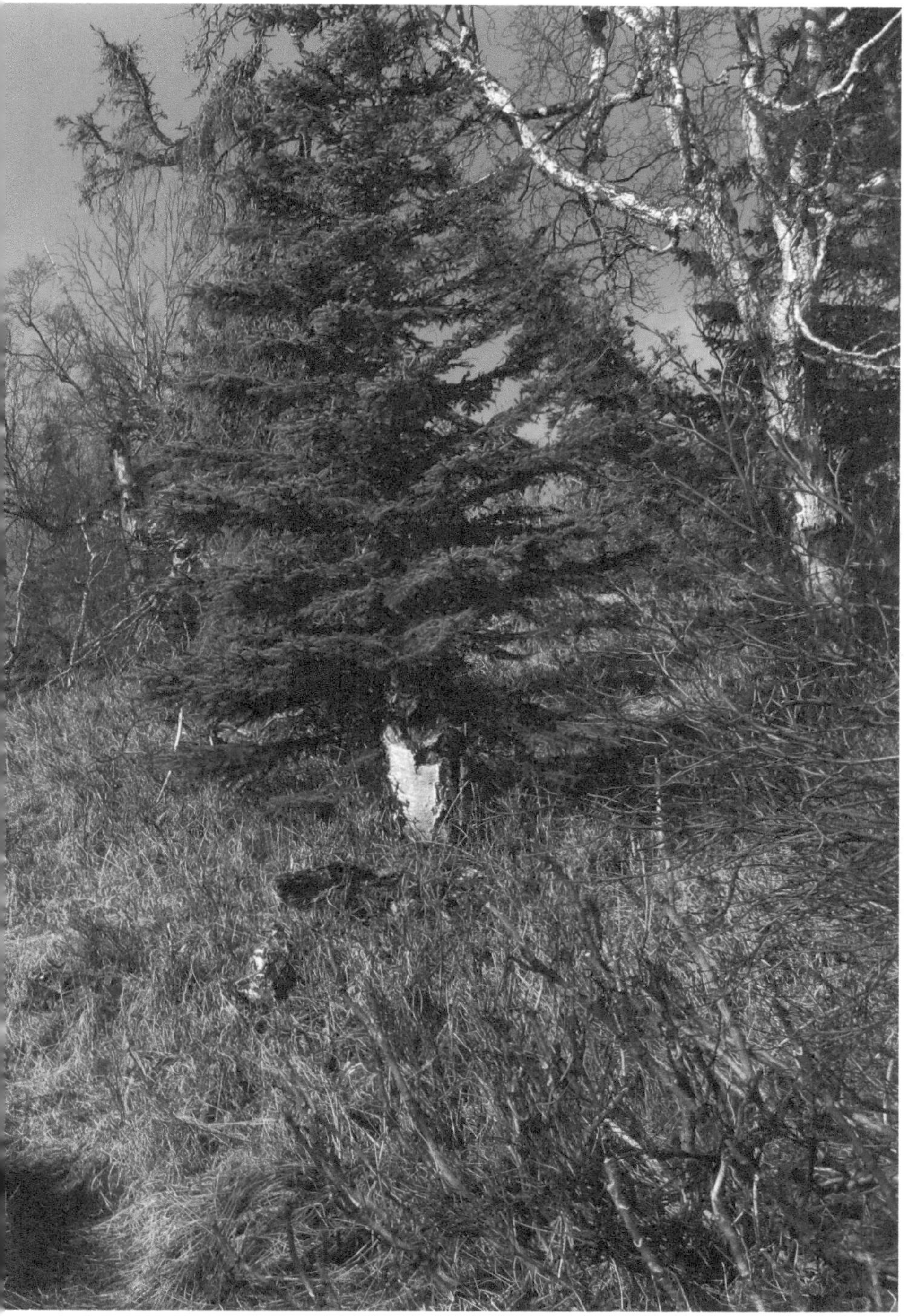

Spring walk in Kincaid Park

## CHAPTER 10

# KINCAID PARK

## OVERVIEW OF KINCAID PARK

Most people know Kincaid Park primarily as a mecca for cross-country skiers. The 30-plus miles of groomed ski trails winding through this 1,400-acre wooded park on the westernmost tip of the Anchorage Peninsula offer a plethora of routes for both novice and advanced skiers. As such, the park hosts some major ski races and meets. It also marks the end of the internationally known Tour of Anchorage ski race which takes place in early March.

Given its reputation as a major ski area, many people remain unaware of the park's possibilities as a location for hiking, biking, and running. When the snow has melted, and the ground has thawed and dried, all those many miles of ski trails open to non-skiers. Of all these trails, three remain most popular in the off-season. These three trails wind through exclusive sections of the park, thus allowing anyone who explores all three to gain an overall familiarity with the park. The first, Lake Loop Trail, winds through the northeast quarter of the park, passing along the way the shore of Little Campbell Lake (also known as Beer-Can Lake), the lowest point in the park. In the summer fishermen and kayakers make the waters of this lake a rarely deserted place. Only late in the evening or early in the morning do the waters have the luxury of stilling to a quiet mirror of the sky and surrounding wooded bluffs. The second, the Mize Loop, the easiest and shortest of the three, circles through the largely open woodlands just north of the Kincaid Chalet. The third popular trail, the 6-mile-long Andrew Lekisch Trail, winds through the hills on the opposite, southwest corner of the park over some of the highest and airiest bluffs in the park over which the winds often blow with a hard chill. As the hilliest competition-certified 10-kilometer ski course in the country, this trail can prove a challenge to hikers, runners, and bikers. Yet as it winds over numerous high hills it offers some especially wide views of Turnagain Arm to the south, Cook Inlet and Fire Island to the west, and the Chugach Mountains to the east.

Besides all its ski trails, Kincaid Park also contains a wide-ranging number of other trails. The most numerous of these trails, a maze of single-track bike trails, remain open all year round not just to bikes, but to foot, and ski travel as well. Weaving back and forth and up and down throughout the length and breadth of the park, these trails accommodate all levels of bikers*. The southernmost miles of the 10.5-mile paved Tony Knowles Coastal Trail also pass through the park before ending at Kincaid Chalet. Other popular destinations in the park include the beach at the westernmost end of the peninsula, and the Kincaid Bluff Trail that traverses the heights above the beach.**

Besides these more popular trails, the park has a large number of other trails that branch off into the woods in seemingly every direction. This seems particularly apparent if one begins hiking or biking from the Stadium, the large open area at the bottom of the hill just east of the chalet. From this point one can follow their whim to all points of the compass.

Admittedly, following one's whim may lead to getting lost. In such cases, one should not feel so much lost as misplaced. Before panicking, remember two things: First no matter what trail you follow, you will rarely find yourself more than 1 mile away from either the road that cuts the park in two or Tony Knowles Coastal Trail. Second, because almost every trail forms a loop, you should simply continue along any trail and you should eventually come out to Kincaid Chalet, Coastal Trail, the road, or some parking area.

------------------------------------------------------------------------

\* For more information about these trails,
  see CHAPTER 12 **Single-Track Biking In Anchorage.**

\*\* For more information about two of the possible hikes one can make in Kincaid Park, see
  [96] **Walk-About Guide to Kincaid Bluff Trail** and [97] **Circumnavgation of Kincaid Park.**

But before venturing out on one's own, most may it helpful to first have familiarity with one or two trails before going out too far or too deep in any direction. With that in mind, and lacking the space to provide detailed descriptions of all the ski trails in the park, the following guides provide descriptions of the three popular trails mentioned earlier—Lake Loop Trail, Mize Loop, and Andrew Lekisch Trail. In addition, to the three trails mentioned above one can find below guides to Kincaid Bluff Trail, Kincaid Beach Trail, and even a circumnavigation of the entire park. Altogether, these three trails should provide fine starting points from which to branch out onto more and more trails inside the park until, with enough exploring, one knows the park intimately.

Sunset on Kincaid Beach

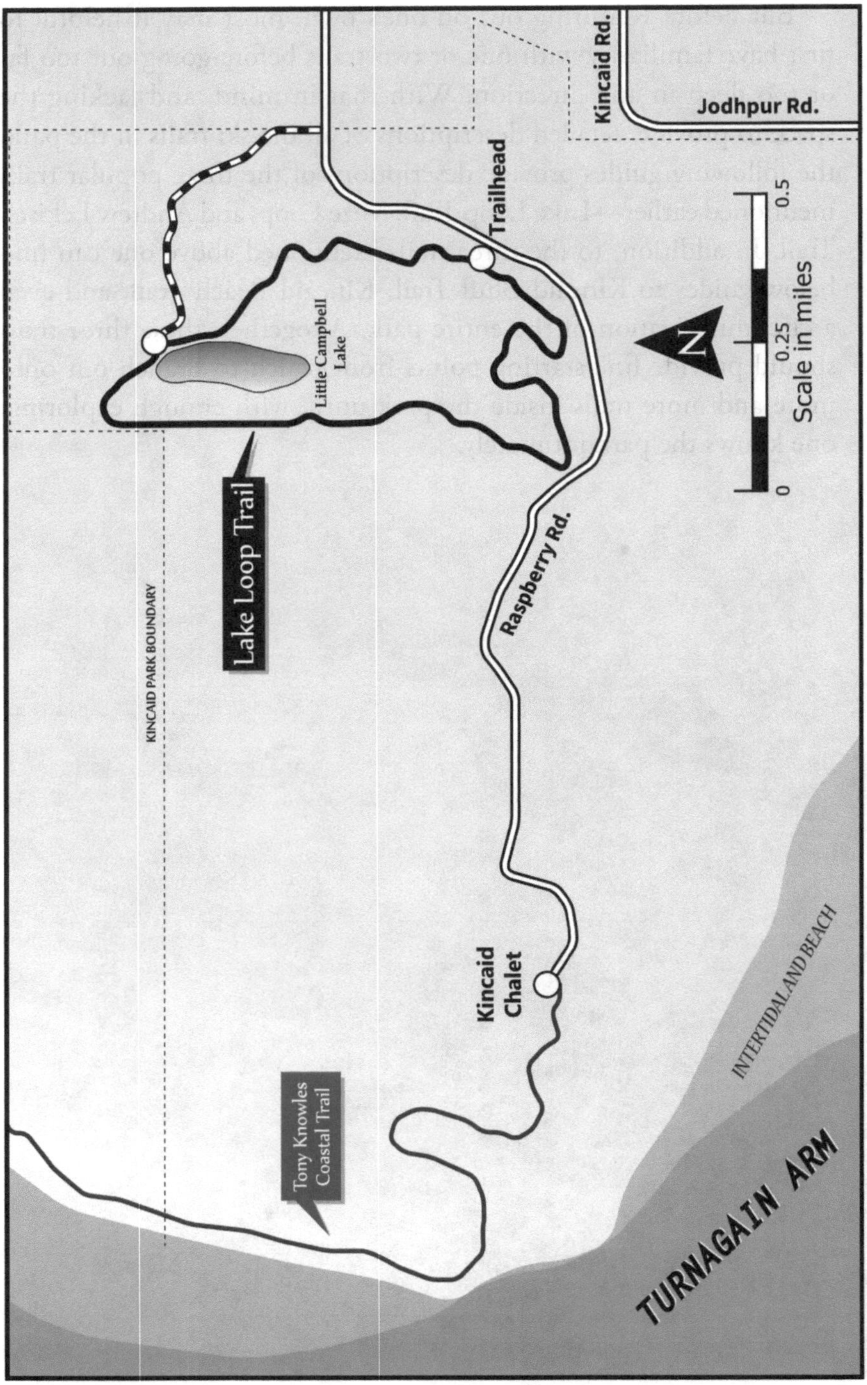
Lake Loop Trail
Little Campbell Lake
Trailhead
Kincaid Rd.
Jodhpur Rd.
N
0
0.25
0.5
Scale in miles
Raspberry Rd.
KINCAID PARK BOUNDARY
Kincaid Chalet
Tony Knowles Coastal Trail
INTERTIDALAND BEACH
TURNAGAIN ARM

# Walk-About Guide to Lake Loop Trail

**TRAIL LOCATION:** Lake Loop Trail begins at Raspberry Road Parking Area. To get there drive 3.5 miles south from downtown Anchorage on L Street and its extension Minnesota Drive. There, turn right off the first Raspberry Road exit. At the bottom of the exit ramp turn right (west) onto Raspberry Road. Follow Raspberry Road for approximately 3.25 miles past the major intersection of Four Corners and Sand Lake Road to the entrance of Kincaid Park.

Continuing straight past the entrance, follow Raspberry Road as it winds up a broad wooded hill and into the park. Approximately 0.5 miles past the entrance the road reaches the Raspberry Road Parking Area on the right (north). Turn into this parking area and park where available. Lake Loop Trail begins beside the information board just up the embankment at the back of the parking area.

Upon climbing the embankment past the information board, turn left (west) and start down the wide ski trail. Less than 0.2 miles from the parking area, Lake Loop merges with Margaux's Loop on the right (north). Continuing straight ahead, climb Margaux's Loop past a crossing Raspberry Road to where the trail bears right (north) and downhill. Approximately 0.6 miles from the parking area, Margaux's Loop reaches a junction with S-Turn which marks the beginning of Lake Loop Trail.

Turn right (north) follow the wide trail as it descends a long hill. At the bottom of the hill, where a number of other trails converge, turn up the trail farthest to the left (northwest) and climb a short hill to the top. Continuing straight ahead, one begins the descent of Big Niagara, a long, straight downhill approximately 1.1 miles from the parking area. At the bottom of Big Niagara the loop climbs over one more small hill just beyond Big Niagara and takes a sharp right turn (southwest) out to the open north shore of Little Campbell Lake. One has completed just over half of the loop.

Continuing straight across the grassy left (north) shore of the lake, follow the dirt trail up into the woods on the far side. Keeping straight, follow the trail across the base of a wooded bluff. At the end of the bluff, follow the trail as it turns up and to the right (south) where it parallels Raspberry Road (which one should see glimpses of through the trees).

From here back to Raspberry Road Parking Area one has a more or less continuous climb. At the top of the first little rise, one reaches a trail junction with a short cut-off. Bear right (west) at this cut-off and start across the slope of the bluff. At the far end of the slope, one should reach another intersection overlooking Little Campbell Lake. Here turn left (south) and uphill to switchback yet higher on the slope of the bluff. At the end of this switchback, one reaches yet another trail junction (the top of the cut-off one passed earlier). Here turn right (south). Within 100 feet one comes to a T-intersection. Turn left (southeast) at this intersection and begin the climb the last short rise to the top of the bluff. Approximately 0.3 miles later the trail arrives back at Raspberry Road Parking Area.

**TRAIL CONDITION:** Despite its many sharp ascents and descents, this wide trail remains in excellent condition.

**TRAIL MILEAGE:** To complete this loop from Raspberry Road Parking Area and back entails approximately 2.9 miles of hiking.

**TOTAL ELEVATION GAIN:** To complete this loop from Raspberry Road Parking Area and back entails a total elevation gain of approximately 650 feet.

**HIGH POINT:** This trail reaches its highest point of approximately 225 feet above sea level approximately 0.3 after starting where the trail passes near the right (north) end of a bridge over Raspberry Road.

**NORMAL HIKING TIME:** To hike from the beginning of this loop at Raspberry Road Parking Area and back should take anywhere from 1 to 2 hours, depending on the condition and ambition of the hiker(s) involved.

**CAMPSITES:** One will find no designated camping areas on this trail. Nor should one need one considering the shortness of the hike.

**BEST TIME:** Most people should find any time during the off-ski season a good time to do this hike. Bikers should, however, wait until the trails dry sufficiently so as not to leave deep ruts.

**USGS MAPS:** Tyonek A-1.

Spring thaw in Kincaid Park

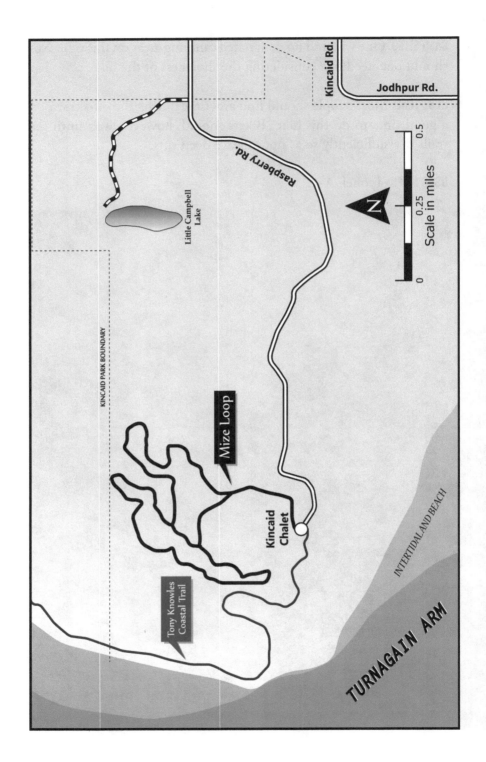

Kincaid Rd.

Jodhpur Rd.

Raspberry Rd.

N

0.5

0.25

0

Scale in miles

Little Campbell Lake

KINCAID PARK BOUNDARY

Mize Loop

Kincaid Chalet

Tony Knowles Coastal Trail

INTERTIDAL AND BEACH

TURNAGAIN ARM

# Walk-About Guide to Mize Loop

This ski trail draws many hikers looking for easily accessed views of Cook Inlet as well as many mountain bikers looking for a wide trail without any overly challenging hills. Many also use it to access the Sisson Loop, a long but easy, and largely deserted, loop that circles between the base of the bluffs and Tony Knowles Coastal Trail.

**TRAIL LOCATION:** Mize Loop begins at the northeast corner of the Stadium below Kincaid Chalet in Kincaid Park. To get there drive 3.5 miles south from downtown Anchorage on L Street and its extension Minnesota Drive. There, turn right off the first Raspberry Road exit. At the bottom of the exit ramp turn right (west) onto Raspberry Road. Follow Raspberry Road for approximately 3.25 miles past the major intersection of Four Corners and Sand Lake Road to the entrance of Kincaid Park.

Continuing straight past the entrance, follow Raspberry Road as it winds up broad wooded hill and into the park. Approximately 0.5 miles past the entrance the road reaches the Raspberry Road Parking Area on the right (north) side of the road. Passing this parking area, continue up the road for another approximately 1.6 miles to where the road makes a dip before a last short uphill to Kincaid Chalet. At the bottom of the dip one reaches a large parking area on the right (north) side of the road. Pull into the parking area and park wherever feasible.

Access to Mize Loop begins at the large information board overlooking the broad and open area, known as the Stadium, at the far end of the parking area. One can recognize the Stadium by the race director's tower on the left (west) side and hilly woods on the right (east). Once on the flats of the Stadium, continue past the tower on the far right (northeast) corner, passing the beginning of Margaux's Loop along the way. Approximately 0.2 miles later, at the far corner of the Stadium bear right (northeast) down a short slope and enter the woods. Almost immediately upon entering the woods Mize Loop reaches a trail junction. At this junction bear left (north). Continuing on the main trail, one next passes straight through a major junction with Sisson Loop on the right (north). Approximately 1.1 miles from the parking area, Mize Loop passes a short-cut on the left (south) that leads back to the Stadium. In another approximately 0.5 miles the trail curves to the south and reaches Pia-Margrethe's Overlook, where the trail begins its traverse across the top of the bluff overlooking Turnagain Arm. Approximately 2.0 miles from the parking area the trail makes a steep climb up to Arlene's Overlook, a good place for a quick rest. For the next 0.4 miles the trail continues left at three successive intersections. Approximately 0.1 miles after the last of these intersections, the trail begins a 0.2 miles climb to the northwest end of the Stadium. In another 0.1 miles one reaches the information board beside the parking area to complete the loop.

**TRAIL GRADE:** This trail rates Grade 1 as a hike.

**TRAIL CONDITION:** This wide trail remains in excellent condition.

**TRAIL MILEAGE:** To complete this loop from the Stadium and back entails approximately 2.7 miles of hiking or biking.

**TOTAL ELEVATION GAIN:** To complete this loop from the Stadium and back entails a total elevation gain of approximately 200 feet.

**HIGH POINT:** This trail reaches its highest point of approximately 200 feet above sea on the trail by Pia-Margrethe's Overlook.

**NORMAL HIKING TIME:** To hike from the beginning of this loop at the Stadium and back should take anywhere from 1 to 2 hours, depending on the condition and ambition of the hiker(s) involved.

**CAMPSITES:** One will find no designated camping areas on this trail. Nor should one need one considering the shortness of the hike.

**BEST TIME:** Most people should find any time during the off-ski season a good time to do this hike. Bikers should, however, wait until the trails dry sufficiently so as not to leave deep ruts.

**USGS MAPS:** Tyonek A-1.

On Andrew Lekisch Trail in Kincaid Park

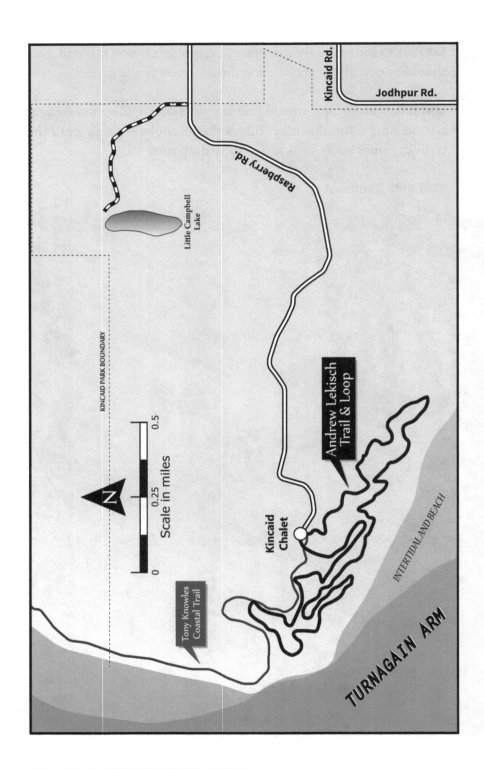

Jodhpur Rd.

Kincaid Rd.

Raspberry Rd.

Little Campbell Lake

KINCAID PARK BOUNDARY

N

0    0.25    0.5
Scale in miles

Andrew Lekisch Trail & Loop

Kincaid Chalet

Tony Knowles Coastal Trail

INTERTIDAL AND BEACH

TURNAGAIN ARM

# Walk-About Guide to Andrew Lekisch Trail

Andrew Lekisch Trail actually consists of three loops of different lengths—1.5 kilometers, 5 kilometers, and 7.5 kilometers. The two longest loops circle over the bluffs rising directly to the south of Kincaid Chalet. In the process they climb many short hills and descend into many narrow vales, passing many wide-ranging views along the way, including more than a couple 360-degree panoramas of the Anchorage bowl and the surrounding bodies of water. On a clear day these views stretch from Kenai Peninsula to the south and Denali to the north.

**TRAIL LOCATION:** Andrew Lekisch Trail begins at the south end of the Stadium below Kincaid Chalet in Kincaid Park. To get there drive 3.5 miles south from downtown Anchorage on L Street and its extension Minnesota Drive. There, turn right off the first Raspberry Road exit. At the bottom of the exit ramp turn right (west) onto Raspberry Road. Follow Raspberry Road for approximately 3.25 miles past the major intersection of Four Corners and Sand Lake Road to the entrance of Kincaid Park.

Continuing straight past the entrance, follow Raspberry Road as it winds up broad wooded hill and into the park. Approximately 0.5 miles past the entrance the road reaches the Raspberry Road Parking Area on the right (north) side of the road. Passing this parking area, continue up the road for another approximately 1.6 miles to where the road makes a dip before a last short uphill to Kincaid Chalet. At the bottom of the dip one reaches a large parking area on the right (north) side of the road. Pull into the parking area and park wherever feasible.

Access to Andrew Lekisch Trail begins at the large information board overlooking the broad and open area, known as the Stadium, at the far end of the parking area. One can recognize the Stadium by the race director's tower on the left (west) side and hilly woods on the right (east).

Upon reaching the flats of the Stadium, turn sharply left (south) and pass through the wide tunnel at that end of the stadium. At the far end of the tunnel one can look and see a bank (blooming with flowers in season) with a big sign reading "Andrew Lekisch Memorial Trail". Turn left (west) at the bank and continue to where a sign for "Andrew's Trail" provides mileage for the three different loops in the Andrew Lekisch Trail System. This guide will describe the 7.5-kilometer loop, the longest of the three.

Bear right at the next intersection beyond the flower bank to begin Andrew Lekisch Trail proper. From this point on, despite the many trail junctions the trail passes, one need only follow the arrows for the 7.5-kilometer loop. As one continues along the loop one reaches a number of spots worthy of mention. These spots can also serve to gauge one's process. At mile 1.5 one reaches overlook above the biathlon range looks out over the chalet and farther north—all the way to Denali on a clear day. At mile 1.9 one reaches an overlook on the right that offers a fine view of Kincaid Beach over 300 feet below and Fire Island, 4 miles to the west.

At mile 3.6 one reaches a junction where the 5-kilometer loop drops off the right (north). At that point Andrew Lekisch Trail begins its final section. After making one more large loop down and to the left (south) the trail passes through a gap and begins the descent down to the flats alongside Tony Knowles Coastal Trail. Here, after paralleling that trail for approximately 200 yards, Lekisch Loop dives into a steep dip. Climbing back toward the Coastal Trail on the far side of this dip the trail then swings sharply to the right to climb high above the soccer field before dropping steeply down on the far side. Upon reaching the bottom of this last hill, turn right (north) and skirt along near side of the soccer field. At the end of the soccer field turn right (east). In approximately 100 feet one should reach the flower bank. Here turn left (north) and pass back through the tunnel to the Stadium and the end of the loop.

**TRAIL GRADE:** This trail, despite its many sharp ascents and descents, still rates Grade 1 as a hike because none of the climbs continue long or high enough to rate the trail higher.

**TRAIL CONDITION:** Despite its many sharp ascents and descents, this wide trail remains in excellent condition.

**TRAIL MILEAGE:** To hike from the beginning of this route at the Stadium and back entails approximately 4.4 miles of hiking or biking.

**TOTAL ELEVATION GAIN:** To hike from the beginning of this route at the Stadium and back entails a total elevation gain of approximately 500 feet.

**HIGH POINT:** This trail reaches its highest point of approximately 380 feet above sea level at the crest of the final bluff before the trail descending to the far end of the soccer field.

**NORMAL HIKING TIME:** To hike from the beginning of this trail at the Stadium and back should take anywhere from 2 to 3 hours, depending on the condition and ambition of the hiker(s) involved.

**CAMPSITES:** One will find no designated camping areas on this trail. Nor should one need one considering the shortness of the hike.

**BEST TIME:** Most people should find any time in the off-ski season a good time to do this hike. Bikers should, however, wait until the trails dry sufficiently so as not to leave deep ruts.

**USGS MAPS:** Tyonek A-1.

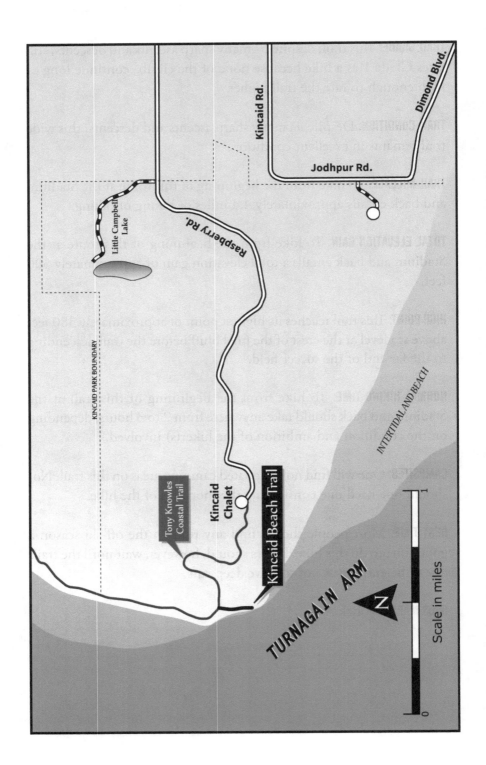

# Walk-About Guide to Kincaid Beach Trail

This beach, located approximately 1.5 miles below Kincaid Chalet in Kincaid Park, deservedly draws people all year round. Hugging an isolated stretch of Anchorage's coast, it offers fine views of the Kenai Peninsula, Fire Island, Mountain Susitna, and the Alaska Range—including Denali. Here, silhouetted by the low late-setting sun, one can enjoy a mid-summer evening walk. In the damp days of autumn one can watch a storm move with ponderous power up Turnagain Arm. Then in winter one can clamber among the great ice cakes that crowd against the shore.

**TRAIL LOCATION:** One can access Kincaid Beach Trail from Tony Knowles Coastal Trail in Kincaid Park. To get there drive 3.5 miles south from downtown Anchorage on L Street and its extension Minnesota Drive. There, turn right off the first Raspberry Road exit. At the bottom of the exit ramp turn right (west) onto Raspberry Road. Follow Raspberry Road for approximately 3.25 miles past the major intersection of Four Corners and Sand Lake Road to the entrance of Kincaid Park. Continuing straight past the entrance, follow Raspberry Road as it winds up broad wooded hill and into the park. Approximately 0.5 miles past the entrance the road reaches the Raspberry Road Parking Area on the right (north) side of the road. Passing this parking area, continue up the road for another approximately 1.75 miles to where the road dead-ends at the parking area in front of Kincaid Chalet. Park wherever convenient.

Access to Kincaid Beach Trail begins on Tony Knowles Coastal Trail that begins just to the left (south) of the chalet. Follow this paved trail as it descends for approximately 1.3 miles to where it reaches the edge of the bluff. Here look for a wooden bench just to the left (south) of the trail and the dirt trail continuing into the woods just beyond it. This bench marks the beginning of Kincaid Beach Trail leading to Kincaid Beach.

Turning onto the dirt trail, follow it along the edge of the bluff for approximately 0.2 miles to a pair of signboards in the trees. Behind the signs another trail, Kincaid Bluff Trail, continues through the woods[*]. At these signs Kincaid Beach Trail bears down and to the right (west) onto

-----------------------------------------------------------------

[*]   For more information about that trail, see [95] **Walk-About Guide to Kincaid Bluff Trail**.

Kincaid Beach

the side of the bluff. Starting down across the bluff, follow the trail as it contours gently downhill to a T-intersection with a steeper dirt trail. Turning sharply right and down onto this steeper trail, follow this trail the last few feet down to Kincaid Beach, where the trail comes to an end.

**TRAIL GRADE:** The bike trails providing access to and from this trail rates Grade 1 as a hike. The dirt trail to the beach also rates grade 1 as a hike.

**TRAIL CONDITION:** Both the bike trail and the dirt trail remain in excellent condition from end to end.

**TRAIL MILEAGE:** To hike to Kincaid Beach from the beginning of this route at Kincaid Chalet and back entails approximately 3 miles of hiking.

**TOTAL ELEVATION GAIN:** To hike to Kincaid Beach from the beginning of this route at Kincaid Chalet and back entails a total elevation gain of approximately 225 feet.

**HIGH POINT:** This trail reaches its highest point of approximately 200 feet above sea level at Kincaid Chalet.

**NORMAL HIKING TIME:** To hike to Kincaid Beach from the beginning of this route at Kincaid Chalet and back should take anywhere from 1.5 to 4 hours, depending on the condition and ambition of the hiker(s) involved, and how long they want to linger on the beach.

**CAMPSITES:** One will find no designated camping areas on this trail. Nor should one need one considering the shortness of the hike.

**BEST TIME:** Most people should find any time of year a good time to do this hike.

**USGS MAPS:** Tyonek A-1.

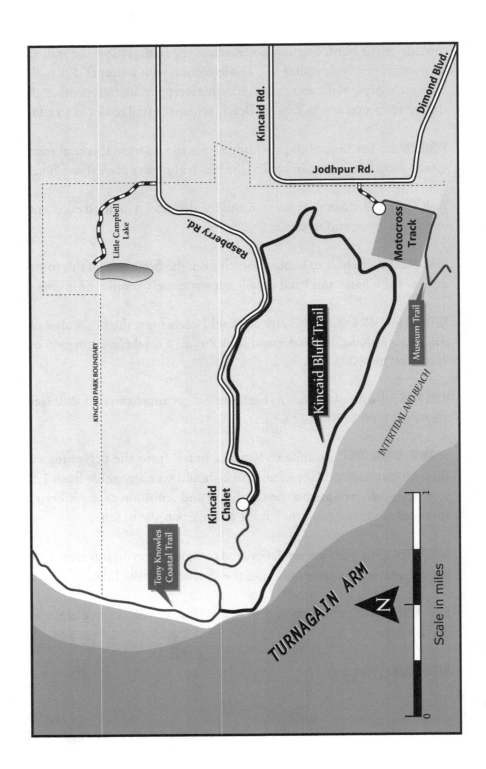

Dimond Blvd.

Kincaid Rd.

Jodhpur Rd.

Little Campbell Lake

Raspberry Rd.

KINCAID PARK BOUNDARY

Motocross Track

Museum Trail

Kincaid Bluff Trail

INTERTIDAL AND BEACH

Kincaid Chalet

Tony Knowles Coastal Trail

TURNAGAIN ARM

N

Scale in miles

1

0

# Walk-About Guide to Kincaid Bluff Trail

This trail stuns a lot of people who hike it for the first time with its magnitude. Not only does it begin on an actual beach (a rarity in Anchorage) but as it climbs off the beach to traverse the bluffs above it offers wide-reaching panoramic views of Denali to the north, Mount Susitna to the northwest, Knik Arm to the west, and Turnagain Arm to the south, as well as glimpses of the Chugach Mountains to the east.

**TRAIL LOCATION:** One accesses Kincaid Bluff Trail via Kincaid Beach Trail in Kincaid Park*. To get there drive 3.5 miles south from downtown Anchorage on L Street and its extension Minnesota Drive. There, turn right off the first Raspberry Road exit. At the bottom of the exit ramp turn right (west) onto Raspberry Road. Follow Raspberry Road for approximately 3.25 miles past the major intersection of Four Corners and Sand Lake Road to the entrance of Kincaid Park.

Continuing straight past the entrance, follow Raspberry Road as it winds up broad wooded hill and into the park. Approximately 0.5 miles past the entrance the road reaches the Raspberry Road Parking Area on the right (north) side of the road. Passing this parking area, continue up the road for another approximately 1.75 miles to where the road dead-ends at the parking area in front of Kincaid Chalet. Park wherever convenient.

To access Kincaid Bluff Trail from the chalet first follow the paved Tony Knowles Coastal Trail from where it begins just to the left (south) of the chalet. After descending for approximately 0.75 miles, this paved trail levels out. Approximately 0.5 miles later the trail reaches

-------------------------------------------------------------------

*   For more information about that trail, see [95] **Walk-About Guide to Kincaid Beach Trail**.

WALK-ABOUT GUIDE TO ALASKA   **505**

the edge of the bluff. At this point, look for a wooden bench to the left (south) and the dirt trail that leads into the trees just beyond it. This bench marks the beginning of Kincaid Beach Trail.

Turning left onto the dirt trail follow it along the edge of the bluff for approximately 200 yards to a pair of signboards. Behind the signs These signboards mark the beginning of Kincaid Bluff Trail. Here, where Kincaid Beach Trail slants down and to the right onto the bluff, Kincaid Bluff Trail begins behind the signs. Squeezing around the signs, follow Kincaid Bluff Trail into the woods beyond. Continue along this trail for another approximately 50 yards as it follows the level crest of the bluff through the trees. At the end of this section the trail pops out of the woods and intersects at a T-intersection with a steep trail on the steep crest of a grass slope. Turning left (east) on this trail follow it as it climbs steeply to the top of open bluff approximately 200 feet above. (Turning left and downhill on this steep trail leads one down to Kincaid Beach.)

From the top of the open and scenic bluff, continue along the main trail as it bears left to follow the crest. Along its turning and twisting way this main trail passes numerous side trails leading back to Andrew Lekisch Trail and Kincaid Chalet. Approximately 1 mile after first climbing onto the crest of the bluff, this turning and twisting trail makes a short, sharp climb to a very well-placed bench overlooking Cook Inlet. Past the bench, the trail winds onward for another approximately 1 mile to where it reaches a perch overlooking the sand dunes above the motocross tracks circling back and forth in the hollow below.

From this perch one has two options. The first option entails dropping down and to the left (northeast) off the perch and following crest of the dunes to where one looks directly down on the woods below. Then look for a trail in the woods below. With this trail in sight, plunge-step down the flank of the dunes towards it. Having reached the trail, follow it for approximately 100 yards, passing a single-track bike trail in the process, out to the nearest ski trail. Turning right (east) on the ski trail continue along it to the next junction. There turn downhill and to the left (north). Approximately 0.4 miles later this trail reaches the paved bike trail on the near side of Raspberry Road.

Turning left (west) on the bike trail, follow it for approximately 1.25 miles back to Kincaid Chalet.

The second option off the perch entails following the crest of the bluff straight down (east) along the right (south) side of the motocross track. Halfway along the bluff side of the motocross track one reaches the uppermost end of Museum Trail*. This trail leads down to a landscape of pristine wetlands dotted with the seemingly contradictory and symbolic remains of wrecked cars. After exploring the wetlands below one can then backtrack up the trail and then continue around the left (west) side of the motocross track to where on can rejoin the first option for the remainder of the hike.

**TRAIL GRADE:** The bike trails providing access to and from this trail rates Grade 1 as a hike. The trail itself, despite its many sharp but short ascents and descents, rates Grade 2 as a hike for its entire length.

**TRAIL CONDITION:** Despite its many sharp but short ascents and descents this trail remains in surprisingly good shape with few rocks and roots along its length and even few muddy spots.

**TRAIL MILEAGE:** To hike from the beginning of this route at Kincaid Chalet and back entails approximately 5.8 miles of hiking.

**TOTAL ELEVATION GAIN:** To hike from the beginning of this route at Kincaid Chalet and back entails a total elevation gain of approximately 400 feet.

**HIGH POINT:** This trail reaches its highest point of approximately 370 feet above sea level at the top of the last rise one climbs before reaching the sand dunes.

**NORMAL HIKING TIME:** To hike from the beginning of this route at Kincaid Chalet and back should take anywhere from 3 to 5 hours, depending on the condition and ambition of the hiker(s) involved.

----------------------------------------------------------------

\*   For more information about that trail, see [98] **Walk-About Guide to Museum Trail**.

**CAMPSITES:** One will find no designated camping areas on this trail. Nor should one need one considering the shortness of the hike.

**BEST TIME:** Most people should find any time from mid-March to late November a good time to do this hike. It makes for a fine outing in winter as well, provided one avoids walking on the ski trail and instead follows single-track bike trails back to the chalet.

**USGS MAPS:** Tyonek A-1.

Snow Geese on the mud flats

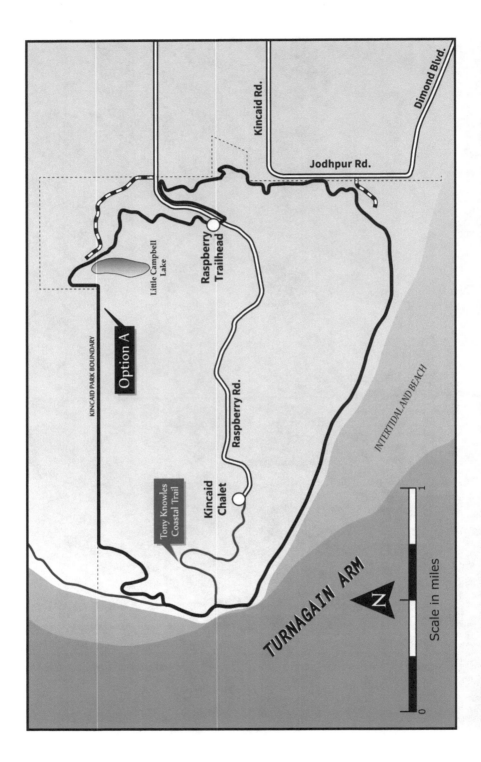

Little Campbell Lake

Raspberry Trailhead

Option A

KINCAID PARK BOUNDARY

Kincaid Rd.

Jodhpur Rd.

Dimond Blvd.

Raspberry Rd.

INTERTIDAL AND BEACH

Tony Knowles Coastal Trail

Kincaid Chalet

TURNAGAIN ARM

N

Scale in miles

1

0

# OPTION A

# Circumnavigation of Kincaid Park

This hike around the entire perimeter of the park crosses many types of terrain, from soggy bottoms to windy heights as it passes along the perimeter of the airport, across gravel pits, and along a section of Kincaid Beach Trail and the entirety of Kincaid Bluff Trail. Along the way, on any given day one might see moose, porcupines, eagles, a fox, a coyote, and even a black bear or two. On any given day one should also, weather permitting, enjoy many far-reaching views.

**TRAIL LOCATION:** This hike begins in the Raspberry Road Parking Area in Kincaid Park\*. From Raspberry Road Parking Area, enter the woods by the information board and turn right (east) on the first major ski trail, which marks the back end of Lake Loop Trail, Staying on the ski trail, follow it as it winds through the woods before turning downhill to a trail junction. Bear right (east) at this junction and follow the trail approximately 100 feet farther to yet another trail junction. Bear right at this junction as well and follow the trail down into the woods.

Approximately 1 mile from the parking area, Lake Loop Trail drops onto the open north end of Little Campbell Lake. Continuing straight across the grassy embankment along the lake, follow the trail into the woods on the far side of the lake. Less than 0.5 miles from the lake, one reaches a trail junction with a non-ski trail that climbs

--------------------------------------------------

\*    To get there see [92] **Walk-About Guide to Lake Loop Trail**.

alongside the fence bordering the airport. Turning right (west) follow this rough trail along the fence for approximately 1.2 miles to where it descends steeply to a T-junction with another ski trail (Arlene's Way). Continuing straight across the ski trail, follow the fence up and over the next steep rise. (One can follow either side of the fence upward.) After descending steeply off the far side of this rise, one reaches a T-junction with another ski trail (Alex Sisson Trail) contouring along the near side of the gravel pits. Turn left (south) on Alex Sisson Trail and follow it for another approximately 1.3 miles to where it reaches a fork. Bearing left (southwest) at this fork follow the trail to where it next swings to the left (southeast). Here look for a narrow foot path on the right (west). Turning right onto this path, follow it out to Tony Knowles Coastal Trail. Turn left (south) on Tony Knowles Coastal Trail and follow it for approximately 0.2 miles to where it swings away from the bluff to begin its climb back to Kincaid Chalet.

Those feeling a bit weary at this point have the option of continuing up Tony Knowles Coastal Trail back to Kincaid Chalet. From there an approximately 1.5 miles hike down the paved bike trail leads back to Raspberry Road Parking Area.

Those wanting to continue along the backside of this circumnavigation should look for a bench and a dirt trail leading straight ahead into the woods behind it. That dirt trail marks the beginning of Kincaid Beach Trail. Turning left onto the dirt trail follow it along the edge of the bluff for approximately 200 yards to a pair of signboards. These signboards mark the beginning of Kincaid Bluff Trail. Here, where Kincaid Beach Trail slants down and to the right onto the bluff, Kincaid Bluff Trail begins behind the signs. Squeezing around the signs, follow Kincaid Bluff Trail into the woods beyond. Continue along this trail for another approximately 50 yards as it follows the level crest of the bluff through the trees. At the end of this section the trail pops out of the woods and intersects at a T-intersection with a steep trail on the steep crest of a grass slope. Turning left (east) on this trail follow it as it climbs steeply to the top of open bluff approximately 200 feet above. (Turning left and downhill on this steep trail leads one down to Kincaid Beach.)

From the crest of the open and scenic bluff, continue along the trail as it bears left to follow the crest. Along its turning and twisting way this trail passes numerous side trails leading back to Andrew Lekisch Trail and Kincaid Chalet. Approximately 1 mile after first climbing onto the crest of the bluff, the turning and twisting trail makes a short, sharp climb to a very well-placed bench overlooking Cook Inlet. Past the bench the trail winds onward for another approximately 1 mile to where it reaches a perch overlooking the sand dunes above the motocross tracks circling back and forth in the hollow below.

From this perch, one has two options. The first, which continues along the circumnavigation, drops onto the dunes and then bears left (northeast) toward the left (north) side of the motocross track. Upon reaching the fence on that side of the track, bear right (east) and follow it to an opening on the left (north). Turning left into this opening in the fence, follow the wide trail behind it out 100 yards to Jodhpur Parking Area. Bearing left across the parking area, continue along Kitchen Sink single-bike trail as it winds south paralleling the oft-visible Jodhpur Road just to the right (east). In approximately 0.5 miles this trail reaches a junction with Tower of Power bike trail. Turn left (northeast) on Tower of Power and follow it across a wide trail leading directly to the right out to a small parking area on Jodhpur Road. On the embankment on the far side Tower of Power reaches a junction with another bike trail on the left (which, for those who wish to shorten the hike, leads directly back to Raspberry Road Parking Area). At this junction turn right (east) and follow Tower of Power as it winds through the woods, crossing Horseshoe Loop ski trail twice along the way, to where it drops onto the paved bike trail at the entrance of Kincaid Park. There turn right (west) up the bike trail to where one crosses Raspberry Road back to Raspberry Road Parking area and the end of the circumnavigation.

The second option off the perch entails following the crest of the bluff straight down (east) along the right (south) side of the motocross track. Halfway along the bluff side of the motocross track one reaches the uppermost end of Museum Trail*. This trail leads down to a landscape of pristine wetlands dotted with the seemingly contradictory

---

\* For more information about that trail, see [98] **Walk-About Guide to Museum Trail**.

and symbolic remains of wrecked cars. After exploring the wetlands below one can then backtrack up the trail and then continue around the left (west) side of the motocross track to where one can rejoin the first option for the remainder of the hike.

**TRAIL GRADE:** This trail, despite its many sharp but short ascents and descents, rates Grade 2 as a hike for its entire length.

**TRAIL CONDITION:** Though the part of this route paralleling the fence bordering the airport can prove quite soggy in the spring, this entire route remains easy to follow, especially when it follows ski trails and bike trails, most of which remain wide as a dirt road.

**TRAIL MILEAGE:** To complete this loop from Raspberry Road Parking Area and back again entails approximately 8.8 miles of hiking.

**TOTAL ELEVATION GAIN:** To hike this loop from Raspberry Road Parking Area and back again entails a total elevation gain of approximately 800 feet.

**HIGH POINT:** This trail reaches its highest point of approximately 325 feet above sea level about halfway along Kincaid Bluff Trail.

**NORMAL HIKING TIME:** To hike this loop from Raspberry Road Parking Area and back again should take anywhere from 4 to 7 hours, depending on the condition and ambition of the hiker(s) involved.

**CAMPSITES:** One will find no designated camping areas on this route. Nor should one need one considering the shortness of the hike.

**BEST TIME:** Most people should find any time from mid-March to late November a good time to do this hike. It would make for a fine outing in winter as well but for the fact that one should avoid walking on groomed ski trails

**USGS MAPS:** Tyonek A-1.

Evening on Kincaid Bluff Trail (OR) Sunday afternoon on Kincaid Bluff Trail

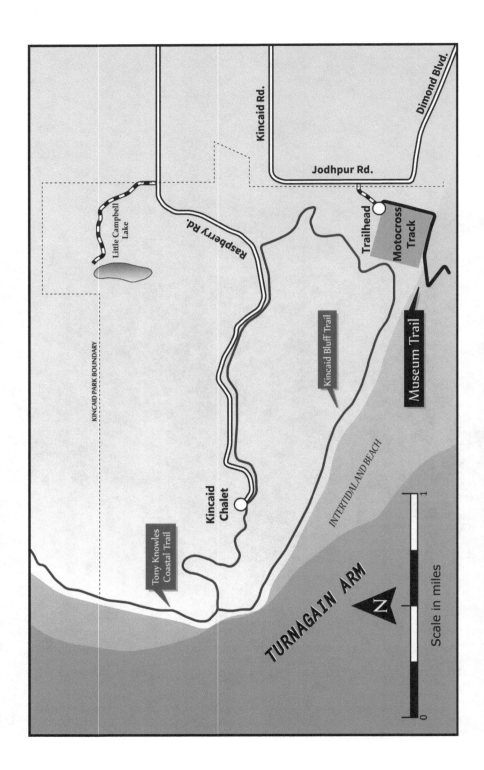

Kincaid Rd.

Dimond Blvd.

Jodhpur Rd.

Little Campbell Lake

Raspberry Rd.

Trailhead

Motocross Track

Kincaid Bluff Trail

Museum Trail

KINCAID PARK BOUNDARY

INTERTIDAL AND BEACH

Kincaid Chalet

Tony Knowles Coastal Trail

TURNAGAIN ARM

N

1

Scale in miles

0

# Walk-About Guide to Museum Trail

Lacking any specific name, this book borrows a name coined by a friend for this rather unique trail with its odd juxtaposition of junked cars and wildlife: Museum Trail. For a period of time the bluff by the motocross track at Kincaid Park which this trail descends served as a popular place to roll off old cars, stolen cars, and wrecked cars. The tangled heaps of the remains of these cars litter both the bluff and the marshy flats below. At some point venturesome souls forged a trail leading straight down the bluff. Perhaps they did so to view or ransack the discarded cars. Perhaps they did so to access the flats below, which can make for some very fine walking or skiing when frozen. Perhaps they did so to view migrating birds. Or perhaps they did so merely out of curiosity. A trail crew has since taken that rough, steep trail and transformed it into a very user-friendly trail and a very unique trail. For though this trail does not descend deep or travel far it does access an often ignored, and relatively wild and wet borderland and its mix of salt and fresh water that makes for such a special and vital environment.

**TRAIL LOCATION:** Museum Trail begins on the crest of the bluff only a few feet south of the motocross track at Kincaid Park. To get there drive 3.5 miles south from downtown Anchorage on L Street and its extension Minnesota Drive. There one reaches the exit for Raspberry Road. Turning right off the first Raspberry Road exit, turn right (west) on Raspberry Road. Then follow Raspberry Road for approximately 2.2 miles past the major intersection of Four Corners to the intersection with Sand Lake Road on the left. Here turn left (south) on Sand Lake Road. Continue along Sand Lake Road for approximately 0.6 miles to an intersection with Kincaid Road. Turn right (west) on Kincaid

Road. Follow this road for 1 mile to where it ends at an intersection with Jodhpur Road. Turn left (south) on Jodhpur Road and follow it for approximately 0.4 miles to a road on the right (west) leading into Kincaid Park. Turn onto this road and follow this road and follow it the short way toward Jodhpur Parking Area. Within 100 feet one reaches a junction with a road leading to the right. The road to the right leads into Jodhpur Parking Area. The road leading straight ahead leads to the grandstands beside the motocross track, which may seem the better road to take. But though driving straight ahead brings one closer to the beginning of the trail, one may not find the gate leading into the motocross track open on a consistent basis. (In fact, one may find it open on the drive in but locked on the drive out.) For this reason it seems best to park at the Jodhpur Parking Area.

Once parked, follow the road back out of the parking area and turn right (south) up the road leading to the motocross track. Upon reaching the grandstands above the track, look for the dirt road dropping off the backside of the opening toward the bluff below. Follow this road for approximately 100 feet down onto the open motocross track below. There, keeping well to the left side of the wide track (to stay out of harm's way) cross to the fence at the crest of the bluff. Then turn right (west) and follow the fence for another approximately 100 feet to where two posts mark an opening in the fence. Pass through the open opening and look for the sign reading "No Camping". This sign marks the upper end of Museum Trail.

Museum Trail, which makes one big switchback down the slope, begins by slanting down to the (west) across the slope of the bluff. Upon reaching the first stand of trees below the bluff, one comes upon the first set of roped posts that help prevent any falls. At this point one also reaches a junction with a trail climbing steeply up to the right (northwest) back toward the bluff. Continuing to slant down the slope the trail soon reaches another stand of trees. There the trail passes above the first visible wrecked car just below to the left. Halfway down this stand of trees the trail turns sharply left (southeast) to switchback down the final section of trail. Emerging from the trees, the trail continues down for another approximately 150 feet to where a plastic wand marks the lower end of the trail.

At this point, one has three primary choices. First, one can turn around and return the way they have come. Second, one can explore the wetlands below and its scenic but odd mix of wrecked cars and wild flora and fauna. Third, adventuresome souls might even consider turning right (west) and following the base of the bluff back to Kincaid Beach and Kincaid Beach Trail. Along the way one may have to negotiate passing (at high tide) over or circling around (at low tide) a substantial landslide*.

**TRAIL GRADE:** This trail rates Grade 1.

**TRAIL CONDITION:** This trail remains excellent condition from end to end, though one expect to slip and slide quite a bit along its length on wet days.

**TRAIL MILEAGE:** To hike from the uppermost end of this trail on the crest of the bluff down to edge of wetlands below entails approximately 0.3 miles of hiking, for a round-trip total of approximately 0.6 miles. This means that to hike from Jodhpur Parking Area down to the wetlands at bottom end of Museum Trail and back entails a round-trip total of approximately 1.6 miles.

**TOTAL ELEVATION GAIN:** To hike from the uppermost end of this trail on the crest of the bluff down to edge of wetlands below entails a total elevation loss of approximately 150 feet. This means that the climb back up to the bluff entails a total elevation gain of approximately 150 feet.

**HIGH POINT:** This trail reaches its highest point of approximately 150 feet above sea at the beginning of the trail.

**NORMAL HIKING TIME:** To walk the entire length of this trail to and from Jodhpur Parking Area and back should take anywhere from 1 to 2 hours, depending on the condition and ambition of the hiker(s) involved.

-------------------------------------------------------------------

\* For more information about that trail, see [95] **Walk-About Guide to Kincaid Beach Trail**.

**CAMPSITES:** One will find no designated camping areas on this trail. Nor should one need one considering the shortness of the hike.

**BEST TIME:** Most people should find any time of year a good time to do this hike, though one can expect icy conditions in winter.

**USGS MAPS:** Tyonek A-1.

Relics along Museum Trail

On the sand dunes above Museum Trail

Moose on an Anchorage bike trail

## CHAPTER 11

# ANCHORAGE BOWL

## OVERVIEW OF THE BIKE TRAILS IN THE ANCHORAGE BOWL

Anchorage can boast many miles of bike trails. As they wind those many miles back and forth across the city these trails pass under or over major roads, allowing the bicyclist to continue without pause or worry for many traffic-free miles. In addition, many of these trails, despite their close proximity to major roads, businesses, and communities, wind many miles through woods, along creeks, around lakes, and by the coast, which makes for many scenic views. They also allow a better chance for the cyclist to come across moose, eagles, porcupines, coyotes, and maybe even a bear. On especially rare occasions one might even catch sight of a wolf, showing that though the trails may wind through the largest city in Alaska they still have a very wild side.

Of all the bike trails in Anchorage, the four longest and most popular—Tony Knowles Coastal Trail, Campbell Creek Trail, Lanie Fleischer Chester Creek Bike Trail, and Ship Creek Bike Trail—all pass through distinct parts of the city, making them all worthy of exclusive mention. In addition, one can combine any and all of these trails in various ways to create longer loop tours of the city, which many will find a pleasant way to spend a morning, an afternoon, or a day.

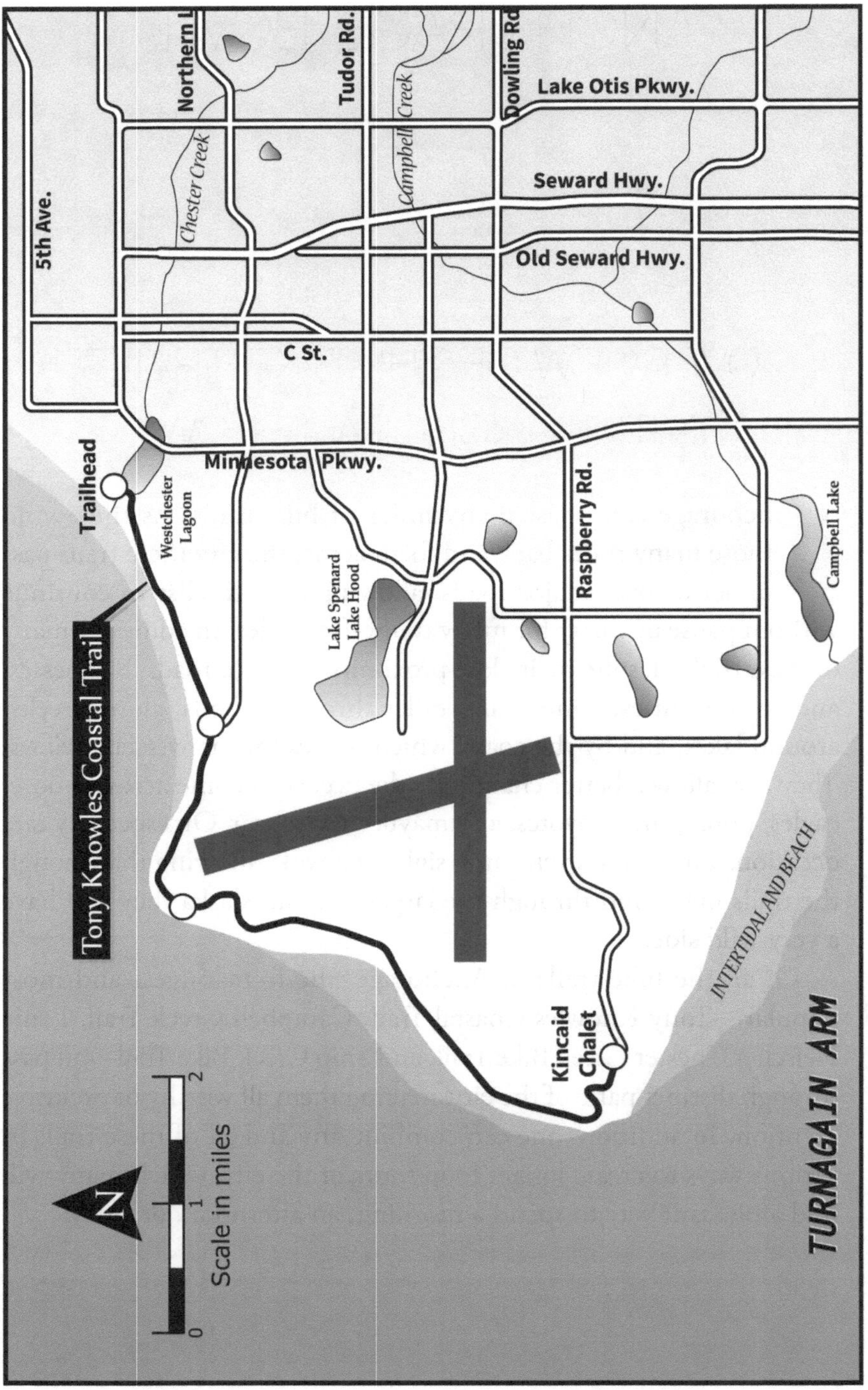
5th Ave.
Northern L
Tudor Rd.
Dowling Rd
Lake Otis Pkwy.
Seward Hwy.
Old Seward Hwy.
C St.
Chester Creek
Campbell Creek
Minnesota Pkwy.
Trailhead
Westchester Lagoon
Tony Knowles Coastal Trail
Lake Spenard
Lake Hood
Raspberry Rd.
Campbell Lake
Kincaid Chalet
INTERTIDAL AND BEACH
TURNAGAIN ARM
N
0
1
2
Scale in miles

# Walk-About Guide to
# Tony Knowles Coastal Trail

Of all the bike trails in Anchorage, this stands out as jewel in the crown. Routed for over half its length around the tip of the peninsula beyond Ted Stevens Airport, a part of town that laid largely fallow, this bike trail passes through some very secluded woodlands. To connect those insular lands with downtown Anchorage, the then Mayor Tony Knowles managed to reconcile the landowners along the planned route closest to the city that such a paved bike trail, crossing some land which had seen no building on them since the earthquake of 1964, would increase the quality of their life. One by one the local landowner agreed to the trail—and it seems nary a one regrets that decision. Consequently, this trail follows the coast around most of the Anchorage Peninsula. Along the way one can marvel at some fine views of the westernmost Talkeetna Mountains rising due north; Denali, Foraker, and Hunter hovering over the horizon to the northwest; and the dominant silhouette of Mount Susitna, with the Alaska Range beyond it, filling the eastern horizon to the west.

Depending on the season one might also see beluga whales, snow geese, Sandhill cranes, bald eagles, and cliff swallows at various points along the trail. Even in the deepest and darkest days of winter on might see a blur of waxwings flittering across the sky, a troupe of ravens playing in the winds ricocheting up the bluffs out at Point Woronzof, or a lone snowshoe rabbit cautiously tip-toeing across the trail.

**TRAIL LOCATION:** This bike trail begins at the northwest corner of Westchester Lagoon in west Anchorage. To get there follow L Street south from West 5th Avenue in downtown Anchorage for just over 1.1 miles to where L Street turns downhill and intersects West 15th Avenue at a set of lights. Turn right (west) on West 15th Avenue and follow it for approximately 0.5 miles to where it ends at an intersection with U Street, where one should see a playground directly ahead. Turn right (north) onto U Street and immediately turn left into the parking area for the playground by Westchester Lagoon. Tony Knowles Coastal Trail begins alongside the lagoon just to the left (south) of the parking area.

From the parking area, walk or bike out to the paved bike trail and the sign marking the beginning of Tony Knowles Coastal Trail and turn right (west). In less than 100 feet Tony Knowles Coastal Trail reaches a fork in the trail. Bear left at this fork and follow the trail along the western shore of Westchester Lagoon. Just past the radio tower at the southwest corner of the lagoon the trail crosses a wooden causeway. At the end of the causeway the trail passes through a tunnel under the railroad tracks. Immediately upon emerging from the far end of the tunnel, the trail arrives on the coast of the peninsula.

Tony Knowles Coastal Trail then follows the coast, only occasionally losing sight of the ocean, for the next 8 miles. Just after milepost 1.0 from the parking area at Westchester Lagoon the trail swings up a short hill and crosses the northern side of Lyn Ary Park. At the far side of the park it starts downhill to again parallel the low bluff. Between milepost 1.5 and 2.0 the trail turns inland and climbs a longer hill. At the top of this hill the trail reaches Earthquake Park on the right (north).

Climbing more gradually, the trail next crosses the entrance to a parking area where during the summer one more often than not passes a tour bus or two. Just after passing this parking area the trail climbs steadily for the next 0.5 miles. Approximately 200 yards past the 3.5 milepost the trail reaches an open shelf along the crest of the bluff. On clear days this viewpoint offers a panoramic view that sweeps from the long, low silhouette of Mount Susitna on the left (west-northwest); past the snow-covered masses of Hunter, Foraker, and Denali to the northwest, and then the long ridge of the westernmost ridges of the Talkeetna Mountains to the north; and then finally to the northwest flank of the Chugach Mountains to the northeast.

Just past this bluff the trail sweeps steeply down around a corner where it passes the parking area for Point Woronzof. Crossing the access road to this parking area, the trail continues downhill to a second, small parking area. Immediately after crossing this parking area the trail makes a short climb into the woods beyond.

For the next almost 5 miles the trail winds through the woods without crossing any road. Though planes of all sizes often come and go overhead as they take off and land at the nearby Ted Stevens Airport, civilization somehow seems distant. The moose, porcupines, and even black bears one often sees on this stretch of trail, as well as the expanse of ocean one often sees through the trees to the right (west) enhances this sensation.

This section of trail also seems to pass more slowly, perhaps because it has few obvious landmarks other than the continually passing mileposts with only a few fine prospects through the trees of the nearby ocean. Nevertheless, along the way it does pass some distinct landmarks. Approximately 200 yards past milepost 4.5 the trail again turns along the coast within sight of Knik Arm. Just after milepost 6.5 it reaches its westernmost end at a steel bridge located just beyond the edge of the airport's east-west runway. Between mileposts 7.0 and 7.5 the trail crosses along the western rim of a large hollow on the left (east). Just before milepost 8.0 it reaches a rest area with a picnic table. This rest area offers one of the more unobstructed views from Fire Island and Knik Arm.

Soon after milepost 8.0 the trail turns inland at the wooden bench marking the beginning of Kincaid Bluff Trail*. This turn inland marks the beginning of the almost 1-mile climb to Kincaid Chalet. Beginning gradually at first, the trail winds up past open cottonwood woodlands on the left and thicker willow thickets on the right. Approximately 0.4 miles from its turn inland, the trail sweeps right (southeast) to make the final steeper climb to Kincaid Chalet. Though two shallower sections offer some respite in this climb, the last 200 hundred yards up and out of the woods require some determined pedaling.

---

\* For more information about this trail, see [96] **Walk-About Guide to Kincaid Bluff Trail** in Chapter 10.

As one emerges out of the woods and comes in sight of the chalet the angle of the trail decreases. Passing Kincaid Chalet the trail comes to end at the 9.0 milepost next to parking area just beyond it.

From the end of Tony Knowles Coastal Trail, one had a number of choices. First, one can rest from the climb. Second, one can immediately turn around and return the way they have come, and thus enjoy the gratification of easily sweeping down the long hill they have just struggled up. Third, also during the summer, one can explore the maze of ski trails and single-track bike trails that crisscross Kincaid Park. Fourth and last, one can continue along the bike trail and complete one of two circumnavigations of the city*.

**TRAIL GRADE:** Despite its hills, this paved trail rates Grade 1 for its entire length.

**TRAIL CONDITION:** Paved for its entire length, this trail remains in excellent shape. Even in winter it often remains packed well enough for anyone choosing to travel by foot or bike along its length.

**TRAIL MILEAGE:** To go from the beginning of this trail at Westchester Lagoon to Kincaid Chalet entails approximately 9 miles of biking, hiking, running, or skiing for a round-trip total of 18 miles.

**TOTAL ELEVATION GAIN:** To go from the beginning of this trail at Westchester Lagoon and back entails a total elevation gain of approximately 600 feet.

**HIGH POINT:** This trail reaches its highest point of approximately 225 feet above sea at the end of the trail at Kincaid Chalet.

**NORMAL HIKING TIME:** To bike from the beginning of this trail at Westchester Lagoon and back should take 2 to 4 hours, depending on the condition and ambition of the biker(s) involved. To hike from the beginning

---

\*   For more information about these routes, one in reverse,
    see [102] **OPTION A—Short Circumnavigation of Anchorage** and
    [105] **OPTION A—Long Circumnavigation of Anchorage**.

of this route at Westchester Lagoon and back entails back should take anywhere from 7 to 12 hours, depending on the condition and ambition of the hiker(s) involved.

**CAMPSITES:** One will find no designated camping areas on this trail. Nor should one need one considering the shortness of the bike ride.

**BEST TIME:** Most people should find any time of year a good time to bike, hike, run, or ski this route.

**USGS MAPS:** Anchorage A-9 and Tyonek A-1.

After a rain on Tony Knowles Coastal Trail

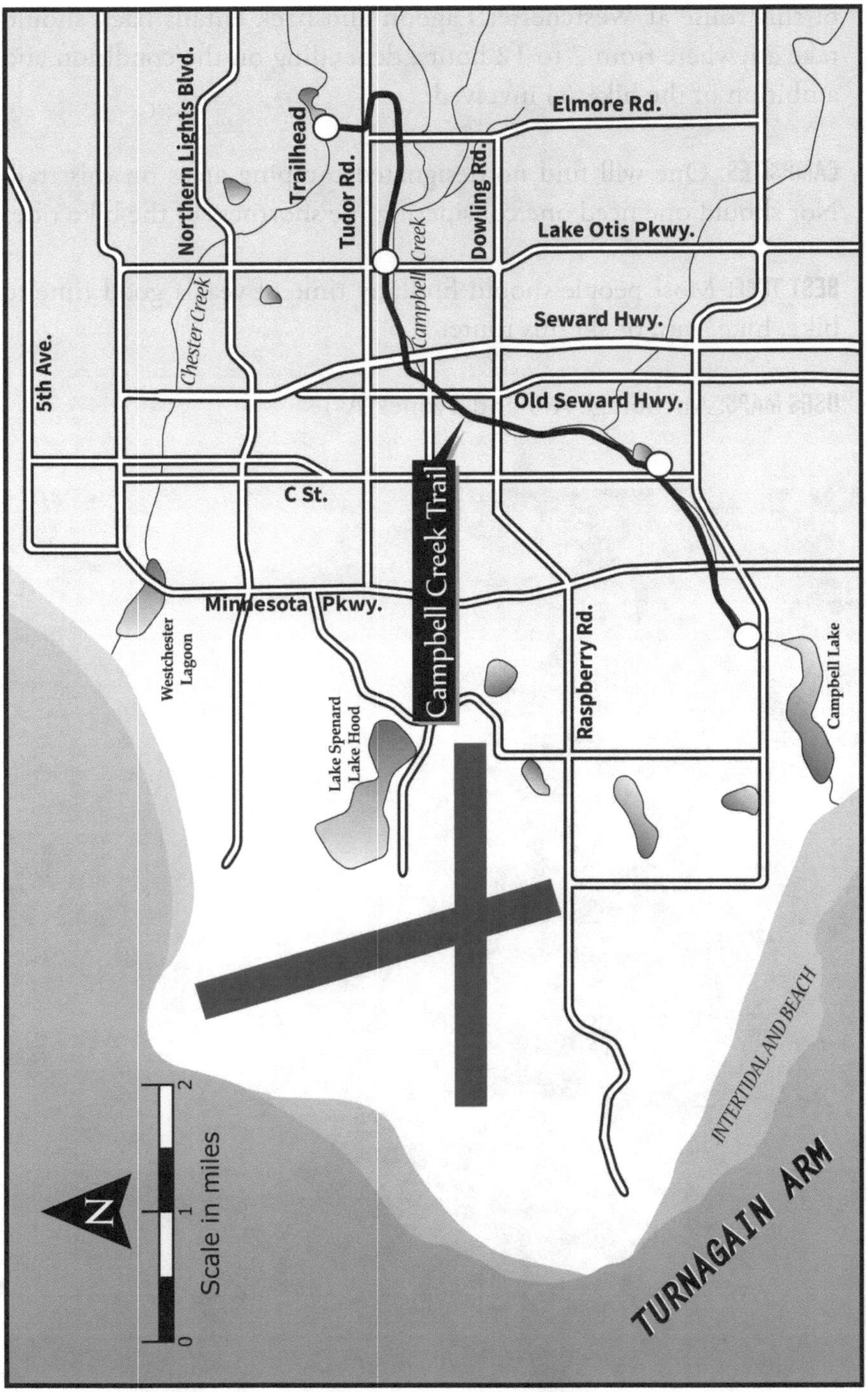
Elmore Rd.
Northern Lights Blvd.
Trailhead
Tudor Rd.
Dowling Rd.
Campbell Creek
Lake Otis Pkwy.
Chester Creek
Seward Hwy.
5th Ave.
Old Seward Hwy.
Campbell Creek Trail
C St.
Minnesota Pkwy.
Westchester Lagoon
Lake Spenard
Lake Hood
Raspberry Rd.
Campbell Lake
INTERTIDAL AND BEACH
TURNAGAIN ARM
N
Scale in miles
0
1
2

# Walk-About Guide to
# Campbell Creek Trail

This bike trail follows Campbell Creek across the Anchorage bowl. Beginning on the central northeast side of the city, it diagonals down across the bowl toward Campbell Lake in the southwest corner. Before 2014 anyone following this route had could only get across New Seward Highway by pulling their bicycles along the rocky shore of Campbell Creek where it crossed under the highway. But since the completion of the bike trail underpass people can pass easily back and forth along the entire length of this trail.

**TRAIL LOCATION:** This bike trail begins at on the south side of University Lake by Alaska Pacific University. To get there drive 3.2 miles south of downtown Anchorage on the Seward Highway. Then, just after Milepost 124, turn right (west) on the Tudor Road exit. At the end of the ramp, turn left (east) cross back over the highway. Continue straight on Tudor Road as it gradually ascends past Lake Otis Parkway. Approximately 1 mile past Lake Otis Parkway, Tudor Road reaches a set of lights with Elmore Drive on the right (south) and Bragaw Street on the left (north). Turn left (north) on Bragaw Street and follow it for approximately 0.4 miles to a parking area in the woods on the right (east). Turn into the parking area. From the parking area one can access the beginning Campbell Creek Trail by following the paved bike trail just to the left (north) of the parking area for less than 100 feet to a bike trail turnaround. Campbell Creek Trail begins on the right (south) side of the turnaround.

Turning right at the turnaround, follow Campbell Creek Trail as it first dips down through a tunnel visible just ahead. On the far side of the tunnel follow the trail up and over Tudor Road (mile 0.1). Continuing straight down the other side of the bridge, follow the main trail toward the mountains. Approximately 0.25 miles from the bridge the trail swings right (south) passes under a road and then swings in a big U-turn back to the west. Just after passing some baseball fields on the left (south) the trail passes under Elmore Drive (mile 1.4).

For the next several miles the trail follows Campbell Creek southeast across the Anchorage Peninsula. In doing so, it has a couple of tricky-to-follow sections. Approximately 1.5 miles after passing under Elmore Drive the trail reaches a playground on Lake Otis Parkway (mile 2.3). Here one must do a little twisting and turning on sidewalks. First, turning left (south) up Lake Otis Parkway, follow it for approximately 0.25 miles to where one can U-turn down into a tunnel that crosses under Lake Otis Parkway. At the far end of the tunnel follow the far side of Lake Otis Parkway back (north) to 47th Avenue. Turn left (west) on 47th Court and follow it the short distance to its very end to the continuation of the Campbell Creek Bike Trail (mile 3.0).

Approximately 1 mile later the trail begins passing under a series of roads in rapid succession. First it passes under the Seward Highway (mile 3.8), then under International Airport Road (mile 4.1), and finally under Old Seward Highway (mile 4.3). Less than 1 mile later the trail follows Campbell Creek under Dowling Road. The trail next crosses back and forth over Campbell Creek before reaching Taku Lake (mile 6.2). After passing under C Street (mile 6.6), the trail turns sharply right (north) and crosses a short and narrow wooden bridge. Immediately after crossing this bridge, the trail makes a sharp turn to the left (west). Continuing in a more or less straight line down the north shore of Campbell Creek the trail crosses under Arctic Boulevard (mile 6.9) and Minnesota Drive (mile 7.5). Not long after passing under Minnesota Drive, the trail swings up to right (northwest) onto E. 88th Avenue (mile 8.1), which marks the end of the trail.

At this point one has one of two options. First, one can turn around and retrace the trail back to University Lake. Second, one can continue up E. 88th Avenue and complete one of two circumnavigations of the city*.

**TRAIL GRADE:** This paved trail rates Grade 1 for its entire length.

**TRAIL CONDITION:** This trail remains in excellent shape.

**TRAIL MILEAGE:** To go from the beginning of Campbell Creek Trail at University Lake to where it ends at E. 88th Avenue entails approximately 8.1 miles of biking, for a round-trip total of 16.2 miles.

**TOTAL ELEVATION GAIN:** To go from the beginning of Campbell Creek Trail at University Lake to where it ends at E. 88th Avenue and back entails a total elevation gain of approximately 100 feet.

**HIGH POINT:** This trail reaches its highest point of approximately 175 feet above sea level just before one passes under the first bridge approximately 0.25 miles beyond the bridge over Tudor Road.

**NORMAL HIKING TIME:** To bike from the beginning of Campbell Creek Trail at University Lake to where it ends at E. 88th Avenue and back should take anywhere from 1.5 to 3 hours, depending on the condition and ambition of the biker(s) involved.

**CAMPSITES:** One will find no designated camping areas on this trail. Nor should one need one considering the shortness of the bike ride.

**BEST TIME:** Most people should find any time of year a good time to do bike, hike, run, or ski this route.

**USGS MAPS:** Anchorage A-8.

-------------------------------------------------------------------------

* For more information about these routes, one in reverse,
  see [102] **OPTION A—Short Circumnavigation of Anchorage** and
  [105] **OPTION A—Long Circumnavigation of Anchorage**.

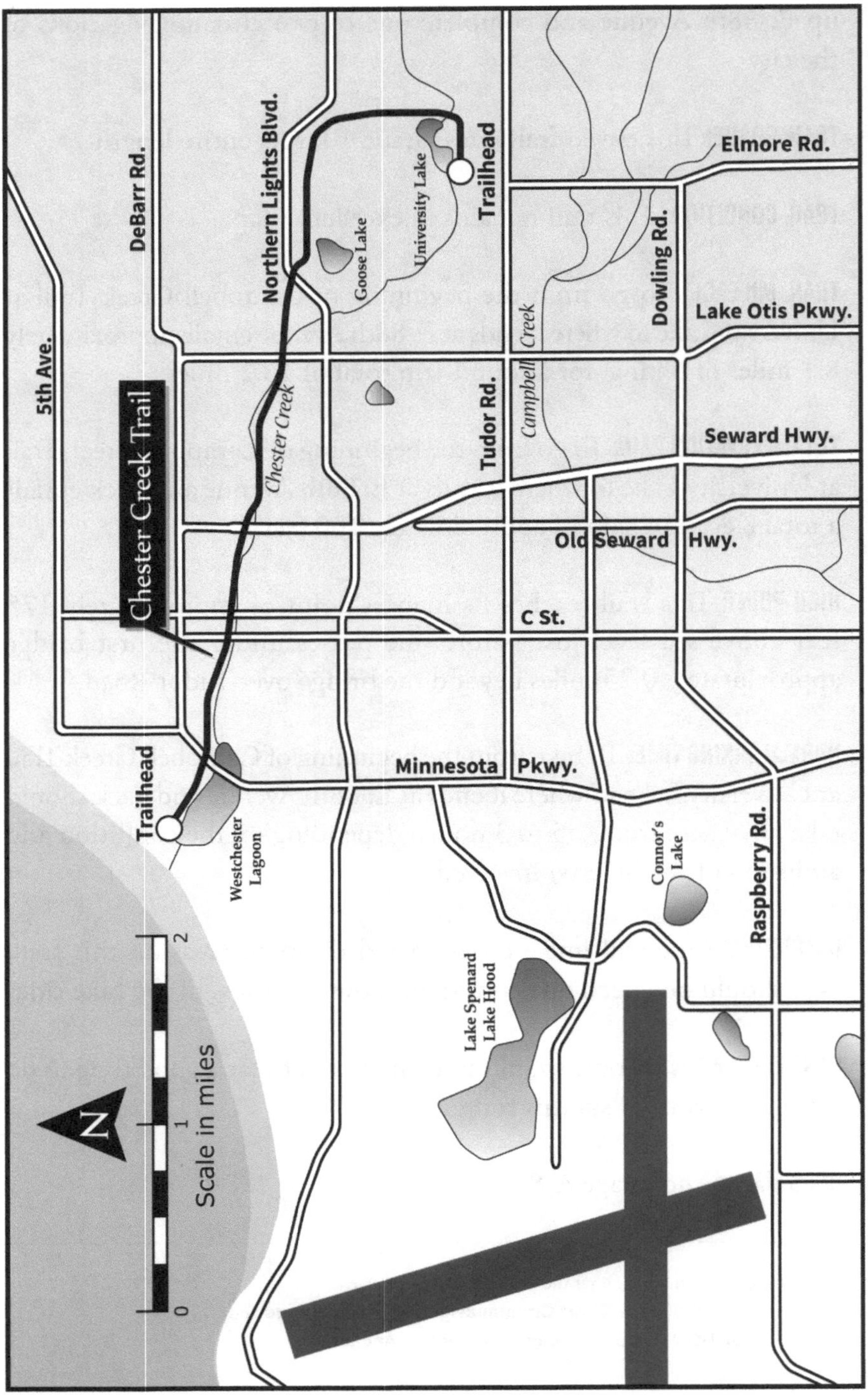
Chester Creek Trail
5th Ave.
DeBarr Rd.
Northern Lights Blvd.
Trailhead
Elmore Rd.
University Lake
Goose Lake
Dowling Rd.
Lake Otis Pkwy.
Campbell Creek
Tudor Rd.
Chester Creek
Seward Hwy.
Old Seward Hwy.
C St.
Minnesota Pkwy.
Trailhead
Westchester Lagoon
Connor's Lake
Raspberry Rd.
Lake Spenard
Lake Hood
N
0
1
2
Scale in miles

# Walk-About Guide to Lanie Fleischer Chester Creek Bike Trail

This bike trail begins at the same location as Tony Knowles Coastal Trail, but in the exact opposite direction. In fact, if not for the milepost 0.0 miles indicating where one starts east and one starts west, one would think them the same trail. Many people do treat them as one and the same trail. Each trail does, however, pass through entirely different terrain. Whereas Tony Knowles Coastal Trail leads out to the ocean, Lanie Fleischer Bike Trail leads up Chester Creek toward the mountains.

**TRAIL LOCATION:** This bike trail begins at the northwest corner of Westchester Lagoon in west Anchorage. To get there follow L Street south from West 5th Avenue in downtown Anchorage for just over 1.1 miles to where L Street turns downhill and intersects West 15th Avenue at a set of lights. Turn right (west) on West 15th Avenue and follow it for approximately 0.5 miles to where it ends at an intersection with U Street, where one should see a playground directly ahead. Turn right (north) onto U Street and immediately turn left into the parking area for the playground by Westchester Lagoon. Tony Knowles Coastal Trail begins on the bike trail running along the lake just to the left (south) of the parking area.

Thus begins the Lanie Fleischer Chester Creek Bike Trail. From the parking area, walk or bike out to the paved bike trail and turn left (east). In a matter of feet the trail passes the boat ramp for Westchester Lagoon. The trail then continues along the left (north) side of Westchester Lagoon. Just past milepost 0.5 miles the trail leaves the edge of the lagoon and passes in quick succession in the next less than 0.5 miles through three tunnels. Past the third tunnel the trail starts up the left (north) shore of Chester Creek, which flows just out of sight on the far side of trees on the right.

The trail follows Chester Creek for most of the remainder of its length. Just before milepost 1.0 the trail passes under Arctic Boulevard and reaches Valley of the Moon Park. Approximately 0.3 miles later the trail passes under C Street and, after a very short climb, crosses a bridge over Chester Creek (mile 1.3).

Bearing left off the bridge, the trail now follows the right (south) side of Chester Creek. After going under A Street (mile 1.5) the trail passes side trails to the left and right before crossing back over Chester Creek (mile 1.8). Just beyond the bridge a side trail to the left (north) leads out to Mulcahy Stadium and Sullivan Arena. (On any given day of the summer or fall one might happen upon a baseball, football, or soccer game at Mulcahy Stadium, which one can watch through the fence.)

Just past milepost 2.0 the trail passes under the Seward Highway. Almost immediately beyond the tunnel, the trail crosses a bridge back to the south side of Chester Creek (mile 2.1). Bearing left at the far end of the bridge, the trail continues up the south side of Chester Creek into the woods beyond. At the far end of the woods the trail bears left up to the edge of a pond that momentarily slows Chester Creek's flow (mile 3.0). A picnic table by the lower end of the pond can offer a fine place for a rest. Just beyond the picnic table the trail crosses over the pond's outlet. After crossing under Lake Otis Parkway (mile 3.1) the trail climbs a low rise to Tikishla Park. Approximately 200 yards past milepost 3.5 the trail bears right and crosses a short and narrow bridge over a dirty creek (mile 3.6). It then climbs steeply to a far more substantial bridge over Northern Lights Boulevard (mile 3.8). At the far side of the bridge, the trail reaches a T-intersection. Here the trail bears left (east) and downhill. (Bearing right at this intersection leads a short way out to the parking area by Goose Lake and a bike trail to the left leading eventually to the University of Alaska.)

For the next approximately 1 mile past this junction the trail climbs slowly through the woods alongside Northern Lights Boulevard. After circling up a wide hill and passing a bridge leading left (north) over

Northern Lights Boulevard (mile 4.8), the trail swings down to the right (southeast) to a roundabout. After passing under some power lines (mile 5.1) the trail swings right (south) along the backside of a neighborhood. Approximately 0.5 miles later the trail crosses a small bridge and turns right again (west) along the backside of a medical complex. In another approximately 0.5 miles the trail reaches a roundabout which marks its junction with Campbell Creek Trail*. This roundabout marks the end of Lanie Fleischer Chester Creek Bike Trail.

At this point one has two major choices. First, one can return the way they have come. Second, one can turn left (south) on Campbell Creek Trail to continue a circumnavigation of Anchorage**.

**TRAIL GRADE:** Despite some short and steep hills, this paved trail rates Grade 1 for its entire length.

**TRAIL CONDITION:** This trail remains in excellent shape.

**TRAIL MILEAGE:** To go from the beginning of Lanie Fleischer Chester Creek Bike Trail at Westchester Lagoon to its intersection with Campbell Creek Trail entails approximately 6.5 miles of biking, hiking, running, or skiing for a round-trip total of approximately 13 miles.

**TOTAL ELEVATION GAIN:** To bike from the beginning of Lanie Fleischer Chester Creek Bike Trail at Westchester Lagoon to its intersection with Campbell Creek Trail and back entails a total elevation gain of approximately 150 feet.

**HIGH POINT:** This trail reaches its highest point of approximately 120 feet above sea as at turns along the backside of the neighborhood at approximately mile 5.5.

------------------------------------------------------------------------

\* For more information about that trail,
   see [100] **Walk About Guide to Campbell Creek Trail.**

\*\* For more information about this route, only in reverse,
   see [102] **OPTION A—Short Circumnavigation of Anchorage.**

**NORMAL HIKING TIME:** To bike from the beginning of Lanie Fleischer Chester Creek Bike Trail at Westchester Lagoon to its intersection with Campbell Creek Trail and back should take 1 to 3 hours, depending on the condition and ambition of the biker(s) involved.

**CAMPSITES:** One will find no designated camping areas on this trail. Nor should one need one considering the shortness of the bike ride.

**BEST TIME:** Most people should find any time of year a good time to do bike, hike, run, or ski this route.

**USGS MAPS:** Anchorage A-8.

Westchester Lagoon

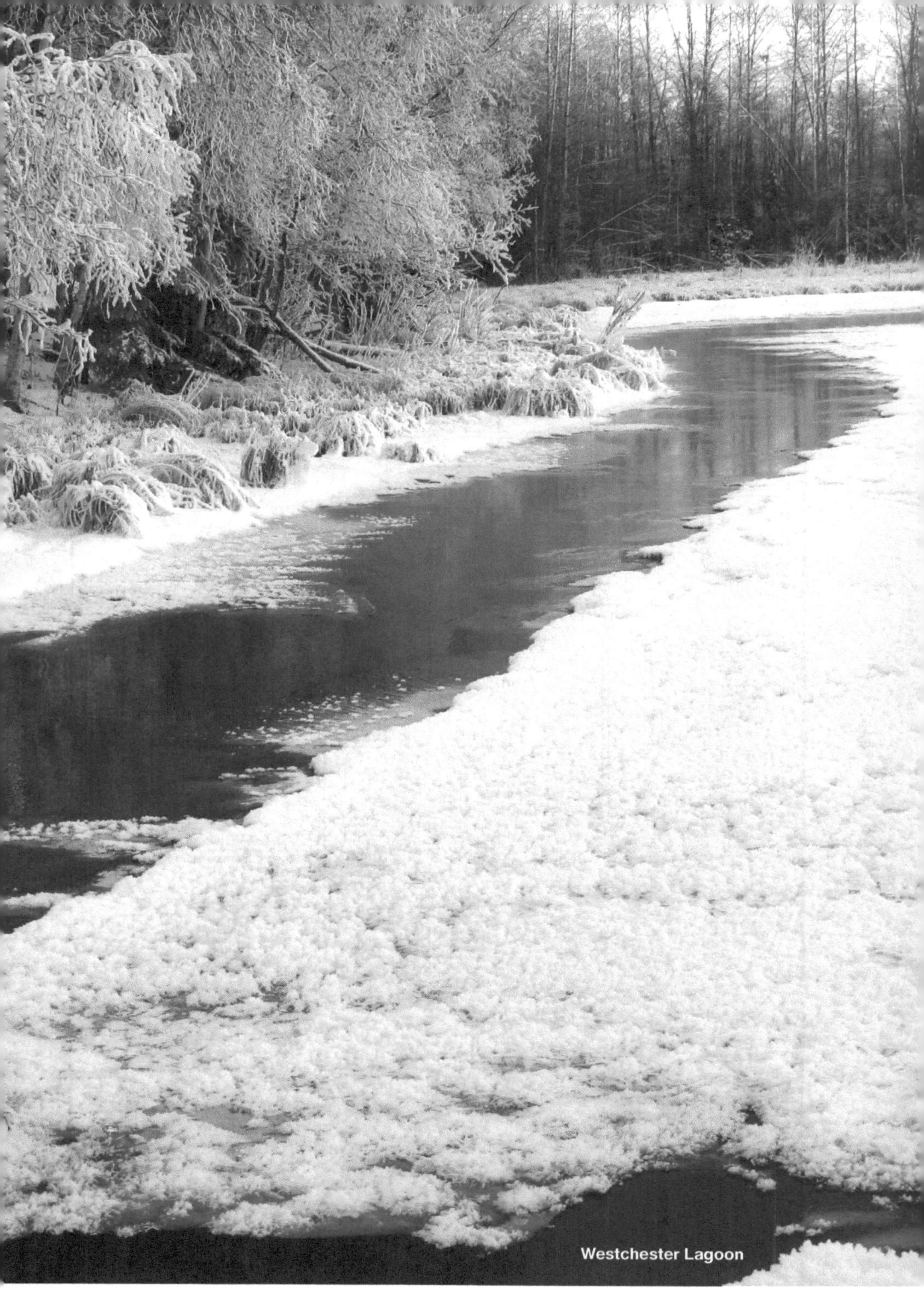

Westchester Lagoon

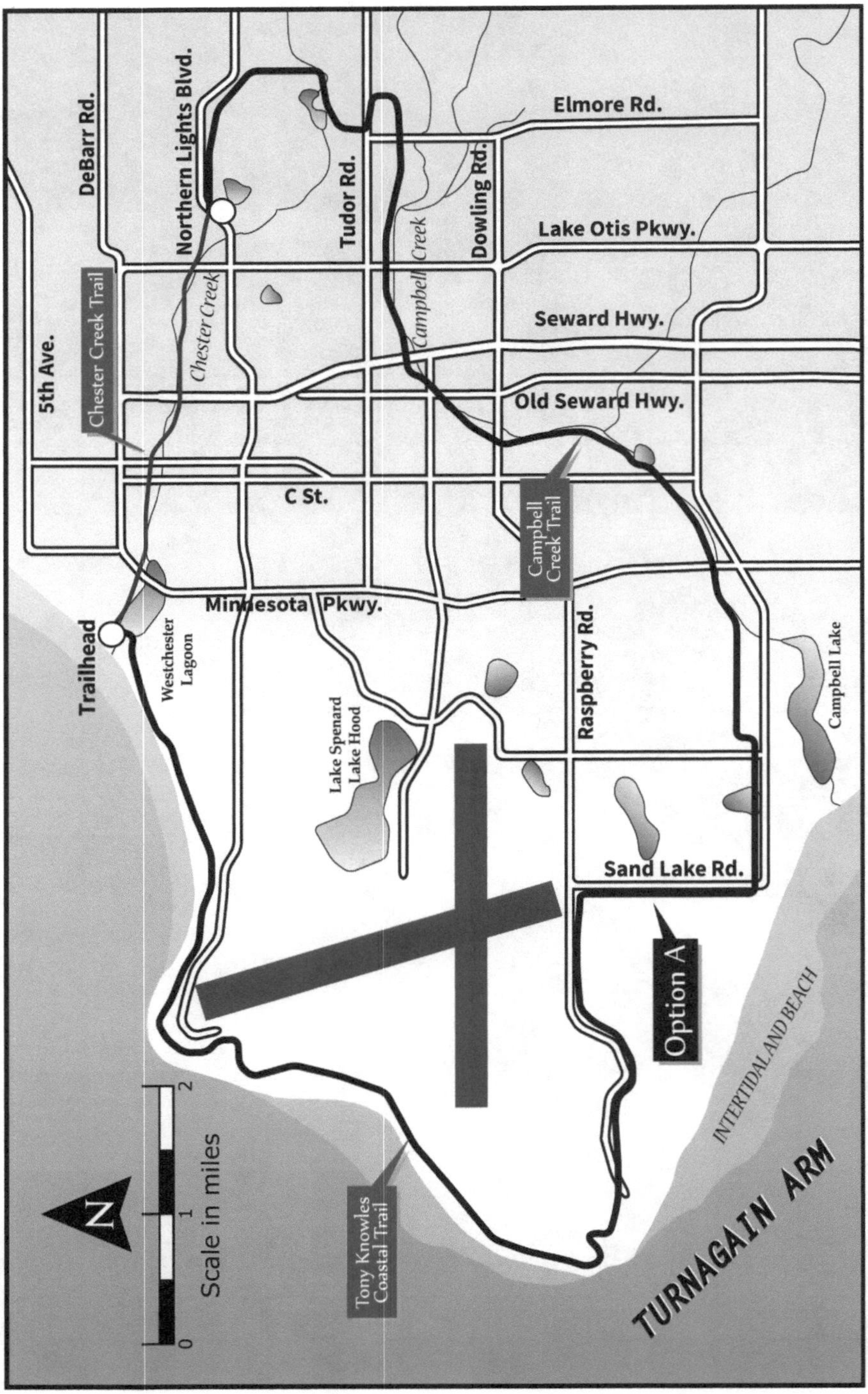

DeBarr Rd.
Northern Lights Blvd.
Elmore Rd.
Tudor Rd.
Dowling Rd.
Lake Otis Pkwy.
Campbell Creek
5th Ave.
Chester Creek Trail
Chester Creek
Seward Hwy.
Old Seward Hwy.
C St.
Campbell Creek Trail
Minnesota Pkwy.
Trailhead
Westchester Lagoon
Lake Spenard
Lake Hood
Raspberry Rd.
Campbell Lake
Sand Lake Rd.
Option A
INTERTIDAL AND BEACH
TURNAGAIN ARM
Tony Knowles Coastal Trail
N
0
1
2
Scale in miles

# OPTION A

# Short Circumnavgation of Anchorage

Apart from the long clockwise circumnavigation of Anchorage mentioned in the introduction to [101] **Walk-About Guide to Lanie Fleischer Bike Trail** above, one also has a choice of a shorter circumnavigation. This shorter route, while following a number of the same trails, encloses a smaller portion of the city. But though not as long, it does remain far more exclusively on bike trails. That, along with the slightly shorter length, makes this tour of Anchorage more popular with local bikers, many of whom find the distance and the route far more appropriate for a day's work out.

**TRAIL LOCATION:** This bike ride begins at the start of Tony Knowles Coastal Trail at the northwest corner of Westchester Lagoon*. One on the bike trail, turn right (west) and follow Tony Knowles Coastal Trail all the way to its end at Kincaid Chalet at Kincaid Park (mile 9.1).

As it progresses toward Kincaid Park, the trail first crosses under the railroad tracks and emerges out on the coast (0.5 mile). It then passes Lyn Ary Park (1.1 mile). Earthquake Park (2.0 miles), entrance to a parking area (2.9 miles), the crest of Point Woronzof (3.5 miles), and Point Woronzof parking area (4 miles). After this parking area, the trail turns away from the water. After passing another parking area, the trail enters the woods beyond where it soon comes in sight of Knik

---

* To get there, see [99] **Walk-About Guide to Tony Knowles Trail**.

Arm again (4.6 miles). As it follows the bluff above Knik Arm the trail next passes a substantial steel bridge at the end airport's east-west runway (6.5 miles), and a rest area with a picnic table (7.9 miles). At mile 8.1, where the trail passes a bench to the right and the beginning Kincaid Bluff Trail the bike trail turns away from the water. From this point it begins climbing the long hill to Kincaid Chalet (8.4 miles), and the end of Tony Knowles Coastal Trail.

Upon reaching the end of Tony Knowles Coastal Trail at Kincaid Chalet, continue straight on the bike trail as it parallels the right (south) side of Raspberry Road through the park. In 2 miles the trail reaches the bottom of a long hill and passes the entrance sign for Kincaid Park (mile 11.1).

For the next 4.7 miles the route hugs roads. Continuing along Raspberry Road, the trail next reaches an intersection with Sand Lake Road (mile 12.1). Turn sharply right (south) and follow the bike trail along Sand Lake Road up and over a hill to its intersection with West Dimond Boulevard (13.6 miles). Turning left (east) at this intersection, follow the bike trail along the left (north) side of West Dimond Boulevard. In 1 mile this trail reaches the intersection at Jewel Lake Road (mile 14.6). Turn left (north) on Jewel Lake Road and follow it to the first set of lights (mile 14.7). Cross Jewel Lake Road at these lights and continues down East 88th Avenue past two schools on the left (north). Just beyond the schools the road passes straight through a 4-way intersection and starts down a short hill. At the bottom of the hill where the road swings left (north) and uphill, the bike trail leaves the road and swings right (south) to the shore of Campbell Creek (mile 16.0).

For the next several miles the trail follows Campbell Creek northwest across the Anchorage Peninsula. In doing so, it first passes under a number of roads. The trail first crosses under Minnesota Drive (16.7 miles) and Arctic Boulevard (17.0). Less than 0.2 miles beyond Arctic Boulevard, the trail turns sharply right (south) and crosses Campbell Creek over a short and narrow bridge. Then it turns sharply left (east) and passes under C Street (17.2 miles). Bearing left up the hill the next reaches the south shore of Taku Lake (17.3 miles). After leaving the north end of Taku Lake the trail crosses back and forth over Campbell Creek a number of times before passing under Dowling Road.

Approximately 1 mile later the trail begins passing under a series of roads. In rapid succession it passes under Old Seward Highway (mile 19.8), International Airport Road (mile 20.0), and the Seward Highway (mile 20.2). After skirting through a neighborhood, by a lake and soccer fields, the trail drops onto 47th Avenue (mile 21.1).

Now one must do a quick back-and-forth to cross Lake Otis Parkway. Begin by following 47th Avenue out to Lake Otis Parkway (mile 21.2). Turn right (south) on Lake Otis Parkway and follow it to the next set of lights. Straight across the road at these lights one reaches a tunnel under Lake Otis Parkway. After passing through the tunnel and coming up on the opposite side, do quick U-turn and follow Lake Otis Parkway north to a park by Campbell Creek (mile 21.8). Cross the parking area and turn right (right) on the bike trail on the far side.

From here to the end of the ride, this circumnavigation remains on bike trails. First, after crossing a long bridge and rolling up and over a few low hills the trail passes under Elmore Drive (mile 23.3). Approximately 0.3 miles later the trail passes under a thoroughfare and comes out to the edge of Tudor Road. Follow Tudor Road west for approximately 0.2 miles to where the trail crosses up and over Tudor Road on a substantial bridge (mile 24.0). Dropping off the far side of the bridge, the trail squeezes between a medical building on the left and a pond on the right and passes through a short tunnel. Just beyond the tunnel it reaches a roundabout (mile 24.1). This roundabout marks the end of Campbell Creek Trail and the beginning of Lanier Fleischer Chester Creek Bike Trail.

Turning right (east) at this roundabout, follow Lanie Fleischer Chester Creek Bike Trail east as it swings up along the back side of more medical buildings. Then, after crossing a bridge the trail turns north passing along the edge of a neighborhood and crossing under some power lines before reaching another roundabout (mile 24.6). Turn left (west) at this roundabout and follow it up past the southern end of a bridge over Northern Lights Boulevard. Passing this first bridge, continue along the trail as it parallels Northern Lights Boulevard for approximately 1 mile to a second bridge (mile 25.6).

Here turn right (north) and cross the bridge over Northern Lights Boulevard. At the bottom of the hill on the far side of northern Lights Boulevard bear left (east) over a much smaller, narrower bridge (mile 25.8). Bear left again at the trail intersection one reaches immediately past the bridge.

As the trail trends slowly downhill it passes under Lake Otis Parkway (mile 26.3), Seward Highway (mile 27.4), followed in the next 1 mile by A Street, C Street and Arctic Boulevard. After three more underpasses in rapid succession, the last of which passes under Minnesota Drive (mile 28.8), the trail reaches the east end of Westchester Lagoon. Now it only remains to follow the right (north) side of Westchester Lagoon back to where one started to the beginning of Tony Knowles Coastal Trail to complete this circumnavigation (mile 29.4).

**TRAIL GRADE:** All the bike trails and roads this route follows rate Grade 1 as both a hike and a bike ride.

**TRAIL CONDITION:** All these trails remain in excellent condition.

**TRAIL MILEAGE:** To complete this entire circumnavigation of Anchorage from the beginning of this route at Westchester Lagoon and back entails approximately 29.4 miles of biking.

**TOTAL ELEVATION GAIN:** To complete this entire circumnavigation of Anchorage from the beginning of this route at Westchester Lagoon and back entails a total elevation gain of approximately 500 feet.

**HIGH POINT:** This trail reaches its highest point of approximately 225 feet above sea level at Kincaid Chalet.

**NORMAL HIKING TIME:** To complete this entire circumnavigation of Anchorage from the beginning of this route at Westchester Lagoon and back should take anywhere from 3 to 5 hours, depending on the condition and ambition of the biker(s) involved.

**CAMPSITES:** One will find no designated camping areas on this route. Nor should one need one considering the shortness of the bike ride.

**BEST TIME:** Most people should find any time from mid-March to early October a good time to do this bike ride. It would make for a fine outing in winter for those who enjoy winter biking.

**USGS MAPS:** Anchorage A-8 and Tyonek A-1.

Anchorage from Tony Knowles Coastal Trail

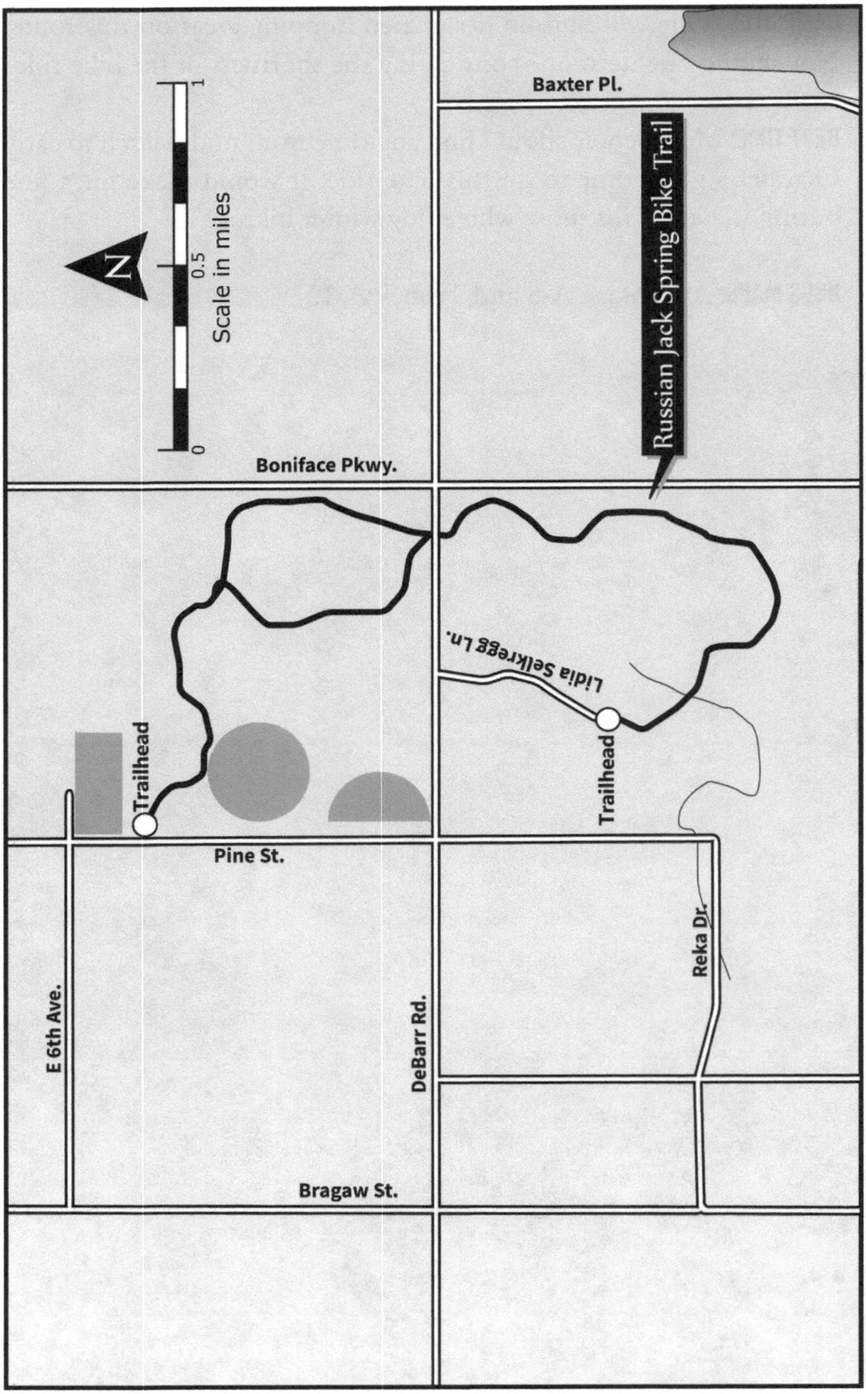
Baxter Pl.
Russian Jack Spring Bike Trail
N
0
0.5
1
Scale in miles
Boniface Pkwy.
Lidia Selkregg Ln.
Trailhead
Trailhead
Pine St.
Reka Dr.
E 6th Ave.
DeBarr Rd.
Bragaw St.

# Walk-About Guide to Russian Jack Springs Bike Trail

**TRAIL LOCATION:** Russian Jack Springs Bike Trail begins at Russian Jack Springs Chalet. To get there follow 6th Avenue east from downtown Anchorage to Gambell Street (the Seward Highway). Turn right (south) on Gambell Street. In less than 1 mile Gambell Street reaches an intersection with 15th Avenue. Turn left (east) on 15th Avenue and follow it to where it turns into DeBarr Road at the intersection with Lake Otis Parkway.

Approximately 2.5 miles from Gambell Street, DeBarr Road passes through an intersection with Pine Street. Approximately 0.25 miles later DeBarr Road reaches a road on the right leading into Russian Jack Springs Golf Course. Turn right (south) on this road and follow it past the greenhouses to the parking area in front of Russian Jack Springs Chalet. Russian Jack Springs Bike Trail begins on the paved bike trail directly to the left (east) of the chalet.

From the parking area, the paved trail immediately drops down a short hill into the woods. Upon entering the woods the trail reaches an intersection (mile 0.1). Turn left (east) here and cross the bridge. After the bridge the trail climbs a slope and swings left (north). Just as the trail straightens out it passes on the right a trail leading to right (east) leading down and under Boniface Parkway (mile 0.3). The trail then bears right where it merges with the outbound single-lane park road (mile 0.4). Soon after that the trail crosses the in-bound single-lane park road with parking area on right (mile 0.6). At the far side of the parking area the trail winds down into the woods where it eventually bears right and goes through tunnel under DeBarr Road (mile 0.9). At the far end of the tunnel, the trail climbs up and over a pair of short sharp hills beside Boniface Parkway before turning left (east) and downhill away from the highway and entering some woods.

It then passes a paved trail leading down to Boniface Parkway (mile 1.2). Beyond the woods, the trail emerges into the open in the midst of some baseball and soccer fields. There the trail comes to an end by a playground on Pine Street (mile 1.6).

At this point one has two major choices. First, one can return the way they have come. One can even do this via an optional dirt trail route. This optional route begins approximately 0.2 miles back along the bike trail. There a dirt trail leads into the woods on the right (south). One in the woods, this trail bears right and downhill. At the bottom of the hill the trail swings to the left (south) and climbs straight past a number of other trails to the crest of a bluff. Just beyond the crest of the bluff the trail swings to the right to head west back over ridge crest.

At bottom the hill the trail swings to the left again to climb back over the ridge. Before reaching the top, however, it climbs onto a parking area. Here bear left (northeast) and turn around the upper right (northeast) corner of the parking area to a covered picnic table. Passing to the right of the picnic hut, follow the trail as it re-enters the woods and turns down sharply to where it re-joins the paved Russian Jack Springs Bike Trail just before the tunnel under DeBarr Road. One need only turn right and follow the paved trail back to Russian Jack Springs Chalet.

Second, one can continue following the long circumnavigation of Anchorage by turning right on Pine Street[*].

**TRAIL GRADE:** Despite some short and steep hills, this paved trail rates Grade 1 for its entire length.

**TRAIL CONDITION:** This trail remains in excellent shape.

**TRAIL MILEAGE:** To go from the beginning of Russian Jack Springs Bike Trail at Russian Jack Springs Chalet to the end of the trail at the playing fields on Pine Street entails approximately 1.2 miles of biking,

------------------------------------------------------------

[*] For more information about that circumnavigation, see [105] **OPTION A—Long Circumnavigation of Anchorage**.

hiking, running, or skiing for a round-trip total of 2.4 miles. Taking the optional route back entails a round-trip total of approximately 3.2 miles.

**TOTAL ELEVATION GAIN:** To bike from the beginning of Russian Jack Springs Bike Trail at Russian Jack Springs Chalet to the end of the trail at the playing fields on Pine Street and back entails a total elevation gain of approximately 100 feet. Taking the optional route back entails total elevation gain of approximately 225 feet.

**HIGH POINT:** This trail reaches its highest point of approximately 200 feet above sea at the crest of the second hill on bluff above Boniface Parkway beyond the tunnel. On the optional route back the trail reaches its highest point of approximately 225 feet on the first pass over the ridge.

**NORMAL HIKING TIME:** To bike from the beginning of Russian Jack Springs Bike Trail at Russian Jack Springs Chalet to the end of the trail at the playing fields on Pine Street and back should take 15 to 30 minutes, depending on the condition and ambition of the biker(s) involved.

**CAMPSITES:** One will find no designated camping areas on this trail. Nor should one need one considering the shortness of the bike ride.

**BEST TIME:** Most people should find any time of year a good time to bike, hike, run, or ski this route.

**USGS MAPS:** Anchorage A-8.

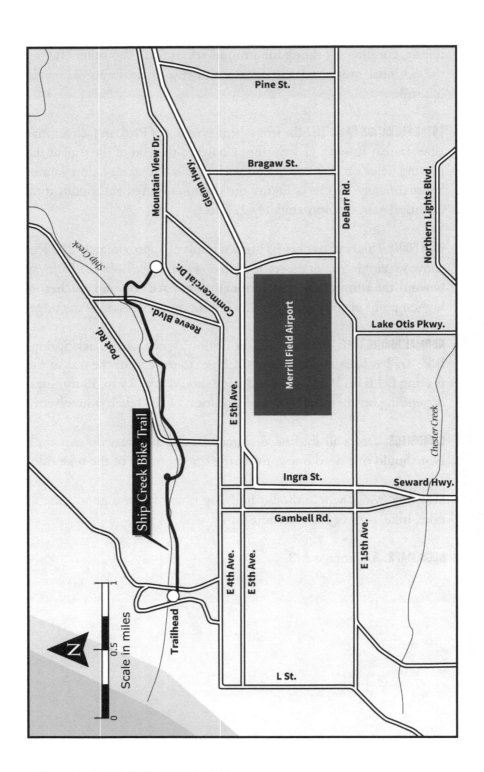

Pine St.

Bragaw St.

Mountain View Dr.

Glenn Hwy.

DeBarr Rd.

Northern Lights Blvd.

Ship Creek

Commercial Dr.

Reeve Blvd.

Post Rd.

Merrill Field Airport

Lake Otis Pkwy.

Chester Creek

Ship Creek Bike Trail

E 5th Ave.

Ingra St.

Seward Hwy.

Gambell Rd.

E 4th Ave.

E 5th Ave.

E 15th Ave.

Trailhead

Scale in miles

1

0.5

0

N

L St.

# Walk-About Guide to
# Ship Creek Bike Trail

Used primarily by fishermen wishing to access Ship Creek, this trail deserves wider use. Though it traverses through the heart of industrial Anchorage, it also at times passes through pleasant woods as it hugs the shores of Ship Creek. It also boasts a wonderfully high bridge that spirals high above the waters of Ship Creek.

**TRAIL LOCATION:** Ship Creek Bike Trail begins on the south shore of Ship Creek just behind the Alaska Railroad Depot. To get there from downtown Anchorage, first turn onto West 3rd Avenue at its westernmost end. Follow West 3rd Avenue east toward the mountains for approximately 100 yards. Then turn downhill to the left (north) onto Christensen Road. Follow Christensen Road as it swings around a corner to the right (east) and turns into 1st Avenue. Stay on 1st Avenue as it passes the front of the Alaska Railroad Depot. Just past the depot turn left (north) onto West C Street and cross the railroad tracks. At this point look for any possible place to park on one of the side streets or in the nearby parking areas.

Then, on bike or on foot, continue along West C Street to the bridge over Ship Creek. Just before crossing the bridge, turn right (east) onto Ship Creek Bike Trail (mile 0.0).

For the next 2.7 miles this trail parallels the creek, crossing back and forth in the process numerous times. Just before its halfway point (mile 0.8) the trail crosses Ship Creek to the left (north) side. It then circles under itself and begins climbing over a surprisingly high bridge. From the top of the bridge (mile 1.0) one looks 50-plus feet directly down to Ship Creek. The bridge also allows juxtaposed wide views of the mountains above and the industrial section of the city below. After circling down the far side of the bridge, the trail continues up the right (south) side of Ship Creek and passes under a road.

One should find this upper end of the trail surprisingly free of many people and more seemingly rural as it passes through more pronounced woods. As it approaches its end, the trail crosses under another road (mile 2.3) and climbs into the woods beyond. At the far end of the woods, the trail emerges onto Richmond Circle beside Tyson Elementary School where it ends (mile 2.7).

At this point, one has two major choices. First, one can return the way they have come. Second, they can continue up Richmond Circle along a bike route that circumnavigates Anchorage*.

**TRAIL GRADE:** This paved trail rates Grade 1 for its entire length.

**TRAIL CONDITION:** This trail remains in excellent shape for its entire length.

**TRAIL MILEAGE:** To go from the Alaska Railroad Depot to Tyson Elementary School entails approximately 2.7 miles of biking for a round-trip total of 5.2 miles.

**TOTAL ELEVATION GAIN:** To bike from the Alaska Railroad Depot to Tyson Elementary School and back entails a total elevation gain of approximately 150 feet.

**HIGH POINT:** This trail reaches its highest point of approximately 150 feet above sea level at the top of the bridge located just after halfway along the trail.

**NORMAL HIKING TIME:** To bike from the Alaska Railroad Depot to its end at Tyson Elementary School and back should take 0.5 to 1 hour, depending on the condition and ambition of the biker(s) involved.

------------------------------------------------------------------------

*   For more about that bike route,
    see [105] **OPTION A—Long Circumnavigation of Anchorage**.

**CAMPSITES:** One will find no designated camping areas on this trail. Nor should one need one considering the shortness of the bike ride.

**BEST TIME:** Most people should find any time of year a good time to do bike, hike, run, or ski this route.

**USGS MAPS:** Anchorage A-8.

Ship Creek

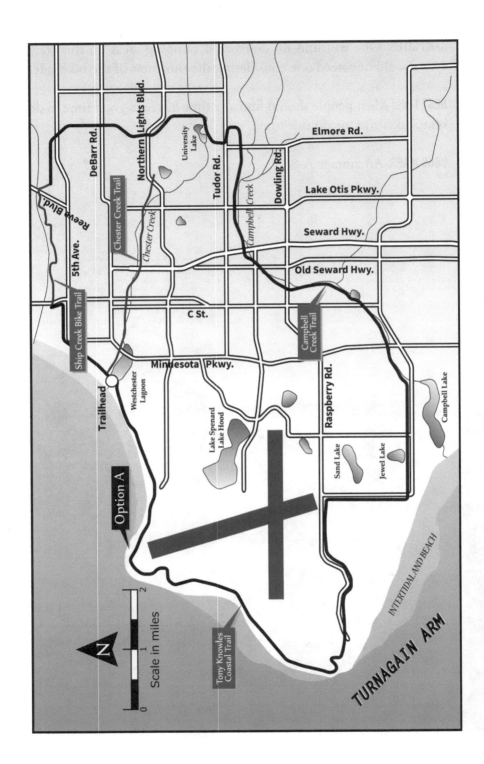

Option A

Ship Creek Bike Trail

Chester Creek Trail

Campbell Creek Trail

Tony Knowles Coastal Trail

Trailhead

Westchester Lagoon

DeBarr Rd.

Reeve Blvd.

5th Ave.

Northern Lights Blvd.

University Lake

Chester Creek

Tudor Rd.

Elmore Rd.

Dowling Rd.

Campbell Creek

Lake Otis Pkwy.

Seward Hwy.

Old Seward Hwy.

C St.

Minnesota Pkwy.

Raspberry Rd.

Campbell Lake

Lake Spenard

Lake Hood

Sand Lake

Jewel Lake

INTERTIDAL AND BEACH

TURNAGAIN ARM

N

Scale in miles

0    1    2

# 105

# OPTION A

# Long Circumnavigation of Anchorage

This circumnavigation of Anchorage encompasses an even larger portion of Anchorage than [102] **OPTION A—Short Circumnavigation of Anchorage** described above. Like that trip this circumnavigation remains best done on bike. This choice of transportation has to do with not only the circumnavigation's length, but also because it follows paves bike trails and roads for its entire length. Though most may not particularly relish biking on a road, at least the roads one rides to complete this circumnavigation have either little traffic or have substantial bike trails beside them. The only exceptions to this general rule come in the section connecting Davis Park and Russian Jack Springs Park and the section connecting the end of Campbell Creek Bike Trail with the bike trail along West Dimond Boulevard. To make up for these sometimes traffic-heavy sections, the route at other times follows completely isolated trails through woods and along bluffs. Altogether, these various sections combine to provide a full tour of the city.

Finally, though others might choose to do this circumnavigation by beginning on Tony Knowles Coastal Trail, this guide describes the route backwards from the way most people would do it. It does so for the simple reason that it saves the best for last in that this description ends with the last 9 miles of the route following Tony Knowles Coastal Trail along the coast of the Anchorage peninsula.

**TRAIL LOCATION:** This bike route begins at the start of Tony Knowles Coastal Trail*. Immediately after starting along Tony Knowles Coastal Trail (mile 0.0) one reaches a fork in the trail. Instead of following Tony Knowles Coastal Trail to the left (southwest) at this fork, bear right (northwest) onto the northern extension of Tony Knowles Coastal Trail. Immediately after bearing left, the trail crosses a wooden bridge and passes through a tunnel under the railroad tracks. On the immediate far side of the tunnel one emerges onto the coast of the Anchorage Peninsula. Continue along this bike trail for its entire length.

At its far end the bike trail slides straight onto 2nd Avenue (mile 1.4). At the first intersection on 2nd Avenue turn left (north) and downhill on Christensen Road. Follow Christensen Road as it swings down and around a corner to the right (east). There it turns into 1st Avenue. Stay on 1st Avenue as it passes the front of the Anchorage Railroad Depot. Just past the depot turn left (north) onto West C Street. Follow this road 0.2 miles straight across the railroad track to the bridge over Ship Creek. Just before crossing the bridge, turn right (east) onto the Ship Creek Bike Trail (mile 2.1).

Follow Ship Creek Bike Trail up-creek for the next 2.7 miles as it snakes back and forth over the creek. (On any given day in the summer one might see the incongruous sight of fishermen back-dropped by factories and warehouses.) At its uppermost end this trail one comes out of the woods on Richmond Circle next to Tyson Elementary School (mile 4.7).

For the next 2-plus miles the route now follows roads. Follow Richmond Street up to the left and through the gate at the top of the hill above the school. Past the gate continue straight for two blocks. There turn left (north) onto Schodde Street (mile 5.1). Follow Schodde Street for three blocks to Thompson Street and turn right (east) (mile 5.3). Follow Thompson Street to its very end. There, where the road turns left, one reaches a gate leading straight ahead to Davis Park. Go through the gate and turn right onto North Pine Street (mile 6.2). Follow North Pine Street for 100 yards to its

---

\* To get there, see [99] **Walk-About Guide to Tony Knowles Coastal Trail.**

intersection with Mount View Drive (mile 6.3). Then turn left (east) on Mountain View and continue for another 100 feet. There turn right and cross Mountain View Drive and continue up McCarrey Street as it crosses over the Glenn Highway. Approximately 0.7 miles later, by which time McCarrey Street has turned into Pine Street, one reaches a four-way stop intersection at the northwest corner Russian Jack Springs Park. Go straight through this intersection and continue to just past the playground to where one can turn left (east) into a parking area for Russian Jack Springs Park (mile 7.2). At the far end of the parking area one should come to a bike trail leading to the right (south).

One now, thankfully, leaves the traffic behind to follow bike trails for the next 12 miles. Just after leaving the parking area, the trail climbs into the woods. At the upper end of the woods, the trail swings left (south) to follow a bluff paralleling Boniface Drive below. Approximately 0.8 miles from the beginning of the bike trail at the playground, one passes through a tunnel under DeBarr Road (mile 8.1). Bearing left at the far end of the tunnel, the trail climbs again and soon reaches a small parking are in the woods. Go straight past the parking area. Approximately 100 feet later where the main trail seems to go straight ahead, turn left onto what seems a side trail (mile 8.5). After next swing around a wide corner, the trail drops down a hill and crosses a wooden bridge where it reaches a T-intersection (mile 8.9). Turning left (south) at this intersection, follow the trail through the woods, across a small stream, and up a short, sharp hill. Coming out of the woods, the trail swings around some apartment buildings and reaches another apparent side trail leading to the left (south) (mile 9.3). Turn onto this side trail and follow it out to a bridge over Northern Lights Boulevard (mile 9.7). At the far side of the bridge the route reaches a T-intersection with Lanie Fleischer Chester Creek Bike Trail*. Turning left (east) on this trail, follow it down to a roundabout (mile 9.8). Bearing right (south) at this roundabout continue following Lanie Fleischer Chester Creek Bike Trail.

---

* For more information about that trail,
see [101] **Walk-About Guide to Lanie Fleischer Bike Trail.**

For the next number of miles one should find the route a bit easier to follow. Approximately 1.5 miles past the roundabout, after making a large half-circle through the woods one reaches another roundabout (mile 11.1). Here turn left (south) and pass through the tunnel visible just ahead. On the far side of the tunnel follow the trail up and over Tudor Road (mile 11.2). Continuing straight down the other side of the bridge, follow the trail directly toward the mountains. Approximately 0.25 miles later, the trail swings right (south) and passes under another road before swinging back to the east. Just after passing some baseball fields on the left (south) the trail passes under Elmore Drive (mile 12.5).

For the next several miles the trail follows Campbell Creek southeast across the Anchorage Peninsula. In doing so, it has a couple of tricky-to-follow sections. Approximately 1.5 miles after passing under Elmore Drive the trail reaches a playground on Lake Otis Parkway (mile 2.3). Here one must do a little twisting and turning on sidewalks. First, turning left (south) up Lake Otis Parkway, follow it for approximately 0.25 miles to where one can U-turn down into a tunnel that crosses under Lake Otis Parkway. From the far end of the tunnel follow the far side of Lake Otis Parkway back (north) to 47th Avenue. Turn left (west) on 47th Court and follow it the short distance to its very end where one will find the continuation of the Campbell Creek Bike Trail (mile 3.0).

Approximately 1 mile later the trail begins passing under a series of roads in rapid succession. First it passes under the Seward Highway (mile 3.8), then under International Airport Road (mile 4.1), and finally under Old Seward Highway (mile 4.3). Less than 1 mile later the trail follows Campbell Creek under Dowling Road. The trail next crosses back and forth over Campbell Creek before reaching Taku Lake (mile 6.2). After passing under C Street (mile 6.6), the trail turns sharply right (north) and crosses a short and narrow wooden bridge. Immediately after crossing this bridge, the trail makes a sharp turn to the left (west). Continuing in a more or less straight line down the north shore of Campbell Creek the trail crosses under Arctic Boulevard (mile 6.9) and Minnesota Drive (mile 7.5). Not long after passing under Minnesota Drive, the trail swings up to right (northwest) onto

E. 88th Avenue (mile 8.1), which marks the end of Campbell Creek Trail, but not the end of the circumnavigation.

For the next 4.7 miles the route follows roads. First, it follows East 88th Avenue uphill and straight through a four-way stop intersection to a set of lights on Jewel Lake Road (mile 20.5). Cross Jewel Lake Road at the lights and turn left (south). Continue down Jewel Lake Road to another set of lights at its intersection with West Dimond Boulevard (20.6 miles). Turn left (west) on West Dimond Boulevard and follow the bike trail alongside it as it climbs gradually past Jewel Lake Road to a roundabout at the intersection with Sand Lake Road (21.6 miles). Cross the roundabout and turn right (north) onto the bike trail that parallels the left side of Sand Lake Road. Follow Sand Lake Road for the next approximately 1.5 miles to its intersection with Raspberry Road (mile 23.1). Turn left (west) onto Raspberry Road and follow it to where a large sign in the middle of the road marks the entrance into Kincaid Park (mile 24.1).

From here to the end of the circumnavigation one follows much more pleasant bike trails through the woods and out along the coast of the Anchorage peninsula. This pleasant section, however, begins by continuing past the entrance sign and climbing a series of climbs to Kincaid Chalet (mile 26.1).

At the chalet, one has reached the southern end of Tony Knowles Coastal Trail*. Beginning just to the left (south) of the chalet, this trail begins by dropping off the far side of the bluff. Approximately 1 mile down from the chalet the trail swings right (north) along the top of the bluffs at the westernmost end of the peninsula. For the next approximately 4 miles the trail winds pleasantly through the woods along the bluff.

It then crosses an access road into a parking area (mile 31.0). A few hundred yards beyond that it crosses the access road into the parking area for Point Woronzof (mile 31.1). A short, steep climb then brings the trail to the top of Point Woronzof from where one can partake of a wide and long view of the entire northern horizon across Knik

---

\*    For more information about that trail,
     see [99] **Walk-About Guide to Tony Knowles Coastal Trail**.

Arm (mile 31.3). This marks the last climb of any consequence on the route.

From Point Woronzof, the trail descends steadily, crossing another parking area, before reaching Earthquake Park (mile 32.7). A downhill ride, followed by a turn to the left (north) brings one back out to the edge of Knik Arm. From here one makes a short climb to pass by Lyn Ary Park. The trail then slides back down to shore again at the far side of the park. In the next 0.6 miles it crosses the bridge over Fish Creek and passes through the tunnel under the railroad tracks after which the trail emerges onto the western end of Westchester Lagoon. A short ride around the shore of the lagoon brings one back to the beginning of Tony Knowles Coastal Trail at the playground and the end of the circumnavigation (mile 35.1).

**TRAIL GRADE:** All the bike trails and roads this route follows rate Grade 1 as both a hike and a bike ride.

**TRAIL CONDITION:** All the trails and roads that make up this circumnavigation remain in excellent shape.

**TRAIL MILEAGE:** To complete this entire circumnavigation of Anchorage from Westchester Lagoon and back entails approximately 35.1 miles of biking.

**TOTAL ELEVATION GAIN:** To complete this entire circumnavigation of Anchorage from Westchester Lagoon and back entails a total elevation gain of approximately 800 feet.

**HIGH POINT:** This route reaches its highest point of approximately 225 feet above sea level at Kincaid Chalet.

**NORMAL HIKING TIME:** To complete this entire circumnavigation of Anchorage from Westchester Lagoon and back should take anywhere from 3 to 7 hours, depending on the condition and ambition of the biker(s) involved.

**CAMPSITES:** One will find no designated camping areas on this route. Nor should one need one considering the shortness of the bike ride.

**BEST TIME:** Most people should find any time from mid-March to early October a good time to do this bike ride. It also makes for a fine outing in winter if one has the proper bike.

**USGS MAPS:** Anchorage A-8 and Tyonek A-1.

Moose near Kincaid Park

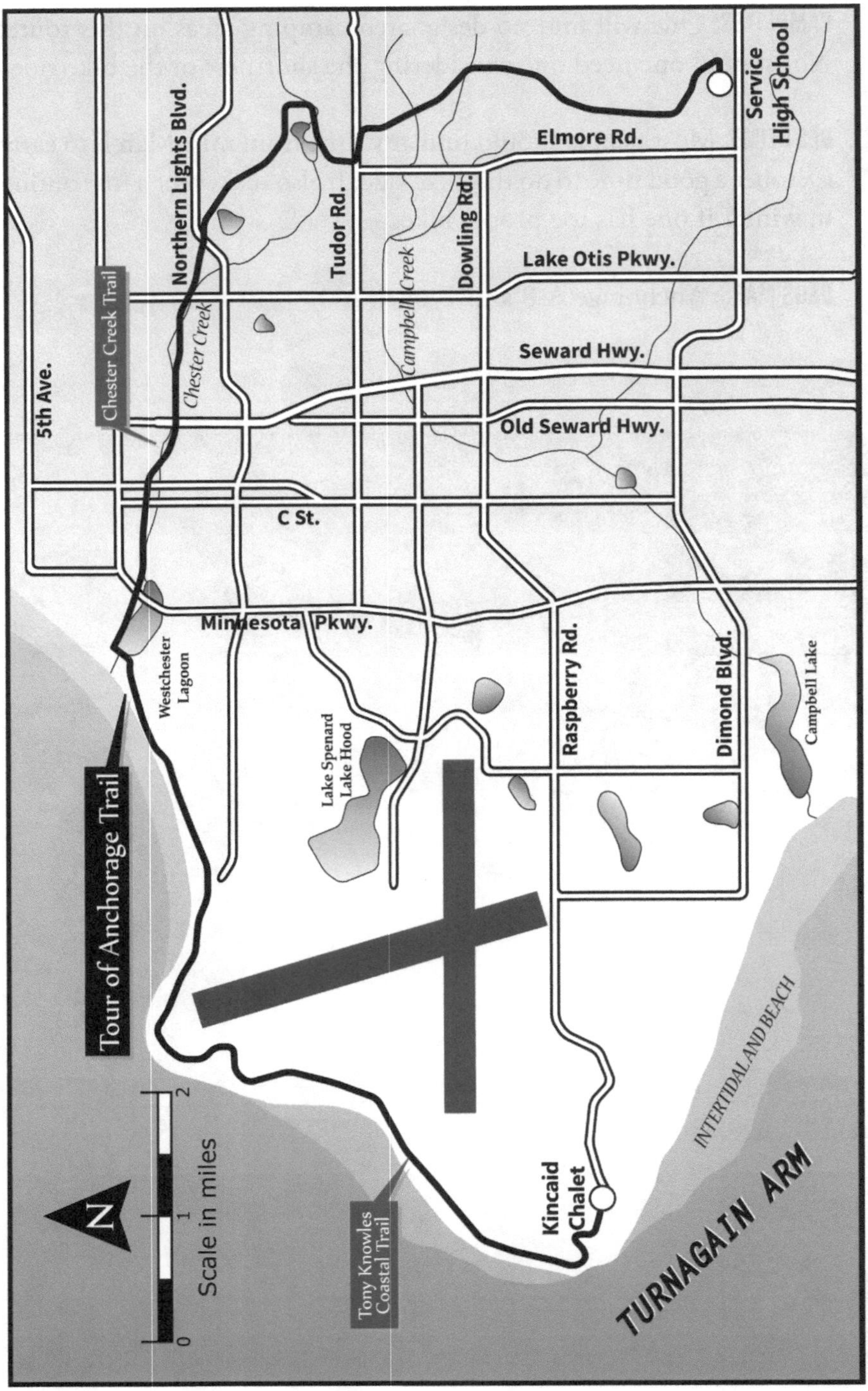

Tour of Anchorage Trail
Chester Creek Trail
Tony Knowles Coastal Trail
Service High School
Kincaid Chalet
5th Ave.
Northern Lights Blvd.
Tudor Rd.
Dowling Rd.
Elmore Rd.
Lake Otis Pkwy.
Seward Hwy.
Old Seward Hwy.
C St.
Minnesota Pkwy.
Raspberry Rd.
Dimond Blvd.
Chester Creek
Campbell Creek
Westchester Lagoon
Lake Spenard
Lake Hood
Campbell Lake
INTERTIDAL AND BEACH
TURNAGAIN ARM
N
Scale in miles
0
1
2

# 106

# Walk-About Guide to Tour of Anchorage Route

Snow conditions allowing, the cross-country ski race Tour of Anchorage takes place each year in the first week of March. This world-renowned ski race draws people not only from all across the United States, but also from many parts of Europe and sometimes even from Russia.

Those who enter this race have three choices of distances. The longest (50 kilometers), which begins at Service High School on lower Hillside, includes Spenser Loop, a trail off-limits to all but skiers in winter. The middle distance (40 kilometers), which also begins at Service High School, bypasses Spenser Loop and utilizes trails that anyone can hike, bike, run, or ski any time of year. The shortest (25 kilometers), which begins at Russian Jack Springs Park, utilizes trails already mentioned above as part of the shorter circumnavigation of Anchorage.

This trail guide will describe the 40-kilometer route for a number of reasons. First, in its traversal of the Anchorage bowl, this route, like the 50-kilometer route, connects the two most popular parks in Anchorage: Far North Bicentennial Park and Kincaid Park. Second, along the way it utilizes many of the most popular biking and hiking trails in the Anchorage bowl, including Viewpoint Trail around Campbell Airstrip, Chester Creek Bike Trail, and Tony Knowles Coastal Trail. Third, the mere fact that the 40-kilometer route not only follows trails open to all form of travel all year round means whether on bike skis, or foot one can follow this route, a route from the foot of the mountains to the shore of the sea, any time.

**TRAIL LOCATION:** The 40-kilometer Tour of Anchorage route begins on an inconspicuous bike trail that originates in the northwest corner of the parking area behind Service High School. To get there drive south on the Seward Highway from 5th Avenue in downtown Anchorage for approximately 5.5 miles to the Dimond Boulevard exit. Turn off the highway at this exit. At the bottom of the ramp, turn left and cross back under the highway. In less than 100 yards Dimond Boulevard turns into Abbott Road as it swings in a broad curve to the left. Follow Abbott Road as it swings first around this curve to the right (south) and then to the (left) north. Approximately 1 mile from the Seward Highway Abbott Road reaches a set of lights at Lake Otis Parkway. Continue straight through these lights and follow Abbott Road uphill toward the mountains for another approximately 1 mile to another set of lights. Continue straight through these lights as well and continue for another 0.75 miles uphill.

At that point one should come in sight of Service High School on the left (north) side of Abbott Road. Continue along Abbott Road past the school's main building to its far end. There turn left (north) into the parking area. Follow this parking area back to the far right (northeast) corner of the school and park where available.

The route begins by turning onto the bike trail that leaves the parking area by slipping down between the football field on the left (east) and sports building on the right (east) (mile 0.0). After dropping down a very short hill the trail climbs into the woods beyond. There, where the bike trail swings right (south), look up to the left to a wide dirt trail entering the woods. Follow this dirt trail up the short embankment. Just past the top of the embankment this trail reaches a 4-way junction with Homestead Trail (mile 0.2). Turn left (north) on Homestead Trail and follow it a short way to another 4-way trail junction (mile 0.3). Continue straight through this junction and follow Homestead Trail down into the trees on the far side. For the next mile the route trends predominantly downhill. After one last, relatively steep downhill the trail flattens out and reaches a T-junction with Coyote Trail (mile 1.3).

Turn right at this junction onto Coyote Trail. In a matter of feet this trail crosses into BLM land. A few steps later it crosses a wide bridge over a shallow stream. Continue past the bridge to where Coyote Trail reaches a junction with Viewpoint Trail on the right (east) (mile 1.4). Here turn right (east) onto Viewpoint Trail.

Follow Viewpoint Trail as it climbs up and over a low rise. Just beyond the far side of this low ride the trail starts climbing more steadily to the top of a hill (mile 1.9). Just after turning left (north) across the crest of this hill, Viewpoint Trail drops steeply off to the right (east). Staying on Viewpoint Trail, follow it as it winds through the woods, passing a number of side trails along the way. Approximately 1.1 miles later the trail eventually emerges from the woods and reaches the left (south) end of a large walking bridge over Campbell Creek (mile 3.1). This bridge leads one out to the parking area on Campbell Airstrip Road*.

Here Viewpoint Trail turns into Old Rondy Trail. Continuing straight past the bridge (east) on Old Rondy Trail, the trail passes through a T-intersection with a sled dog trail (mile 3.2). In approximately 0.1 miles Old Rondy Trail reaches another intersection where it bears right. In less than 0.1 miles later the trail reaches another T-intersection with a trail leading out to Campbell Science Center on the left and Campbell Creek on the right (mile 3.5). For the next 1.6 miles Old Rondy Trail winds down through the woods crossing one major bridge over Campbell Creek in the process before emerging out of the woods onto a paved bike trail (mile 5.1).

Turn right (north) on this paved trail as it immediately passes under one road and continues to swing left (east) to parallel Tudor Road. A short way down Tudor Road the trail swings up and over a substantial footbridge that crosses the road (mile 5.6). Having crossed Tudor Road, continue down between the large medical building on the left and a reflection pond on the right and into a tunnel. Just past the tunnel the trail rises slightly to a roundabout (mile 6). This roundabout marks the beginning of Lanie Fleischer Chester Creek Bike Trail**. At this

---

\* For more information on that trailhead,
see [85] **Walk-About Guide to Rover's Run** in Chapter 9.

\*\* For more information about that trail,
see [101] **Walk-About Guide to Lanie Fleischer Bike Trail**.

roundabout turn right (east) and follow Lanie Fleischer Chester Creek Bike trail east as it swings up along the back side of more medical buildings. Then, after crossing a bridge the trail turns north passing along the edge of a neighborhood and crossing under some power lines before reaching another roundabout (mile 7.3). Turn left (west) at this roundabout and follow it up past the southern end of a bridge over Northern Lights Boulevard (mile 7.5). Passing this first bridge, continue along the trail as it parallels Northern Lights Boulevard for approximately 1 mile to a second bridge (mile 8.3).

Here turn right (north) and follow Lanie Fleischer Bike Trail across the bridge over Northern Lights Boulevard. At the bottom of the hill on the far side of northern Lights Boulevard bear left (east) over a much smaller, narrower bridge (mile 8.4). Bear left again at the trail intersection one reaches immediately past the bridge.

As the trail trends slowly downhill it passes under Lake Otis Parkway (mile 9), Seward Highway (mile 27.4), followed in the next 1 mile by A Street, C Street and Arctic Boulevard. After three more underpasses in rapid succession, the last of which passes under Minnesota Drive (mile 11.6), the trail reaches the east end of Westchester Lagoon. Now follow the right (north) side Westchester Lagoon to the beginning of Tony Knowles Coastal Trail (mile 12.2).

For the next approximately 9.5 miles from Westchester Lagoon to Kincaid Chalet the route follows Tony Knowles Coastal Trail*. Just past the playground at the far end of Westchester Lagoon, this trail reaches its first intersection. Here bear left (south) and continue around the lagoon toward the radio tower. Continuing past the radio tower, the trail swings right (west) and follows a boardwalk across a marsh. At the end of the marsh the trail passes through a tunnel under the railroad tracks. Immediately upon emerging from the far end of the tunnel, one arrives on the coast of the Anchorage peninsula.

The route now continues for the next 8 miles along the coast, with only occasional stretches during which one loses sight of the ocean. Just after milepost 1.0 of the Tony Knowles Coastal Trail the route

---

\* For more information about that trail,
  see [99] **Walk-About Guide to Tony Knowles Coastal Trail**.

reaches Lyn Ary Park (mile 13.1). Just before milepost 2 the trail passes Earthquake Park (mile 14). Less than 0.5 miles later, just after over the entrance to a parking area, the trail begins a long and steady climb to the crest of Point Woronzof (mile 16.0) and its wide and long view to the north. Just past this bluff the trail sweeps steeply down around a corner and passes the parking area for Point Woronzof. After crossing the entrance for yet another parking area, the trail climbs back into the woods (mile 16.4).

For the next almost 5 miles the trail winds through these woods without crossing any road and without seeing any cars. Approximately halfway through this stretch the trail reaches a substantial steel bridge (mile 18.9). (Just after the bridge the race route turns onto a variety of ski trails, which remain closed to non-skiers in winter months. For that reason, this description offers an alternative route that continues along the bike trail.) Approximately 1.7 miles later, the bike trail turns inland at the wooden bench marking the beginning of Kincaid Bluff Trail (mile 20.6)*.

This turn inland marks the beginning of the almost 1-mile climb to Kincaid Chalet and the end of the Tour of Anchorage. Beginning gradually for the first 0.4 miles of the climb, the trail then sweeps up to the right (southeast) and climbs more steeply. As the trail emerges out of the woods at the uppermost end of this climb, it comes in sight of Kincaid Chalet. Just after passing milepost 9 Tony Knowles Coastal Trail reaches its southernmost end (mile 21.2).

Though the tour officially ends on a large field just beyond the chalet, one can consider the end of Tony Knowles Coastal Trail beside the chalet as fine a place to finish as any.

**TRAIL GRADE:** All the bike trails and roads that join together to make up this route rate Grade 1 as a hike.

**TRAIL CONDITION:** Despite its many twist and turns almost the entire length of this trail remains in fine shape. Even the off-pavement sections of

---

\* For more information about this trail, see [96] **Walk-About Guide to Kincaid Bluff Trail.**

the route remain excellent for all sorts of travel. Only in the lower part of the section between Campbell Tract and Tudor Road does the trail have any substantial roots and mud holes.

**TRAIL MILEAGE:** To complete this entire route from Service High School to Kincaid Chalet entails approximately 21.2 miles of hiking, biking, running, or skiing.

**TOTAL ELEVATION GAIN:** To complete this entire route from Service High School to Kincaid Chalet entails a total elevation gain of approximately 700 feet.

**HIGH POINT:** This route reaches its highest point of approximately 350 feet above sea level where it starts at Service High School.

**NORMAL HIKING TIME:** To complete this entire route from Service High School to Kincaid Chalet should take anywhere from 2 to 4 hours on bike and 6 to 10 hours on foot, depending on the condition and ambition of the biker(s) and hiker(s) involved.

**CAMPSITES:** One will find no designated camping areas on this route. Nor should one need one considering the shortness of the route and its proximity to civilization.

**BEST TIME:** Most people should find any time from mid-March to early October a good time to do this bike ride. It also makes a fine outing in winter for any form of self-propelled travel.

**USGS MAPS:** Anchorage A-8 and Tyonek A-1.

Hiking in January on Hillside (OR) January on Tony Knowles Coastal Trail

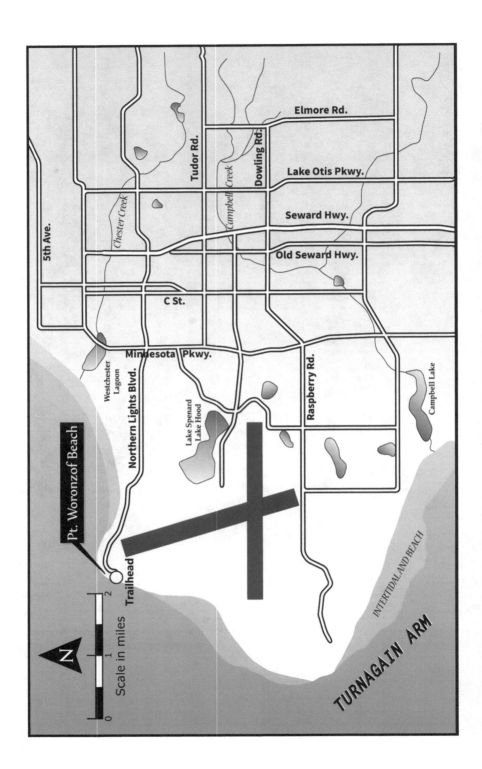

Elmore Rd.

Tudor Rd.

Dowling Rd.

Campbell Creek

Lake Otis Pkwy.

Chester Creek

Seward Hwy.

5th Ave.

Old Seward Hwy.

C St.

Minnesota Pkwy.

Westchester Lagoon

Raspberry Rd.

Campbell Lake

Northern Lights Blvd.

Lake Spenard

Lake Hood

Pt. Woronzof Beach

Trailhead

Scale in miles

N

0    1    2

INTERTIDAL AND BEACH

TURNAGAIN ARM

# 107

# Walk-About Guide to Point Woronzof Beach Walk

Many make the short drive out to Point Woronzof for a respite from their usual day-to-day existence. Some go out to watch a sunset, some go out to socialize (especially students just let out from school), and some go out to meander along the beach just below Point Woronzof.

Those who have yet to walk this beach should find it a unique experience offering a sea-level view of Knik Arm. Mount Susitna, and, upon turning the corner of the bluffs to the northeast, Anchorage and the Chugach Mountains framing it.

**TRAIL LOCATION:** Access to the beach at Pointy Woronzof begins at the parking area at Point Woronzof. To get there go west on 5th Avenue to where it ends on L Street. There turn left (south) on L Street and follow it approximately 1 mile to where it starts downhill. At that point L Street turns into Minnesota Drive. Staying on Minnesota Drive follow it down and across the Chester Creek trough to where approximately 2.1 miles from downtown it reaches a major intersection with Northern Lights Boulevard. Turn right (west) on Northern Lights Boulevard and follow it for approximately 2 miles to where, just past the last homes, one reaches Aircraft Drive on the left (south).

At this point Northern Lights Boulevard turns into Woronzof Drive. Passing the parking area for Earthquake Park on the right (north), continue on Woronzof Drive. Approximately 0.5 miles later Woronzof Drive passes Postmark Drive on the left (south) and a parking area on the right (north). Just after the parking area the road begins climbing up and over the bluff ahead. At the far side of the bluff the road swings down and around a wide curve.

At the bottom of the curve one reaches the entrance to the parking area for Point Woronzof on the right (west). Turn into this road and follow it down to the parking area. Park where available. The trail leading down to the beach begins on the back (west) side of the parking area.

Upon leaving the parking area the wide trail drops at a short angle down to the shingled beach below. Once on the beach one can walk in either direction. Beware, however, that one can walk but a short distance (approximately 0.5 miles) to the right (south) before signs warn one not to go further. Even if one chooses to ignore the signs, one must cross the rock shelf below the sewage treatment plant. Beyond that point the beach soon comes to some dangerous marshy and muddy flats.

If one chooses to walk the beach in the other direction (north), however, the beach continues on for quite a distance (almost 1 mile). On this end of the beach one also passes directly below the towering bluffs of Point Woronzof, which strike some as more impressive when looking up from the bottom than when looking down from the top. But beware of the tides. On especially high tides one can find themselves hugging the base of the bluffs far more dearly than one would wish if they don't remain wary.

**TRAIL GRADE:** Despite some loose shingle, this walk rates Grade 1 as a hike.

**TRAIL CONDITION:** The conditions for this walk depend on the tides and the season. In winter on can expect much ice, often in the form of long shelves and big blocks. Generally, though, the beach remains quite firm underfoot especially on the walk around to the north of the bluffs.

**TRAIL MILEAGE:** To go from the parking area at Point Woronzof down to the beach entails approximately 100 feet of hiking. On the beach, one can walk approximately 0.5 miles to the left (south) and approximately 1 mile to the right (north).

**TOTAL ELEVATION GAIN:** To hike from the parking area at Point Woronzof down to the beach and back entails a total elevation gain of approximately 40 feet.

**HIGH POINT:** This trail reaches its highest point of approximately 50 feet above sea at the parking area at Point Woronzof.

**NORMAL HIKING TIME:** To hike from the parking area at Point Woronzof down to the beach and back should take 0.25 to 2 hours, depending on the condition and ambition of the hiker(s) involved.

**CAMPSITES:** One will find no designated camping areas on or near the beach. Nor should one need one considering the shortness of the hike.

**BEST TIME:** Most people should find any time of year a good time to do this walk. Just beware of the ice in winter and the varying tides in all seasons.

**USGS MAPS:** Tyonek A-1.

September on the beach at Point Woronzof

Single-track biking in Kincaid Park

## CHAPTER 12

# SINGLE-TRACK BIKING IN THE ANCHORAGE BOWL

## OVERVIEW OF SINGLE-TRACK BIKING IN THE ANCHORAGE BOWL

Though one can bike many places in the Anchorage bowl, including along many biking, hiking, and ski trails, only Hilltop Ski Area and Kincaid Park have established a network of single-track trails devoted to biking. In these two areas anyone wanting to single-track bike will find not only trails for all levels of bikers, but many miles of trails to bike. Many of these trails offer profoundly unique views. Some of the trails at Kincaid Park, for instance, skirt along the top of bluffs that offer extensive views of Cook Inlet but all the mountains on the surrounding horizons, while some of the trails on Hillside offer wide views of the Anchorage bowl. Nor, despite the plethora of trails, need one fear losing their way. Both Hilltop Ski Area and Kincaid Park have posted detailed maps at all major trailheads and junctions in their respective trail systems that should prevent almost anyone from losing their way.

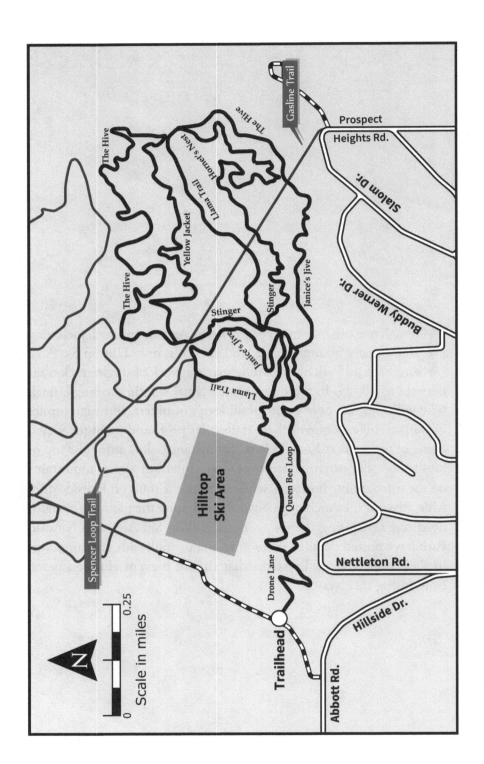

Gasline Trail

Prospect
Heights Rd.

Slalom Dr.

The Hive

The Hive

The Hive

Hornet's Nest

Llama Trail

Yellow Jacket

Janice's Jive

Stinger

Stinger

Stinger

Buddy Werner Dr.

Janice's Jive

Llama Trail

Spencer Loop Trail

Hilltop
Ski Area

Queen Bee Loop

Nettleton Rd.

Drone Lane

N

0.25

Scale in miles

0

Trailhead

Hillside Dr.

Abbott Rd.

# 108

# Walk-About Guide to Single-Track Biking In Hilltop Ski Area

**TRAIL LOCATION:** One can find the best point of access to the single-track bike trails on Hillside at a trailhead at Hilltop Ski Area. To get there drive south on the Seward Highway from 5th Avenue in downtown Anchorage for approximately 5.5 miles to the Dimond Boulevard exit. Turn off the highway at this exit. At the bottom of the ramp, turn left and cross back under the highway. In less than 100 yards Dimond Boulevard turns into Abbott Road as it swings in a broad curve to the left. Follow Abbott Road as it swings first around this curve to the right (south) and then to the (left) north. Approximately 1 mile from the Seward Highway Abbott Road reaches a set of lights at Lake Otis Parkway. Continue straight through these lights and follow Abbott Road uphill toward the mountains for another approximately 1 mile to another set of lights. Continue straight through these lights as well and continue for another 0.75 miles uphill.

At that point one should come in sight of Service High School on the left (north) side of Abbott Road.

Continuing straight past Service High School, follow Abbott Road as it passes under a walking bridge. Approximately 0.5 miles after the bridge, the road reaches a parking area for the lighted cross-country ski loop of Hillside Park. Continue along Abbott Road to the far end of the parking area. There one should reach a road on the left (north) marked by a large sign for Hilltop Ski Area. Turn left onto this road. Follow this road for approximately 0.1 miles to the second road on the right (east). Turn into this road and park near the right (south) end. Park where available. Access to the single-track bike trails begins at the large billboard at the back right side of the parking area. The billboard contains a map of all the singe-track bike routes that weave up and down and across the slopes of the upper end of Campbell Tract for a total of 7.7 miles.

One notices two characteristics about these trails on first looking at the map. First, that all but one (Janice's Jive) have name's associated with the wasp family: Drone, Queen Bee Loop, Yellow Jacket, Hornet's Nest, and Stinger, the last two of which don't sound particularly inviting. Second, one can climb away from the parking area on one trail only—Drone Trail. This trail continues up to an intersection with Queen Bee Loop. Both of these trails continue climbing the slope to intersections with Janice's Jive. This trail swings in a wide circle across the slope above the ski area, crossing Lower Gasline Trail twice along the way*. This hints at a truth about many of these trails: that most have some arduous ascents and thrilling descents. This seems especially true of the longest trail, the 1.9-mile-long The Hive, located on the north side of Lower Gasline Trail, which one can form a large loop with Janice's Jive, located on the south side of Lower Gasline Trail. Together these two trails form a 3-mile loop enclosing almost every other trail on the slope.

For those looking for especially technical routes, try Hornet's Nest and Stinger, both of which make detours off Janice's Jive only to rejoin it farther down the trail.

---

\* For more information about that trail,
   see [79] **Walk-About Guide to Lower Gasline Trail** in Chapter 8.

**Single-Track Biking on Hillside**

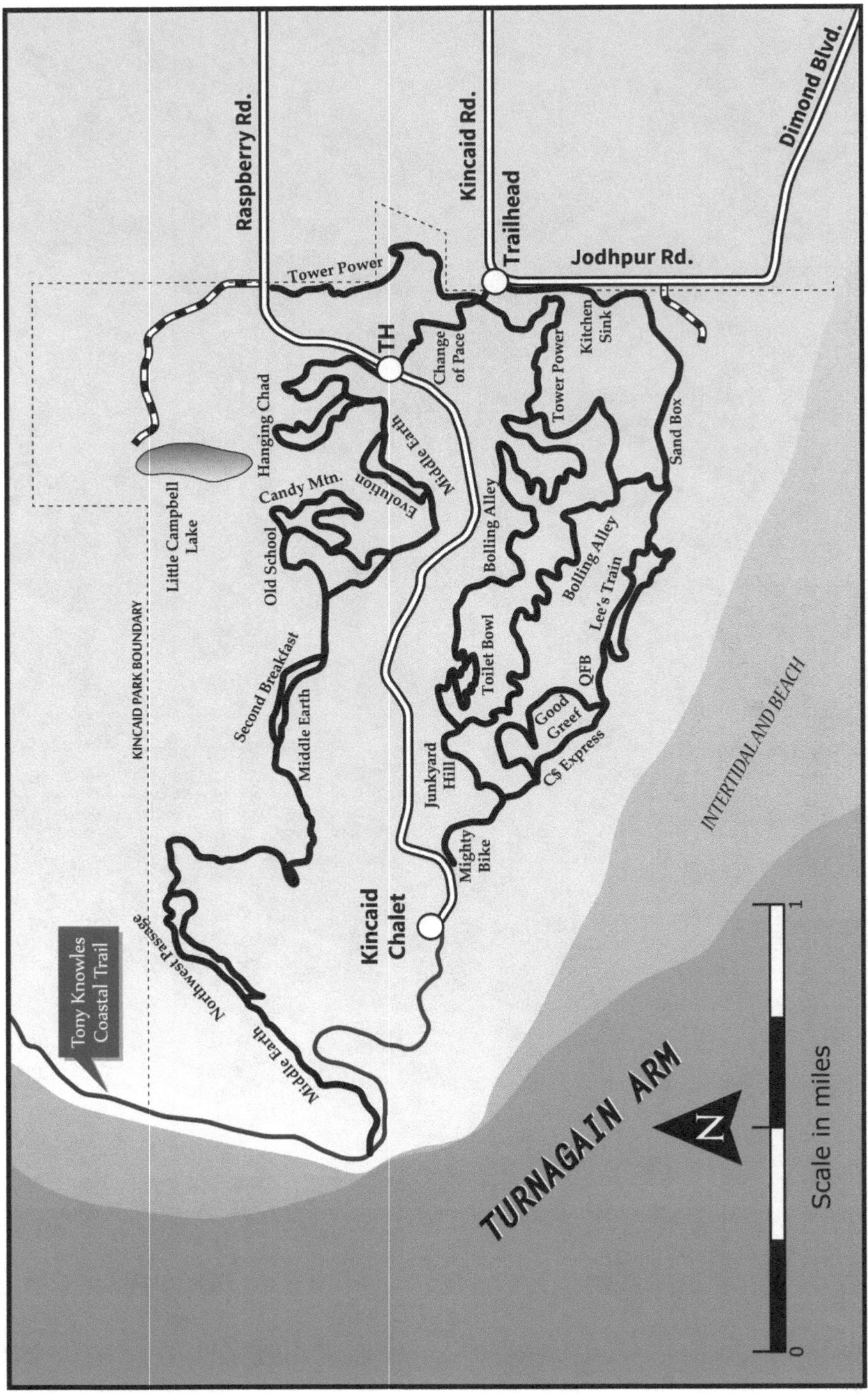
Raspberry Rd.
Kincaid Rd.
Dimond Blvd.
Trailhead
Jodhpur Rd.
Tower Power
TH
Change of Pace
Kitchen Sink
Tower Power
Hanging Chad
Middle Earth
Evolution
Candy Mtn.
Old School
Little Campbell Lake
KINCAID PARK BOUNDARY
Second Breakfast
Middle Earth
Bolling Alley
Bolling Alley
Sand Box
Lee's Train
Toilet Bowl
QFB
Good Greef
C$ Express
Junkyard Hill
Mighty Bike
INTERTIDAL AND BEACH
Kincaid Chalet
Northwest Passage
Middle Earth
Tony Knowles Coastal Trail
TURNAGAIN ARM
N
Scale in miles
0
1

# 109

# Walk-About Guide to Single-Track Biking In Kincaid Park

Though Hilltop Ski Area can boast some spectacular single-track trails, Kincaid Park on the western end of the peninsula remains the mecca of single-track biking in the Anchorage bowl. A network of trails totaling 17.1 miles wind through all corners of the park, at times topping out at 360-degree views of the Anchorage bowl and Knik Arm Kincaid Park and at other times weaving through deep green shadows.

Of the total miles of trails in the park, one can divide them into two large sections separated by Raspberry Road, the paved road running up the center of the park. To the south of this road wind 10 total miles of trails. Of these, the 3.6-mile-long Boiling Alley remains the longest. To the north of this trail wind another 7-plus total miles of trails. Of these the 4-mile-long Middle Earth Trail remains not only the longest and roughest, but in its windings it crosses the entire east-west length of the park. One can, of course, cross the road via a number of ski bridges tunnels, and cross-walks to connect both bodies of trails, but no single-track trail crosses the road.

Finally, though space does not allow discussion of all the trails in Kincaid Park, the guides below describe the numerous places around the park where one can access a variety of single-track trails that eventually connect to all the other trails on that side of Raspberry Road. Each of these four access points has a large map of all the trails in the park as well as a board listing some of the etiquette one should try to practice while on these trails.

[1] **RASPBERRY ROAD PARKING AREA:** The first begins at a parking area approximately 0.5 miles inside the park on Raspberry Road. To get there drive 3.5 miles south from downtown Anchorage on L Street

and its extension Minnesota Drive. There, turn right off the first Raspberry Road exit. At the bottom of the exit ramp turn right (west) onto Raspberry Road. Follow Raspberry Road for approximately 3.25 miles past the major intersection of Four Corners and Sand Lake Road to the entrance of Kincaid Park.

Continuing straight past the entrance, follow Raspberry Road as it winds up a broad wooded hill and into the park. Approximately 0.5 miles past the entrance the road reaches the Raspberry Road Parking Area on the right (north). Turn into this parking area and park where available. Lake Loop Trail begins beside the information board just up the embankment at the back of the parking area.

From the parking on the right (north) side of the road one can access Middle Earth (4.0 miles), the longest continuous single-track bike trail in Kincaid Park. Upon crossing to the left (south) side of the road one can also access Change of Pace (0.4 miles). One can also access Tower Power by riding a short way down the paved bike trail paralleling the south side of Raspberry Road. Approximately 0.6 miles from the parking area, the bike trail passes through some posts to a small paved loop by the park's entrance. Just beyond this loop look up and to the right (south) where another access point for Tower Power begins at the top of the embankment. From this access point Tower Power (1.4 miles), which, as its name implies, climbs for most of its length to where it ends at a T-junction with Boiling Alley, a very popular loop trail that circles though the center of Kincaid Park.

[2] **JODPHUR ROAD PARKING AREA:** The second means of access begins in the southeast corner of the park at Jodhpur Parking Area. To get there drive 3.5 miles south from downtown Anchorage on L Street and its extension Minnesota Drive. There one reaches the exit for Raspberry Road. Turning right off the first Raspberry Road exit, turn right (west) on Raspberry Road. Then follow Raspberry Road for approximately 2.2 miles past the major intersection of Four Corners to the intersection with Sand Lake Road on the left. Here turn left (south) on Sand Lake Road. Continue along Sand Lake Road for approximately 0.6 miles to an intersection with Kincaid Road. Turn right (west) on Kincaid Road. Follow this road for 1 mile to where it ends at an intersection

with Jodhpur Road. Turn left (south) on Jodhpur Road and follow it for approximately 0.4 miles to a road on the right (west) leading into Kincaid Park. Turn onto this road and follow this road and follow it the short way into Jodhpur Parking Area.

One can find two starting points for single-track bike trails in this parking area. The trailhead on the right (north) side of the parking area accesses Kitchen Sink (0.6 miles), which ends at a T-junction with Tower Power. The trailhead on the left (south) side of the parking area accesses Sand Box (0.6 miles).

[3] **KINCAID CHALET:** The third access point begins just southeast of Kincaid Chalet. To get there drive 3.5 miles south from downtown Anchorage on L Street and its extension Minnesota Drive. There one reaches the exit for Raspberry Road. Turning right off the first Raspberry Road exit, turn right (west) on Raspberry Road. Then follow Raspberry Road for approximately 3.25 miles past the major intersection of Four Corners and Sand Lake Road to the entrance of Kincaid Park.

Continuing straight past the entrance, follow Raspberry Road as it winds up broad wooded hill and into the park. Approximately 0.5 miles past the entrance the road reaches the Raspberry Road Parking Area on the right (north) side of the road. Passing this parking area, continue up the road for another approximately 1.6 miles to where the road makes a dip before a last short uphill to Kincaid Chalet. There one reaches a large parking area on the right (north) side of the road. Pull into the parking area.

From there the access point begins at the edge of the woods on the other side of Raspberry Road. One can get there by riding under the tunnel just to the left (west) of the parking area. After passing through the tunnel turn left (east). Then continue straight past the beginning of Andrew Lekisch Trail to the signboard and map by the edge of the trees just beyond. From this trailhead one can access Mighty Bike (0.6 miles), which connects with a number of loops through the park.

[4] **TONY KNOWLES COASTAL TRAIL:** The fourth and last point of access begins on approximately 1 mile down Tony Knowles Bike Trail from Kincaid Chalet. To get there drive 3.5 miles south from downtown Anchorage

on L Street and its extension Minnesota Drive. There one reaches the exit for Raspberry Road. Turning right off the first Raspberry Road exit, turn right (west) on Raspberry Road. Then follow Raspberry Road for approximately 3.25 miles past the major intersections of Four Corners and Sand Lake Road. Continuing past Sand Lake Road, follow Raspberry Road to the entrance of Kincaid Park.

Continuing straight on Raspberry Road past the entrance, follow it as it wind up and into the park. Approximately 2 miles into the park, the road reaches a dead-end at the parking area in front of Kincaid Chalet. Park wherever possible.

From this parking area bike down Tony Knowles Coastal Trail that begins just to the left (south) of the chalet. After descending a half-mile-plus long hill the trail levels out. From that point continue for another approximately 0.4 miles reaches the edge of the bluff overlooking the ocean and swings left (north). Between miles 8.5 and 8.0, just as the bike trail swings right, look for the marked beginning of Middle Earth single-track bike trail marked by a large map showing all the trails in Kincaid Park.

Turning onto Middle Earth follow it across the flats and up across the face the bluffs and into the woods beyond. After climbing a second bluff in the woods, the trail continues through the woods and eventually cross almost the entire length of the park before reaching its far end at the Raspberry Road Parking Area.

Single-track biking in Kincaid Park

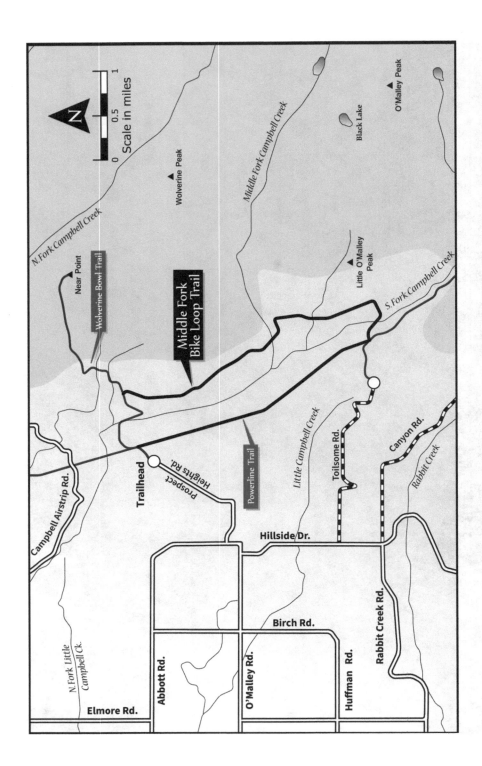

N

Scale in miles
0    0.5    1

N. Fork Campbell Creek

Wolverine Peak

Near Point

Wolverine Bowl Trail

Middle Fork Campbell Creek

Middle Fork
Bike Loop Trail

Black Lake

O'Malley Peak

Little O'Malley
Peak

S. Fork Campbell Creek

Little Campbell Creek

Canyon Rd.

Rabbit Creek

Toilsome Rd.

Powerline Trail

Campbell Airstrip Rd.

Trailhead

Prospect Heights Rd.

Hillside Dr.

N. Fork Little
Campbell Ck.

Birch Rd.

Abbott Rd.

O'Malley Rd.

Huffman Rd.

Rabbit Creek Rd.

Elmore Rd.

# 110

# Walk-About Guide to Biking on Hillside in Winter

For many bikers Hillside makes for one of the finest places to bike in the winter. Popular destinations include Wolverine Bowl Trail, Powerline Trail, and Middle Fork Trail. Of all the possible routes one could bike in winter on Hillside, the large loop that circles up and back to Prospect Heights via Middle Fork Loop Trail remains the most popular.

During the summer months much of Middle Fork Loop Trail requires a permit for travel by bicycle, which makes sense considering the muddy ground and delicate fauna the trail crosses. In winter, however, it requires no permit. The winter also makes for better biking. Not only does the snow blanket the mud and fauna, but it also covers many of the boulders and roots along the trail. No wonder that on most weekends in winter one usually sees far more bikers than hikers or skiers on the trail.

The availability of Middle Fork Loop to bikers in winter also makes it possible for them to complete the loop that circles from Prospect Heights across Hillside and back again along three different trails— Wolverine Bowl Trail, Middle Powerline Trail, and Middle Fork Loop Trail—as it first climbs through the woods onto the tundra above, then after circling below the fronts of Wolverine Peak, O'Malley Peak, and Flattop it descends down the power lines and back into the woods to Prospect Heights.

**TRAIL LOCATION:** This loop begins at Prospect Heights parking area. To get there drive 6.2 miles south from Anchorage on the Seward Highway. There, just after Milepost 121, take a right (west) on the O'Malley Road exit. At the end of the ramp, turn left (east) and cross back under the highway. Continue straight on this road as it ascends past Lake Otis Parkway and the Anchorage Zoo. Approximately 3 miles from the Seward Highway one passes Hillside Road leading right (south) toward Glen Alps. Staying on O'Malley Road, follow it as it swings in less than 100 yards to the left (north) where it changes to Hillside Drive. Almost immediately after Hillside Drive straightens out, it reaches a junction with Upper O'Malley Road on the right (east). Turn right (east) onto Upper O'Malley Road on the right (east). After an approximately 0.5-mile winding climb, this road ends at a T-intersection with Prospect Drive. Turn left (north) on Prospect Drive and follow it for 1 mile to a stop sign. Bear left through the stop sign onto Siderof Lane. Approximately 200 yards beyond the Stop sign this road crosses the boundary Chugach State Park where it reaches an access road leading into a parking area on the right (north). Turn into this parking area and park wherever convenient. Wolverine Bowl Trail, the trail that begins this loop, starts at the gate just to the right of the outhouse at the far end of the parking area[*].

Begin the loop by following Wolverine Bowl Trail for approximately 1 mile to where, just after crossing Campbell Creek, it makes a wide switchback up to a junction with Middle Fork Loop Trail on the right (south)[**].

Here turn right (southeast) onto Middle Fork Loop Trail. Follow this trail as it climbs steadily for approximately 1 mile. At that point the wide, relatively straight trail passes a bench and a sign indicating no (summer) biking beyond this point. Less than 200 feet past the bench the trail begins to twist and turn up a series of short climbs as it continues to wind around the southwest ridge of Wolverine Peak

---

[*]    For more information about that trail,
     see [57] **Walk-About Guide to Wolverine Bowl Trail** in Chapter 5.

[**]    For more information about that trail,
     see [41] **Walk-About Guide to Middle Fork Loop Trail** in Chapter 3.

towering above and to the left (east). For the next approximately 0.9 miles the trail trends upwards, at times quite dramatically, as it climbs over the base of the ridge.

After one last sharp climb the trail begins to contour the south flank of Wolverine Peak to where it soon reaches a bridge over Middle Fork Campbell Creek. Just beyond the bridge the trail climbs an embankment and crosses a wide, level area. At the far side of this flat area, it bears left and contours down to an intersection with Middle Fork Trail. Beyond this intersection the trail climbs up and over one last small hill. At that point, approximately 0.5 miles past the bridge, the trail starts the final 1-mile traverse over to South Fork Campbell Creek. After dropping to cross South Fork Campbell Creek the trail climbs steadily up to Powerline Trail*.

Then the route follows Powerline Trail straight up and over the next rise and then straight past Powerline Access Trail leading left (southwest) to Glen Alps. Continuing straight over the rise, continue down the far side where it turns into Middle Powerline Trail. Near the bottom of the hill at a junction with Upper Gasline Trail, follow Middle Powerline Trail to the right (northwest). For the next approximately 3 miles Middle Powerline Trail trends downward, passing numerous side trails along the way, many of which, like the South Fork Rim Trail, make for some scenic, though indirect, optional ways down**. At its very end it intersects with Wolverine Bowl Trail—and the end of the loop. At this last intersection turn left (southwest) on Wolverine Bowl Trail and follow it 0.1 miles back to Prospect Heights parking area where one started.

**TRAIL GRADE:** This trail rates Grade 2 as a bike ride.

**TRAIL CONDITION:** The conditions along this trail vary depending on snowfall and thaws. On one day one might find the trail well-packed

--------------------------------------------------------------------------

\*    For more information about that trail,
     see [31] **Walk-About Guide to Powerline Trail** in Chapter 3.

\*\*   For more information about these trails, see various **Walk-About guides** in Chapter 4.

and firm. On another day one might find it slushy. And yet one another day one might find it icy. These conditions may also vary from section to section on any given day.

**TRAIL MILEAGE:** To complete this entire loop from Prospect Heights parking area and back again entails approximately 8 miles of biking.

**TOTAL ELEVATION GAIN:** To complete this entire loop from Prospect Heights parking area and back again entails a total elevation gain of approximately 1,600 feet.

**HIGH POINT:** This hike reaches its highest point of approximately 2,200 feet above sea level where Powerline Trail turns into Middle Powerline Trail at junction with Powerline Access Trail leading out to Glen Alps parking area.

**NORMAL HIKING TIME:** To bike from Prospect Heights parking area and back should take anywhere from 1 to 3 hours, depending on the condition, ambition, and ability of the biker(s) involved.

**CAMPSITES:** One will find no designated campsites on this climb. Nor should one need any considering the shortness of the bike ride.

**BEST TIME:** Most people should find any time from the first substantial snowfall to the spring melt a good time to do this bike ride.

**USGS MAPS:** Anchorage A-8 and A-7.

Biking on Middle Fork Loop Trail

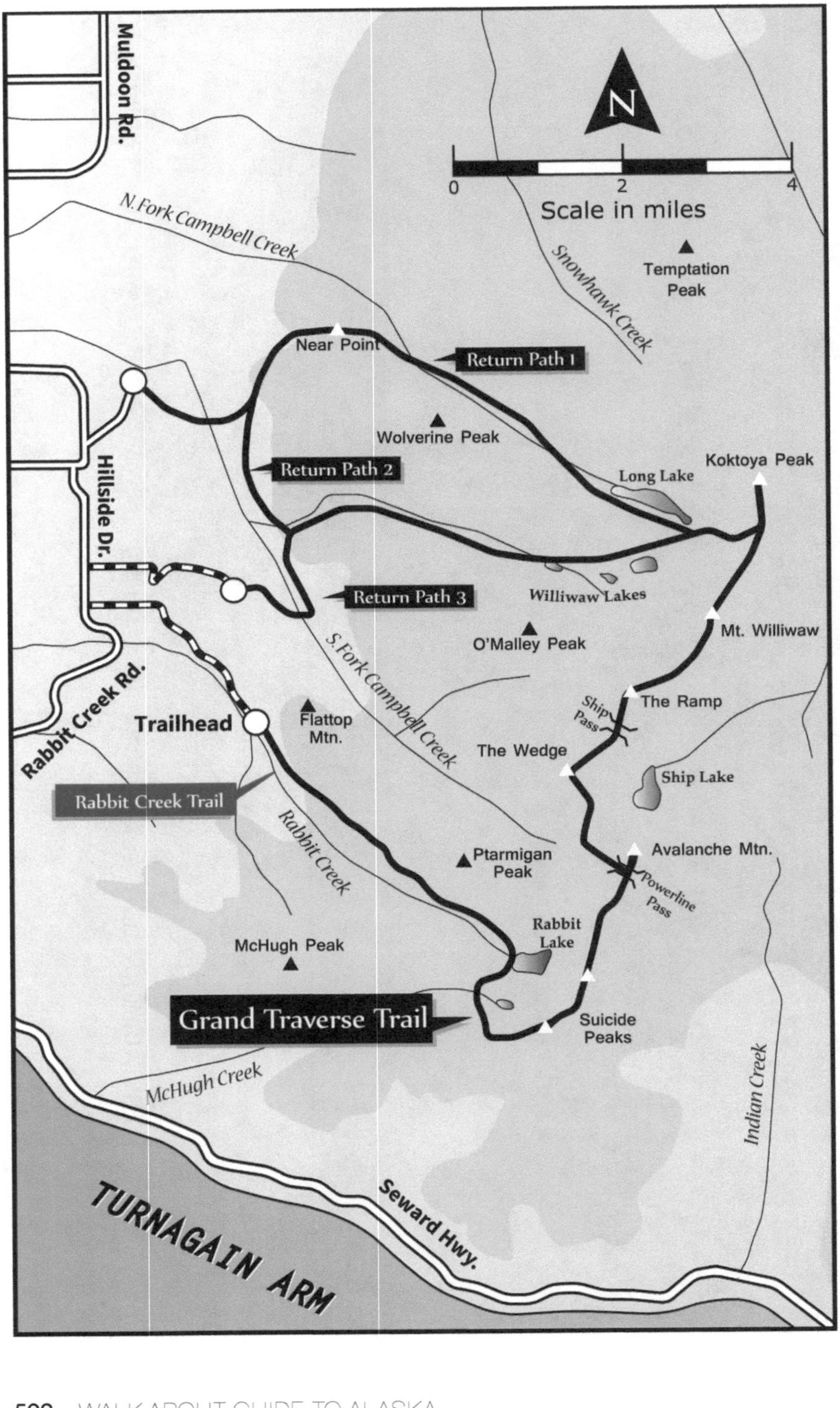

Muldoon Rd.
N
0
2
4
Scale in miles
N. Fork Campbell Creek
Snowhawk Creek
Temptation Peak
Near Point
Return Path 1
Wolverine Peak
Return Path 2
Long Lake
Koktoya Peak
Hillside Dr.
Williwaw Lakes
Return Path 3
Mt. Williwaw
O'Malley Peak
S. Fork Campbell Creek
Rabbit Creek Rd.
Trailhead
Flattop Mtn.
Ship Pass
The Ramp
The Wedge
Ship Lake
Rabbit Creek Trail
Rabbit Creek
Ptarmigan Peak
Avalanche Mtn.
Powerline Pass
Rabbit Lake
McHugh Peak
Grand Traverse Trail
Suicide Peaks
McHugh Creek
Indian Creek
TURNAGAIN ARM
Seward Hwy.

## CHAPTER 13

# GRAND TOUR OF THE FRONT RANGE

## Walk-About Guide to Traverse from South Suicide Peak to Koktoya Peak

This traverse, which includes passing over the summits of six of the twelve 5,000-foot peaks in the Front Range, should give one pause before undertaking it. Not only does it require much time and stamina, but it also requires some serious hand-over-hand scrambling up many steep gullies and along many exposed ridges. With that said, those capable of undertaking this traverse should find it memorable not only for its difficulties, but also the airiness of the route and the expansiveness of the views. This results from the fact that one can stay on the ridge that forms the backbone of the Front Range from South Suicide Peak to Koktoya Peak for most of the way. Only between Avalanche Mountain and The Wedge should one have to descend off the ridge to go around the base of Avalanche Mountain before again climbing back onto the ridge for the remainder of the traverse. But even experienced mountaineers may find it possible to down-climb this steep northwest spine on the way to The Wedge.

**TRAIL LOCATION:** This traverse begins by hiking the length of Rabbit Creek Trail to Rabbit Lake*. To get there drive 8.5 miles south on the Seward

---

\* For more information about that trail, see [17] **Walk-About Guide to Rabbit Creek Trail** in Chapter 2.

Highway to just past Milepost 119 where one reaches the DeArmoun Road exit. Take this exit and at the end of the exit ramp turn left (east) and cross back over the highway toward the mountains. After approximately 3.5 miles of steady climbing, DeArmoun Road reaches the lights at the intersection with Hillside Road. Continuing straight through the lights, follow Upper DeArmoun Road as it continues uphill. Approximately 1 mile later the road reaches an intersection with Canyon Road on the right. (One will recognize this road by the row of mailboxes at this junction.) Turning down Canyon Road, follow it for the next 2 miles as it snakes up valley, passing many side streets, along the way. Continuing up valley on Canyon Road, follow it until, after passing one open gate, it dead-ends at a closed gate. This second gate marks the beginning of Rabbit Creek Trail. (Owing to the roughness of the road, some vehicles may have trouble reaching as far as this second gate. If so, one can park at the wide turnaround just below the first gate and walk the short distance up and around the next corner in the road to the second gate.)

The trail begins by passing around the second gate and continuing up the road beyond it. Within 1 mile the trail reaches the section torn up by the previous owner. Past this section the trail continues to follow the same road on which it started up valley. After one long and gradual climb the trail finally reaches tree line. From the top of this climb the trail, from which one can now enjoy a wide view of the terrain ahead, then descends onto the flat upper stretches of the valley. Approximately 2 miles later it reaches the west shore of Rabbit Lake (3,000-plus feet) spread out beneath the imposing face of North Suicide Peak. There the trail comes to an end.

From the shore of Rabbit Lake turn right (south) and cross Rabbit Creek. Then climb over the low hump directly ahead and descend to McHugh Lake. Turning right (south) along the shore of McHugh Lake follow the shore to where McHugh Creek leaves the lake and look for a wide slow place in the current to cross to the far shore.

This far side of McHugh Creek marks the beginning of the climb up South Suicide Peak proper. After picking a route up the broad but steep tundra slope leading to the buttress towering approximately 1,200 feet above, begin climbing. Once on the buttress, bear left (east-northeast) and follow the crest of the ridge to where it drops into a wide tundra saddle below the summit cone. At the far side of the saddle follow the right side of the ridge's crest for the final approximately 600-foot climb to the summit.

On this climb make sure to stay as close as possible to the crest of the ridge, keeping the precipitous west face of the mountain on your left. For those who don't want to look down the sheer west face, they can corkscrew up and to the right, making sure not to stray far from the crest of the ridge. At the very top of this climb, one reaches the steep crown of the summit. A few scrambling steps to the right one should find a spot to clamber up and over onto the summit (5,005 feet).

Having reached this first summit, continue down the far side into the very appropriately named Windy Gap (so named because of the ferocious south winds that funnel through it). From the bottom of the gap continue up the broad open slope on the opposite side. At the top of the slope, the ridge narrows dramatically, requiring one exposed move to reach the summit of North Suicide Peak (5,065 feet).

From the top of North Suicide Peak continue the traverse by down-climbing the steep and rocky north ridge on the far side of the summit. At the base of the ridge, the route continues across the knife-edged saddle toward next buttress in the ridge. (One wide notch in this saddle may compel some people to descend the few dozen feet it takes to get around it. Others might hop this short gap with surprising ease.)

Once across the saddle, follow the sheep trail on the far side up and around the back of the next buttress in the ridge. At north end of the buttress the route comes to a broad scree slope dropping into Powerline Pass. Descend this wide slop toward the power station on the right (northwest) end of the pass. Upon reaching the power station, pass directly to its right (east) and begin climbing the broad tundra and scree slope directly behind it. Staying relatively close to the ridge line on the left (east), continue to the top of ridge (4,600 feet) There turn right (east) and continue down the long ridge crest as it swings to the left (north). As one continues down the ridge, passing over a number of smaller knolls and false summits along the way, one should have fine views in all directions. For instance, far below to the left, at the base of the precipitous north wall of the mountain one should see the turquoise waters of Ship Lake while far below to the right (south) one can see both Indian Creek Pass and Turnagain Arm beyond that. Approximately 1 mile after reaching the top of the ridge a short sharp climb brings one to the spired true summit of Avalanche Mountain (5,050 feet).

To continue the route from this summit one must first backtrack to Powerline Pass. (Experienced climbers may want to try to down-climb the northwest ridge leading toward The Wedge, but most will find it easier and safer to go down and around the base of the mountain.) In Powerline Pass turn right (west) and follow Powerline Trail down toward Glen Alps for approximately 0.25 miles to where one can traverse the boulder-covered slope back up to the narrow ridge that forms a saddle leading over toward The Wedge. Then turn left onto the sheep trail that leads across the ridge's length. (But do not lapse lackadaisical on this trail. People have fallen to their death on this short traverse connecting one peak to another.) At the far end of the saddle, one can either climb up the crest of the ridge to the summit of The Wedge (4,660 feet) and down to Ship Pass or continue along the sheep trail that contours across the backside of The Wedge over to Ship Pass. Either way, having reached Ship Pass, continue straight across its crest and start up the faint trail leading to the summit of The Ramp. As the ridge narrows near the top the trail passes along some marvelously exposed ledges to where after a last little scramble one reaches the summit of The Ramp (5,240 feet).

From The Ramp to the end of the traverse on Koktoya Peak one follows the crest of the 4,000-foot-plus ridge the entire way. From the summit of The Ramp continue along the rocky crest as it winds by exposed notches and ledges, and around boulders and spires. As one nears Mount Williwaw a sheep trail will slowly appear. This sheep trail makes itself more readily apparent as it climbs along a line of spires and descends to a broad shelf directly below the broad summit cone of Mount Williwaw. At this point turn up and follow the trail up the wide crest of the ridge to the summit (5,545 feet).

Continuing straight down the slope on the far side of Mount Williwaw, follow the pronounced sheep trail to Ship Creek Overlook (4,445 feet) the broad saddle below Koktoya Peak. From this overlook one can look both up and down the length of the Ship Creek valley as well as farther inland to the great peaks and perpetual snowfields of the inner Chugach. On a really clear day, one can even see as far as Mount Marcus Baker, the highest peak in the Chugach Mountains.

One now need only a little more effort to reach the summit of Koktoya Peak located approximately 1 mile further up the ridge from the Overlook. Begin this last climb by first continuing straight ahead (north) across the crest of the saddle. At the far side of the saddle, turn up the ridge's crest toward the summit. The higher one climbs, the more rock gendarmes and cliffs one has to maneuver around. By drifting toward the shallower slopes on the left (west), however, one can avoid most of the more dangerous obstacles. Nevertheless, one still has to clamber up much scree the higher one climbs. Eventually the ridge rounds off for the final stretch to the summit (approximately 5,150 feet).

From the summit of Koktoya Peak one still has a long hike back to civilization. In making this hike, one has three choices. First, the longest route one can take leads to Prospect Heights parking area via Near Point. To get there descend to the left (south) shore of Long Lake and follow the faint trail that leads down the North Fork Campbell Creek Valley. Just before reaching brush line, bear up and to the left (southwest) toward the saddle just before Near Point. Once on the saddle follow the trail up and over the summit and down Wolverine Bowl Trail to Prospect Heights parking area*.

Second, one can also reach Prospect Heights parking area via Williwaw Lakes Trail, Middle Fork Loop Trail, and Wolverine Bowl Trail**. Begin this hike out by first following the ridge back toward Mount Williwaw. Once in the saddle between the two peaks bear down and to the right toward the pass separating the headwaters of Middle Fork Campbell Creek and the headwaters of North Fork Campbell Creek. Having reached this pass, next look for the faint trail

--------------------------------------------------------------------

\*    For more information about that trail,
see [57] **Walk-About Guide to Wolverine Bowl Trail** in Chapter 5.

\*\*   For more information about these trails, see [41] **Walk-About Guide to Middle Fork Loop Trail** in Chapter 3 and [61] **Walk-About Guide to Williwaw Lakes Trail** and [57] **Walk-About Guide to Wolverine Bowl Trail** in Chapter 5.

that leads down to the uppermost end of Williwaw Lakes Trail where it circles around the uppermost of the Williwaw Lakes. Then follow Williwaw Lakes Trail down to its intersection with Middle Fork Loop Trail. Turn right (northwest) on Middle Fork Loop Trail and follow it down to its intersection with Wolverine Bowl Trail. There, turn left (southwest) on Wolverine Bowl Trail and follow it out to Prospect Heights parking area.

The third and shortest route leads out to Glen Alps parking area. One begins this hike by first following the same trails as the second route, namely Williwaw Lakes Trail and Middle Fork Loop Trail. In doing so, follow the same route as described above to where Williwaw Lakes Trail reaches an intersection with Middle Fork Loop Trail. At that intersection, turn left (south), instead of right on Middle Fork Loop Trail. Then follow Middle Fork Loop Trail back to Powerline Trail. Turn right (west) on Powerline Trail and follow it for approximately 100 yards up to the access trail bearing left (west) to Glen Alps parking area.

For those who want to return all the way to Rabbit Creek Trail parking area, they must first reach Glen Alps. From there one must climb Flattop Mountain Trail up the front of the mountain and descent Flattop Trail down the back of the mountain[*].

**TRAIL CONDITION:** Rabbit Creek Trail, where one begins this traverse, rates Grade 2 as a hike for much its length, with long stretches of Grade 1 hiking as it approaches Rabbit Lake. Once one begins climbing South Suicide Peak, however, the route rates Grade 5 to 6 for most its length. Along the way one does receive some respite with Grade 4 sections in the traverse of Ship Pass as well as across the wide saddle between Mount Williwaw and Koktoya Peak. From Koktoya Peak all routes back to trailheads rate Grade 4 initially. On reaching trail again the remainder of the routes out rate Grade 2 as hikes.

**TRAIL MILEAGE:** To hike from the beginning of Rabbit Creek Trail to the summit of South Suicide Peak entails 8.2 miles of hiking. To hike the

---

[*]    For more information about those trails, see [26] **Walk-About Guide to Flattop Mountain Trail** in Chapter 3 and [25] **Walk-About Guide to Flattop Trail** in Chapter 2.

entire spine of the Front Range from the summit of South Suicide Peak to the summit of Koktoya Peak entails approximately 12.5 miles of hiking. To hike from the summit of Koktoya Peak out to Prospect Heights via Near Point entails approximately 10.5 miles of hiking.

To hike from the summit of Koktoya Peak out to Prospect Heights parking area via Williwaw Lakes Trail entails approximately 9.5 miles of hiking. To hike from the summit of Koktoya Peak out to Glen Alps parking area entails approximately 8 miles of hiking.

This means that the entire hike from Rabbit Creek Trail to the summit of Koktoya Peak and back via Near Point to Prospect Heights parking area entails approximately 30.7 miles of hiking, that the entire hike from Rabbit Creek Trail to the summit of Koktoya Peak and back via Williwaw Lakes Trail to Prospect Heights parking area entails approximately 29.7 miles of hiking, and that the entire hike from Rabbit Creek Trail to the summit of Koktoya Peak and back to Glen Alps parking area entails approximately 29.2 miles of hiking. The mileage for each section of this traverse breaks down to the following:

➤ From Rabbit Creek parking area to the summit of South Suicide Peak: **8.2 MILES.**

➤ From the summit South Suicide Peak to North Suicide Peak: **1.0 MILES.**

➤ From North Suicide Peak to Powerline Pass: **2.0 MILES.**

➤ From Powerline Pass to Avalanche Mountain: **2.0 MILES.**

➤ From Avalanche Mountain to The Wedge: **2.0 MILES.**

➤ From The Wedge to the summit of The Ramp: **1.5 MILES.**

➤ From The Ramp to the summit of Mount Williwaw: **1.8 MILES.**

➤ From Mount Williwaw to the summit Koktoya Peak: **2.0 MILES.**

➤ Total mileage in just the end-to-end hike of the peaks: **12.3 MILES.**

The additional mileage for each of the routes from the summit of Koktoya Peak out to one of the parking areas breaks down as follows:

➤ From Koktoya Peak to Prospect Heights parking area via Near Point: **10.5 MILES.**

➤ From Koktoya Peak to Prospect Heights parking area via Williwaw Lakes Trail: **9.5 MILES.**

➤ From Koktoya Peak to Glen Alps parking area: **8 MILES.**

**TOTAL ELEVATION GAIN:** To hike from the beginning of Rabbit Creek Trail to the summit of Koktoya Peak entails a total elevation gain of approximately 11,900 feet. This means that the entire hike from Rabbit Creek Trail to the summit of Koktoya Peak and back via Near Point to Prospect Heights parking area entails a total elevation gain of approximately 12,900 feet, that the entire hike from Rabbit Creek Trail to the summit of Koktoya Peak and back via Williwaw Lakes Trail to Prospect Heights parking area entails a total elevation gain of approximately 12,400 feet, and that the entire hike from Rabbit Creek Trail to the summit of Koktoya Peak and back to Glen Alps parking area entails a total elevation gain of approximately 12,600 feet. The elevation gain for each section of this traverse breaks down to the following:

➤ Rabbit Creek Trail parking area (2,000 feet above sea level) to the summit of South Suicide (5,005 feet): **3,005 FEET.**

➤ From South Suicide to North Suicide (5,065 feet): **1,000 FEET.**

➤ From North Suicide to Avalanche Mountain (5,050 feet): **2,300 FEET.**

➤ From Avalanche Mountain over The Wedge (4,660 feet) to The Ramp (5,240 feet): **2,600 FEET.**

➤ From The Ramp to Mount Williwaw (5,545 feet): **1,200 FEET.**

➤ From Mount Williwaw to Koktoya Peak (approximately 5,150 feet): **700 FEET.**

**HIGH POINT:** This traverse reaches its highest point of 5,545 feet above sea level at the summit of Mount Williwaw, the highest peak in the Front Range.

**NORMAL HIKING TIME:** No matter what route out one takes from the summit of Koktoya Peak out to a parking area, this hike should take anywhere from 20 hours to 3 days.

**CAMPSITES:** One will find no designated campsites along this route. One can find many fine places upon which to pitch a tent in almost of the saddles and passes one crosses in the process of completing this traverse. Powerline Pass, Ship Pass, and Ship Creek Overlook make particularly fine spots for camping. None of these spots, however, have any reliable water sources, especially later in the season when even the most persistent snowfield has probably melted. In order to find water one must descend at least partially into the valleys below.

**BEST TIME:** Most people should find any time from mid-June to mid-September a good time to do this traverse.

**USGS MAPS:** Anchorage A-8 and A-7.

On the summit

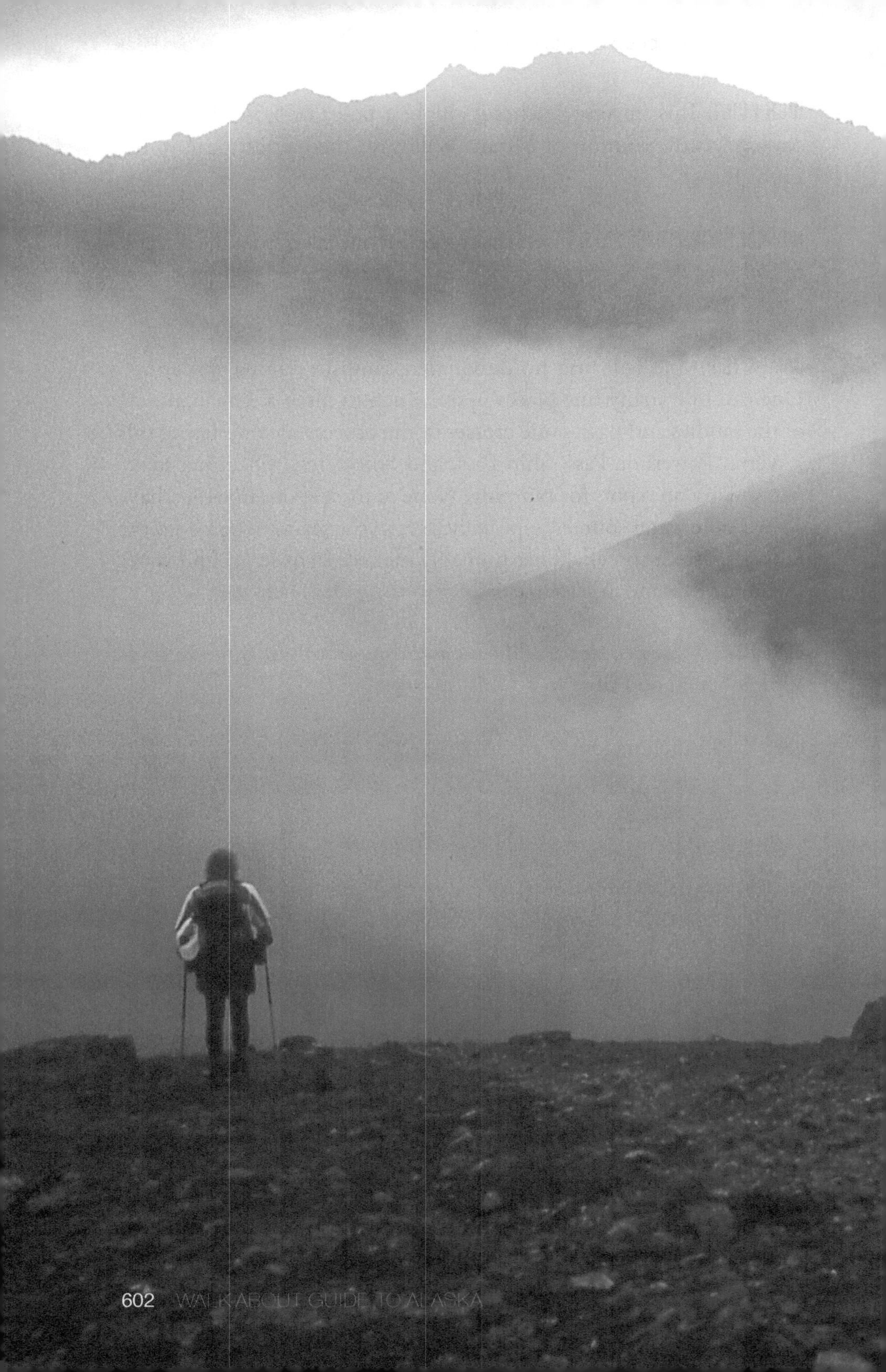

# APPENDICES

## APPENDIX 1:
## INFORMATION SOURCES

### Alaska Public Lands Information Center
605 West Fourth Avenue
Anchorage, AK 99501

(907) 271-2737

http://www.alaskacenters.gov/anchorage.cfm

### Alaska Department Of Fish And Game
P.O. Box 115526
1255 W. 8th Street
Juneau, AK 99811-5526

http://www.adfg.alaska.gov/index.cfm?adfg=home.main

**Anchorage Area Office**

333 Raspberry Road
Anchorage, AK 99518

(907) 267-2100

### Bureau Of Land Management
**Alaska State Office**

222 West Seventh Ave. #13
Anchorage, Alaska 99513-7504

Public Room: 907-271-5960

Office of Communications: 907-271-5555

TTY/Federal Relay System: 1-800-877-8339

http://www.blm.gov/ak/st/en.html

Email:
BLM_AK_AKSO_Public_Room@blm.gov

### Chugach State Park
http://dnr.alaska.gov/parks/units/chugach/

### Chugach State Park Headquarters
Potter Section House
Mile 115 Seward Highway
HC 52, Box 8999
Indian, AK 99540

(907) 345-5014

### Chugach National Forest
3301 C Street, Suite 300
Anchorage, AK 99503

(907) 271-2500

TDD (907) 271-2504

Cabin Reservations: Alaska Public Lands Information Center, (907) 271-2599 or through any U.S. Forest Service district office in the state.

**Girdwood District Office**

P.O. Box 129
Girdwood, AK 99587

(907) 783-3242

## Alaska Department Of Natural Resources

550 W. 7th Ave, Suite 1260

Anchorage, AK 99501-3557

Phone: 907-269-8400

Fax: 907-269-8901

TTY: 907-269-8411

http://dnr.alaska.gov/

## Eagle River Nature Center

(managed by the non-profit Friends of Eagle River Nature Center, Inc.)

32750 Eagle River Road
Eagle River, AK 99577

Phone: 907-694-2108

Fax: 907-694-2119

http://www.ernc.org/

## Alaska Department Of Transportation And Public Facilities

P.O. Box 196900
Anchorage, AK 99519-6900

Numbers to call for highway and road conditions:

Anchorage: (907) 243-7675

Main Number (Maintenance Division): (907) 266-1735

Matanuska-Susitna District: (907) 745-2159

## Alaska Division Of Tourism

P.O. Box 110801-0801
Juneau, AK 99811

Juneau: (907) 465-2010

Anchorage: (907) 563-2167

Ask for the "Vacation Planner," an annually revised publication that lists names, addresses, and phone numbers of businesses and services that cater to any and all who visit Alaska, whether they want to just rent a car or take a ten day rafting trip.

## U.S. Geological Survey

Earth Science Information Center

4230 University Drive
Anchorage, AK 99508-4664

(907) 786-7011

Alaska topographical maps are available to the public through this office.

## Alaska Mountaineering Club

P.O. Box 102937
Anchorage, AK 99510

## Alaska Avalanche School

Alaska Mountain Safety Center

9140 Brewster Drive

Anchorage, AK 99516

(907) 345-3566

## Nordic Skiing Association

203 West 15th Avenue, Suite 204
Anchorage, AK 99501

(907) 276-7609

# APPENDIX 2
# CABIN RENTALS

Three separate groups maintain the cabins in Chugach State Park and State Forest. For the most part, the location of the cabin—whether on State Park land or State Forest Land—determines what office to contact. The exceptions to this rule include the cabin and yurt run by the Friends of Eagle River Nature Center, Inc. Because of the popularity of all the cabins in the Chugach Mountains, one should make reservations early. Rental fees may vary from organization to organization.

## Alaska Department Of Natural Resources
### Public Information Center
Frontier Building
3601 C Street, Suite 200
Anchorage, AK 99503

(907) 269-8400

Reservations for cabins in Chugach State Park may be made through this office or at the nearest State Park office (see their park headquarters address and phone number listed in Appendix 1).

http://dnr.alaska.gov/parks/cabins/index.htm

## Alaska Hut Association
(For reservations at Manitoba Cabin)
http://www.alaskahuts.org/index.html

## Alaska Public Lands Information Center
605 West 4th Avenue, Suite 105
Anchorage, AK 99501

(907) 644-3661

Reservations for cabins located on National Forest land may be made through this office.

http://www.alaskacenters.gov/cabins.cfm

## Eagle River Nature Center
(managed by the non-profit Friends of Eagle River Nature Center, Inc.)

32750 Eagle River Road
Eagle River, AK 99577

Phone: 907-694-2108

Fax: 907-694-2119

http://www.ernc.org/

Reservations for their new privately owned cabin and yurt located within a few miles of the Center along the Eagle River Trail and Albert Loop Trail respectively can be made through this organization.

# APPENDIX 3
# PARKING AND HIKING PERMITS

For permission to hike and camp on military lands one should contact the Military Police at the following number:

(907) 384-0823

For a far easier way to receive permission, Fort Richardson has established a very efficient website through which one can obtain a day permit or, even better, purchase a year-long pass. The following web address accesses this site:

https://jber.isportsman.net/

At this site one can even create a personal account. Through such an account one can quickly check status and sign in and sign out of the various designated recreation areas on military land. One can also check to see if the military has temporarily closed any areas for maneuvers. Maps on the website indicate the sections of various areas that the military has designated for recreational use. One then signs in to enter that area. For most people reading this book, the Snow Hawk Valley Trail and Temptation Peak all lie inside sections 428, 431, and 427, whereas Ice Cream Cone Trail, Knoya Peak, Kanshee Peak, and Tikishla Peak lie inside sections 439, 430, and 431.

## CHUGACH STATE PARK PERMITS

As of March, 1998, one must pay a parking fee at all but one of the Chugach State Park trailheads, campgrounds and picnic areas. (The parking area outside the privately leased Eagle River Nature center remains the one exception. One will find their policy described below.) As an alternative to this pay-when-you-park routine one can buy a season pass, good for all but the parking area at Eagle River Nature Center. One can purchase this season pass at Chugach State Park Headquarters (the address of which can be found in Appendix 1). If one buys more than one permit one can request a discount for the second permit.

Eagle River Nature Center, managed by the non-profit organization Friends of Eagle River Nature Center, Inc., also charges a fee for parking outside their facility (the address of which one can find in Appendix 1). Unlike the State Park, one cannot buy a season parking ticket. However, for the cost of signing as a member of the Friends of Eagle River Nature Center, one not only gets free year-round parking, but a newsletter and regular updates on special affairs taking place at the center.

Nordic Skiing Association, which manages and maintains a section of Arctic Valley Road, has also initiated parking fees for Alpenglow Parking Area. A seasonal permit can also be purchased through the Ski Association, whose address can be found in APPENDIX 2.

# ABOUT THE AUTHOR

Shawn Lyons, by vocation and avocation, lives a life of many parts. As a professional classical guitarist, he plays dinner music every Thursday through Saturday at Villa Nova Restaurant in Anchorage. When not playing guitar at Villa Nova, Shawn gives private guitar at the University of Alaska in Anchorage. There he also teaches Music Appreciation, English Composition, and Literature. Most know him, however, as an avid hiker and hill scrambler. So much so that after many long hikes through many a valley and over many a summit, many consider him the hiking guru of South Central Alaska. In addition, as an ultra-athlete, he has won the Iditashoe wilderness snowshoe race times, and the 100-mile Coldfoot Classic, held each year on Halloween above the Arctic Circle, three times. For many years Shawn's narratives about his hikes and races often appeared in a weekly hiking/climbing column that he writes for *The Anchorage Daily News.*